ENGLISH BOOKS
WITH
COLOURED PLATES

ENGLISH BOOKS

WITH

COLOURED PLATES

1790 TO 1860

A Bibliographical Account of
the most Important Books
illustrated by English Artists
in Colour Aquatint and
Colour Lithography

R. V. Tooley

1973
DAWSONS OF PALL MALL
Folkestone & London

This reprint authorised by B. T. Batsford Ltd
First published in 1954
Reprinted 1973

DAWSONS OF PALL MALL
CANNON HOUSE
FOLKESTONE, KENT, ENGLAND

ISBN: 0 7129 0583 9

MADE AND PRINTED IN GREAT BRITAIN BY
UNWIN BROTHERS LIMITED
THE GRESHAM PRESS, OLD WOKING, SURREY, ENGLAND
A MEMBER OF THE STAPLES PRINTING GROUP

PREFACE

THE first half of the nineteenth century is one of the most active periods in English History: an era of expansion, of travel, conquest, invention, trade; and political asylum, personal freedom and national success. Fashion was the prime arbiter, and fashion decreed that the wealthy and leisured should have a knowledge of architecture, the classics and the arts: drawing and watercolour painting were taught as much as dancing and deportment. All these factors combined made a great impact upon, and were reflected in, the art of the period. Thus a spate of books appeared on Travel and Antiquities. The national and personal ego was titillated by illustrations of the mansions of the nobility and gentry; by a graphic record of military exploits; by sport in all its branches and the English way of life; from books on landscape gardening to the latest invention, the steam engine; and particularly by a caricature untrammelled by late Victorian conventions. The wealth of a substantial part of the community and a well-informed public enabled publishers to employ the foremost artists of their day in book illustration, and they were supported by a number of remarkably fine craftsmen, engravers and colourists.

Two processes were mainly employed for the reproduction of colour: aquatint and lithography. Aquatint illustrations were printed in one, two and occasionally three colours, and the tinting finished by hand. It was fortunate that such a process, more suitable than any other for the reproduction of watercolour drawings, came into general use when England was peculiarly rich in artists working in this medium. In the larger ventures where a thousand copies of a book with a hundred or more illustrations were proposed (necessitating the colouring of over a hundred thousand prints), master colourists, or the artist himself, made specimens which were then given to numerous copyists. In the early days many political refugees made a meagre existence in this manner. But this mode of production was expensive: for example, the Microcosm was issued at 13 guineas; Daniell's Voyage for £60 (or 96 guineas for large-paper copies); Naylor's Coronation for £200. It must be remembered that this was in a period when the cost of living was a fraction of what it is today, so that in effect many volumes can be bought now at less than they cost their contemporary purchasers. For this reason aquatint engraving gradually gave way to lithography as this was perfected. It was a far cheaper process and, moreover, it excelled in the reproduction of crayon drawings.

The following work is an attempt to record this remarkable flowering in

English Book Illustration. It is not exhaustive, but an endeavour has been made to include all the more important books and many minor items. Two subjects have, however, been excluded: Botany and Ornithology, as they alone would need a volume each if described in a comparable manner.

This work was first published in 1935, listing just under 300 titles, covering 400 volumes. The present edition has been extended to 517 titles, covering 700 volumes, listing several thousand engravings. With one or two exceptions, which have been noted, I have personally examined each work. Of the rarer items five or six copies have been scrutinised, and up to 30 or 40 copies of the more common works, to check and re-check collations, discover variations and ensure accuracy. This has entailed several years' research. Nevertheless, as no large bibliographical work has appeared entirely free from blemish, I would be pleased to receive any corrections or suggested additions, which should be addressed to me c/o Messrs. B. T. Batsford, Ltd.

R. V. TOOLEY

London, 1954.

ACKNOWLEDGMENT

I WISH to record my acknowledgment to previous writers on the subject or on particular artists: Cohn, Cruikshank, Grego, Hardie, Lewine, Lowndes, Neville, Oviedo, Prideaux, Schwerdt, Slater and the compilers of Book Auction Records and Book Prices Current, whose statements have been verified. My thanks are also due to the staffs of the National and Public Institutions, the British Museum, South Kensington Library, Guildhall, and Bishopsgate Institution for their kindness and help. Also to the following individuals for assistance or permission to see particular copies: T. D. Burrows, Miss J. Clark, D. A. Colman, Mrs. Barton Day, J. L. Douthwaite, C. W. F. Goss, Graham Watson, H. Harvey Frost, W. Harris, Dr. Jefferys, G. Plummer and J. Watson; and lastly to my numerous friends in the bookselling fraternity—Messrs. Bain, Batsford, Bumpus, Francis Edwards, Joseph, Maggs, Marks, Myers, Quaritch, Robinson, Robson, Sawyer, Spencer, Stevens and Brown, Suckling and Thorp, whose aggregate stock is the backbone of any comparative research and who have generously allowed me to examine their volumes at my leisure.

ARRANGEMENT

The arrangement is alphabetical, firstly under authors, and if anonymous, under titles. There are however some exceptions: Rowlandsons have been grouped together for ease of reference and some works, such as Ackermann's Westminster Abbey, placed under the name by which they are known rather than under the writer of the text; but in all such cases cross references have been supplied.

1 ABEL (C.)

Narrative of a Journey in the interior of China, and of a Voyage to and from that Country, in the years 1816 and 1817; containing an account of the most interesting transactions of Lord Amherst's Embassy to the Court of Pekin, and observations on the countries which it visited (rule). By Clarke Abel, M.D. F.R.S. F.L.S. and Member of the Geological Society, Chief Medical Officer and Naturalist to the Embassy (rule). Illustrated by Maps and other Engravings. London: Printed for Longman, Hurst, Rees, Orme and Brown, Paternoster Row.

Quarto   1819

COLLATION.—Title as above (v. Printed by A. Strahan, Printers Street, London) + Ded. 1 leaf. + Pref. pp. 5–10 + Contents pp. 11–16 + pp. 1–420 (including Index) + Errata slip, + 4 maps + coloured plates + uncoloured plates.

1. Exocoetus Splendens. Drawn from a sketch by W. Havell Esq. Engraved by T. Fielding. Coloured.
2. The Waterfall at Hong Cong. T. Fielding sculpt. Coloured.
3. Nan Wang Hoo. Drawn from a Sketch by Lieut. J. Cooke, R.M. Engraved by T. Fielding. Coloured.
4. View of the Landing Place at Pulo Leat. Drawn from a sketch by H. Roper Esq. T. Fielding sculpt. Coloured.
5. View of the Central Spring at Epetan in Java. T. Fielding sculpt. Coloured.
6. The Crater (and Ascent) of Gonong Karang. Drawn by C. Abel Esq. Engraved by T. Fielding. Coloured.
7. The Great Snake of Java. Sydenham Edwards delt. Engraved by T. Fielding. Coloured.
8. Temple of Quong Ying. Uncoloured.
9. Geological Views, Cape of Good Hope. Uncoloured.
10. Geological Views, Cape of Good Hope. Uncoloured.
11. Geological Views in China. Uncoloured.
12. (Monkey.) Sydenham Edwards delt. T. Fielding sculpt.
13. Shark's Eye.
14–19. Six plates of plants without titles.
20. Track of the Alceste.
21. Map of Route on Yang-Tse–Kiang.
22. Chart of China and Yellow Seas.
23. Map of China.

2 ACKERMANN (Rudolph)

The History of the Abbey Church of St. Peter's Westminster, Its Antiquities and Monuments (thick and thin rule) In Two Volumes Vol. I (II) (thick and thin rule) London: Printed for R. Ackermann, 101, Strand, by L. Harrison and J. C. Leigh, 373, Strand (short rule)

2 vols. Quarto.   1812

COLLATION VOL. I.—Half-title, "The History of St. Peter's Westminster (swelled rule) Vol. I" [II] (v. blank) + Title as above (v. blank) + Dedication to William Vincent D.D. Dean of the Abbey 1 p. (v. blank) + List of Subscribers pp. vii–xiii (p. xiv blank) + Introduction pp. xv–xviii + Arrangement of the Plates in both volumes 2 pp. (unnumbered) + Text pp. 1–292 + Appendix pp. 293–330 + Index to First Volume 6 pp. (unnumbered) + plan, portrait, and 1 coloured plate.

The coloured plates all bear imprint, "Published [date] for R. Ackermann's Westmr. Abbey at 101 Strand London."

Ackermann's Abbey (*contd.*)

1. To front title. Plan of Westminster Abbey. London Pub. Decr. 1 1812, at R. Ackermann's Repository of Arts 101 Strand (uncoloured).
  (No number, to face ded.) William Vincent D.D. Dean of Westminster Painted by Wm. Owen, R.A. Engraved by Henry Meyer Feb. 4 1812 (uncoloured).
2. p. 1. West Front of Westminster Abbey. A. Pugin delt. J. Bluck sculpt. Augt. 1 1812.

VOL. II.—Half-title as before + Title as before + Text pp. 1–275 (p. 276 blank) (pp. 204–5 are repeated with asterisks) + Index to Second Volume 4 pp. (unnumbered) + 80 coloured aquatint plates with imprint as before.

1. Front. Aymer de Valance, Earl of Pembroke. A. Pugin delt. S. Mitan sculpt. (serving as an engraved title).
2. p. 1 [marked plate 3]. North East View of Westminster Abbey. F. Mackenzie delt. J. Bluck sculpt. Octr. 1 1811.
3. p. 6 [marked plate 4]. Henry Seventh Chapel Shewing two renovated Pinacles. A. Pugin delt. J. Bluck sculpt. May 1 1811.
4. p. 6 [marked plate 12]. Fragments & Parts of the Exterior of Henry the Seventh Chapel, Westminster Abbey. F. Mackenzie delt. T. Sutherland sculpt. Octr. 1 1811.
5. p. 9. Interior view of Westminster Abbey, from the West Gate. F. Mackenzie delt. J. Bluck sculpt. June 1 1811.
6. p. 14. Interior View of Westminster Abbey, looking towards the West Entrance. F. Mackenzie delt. J. Bluck sculpt. July 1 1811.
7. p. 14 [marked plate C]. West Windows, Westminster Abbey. J. White delt. J. Hamble sculpt. 1 July 1812.
8. p. 15 [marked plate 7]. The Choir Westminster Abbey. F. Mackenzie delt. J. Bluck sculpt. Novr. 1 1811.
9. p. 18 [marked plate A]. Mosaic Pavement Before the Altar, Westminster Abbey. White delt. & sculpt. 1 June 1812.
10. p. 24 [marked plate D]. North Window. W. J. White delt. F. C. Lewis sculpt. 1st April 1812.
11. p. 28 [marked plate 16]. West Entrance, Turning to the right—Westminster Abbey. H. Villiers delt. J. Bluck sculpt. Decr. 1 1811.
    (with the monuments of) 1. Captain James Cornwall 2. Rt. Hble. James Craggs 3. Henry Wharton 4. Wm. Congreve 5. John Friend, M.D.
12. p. 28 [marked plate 11]. Fragments & Arches in Westminster Abbey. A. Pugin delt. T. Sutherland sc. Augt. 1 1811.
13. p. 28 [marked plate 15]. Fragments of Ceilings &c. &c. &c. F. Mackenzie delt. T. Sutherland sculpt. 1st Febr. 1812.
14. p. 28. Fragments. Parts. Windows. Pillars &c &c. Westminster Abbey. A. Pugin delt. T. Sutherland sculpt. 1 Decr. 1811.
15. p. 28 [marked plate 13]. Fragments. Windows. Doors &c. Westminster Abbey. A. Pugin delt. T. Sutherland Aquat. Novr. 1 1811.
16. p. 33 [marked plate 17]. 2nd & 3rd Window, South Aisle. H. Villiers delt. J. Bluck sculpt. 1 Jan. 1812.
    (with the monuments of) 6. Admiral Tyrell 7. Ld. Vist. Howe 8. Sir L. Robinson Br. 9. Dr. Thos. Sprat 10. Dr. Js. Wilcocks 11. Dr. Z. Pearce 12. Mrs. K. Bovey 13. Dr. I. Thomas.
17. p. 37 [marked plate 18]. 4th & 5th Window, South Aisle. A. Pugin delt. F. C. Lewis sculpt. 1st March 1812.
    14. General Fleming 15. General Wde 16. Mrs. Ann Fielding 17. John Smith 18. Mrs. Harsnet 19. Col. Davis 20. Robt. Cannon.
18. p. 40 [marked plate 19]. 6th & 7th Window South Aisle. A. Pugin delt. J. Bluck sculpt. 1st April 1812.
    21. Sir I. Chardin Bart. Tablet on the Right Mrs. B. Radley 22. Major André 23. Sir P. Fairborne. 24. Col. R. Townshend 25. Willm. Hargrave 26. Sidney Earl Godolphin 27. Sir C. Harbord & C. Cottrell 28. Diana Temple.
19. p. 45 [marked plate 20]. Entrance into the Choir. West Entrance. T. Uwins delt. J. Bluck sculpt. March 1 1812.

Ackermann's Abbey (*contd.*)

29. Sir Isaac Newton   30. Earl of Stanhope   31. Sir Thos. Hardy   32. John Conduitt Esqr.

20. p. 50 [marked plate 21]. 8th & 9th Window, South Aisle. G. Shepherd delt. F. C. Lewis sculpt. 1 May 1812.
33. John Methuen Esqr. 34. Thos. Knipe 35. G. Stepney Esq. 36. Dr. Is. Watts 37. Martin Folkes 38. Sir R. Bingham 39. Major R. Creed 40. G. Churchill Esqr. 41. Capt. Wm. Julius 42. Genl. Strode.

21. p. 58 [marked plate 22]. 10th Window & Entrance to the Cloister. Thomson delt. J. Bluck sculpt. 1 July 1812.
43. Rear Adml. John Harrison   44. (numbered 45) Mrs. Ann Wemyss 45. (numbered 44) Sophia Fairholm 46. Wm. Dalrymple 47. Sir J. Burland Knt. 48. Sir Cloudesly Shovell 49. Wm. Wragg Esqr.

22. p. 63 [marked plate 23]. South Aisle. G. Shepherd delt. T. Sutherland sculpt. Feb. 1st 1812.
50. Thos. Thynn Esqr. 51. Thos. Owen Esq. 52. Dame Grace Gethin 53. Eliz. & Judith Freke 54. Sir Thos. Richardson. 55. Genl. de Paoli 56. Jas. Kendall Esqr. 57. Wm. Thynne Esqr.

23. p. 66 [marked plate 24]. West Side of Poets Corner. H. Villiers delt. J. Bluck sculpt. June 1 1811.
58. Stepn. Hales D.D. 59. Ed. Wetenhall M.D. 60. Sr. J. Pringle Bart. 61. Sr. Robt. Taylor Knt. 62. J. Ernest Grabbe 63. David Garrick 64. Wm. Outram D.D. 65. Isc. Barrow D.D. 66. Thos. Triplett D.D. 67. Sr. Richd. Coke 68. Isc. Casaubon 69. Wm. Camden.

24. p. 74 [marked plate 25]. West side of Poets Corner. H. Villiers delt. J. Bluck sculpt. Augt. 1 1811.
70. Mrs. My. Hope. 71. Major Genl. Sr. A. Campbell 72. G. F. Handel 73. Rt. Hon. J. S. Mackenzie 74. Sr. E. Atkyns 75. Eliz Dowr. Barons. Lechmere 76. Wm. Anne Villettes 77. Richard Busby D.D. 78. Bishop Duppa 79. Mrs. Christn. Ker 80. Robt. South D.D. 81. Sr. Js. Adols. Oughton.

25. p 89 [marked plate 26]. Entrance into Poets Corner, Westminster Abbey. A. Bugin delt. J. Bluck Aquata. Novr. 1 1811.
82. John Dryden 83. Martha Birch 84. A. Cowley 85. I. Roberts 86. G. Chaucer 87. I. Phillips 88. R. Booth 89. M. Drayton 90. Ben Johnson 91. S. Butler 92. E. Spencer 93. I. Milton 94. Gray 95. C. Anstey.

26. P. 98 [marked plate F]. Poets Corner, Westminster Abbey. J. White delt. J. Bluck sculpt. 1 Sepr. 1812.
96. Thos. Shadwell 97. Willm. Mason 98. Mattw. Prior 99. St. Evremond 100. John Phillips A. John Milton 100. Abm. Cowley.

27. p. 103. South View of Poet's Corner. Pugin & H. Villiers delt. Bluck sculpt. May 1 1811.
101. Mrs. Prichard 102. Shakespeare 103. Thomson 104. Rowe 105. Gay 106. Goldsmith 107. Duke of Argyle 108. Addison.

28. p. 108 [marked plate 9]. North View, across the Transept from Poets Corner, Westminster Abbey. F. Mackenzie delt. J. Bluck sculpt. Septr. 1 1811.

29. p. 109 [marked plate 28]. Chapel of St. Benedict. F. Mackenzie delt. J. Bluck sculpt. July 1 1811.
107. T. Counts. of Hertford 108. Dr. Gabriel Goodman 109. George Sprat 110. Archbp. of Langham 111. Earl and Countess of Middlesex 112. Dr. Wm. Bill.

30. p. 112 [marked plate 29]. East View of St. Edmund's Chapel. A. Pugin delt. J. Bluck sculpt. Septr. 1 1811.
113. Countess of Stafford 114. Earl of Stafford 115. Nicholas Monck 116. Dutchess of Suffolk 117. Francis Hollis 118. Lady K. Knollys 119. Lady Jane Seymour 120. Lady E. Russell 121. Lord John Russell 122. John of Eltham second Son of King Edward the Second 123. Two children of Edward the Third.

31. p. 116 [marked plate 30]. West View of St. Edmund's Chapel. A. Pugin delt. J. Bluck sculpt. June 1 1811.
125. Sr. Barnard Brocas 126. Sir. Richard Pecksall 127. Ed. 8th Earl of Shrewsbury 128. Earl of Pembroke 129. Ed. Lord Herbert 130. Sr. Humphrey Bourchier 131. Robt. de Waldeby 132. Dutchess of Gloucester 133. The Counts. of Stafford 134. Henry Ferne.

Ackermann's Abbey (*contd.*)

32. p. 119 [marked plate 31]. St. Nicholas Chapel Westminster Abbey. F. Mackenzie delt. J. Bluck sculpt. 1 Jany. 1812.
   135. Lady Jane Clifford 136. Anne Duchess of Somerset 137. Sr. George & Lady Fane 138. Lady Burleigh 139. Lady Cecil 140. Sr. Humphrey Stanley 141. Baron Carew 142. Nicholas Bagenall.
   A. Entrance to the Duke of Northumberland Vault. B. Mrs. Amy Blois.

33. p. 121 [marked plate 32]. West View of St. Nicholas Chapel. A. Pugin delt. J. Bluck sculpt. 1 July 1812.
   143. Sir George Villiers 144. Wm. de Dudley 145. Anna Sophia Harley 146. The Marchs. of Winchester 147. Lady Ross 148. The Duchs. of Northumberland 149. Philippa Daughter of Lord Mohun.

34. p. 124. [marked plate 33]. South East Area, Westminster Abbey. F. Mackenzie delt. J. Bluck sculpt. Jany. 1 1812.
   153. King Sebert 154. Richard Tufton 155. Sir Robt. Aiton 156. Grave Stone of the Earl of Middlesex 157. Children of Henry III and Edward I 158. Sir Thos. Ingram.

35. p. 128. [marked plate B]. Interior of King Sebert's Monument. Pugin & Mackenzie delt. J. Bluck sculpt. 1st Feby. 1812.

36. p. 134 [marked plate Q]. Porch of Henry 7th Chapel. Thompson delt. J. Bluck sculpt. 1 Novr. 1812.

37. p. 134 [marked plate 8]. Henry the Seventh Chapel, Westminster Abbey (interior). F. Mackenzie delt. J. Bluck sculpt. Octr. 1 1811.

38. p. 134 [marked plate 10]. Fragments of Henry the Seventh Chapel. Mackenzie delt. Sutherland sculpt. July 1 1811.

39. p. 136 [marked plate 35]. Henry Seventh Monument: Henry Seventh Chapel. Mackenzie delt. Bluck sculpt. May 1 1811.

40. p. 138 [marked plate H]. 162. Interior of Henry the Seventh's Monument. Remaining figures on the Screen of Henry the Seventh's Monument. F. Mackenzie delt. J. Bluck sculpt. 1 June 1812.

41. p. 152 [marked plate 36]. Lewis Stuart, Duke of Richmond Henry the Seventh's Chapel. T. Uwins delt. J. Bluck sculpt. 1 Octr. 1812.

42. p. 153 [marked plate R]. Henry 7th Chapel. T. Uwins delt. J. Bluck sculpt. 1 Decr. 1812.
   164. John Sheffield, Duke of Buckingham.

43. p. 155 [marked plate 37]. George Villiers, Duke of Buckingham. Mackenzie delt. Bluck & Hopwood sculpt. 1 Augt. 1812.

44. p. 157 [marked plate 38]. East End of South Aisle. F. Mackenzie delt. J. Bluck sculpt. Octr. 1 1811.
   166. Lady Walpole 167. Duke of Albemarle 168. Countess of Richmond.

45. p. 159 [marked plate 39]. 169. Queen Elizabeth 170. Mary Queen of Scots. Mackenzie delt. Sutherland Aquat. May 1 1811.

46. p. 163 [marked plate 40]. North Aisle Henry 7th Chapel. Thompson delt. Sutherland sculpt. 1 Novr. 1812.
   171. Mary, Third Daughter of James I 172. Sophia, Fourth Daughter of James I 173. Edward 5th and his Brothers 174. Sir George Savile 175. C. H. Montague.

47. p. 170 [marked plate 41]. West Side of the Chapel of St. Paul. Mackenzie delt. Bluck sculpt. Augt. 1 1811.
   177. Sr. John Buckering Miles Knt. 178. Sr. Js. Fullerton Knt. 179. Sir Thos. Bromley Knt.

48. p. 172 [marked plate 40]. East Side of the Chapel of St. Paul, from an elevated situation. F. Mackenzie del. J. Bluck Aquat. July 1 1811.
   180. Lord Dudley Carleton Viscount of Dorchester 181. Frances Countess of Sussex 182. Lady Anne Cottington and 183. Francis Lord Cottington 184. Lewis Robert Lord Bourchier and his Lady 185. Sir Giles Dawbeney and his Lady 186. Lieut. Gen. Sr. Hy. Bellayse.

49. p. 176 [marked plate 43]. West Side of St. Erasmus Chapel. A. Pugin delt. J. Bluck sculpt. March 1st 1812
   186. George Fascet 187. Mary Kendal 188. Thos. Vaughan 189. Ed. Popham.

Ackermann's Abbey (*contd.*)

50. p. 179. [marked plate 44]. East Side of St. Erasmus's Chapel. F. Mackenzie delt. J. Bluck sculpt. Feby. 1 1812.
    190. Thos. Carey 191. Hugh de Bohun 192. Henry Carey 193. Thos. Cecil Earl of Exeter 194. William of Colchester 195. Thos. Ruthell.

51. p. 183 [marked plate U]. Islip Chapel. F. Mackenzie delt. J. Bluck sculpt. 1 Decr. 1812.
    196. Sir C. Hatton.

52. p. 184 [marked plate P]. The Screen of Abbot Islip's Chapel, and the Entrance to the Chapel of St. Erasmus. F. Mackenzie delt. J. Bluck sculpt. 1 Decr. 1812.
    A. Wm. Barnard, Bishop of Derry. B. Juliana Crewe. C. Lady Jame Crewe.

53. p. 187 [marked plate 45]. Chapel of St. Andrew. A. Pugin delt. J. Bluck sculpt. 1 Novr. 1812.
    c *sic* Earl & Countess of Mountrath 197. Admiral Totty 198. Countess of Kerry A. Lord & Lady Norris from the North Side (second view) Chapel of St. John the Evangelist 199. Sir Geo. Pocock 200. Sir Geo. Holles 201. Sir Francis Vere B. Captn. Cooke.

54. p. 193 [marked plate 46]. Chapel of St. John the Evangelist. Mackenzie delt. Lewis sculpt. 1 Decr. 1812.
    202. The Earl and Counts. of Montrath 203. Susa. Jane Davidson 204. Lord & Lady Norris 205. Dutchess of Somerset 206 Lady Nightingale.

55. p. 194 [marked plate 47]. North Area. T. Uwins delt. J. Bluck sculpt. 1 Septr. 1812.
    207. General Wolfe 208. Lt. Genl. Villettes 209. Genl. Stuart 210. B. J. Forbes and R. G. Forbes 211. R. Kempenfelt A. Sir J. A. Oughton. B. Bishop Duppa.

56. p. 196 [marked plate N]. North East Area. F. Mackenzie delt. J. Bluck sculpt. 1 Augt. 1812.
    212. K. Henry the 3rd A. Lady Anne Cottington. B. Lord Bourchier C. Henry the 3rd.

57. p. 198 [marked plate 49]. North Aisle. H. Villiers delt. Bluck sculpt. June 1 1811.
    213. Admiral Holmes 214. Wm. Pulteney Earl of Bath 215. Lord Ligonier 216. Captain Edward Cooke.

58. p. 200 [marked plate 50]. 218 Edmund Crouchback A. Part of the Screen of Edward the Confessor. F. Mackenzie delt. T. Sutherland Sculpt. Septr. 1 1811.

59. p. 201 [marked plate 51]. 119 Queen Phillipa 120. Queen Eleanor. F. Mackenzie delt. J. Bluck sculpt. 1 June 1812.

60. p. 202 [marked plate L]. Edward the Confessor's Chapel. F. Mackenzie delt. J. Bluck sculpt. 1 Novr. 1812.
    221. De la Tour de Gouvernett 222. Edward 1st Longshanks 223. Elizh. Tudor 224. Margaret A. John Waltham Bishop of Salisbury.

61. p. 204* [marked plate 34]. Richard the Second. Edward the Third. F. Mackenzie delt. J. Bluck sculpt. 1st Dec. 1811.

62. p. 207 [marked plate 53]. The Screen of Edward the Confessor. F. Mackenzie delt. G. Lewis sculpt. March 1 1812.

63. p. 207 [marked plate M]. Edward the Confessor's Monument Edward the Confessor's Chapel. A. Pugin delt. J. Bluck sculpt. May 1 1812.

64. p. 208 [marked plate 52]. Henry the Fifth Chapel. F. Mackenzie delt. J. Bluck sculpt. June 1 1811.

65. p. 210 [marked plate O]. Screen over the Chantry of Henry Vth. F. Mackenzie delt. J. Bluck sculpt. June 1 1811.

66. p. 211 [marked plate E]. East Windows. W. J. White delt. F. C. Lewis sculpt. May 1 1812.

67. p. 213 [marked plate G]. Aveline, First Wife of Edmund Crouchback, Earl of Lancaster, on the North side of the Altar in Westminster Abbey. F. Mackenzie delt. J. Bluck sculpt. 1 April 1812.

68. p. 218 [marked plate 54]. North Cross. A. Pugin delt. J. Hamble sculpt. 1 Sepr. 1812.
    229. Sir Peter Warren 230. Hannah Vincent 231. Adl. Storr 232. Sir Gilbert Lort 233. Grace Scott. A. Clemt. Saunders Esq. 248. Percy Kirk Esq. 249. Ld. Beauclerk 250. John Warren D.D. 251. Sir John Balchen Knt. 252. Genl. Guest.

69. p. 220 [marked plate 55]. North Entrance Westminster Abbey. Mackenzie & H. Villiers delt. Bluck & Williamson sculpt. Novr. 1 1811.
    234. Capts. Manners, Blair & Bayne 235. Earl of Chatham 236. Sr. Chas. Wager 237. Adml. Vernon 238. John Holles, Duke of Newcastle 239. Duke & Dutchs. of Newcastle.

Ackermann's Abbey (contd.)

70. p. 221 [marked plate I]. Lord Chatham. H. Villiers delt. Williamson & Sutherland sculpt. 1 Septr. 1812.

71. p. 225 [marked plate 56]. Duke of Argyle. 240. Lord Mansfield. H. Villiers delt. Williamson & Sutherland sculpt. 1 Decr. 1811.

72. p. 226 [marked plate 57]. North Transept. A. Pugin delt. Hamble sculpt. 1 Novr. 1812.
241. Adml. Charles Watson 242. Sir Willm. Sanderson 243. Earl of Halifax 244. Sir Clifford Wintringham 245. Jonas Hanway 246. Genl. Hope 247. Sir Eyre Coote.

73. p. 237 [marked plate 58]. 253. Richd. Kane 254. Dr. Saml. Bradford 255. Dr. Hugh Boulter 256. Philip de Saumarez Esqr. 257. John Blow 258. Wm. Croft 259. Temple West Esq. 260. Richd. Le Neve Esq. 261. Sir Edmund Prideaux 262. Chs. Williams 263. Dr. Peter Heylin 264. Lord Dunbar. G. Shepherd delt. Josh. Hamble sculpt. 1 June 1812.

74. p. 241 [marked plate 59]. North Aisle. G. Shepherd delt. T. Sutherland sculpt. 1 Aug. 1812.
268. Sir Thos. Duppa 269. Dame Elizh. Carteret 270. Dr. S. Arnold 271. Almericus De Courcy 272. H. Purcell Esqr. 273. Hugh Chamberlen 274. Sir Thos. Heskett 275. Dame Mary James.

75. p. 245 [marked plate 60]. 4th & 5th Window, North Aisle. G. Shepherd delt. F. C. Lewis sculpt. 1 May 1812.
275. Thos. Livingston 276. Ed. De Carteret 277. Philip Carteret 278. Jas Stewart Denham Bart. 279. Henry Priestman 280. John Baker Esqr.

76. p. 247 [marked plate 61]. 6th 7th & 8th Window, North Aisle. W. J. White delt. J. Hamble sculpt. 1 Oct. 1812.
281. R. Mead 282. Rt. and Rd. Cholmondeley 283. Ed. Mansell 284. G. Thornburgh 285. Ed. Herbert 286. Ann Whytell 287. Gideon Loten 288. Thos. Mansell and Wm. Morgan 289. Jane Hill 290. Mary Beaufoy 291. Josiah and John Twysden 292. Thos. Banks. 293. Wm. Levintz 294. Robt. Killigrew 295. Js. Bringfield 296. H. Twisden.

77. p. 254 [marked plate 62]. 9th 10th & 11th Windows North Aisle. J. White delt. J. Bluck sculpt. Octr. 1 1812.
297. Capts. Hervey & Hutt 298. Fred Lake 299. Jno. Woodward 300. Martha Price 301. Anne Counts. of Clanrickard 302. James Egerton 304. Genl. Lawrence 305. Penelope Egerton 306. Sir Godfrey Kneller 307. Wm. Horneck Esqr.

78. p. 256 [marked plate 63]. 303. Capt. Montague. West Entrance. Addison, Poets Corner. T. Uwins delt. Hopwood & Hamble sculpt. Augt. 1812. A. Handel B. Lechmore C. Hales D. Outram.

79. p. 260 [marked plate T]. South East Angle of the Cloisters. Thompson delt. Hamble sculpt. 1 Decr. 1812.

80. p. 263 [marked plate S]. Monuments in the Cloisters viz. 1. Rebecca Broughton 2. Daniel Pulteney. 3. James Mason 4. Mary Peters 1668—— 5. Ann Winchcombe 6. George Walsh Esq. 1747—— 7. Edwd. Tufnel Archt. 8. Ann Palmer 9. Wm. Wollet Engr. 10. Revd. James Field 11. Christr. Chapman & Daughter 12. Elizh. Abrahal 13. Bonnell Thornton. J. White del. T. Sutherland sc. 1 Octr. 1812.

RÉSUMÉ.—83 plates in all (viz. 1 plan and 1 portrait uncoloured, 1 coloured line engraving and 80 coloured aquatint plates), after F. Mackenzie (32 or 33), Mackenzie & Villiers, (1) Mackenzie & Pugin (1), A. Pugin (17 or 16), Pugin & Villiers (1), W. J. White (8), H. Villiers (7), T. Uwins (5), G. Shepherd (5), Thompson (4); by J. Bluck (49), Bluck & Williamson (1), Bluck & Hopwood (1), T. Sutherland (12), Sutherland & Williamson (2), Hamble (6), F. C. Lewis (5), G. Lewis (1), Lewis (no initial) (1), Mitan (1), Hopwood & Hamble (1), White (1).

ISSUES.—There are two issues of Ackermann's " Abbey." The second and most usual issue is as above (see B.M. and V. & A. Mus.), the first issue differs from the above in that the first plate of Vol II Aymer de Valence is marked F. Mackenzie (not Pugin) delt. (see Guildhall Library and West. Abbey Library). The List of Plates also varies, the plates being given in a different order, e.g. plate 28 being listed for p. 23 instead of 108 as above, plates 37 and 38 at p. 168 instead

Ackermann's Abbey (*contd.*)

of 134, and plate 56 at p. 133 instead of 196 &c. in Vol. II, and in Vol. I the portrait of Wm. Vincent is given as facing the half-title.

SIZE.—14¼ × 11½ inches full size. The plate marks average 11¾ × 9¼–9½ inches, and the engraved surface of the plates from 10⅛ × 7¼ inches to 11¾ × 8¼ inches. Watermark—J. Whatman 1808 on plates.

REMARKS.—Issued in paper wrappers in 16 monthly parts and on completion in boards at £15. The text is by W. Combe. Large-paper copies have the portrait of William Vincent on India paper. The finest copy is preserved and may be seen in a glass case in Westminster Abbey; the letterpress is printed on vellum, with all the original drawings mounted and bound in.

3 ACKERMANN (Rudolph)

The History of the Colleges of Winchester, Eton, and Westminster; with the Charter-House, the Schools of St. Paul's, Merchant Taylors, Harrow, and Rugby, and the Free-School of Christ's Hospital. (thick and thin rule) London: Printed for and Published by R. Ackermann, 101, Strand. L. Harrison, Printer, 373, Strand (short rule)

Quarto. 1816

COLLATION.—Title as above (v. blank) + Introduction 1 leaf (iii–iv) + List of Subscribers 1 leaf (v. vi) + Arrangement of the Plates 1 page (v. blank) + Winchester pp. 1–56 with 10 coloured plates.

1. p. 1. Winchester College Entrance, with the Warden's House. W. Westall delt. D. Havell sculpt. Feby. 1 1816.
2. p. 24. Nave of Winchester Cathedral, with William of Wykeham's Tomb. F. Mackenzie delt. D. Havell sculpt. Feby. 1 1816.
3. p. 30. Winchester College, from the Warden's Garden. W. Westall delt. J. C. Stalder sculpt. Jany. 1 1816.
4. p. 31. Winchester College Chapel, From the Great Court. W. Westall delt. J. Bluck sculpt. Feby. 1 1816.
5. p. 32. Cloisters of Winchester College. F. Mackenzie delt. D. Havell sculpt. Jany. 1. 1816.
6. p. 36. Winchester College, from the Meadow. W. Westall delt. J. C. Stadler sculpt. Jany. 1 1816.
7. p. 38. Winchester College Chapel (interior). F. Mackenzie delt. W. Bennett sculpt. Feb. 1 1816.
8. p. 40. Library of Winchester College. F. Mackenzie delt. W. Bennett sculpt. March 1 1816.
9. p. 42. School Room of Winchester College. F. Mackenzie delt. J. Stadler sculpt. March 1 1816.
10. p. 55. Winchester Scholar. T. Uwins delt. J. Agar sculpt. Jany. 1 1816.

+ History of Eton College pp. 1–72 with 10 coloured plates

11. p. 1. Eton College, from the River. W. Westall delt. J. C. Stadler sculpt. March 1 1816.
12. p. 31. Eton College Great Court. W. Westall delt. J. Bluck sculpt. April 1 1816.
13. p. 32. Cloisters of Eton College. W. Westall delt. J. Bluck sculpt. May 1 1816
14. *ibd.* Eton College Chapel. F. Mackenzie delt. J. Stadler sculpt. April 1 1816.
15. p. 33. Ante-Chapel of Eton College. A. Pugin delt. D. Havell sculpt. June 1 1816.
16. p. 34. Eton College Chapel [interior]. F. Mackenzie delt. D. Havell sculpt. May 1 1816.
17. p. 35. Eton School Room. A. Pugin delt. J. Stadler sculpt. May 1 1816.
18. p. 36. Hall of Eton College. A. Pugin delt. J. Stadler sculpt. March 1 1816.
19. p. 37. Eton College Library. F. Mackenzie delt. W. Bennett sculpt. April 1 1816.
20. p. 66. Eton Scholar. T. Uwins delt. J. Agar sculpt. April 1 1816.

+ History of Westminster School pp. 1–27 + 4 coloured plates.

21. p. 8. Westminster Scholar. T. Uwins delt. J. Agar sculpt. Septr. 1 1816.
22. p. 21. Hall of Westminster School. A. Pugin delt. J. Stadler sculpt. Augt. 1 1816.
23. p. 22. Westminster School Room. A. Pugin delt. J. C. Stadler sculpt. Augt. 1 1816.

Ackermann's Public Schools (*contd.*)

24. p. 24. Dormitory of Westminster School. A. Pugin delt. J. Bluck sculpt. Septr. 1 1816.

+ History of Charterhouse pp. 1–32 with 5 coloured plates.

25. p. 21. Charter House, from the Square. W. Westall delt. J. C. Stadler sculpt. July 1 1816.
26. p. 22. Charter House, from the Playground. W. Westall delt. W. Bennett sculpt. July 1 1816.
27. p. 24. Hall of Charter House. A. Pugin delt. D. Havell sculpt. Augt. 1 1816.
28. p. 25. Dr. Fisher's Apartments, Charter House. A. Pugin delt. J. Stadler sculpt. July 1 1816.
29. p. 31. Charter House School Room. A. Pugin delt. J. Bluck sculpt. Decr. 1 1816.

+ History of St. Paul's School pp. 1–34 with 2 coloured plates.

30. p. 1. St. Paul's School. A. Pugin delt. J. Stadler sculpt. Decr. 1 1816.
31. p. 27. The School Room of St. Paul's. F. Mackenzie delt. J. Bluck sculpt. Decr. 1 1816.

+ History of Merchant Taylors' School pp. 1–22 with 2 coloured plates.

32. p. 19. The Merchant Taylors' School Room. A. Pugin delt. J. Stadler sculpt. Decr. 1 1816.
33. p. 20. Examination Room of Merchant Taylors' School. F. Mackenzie delt. D. Havell sculpt. Decr. 1. 1816.

+ History of the Free School of Harrow pp. 1–40 with 5 coloured plates.

34. p. 1. Harrow Church & School, from near the Cricket Grounds. W. Westall delt. J. Stadler sculpt. June 1 1816.
35. p. 2. Interior of Harrow Church. F. Mackenzie delt. J. Stadler sculpt. May 1 1816.
36. p. 16. Harrow School Room. A. Pugin delt. D. Havell sculpt. July 1 1816.
37. p. 17. Harrow School. W. Westall delt. J. Stadler sculpt. June 1 1816.
38. p. 18. First Master's House, Harrow School. F. Mackenzie delt. J. Stadler sculpt. June 1 1816

+ History of Rugby School pp. 1–34 with 5 coloured plates.

39. p. 1. View of Rugby School from the Northampton Road. W. Westall delt. D. Havell sculpt. Novr. 1 1816.
40. p. 14. View of the Southern Schools & Dormitories of Rugby School—from the Playground. W. Westall delt. J. Stadler sculpt. Novr. 1 1816.
41. p. 20. The Head Master's House, Rugby School. W. Westall delt. J. Stadler sculpt. Oct. 1 1816.
42. p. 21. Great School Room of Rugby. J. Gendall delt. D. Havell sculpt. Novr. 1 1816.
43. p. 22. View from the Quadrangle, Rugby School. W. Westall delt. D. Havell sculpt. Novr. 11816.

+ History of Christ's Hospital pp. 1–43 with 5 coloured plates.

44. p. 19. Hall of Christ Hospital. A. Pugin delt. J. Stadler sculpt. Octr. 1 1816.
45. p. 23. Writing School, Christ's Hospital. F. Mackenzie delt. J. Stadler sculpt. Oct. 1 1816.
46. *ibd.* Grammar School of Christ Church. A. Pugin delt. J. Stadler sculpt. Sepr. 1 1816.
47. p. 31. Interior of Christ Church. F. Mackenzie delt. D. Havell sculpt. Septr. 1 1816.
48. p. 32. A Scholar of Christ Hospital. T. Uwins delt. J. Agar sculpt. Oct. 1 1816.

RÉSUMÉ.—48 *coloured engravings (44 being coloured aquatint views and 4 being coloured line engravings of costume), the artists being Westall (15), Mackenzie (14), Pugin (14), Uwins (4), and Gendall (1); the engravers Stadler (22), Havell (12), Bluck (6), Bennett (4), and Agar (4).*

A VARIANT?—I *have seen a copy with 2 titlepages, the words Vol I and Vol. II being printed insertions immediately above the thick and thin rule on the titlepage. As I have only observed a solitary example in this condition, I am inclined to class this as purely the whim of its erstwhile owner. I have also noted copies bound up with a series of mezzotint portraits of the founders, viz. William of Wykeham, Henry VI, Henry VIII, Thomas Sutton, John Colet and Edward VI. These in no wise belong to the book and do not add to its beauty or value.*

REMARKS.—1000 *copies were printed on large wove elephant paper. Originally issued in 12 monthly parts, with 4 plates to each part, the first appearing 1 Jan. 1816. (The work was advertised to appear on 1 Sept. 1815, but publication was delayed till the following year.) The price per part was 12s. each for the first 500 copies and 16s. per part for the remainder. On completion it was issued in quarto boards at 7 guineas or in the parts complete for £7 4s. Fifty copies were printed on large paper at 1 guinea per part and on completion issued in atlas*

8

Ackermann's Public Schools (*contd.*)

quarto for 12 *guineas. Twenty-five copies were printed with the plates uncoloured India proof impressions.*

The text is by Combe with the exception of Winchester, Eton and Harrow, W. H. Pyne writing the descriptive notes to these. Ackermann's " Schools" is more popular than this "Oxford" and "Cambridge" and occurs less frequently for sale, not more than one or two copies appearing each year in the auction rooms on an average. The two states of the first issue, and the second issue are all desirable (see infra).

The various schools also occur separately for sale, with specially printed titles. They are almost invariably late issues.

SIZE.—Printed on large and small paper, the full size of small-paper copies is 14¼ × 11½ *inches. Copies* 13¼ *inches or over may be described as "tall." Large-paper copies measure* 16½ × 13 *inches.*

Plate marks range from 10⅛ × 12 *inches to* 11¾ × 8 *inches, and the average size of the engraved surface of the plates is* 10 × 8 *inches.*

ISSUES.—There are three issues, with two states of the first, in addition to later reprints.

1st Issue, 1st State.—Charterhouse plate 26, p. 22 is lettered "Charter House School from the Playground." It depicts 2 washerwomen with basket laying out linen on the lawn, with 11 *figures on the paths. Westminster, plate 23, p. 22, "Westminster School Room." The masters are bareheaded.*

The watermark is Whatman 1812. *Extraordinarily rare. I have only seen one copy in this state.*

1st Issue, 2nd State.—P. 22, Charter House, is lettered by means of a printed overslip "Charter House from the Playground," the word "School" being omitted. The original lettering, being longer than the printed overslip, was erased by the publisher before the label was applied. The view still depicts the washerwomen.

Plate 23, p. 22, "Westminster School Room." The masters bareheaded. Watermark Whatman 1812. *Also very rare. Copies in Guildhall and in H. Harvey Frost Esq.'s collection.*

2nd Issue.—P. 22, "Charter House from the Playground." The plate is entirely changed, the original foreground being cut away and a view of 13 boys and masters playing cricket, with 13 figures in the paths, taking the place of the washerwomen. The lettering under the plate is, of course, printed direct with no overslip.

P. 22, Westminster School Room as before, the masters bareheaded.

3rd Issue.—The plate p. 22, Charter House as before; that is, with the boys playing cricket.

Plate p. 23, "Westminster School Room." This plate is reworked, hats have been added to the masters' heads, and the fine lighting of the plate in the first state is destroyed by rebiting the names on the right-hand wall to make them stand out clearly (in the first state these names, being under or at the side of the windows, are left in the shadow, the full light being thrown against the opposite wall). This second state of the plate is definitely inferior.

Plate 6, p. 36, Winchester College, from the Meadow also exists in two states, the first dated Jan. 1st 1815 and second dated Jany. 1 1816.

Later Issues.—The plates were reissued at various times. I have seen copies with the watermarks as late as 1827.

4 ACKERMANN (R.)

A History of the University of Cambridge, its Colleges, Halls, and Public Buildings (thick and thin rule) In Two Volumes. Vol. I [II] (thick and thin rule) London: Printed for R. Ackermann, 101, Strand, by L. Harrison and J. C. Leigh, 373, Strand (short rule)

Ackermann's Cambridge (*contd.*)

2 vols.   Quarto.   1815

COLLATION VOL. I.—Half-title, "A History of the University of Cambridge, &c. &c. &c. (swelled rule) Vol. I" [II] (v. blank) + Title as above (v. blank) + Dedication to Duke of Gloucester 1 p. (v. blank) + Introduction 2 pp. (vii–viii) + List of Subscribers 4 pp. (ix–xii) + List of Plates to both vols. 2 pp. (unnumbered) + pp. 1–296 + Index to First Volume 3 ll. + 26 coloured plates.

Each plate bears imprint, "London Pub. [date] at 101 Strand, for R. Ackermann's History of Cambridge."

1. Frontispiece.   Cambridge from the Ely Road.   Wm. Westall delt.   J. C. Stadler sculpt.   March 1 1815.

    face dedication (Portrait of) His Royal Highness the Dule of Gloucester, Chancellor of the University of Cambridge.   Drawn by R. W. Satchwell from a Painting by J. Opie, R.A.   Engraved by Henry Meyer.   Decr. 1 1815.

  p.   1. Hugh de Balsham, Founder of St. Peter's College.

2. p.   2. Part of St. Peter's College from the Private Garden.   W. Westall delt.   J. Stadler sculpt. Augt. 1 1815.

3. p.   9. Court of Peter House.   F. Mackenzie delt.   J. C. Stadler sculpt.   Feby. 1 1815.

4. p. 10. Chapel of St. Peter's College.   A. Pugin delt.   D. Havell sculpt.   Novr. 1 1815.

5. p. 12. St. Peter's College.   A. Pugin delt.   J. C. Stadler sculpt.   June 1 1814.

  p. 27. Elizabeth de Clare, Foundress of Clare Hall.

6. p. 34. Clare Hall.   A. Pugin delt.   J. Bluck sculpt.   July 1 1814.

7. p. 35. Clare Hall Chapel.   F. Mackenzie delt.   J. Stadler sculpt.   Aug. 1 1815.

8. p. 36. Entrance to the Avenue, from Clare Hall Piece, with the New Buildings of King's.   W. Westall delt.   J. Stadler sculpt.   Jany. 1 1815.

  p. 51. Mary Countess of Pembroke, Foundress of Pembroke College.

9. p. 52. Pembroke Hall &c. from a window at Peterhouse.   F. Mackenzie delt.   J. C. Stadler sculpt. Oct. 1 1814.

10. p. 56. Pembroke College.   A. Pugin delt.   J. Stadler sculpt.   May 1 1814.

  p. 81. John Caius, Founder of Caius College.

11. p. 82. Caius College.   A. Pugin delt.   D. Havell sculpt.   Augt. 1 1814.

12. p. 92. Chapel of Caius College.   F. Mackenzie delt.   J. Stadler sculpt.   Octr. 1 1815.

  p. 119. William Bateman, Bishop of Norwich, Founder of Trinity Hall.

13. p. 131. Front of Trinity Hall.   A. Pugin delt.   J. C. Stadler sculpt.   March 1 1815.

  p. 155. Henry Duke of Lancaster, Founder of Corpus Christi or Benett's College.

14. p. 170. Chapel of Benet College.   W. Westall delt.   D. Havell delt (*sic*).   April 1 1815.

  p. 195. King Henry VI.   Founder of King's College.

15. p. 196. Plan & Section of the Roof of King's College Chapel.   F. Mackenzie delt.   J. Bluck sculpt. Aug. 1 1815.

16. p. 197. Chapel of King's College [Interior].   A. Pugin delt.   J. C. Stadler sculpt.   Dec. 1 1815.

17. p. 198. The Choir, King's Chapel.   F. Mackenzie delt.   J. C. Stadler sculpt.   Sept. 1 1815.

18. p. 199. West Entrance to King's College Chapel.   F. Mackenzie delt.   J. C. Stadler sculpt.   Dec. 1 1815.

19. p. 200. South Porch of King's College Chapel.   A. Pugin delt.   J. Bluck sculpt.   May 1 1814.

20. p. 203. South Side of King's College Chapel.   F. Mackenzie delt.   D. Havell sculpt.   Decr. 1 1815.

21. p. 204. West End of King's College Chapel.   F. Mackenzie delt.   D. Havell sculpt.   March 1 1815.

22. p. 205. Court of King's College.   F. Mackenzie delt.   D. Havell sculpt.   Septr. 1 1814.

  p. 243. Margaret, Wife of King Henry VI, Foundress of Queen's College.

23. p. 244. Queen's College.   W. Westall delt.   J. C. Stadler sculpt.   July 1st 1814.

24. p. 250. Queen's College from the Private Walk.   W. Westall delt.   J. Bluck sculpt.   Decr. 1 1814.

25. p. 252. Hall of Queen's College.   A. Pugin delt.   J. Bluck sculpt.   April 1 1815.

  p. 277. Robert Woodlark, Founder of Catharine Hall.

26. p. 282. Chapel of Catharine Hall.   F. Mackenzie delt.   J. Bluck sculpt.   Novr. 1 1815.

VOL. II.—Half-title as before + Title as before + pp. 1–324 + Index to Second Volume 4 ll. (unnumbered) + 53 coloured plates.

Ackermann's Cambridge (*contd.*)

27. Frontispiece. Colonnade under Trinity Library. W. Westall delt. J. Stadler sculpt. May 1 1815.
    p.   1. John Alcock, Founder of Jesus College.
28. p.   10. Jesus College, from the Close. W. Westall delt. J. Stadler sculpt. Aug. 1 1814.
29. p.   12. Ante Chapel of Jesus College. F. Mackenzie delt. J. Bluck sculpt. Novr. 1 1814.
    p.   45. Margaret Countess of Richmond, Foundress of Christ College.
30. p.   49. Christ College, from the Street. W. Westall delt. J. Bluck sculpt. June 1 1815.
31. p.   50. Chapel of Christ College. A. Pugin delt. J. C. Stadler sculpt. Oct. 1 1815.
    p.   79. Margaret, Countess of Richmond, Foundress of St. John's College (the portrait the same as that at p. 45 but with a different background).
32. p.   81. Second Court of St. John's College. W. Westall delt. J. C. Stadler sculpt. Novr. 1 1814.
33. p.   83. St. John's College, from Fisher's Lane. W. Westall delt. J. C. Stadler sculpt. Octr. 1 1814.
34. p.   91. Chapel of St. John's College. F. Mackenzie delt. J. C. Stadler sculpt. Septr. 1 1815.
35. p.   91. St. John's Library. W. Westall delt. D. Havell sculpt. Septr. 1 1815.
36. p.   92. St. John's College, from the Gardens. F. Mackenzie delt. R. Reeve sculpt. Augt. 1 1814.
    p. 147. Edward Stafford, Duke of Buckingham, Founder of Magdalen College.
37. p. 151. Chapel of Magdalen College. F. Mackenzie delt. J. Bluck sculpt. Novr. 1 1815.
38. p. 152. Magdalen College Library. W. Westall delt. J. Stadler sculpt. Aug. 1 1815.
    p. 169. King Henry VIII, Founder of Trinity College.
39. p. 176. Trinity Gate. W. Westall delt. J. Stadler sculpt. April 1 1815.
40. p. 180. Hall of Trinity College. A. Pugin delt. J. Bluck sculpt. Jany. 1 1815.
41. p. 181. Quadrangle of Trinity College. W. Westall delt. J. Bluck sculpt. May 1 1815.
42. p. 182. Chapel of Trinity College. F. Mackenzie delt. J. Bluck sculpt. Septr. 1 1814.
43. p. 183. Kitchin of Trinity College. W. H. Pyne delt. J. C. Stadler sculpt. Septr. 1 1815.
44. p. 184. Library of Trinity College (Interior). A. Pugin delt. D. Havell sculpt. Decr. 1 1814.
45. p. 185. Trinity College Bridge. W. Westall delt. J. Stadler sculpt. July 1 1815.
46. p. 190. Trinity Library from St. John's Gardens. W. Westall delt. J. Stadler sculpt. Augt. 1 1814.
    p. 227. Sir Walter Mildmay, Founder of Emmanuel College.
47. p. 228. Emanuel College. F. Mackenzie delt. J. C. Stadler sculpt. June 1 1814.
48. p. 232. Front of Emanuel College. A. Pugin delt. J. C. Stadler sculpt. May 1 1815.
49. p. 235. Chapel of Emanuel College. A. Pugin delt. J. C. Stadler sculpt. June 1815.
50. p. 236. Hall of Emanuel College. A. Pugin delt. J. Bluck sculpt. Feby. 1 1815.
    p. 261. Frances Sidney, Countess of Sussex, Foundress of Sidney College.
51. p. 268. Hall of Sidney College. A. Pugin delt. D. Havell sculpt. Jany. 1 1815.
52. p. 283. Downing College. W. Westall delt. D. Havell sculpt. Decr. 1 1814.
53. p. 289. Law School. F. Mackenzie delt. J. C. Stadler sculpt. Augt. 1 1814.
54. p. 290. Theatre of Anatomy. A. Pugin delt. J. C. Stadler sculpt. Novr. 1 1815.
55. p. 291. [Exterior of] Public Library & Senate House. F. Mackenzie delt. J. Stadler sculpt. July 1 1814.
56. p. 292. [Interior of] Public Library. F. Mackenzie delt. Dl. Havell sculpt. June 1 1814.
57. p. 293. Senate House [Interior]. A. Pugin delt. D. Havell sculpt. Feby. 1 1815.
58. p. 294. [Exterior of] St Mary's Church. A. Pugin delt. D. Havell sculpt. June 1 1815.
59. p. 296. Interior of St. Mary's Church. W. Westall delt. J. Stadler sculpt. July 1 1815.
60. p. 297. Botanic Garden. W. Westall delt. J. Stadler sculpt. July 1 1815.
61. p. 312. Doctor in Divinity in the ermined robe, or cope. T. Uwins delt. J. Agar sculpt. Dec. 1st 1814.
62. *ibd.*   Doctor in Divinity, in the Scarlet Gown. T. Uwins delt. J. Agar sculpt. Jany 1 1815.
63. *ibd.*   Doctor in Law or Physic, in Congregation Robes. T. Uwins delt. J. Agar sculpt. Novr. 1 1814.
64. *ibd.*   Doctor in Physic. T. Uwins delt. J. Agar sculpt. Septr. 1 1814.
65. p. 313. Doctor in Music. T. Uwins delt. J. Agar sculpt. Feby. 1 1815.
66. *ibd.*   Master of Arts, of the Non Regent, or Lower House. T. Uwins delt. J. Agar sculpt. June 1 1814.
67. *ibd.*   Bachelor of Arts. T. Uwins delt. J. Agar sculpt. May 1 1814.
68. *ibd.*   Nobleman. T. Uwins delt. J. Agar sculpt. March 1 1815.
69. *ibd.*   Fellow Commoner. T. Uwins delt. J. Agar sculpt. July 1 1814.

Ackermann's Cambridge (*contd.*)

70. *ibd.*   Pensioner. T. Uwins delt. J. Agar sculpt. Octr. 1 1814.
71. *ibd.*   Proctor. T. Uwins delt. J. Agar sculpt. April 1 1815.
72. p. 314. Pensioner of Trinity Hall.—Common Dress of the Doctor in Law, & Doctor in Physic. T. Uwins delt. J. Agar sculpt. July 1 1815.
73. *ibd.*   Fellow Commoner of Emanuel College. Nobleman. Fellow Commoner of Trinity College. T. Uwins delt. J. Agar sculpt. May 1 1815.
74. *ibd.*   Pensioner of Trinity College.—Master of Arts with the hood squared. Sizar. Master of Arts, of the Regent, or Upper House. T. Uwins delt. J. Agar sculpt. June 1 1815.
75. *ibd.*   Doctor in Divinity in his Ordinary Dress. Doctor in Divinity in the Surplice. Esquire Beadle. Yeoman Beadle. T. Uwins delt. J. Agar sculpt. Oct. 1 1815.
76. p. 316. [Exterior of] St. Sepulchres The Round Church. A. Pugin delt. J. Hill sculpt. May 1 1814.
77. *ibd.*   [Interior of] St. Sepulchres, The Round Church. A. Pugin delt. J. Hill sculpt. Novr. 1 1814.
78. p. 317. Trinity Church. A. Pugin delt. D. Havell sculpt. Octr. 1815.
79. p. 318. Prison and Castle, from the Huntingdon Road. W. Westall delt. J. C. Stadler sculpt. Oct. 1 1814.

RÉSUMÉ.—*Portrait of Duke of Gloucester and 79 coloured aquatint plates by Pugin (22), Westall (20), Mackenzie (20), Uwins (15), and Pyne (1); engraved by Stadler (34), Havell (14), Agar (15), Bluck (13), Hill (2), Reeve (1). In addition some copies have the series of 16 portraits of the Founders.*

SIZE.—*Issued in two ways with the Founders of the colleges and without. On large paper 16½ × 13 inches and on small paper 14 × 11½ inches. Size of plate marks 10 × 11¾ inches, and of engraved surface of the plates 8 × 10½ inches average. Watermark J. Whatman 1811.*

ISSUES.—*I have discovered no essential differences in the various copies I have examined. There is a variant in plate 56, p. 292, [Interior of the] "Public Library," the engraver's Christian name "Dl." being omitted. This I have only observed in large-paper copies [B.M. King's Library]. There are, however, later issues of the plates, with watermarks posterior to the date of publication [Guildhall Lib. Watermarks 1825].*

REMARKS.—*1000 copies were printed on large wove elephant paper, in 20 monthly parts, the first appearing 1 May 1814. The first 500 parts were sold at 12s. per part, the remainder at 16s. per part. A series of portraits of the Founders was printed separately to be bound up with the work if so desired. On completion the work was issued in 2 vols. elephant quarto in boards for £16, 50 copies being on large paper atlas quarto for £27, 25 India paper proofs. The plates of the Founders were optional, and though copies with these portraits naturally fetch a higher price, in my purely personal opinion I do not think they harmonise well with the other plates, and I find copies without the Founders most desirable: the visual pleasure given by the beautiful aquatint views is not interrupted by the inferior rendering of the portraits. This, of course, does not apply to the 15 costume plates which form an integral part of the book. Large-paper copies are the finest but are very difficult to procure; they gave a gloss, an incomparably rich glow absent from small-paper copies, fine as the latter are in early impressions; their text is also on thick Whatman paper and the portrait of the Duke of Gloucester on India paper. Ackermann's "Cambridge" occurs less frequently for sale than the "Oxford."*

The finest example of Ackermann's "Cambridge" I have seen is a copy in original parts with the Founders also in original wrappers in the possession of H. Harvey Frost, Esq. I am indebted to his courtesy for the following particulars.

Size 14½ × 11¾ inches, 20 monthly parts in yellow buff paper wrappers.

Part 1, p. 1 of wrappers depicts an architectural doorway design, with the title of the work on the door, p. 2 Advertisement of the Microcosm, Westminster Abbey, Poetical Illustrations, Blair's Grave, Antiquities of York &c., p. 3 of wrappers advertisement of Ackermann's "Oxford," p. 4 of wrappers ditto "Cambridge."

Ackermann's Cambridge (*contd.*)

pp. 1–24 and 4 plates, S. Porch King's College Chapel, Pembroke College, St. Sepulchres, Bachelor of Arts, May 1 1814.

Part 2. No change in wrappers.

pp. 25–48 & 4 plates, Masters of Arts, St. Peter's College, Public Library, Emanuel College, June 1 1814.

Part 3. No change in wrappers.

pp. 49–72 & 5 plates, Law School (dated Aug. 1 1814), Clare Hall, Queen's College, Public Library, Fellow Commoner, July 1 1814.

Part 4. No change in wrappers.

pp. 73–104 & 4 plates, Jesus College, St. John's College, Trinity Library, Caius College, Aug. 1 1814.

Part 5. No change in wrappers.

pp. 105–136 & 3 plates Doctor in Physic, Chapel of Trinity College, Court of King's College, Sept. 1 1814.

Part 6, p. 1 of wrappers as before, p. 2 blank, p. 3 advert. of "Cambridge," p. 4 advert. of Historical Sketches of Russia, Portraits of Illustrious Visitors and Repository Vol. II.

pp. 137–160 & 4 plates, Pensioner, Prison & Castle, Pembroke Hall, St John's College from Fisher's Lane, Oct. 1 1814.

Part 7, p. 1 of wrappers as before, p. 2 Advert. of "Oxford," pp. 3 & 4 as in part 6.

pp. 161–184 and 4 plates, Court of St. John's College, Dr in Law or Physic, St. Sepulchres (int), Antechapel Jesus College, No. 1 1814.

Part 8. No change from part 7 in wrappers.

pp. 185–216 & 4 plates, Doctor of Divinity, Downing College, Library of Trinity College, Queen's College from Private Walk, Dec. 1 1814.

Part 9, p. 1 of wrappers as before, p. 2 advert. of Microcosm &c. as in part 1, p. 3 advert. of proposed issue of portraits of the Founders of the Oxford Colleges and advert. of the volumes on Cambridge, p. 4 advert. for Ackermann's Schools—to be published 13th Sept. 1815.

Part 10. No change from part 9 in wrappers.

pp. 241–264 & 4 plates, Doctor in Music, Court of Peter House, Senate House, Hall of Emanuel College, Feb. 1 1815.

Part 11. No change from part 9 in wrappers.

pp. 265–296 & 4 plates, Nobleman, W. End King's College Chapel, Front Trinity Hall, Cambridge from Ely Road, March 1 1815.

Part 12, p. 1 of wrappers as before, p. 2 Advert. of Costume of Yorks., 12 views of Moscow, New Drawing Book . . . and Young's Portraits of the Emperors of Turkey, p. 3 as in part 9 but with advert. of Abbey and Illusts. of H.R.H. Princess Eliza added, p. 4 as in part 9 but with advert. of Ackermann's superficial water colours added.

pp. 1–32 & 4 plates, Proctor, Hall of Queen's College, Chapel of Benet College, Trinity Gate, April 1 1815.

Part 13. No change from part 12 in wrappers.

pp. 33–56 & 5 plates, Fellow Comm. Emanuel College, Trinity College, Colonnade Trinity Library, Front of Emanuel College, Quadrangle of Trinity College, May 1 1815.

Part 14, p. 2 of wrapper blank, otherwise no change.

pp. 57–88 & 4 plates, Pensioner of Trinity College &c. St. Mary's Church, Chapel of Emanuel College, Christ College from Street, June 1 1815.

Part 15. No change from part 14 in wrappers.

pp. 89–120 & 4 plates, Pensioner of Trinity Hall &c., Botanic Garden, Int. of St. Mary's Church, Trinity College Bridge, July 1 1815.

Part 16, p. 1 of wrapper as before, p. 2 as in part 12, no change in pp. 3 & 4.

pp. 121–152 & 4 plates, Clare Hall Chapel, Magdalen College Library, Roof King's College, Part St. Peter's College, Aug. 1 1815.

Part 17. No change from part 16 in wrappers.

pp. 153–184 & 4 plates, Kitchen of Trinity College, St. John's Library, Chapel of St. John's College, Choir King's Chapel, Sept. 1 1815.

Part 18. No change from part 16 in wrappers.

pp. 185–216 & 4 plates, Doctor in Divinity &c., Trinity Church, Chapel of Christ College, Chapel of Caius College, Oct. 1 1815.

Ackermann's Cambridge (*contd.*)

Part 19, p. 1 of wrappers as before, p. 2 advert. of Young's Turkish Portraits replaced by advert. of Portrait of Blucher, 6th edn. of Syntax Tour &c., p. 3 as in part 12, p. 4 advert. for proposed publication of a series of "Founders" for Ackermann's Cambridge and advert. for Ackermann's Schools, the date for publication being altered to Jan. 1 1816.

    pp. 217–248 & 4 plates, Chapel of Catherine Hall, Chapel of St. Peter's College, Theatre of Anatomy, Chapel Magdalen College, Nov. 1 1815.

Part 20. No change from part 19 in wrappers.

    pp. 249–324 + Half-title to Vol. I. Title to Vol. I, Portrait of Duke of Gloucester, Dedication 1 lf., Intro. 1 lf., Index Vol. I. 3 ll. Arrangements of the Plates 1 lf. + Half-title to Vol. II + Title to Vol. II + Index to Vol. II 4 ll. and 3 plates, South Side King's College Chapel, W. Entrance ditto, Chapel of King's College.

FOUNDERS.—A Series of Portraits of those Distinguished Persons who were the Founders of Colleges and Public Buildings in the University of Cambridge from Pictures in that University (thick and thin rule) London: Published January 1st 1816, by R. Ackermann, Repository of Arts, 101, Strand; and to be had of all the Book and Printsellers in the United Kingdom.

  Issued in printed paper wrappers at £2 to subscribers and £3 for large-paper copies.

    P. 1 of wrappers as above, pp. 2, 3 and 4 as in part 19 of "Cambridge," a 2 pp. printed slip advertising Ackermann's "Schools" and Founders of Cambridge and 16 portraits.

Hugh de Balsham.	Robert Woodlark.
Elizabeth de Clare.	John Alcock.
Mary Countess of Pembroke.	Margaret Countess of Richmond.
Henry Duke of Lancaster.	ditto. different background.
Wm. Bateman, Bishop of Norwich.	Edward Stafford, Duke of Buckingham.
John Caius.	King Henry VIII.
King Henry VI.	Sir Walter Mildmay.
Margaret wife of King Henry VI.	Frances Sidney, Countess of Sussex.

  Fine copies with brilliant early impressions of the plates, free from "foxmarks" and "offset," are rarities, especially if on large paper, with early watermark.

5 ACKERMANN (Rudolph)

A History of the University of Oxford, its Colleges, Halls and Public Buildings (thick and thin rule) In Two Volumes. Vol. I [II] (thick and thin rule) London: Printed for R. Ackermann, 101, Strand, By L. Harrison and J. C. Leigh, 373, Strand (short rule)

2 vols. Quarto.   1814

  COLLATION VOL. I.—Half-title, "A History of the University of Oxford, &c. &c. &c. (swelled rule) Vol. I" [II] (v. blank) + Title as above (v. blank) + Dedication to William Wyndham Grenville Lord Grenville 1 p. (v. blank) + Introduction 2 pp. (vii–viii) + List of Subscribers 6 pp. (ix–xiv) + Arrangement of the Plates to both vols. 2 pp. (unnumbered) + pp. i–xxv (xxvi blank) + pp. 1–275 (p. 276 blank) + Index to First Volume 6 pp. (unnumbered) + portrait + 30 coloured aquatint plates.

  Each plate bears imprint, "London Pubd. [date] at 101 Strand for R. Ackermann's History of Oxford."

   1. Frontispiece. View of Oxford taken from New College Tower. W. Westall delt. J. Bluck sculpt. Sept. 1 1814.

   Face Dedication. Stipple portrait, The Right Honourable William Wyndham Grenville, Lord Granville, Chancellor of the University of Oxford. Willm. Owen Esqr. R.A. pinxt. Henry Meyer sculpt. November 21 1814 (uncoloured).

Ackermann's Oxford (*contd.*)

2. p.   i [or page ii]. Hight Street, Looking West. A. Pugin delt. J. Bluck sculpt. Oct. 1 1814.

3. p.   iii [or page i]. Entrance to Oxford, from the London Road. F. Nash delt. F. C. Lewis sculpt. June 1 1813.

4. *ibd.*   [or vol. II, p. 243]. Porch of St. Mary's Church. A. Pugin delt. D. Havell sculpt. Novr. 1814.   } together on
          Stair Case of Christ Church. A. Pugin delt. D. Havell sculpt. Novr. 1814. } 1 plate.

5. *ibd.*   [or vol. II, p. 242]. St. Mary's Church, taken from the top of Radcliffe Library. F. Nash delt. F. C. Lewis sculpt. 1st Novr. 1813.

6. p.   x. The Old Tower. A. Pugin delt. J. Bluck sculpt. March 1 1814.

7. p. xiii. St. Aldate's from Carfax. A. Pugin delt. J. Hill sculpt. Novr. 1st 1813.

8. p.   xv. St. Peter's Church. A. Pugin delt. R. Reeve sculpt. July 1 1814.

9. *ibd.*   Crypt of St. Peter's Church. F. Nash delt. J. Bluck sculpt. July 1 1813.

   p.   1. Walter de Merton, Bishop of Rochester, Founder of Merton College.

10. p.   1 [or page 10]. Merton College, North Window of the Ante Chapel. A. Pugin delt. T. Sutherland sculpt. May 1 1813.

11. p.   9. Merton Chapel. A. Pugin delt. J. Bluck sculpt. 1 May 1813.

12. p. 12 [or page 11]. Magpie Lane. A. Pugin delt. J. Bluck sculpt. Augt. 1 1813.

   p. 25. King Alfred, Founder of University College.

13. p. 25. University & Queen's Colleges, High Street. Pugin delt. J. Hill sculpt. June 1 1813.

14. p. 39. Hall of University College. A. Pugin delt. J. Hill sculpt. Jany. 1 1814.

   p. 51. John Baliol, Cofounder with Devorguilla his Wife of Baliol College.

   p. 52. Devorguilla Baliol, Cofounder with John Baliol of Baliol College.

15. p. 61. Quadrangle of Balliol College. F. Mackenzie delt. J. Bluck sculpt. Augt. 1 1814.

   p. 73. Walter Stapledon, Founder of Exeter College.

16. p. 81. Hall of Exeter College. A. Pugin delt. J. Bluck sculpt. March 1 1814.

   p. 93. King Edward IInd, Founder of Oriel College.

17. p. 93 [or page 98]. Oriel College. F. Nash delt. F. C. Lewis. sculpt. Decr. 1 1813.

   p. 109. Robert Egglesfield, Founder of Queen's College.

   p. 123. Sir Joseph Williamson Knt. Found of the present Edifice of Queen's College.

18. p. 125. Queen's College Chapel. A. Pugin delt. J. C. Stadler sculpt. Octr. 1 1814.

   p. 135. William of Wykeham, Bishop of Winchester, Founder of New College.

19. p. 156. New College, Entrance Gate. A. Pugin delt. J. Hill sc. Novr. 1 1814.   } together on
          Magdalen College Entrance Gate. A. Pugin delt. D. Havell sculpt. Nov. 1 1814. } 1 plate.

20. p. 159. Chapel of New College. F. Mackenzie delt. J. C. Stadler sculpt. Dec. 1 1814.

21. p. 162. Window of New College Chapel. Designed by Sir J. Reynolds. Painted on Glass by Jervas. Engraved by G. Lewis. June 1 1814.

   p. 175. Richard Flemming, Bishop of Lincoln, Founder of Lincoln College.

   p. 178. Thomas Rotheram, Cofounder with Richd. Flemming, of Lincoln College.

22. p. 186. Chapel of Lincoln College, from the Ante Chapel. F. Mackenzie delt. G. Lewis sculpt. Jany. 1 1814.

   p. 195. Henry Chichely, Archbishop of Canterbury, Founder of All Souls College.

23. p. 210 [or page 209]. All Souls, taken from the top of the Radcliffe Library. A. Pugin delt. J. Bluck sculpt. Jany. 1 1814.

24. p. 215. Library of All Souls College. A. Pugin delt. J. Bluck sculpt. 1 June 1814.

25. p. 218. Chapel of All Souls College. F. Mackenzie delt. J. C. Stadler sculpt. Decr. 1 1814.

   p. 233. Willm. Patten of Wainfleet, Bishop of Winchester, Founder of Magdalen College.

26. p. 24 [sometimes misplaced p. 156]. Old Gate of Magdalen College. A. Pugin delt. J. Bluck sculpt. Septr. 1 1814. (This plate is lettered by means of a small slip pasted over the original lettering which reads New College Entrance Gate.)

27. p. 248. Cloister of Magdalen College. A. Pugin delt. J. Bluck sculpt. Feby. 1 1814.

28. p. 250. Magdalen Tower. F. Nash delt. G. Lewis sculpt. Agut. 1 1814.

29. p. 258. Chapel of Magdalen College. A. Pugin delt. G. Lewis sculpt. April 1 1814.

30. p. 261. West Entrance to the Chapel of Magdalen College. F. Mackenzie delt. D. Havell sculpt. Nov. 1 1814.

VOL. II.—Half-title as before (changing Vol. I to Vol. II) + Title as in Vol. I (changing

Ackermann's Oxford (*contd.*)

Vol. I to Vol. II) + pp. 1–262 + Index to second volume 6 pp. (unnumbered) + 51 coloured aquatint and stipple plates.   Each plate bearing imprint as in Vol. I.

31. Frontispiece. View of Oxford, from the Gallery in the Observatory.   W. Turner delt.   J. Bluck sculpt. July 1st 1814.

p.   1. William Smith, Cofounder with Richard Sutton, of Brazen Nose College.

p.   2. Richard Sutton Knt.   Cofounder of Brazen Nose College.

32. p.   1 [or page 25].   Brazen-Nose College & Radcliffe Library.   A. Pugin delt.   J. Bluck sculpt. Feby. 1 1814.

33. p.   25. [or page 26].   Brazen-Nose College, Part of the Schools &c. taken from the top of Radcliffe Library.   F. Mackenzie delt.   J. Hill aquat.   Aug. 1 1813.

p.   35 Richard Fox, Bishop of Winchester, Founder of Corpus Christi College.

34. p.   35 [or page 44].   Corpus Christi College and Christ Church Cathedral.   W. Westall delt.   J. C. Stadler sculpt.   May 1 1814.

35. p.   55 [or page 58].   Chapter House.   Mackenzie delt.   J. Bluck sculpt.   Novr. 1 1814.

p.   55. Cardinal Wolsey, Founder of Christ Church College.

p.   57. King Henry 8th, Cofounder with Cardinal Wolsey, of Christ Church College.

36. p.   72. Part of Christ Church Cathedral.   W. Westall delt.   W. Bennett sculpt.   June 1 1814.

37. p.   74. Choir of the Cathedral.   F. Nash delt.   F. C. Lewis sculpt.   Oct. 1 1813.

38. p.   76. The Kitchen at Christ Church.   A. Pugin delt.   F. C. Lewis sculpt.   Dec. 1 1813.

39. p.   78. Gate of Christ Church—from Pembroke College.   F. Mackenzie delt.   J. Reeves sculpt. May 1 1814.

40. p.   80. Hall of Christ Church.   A. Pugin delt.   J. Bluck sculpt.   Augt. 1 1814.

41. p.   82. Library of Christ Church.   F. Mackenzie delt.   J. C. Stadler sculpt.   Decr. 1 1814.

42. p.   85. Christ Church Library, Peckwater.   F. Mackenzie delt.   F. C. Lewis sculpt.   May 1 1813.

p. 101. Sr. Thomas Pope Knt.   Founder of Trinity College.

43. p. 115. Trinity College Chapel.   A. Pugin delt.   J. Bluck sculpt.   Septr. 1 1813.

p. 121. Sir Thomas White, Founder of St. John's College.

44. p. 121 [or page 130].   St. John's College, from the Garden.   F. Mackenzie delt.   J. Hill sculpt. Sept. 1st 1813.

45. p. 130 [or page 129].   Quadrangle of St. John's College.   A. Pugin delt.   J. Hill sculpt.   Octr. 1 1813.

p. 141. Queen Elizabeth, Founder of Jesus College.

46. p. 149. Jesus College Chapel.   W. Westall delt.   W. Bennett sculpt.   Octr. 1 1814.

p. 155. Nicholas Wadham, Founder of Wadham College.

p. 156. Dorothy Wadham, Foundress of Wadham College.

47. p. 161. Wadham College, from the Parks.   A. Pugin delt.   J. Hill sculpt.   Novr. 1 1813.

48. p. 163. Wadham College Chapel.   F. Mackenzie delt.   J. Bluck sculpt.   July 1 1813.

p. 169. Thomas Tesdale, Cofounder of Pembroke College.

p. 170. Richd. Wightwick S.T.B. Cofounder of Pembroke College.

p. 179. Sir Thomas Cookes, Founder of Worcester College.

49. p. 179 [or page 184].   Worcester College.   W. Westall delt.   J. Stadler sculpt.   Septr. 1814.

50. p. 189 [or page 173].   Hertford College (on left-hand side of plate).   W. Westall delt. ⎱ together on 1 plate.

Pembroke College (on right-hand side)   J. C. Stadler sculpt.   May 1 1814. ⎰

(These two views are lettered by means of printed slips pasted over the original lettering; without the slips the lettering is reversed, Pembroke being on the left and Hertford on the right.)

p. 189. Dr. Richard Newton, Founder of Hertford College.

51. p. 201 [or page 200].   Alban Hall.   F. Mackenzie delt.   J. Hill sculpt.   June 1 1813.

52. p. 209. Door of the Divinity School.   A. Pugin delt.   D. Havell sc. ⎱ together on 1 plate.

St. Mary's Hall.   A. Pugin delt.   Lewis sculpt. ⎰ Decr. 1 1814.

53. p. 218. Magdalen Hall ⎱ together on 1 plate.   F. Mackenzie delt.   J. Bluck sculpt.   July 1 1814.
New Inn Hall ⎰

54. p. 223 [or Vol. I p. 80].   The Public Schools, & Part of Exeter College Library, from the Garden. F. Nash delt.   J. Hill sculpt.   Augt. 1 1813.

55. p. 224. The Statute Gallery.   W. Westall delt.   Lewis sculpt.   Septr. 1 1814.

p. 226. Humphrey, Duke of Gloucester, Founder of the Divinity School.

Ackermann's Oxford (*contd.*)

56. p. 226. Divinity School. F. Mackenzie delt. F. C. Lewis sculpt. June 1st 1813.
    p. 227. Sir Thomas Bodley, Founder of Bodleian Library.
57. p. 229. Bodleian Library. A. Pugin delt. J. C. Stadler sculpt. March 1 1814.
    p. 233. Gilbert Sheldon, Archbishop of Canterbury, Founder of the Theatre.
    p. 235. Elias Ashmole, Founder of the Ashmolean Museum.
    p. 237. Edwd. Hyde—Earl of Clarendon, Founder of the Clarendon Printing House.
58. p. 237. The Clarendon Printing House, Theatre, & Museum. F. Mackenzie delt. J. C. Stadler
        sculpt. April 1 1814.
    p. 238. Dr. Radcliffe, Founder of the Radclivian Library.
59. p. 238. Radcliffe Library. F. Mackenzie delt. J. Bluck sculpt. Octr. 1 1813.
60. *ibd.* [or page 239]. The Radcliffe Library (interior). F. Mackenzie delt. J. Bluck sculpt.
        Septr. 1 1813.
61. *ibd.* [or page 239]. The Vestibule of Radcliffe Library. F. Mackenzie delt. J. Hill sculpt.
        Decr. 1813.
62. p. 240. Astronomical Observatory. W. Westall delt. J. C. Stadler sculpt. April 1 1814.
63. *ibd.* [or page 241]. Astronomical Observatory (interior). F. Mackenzie delt. J. Bluck sculpt.
        Feby. 1 1814.
64. p. 241 [or page 204]. Botanic Garden. A. Pugin delt. D. Havell sc. } together on 1 plate.
        St. Edmund's Hall. A. Pugin delt. J. Hill sculpt. } Decr. 1 1814.
65. p. 259. Doctor in Divinity. T. Uwins delt. J. Agar sculpt. Octr. 1 1813.
66. *ibd.* Doctor in Divinity, in Convocation. T. Uwins delt. J. Agar sculpt. June 1 1814.
67. *ibd.* [on page 260]. Doctor in Physic, Full Dress. T. Uwins delt. J. Agar sculpt. Dec. 1 1813.
68. *ibd.* [or page 260]. Doctor in Physic. T. Uwins delt. J. Agar sculpt. June 1st 1813.
69. *ibd.* [or page 260]. Bachelor of Laws. T. Uwins delt. J. Agar sculpt. Septr. 1 1813.
70. *ibd.* [or page 260]. Doctor in Music. T. Uwins delt. J. Agar sculpt. Augt. 1 1813.
71. *ibd.* [or page 261]. Master of Arts. T. Uwins delt. J. Agar sculpt. April 1 1814.
72. *ibd.* [or page 261]. Bachelor of Arts. T. Uwins delt. J. Agar sculpt. May 1st 1813.
73. *ibd.* [or page 261]. Nobleman. T. Uwins delt. J. Agar sculpt. Novr. 1 1813.
74. *ibd.* [or page 261]. Gentleman Commoner. T. Uwins delt. J. Agar sculpt. March 1 1814.
75. *ibd.* [or page 261]. Commoner. T. Uwins delt. J. Agar sculpt. July 1 1813.
76. *ibd.* [or page 261]. Student in Civil Law. T. Uwins delt. J. Agar sculpt. Jany. 1 1814.
77. *ibd.* [or page 261]. Scholar. T. Uwins delt. J. Agar sculpt. May 1 1814.
78. *ibd.* [or page 262]. Proctor. T. Uwins delt. J. Agar sculpt. Feby. 1 1814.
79. *ibd.* [or page 262]. Gentleman Commoner & Nobleman, Undress Gowns—Pro Proctor. T.
        Uwins delt. J. Agar sculpt. July 1 1814.
80. *ibd.* [or page 262]. Servitor. Bachelor of Divinity. Collector. T. Uwins delt. J. Agar sculpt.
        Aug. 1 1814.
81. *ibd.* [or page 262]. Vice Chancellor. Esquire Beadle. Yeoman Beadle. Verger. T. Uwins
        delt. J. Agar sculpt. Octr. 1 1814.

RÉSUMÉ.—*82 plates in all, or if with portraits of the Founders 115 plates, viz. an uncoloured portrait of Lord Grenville, 64 coloured aquatint plates (containing 67 views, 6 of the plates containing 2 views each) and 17 coloured plates in line and stipple of the costume of the University. The artists are: Pugin (31 or 30), Mackenzie (20), Westall (8), Nash (7 or 8), Turner (1), Reynolds (1). The engravers are: Bluck (22 or 23), Hill (11 or 12), Stadler (10), F. C. Lewis (7), G. Lewis (4), Lewis without initial (2), Havell (7), Bennett (2), J. Reeve (1), R. Reeve (1), Sutherland (1). The 17 costume plates are all by Agar after Uwins. The 33 "Founder" plates bear no artist's or engraver's name.*

SIZE.—*Printed on large and small paper. Full size of small paper 14 × 11½ inches, of large paper 16½ × 13 inches. Size of plate marks 11¾ × 10 inches, engraved surface of the plates 8 × 10½ inches average. Portraits of the Founders 5 × 6 inches. Watermark J. Whatman 1811.*

Copies were sold without, and with, "Portraits of the Founders of the Colleges."

ISSUES.—*The following variations occur:*

(a) There are two issues of the List of Plates. The first issue without the Founders, the second issue with the Founders. The order of the plates, even the volume order, is different in these two

Ackermann's Oxford (*contd.*)

lists. In the collation above, the plates are indicated in the order they come in the first state, the correct pages for copies with the Founders being given in square brackets. (The second issue of the list of plates is sometimes found in copies in otherwise early state.)

(*b*) Vol. I, pl. I, front. "View of Oxford from New College Tower." 1st state, the imprint reads, Pub. Sept. 1 1814 for R. Ackermann's History of Cambridge. 2nd state, the misprint is corrected to Oxford.

(*c*) Large-paper copies have the portrait of the Chancellor on India paper.

(*d*) Vol. I, p. x. "The Old Tower." 1st state, imprint dated Dec. 1813 (V. & A.). 2nd state, imprint dated March 1 1814 (B.M. and Guildhall).

(*e*) Vol. I, p. 25. "University & Queen's Colleges." 1st state, F. Nash delt. R. Hills sculpt. (a very rare state, B.M. large-paper copy). 2nd state, Pugin delt. J. Hill sculpt.

(*f*) Vol. I, p. 247. Without overslip lettered "New College Entrance Gate," with small printed overslip lettered "Old Gate of Magdalen College."

(*g*) Vol. II, p. 35 (or p. 44). "Corpus Christi College." 1st state, imprint dated May 1 1814 (B.M. and Guildhall). 2nd state, imprint dated June 1 1814 (V. & A.).

(*h*) Vol. II, p. 121 (or p. 130). "St. John's College from the Garden." 1st state, imprint dated Aug. 1 1813 (V. & A.). 2nd state, imprint dated Sept. 1 1813 (B.M. and Guildhall).

(*i*) Vol. II, p. 189 (or p. 173). "Hertford & Pembroke College." 1st state, the space between the two views is filled in with aquatint (B.M. and V. & A.). 2nd state, the space between the two views is cleaned and left white. This plate is also lettered by means of small printed overslips, Hertford on left- and Pembroke on right-hand side of the plate. Without the overslips these positions are reversed.

(*j*) Vol. II, p. 201 (or p. 200). "Alban Hall." 1st state, imprint dated June 1 1813 (B.M. and V. & A.). 2nd state, imprint dated July 1 1813 (Guildhall).

(*k*) Vol. II, p. 226. "Divinity School." 1st state, F. Mackenzie delt. J. Bluck sculpt. (B.M. and V. & A.). 2nd state, F. Mackenzie delt. F. C. Lewis sculpt. (Guildhall).

(*l*) Vol. II, p. 239. "The Vestibule." 1st state, imprint dated Nov. 1813 (B.M. and V. & A.). 2nd state, imprint dated Dec. 1813 (Guildhall).

(*m*) I have also seen copies with the spelling Bedel instead of Beadle in last plate of Vol. II.

Of the forty or fifty copies I have examined, not one has contained all the above plates in the first state. The B.M. copy has all but two in the first state, and the Victoria & Albert Museum copy has likewise all but two, though a different two in the first state. Too great importance need not be attached to the List of Plates being in the first or second state, as some original owners of first impressions undoubtedly substituted a second issue of the List of Plates when they added the Founders to their copies. It is moreover pleasant to have the List of Plates agreeing with the copy actually possessed. In the same way it is unwise to place much reliance on the small printed pasteover slips (plates f and i). It is possible to wash off these slips, or they may even have worn off, through being incorrectly applied or through the perishing of the adhesive used.

I have examined several where they have been loose. The "Oxford" printed overslips do not form a parallel with overslip in the "Public Schools"; in the latter case the plate had to be definitely "treated" before issue. Really choice copies of Ackermann's "Oxford," however, should have the following 5 points:

(1) *The half-titles should be present (with the rest of prelim. ll.).*

(2) *Plate I, Vol. I, should have misprint "Cambridge."*

(3) *Plate 50, Vol. II, p. 189 or 173, should have aquatinting between the views of Pembroke and Hertford.*

(4) *Plate 56, Vol. II, p. 226, "Divinity School," should be engraved by Bluck.*

(5) *Watermarks should not be later than the year of publication.*

As many as possible of the 5 plates that exist with the earliest imprint date should be secured, and if Plate 13, Vol. I, p. 25, "University & Queen's Colleges," by Nash is obtained, the purchaser will be fortunate, for this state is rare.

Ackermann's Oxford (*contd.*)

There are later issues of the plates with watermarks dated after the date of publication of the work. Such copies should be avoided by the collector.

REMARKS.—1000 *copies were printed on large wove elephant paper, in 20 monthly parts, the first appearing 1 May 1813. The first 500 copies at 12s. per part (these were subscribed by 1st April 1814), the remaining 500 were raised to 16s. per part. The large-paper copies were priced £1 1s. per part. On completion the work was issued in 2 vols. elephant quarto boards for £16 or atlas quarto (i.e. L.P.) for £27. There were 50 copies on large and thick paper, 25 copies being issued uncoloured, the plates on India paper, proof impressions. The series of the "Founders' Portraits" was not issued till a later date, viz. 1st April 1815: their inclusion is optional, and as I have stated in the "Cambridge," copies are complete, and in my opinion preferable without the Founders, and for the same reason: they may add slightly to the interest, but they are not the equal of the other plates. They may be secured in a separate volume as they were issued (see next item). The "Costume of Members of the University of Oxford" was also issued separately in elephant quarto for £3 13s. 6d. These, however, form an integral part of the work and must be present. As in the Cambridge, large-paper copies are definitely superior in finish, owing to the extra care and fine paper on which they were pulled. Large-paper impressions of the Oxford plates have an incomparably beautiful sheen, a suffused rich glow and "bloom," that is absent from ordinary copies. Large-paper copies have not so far been estimated at their just worth; only one copy on large paper was printed for 20 on small paper.*

6 ACKERMANN (Oxford Founders)

A Series of Portraits of those Distinguished Persons who were the Founders of Colleges and Public Buildings in the University of Oxford; from Pictures in that University and from Private Collections. London: Published April 1st, by R. Ackermann, Repository of Arts, 101, Strand.

COLLATION.—Title as above + Directions for placing the Plates in the History of Oxford + 33 plates.
Engraved by R. Cooper and T. Williamson.

1. King Alfred.
2. Walter de Merton.
3. John Baliol.
4. Devorguilla Baliol.
5. Walter Stapledon.
6. King Edward IInd.
7. Sir Joseph Williamson. Knt. Founder of Present Edifice of Queens College.
8. Robert Egglesfield.
9. William of Wykeham.
10. Richard Fleming, Bishop of Lincoln.
11. Thomas (de) Rotherham.
12. Archbishop Chichely.
13. William Patten of Wainfleet, Bishop of Winchester.
14. William Smith.
15. Sir Richard Sutton, Knt.
16. Bishop Fox.
17. Cardinal Wolsey.
18. King Henry VIII.
19. Sir Thomas Pope, Knt.
20. Sir Thomas White, Knt.
21. Queen Elizabeth.
22. Nicholas Wadham.
23. Dorothy Wadham.
24. Thomas Tesdale.
25. Richard Wightwick, S.T.B.
26. Sir Thomas Cookes, Worcester College.
27. Dr Richard Newton, Hertford College.
28. Humphrey Duke of Gloucester, Divinity School.
29. Sir Thomas Bodley, Bodleian Library.
30. Archbishop Sheldon, The Theatre.
31. Elias Ashmole, Ashmolean Museum.
32. Edward Hyde, Earl of Clarendon Printing Office.
33. Dr. Radcliffe, Radclivian Library.

Issued in elephant quarto boards for £3 13s. 6d. and in atlas quarto for £4 14s. 6d.

7 ACKERMANN (Rudolph)

The Microcosm of London (or London in Miniature) In Three Volumes London, Printed for R. Ackermann, Repository of Arts, No. 101, Strand, by T. Bensley, Bolt Court, Fleet Street.

3 vols. Quarto.   1808–10

COLLATION VOL. I.—A composition title engraved on wood (consisting of an architectural background, Dome of St. Paul's, Towers of Abbey &c., shipping at foot) with imprint, T. Bensley, Printer, Bolt Court, Fleet Street, London. (v. blank) + Engraved dedication to H.R.H. the Prince of Wales Thos. Tomkins Script. Robt. Ashby Sculpt., with a fine stipple vignette at head E. F. Burney del. Thos. Williamson sculp. (consisting of a central female with Apollo as a cherub driving his chariot on either side) v. blank + Contents (being list of plates) 1 p. (v. blank) + Introduction 4 pp. (i–iv) + sub-title "The Microcosm of London; or, London in Miniature (swelled rule) Vol. I" [II, III] (v. blank) + pp. 3–321 [L. Harrison, Printer, 373, Strand] + 32 coloured plates.

All the plates in each volume are marked Rowlandson and Pugin, or Pugin and Rowlandson delt. et sculpt. and all bear Ackermann's imprint as follows: London Pubd. [date] at R. Ackermann's Repository of Arts, 101, Strand.

1. p.   9. Drawing from Life at the Royal Academy, (Somerset House) Bluck Aquat.   1 Jany. 1808.
2. p.   10. Exhibition Room, Somerset House, Hill Aquatin   1 Jany. 1808.
3. p.   16. Board Room of the Admiralty.   Hill Aquatin   1 Jany. 1808.
4. p.   23. Astley's Amphitheatre.   Hill Aquat.   Jany. 1 1808.
5. p.   25. Dining Hall, Asylum.   Hill Aquat.   Feb. 1 1808.
6. p.   33. Christie's Auction Room.   J. Bluck Aquat.   Feb. 1 1808.
7. p.   40. The Great Hall, Bank of England.   Hill Aquat.   Feb. 1 1808.
8. p.   52. Bartholomew Fair.   J. Bluck Aquat.   Feb. 1 1808.
9. p.   63. Billingsgate Market.   J. Bluck Aquat.   1 March 1808.
10. p.   69. The Hall, Blue Coat School.   Hill Aquat.   1 March 1808.
11. p.   82. Bow Street Office.   Hill aquat.   1 March 1808.
12. p.   92. Pass-Room Bridewell.   Hill aquat.   1 March 1808.
13. p.   98. British Institution, (Pall Mall).   J. Bluck aquat.   1st April 1808.
14. p. 101. The Hall and Stair Case, British Museum.   J. Bluck Aquat.   1 April 1808.
15. p. 107. The Hall Carlton House.   J. Bluck aquat.   1st April 1808.
16. p. 114. The Roman Catholic Chapel, (Lincolns Inn Fields).   J. Bluck aquat.   1st April 1808.
17. p. 119. Coal Exchange.   Hill Aquat.   1 May 1808.
18. p. 123. Royal Cock Pit.   Bluck Aquat.   1 May 1808.
19. p. 126. Water Engine, Cold-Bath-Field's Prison.   J. Bluck Aquat.   May 1 1808.
20. p. 135. The College of Physicians.   Bluck aquat.   1 May 1808.
21. p. 190. House of Commons.   J. Bluck Aquat.   1st June 1808.
22. p. 193. Court of Chancery, Lincoln's Inn Hall.   J. C. Stadler Aquat.   1st June 1808.
23. p. 203. Court of Common Pleas, Westminster Hall.   J. C. Stadler Aquat.   1st June 1808.
24. p. 205. Court of Kings Bench. Westminster Hall.   J. Bluck Aquat.   1st June 1808.
25. p. 207. Court of Exchequer, Westminster Hall.   J. C. Stadler Aquat.   July 1 1808.
26. p. 209. Covent Garden Market Westminster Election.   Bluck Aquat.   1 July 1808.
27. p. 212. Covent Garden Theatre, J. Bluck Aquat.   1 July 1808.
28. p. 217. [marked plate 29].   Custom House.   From the River Thames, J. Bluck Aquat.   1 Augt. 1808.
29. p. 218. [marked plate 28].   The Long Room, Custom House.   J. C. Stadler Aquat.   1st July 1808.
30. p. 223. [marked plate 29].   Debating Society, Piccadilly.   J. C. Stadler sculpt.   Augt. 1 1808.
31. p. 224. Doctors Commons.   Stadler Aquat.   1 Augt. 1808.
32. p. 228. Drury Lane Theatre.   Bluck Aquat.   1st Augt. 1808.

VOL. II.—Title as before + Dedication as before, with the exception of the stipple vignette, the design of which is altered to cherub with palette and brushes, female figure with globe

Ackermann's Microcosm (*contd.*)

and triangle, and cherub with compass and lead. E. F. Burney del, no engraver given, but the solitary word sculp. + Contents of Vol. II [i.e. list of plates] v. blank + Introduction pp. iii–vi + sub-title as before + pp. 1–239 [Harrison and Rutter, Printers, 373 Strand.] + 32 coloured plates.

33. p. 13. Corn Exchange, Mark Lane. J. Bluck Aquat. 1st Sept. 1808.
34. p. 25. Exhibition of Water Coloured Drawings, Old Bond Street. Stadler Aquat. 1st Septr. 1808.
35. p. 36. Fire in London. J. Bluck Aquat. 1st Septr. 1808.
36. p. 44. Fleet Prison. Stadler Aquat. 1st Septr. 1808.
37. p. 61. Foundling Hospital, The Chapel. J. Bluck Aquat. 1st Oct. 1808.
38. p. 79. Freemasons Hall, Great Queen Street. Stadler Aquat. 1st Octr. 1808.
39. p. 94. Great Subscription Room at Brooke's St. James's Street. Stadler Aquat. 1st Octr. 1808.
40. p. 103. Guildhall. J. Bluck Aquat. 1st Octr. 1808.
41. p. 115. [marked plate 42]. Common Council Chamber, Guildhall. J. Bluck aquat. 1st Novr. 1808.
42. p. 124. [marked plate 41]. Guildhall. Examination of a Bankrupt before his Creditors-Court of Kings Bench. J. Bluck Aquat. 1st Novr. 1808.
43. p. 125. Herald's College, The Hall. J. Bluck Aquat. 1st Novr. 1808.
44. p. 133. Hospital, Middlesex. Stadler Aquat. 1st Novr. 1808.
45. p. 139. India House, The Sale Room. Stadler Aquat. 1st Decr. 1808.
46. p. 161. Kings Bench Prison. J. C. Stadler Aquat. 1st Decr. 1808.
47. p. 162. Kings's Mews, Charing Cross. J. C. Stadler aquat. 1st Decr. 1808.
48. p. 163. Lambeth Palace. J. C. Stadler aquat. 1st Decr. 1808.
49. p. 174. Lloyd's Subscription Room. J. C. Stadler aquat. 1st Jany. 1809.
50. p. 176. Leaden Hall Market. J. C. Stadler aquat. 1st Jany. 1809.
51. p. 181. Egyptian Hall, Mansion House. J. Bluck aquat. 1st Jany. 1809.
52. p. 183. House of Lords. J. Bluck aquat. 1st Jany. 1809.
53. p. 193. Lottery Drawing: Coopers Hall. Stadler aquat. 1st Feby. 1809.
54. p. 196. Magdalen Chapel. Bluck aquat. 1st Feby. 1809.
55. p. 203. The Mint. J. Bluck aquat. 1st Feby. 1809.
56. p. 206. Mounting Guard, St. James's Park. J. Bluck aquat. 1st Feby. 1809.
57. p. 209. Newgate Chapel. Stadler aquat. 1st March 1809.
58. p. 212. Old Bailey. Stadler aquat. 1st March 1809.
59. p. 213. Opera House. J. Bluck aquat. 1st March 1809.
60. p. 215. Pantheon Masquerade. Bluck aquat. 1st March 1809.
61. p. 222. Philanthropic Society, The Chapel. J. Bluck aquat. 1st April 1809.
62. p. 226. Pillory, Charing Cross. Bluck aquat. 1st April 1809.
63. p. 230. The Post Office. (No aquatinter given, the word aquat. only.) 1st April 1809.
64. p. 236. Quakers Meeting. Stadler aquat. 1st April 1809.

VOL. III.—Title as before + Dedication as before, with the exception of the stipple vignette, the design of which is altered to cherub setting bird free, female figure of justice, cherub with cap, wand, and scroll. E. F. Burney del. Thos Williamson sculp. + Contents of Vol. III [being list of plates] (v. Note to Patrons) + Introduction 2 pp. (iii–iv) + Half-title as before (v. blank) + pp. 1–280 [Harrison and Rutter, Printers, 373, Strand] + Index and Errata 3 ll. unnumbered, and 40 coloured plates.

65. p. 1. Queen's Palace, St. James's Park. Bluck aquat. 1st May 1809.
66. p. 13. Royal Circus. Bluck aquat. 1st May 1809.
67. p. 17. Royal Exchange. Hill aquat. 1st May 1809.
68. p. 32. Royal Institution, Albemarle Street. Stadler aquat. 1st May 1809.
69. p. 41. Sadlers Wells Theatre. Bluck aquat. June 1st 1809.
70. p. 45. Session House, Clerkenwell. J. Bluck aquat. June 1st 1809.
71. p. 67. Society for the Encouragement of Arts, &c. Adelphi. J. Bluck. aquat. July 1st 1809.
72. p. 73. Society of Agriculture. J. G. Stadler aquat. June 1st 1809.
73. p. 86. Somerset House, Strand. Bluck aquat. 1st June 1809.

Ackermann's Microcosm (*contd.*)

74. p. 99. Stamp Office, Somerset House. J. C. Stadler aquat. July 1st 1809.
75. p. 101. New Stock Exchange. J. C. Stadler aquat. July 1st 1809.
76. p. 113. Drawing Room St. James's. J. Bluck aquat. July 1st 1809.
77. p. 121. St. Luke's Hospital. J. C. Stadler aquat. Augt. 1st 1809.
78. p. 127. St. Margarets, Westminster. J. Bluck aquat. Augt. 1st 1809.
79. p. 130. St. Martins, in the Fields. Stadler aquat. Augt. 1st 1809.
80. p. 145. St. Paul's Cathedral. J. Bluck aquat. Augt. 1st 1809.
81. p. 158. Surrey Institution. J. C. Stadler aquat. Septr. 1st 1809.
82. p. 167. Synagogue, Dukes Place, Hounsditch. Sunderland aquat. Septr. 1st 1809.
83. p. 172. Tattersall's Horse Repository. Sunderland aquat. Septr. 1st 1809.
84. p. 174. Temple Church. Bluck aquat. Septr. 1st 1809.
85. p. 185. [marked plate 85 Second]. View of the Tower. Sunderland aquat. Octr. 1st 1809.
86. p. 188. [marked plate 101]. Horse Armoury, Tower. Sunderland aquat. Novr. 1st 1809.
87. p. 197. [marked plate 86]. Board of Trade. Sunderland aquat. Octr. 1st 1809.
88. p. 201. [marked plate 87]. Trinity House. Sutherland aquat. Oct. 1st 1809.
89. p. 204. [marked plate 88]. Vauxhall Garden. J. Bluck aquat. Octr. 1st 1809.
90. p. 208. St. Stephen's, Walbrook. Bluck aquat. Nov. 1st 1809.
91. p. 217. Watch House, St Mary Le Bone. J. Bluck aquat. Sept. 1st 1809.
92. p. 218. West India Docks. Bluck aquat. Jany 1st 1810.
93. p. 229. Westminster Abbey. Bluck aquat. Decr. 1st 1809.
94. p. 235. Westminster Hall. J. Bluck aquat. Decr. 1st 1809.
95. p. 239. Whitehall. [Chapel]. J. Bluck aquat. Decr. 1st 1809.
96. p. 242. Workhouse, St. James's Parish. Sunderland aquat. Decr. 1st 1809.
97. p. 246. Greenwich Hospital, the Painted Hall. Bluck aquat. Jany. 1 1810.
98. p. 252. Chelsea Hospital. J. Bluck aquat. Jany. 1st 1810.
99. p. 256. Military College, Chelsea. Sunderland aquat. Jany. 1 1810.
100. p. 263. New Covent Garden Theatre. Bluck aquat. Jany. 1 1810.
101. p. 267. [marked plate 102]. South Sea House Dividend Hall. Sutherland aquat. Feb. 1 1810.
102. p. 269. [marked plate 103]. Excise Office, Broad Street. Sutherland aquat. Feb. 1 1810.
103. p. 278. [marked plate 104]. View Westminster Hall and Bridge. J. Bluck aquat. Feb. 1 1810.
104. p. 279. [marked plate 89]. View of London from the Thames taken opposite the Adelphi. J. Bluck aquat. Novr. 1st 1809.

RÉSUMÉ.—104 *coloured aquatint plates after Rowlandson and Pugin by Bluck (53, 54 or 55), Hill (10), Stadler (28 or 29), Sutherland (10), Not given (1), Harraden (1 or none).*

Size of text 14¼ × 11½ *inches. Size of plate marks* 11 × 9¾ *inches and of engraved surface of plates average* 10 × 7¾ *inches.*

GENERAL REMARKS.—*The "Microcosm of London" is one of the great colour-plate books, and a carefully selected copy should form the corner stone of any collection of books on this subject. The plates by Rowlandson and Pugin present an unrivalled picture of London in early 19th century, of historic value, as many of the buildings no longer exist. From a bibliographical point of view the work presents many absorbing and intricate problems. Of the sixty or seventy copies I have examined in the last few years, not one has been in the first state throughout. Should such a copy ever occur for sale, it should realise a very high figure. There are different issues of the plates, of the text, and of the paper. These variations are further complicated by the fact that they are not necessarily uniform. Late impressions of some plates frequently occur with early impressions in the same volume, and the first issue of the text does not necessarily accompany first issue of the plates. As a picture book alone the work will always command a good price, but the discriminating collector will exercise much care and thought before making a final selection, and endeavour to secure as many of the following salient points in the first state as possible.*

N.B.—*It is useful to remember that the plates are roughly arranged alphabetically throughout the* 3 *volumes.*

ISSUES.—*TEXT. 1st State.*—*The Errata entirely uncorrected. (I have seen four copies,*

Ackermann's Microcosm (*contd.*)

one formerly in the possession of Messrs. Maggs Bros. in this state, but cannot refer to any in a public library.)

2nd State.—*The text remains uncorrected with the exception of Vol. I, p. 218, line 13, Coustum House being corrected to Custom House* [B.M., Guildhall, Bishopsgate Inst.]

3rd State.—*The text reset, and the Errata to Vol. I corrected* [Guildhall 2nd copy].

WATERMARKS.—*These must all be pre-publication. The plates were reissued without the imprints being changed, and copies exist purporting to be 1808–10, but bearing later watermarks, the plates being reprinted to 1836 at least. The same scrutiny must be applied to the text. The paper was mainly supplied by J. Whatman and L. & D.*

PRELIMINARY LEAVES.—*All the preliminary leaves must be present, and the 3 dedications must each have a different vignette heading. There are two states to the contents leaf of Vol. I.*

> 1st state lettered "*Contents*"
> 2nd state   ,,   "*Contents Vol. I*"

The number of the volume in the composition woodcut title should be clearly printed [I, II and III] *and not inserted by hand. In the correct woodcut title to Vol. I, there is a comma after Bensley in the imprint, but not in Vols. II and III.*

Variations of the Plates

VOL. I

Plate 1, p. 9. Drawing from Life at the Royal Academy (Somerset House).
   (*a*) *Aquatinted by Harraden* [B.M. King's Lib., S. Ken., Guildhall, Harvey Frost]
   (*b*) *Aquatinted by Bluck* [B.M. Print Room, Guildhall 2nd copy].
   The first state is the finer; in the second state the plate was reworked, the features and even the positions of the students being altered.

Plate 3, p. 16. Board Room of the Admiralty.
   (*a*) *No artist or engraver given.*
   (*b*) *Hill aquatin.*
   The first state is rare. Noted in 3 copies only.

Plate 4, p. 23. Astley's Amphitheatre.
   (*a*) *Ceiling clear wash, design showing in opening, figures sharply drawn.*
   (*b*) *Ceiling aquatinted, opening very dark, figures particularly in orchestra do not stand out, the under supports of the tiers indicated only by aquatint, and arena equally aquatinted all over.*

Plate 5, p. 25. Dining Room Asylum.
   (*a*) *Floor is flagged up to the fireplace.*
   (*b*) *Aquatint in floor before fireplace, flagging in foreground only.*

Plate 8, p. 52. Bartholomew Fair.
   (*a*) *All small figures stand out sharply and clearly the name Richardson easily readable on both sides of the marquee, the shadows in the foreground worked in clear washes* [B.M., Guildhall, Harvey Frost].
   (*b*) *Shadows of figures in foreground worked in small engraved lines, the whole plate darkened, figures particularly on roundabout in left-hand corner blurred* [Guildhall 2nd copy].

Plate 9, p. 63. Billingsgate Market.
   (*a*) *The crowd under the verandah cleverly shown with an occasional figure picked out,*

Ackermann's Microcosm (*contd.*)

the letters of the bill on the buttress readable, the middle foreground treated with light wash.

(b) *Middle foreground aquatinted, the dog eating the fish aquatinted all over, figures on verandah all of equal tone value, bill on buttress unreadable.*

Plate 10, p. 69. *The Hall, Blue Coat School.*

(a) *The shading on the ceiling and walls effected by finely engraved parallel lines. The hands in the picture on the wall and the brackets stand out in the thick lines as if superimposed on the plate* [B.M., Guildhall, S. Ken., Harvey Frost].

(b) *The shading achieved by heavy aquatint, the hands and brackets show normally in the design.*

Plate 11, p. 82. *Bow Street Office.*

(a) *A mirror under the clock, plain wash sky showing through ceiling window, outlines of bust on back wall clearly defined.*

(b) *A framed proclamation takes the place of the mirror, the sky shaded in aquatint, bust dark with blurred outlines.*

Plate 12, p. 92. *Pass Room, Bridewell.*

(a) *The notice on right-hand wall, "Those who dirts their bed will be punished," easily readable. Figures and their shadows in foreground shaded by line.*

(b) *The notice on wall illegible and the figures shaded in aquatint.*

Plate 17, p. 119. *Coal Exchange.*

The foreground of this plate should be light and notice on back wall Coal Sales &c. very clear. Sometimes this plate is very dark with heavy aquatinting in foreground and notice on back wall almost illegible.

Plate 18, p. 123. *Royal Cock Pit.*

(a) *Royal Arms in central background drawn in sketchy manner, the spectator fifth from the left of the right-hand doorway resting his head on his hand* [B.M. Print Room, S. Ken, Guildhall, Harvey Frost].

(b) *Royal Arms executed in conventional manner. The spectator fifth from the left of right-hand doorway does not rest his head on his hand* [Guildhall 2nd copy].

Plate 21, p. 190. *House of Commons.*

(a) *All figures stand out clearly including the back benches. A figure appears as if coming out of the box behind the Speaker.*

(b) *The distant figures rather blurred, and the figure appearing from box behind Speaker almost obliterated with heavy aquatint.*

Plate 28, p. 217 [marked plate 29]. *Custom House.*

(a) *Side of ship by quayside clear wash only.*

(b) *Side of ship aquatinted.*

VOL. II

Plate 39, p. 94. *Great Subscription Room at Brooke's.*

(a) *Aquatinted by Bluck* [B.M. Print Room, Guildhall and one other].

(b) *Aquatinted by Stadler* [B.M. King's Lib., S. Ken. Guildhall 2nd copy].

The first state is rare.

VOL. III

Plate 91, p. 217. *Watch House, St. Mary le bone.*

(a) *Lettered Watch House St. James.*

Ackermann's Microcosm (*contd.*)

(*b*) *Lettered Watch House only, St. James being erased.*

(*c*) *Lettered Watch House St. Marylebone.*

The first state is perhaps the rarest of the Microcosm plates. It was two years before I finally located this issue in a copy at Francis Edwards Ltd.

FINAL REMARKS.—The finest copy of the "Microcosm" I have seen is in the possession of H. Harvey Frost Esq., who with great courtesy permitted me to examine it. It measures $14\frac{1}{16} \times 11\frac{1}{2}$ inches, and contains the original wrappers bound in at the end. The "Microcosm" was advertised to be issued in monthly parts, on the first day of each month, at 7 shillings per part, in 4 volumes of 24 numbers, printed on "large 4to Royal Elephant Vellum paper hot pressed." This was found to be unremunerative, and the price was advanced to 10s. 6d. to non-subscribers after the 8th number and the work to be completed in 3 volumes instead of 4 as intended, but the number of parts increased to 26, a slip note to this effect being inserted in part 17, and it was published in 3 vols. for £13 13s.

8 ACKERMANN (R.)

The Repository of Arts, Literature, Commerce, Manufactures, Fashions and Politics. This work already honoured by His approbation is most humbly dedicated by permission to his Royal Highness the Prince of Wales by his grateful and obedient servant R. Ackermann.

40 vols. Octavo. 1809–28

COLLATION VOL. 1.—Engraved title as above with vignette at head (v. blank) + Text pp. 1–503 + 7 pp. index (unnumbered). In addition there are 7 leaves not included in the pagination (that is, a sub-title with contents below, one for each month and one for the supplement).

Part 1, Jan 1809
  Walking Dress.
  Evening Full Dress.
  Ackermann's Repository of Arts 101 Strand
    Pugin & Rowlandson dclt.
  Chaise longue . . . Window seat. G. Smith
    delt.
  British Sports by Howitt.
  4 cloth patterns.

Part 2, Feb 1809
  Pointers. Howitt.
  Wedgwood & Byerley York Street, St. James's
    Square.
  Half Dress.
  Dancing Dress.
  Patent Landau.
  4 cloth patterns.

Part 3, Mch 1809
  Setters. Howitt.
  Walking Dress.
  Opera Dress.
  Messrs. Harding Howell & Co. 89 Pall Mall.
  Ladies Secretaire (and) Parlor Chair. G.
    Smith.
  4 cloth patterns.

Part 4, Apr 1809
  Spaniels. Howitt.

Part 4, Apr 1809 (*contd.*)
  Full Dress.
  Walking Dress.
  Messrs. Lackington Allen & Co. Temple of
    the Muses, Finsbury Square.
  Window Curtain.
  3 cloth patterns.

Part 5, May 1809
  Water Spaniels. Howitt.
  Ball Dress.
  Walking Dress.
  Messrs. Pellatt & Green, St. Pauls Church
    Yard.
  Sofa Bed.
  4 cloth patterns.

Part 6, Jun 1809
  Red Grouse. Howitt.
  Walking Dresses.
  Walking Dress.
  Carleton House.
  Tabouret, Table, Chair, Footstool.
  3 cloth patterns.

Supplement 1809
  A Plan of Martinique.
  Fashionable Head Dresses.
  Lord Cochrane. R. Cooper sc. (uncoloured).

Ackermann's Repository of Arts (*contd.*)

Two other illustrations are sometimes found here, viz. Price & Co. chemists, and Furniture Warehouse, Pall Mall.   They are uncoloured, not called for in the List of Plates and come with the advertisements.   The volume can be considered complete without them.

VOL 2.—Engraved frontispiece + Text pp. 1–521 + 5 pp. index unnumbered + 7 sub-titles.

Part 7, Jul 1809
    Black Grouse. Howitt.
    Opera Dress.
    Promenade Dress.
    Somerset House and New Church, Strand.
        Taken from the Morning Post Office.
    Library Sofa and Candelabra.
    4 cloth patterns.

Part 8, Aug 1809
    Archduke Charles of Austria. Robt Cooper
        scut. (uncoloured).
    Partridge. Howitt.
    2 medals. E. F. Burney delt. S. Mitan sculpt.
        (uncoloured).
    Walking Costume.
    Promenade Dresses.
    Messrs. Morgan and Sanders, Catherine St.
        Strand.
    Ladies Toilette Fauteuil, Footstool &c.
    4 cloth patterns.

Part 9, Sep 1809
    Pheasant. Howitt.
    Mourning Dresses.
    Promenade Dress.
    Bank of England from Cateaton Street. Pugin
        delt. S. Mitan sculpt.
    Child's Cot Bed, Nursery Chair.
    3 cloth patterns.

Part 10, Oct 1809
    A Curious Specimen from Agrigentum.
    Woodcock. Howitt.
    Ball Dress.
    Walking Dress.
    Theatre Royal Covent Garden from Bow
        Street.
    French Window Curtain & Grecian Settee.
    4 cloth patterns.

Part 11, Nov 1809
    Wild Duck. Howitt.
    Morning Dress.
    Morning Walking Dress.
    South View of the Bank.
    Patent Chariot.
    4 cloth patterns.

Part 12, Dec 1809
    Commandant Schoenecher. T. Uwins delt.
    Major Muller. T. Uwins delt.
    Hare. Howitt.
    Tyrolese Walking Dress.
    Evening Dress.
    Drawing Room Chairs.
    4 cloth patterns.

Supplement 1809
    Andreus Hoffer, Commander in chief of the
        Tyrolese.

R. Ackermann's Patent Card (4 leaves) is sometimes found in Part 8.

VOL. 3.—Engraved title + Text pp. 1–490 + 5 pp. index unnumbered + 7 sub-titles.

Part 13, Jan 1810
    Going Out. Howitt.
    Evening Dress.
    Carriage or Promenade Dress.
    Westminster Abbey & St. Margarets.
    Cabinet Writing Table & Chair.
    3 cloth patterns.

Part 14, Feb 1810
    Major von Schill.
    Grouse Shooting. Howitt.
    Pitt's Cabinet Globe Writing Table.
    Saloon to the Private Boxes, Covent Garden
        Theatre.
    Evening or Full Dress.
    Opera Dress.
    4 cloth patterns.

Part 15, Mch 1810
    Meteorological Diagrams (folding)
    Partridge Shooting. Howitt.

Part 15, Mch 1810 (*contd.*)
    Circular Moveable Bookcase.
    North View of the India House, Leadenhall
        Street
    Ball Dress.
    Morning Dress.
    7 paper patterns.
    3 cloth patterns.

Part 16, Apr 1810
    Duke of Brunswick Oels.
    Pheasant Shooting. Howitt.
    A Patent Sideboard.
    British Museum New Building.
    Ladies Evening or Opera Dress.
    Full Dress of a Gentleman.
    4 cloth patterns.

Part 17, May 1810
    Hall at the Royal Academy Sommerset (*sic*)
        House.

Ackermann's Repository of Arts (*contd.*)

Part 17, May 1810 (*contd.*)
Woodcock Shooting. Howitt.
Walking Dress.
Promenade or Opera Dress.
Salon Chair, Library Chair.
4 cloth patterns.

Part 18, Jun 1810
Duck Shooting. Howitt.
Bullock's Museum, 22 Piccadilly.

Part 18, Jun 1810 (*contd.*)
Walking Dress.
Evening or Full Dress.
Gothic Sopha, Table, Chair & Footstool for a Library.
R. Ackermanns Pattern Card (8 pages).
3 cloth patterns.

Supplement, 1810
Bishop of Oporto. Robt. Cooper sculpt.

VOL. 4.—Engraved title + Text pp. 1–472 + 4 pp. index unnumbered + 7 sub-titles not included in the pagination.

Part 19, Jul 1810
Snipe Shooting. Howitt.
Ball Dress.
Promenade Dresses.
View of Piccadilly from Hyde Park Corner Turnpike.
Mahogany Sideboard & Dining Room Chair.
4 paper patterns.
4 cloth patterns.

Part 20, Aug 1810
Michaels Palace & the Imperial Palace Vienna.
Coming Home. Howitt.
Walking Dress.
Morning Dress.
Banquette.
3 cloth patterns.

Part 21, Sep 1810
Dartmoor Prison & English Barracks (folding).
Patent Still (uncoloured). Invented by J. Stancliffe.
Full Dress.
Walking Dress.
View of Cornhill, Lombard St. & Mansion House.
Library Reading Chairs.
4 cloth patterns.

Part 22, Oct 1810
Map of Island of Capri. E. Gullan sculp.
Perch Shad & Barbel.
Morning Dress.
Evening Promenade or Sea Beach Costumes.
The Bason in the Green Park, St. James's.
Window Curtains.
3 cloth patterns.

Part 23, Nov. 1810
Roach & Salmon Trout.
Half Dress.
Walking & Morning Dress.
Lincolns Inn Fields coming in from Gt. Queen Street.
Royal Patent Invalid Chair.
4 cloth patterns.

Part 24, Dec 1810
Straits of Messina. E.W. delt.
General Statistical View (folding).
Gudgeons.
Morning Walking or Carriage Costume.
Evening Mourning Dress.
A Sideboard.
4 cloth patterns.

Supplement, 1810
Maria Louisa Empress of France. Guerard pinxt. A. Cardon sculpt. (uncoloured).

VOL. 5.—Engraved title + Text pp. 1–386 + 4 pp. index unnumbered + 6 sub-titles not included in the pagination.

Part 25, Jan 1811
Carp & Eels.
Evening Dresses.
Walking Dress.
Whitehall Yard (from the Street opposite the Horse Guards).
Imperial Turkey Ottoman or Circular Sofa.
3 cloth patterns.

Part 26, Feb 1811
Tench Chub & Bleak.

Part 26, Feb 1811 (*contd.*)
Charing Cross looking up the Strand.
Meteorological Diagrams, 1810.
Walking Dress or Carriage Costume.
Opera Dresses.
Drawing Room Chairs.
3 cloth patterns.

Part 27, Mch 1811
Pike and Flounders.
A Library Couch.

Ackermann's Repository of Arts (*contd.*)

Part 27, Mch 1811 (*contd.*)
Carriage Dress.
Opera Dress.
Ironmonger Hall.
3 cloth patterns.

Part 28, Apr 1811
Nelson's Monument on Carlton Hill, Edinburgh.
Lamprey & Salmon.
A Military Couch Bed.
Ball Dress.
Walking Dress.
Jewellery (folding). Designed & Manufactured
   by J. H. Barlow (uncoloured).
3 cloth patterns.

Part 29, May 1811
Sturgeon & Smelts.
Full Dress.
Opera Dress.
Lansdowne House, Berkley Square.
The Cradle of King of Rome & His Majesty.
4 cloth patterns.

Part 30, Jun 1811
Shell Fish.
A View of Whitehall & the Horse Guards.
Ladies Work Table.
Promenade Dresses.
Fashionable Head Dresses.
4 cloth patterns.

VOL. 6.—Engraved title + Text pp. 1–372 + 4 pp. index unnumbered + 6 sub-titles not included in the pagination.

Part 31, July 1811
Rt. Hble. Lord Visct Wellington. Drawn by
   A. Buck (uncoloured).
Whitehall Chapel.
Metamorphic Library Chair.
Opera Dress.
Promenade Dress.
3 cloth patterns.

Part 32, Aug 1811
The Geyser in Iceland.
The Hall of the Auction Mart.
A French Window Curtain.
Walking Dress.
Evening Dress.
4 cloth patterns.

Part 33, Sep 1811
Interior View of the Bank.
A Bookcase.
The Conservatory at Carlton House (folding).
Promenade Costume.
Morning Dress.
3 cloth patterns.

Part 34, Oct 1811
Auction Mart Coffee Room.

Part 34, Oct 1811 (*contd.*)
Merlin's Mechanical Chair.
Carlton House (folding).
Walking Dress.
Evening Dress.
4 cloth patterns.

Part 35, Nov 1811
Old House formerly the occasional residence
   of Henry the Eighth at Newington Green
   Middlesex.
Russell Institution Great Coram Street.
A Sett of Continued French Drapery Window
   Curtains.
Walking Dress.
Carriage Dress.
4 cloth patterns.
A Border and Pattern of Veil (uncoloured).

Part 36, Dec 1811
Warwick House. The residence of Her Royal
   Highness Princess Charlotte of Wales.
Riding Habit.
Mourning Dress.
Sofa Writing Table.
4 cloth patterns.
Pattern for Needlework (uncoloured).

VOL. 7.—Engraved title + Text pp. 1–374 + 4 pp. index not numbered + 6 sub-titles not included in the pagination.

Part 37, Jan 1812
The Staircase at Carlton House (folding).
Leicester Square from Leicester Place.
Half Dress.
Polish Walking Pelisse.
Four Posted Bed.
4 cloth patterns.
Pattern of Needlework (uncoloured).

Part 38, Feb 1812
Punishment of Criminals in Switzerland.
A View of St. Dunstans Church, Fleet Street.
Messrs Wilkinson & Wornums Upright Patent
   Piana Forte.
Ball Dress.
Walking Dress.
Pattern for Needlework.
3 cloth patterns.

Ackermann's Repository of Arts (*contd.*)

Part 39, Mch 1812
  Port Patrick.   E. Walsh Esqr. delt.
  Tottenham Court Road Turnpike & St. James's
  Indoor Morning Dress.   [Chapel.
  Evening Full Dress.
  A Library Bookcase.
  Pattern of Needlework (uncoloured).
  4 cloth patterns.

Part 40, Apl 1812
  Meteorological Diagrams.
  Southwark Bridge (folding).
  The Monument.
  A Toilette Dressing Case.
  Morning Dress.
  Ball Dress.
  3 cloth patterns.

Part 41, May 1812
  High Street Southampton taken from Bar
  Gate.
  Bridge Street Blackfriars.
  Library Table & Chair.
  Morning Dress.
  Walking Dress.
  4 cloth patterns.

Part 42, Jun 1812
  St. James's Palace.
  Walking Dress.
  Morning Dress.
  French Sofa & Drawing Room Chair.
  3 cloth & 1 paper pattern.
  Pattern of Needlework (uncoloured).

Two plates are sometimes found in this volume that are not included in the List of Plates, viz. London Female Penitentiary Pentonville (folding) and a pattern of needlework uncoloured at end of May part.

VOL. 8.—Engraved title + Text pp. 1–364 + 4 pp. index unnumbered + 6 sub-titles not included in the pagination.

Part 43, Jul 1812
  Maidstone Kent.   F.W.L. Stockdale fecit.
  Polito's Royal Menagerie, Exeter Change
  Strand.
  Evening Dress.
  Promenade Dress.
  French Library Curtain.
  4 cloth patterns.
  Pattern of Needlework (uncoloured).

Part 44, Aug 1812
  Treaty House Uxbridge.
  St. James's Square.
  Evening Dress.
  Promenade Dress.
  French Sofa.
  4 cloth patterns.
  Pattern of Needlework (uncoloured).

Part 45, Sept 1812
  Queen Square.
  Napoleon, Maria Louisa & King of Rome (un-
  coloured medallions).
  Evening Dress.
  Walking Dress.
  Drawing Room Window Curtain.
  4 cloth patterns.
  Pattern of Needlework (uncoloured).

Part 46, Oct 1812
  Soho Square.
  Promenade Costume.
  Morning Costume.
  A Verandah.   J. Papworth delt.
  Figures for Landscapes (sepia).
  Figures for Landscapes (sepia).
  Pattern for Needlework (uncoloured).

Part 47, Nov 1812
  George Street, Hanover Sqre.
  New Drury Lane Theatre.
  Candelabrum Stool & Reading Table.
  Evening Dress.
  Parisian Opera Dress.
  3 cloth patterns.
  Pattern for needlework (uncoloured).

Part 48, Dec 1812
  Figures for Landscape (after Pyne, un-
  coloured).
  Figures for Landscape (after Pyne, un-
  coloured).
  Royal Exchange.   T. Sutherland sc.
  A Bookcase.
  Evening Dress.
  Morning Dress.
  Pattern for Neelework (uncoloured).

VOL. 9.—Engraved title + Text pp. 1–374 + 4 pp. index unnumbered + 6 sub-titles not included in the pagination.

Part 49, Jan 1813
  Alexander the First Emperor of all the Russias.
  Engraved J. Minasi (uncoloured).

Part 49, Jan 1813 (*contd.*)
  View of Windsor.   J. Varley delt.   J. Bluck sc.
  Plan of a Cottage Ornee.

Ackermann's Repository of Arts (*contd.*)

Part 49, Jan 1813 (*contd.*)
Morning Walking Dress.
Opera Dress.
Pattern for Needlework.
3 Paper Patterns.

Part 50, Feb 1813
[Pynes Rustic Figures.]
[Pynes Rustic Figures.]
Tyburn Turnpike.
Cabinet and Dwarf Table.
Gothic Hall.
Opera Dress.
Morning Dress.
2 cloth and 1 paper pattern.
Pattern for Needlework (uncoloured).

Part 51, Mch 1813
Gothic Staircase and Vestibule.
Portions of Roman and Gothic Cathedrals (uncoloured).
Half Dress.
Opera Dress.
Pococks Reclining Patent Chair.
Cavendish Square, North Side.
4 cloth patterns.
Pattern for Needlework (uncoloured).

Part 52, Apr 1813
Meteorological Chart.
Meteorological Chart.

Part 52, Apr 1813 (*contd.*)
Pynes Figures.
Pynes Figures.
Gothic Conservatory.
Ackermanns Library for works of Art. A. Pugin delt. J. Bluck sculpt (folding.)
Carriage Dress.
Morning Dress.
Pattern for Needlework (folding, uncoloured).

Part 53, May 1813
Gothic Bed Room.
London Commercial Sale Rooms, Mark Lane.
A State Bed.
Morning Dress.
Full Dress.
4 cloth patterns.
Pattern for Needlework (uncoloured).
Rustic Figures.
Rustic Figures.

Part 54, June 1813
Gothic Library.
Cheapside.
Section of the Common Sewers.
A Hamburger Volunteer.
Promenade Dress.
Ball Dress.
3 cloth patterns.
Pattern for Needlework (uncoloured).

An extra coloured plate Tyburn Turnpike not in List of Plates is sometimes found in this volume though called for on text p. 88.

VOL. 10.—Engraved title + Text pp. 1–376 + 4 pp. index unnumbered + 6 sub-titles not included in pagination.

Part 55, July 1813
Alexander Zemlenutin Kossack of the Don Regiment Sulin the 9th
French Window Curtain.
A Library.
Manchester Square. North Side.
Morning Walking Dress.
Full Dress.
3 cloth and 1 paper pattern.

Part 56, Aug 1813
Monument of Mr. Pitt, Guildhall (uncoloured).
Portman Square, North Side.
Antique Sofa and Table.
Evening Dress.
Morning Dress.
3 Cloth patterns.
Pattern for Needlework (uncoloured).

Part 57, Sep 1813
Berkeley Square.
Bed Room Chair. Cottage Chair.

Part 57, Sep 1813 (*contd.*)
Evening Dress.
Promenade Dress.
3 cloth patterns.
Rustic Figures.
Rustic Figures.

Part 58, Oct 1813
A View of Fort George, Upper Canada from Old Fort Niagara. E.W. in locum delin.
The Indian Jugglers.
Footstools.
Evening Dress.
Morning Dress.
3 cloth patterns.
Pattern for Needlework (uncoloured)

Part 59, Nov 1813
Colossal Column of French Ordnance.
North Side of Grosvenor Square.
Morning Dress.
Evening Dress.

Ackermann's Repository of Arts (*contd.*)

Part 59, Nov 1813 (*contd.*)
4 cloth patterns.
Rustic Figures.
Pattern for Needlework (uncoloured).

Part 60, Dec 1813
Montague House now British Museum.

Part 60, Dec 1813 (*contd.*)
Patent Montgolfier Smoke Conductor. J. Gregson delt.
Morning Dress.
Evening Dress.
Rustic Figures.
3 cloth patterns.
Pattern for Needlework (uncoloured).

The pattern for needlework listed in the September 1813 was not issued. The descriptive text to the French Window Curtain which is called for in part 55 was not given until part 57 and the plate is consequently sometimes found in this position.

VOL. 11.—Engraved title + Text pp. 1–371 + 3 pp. index unnumbered + 6 sub-titles not included in the pagination.

Part 61, Jan 1814
Wolfgang Amadeus Mozart. uncoloured.
The Pantheon.
Death and Bonaparte. T. Rowlandson del. (folding).
Library Table & Chair.
Promenade Dress.
Morning Dress.
[Pattern for Needlework] Half a Collar.

Part 62, Feb 1814
St. Clement Danes.
Writing & Back Gammon Table.
Ball Dress.
Walking Dress.
Isabella Moreau (uncoloured).
Needlework Patterns.

Part 63, Mch 1814
St Stephen's Church Walbrook.
Secretaire Bookcase.
Evening Dress.
Walking Dress.
Rustic Figures. uncoloured.

Part 63, Mch 1814 (*contd.*)
Rustic Figures. Uncoloured.
Needlework Patterns.

Part 64, Apr 1814
Meteorological Diagrams.
St Paul's Cathedral, West Front.
Carlton House Table & Chair.
Walking Dress.
Morning Dress.
Needlework Patterns.

Part 65, May 1814
St Leonards Shoreditch.
Design for Window Curtains.
G. L. von Blucher (uncoloured).
Opera Dress.
Walking Dress.
Needlework Patterns.

Part 66, Jun 1814
Salt Mine. R. H. Martin delt. J. Bluck sc.
The Old Bailey.
4 cloth patterns.
Walking Dress.
Full Dress.

VOL. 12.—Engraved title + Text pp. 1–372 + 3 pp. (iv blank) index unnumbered + 6 sub-titles not included in the pagination.

Part 67, Jul 1814
View of London Bridge.
Design for an Ottoman Couch.
Evening Dress.
Morning Dress.
Needlework Pattern.
Rustic Figures. W. H. Pyne. uncoloured.

Part 68, Aug 1814
Cold Baths Fields Prison.
Bed Room Chairs.
Walking Dress.
Evening Dress.
Rustic Figures. W. H. Pyne. uncoloured.
Needlework Patterns.

Part 69, Sep 1814
Ackermanns Transparency (folding).
Hall Chairs.
Morning Dress.
Evening Half Dress.
Needlework Pattern.

Part 70, Oct 1814
View of the Bridge & Pagoda, St. James Park. A. Pugin delt. J. R. Hamble aquat. (folding).
Parlour Chairs.
Promenade Dress.
Walking Dress.
Needlework Pattern.

Ackermann's Repository of Arts (*contd.*)

Part 71, Nov 1814
View of the Temple of Concord in the Green Park.
  A. Pugin delt. J. C. Stadler aquat. (folding.)
Queenston, or the landing between Lake
  Ontario & Lake Erie.
Walking Dress.
Half Dress.
Needlework Pattern.

Part 72, Dec 1814
Buckingham Stairs Water Gate from the
  River.
Head Dresses.
Walking Dress.
Drawing Room Chairs.
4 cloth patterns.

Pynes rustic figures listed for September was not published.

VOL. 13.—Engraved title + Text pp. 1–370 + 2 pp. index + 6 sub-titles not included in the pagination.

Part 73, Jan 1815
Lunatic Hospital of St Lukes.
Library Window Curtain.
Evening Dress.
Opera Dress.
3 cloth patterns.

Part 74, Feb 1815
St Martin's in the Fields.
Morning Dress.
Evening Dress.
French Cottage Bed.
Needlework Pattern.

Part 75, Mch 1815
Oxford Street & Entrance into Stratford Place.
Drawing Room Window Curtain.
Walking Dress.
Morning Dress.
Needlework Patterns.

Part 76, Apr 1815
A Labyrinth.
A French Sofa.
Portland Place.
Evening Dress.
Morning Dress.
Needlework Patterns.

Part 77, May 1815
Meteorological Diagrams.
French Bed Chamber (folding).
Walking Dress.
Evening Dress.
4 cloth patterns.

Part 78, Jun 1815
Town Hall Southwark.
Ball Dress.
Carriage Dress.
Violettes du 20 Mars 1815. Canu fecit.
Needlework Patterns.

VOL. 14.—Engraved title + Text pp. 1–439 (p. 440 blank) including index + 6 sub-titles not included in the pagination. The text to Vol. 14. finishes on p. 368, followed by 4 pp. of index, the penultimate marked "end of vol. XIV," but this is followed by a Supplement and Index paged 373–439.

Part 79, Jul 1815
Glaciers of Canton Berne Drawn from a model
  in alto relief by Meyer.
Mercers Hall.
Furniture for an Artist's or Amateurs Aparte-
  ment.
Walking Dress.
Evening Dress.
Needlework Patterns.

Part 80, Aug 1815
Town & Port of Ostend from the East. E.
  Walsh Esq delt. 1815.
Bullock's Museum Piccadilly.
Furniture for a Music Room.
Evening Dress.
Promenade Dress.
Needlework Patterns.

Part 81, Sep 1815
Theodore Koerner's Monument.
St Stephens Chapel & Speakers House from
  Westminster Bridge.
Boudoir Window Curtains.
Dinner Dress.
Carriage Dress.
Needlework Pattern.

Part 82, Oct 1815
La Belle Alliance Taken on the Spot June
  25th by E. Walsh. J. C. Stadler sculpt.
  (folding).
Blackfriars Bridge from the Strand Bridge.
Dining & Drawing Room Chairs.
Morning Dress.
Walking Dress.
Needlework Patterns.

Ackermann's Repository of Arts (*contd.*)

Part 83, Nov 1815
  Christ Church Spitalfields.
  Fashionable Furniture.
  St. Helena.
  Morning Dress.
  Promenade Dress.
  Muslin Patterns.

Part 84, Dec. 1815
  St. Johns Church Westminster from the River.
  Firescreens.
  Evening Dress.
  Walking Dress.
  Needlework Patterns.

SERIES 2.

VOL. 1.—Title (white lettering on black design) + Text pp. 1–367 + 5 pp. index un-numbered + 6 sub-titles not included in the pagination.

Part 1, Jan 1816
  Cottage Ornee.
  Chimney Piece of Mona Marble.
  Mr. Ross's Room, Bishopsgate Street.
  Carriage Dress.
  Evening Dress.
  Muslin Patterns.

Part 2, Feb 1816
  Gothic Cottage.
  Bonaparte's Carriage.
  Evening Dress.
  Walking Dress.
  Drawing Room Window Curtain.
  Muslin Pattern.

Part 3, Mch 1816
  Park Lodge & Entrance.
  A Winter Sledge.
  Evening Dress.
  Carriage Dress.
  French Sofa Bed.
  Muslin Pattern.

Part 4, Apr 1816
  Cottage Ornee.
  An Imperial Sledge.
  Morning Dress.
  Opera Dress.
  A French Bed.
  Muslin Patterns.

Part 5, May 1816
  A Hunting Lodge.
  J. Brutus. G. Guillon le Thiere P. Rome 1810 Pinelli incise. (uncoloured, folding)
  Evening Dress.
  Morning Dress.
  Grecian Furniture.
  Muslin Patterns.

Part 6, Jun 1816
  A Diary.
  Bridal Dress.
  Evening Dress.
  Dining Room.
  Muslin Patterns.

VOL. 2.—Title + Text pp. 1–368 + 4 pp. index not numbered + 6 sub-titles not included in the pagination.

Part 7, Jul 1816
  A Gothic Conservatory.
  The New Custom House.
  Opera Dress.
  Morning Dress.
  A Saloon.
  Muslin Pattern.

Part 8, Aug 1816
  Gardener's Cottage.
  His Serene Highness Prince Leopold George.
  Evening Dress.
  Walking Dress.
  Dining Room.
  Muslin Patterns.

Part 9, Sep 1816
  Garden Seats.
  The Banqueting House.
  Half Dress.

Part 9, Sep 1816 (*contd.*)
  Evening Dress.
  A Small Bed.
  Muslin Patterns.

Part 10, Oct 1816
  A Vicarage House.
  Part of the Ruins of Savoy in 1816 taken from the Strand Bridge.
  Half Dress.
  Ball Dress.
  A Mona Marble Chimney Piece.
  Muslin Patterns.

Part 11, Nov. 1816
  Cottage Ornee.
  Plan and Elevation of the New Bridge now building over the Thames. J. Rennie Civil Engineer F.R.S. &c. (uncoloured).
  Morning Dress.

Ackermann's Repository of Arts (*contd.*)

Part 11, Nov 1816 (*contd.*)
Evening Dress.
An English Bed.
Muslin Patterns.

Part 12, Dec 1816
A Park Entrance.
Plan and Elevation of the Savoy Reduced from

Part 12, Dec 1816 (*contd.*)
a View taken in the year 1736 by G. Vertue
(uncoloured).
Promenade Dress.
Carriage Dress.
Drawing Room Window Curtains.
Ornaments for Painting on Wood & Fancy
Work (uncoloured).

The portrait of Prince Leopold is sometimes found in part 7.

VOL. 3.—Title + Text pp. 1–368 + 4 pp. index unnumbered + 6 sub-titles not included in
the pagination.

Part 13, Jan 1817
Fishing Lodge.
Table D'Hote.
A View and Plan of Longwood House St.
Helena the Residence of Napolean Bona-
parte.
Full Dress.
Parisian Head Dresses.
Ornaments for Painting on Wood & Fancy
Work (uncoloured).

Part 14, Feb 1817
A Cottage.
Searched by the Douaniers on the French
Frontiers.
Dottator et Lineator Loquitur (uncoloured).
Carriage Dress.
Evening Dress.
Ornaments for Painting on Wood & Fancy
Work (uncoloured).

Part 15, Mch 1817
A Villa.
Consulting the Prophet.
The Westminster Penitentiary.
Opera Dress.
Evening Dress.
Needlework Patterns.

Part 16, Apr 1817
A Cottage.
The Prophet discovering himself and exposing
the deception.
Specimen of R Ackermanns Lithographic Art.
St Elizth. Castle Jersey. S. Prout delt.
(uncoloured).
Parisian Ball Dress.
Walking Dress.
Drawing Room Window Curtain.
Muslin Patterns.

Part 17, May 1817
A Villa.
The Arrival in Paris.
Specimen of R Ackermanns Lithography. May
1817 (uncoloured).
Vauxhall Bridge.
Evening Dress.
Morning Dress.

Part 18, Jun 1817
An Ice House.
Liberality to Infirm Beggars on leaving Yvry.
Specimen of Ackermann Lith. (folding, un-
coloured).
Evening Dress.
Morning Dress.
Chimney Piece of Mona Marble.

*In addition to the specimen of Ackermann's Lithography a second plate "Lithographic Orna-
mental Pattern" is called for in the List of Plates, but this was never issued.*

VOL. 4.—Title + Text pp. 1–368 + 4 pp. index not numbered + 6 sub-titles not included
in the pagination.

Part 19, July 1817
A Villa.
Rural Happiness at Caverac.
Concert of Cats.   R. Ackermann's Lithography
July 1817   Painted by P. Breughal.   Etched
on stone by an amateur (uncoloured).
Dinner Dress.
Evening Dress.

Part 20, Aug 1817
A Cottage Orne.

Part 20, Aug 1817 (*cont.*)
Pleasures of a Poste aux Anes.
New Bethlem Hospital, St. Georges Fields.
Parisian Bonnets.
Walking Dress.
Needlework Patterns.

Part 21, Sep 1817
Four Cottages.
The Embrace.
Brighton Walking Dress.

Ackermann's Repository of Arts (*contd.*)

Part 21, Sep 1817 (*contd.*)
 The Glengary Habit.
 Fashionable Chairs.
 Muslin Patterns.

Part 22, Oct 1817
 A Gothic Cottage.
 [Durers Prayer Book] (*Specimen* 1 *leaf without title*).
 Evening Dress.
 Promenade Dress.
 A French Bed.
 Muslin Patterns.

Part 23, Nov 1817
 A Bailiffs Cottage.
 Views of the Schloss, Nearer View of the

Part 23, Nov 1817 (*contd.*)
 Schloss, The New House of Her Serene Highness the Duchess Regent of Saxe Meiningen at Liebenstein.
 Ball Dress.
 Walking Dress.
 An Ottoman for a Gallery.
 Muslin Patterns.

Part 24, Dec 1817
 [Memorial to Charlotte Augusta Princess of Wales] No title (uncoloured).
 At Avignon First Sight of Clara.
 Evening Dress.
 Walking Dress.
 A Domestic Chapel.
 Muslin Patterns.

VOL. 5.—Title + Text pp. 1–380 + 4 pp. index unnumbered + 6 sub-titles not included in the pagination.

Part 25, Jan 1818
 View of the Banks of the Lake of Geneva near St. Gingough.
 At the Tomb of Laura.
 An Universal Fish Table. R. Ackermann's lithographic Press (uncoloured).
 Pictorial Cards.
 Evening Dress.
 Carriage Dress.

Part 26, Feb 1818
 View of the Extremity of Lake of Geneva.
 Auction of Relics at Avignon.
 Pictorial Cards.
 Evening Dress.
 Walking Dress.
 Muslin Patterns.

Part 27, Mch 1818
 View of the Bridge of St. Maurice.
 Pictorial Cards.
 Bridal Dress.
 Walking Dress.
 Muslin Pattern.

Part 28, Apr 1818
 Waterfall of Pissevache.
 A Prisoner at Avignon.
 Sections of Carriage. Ackermann's lithographic Press.
 Plan of Carriage. Ackermann's lithographic Press.
 Elevation of Carriage.
 Pictorial Cards.
 Walking Dress.
 Evening Dress.

Part 29, May 1818
 West View of Sion.
 Pictorial Cards.
 Muslin Patterns.
 Dinner Dress.
 Morning Dress.

Part 30, Jun 1818
 East View of Sion.
 A Tragic Story at Avignon.
 A Verandah.
 Pictorial Cards.
 Walking Dress.
 Evening Dress.

The Tragic Story of Avignon is sometimes found in the May number—it should be in June.

VOL. 6.—Title + Text pp. 1–368 + 4 pp. index unnumbered + 6 sub-titles not counted in the pagination.

Part 31, Jul 1818
 View of Brieg.
 Before the Tribunal at Avignon.
 Pictorial Cards.
 Walking Dress.
 Riding Dress.
 Muslin Patterns.

Part 32, Aug 1818
 View of the Gallery and Bridge of the Ganther.
 Pictorial Cards.
 Morning Dress.
 Evening Dress.
 A Pier Table and Grecian Pedestal.
 Muslin Patterns.

Ackermann's Repository of Arts (*contd.*)

Part 33, Sep 1818
View from the Entrance of the Gallery of Schalbet.
Sacred Page Displayed.
Walking Dress.
Evening Dress.
Pictorial Cards.
Muslin Patterns.

Part 34, Oct 1818
View of Gallery of Schalbet from the Italian Side.
Residence of Prince Homburg near Frankfurth.
Pictorial Cards.
Evening Dress.
Walking Dress.
Muslin Patterns.

Part 35, Nov 1818
View of Gallery of Glaciers.
Pictorial Cards.
Morning Dress.
Walking Dress.
Muslin Patterns.
Commode Pier Glass & Tabourets.

Part 36, Dec 1818
View of the Site of the Monastery of Simplon & of Mount Rosa.
Pictorial Cards.
Evening Dress.
Walking Dress.
Drawing Room Window Curtain.
Muslin Patterns.

VOL. 7.—Title + Text pp. 1–368 + 4 pp. index unnumbered + 6 sub-titles not included in the pagination.

Part 37, Jan 1819
A Woodland Seat.
View of the Village of Simplon.
Pictorial Cards.
The Isabella & Alexander under Capt Ross passing a remarkable Iceberg July 1818 (uncoloured).
Half Mourning Walking Dress.
Half Mourning Evening Dress.

Part 38, Feb 1819
An Aviary.
View of the Exterior of Gallery of Algaby.
Pedestrian Hobbyhorse.
Walking Dress.
Evening Dress.
Muslin Patterns.

Part 39, Mch 1819
A Landaulet with Birch's Patent Roof and Ackermanns patent moveable axles. Drawn by Blunt. Engravd by S. Mitan.
View from the Interior of the Gallery of Algaby.
Walking Dress.
Evening Dress.
Drawing Room Window Curtain & Jardiniere.
Muslin Patterns.

Part 40, Apr 1819
Alto Bridge.
A Bridge & Boat House.
Ackermanns Lithography.
Walking Dress.
Evening Dress.
Gothic Furniture.
Muslin Patterns.

Part 41, May 1819
A Polish Hut.
4 samples metallick paper Brunells Patent.
View of the New Road near the Grand Gallery.
Morning Dress.
Walking Dress.
Dining Room Suit. (*sic*)

Part 42, Jun 1819
An Aviary.
Morning Dress.
Evening Dress.
Royal Waterloo Bath.
View of the Interior of the Grand Gallery.
Muslin patterns.

VOL. 8.—Title + Text pp. 1–368 + 4 pp. index unnumbered + 6 sub-titles not included in the pagination.

Part 43, Jul 1819
A Bridge Adapted to Park Scenery.
A Light Pheaton with Ackermanns Patent Moveable Axles. Drawn by C. Blunt. Engraved by S. Mitan.
Patterns.
View of the End of the Grand Gallery towards Italy.

Part 43, Jul 1819 (*contd.*)
Walking Dress.
Evening Dress.

Part 44, Aug 1819
The London Engineer (steam yacht).
A View near Gondo.
Morning Dress.

Ackermann's Repository of Arts (*contd.*)

Part 44, Aug 1819 (*contd.*)
  Evening Dress.
  Drawing Room Window Curtain & Work Table
  Black and White Pattern.

Part 45, Sep 1819
  A Swiss Cottage.
  View of the Gallery of Issel.
  Interior of the Great Room at Egyptian Hall
    (uncoloured).
  Walking & Morning Dress.
  Evening Dress.
  Drawing Room Window Curtains.
  Black and White Pattern.

Part 46, Oct 1819
  A Fountain.
  Entrance of Valley of Dovedro.
  Walking Dress.
  Evening Dress.

Part 46, Oct 1819 (*contd.*)
  Library Window Curtains.
  Black and White Pattern.

Part 47, Nov. 1819
  Park Entrances.
  View of a Bridge over the Cherasca.
  A Light Pheaton.
  Walking Dress.
  Evening Dress.
  Muslin Pattern.
  Urlings Lace (and leaf of text). Usually missing.

Part 48, Dec 1819
  Coppice wood Fences Gates and Hurdles.
  View of the Entrance of the Last Gallery.
  Walking Dress.
  Morning Dress.
  Three Designs for Window Draperies.
  Muslin Pattern.

VOL. 9.—Title + Text pp. 1–368 + 4 pp. index unnumbered + 6 sub-titles not included in the pagination.

Part 49, Jan 1820
  A Garden Seat.
  View of the Bridge of Crevola and the Valley
    of Domo D'ossola.
  Barouche with Ackermanns Patent Moveable
    Axles Drawn by C. Blunt. Engraved by
    S. Mitan.
  Half Dress.
  Evening Dress.
  Chinese Pattern.

Part 50, Feb 1820
  An Alcove.
  Bridge of Crevola.
  Draperies for Circular Windows.
  Carriage Dress.
  Evening Dress.
  Muslin Pattern.

Part 51, Mch 1820
  A Cenotaph.
  Villa.
  Walking Dress.
  Evening Dress.
  Drawing Room Window Curtains.
  Muslin Patterns.

Part 52, Apr 1820
  A Venetian Tent.
  The Royal Vault St. Georges Chapel Windsor.
    F. Nash delt. D. Havell sculpt (folding).
  View of the Lago Maggiore and the Boromeo
    Islands.
  Carriage Dress.
  Evening Dress.
  Muslin Pattern.

Part 53, May 1820
  An Apiary.
  View of the Island of Bella.
  Walking Dress.
  Evening Dress.
  Window Draperies.
  Black and White Pattern.

Part 54, Jun 1820
  A Garden Seat.
  View of Arona.
  Walking Dress.
  Evening Dress.
  Window Draperies.
  Black and White Borders.

VOL. 10.—Title + Text pp. 1–376 including index + 6 sub-titles not included in the pagination.

Part 55, Jul 1820
  A Garden Fountain.
  View from Stresa of the Beautiful Island.
  Walking Dress.
  Court Dress.
  Window Draperies.
  Black and White Pattern.

Part 56, Aug 1820
  An Ice Well.
  View of Pliniana on the Lake of Como.
  Walking Dress.
  Evening Dress.
  A Droschki.
  Black and White Borders.

Ackermann's Repository of Arts (*contd.*)

Part 57, Sep 1820
  A Bath.
  View of Sesto.
  Cottage Dress.
  Ball Dress.
  Window Drapery.
  Black and White Borders.

Part 58, Oct 1820
  A Rustic Bridge.
  The Inn at Marseilles.
  View of the Bridge of Baveno & of the Madre
    Islands.
  Walking Dress.
  Evening Dress.
  Black and White Pattern.

Part 59, Nov 1820
  A Conservatory.
  View of Milan.
  Siderographia Banknote: Patent Harland Steel
    Plate.
  Walking Dress.
  Evening Dress.
  Muslin Patterns.

Part 60, Dec 1820
  A Garden Fountain.
  An Academy for Young Gentlemen near
    Dresden.
  Walking Dress.
  Full Dress.
  View of Geneva.
  Black and White Pattern.

Siderographia Bank Note and Harland Steel Plate are printed on 2 sides of 1 leaf and counted as 1 plate.

VOL. 11.—Title + Text pp. 1–380 including index + 6 sub-titles not included in the pagination.

Part 61, Jan 1821
  A Picturesque Dairy.
  The New French Violins & Acoustic Experi-
    ments of Dr. Savart (uncoloured).
  Bern.
  Design for an Ottoman Painted on a large scale
    by Miss Welch for the King of Persia (un-
    coloured).
  Promenade Dress.
  Evening Dress.

Part 62, Feb 1821
  Gamekeeper's Lodge.
  The Tea Plant.
  Morning Dress.
  Evening Dress.
  A Dress Sofa. J. Taylor del. Duvall sc.
  Black and White Borders.

Part 63, Mch 1821
  View of a Lodge.
  The Water Ram.
  View near Thun.
  Heating & Rolling Tea Leaves.
  Head Dresses.
  Evening Dress.

Part 64, Apr 1821
  A Poultry House.
  View of Thun.
  Preparing the Lead for the Packing of Tea.
  Bulbous Roots.
  Promenade Dress.
  Full Dress.

Part 65, May 1821
  Gardener's Cottage.
  Tea Warehouse.
  View of Castle of Spiez.
  Fancy Ball Dress.
  Head Dresses.
  Black and White Pattern.

Part 66, Jun 1821
  A Fountain.
  Making of Tea Chests.
  View of Unterseen.
  Morning Dress.
  Evening Dress.
  Muslin Pattern.

An advertisement for Urling's lace and cotton with 4 patterns can be found in January number.

VOL. 12.—Title + Text pp. 1–372, including index + 6 sub-titles not included in the pagination.

Part 67, Jul 1821
  Garden Railing.
  Treading the Tea in Baskets.
  View of Interlaken.

Part 67, Jul 1821 (*contd.*)
  Walking Dress.
  Evening Dress.
  A Gothic Side Table. J. Taylor invt. et delt.

Ackermann's Repository of Arts (*contd.*)

Part 68, Aug 1821
Gothic Dairy.
Method of gathering Tea by means of Monkeys.
Walking Dress.
Evening Dress.
View of Westminster Abbey shewing the manner in which it was fitted up at the Coronation.
Black and White Pattern.

Part 69, Sep 1821
A Bridge & Temple.
View of the Jungfrau.
Fall of the Staubbach.
Walking Dress.
Evening Dress.
Patterns for Corners of Handkerchiefs.

Part 70, Oct 1821
Plan of a Garden (tinted).
View of the Glaciers of Grindelwald.

Part 70, Oct 1821 (*contd.*)
Walking Dress.
Court Dress.
Library, Side, & Pier Tables.
Muslin Pattern.

Part 71, Nov 1821
A Laundry.
View of the Glaciers of Roselouvi.
Promenade Dress.
Evening Dress.
Chimney Piece of Mona Marble.
Muslin Pattern.

Part 72, Dec 1821
A Small Garden.
Meyringen.
Promenade Dress.
Full Dress.
Girandole.
Black and White Pattern.

VOL. 13.—Title + Text pp. 1–376 including index + 6 sub-titles not included in the pagination.

Part 73, Jan 1822
View of the Quadrant, Regent Street.
The Fall of Olstenbach & the Bridge of Wyler.
Morning Dress.
Full Dress.
Drawing Room Lustre.
Muslin Patterns.

Part 74, Feb 1822
Charles Street.
View of the Village of Brienz.
Head Dresses.
Full Dress.
Fashionable Furniture.
Muslin Patterns.

Part 75, Mch 1822
Charles Street Looking East.
Provincial Bank.
Whitby Old Bank.
Deal Bank.
View of the Castle of Rinkenburg.
Walking Dress.
Evening Dress.
Patterns for the corners of Handkerchiefs.

Part 76, Apr 1822
Regent Street.

Part 76, Apr 1822 (*contd.*)
View of the Cavern of St. Beat near the Lake of Thun.
Walking Dress.
Evening Dress.
Secretaire Bookcase.
Muslin Patterns.

Part 77, May 1822
Langham Place & Portland Place.
Wetzlar.
View on the Lake of Thun from Upper Island.
Morning Dress.
Full Dress.
Muslin Patterns.

Part 78, Jun 1822
The Crescent Portland Place.
The Environs of Thun.
Commercial Bank.
Commercial Bank.
The Picture Gallery of Sir J. Leicester Bart. (uncoloured).
[Monument to late King]. M. Wyatt invt. et sculpt. (uncoloured).
Court Dress.
Evening Dress.

A further illustration in the March Number, Mersey Bank Liverpool, was issued though not called for in the List of Plates.

VOL. 14.—Title + Text pp. 1–372 including index + 6 sub-titles not included in the pagination.

Ackermann's Repository of Arts (*contd.*)

Part 79, Jul 1822
Regent Street looking towards the Quadrant.
The Castle of Wufflens.
Morning Dress.
Evening Dress.
Clock Stand & Flower Stand.
Pattern for Watchstand.

Part 80, Aug 1822
Regent Street from Waterloo Place.
View of a Natural Bridge.
Walking Dress.
Evening Dress.
Flower Stand.
Muslin Pattern.

Part 81, Sept 1822
View of the Italian Opera House.
West Entrance to Tunnel Regents Canal Islington.
Ball Dress.
Court Dress.
Secretaire Bookcase.
Muslin Patterns.

Part 82, Oct 1822
Waterloo Place looking towards Carlton Place.
The City Basin, Regents Canal.
Morning Dress.
Evening Dress.
Sideboard & Cellaret.
Muslin Pattern.

Part 83, Nov 1822
Pall Mall.
Highgate Archway.
Walking Dress.
Evening Dress.
French Sofa Bed.
Muslin Pattern.

Part 84, Dec 1822
The New Street looking towards the Quadrant.
Bishop's College near Calcutta.
Promenade Dress.
Evening Dress.
An Egyptian Chimney Front.
Muslin Pattern.

SERIES 3

VOL. 1.—Title + Text pp. 1–380 including index + 6 sub-titles not included in the pagination.

Part 1, Jan 1823
Entrance Front of His Majestys Cottage Windsor Great Park.
His Majestys Cottage as seen from the Lawn.
Royal Military Trophy and Candelabrum. R. Cooper sct. (uncoloured).
Morning Dress.
Ball Dress.
Muslin Patterns.

Part 2, Feb 1823
Cranburn Lodge. J. Gendall delt.
Cranburn Lodge (Back Front) J. Gendall delt.
Evening Dress.
Head Dresses.
Lady's Work Table.
Muslin Pattern.

Part 3, Mch 1823
Front View of Frogmore House. J. Gendall delt.
The Ruins, Frogmore. J. Gendall delt.
The Hermitage Frogmore. J. Gendall delt.
German Waltz by Beethoven (folding).
Walking Dress.
Evening Dress.
Muslin Pattern.

Part 4, Apr 1823
Chiswick House (Principal Front) J. Gendall delt.
Chiswick House Garden Front. J. Gendall delt.
Mr. Blades' Upper Show Room. J. Gendall delt.
Morning Dress.
Evening Dress.
Needlework Pattern.

Part 5, May 1823
Sion House. J. Gendall delt.
The Park Entrance Sion House. J. Gendall delt.
Promenade Dress.
Evening Dress.
Cabinet Bookcase.
Needlework Pattern.

Part 6, Jun 1823
Deepdene the Seat of T. Hope Esq. J. Gendall delt.
The Rookery Seat of R. Fuller Esq. J. Gendall delt.
Carriage Dress.
Ball Dress.
Fashionable Furniture.
Muslin Pattern.

Ackermann's Repository of Arts (*contd.*)

VOL. 2.—Title + Text pp. 1–372 including index + 6 sub-titles not included in the pagination.

Part 7, July 1823
Tabley House. J. Gendall delt.
Scene in Tabley Park.
Morning Dress.
Ball Dress.
Fashionable Furniture.
Muslin Patterns.

Part 8, Aug 1823
Ditton Seat of Lord Montagu. J. Gendall delt.
Holly Grove House the Seat of Theodore Henry Broadhead Esq. J. Gendall delt.
Fonthill Abbey. The Pavilion (now used as a dormitory for the Visitors) and the Lake in the Old Park. W. Finley del. J. Cleghorn lithd.
National Polonaise (folding).
Evening Dress.
Ball Dress.

Part 9, Sep 1823
Tatton Hall Seat of—Egerton Esq. J. Gendall delt.
Bury Hill Seat of Robert Barclay Esq. J. Gendall delt.
Morning Dress.
Evening Dress.
State Bed.
Muslin Patterns.

Part 10, Oct 1823
Eaton Hall Entrance Front. J. Gendall delt.

Par 10, Oct 1823 (*contd.*)
Eaton Hall (West or Garden Front). J. Gendall delt.
The Temple Lord Grosvenors. J. Gendall delt.
Morning Dress.
Ball Dress.
Muslin Pattern.

Part 11, Nov 1823
Sophia Lodge the seat of Wm. Dawson Esq. View from the Lawn. J. Gendall delt.
Sophia Lodge the seat of Wm. Dawson Esq. J. Gendall delt.
Woodside the Seat of John Ramsbottom Esq. M.P. J. Gendall delt.
Full Dress.
Head Dreses. (*sic*)
Muslin Pattern.

Part 12, Dec 1823
Dropmore Seat of Earl Grenville. View of the Entrance Front. J. Gendall delt.
Dropmore Seat of Earl Grenville. View of the Garden Front. J. Gendall delt.
Beaumont Lodge Seat of Viscount Ashbrooke. J. Gendall delt.
Full Dress.
Evening Dress.
Self Importance. Grattan del. Printed by C. Hullmandel.

VOL. 3.—Title + Text pp. 1–374 including index + 6 sub-titles not included in the pagination.

Part 13, Jan 1824
Princess Elizabeth's Cottage Old Windsor. J. Gendall delt.
Stoke Farm Seat of the Earl of Sefton. J. Gendall delt.
Morning Dress.
Promenade Dress.
Bookcase for a Study.

Part 14, Feb 1824
Pelling Place Lawn Front. J. Gendall delt.
Pelling Place Garden Front. J. Gendall delt.
Promenade Dress.
Evening Dress.
Cabinet Dressing Case.
Muslin Pattern.

Part 15, Mch 1824
St. Leonard's Hill Seat of the Earl of Harcourt. J. Gendall delt.
Iver Grove Seat of the Rt. Honble Lord Gambier. J. Gendall delt.

Part 15, Mch 1824 (*contd.*)
Morning Dress.
Evening Dress.
Decorations of a Chamber and French Bed.
Pattern for Needlework.

Part 16, Apr 1824
St Margarets (View from the Thames) J. Gendall delt.
St. Margaret's (entrance front) Seat of the Earl of Casillis. J. Gendall delt.
Dinner Dress.
Ball Dress.
Cabinet Glass.
Muslin Pattern.

Part 17, May 1824
Wanstead House the Seat of Wm Pole Tilney Long Wellesley Esq. J. Gendall delt.
Delaford Park the Seat of C. Clowes Esq. J. Gendall delt.
Morning Dress.

Ackermann's Repository of Arts (*contd.*)

Part 17, May 1824 (*contd.*)
    Dinner Dress.
    Astronomical Clock.
    Muslin Pattern.

Part 18, Jun 1824
    Stoke Pogis the Seat of John Penn Esq. J.
    Gendall delt.

Part 18, Jun 1824 (*contd.*)
    Gray's Monument at Stoke Pogis the Seat of
    John Penn Esq. J. Gendall delt.
    Promenade Dress.
    Ball Dress.
    Drawing Room Table Chairs and Footstools.
    J. Thomson delt.

VOL. 4.—Title + Text pp. 1–368 including index + 6 sub-titles not included in the pagination.

Part 19, July 1824
    Trentham Hall the Seat of the Marquis of
    Stafford. J. Gendall delt.
    Mausoleum at Trentham the Seat of the Mar-
    quis of Stafford. J. Gendall delt.
    Promenade Dress.
    Opera Dress.
    Alcove Window Curtains.
    Muslin Pattern.

Part 20, Aug 1824
    Hampton House the Residence of the late Mrs.
    Garrick. J. Gendall delt.
    Riching's Lodge seat of the Right Honble. John
    Sulivan. J. Gendall delt.
    Morning Dress.
    Ball Dress.
    Muslin Pattern.

Part 21, Sept 1824
    Stoke Place the Seat of Col. Vyse. J. Gendall
    delt.
    Mrs. Palmer's Villa, Richmond. J. Gendall delt.
    Morning Dress.
    Evening Dress.
    A Sofa. Taylor del.
    Muslin pattern.

Part 22, Oct 1824
    The New Lodge Richmond Park the Seat of
    Viscount Sidmouth. J. Gendall delt.
    Flamstead House. T. H. Shepherd delt.
    Promenade Dress.
    Dinner Dress.
    Fashionable Furniture.
    Muslin Pattern.

Part 23, Nov 1824
    Woburn Abbey Seat of the Duke of Bedford.
    Newstead Abbey the Seat of Lieut Col Wild-
    man.
    Morning Dress.
    Evening Dress.
    [Two Designs for Chairs] J. Taylor del.
    Muslin Pattern.

Part 24, Dec 1824
    Nutwell Court the Seat of Sir Thomas Trayton
    Fuller Eliott Drake Bart. J. Gendall delt.
    Nutwell Court [from River] ditto. J. Gendall
    delt.
    Sicre Gully Pass between Bengal and Bahar.
    Evening Dress.
    Morning Dress.
    Muslin Pattern.

VOL. 5.—Title + Text pp. 1–372 including index + 6 sub-titles not included in the pagination.

Part 25, Jan 1825
    Bicton Seat of the Right Honble Lord Rolle.
    J. Gendall delt.
    Bunney Hall the Residence of Lord Rancliffe.
    [Head Dresses.]
    Evening Dress.
    Group of Villas on Herne Hill, Camberwell.
    J. Thomson delt.
    Muslin Patterns.

Part 26, Feb 1825
    Wimbledon Park the Seat of Earl Spencer.
    T. H. Shepherd delt.
    Pynes the Seat of Sir Stafford Northcote Bart.
    J. Gendall delt.
    Promenade Dress.
    Evening Dress.

Part 26, Feb 1825 (*contd.*)
    A Sofa &c.
    Muslin Pattern.

Part 27, Mar 1825
    Belvoir Castle the Seat of His Grace the Duke
    of Rutland K.G. W. Westall delt.
    Moor Park the Seat of Robert Williams Esq.
    T. H. Shepherd delt.
    Promenade Dress.
    Ball Dress.
    Fashionable Chairs.
    Muslin Pattern.

Part 28, Apr 1825
    Burghley House Seat of the Marquess of
    Exeter. W. Westall delt.

Ackermann's Repository of Arts (*contd.*)

Part 28, Apr 1825 (*contd.*)
Pawderham Castle the Seat of Vist. Lord
  Courtenay. J. Gendall delt.
Morning Dress.
Dinner Dress.
A Sideboard.
Muslin Pattern.

Part 29, May 1825
Dunster Castle Seat of J. F. Luttrell Esq.
Swainston Seat of Sir FitzWilliam Barrington
  Bart. J. Gendall delt.
Morning Dress.

Part 29, May 1825 (*contd.*)
Evening Dress.
Fashionable Furniture.
Muslin Pattern.

Part 30, Jun 1825
Caen Wood the Seat of Earl Mansfield. F. W.
  Stockdale delt.
Piercefield Seat of Nathaniel Wells Esq. F. W.
  Stockdale delt.
Dinner Dress.
Ball Dress.
Gothic Fire Place.

VOL. 6.—Title + Text pp. 1–372 including index + 6 sub-titles not included in the pagination.

Part 31, Jul 1825
Saltram the Seat of Earl Morley. F. W. Stock-
  dale delt.
St. Pierre the Seat of Charles Lewis Esq., F. W.
  Stockdale delt.
Promenade Dress.
Evening Dress.
A Camp Bedstead.
Muslin Pattern.

Part 32, Aug 1825
Southill Park the Seat of Willm Henry Whit-
  bread Esq. F. W. Stockdale delt.
Watermouth, the Seat of Joseph Davie Bassett.
  F. W. Stockdale delt.
Morning Dress.
Dinner Dress.
Gothic Lamp for a Hall.
Muslin Pattern.

Part 33, Sept 1825
Hackwood Park Seat of Lord Bolton.
Broadlands Seat of Rt Hon Lord Visct. Palmer-
  ston.
Morning Dress.
Evening Dress.
Fire Place.
Muslin Pattern.

Part 34, Oct 1825
Stratton Park the Seat of Sir Thos Baring Bart.
  Hewetson delt.
The Vine Seat of Wm John Chute Esq.
  Hewetson delt.
[Head Dresses]
Evening Dress.
Book Case.
Muslin Pattern.

Part 35, Nov 1825
Stoneham Park the Seat of John Fleming Esq.
  M.P. Hewetson delt.
The Grange the seat of Alexander Baring
  Esq. M.P. I. Hewetson delt.
Garden Costume.
Evening Dress.
Gothic Furniture.
Muslin Patterns.

Part 36, Dec 1825
Avington the Seat of His Grace the Duke of
  Buckingham and Chandos K.B. Hewettson
  delt.
Worthy House the Seat of Sir Charles Ogle
  Bart Hewettson delt.
Morning Dress.
Evening Dress.
A Gothic Sofa.
Muslin Pattern.

VOL. 7.—Title + pp. 1–372 including index + 6 sub-titles not included in the pagination.

Part 37, Jan 1826
Guy's Cliff Seat of Bertie Greatheed Esq.
  W. Westall delt.
Colcorton Hall the Seat of Sir Geo. Beaumont
  Bart. W. Westall delt.
Promenade Dress.
Evening Dress.
Side Board.
Muslin Patterns.

Part 38, Feb 1826
Clumber Seat of the Duke of Newcastle. W.
  Westall delt.
Belhus Seat of Sir Thos B. Lennard Bart.
  M.P. F. Stockdale delt.
Dinner Dress.
Evening Dress.
A Gothic Window.
Muslin Pattern.

Ackermann's Repository of Arts (*contd.*)

Part 39, Mch 1826
Aston Hall the Seat of James Watt Esq. W. Westall A.R.A. delt.
Pencarrow the Seat of Lady Molesworth. F. Stockdale delt.
Dinner Dress.
Ball Dress.
Gothic Table.
Needlework Patterns.

Part 40, Apr 1826
Mount Edgcumbe Seat of the Rt. Honble Earl of Mount Edgcumbe. J. Gendall delt.
Orchard Cottage the Seat of Sir Willoughby Gordon. J. Gendall delt.
Carriage Costume.
Evening Dress.
A Gothic Bed.
Muslin Pattern.

Part 41, May 1826
East Cowes Castle the seat of J. Nash Esq.
Enmore Castle Seat of the Earl of Egmont.
Morning Dress.
Ball Dress.
Gothic Chairs.
Muslin Patterns.

Part 42, Jun 1826
Northcourt the Seat of Mrs Bennett. J. Gendall delt.
St. Jermain the seat of Lord Elliot. J. Gendall delt.
Dinner Dress.
Ball Dress.
Gothic Window Curtains.
Muslin Pattern.

VOL. 8.—Title + Text pp. 1–372 including index + 6 sub-titles not included in the pagination.

Part 43, Jul 1826
Norris Seat of the Rt Hon Lord Henry Seymore. J. Gendall delt.
Appuldurcombe Seat of the Earl of Yarborough. J. Gendall delt.
Walking Dress.
Evening Dress.
An Horizontal Grand Piano Forte.
Muslin Pattern.

Part 44, Aug 1826
Wimbledon House the Residence of Mrs. Marriott. T. H. Shepherd delt.
West Farm the Seat of—Bevan Esq.
Promenade Dress.
Evening Dress.
Flower Stands.
Muslin Patterns.

Part 45, Sep 1826
Pentilly Castle the Seat of John Tilly Coryton Esq.
Mitcham Grove the Seat of Henry Hoare Esq.
Carriage Costume.
Evening Dress.
Candelabras.
Muslin Pattern.

Part 46, Oct 1826
Maristow Seat of Sir Manasseh Lopes Bart. F. W. L. Stockdale delt.
Fulford House Seat of Colonel Fulford. J. Gendall delt.
[Head Dresses].
Evening Dress.
Gothic Furniture.
Muslin Patterns.

Part 47, Nov 1826
Oaklands the Seat of Albany Saville Esq. J. Gendall delt.
Crete Hall the Residence of Jeremiah Rosher Esq.
Promenade Dress.
Evening Dress.
A Gothic Sofa.
Muslin Pattern.

Part 48, Dec 1826
Cobham Hall Seat of the Earl of Darnley. T. H. Shepherd delt.
Midgham House the Seat of W. S. Poyntz Esq. M.P. F. W. L. Stockdale delt.
Morning Dress.
Evening Dress.
Gothic Chairs.
Muslin Patterns.

VOL. 9.—Title + Text pp. 1–372 including index + 6 sub-titles not included in pagination.

Part 49, Jan 1827
Sutton Hall the Seat of Richard Arkwright Esq., F. W. L. Stockdale delt.
Clowance the Seat of Sir John St. Aubyn Bart. Stockdale delt.

Part 49, Jan 1827 (*contd.*)
Promenade Dress.
Wedding Dress.
Gothic Furniture.
Muslin Patterns.

Ackermann's Repository of Arts (*contd.*)

Part 50, Feb 1827
Roehampton Priory the Seat of Colthurst Swinton Holland Esq. Stockdale delt.
Trelissick the Seat of Thomas Daniell Esq. T. H. Shepherd delt.
Opera Costume.
Evening Dress.
A Gothic Bed.
Muslin Patterns.

Part 51, Mch 1827
Ham House Seat of the Countess of Dysart. F. W. L. Stockdale delt.
Elvills the Seat of Hon. W. Freemantle M.P. F. W. L. Stockdale delt.
Evening Dress.
Morning Dress.
A Gothic Bookcase.
Muslin Patterns.

Part 52, Apr 1827
Burford Priory Seat of W. S. Lenthall Esq. F. C. L. Stockdale delt.
Offley Place Seat of the Rev. L. Burroughs. G. Shepherd delt.

Part 52 Apr 1827 (*contd.*)
Carriage Costume.
Ball Dress.
A Gothic Cabinet.
Needlework Patterns.

Part 53, May 1827
Ashburnham Park Seat of the Earl of Ashburnham. Stewartson delt.
Eridge Park Seat of the Earl of Abergavenny. Hewetson delt.
Dinner Dress.
Evening Dress.
Gothic Bureau.
Muslin Patterns.

Part 54, Jun 1827
West dean House the Seat of Lord Selsey. Hewetson delt.
R. Ackermann's Repository of Arts 96 Strand.
Promenade Dress.
Evening Dress.
Gothic Furniture.
Muslin Patterns.

VOL. 10.—Title + Text pp. 1–372 including index + 6 sub-titles not included in the pagination.

Part 55, Jul 1827
Michael Grove Seat of Thomas Walker Esq. Hewetson delt.
Poltimores Seat of Sir George Warwick Bamfylde Bart. Stockdale delt.
Carriage Costume.
Ball Dress.
Gothic Furniture.
Muslin Patterns.

Part 56, Aug 1827
Follaton House Seat of Stanley Carey Esq.
Lanhydrock House Seat of the Hon Mrs. Agar. J. W. Stockdale delt.
Promenade Dress.
Evening Dress.
Gothic Furniture.
Muslin Patterns.

Part 57, Sep 1827
Shavington Hall Seat of the Earl of Kilmorey.
Whitmore Lodge the Seat of Robt Mangles Esq.
Sea-Side Costume.
Evening Dress.
Gothic Furniture.
Muslin Pattern

Part 58, Oct 1827
South Hill House. Seat of Thomas Chetham Strode Esq.
Oxton House the Seat of J. Beaumont Sweet Esq.
Promenade Dress.
Ball Dress.
Pugin's Gothic Furniture.
Muslin Pattern.

Part 59, Nov 1827
Wonham Seat of the Rt. Honble Lord Templeton. F. W. L. Stockdale delt.
Buckland Filleigh the seat of John Inglett Fortescue Esq.
Morning Dress.
Dinner Dress.
Pall Mall East. A. Pugin delt.
Muslin Pattern.

Part 60, Dec 1827
Perridge House the Seat of Henry Linbrey Toll Esq.
Marine Villa Seat of the late Sir J. Cox Hippesley Bart. J. Gendall delt.
Carriage Dress.
Ball Dress.
Cockspur Street looking towards the Haymarket. A. Pugin delt.
Muslin patterns.

Ackermann's Repository of Arts (*contd.*)

VOL. 11.—Title + Text pp. 1–376 including index + 6 sub-titles not included in the pagination.

Part 61, Jan 1828
Ashbridge House Seat of the Countess of Bridgewater.
Rockbear House Seat of Thos Porter Esq.
Royal Hospital of St. Catherines Regents Park.
Head Dresses.
Ball Dress.
Muslin Patterns.

Part 62, Feb 1828
Kitley Seat of E. F. Bastard Esq. M.P.
Selsdon the Seat of G. Smith Esq. M.P. F. W. L. Stockdale delt.
Promenade Dress.
Evening Dress.
Drawing Room Chairs.
Muslin Patterns.

Part 63, Mch 1828
Bishops Court Seat of the Right Honble Lord Graves.
Clandon Park Seat of the Rt Honble Earl of Onslow. F. W. L. Stockdale delt.
Dinner Dress.
Ball Dress.
Tete a Tete Stool &c.
Muslin Pattern.

Part 64, Apr 1828
Widey Seat of Anderson Morshead Esq. F. W. L. Stockdale delt.
Hawley House the residence of T. Champion Esq. W. Delamotte Junr. delt.
Carriage Costume.
Evening Dress.
Toilet Table.
Muslin Pattern.

Part 65, May 1828
Killerton Seat of Sir Thos Dyke Acland Bt. M.P.
Huish Seat of the Rt Honble Lord Clinton.
Promenade Dress.
Evening Costume.
A Sideboard.
Muslin Pattern.

Part 66, Jun 1828
Tor Abbey Seat of George Cary Esq (by over-slip)
Muskaw the Residence of Prince Pickler.
Morning Dress.
Ball Dress.
A Sofa.
Muslin Pattern.

VOL. 12.—Title + Text pp. 1–372 including index + 6 sub-titles not included in the pagination.

Part 67, July 1828
Belmont House Seat of J. Norman Esq.
Endsleigh the Seat of His Grace the Duke of ● Bedford. F. W. L. Stockdale delt.
Morning Dress.
Fancy Ball Dress.
A Fire Place.
Muslin Pattern.

Part 68, Aug 1828
Harefield Seat of Gattey Esq.
Lifton Park Seat of W. Arundell Esq.
Carriage Costume.
Evening Dress.
Drawing Room Table.
Muslin Patterns.

Part 69, Sep 1828
Leeds Castle Seat of F. W. Martin Esq. Crouch delt.
Lantarnam Abbey Seat of Sir Henry Protheroe Bart.
Morning Dress.
Evening Full Dress.
Pier Table.
Muslin Pattern.

Part 70, Oct 1828
The Holme the Seat of J. Burton Esq.
Seat of G. B. Greenhough Esq., Regents Park.
Head Dresses.
Evening Dress.
A Bed.
Muslin Pattern.

Part 71, Nov 1828
Knole Seat of the Earl of Plymouth.
Luscombe Seat of Chas Hoare Esq.
Promenade Dress.
Dinner Dress.
A Flower Stand.
Muslin Pattern.

Part 72, Dec 1828
Chevening Seat of the Earl Stanhope.
Holwood Park Seat of John Ward Esq.
Promenade Dress.
Evening Dress.
A Cabinet.
Muslin Patterns.

Ackermann's Repository of Arts (*contd.*)

The Repository is a remarkable publication, enshrining several works that were reprinted later in book form on their own account such as Papworth's Select Views of London (all taken from the Repository except one), Views of Country Seats, Journal of Sentimental Travels in Southern Provinces of France, Picturesque Tour through the Oberland, Rural Residences &c. The Repository embraced most forms of engraving woodcut, line, stipple, aquatint and after 1817 lithograph. The costume plates, which are the only illustrations uniform throughout the whole work, make a magnificent series. As will be seen above many plates have exactly the same titles, e.g. the costume plates and the patterns, but these may be checked by the imprint which gives both the year and the month, and by the volume and plate number.

9 ACKERMANN (R.)

Repository of Fashions containing Elegant Coloured Engravings with Descriptions of Fashionable Female Costumes English and French. Published at R. Ackermann's 96 Strand and sold by all booksellers (rule)

Octavo. 1829

COLLATION.—Title + Text pp. 3–80 + 42 plates.

Part I, Jan 1829
1. Walking Dress.
2. Evening Dress.
3. Parisian Dinner Dress.
4. Parisian Ball Dress.
5. Muslin Pattern (uncoloured).

Part II, Feb 1 1829
6. Morning Dress.
7. Dinner Dress.
8. Parisian Dinner Dresses.
9. Italian Costumes for Fancy Ball & Masquerade Dresses.
10. Muslin Pattern (uncoloured).

Part III, March 1 1829
11. Dinner Dress.
12. Opera Dress.
13. Parisian Carriage Dress.
14. Fancy Ball Dresses of the Sixteenth & Eighteenth Centuries.
15. Muslin Pattern (uncoloured).

Part IV, April 1 1829
16. English Dinner Dress.
17. English Ball Dress.
18. Sultana Fancy Ball Dress.
19. Parisian Ball Dress.
20. Muslin Pattern (uncoloured).

Part V, May 1 1829
21. English Morning Dress.

Part V, May 1 1829 (*contd.*)
22. English Dinner Dress.
23. Parisian Evening Dress.
24. Costume of Henry VII Reign.
25. Muslin Pattern (uncoloured).

Part VI, June 1 1829
26. English Evening Dress.
27. English Dinner Dress.
28. Parisian Evening Dress.
29. Costume of Henry VIIIth Reign.
30. Muslin Pattern (uncoloured).

Part VII, July 1 1829
31. Evening Dress.
32. Walking Dress.
33. Evening Dress. Carriage Dress.
34. Public Promenade Dress.

Part VIII, August 1 1829
35. Wedding Dress.
36. Dinner Dress.
37. Evening Dress. Dinner Party Dress.
38. Morning Dress. Public Promenade Dress

Part IX, Sep. 1 1829
39. Evening Dress.
40. Walking Dress.
41. Full Dress Evening Costume. Ball Dress.
42. Walking Evening & Carriage Dress.

Issued as a supplement to the Repository of Arts being in effect Vol. XIII of the third series. It only ran for 9 months. Rare.

10 ACKERMANN & Co.

The Royal Navy.   A Series of 6 plates numbered 1–6 by R. H. C. Ubsdell, aquatinted by J. Harris, each bearing Ackermann's imprint, London, Published . . . 1848 by Ackermann & Co., 96 Strand.

1. Captain, Lieutenant.
2. Commander, Captain, Midshipman, Admiral.
3. Doctor, Boatswain, Master.
4. Mate, 2nd class Boy, Commodore.
5. Paymaster, Cadet, Assistant Surgeon.
6. Clerk, Second Master, A.B. Seaman.

11 ACKERMANN

Six Progressive Lessons for Flower Painting: with Directions for Drawing and Colouring of Flowers, upon Botanical Principles. (thick and thin rule) The Third Edition. (thin and thick rule) London Published by R. Ackermann, at his Repository of Arts, No. 101, Strand.   1810 (rule) Harrison and Rutter, Printers, 373, Strand.

Oblong folio.   1810

COLLATION.—Title as above (v. blank) + pp. 3–16 + 6 plates (the first 4 plates in 3 states, the last 2 plates in 2 states, 16 in all). Plain, partly coloured and fully coloured, Lettered Lessons 1–6 and bearing Ackermann's imprint dated June 1st 1810.

12 ACKERMANN

Swiss Costume.

Quarto.   1817

A series of 15 coloured aquatint plates numbered 1–15. Each plate bearing imprint; Published Nov. 1st 1817 at R. Ackermann's, 101 Strand (in last 7 plates, date changed to Dec. 1st 1817).

1. A Servant Maid of Zurich.
2. A Farmer of Appenzell.
3. A Country Girl of Lucerne.
4. Mother and Daughter of Lucerne.
5. A Farmer's Servant of Argovie.
6. A Dairy Maid of Lauter Brunnen.
7. A Nurse of Gouggisberg carrying an Infant.
8. A Cowherd of Oberhasll.
9. A Kitchen Maid of Soleure.
10. A Market Farmer of Appenzell.
11. A Country Girl of Lucerne, going to Market.
12. A Dairy Maid of Oberhasli.
13. A Fisherman of Morat.
14. A Country Girl of Berne.
15. A Milkman of Berne.

These plates were taken by Ackermann from Lory and re-engraved on a slightly larger scale, two of Lory's plates being combined to make 1 plate in the case of No. 4.

13 ACKERMANN (R.)

Views of Country Seats of the Royal Family, Nobility and Gentry of England, in one hundred and forty-six coloured engravings, after original designs by W. Westall, J. Gendall, and other artists: with particulars, historical and descriptive (rule) In Two

48

Ackermann's Country Seats (*contd.*)

Volumes vol. I (rule) London: Published by R. Ackermann and Co., Strand and to be had of all booksellers (rule)

2 vols.   Octavo.   1830

COLLATION VOL. I.—Title as above (v. London F. Shoberl, Jun., Lazenby Court, Long Acre) + Preface 1 leaf + Contents of First Vol. 2 ll. + pp. 1–136 + 72 coloured aquatint plates.

Each plate marked, R Ackermanns Repository of Arts &c.

1. Front. Entrance Front of His Majesty's Cottage Windsor Great Park.
2. p. 3. His Majesty's Cottage as seen from the Lawn.
3. p. 4. Frogmore House. J. Gendall delt.
4. p. 8. The Ruins Frogmore. J. Gendall delt.
5. p. 9. The Hermitage Frogmore. J. Gendall delt.
6. p. 11. Cranburn Lodge. J. Gendall delt.
7. p. 12. Cranburn Lodge (Back Front). J. Gendall delt.
8. p. 13. Princess Elizabeth's Cottage Old Windsor. J. Gendall delt.
9. p. 15. East Cowes Castle The Seat of J. Nash Esqre.
10. p. 16. Enmore Castle Seat of the Earl of Egmont.
11. p. 19. Lanhydrock House Seat of Hon Mrs. Agar. J. W. Stockdale delt.
12. p. 21. Perridge House The Seat of Henry Limbrey Toll Esq.
13. p. 23. Eaton Hall (Entrance Front). J. Gendall delt.
14. p. 29. Eaton Hall (West or Garden Front). J. Gendall delt.
15. p. 31. The Temple Lord Grosvernor's. J. Gendall delt.
16. p. 33. Southill Park the Seat of Willm. Henry Whitbread Esqr. F. W. Stockdale delt.
17. p. 35. Trellissick, the Seat of Thomas Daniell Esq. T. H. Shepherd delt.
18. p. 37. Chiswick House (Principal Front). J. Gendall delt.
19. p. 41. Chiswick House Garden Front J. Gendall delt.
20. p. 43. Tatton Hall Seat of — Egerton Esq. J. Gendall delt.
21. p. 45. Pynes The Seat of Sir Stafford Northcote Bart. J. Gendall delt.
22. p. 48. Bury Hill Seat of Robert Barclay Esq. J. Gendall delt.
23. p. 51. Offley Place Seat of the Revd L. Burroughs. G. Shepherd delt.
24. p. 52. Midgham House the Seat of W. S. Poyntz Esq. M.P. F. W. L. Stockdale delt.
25. p. 53. Pelling Place (Lawn Front). J. Gendall delt.
26. p. 54. Pelling Place (Garden Front). J. Gendall delt.
27. p. 55. Cobham Hall Seat of the Earl of Darnley. T. H. Shepherd delt.
28. p. 57. Roehampton Priory the Seat of Colthurst Swinton Holland Esq. Stockdale delt.
29. p. 58. Watermouth the Seat of Joseph Davie Bassett Esq. F. W. Stockdale delt.
30. p. 60. Ashburnham Park Seat of the Earl of Ashburnham. Hewetson delt.
31. p. 61. Bunney Hall the Residence of Lord Rancliffe.
32. p. 63. Follaton House Seat of Stanley Carey Esq.
33. p. 64. Wimbledon Park the Seat of Earl Spencer. T. H. Shepherd delt.
34. p. 66. Burford Priory Seat of W. J. Lenthall Esq. F. C. L. Stockdale delt.
35. p. 68. Oaklands the Seat of Albany Saville Esqre. J. Gendall delt.
36. p. 70. The Holme, the Seat of J. Burton Esq.
37. p. 71. Guy's Cliff Seat of Bertie Greatheed Esq.
38. p. 73. Pentilly Castle the Seat of John Tilly Coryton Esq.
39. p. 75. Clumber Castle Seat of the Duke of Newcastle. W. Westall delt.
40. p. 76. Colcorton Hall the Seat of Sir Geo. Beaumont Bart. W. Westall delt.
41. p. 77. Fulford House Seat of Colonel Fulford. J. Gendall delt.
42. p. 78. Belhus Seat of Sir Thos. B. Lennard Bart. M.P. F. Stockdale delt.
43. p. 79. Mitcham Grove the Seat of Henry Hoare Esq.
44. p. 80. Maristow Seat of Sir Manasseh Lopes Bart. F. W. L. Stockdale delt.
45. p. 82. Mount Edgecumbe Seat of Rt Honble. Earl of Mount Edgecumbe. J. Gendall delt.
46. p. 86. Lantarnam Abbey Seat of Sir Henry Protheroe Bart.
47. p. 87. Lifton Park Seat of W. Arundell Esqre.

Ackermann's Country Seats (*contd.*)

48. p. 89. Orchard Cottage the Seat of Sir Willoughby Gordon.   J. Gendall delt.
49. p. 91. Appuldurcombe Seat of the Earl of Yarborough.   J. Gendall delt.
50. p. 94. Avington the Seat of His Grace the Duke of Buckingham & Chandos.   Hewettson delt.
51. p. 95. Harefield Seat of Gattey Esqre.
52. p. 97. Norris Seat of Rt Hon Lord Henry Seymour.   J. Gendall delt.
53. p. 99. Worthy House the Seat of Sir Charles Ogle Bart.
54. p. 100. Leeds Castle Seat of F. W. Martin Esq.   Crouch delt.
55. p. 102. Crete Hall, the Residence of Jeremiah Rosher Esq.
56. p. 103. Aston Hall the Seat of James Watt Esq.   Crouch delt.
57. p. 105. Pencarrow the Seat of Lady Molesworth.   F. Stockdale delt.
58. p. 107. Eridge Park Seat of the Earl of Abergavenny.   Hewetson delt.
59. p. 108. Holwood Park Seat of John Ward Esq.
60. p. 110. St. Jermain the Seat of Lord Elliot.   J. Gendall delt.
61. p. 112. Marine Villa Seat of the Late Sir J. Cox Hippisley Bart.   J. Gendall delt.
62. p. 115. South-Hill House Seat of Thomas Chetham Strode Esq.
63. p. 116. Oxton House the Seat of J. Beaumont Sweet Esq.
64. p. 120. West Farm the Seat of — Bevan Esq.
65. p. 121. Wimbledon House the Residence of Mrs. Marryat.   T. H. Shepherd delt.
66. p. 123. Chevening Seat of the Earl of Stanhope.
67. p. 126. The Seat of G. B. Greenough Esq.
68. p. 127. North Court the Seat of Mrs. Bennett.   J. Gendall delt.
69. p. 129. Stoke Pogis the Seat of John Penn Esq.   J. Gendall delt.
70. p. 133. Grays Monument.   J. Gendall delt.
71. p. 134. Tor Abbey Seat of George Cary Esq.
72. p. 135. Endsleigh the Seat of His Grace the Duke of Bedford.   F. W. L. Stockdale delt.

VOL. II.—Title as before (v. London F. Shoberl, Jun. Lazenby-Court, Long Acre) + Contents of Second Volume 2 ll. + pp. 1–136 + Directions for Placing the Plates (in both volumes) 1 leaf + 74 coloured aquatint plates.

73. Front. Sion House.   J. Gendall delt.
74. p. 7. The Park Entrance Sion House.   J. Gendall delt.
75. p. 8. St Leonards Hill Seat of the Earl of Harcourt.   J. Gendall delt.
76. p. 10. The Vine Seat of Wm. John Chute Esq.   Hewetson delt.
77. p. 11. Iver Grove Seat of the Rt Honble.   Lord Gambier.   J. Gendall delt.
78. p. 12. Knole Seat of the Earl of Plymouth.
79. p. 17. Hackwood Park Seat of Lord Bolton.   Hewetson delt.
80. p. 18. Flamstead House.   T. H. Shepherd delt.
81. p. 22. Broadlands Seat of the Rt Hon Lord Visct Palmerston.   Hewetson delt.
82. p. 23. Deepdene the Seat of Thomas Hope Esq.   J. Gendall delt.
83. p. 27. Ditton Seat of Lord Montagu.   J. Gendall delt.
84. p. 29. Stoneham Park the Seat of John Fleming Esq. M.P.   Hewetson delt.
85. p. 31. Sutton Hall the Seat of Richard Arkwright Esq.   F. W. L. Stockdale delt.
86. p. 32. Trentham Hall, the Seat of the Marquis of Strafford.   J. Gendall delt.
87. p. 34. Mausoleum at Trenton (the Seat of the Marquis of Strafford).   J. Gendall delt.
88. p. 35. Stoke place the Seat of Col. Vyse.   J. Gendall delt.
89. p. 37. Westdean House the Seat of Lord Selsey.   Hewetson delt.
90. p. 38. The Rookery Seat of R, Fuller Esq.   J. Gendall delt.
91. p. 41. Saltram the Seat of Earl Morley.   F. W. Stockdale delt.
92. p. 42. Widey the Seat of Anderson Morshead Esq.   F. W. L. Stockdale delt.
93. p. 43. St Pierre the Seat of Charles Lewis Esq.   F. W. Stockdale delt.
94. p. 45. Beaumont Lodge Seat of Viscount Ashbrooke.   J. Gendall delt.
95. p. 47. Kitley Seat of F. P. Bastard Esq. M.P.
96. p. 48. Wonham Seat of the Rt Honble Lord Templeton.   F. W. L. Stockdale delt.
97. p. 50. Woburn Abbey Seat of the Duke of Bedford.
98. p. 52. Whitmore Lodge the Seat of Robt. Mangles Esq.   W. Delamotte Junr. delt.
99. p. 53. Stratton Park the Seat of Sir Thos. Baring Bart.   Hewetson delt.
100. p. 54. Belvoir Castle the Seat of His Grace the Duke of Rutland K.G.   W. Westall delt.

Ackermann's Country Seats (*contd.*)

101. p. 57. Selsdon the Seat of G. Smith Esq. M.P. F. W. L. Stockdale delt.
102. p. 58. The New Lodge Richmond Park the Seat of Viscount Sidmouth. J. Gendall delt.
103. p. 61. Holly Grove House the Seat of Theodore Henry Broadhead Esq. J. Gendall delt.
104. p. 63. Picton the Seat of the Rt Honble Lord Rolle. J. Gendall delt.
105. p. 67. Poltimores Seat of Sir George Warwick Bamfylde Bart. Stockdale delt.
106. p. 68. St Margarets View from the Thames Seat of the Earl of Cassillis. J. Gendall delt.
107. p. 71. St Margarets Entrance Front. Seat of the Earl of Cassillis. J. Gendall delt.
108. p. 72. Clowance the Seat of Sir John St Aubyn Bart. Stockdale delt.
109. p. 73. Newstead Abbey the Seat of Lieut. Col. Wildman.
110. p. 75. Shavington Hall Seat of the Earl of Kilmorey.
111. p. 76. Caen Wood the Seat of Earl Mansfield. F. W. Stockdale delt.
112. p. 78. Luscombe Seat of Chas. Hoare Esq.
113. p. 79. Michel Grove Seat of Thomas Walker Esq. Hewetson delt.
114. p. 80. Dunster Castle Seat of J. F. Luttrell Esq.
115. p. 82. Swainston Seat of Sir Fitz-William Barrington Bart. J. Gendall delt.
116. p. 84. Delaford Park the Seat of C. Clowes Esq. J. Gendall delt.
117. p. 86. Buckland Filleigh the Seat of John Inglett Fortescue Esq.
118. p. 89. Huish Seat of the Rt Honble Lord Clinton.
119. p. 90. Dropmore Seat of Earl Grenville View of Entrance Front. J. Gendall delt.
120. p. 92. Dropmore Seat of Earl Grenville View of the Garden Front. J. Gendall delt.
121. p. 94. Hampton House the Residence of the late Mrs. Garrick. J. Gendall delt.
122. p. 96. Killerton Seat of Sir Thos Dyke Acland Bt. M.P.
123. p. 98. Mrs. Palmers Villa Richmond. J. Gendall delt.
124. p. 100. Burghley House Seat of the Marquis of Exeter. W. Westall delt.
125. p. 104. Elvills the Seat of the Hon W. Freemantle M.P. F. W. L. Stockdale delt.
126. p. 105. Woodside the Seat of John Ramsbottom Esq. M.P. F. W. L. Stockdale delt.
127. p. 106. Clandon Park Seat of Rt Honble Earl of Onslow. F. W. L. Stockdale delt.
128. p. 107. Wanstead House the Seat of Wm Pole Tilney Long Wellesley Esq. J. Gendall delt.
129. p. 109. Hawley House the Residence of T. Champion Esq. W. Delamotte Jun. delt.
130. p. 110. Powderham Castle the Seat of Vist. Lord Courtenay. J. Gendall delt.
131. p. 113. Ham House Seat of the Countess of Dysart. F. W. L. Stockdale delt.
132. p. 114. Stoke Farm Seat of the Earl of Sefton. J. Gendall delt.
133. p. 115. Nutwell Court the Seat of Sir Thomas Trayton Fuller Eliott Drake Bart. J. Gendall delt.
134. p. 117. Nutwell Court the Seat of Sir Thomas Trayton Fuller Eliott Drake Bart. J. Gendall delt.
135. p. 119. Bishops Court Seat of the Rt Honble Lord Graves.
136. p. 120. Tabley House. J. Gendall Delt.
137. p. 122. Scene in Tabley Park.
138. p. 123. Belmont House Seat of J. Norman Esq.
139. p. 124. Moor Park the Seat of Robert Williams Esq. T. H. Shepherd delt.
140. p. 126. Rockbear House Seat of Thos. Porter Esq.
141. p. 127. The Grange the Seat of Alexander Baring Esq. M.P. I. Hewetson delt.
142. p. 129. Richings Lodge Seat of Right Honble John Sulivan. J. Gendall delt.
143. p. 130. Ashbridge House Seat of the Countess of Bridgewater.
144. p. 131. Sophia Lodge the Seat of Wm. Dawson Esq. View from the Lawn. J. Gendall delt.
145. p. 133. Sophia Lodge the Seat of Wm. Dawson Esq. J. Gendall delt.
146. p. 134. Piercefield Seat of Nathaniel Wells Esq. F. W. Stockdale delt.

The above series of views first appeared in Ackermann's Repository. They were then collected together and issued as above in book form. They were reissued in 1832, again in an undated edition, and later impressions of the plates were published with Nattali's imprint.

14 ADOLPHUS (J. H.)

A Correct, Full, and Impartial Report of the Trial of Her Majesty, Caroline, Queen Consort of Great Britain, Before the House of Peers; on the Bill of Pains and Penalties,

Adolphus' Trial of Queen Caroline

with Authentic Particulars, embracing every Circumstance connected with, and illustration of the Subject of this momentous event, interspersed with Original Letters, and other Curious and Interesting Documents, not generally known, and never before Published, including at large, Her Majesty's Defence. (rule) The whole, collected, arranged, and edited by J. H. Adolphus Esq. (rule) London: Printed and Published by Jones & Co. 1 Oxford Arms Passage, Warwick Lane, and sold by all Booksellers and Newsmen. (sm. rule) Entered at Stationers Hall.

Octavo. 1820

COLLATION.—Title as above (v. blank) + pp. i–xviii + pp. 1–459 + 6 coloured plates.

1. Front. View of the House of Lords during Her Majesty's Trial.
2. p.   1. Bartolomo Bergami   Copied by permission from an Original Drawing in possession of Mr. Smeeton.   London.   Published Aug. 25th 1820.
3. p. 72. Theodore Majochi Barbara Krautz.   Published Sep. 12th, 1820.
4. p. 126. Louisa Dumont Guiseppi Sacchi.
5. p. 181. Henry Brougham Esq. M.P.   Her Majesty's Attorney General.   Engraved from an Original Drawing.   July 28th 1820.
6. p. 419. Lord Erskine.

15 Adolphus (J. H.)

Memoirs of Caroline Queen Consort of Great Britain.   By J. H. Adolphus Esq.   Author of the Reign of George III. etc. London: Published by Jones & Co. Warwick Square. 1821 (the above lettering on a plaque, supported by figures of Justice, Truth, Royal insignia above, View of Naples below).

2 vols.   Octavo.

COLLATION VOL. I.—Coloured engraved title as above + Contents Vol. I, 4 pp. (iii–iv) + pp. 1–600 + coloured plates.

1. Front. (port.) Caroline Queen of England.   From an original Picture taken from Life, in the Possession of the Publishers London.   Published by Jones & Co.   Oct 28th. 1820.
2.   Engraved Title as above.
3. p. 71. His Late R.H. the Duke of Kent.   Copied by permission from an original Painting.
4. p. 137. His Late Majesty, King George III.   From a Sketch taken at Windsor during his illness.
5. p. 161. Sir Sidney Smith.   Engraved from an Original Drawing.   Oct. 1820.
6. p. 444. The Rt. Honourable Spencer Percival, the able Defender of Her Majesty, in 1806.   London Published by Jones & Co. Warwick Square.   1820.   W. Read, sculpt.
7. p. 549. The Late Samuel Whitbread Esq. M.P.   Engraved from an Original Drawing.   Aug. 16 1820.
8. p. 579. The Villa d'Este, Her Majesty's Residence on the Lake of Como.
9. p. 593. Her Royal Highness the Princess Charlotte of Wales and Saxe Coburg.

VOL. II.—Coloured engraved title as in Vol. I + Contents 3 pp. (5–7) p. 8 blank + pp. 1–526 (pp. 399–400 repeated).

10. Front. His present Majesty George the Fourth, from the latest correct likeness.
11.   Engraved Title.
12. p. 157. Wm. Wilberforce Esq. M.P.   London Published by Jones & Co. Jan. 24th, 1821.
13. p. 259. Sir Francis Burdett Bart. M.P.
14. p. 259. Alderman Wood, M.P.   Engraved from an original Drawing July 1820.
15. p. 411. Dr. Lushington.   Sketched during Her Majesty's Trial   London Published by Jones & Co. March 12th 1821.
16. p. 465. Lady Ann Hamilton.   Copied by Permission, from an Original Drawing for Adolphus's Memoirs of the Queen.   London Published by Jones & Co. Dec. 11th 1820.

Adventures of a Post Captain. See under Thornton (A.).

Adventures of Johnny Newcome in the Navy. See under Rowlandson (T.).

Advice to Sportsmen 1809. See under Rowlandson (T.).

16 AINSLIE (Sir R.)

Interesting Views in Turkey, selected from the original drawings, taken for Sir Robert Ainslie, by Luigi Mayer, F.S.A. (short rule) with Descriptions Historical and Illustrative (rule) London: Printed for Robert Bowyer, 80 Pall Mall; by Bensley & Son, Bolt Court, Fleet Street (short rule)

Quarto. 1819

COLLATION.—Title as above (v. blank) + Text pp. 3–13 + coloured aquatint plates, each with 1 page of Text.

Each plate marked, Published by M. Parker, 22 Golden Square, London 1836.

1. Pera.
2. Aqueduct near Belgrade.
3. View on the Aluta (in Walachia).
4. Ciala Karak (in Bulgaria).
5. Port of Latachia (in Syria).
6. Road over the Balkan Mountain. Piccolo Bent in Romania.
7. Island of Tortosa (in Syria).
8. Eski Estamboul (in Romania) (Mount Balkan).
9. Kaskerat (in Romania).
10. Borgas (in Romania).
11. (Ponte Piccolo in Romania). Tchiurluk (in Romania).
12. Mosque at Latachia (in Syria).
13. Terapia (in Romania).

17 ALEXANDER (J. E.)

Travels from India to England; comprehending a Visit to the Burman Empire, and a journey through Persia, Asia Minor, European Turkey, etc. in the years 1825–26 (rule) containing a Chronological Epitome of the late Military Operations in Ava; an Account of the Proceedings of the present Mission from the Supreme Government of India, to the Court of Tehran, and a Summary of the Causes and Events of the existing War between Russia and Persia; with Sketches of Natural History, Manners and Customs, and illustrated with Maps and Plates. (rule) By James Edward Alexander Esq., Lieut., Late H. M's 13th Light Dragoons, and attached to the suite of Colonel Macdonald Kinneir, K.L.S. Envoy Extraordinary to the Court of Tehran. (thick and thin rule) London: Printed for Parbury, Allen, & Co., Leadenhall Street. (rule)

Quarto. 1827

COLLATION.—Half-title, Travels from India to England (v. blank) + title as above (v. Printed by J. L. Cox, Great Queen Street, Lincolns Inn Fields) + Dedication 1 p. (v. blank) + Preface pp. 7–10 + Contents 11–15 + Illustrations 1 p. + Text pp. 1–301. (Printer's imprint p. 302.)

Front portrait James Edward Alexander. R. J. Lane lith. delt. C. Hullmandel imprt.
p. 1. Map Burman Empire.
p. 14. Shore Dragoon Praw. J. E. A. pinxit. T. Baynes litho delt.
1. p. 22. Burmans. J. E. A. pinxit. W. Sharp litho delt. Coloured.

Alexander's Travels (*contd.*)

p. 32. Prome. J. E. A. pinxit. T. Baynes litho delt.
2. p. 40. Madras Troops in Ava. J. E. A. pinxit. A. Hoffay litho delt. Coloured.
p. 76. Map Persia.
p. 126. Shiraz. J. E. A. pinxit. T. M. Baynes litho delt.
p. 136. Persepolis. J. E. A. pinxit. T. M. Baynes litho delt.
p. 140. Griffin King. J. E. A. pinxit. W. Sharp litho delt.
ibd. Persepolitan Procession. J. E. A. pinxit. W. Sharp litho delt.
3. p. 154. Trooper of the Escort. J. E. A. pinxit. W. Sharp litho delt. Coloured.
p. 178. Palace of Sultaneah. J. E. A. pinxit. W. Gauci, litho delt.
p. 190. Pillars of Heads. J. E. A. pinxit. T. M. Baynes litho delt.
4. p. 200. Persian Troops. J. E. A. pinxit. W. Sharp litho delt. Coloured.
5. p. 238. Turkish Troops. J. E. A. pinxit. A. Hoffay litho delt. Coloured.
p. 254. Quarantine at Rothen Thurn J. E. A. pinxit. T. M. Baynes litho delt.
p. 294–300 Contain woodcut vignettes separately printed (verso of each page being blank).

18 Alexander (W.)

The Costume of China, illustrated in Forty-Eight coloured Engravings. (thick and thin rule) By William Alexander (thin and thick rule) London: (thin and thick rule) Published by William Miller, Albemarle Street.

Quarto.   1805

COLLATION.—Half-title "The Costume of China" the Letter Press by W. Bulmer and Co, Cleveland Row, St James's (v. blank) + Title as above (v. blank) + Engraved Pictorial Title (v. blank) + List of Subscribers 2 ll. + 48 coloured plates + index 2 pp. + Advertisement of Pyne costume of Gr. Brit. 1 p. (v. blank).

Each plate marked, W. Alexander fecit, plate 1–20 London Published [Date] by G. Nicol, Pall Mall, 21–35 by G. & W. Nicol, 37–48, by W. Miller Old Bond St, plate 37 bears no imprint, and each with 1 p. of text.

1. Van-Ta Zhin	July 20 1797	25. Standard Bearer	Oct. 19 1800
2. Peasant	,,	26. Sacrifice at Temple	,,
3. Pagoda	,,	27. Military Station	,,
4. Travelling Barge	,,	28. Fishing Boat	,,
5. Chinese Soldier	Oct. 12 1797	29. Chinese Comedian	Aug. 10 1801
6. Group Of Trackers	,,	30. Group of Chinese	,,
7. View of Bridge	,,	31. Pagoda	,,
8. Trading Ship	,,	32. Ship of War	,,
9. Purveyor	May 1 1798	33. Soldier in Common Dress	Jan. 1 1802
10. Punishment of Cangue	,,	34. Bastinado	,,
11. S. Gate of Ting Hai	,,	35. Triumphal Arch	,,
12. 3 Vessels at Anchor	,,	36. Vessels passing Sluice	,,
13. Portrait of Lama	Sept. 1 1798	37. Mandarin	Oct. 1 1803
14. Chinese Lady	,,	38. Small Idol Temple	,,
15. Burying Place	,,	39. Chinese Gamblers	Sept. 1 1803
16. Front View of Boat	,,	40. Sea Vessels	,,
17. Portrait of Soldier	March 1 1799	41. Soldier of Chu San	Jan. 1 1804
18. Group of Peasantry	,,	42. Examination of Culprit	,,
19. View of Castle	,,	43. Yang Tcheoa	Jan. 1 1803
20. Sea Vessel	,,	44. Temp. Bldg. Tien Sin	Jan. 1 1804
21. Chow Ta Zhin	Dec. 1 1799	45. Tradesman	Nov. 1 n.y.
22. Chinese Porter	,,	46. Funeral Procession	Nov. 1 1804
23. Habitation of Mandarin	,,	47. Stone Building	,,
24. Mandarin's Boat	,,	48. Fisherman and his Family	,,

Alexander. See also under Barrow Cochin China.

19 ALKEN

Alken's Characteristic Sketches of Hunting, with Caricatures of Middlesex Sporting. (sm. rule) Twelve Plates. Fifteen Shillings.

Oblong Quarto.   1825

A series of 12 plates issued in wrappers with printed label (gold on black ground) as above. Each plate is marked, Published (date) by J. Dickinson, 114 New Bond Street.

1. Putting your horse to a brook.   May 1825
2. Going to Cover.   May 1825
3. Topping a Stone Wall.   June 1825
4. Doing the in and out. This is not exactly the way it ought to be-done.   June 1825
5. Doing the in and out. This should never be half done.   May 1825
6. Going to Cover. Having screw'd yourself up for a toutchaat a rail and Ditch.   June 1825
7. Topping a stile with a footboard.   May 1825
8. Going at a swishing pace. To be able to catch the Hounds at their best pace   June 1825
9. Going at a swishing pace. To go a swishing pace you must be able to catch the hounds
    from a bad start.   May 1825
10. Topping a Stone Wall and Coming well into the next Field.   May 1825
11. Doing a Strong Timber Fence.   June 1825
12. At a Brook with the rail to you.   June 1825

20 Alken (H.)

The Beauties and Defects in the Figure of the Horse Comparatively Delineated by H. Alken in a series of Coloured Plates (the above engraved within a circle surrounded by horses and vehicles proceeding round the outer ring) London: Published by S. and J. Fuller, at the Temple of Fancy, 34 Rathbone Place.

Royal octavo.   1816

COLLATION.—Engraved title as above (v. blank) + Introduction 2 pp. (1–2) + pp. 3–29 + 18 coloured plates, each plate with publisher's name and date, July 1, 1816.

First Edition and the first work by Alken to bear his name. Published in boards. Also issued as above with the imprint of James Toovey, 177 Piccadilly. Reprinted in 1821.

21 ALKEN (H.)

British Proverbs.

6 coloured plates all marked Henry Alken del et sculp. London: published by E. & C. M. McLean.   1824

1. The horse thinks one thing and the man that rides him another &c.
2. He that would have a hare for breakfast must hunt overnight &c.
3. Good to begin well better to end well &c.
4. They who love must at least set by &c.
5. All things are soon prepar'd in a well ordered House &c.
6. Life without a friend is death a witness &c.

Issued in paper wrappers with printed title on front wrapper.

22 ALKEN (H.)

A Cockney's Shooting Season in Suffolk. By Henry Alken. Containing the Remarkable Adventures that actually occured to a young Cit on a visit to his friends in the Country. London: Published by Thomas McLean, 26 Haymarket.

Alken's Cockney's Shooting Season (*contd.*)

Folio.   1822

Each plate is marked Henry Alken delt. and bears publisher's imprint and date.   Sixteen pages of letterpress were printed to accompany the plates, but they are usually missing.

1. First View of a Point.   "What makes the stupid Dog stand so?"
2. First View of a Woodcock.   "Mark that thing there, with the long bill!"
3. First Shot Flying.   "He flies off his Charger, and the Birds fly away."
4. Ox Bird or Stint Shooting.   "A Signal of Distress."
5. First Shot at a Hare.   "I've hit one of them, by George."
6. The Best Shot of All.   "I'll never touch a Gun more I give you my Pledge."

Issued in printed wrappers at one guinea.   Rare.

23 ALKEN (H.)

Comparative Meltonians, as they are, and as they were. (rule) "All alike good,—but Time makes strange alterations." (rule) By Ben Tally-Ho (2 line rule) London: Published by Thomas M'Lean, Repository of Wit and Humour, 26, Haymarket.

Oblong Folio.   1823

Title as above (v. blank) and 6 coloured plates.   Each plate marked, Hy. Alken Delt. and G. Hunt Sculpt., and bearing the publisher's imprint and date 1823.

No. 1. A Meltonian, as he was "Going to cover. . . .   Steady, Steady, my pretty fellow, plenty of time."
No. 2. A Meltonian, as he is.   "Going to Cover. . . .   Along, Along, rot your crawling, am I to be all day getting there?"
No. 3. Gone away, A Meltonian as he us'd to be "Forward, Forward, . . .   Thank you my good Friend."
No. 4. Gone away, A Meltonian as he is "Cu's me fell'er but you will get hurt one day if you git so much in the way."
No. 5. Going home, Meltonians as they were "The Grey has carried you in excellent style today."
No. 6. Going home, Meltonians as they are "By the living George . . . B . . . it is all up."

Issued in pinkish wrapper with printed title as above, but with addition of words Price Two Guineas after the date.   A very rare series, among the largest and finest of Alken's plates.

24 ALKEN (H.)

Doing the Thing and the Thing Done.   By Ben Tally HO!   1818

A Series of 6 (or 8) plates, all marked London Published (date) by S. and J. Fuller, 34 Rathbone Place.

1. Morning   { Turning out in Prime Twig / doing the least you can.
2. Afternoon   { Returning home in fine Trim / doing the most you can.
3. Doing it nohow.
4. Doing it somehow.
5. Doing it furiously.
6. Doing the Down leap.
7. The Down leap Done.
8. Doing the Thing well—Giving Dribbler the gobye.

Strictly speaking the last 6 plates only (dated March 2 1818) belong to the set, being all called for in contemporary advertisements, but the first 2 plates (dated April 5th 1818) frequently accompany the other six.

Size of engraved surface $8\frac{3}{4} \times 6\frac{1}{4}$ inches.

25 ALKEN (H.)

Driving Discoveries.

Oblong Quarto. 1817

A Series of 7 coloured plates, all bearing publisher's imprint, London Pub. Jany. 1. 1817 by S. & J. Fuller 34 Rathbone Place.

1. You Discover you have obtained a steady one.
2. You Discover that the reins are under his tail.
3. Up and Down, or the Endeavour to discover which way your horse is inclined to come down backwards or forwards.
4. You Discover you have overlooked a small Post on your whip hand.
5. You Discover a new way of bringing your Equipage into a small compass.
6. Trying a new match you Discover that they are not only alike in colour, weight and action, but in disposition.
7. Breaking up the most expensive part of your Establishment the last Discovery but one, viz. a five and forty foot Gravel Pitt on your off side.

26 ALKEN (H.)

A Few Ideas being Hints to all Would-be Meltonians (rule) All is not Gold that Glitters; neither does keeping Horses at Melton, and mounting the Scarlet make the Real Meltonian (rule) London: Published by Thomas M'Lean 26, Haymarket. 1825

COLLATION.—Title as above on wrapper within Etruscan border (v. blank) and 6 coloured plates each marked, Hy. Alken Delt., and bearing imprint as on title.

1. I say my good Woman, have you any Idea how they manage here, to get a horse out of a Brook.
2. They may call this pleasure, but I have an Idea that it has brought me into considerable trouble.
3. I say my good fellow, have you not an Idea that this Hunting is exceedingly dangerous.
4. I say my hearty fellow, have you any Idea where I can get a personal conveyance to Melton.
5. I say old Furnace have you any Idea how far it is to Melton? Yes I have, it is better than 22 miles I take it.
6. I say my dear fellow, I have an Idea, that it will make a considerable alteration in your personal appearance.

The above and the two following parts were reissued as part of " Ideas, Accidental and Incidental to Hunting," see p. 60.

A Few Ideas being Hints to all Would-be Meltonians. Title as before and 6 coloured plates.

1. I say old Buck, have you any Idea where I can find the Hounds?
2. I had not the most distant Idea of what was on the other side.
3. I say my hearty chap have you any Idea what ought to be done.
4. I shall soon lose all my Ideas.
5. I have an Idea he is going and with him my 150 guineas.
6. I do not think he has an Idea left.

Numerous reissues 1826, 1827 and 1828.

27 ALKEN (H.)

A Few Ideas being Hints to all Would-be whips (rule) 6 line verse signed Ben Tally ho. (rule) London: Published by Thomas M'Lean, 26 Haymarket.

Alken's Few Ideas (*contd.*)

Oblong Foolscap. 1827

COLLATION.—Title on wrapper as above within a decorated border (v. blank) + 6 coloured plates each plate marked, Hy. Alken Delt. London Published by Thos. M'Lean 26 Haymarket.

1. I have an Idea its ten to one but we are down now—but I'll take nine to three that the horses all go over.
2. I have an Idea my Lord that nothing but time or a stone wall will stop them—and I'll bet a cool hundred that Frank will not head them for the next mile.
3. I say Captain I have an Idea we have run foul of several things in our passage.
4. I say my clever feller, have you an Idea you can make this thing capable of progression.
5. I have an Idea that I have got them rather too much together now.
6. I say my dear Sir, have you not an Idea, that there is considerable danger in the present case.

The work was completed with a Fourth Series. A Few Ideas, Caught on Easter Monday, also with 6 plates. This I have been unable to examine.

28 ALKEN (H.)

Field Sports and Pastimes. By Henry Alken, Senr. Six Plates. Price Ten Shillings and Sixpence. London: Thomas M'Lean, 26, Haymarket N.D.

Folio.

COLLATION.—6 coloured plates, marked B. T. Esqr. Delt. (i.e. Ben Tallyo Ho or Henry Alken) London: Published by Thos. M'Lean 26 Haymarket.

1. Going out in the morning. September 1st.
2. Charging.
3. The Shot.
4. Down Charge.
5. Refreshment.
6. Returning Home.

Published in brown paper wrappers.

29 ALKEN (H.)

How to Qualify for a Meltonian: addressed to All Would-be Meltonians By Ben Tally-Ho, Author of "Qualified Horses and Unqualified Riders"; "Sporting Discoveries, or, the Miseries of Hunting"; &c. &c. &c. London: Published by S. and J. Fuller, at the Temple of Fancy, Rathbone Place: And may be had of all Booksellers in the United Kingdom.

Oblong Folio. 1819

COLLATION.—3 leaves of text and 6 coloured plates. Each plate numbered and bearing imprint, London Pub. July 16, 1819 by S. & J. Fuller at their Sporting Gallery 34 Rathbone Place.

(1) How to go to Cover.
(2) How to appear at Cover.
(3) How to ride downhill.
(4) How to take your leap.
(5) How to go thro' an Overflow.
(6) How to take the Lead.

REMARKS.—The text is rare and frequently missing. Issued in brown paper wrappers with title, and advertisements on the reverse.

Size of engraved plate $12\frac{1}{2} \times 8\frac{3}{4}$ inches.

30 ALKEN (H.)

Humourous Miscellanies by Henry Alken. London: Published by Thos. McLean, Repository of Wit and Humour No. 26 Haymarket. 1823

Each plate marked, Hy. Alken Delt. London Published by Thos. McLean Repository of Wit & Humour 26 Haymarket 1823.

1. The Prospect of Hunting . . . all Right.
2. The Reality of Hunting . . . all Wrong.
3. Learning to drive a Dennett.
4. Learning to drive Tandem.
5. Give me another Horse—bind up my wounds—The lights burn blue Vy—that ere's the Moon mix'd with Gash light.
6. A Horse! A Horse! my Kingdom for a Horse! I don't know nothing about that ere—but here's one you shall have for Forty shillings.

Issued in brown paper wrappers as above at 12s.

31 ALKEN (H.)

Hunting Discoveries.

Oblong Folio. 1817

A series of 7 plates, each plate with imprint, London Published March 1 1817 by S. and J. Fuller, Temple of Fancy 34 Rathbone Place.

1. . . . you Discover the whole face of the country covered with snow.
2. . . . you dash over in great style, but Discover when half over the next field that a bough of a tree has taken off your hat.
3. . . . you Discover that your girts are broken.
4. . . . you Discover that it would have been prudent to have had a stronger throat lash.
5. Having frequently boasted of the excellence of your Grey at a Standing timber leap . . . you then Discover . . . it will be necessary to procure a horse somewhat longer in the legs.
6. . . . ditch your horse, you then Discover that the only means you can adopt to preserve him from being drowned is to hold his head up by main strength.
7. . . . you at length perceive a light which you discover is determined if possible to avoid you.

Size of engraved surface $10\frac{1}{4} \times 7\frac{1}{4}$ *inches.*

32 ALKEN (H.)

Hunting, or Six Hours' Sport, by Three Real Good Ones, from the East End, and without seeing a Hound (rule) "Its true—upon my soul, its true." (rule) By Henry Alken. London: Published by Thomas M'Lean, Repository of Wit and Humour, No. 26, Haymarket.

Oblong Folio. 1823

COLLATION.—Title as above (v. blank) and 6 coloured plates. Each plate marked, Hy. Alken Delt. London, Published by Thos. McLean, Repository of Wit & Humour, 26 Haymarket 1823.

1. Hunting, or Six Hour's Sport. " Going to Hunt . . . 8 o'clock . . . an Easy Job."
2. ,, ,, ,, "Throwing off . . . 9 o'clock . . . not so Easy."

Alken's Hunting (*contd.*)

3. Hunting, or Six Hour's Sport.   "Breaking Cover . . . 10 o'clock . . . Rather difficult."
4.   „   „   „   "In full Cry . . . 11 o'clock . . . Hard Work."
5.   „   „   „   "A Check . . . 12 o'clock . . . Tipping for the Swine."
6.   „   „   „   "Going Home . . . making a good Blunt . . . Apology for damage done.

Issued in buff printed wrappers, with title as above, but with addition of words. Price one guinea. Size of engraved surface 12½ × 8½ *inches.*

33 ALKEN (H.)

Hunting Qualifications, in a series of six plates, drawn and engraved by Henry Alken and dedicated without permission, to all Fox-Hunters (2 line verse). London: Published by R. Ackermann Junior at his Sporting Gallery and Repository of Arts, 191, Regent Street, Printed by L. W. Harrison, 5 Princes Street, Leicester Square 1829

Six plates, each with imprint, London Published Augt. 1st 1829 by R. Ackermann, Junr. 191 Regent St. Some copies have 8 leaves of text, but this is uncommon.

1. The Appointment.
2. Getting away.
3. A Slap at a Park Fence.

4. Getting over.
5. Slap at a Brook.
6. Creeping a Finish.

34 ALKEN (H.)

Hunting Sketches.

Oblong Folio.   1821

A series of 7 plates.

How to appear at cover.
Going at a fence.
How to stop your horse.
Going at a chalk pit &c.

Going at a Gate.
Going at a stone wall.
Going home.

35 ALKEN (H.)

Hunting Sketches.

Folio.   1822

Another series of 14 plates.

1. Off to Melton.
2. I fancy he can go.
3. Doing a bit of City.
4. Bull and mouth Inn.
5. Coaching Accident.
6. These came Hopping.
7. Non Effectives.

8. Frogs and Cranes.
9. Eager for the Field.
10. Struggle for a start.
11. Candidates for Brookes.
12. A Check.
13. Death and the Doctors.
14. Dulce Domun.

36 ALKEN (H.)

Ideas, Accidental and Incidental to Hunting, and other Sports; Caught in Leicestershire, &c. (thick and thin rule) By Henry Alken (thin and thick rule) London: Published by Thomas M'Lean, 26 Haymarket

Alken's Ideas (*contd.*)

Folio. [1826–30]

COLLATION.—Title as above (v. blank) + 42 coloured plates all marked, Hy. Alken Delt. London Published by Thos. McLean, 26 Haymarket and date.

1. I say my hearty fellow, have you any Idea where I can get a personal conveyance to Melton [1826].
2. They may call this pleasure, but I have an Idea that it has brought me into considerable trouble [1826].
3. I say my good woman have you any Idea how they manage here to get a horse out of a Brook [1826].
4. I say my good fellow have you not an Idea that this Hunting is exceedingly dangerous [1826].
5. I say my dear fellow I have an Idea that it will make a considerable alteration to your personal appearance [1826].
6. I say old Furnace, have you any Idea how far it is to Melton? [1826].
7. I say old Buck, have you any Idea where I can find the Hounds? [1827].
8. I had not the most distant Idea of what was on the other side [1827].
9. I shall soon lose all my Ideas.
10. I have an Idea he is going and with him my 150 Guineas [1827].
11. I do not think he has an Idea left [1827].
12. I say my hearty chap have you any Idea what ought to be done in the present case [1827].
13. I have an Idea that I have got them rather too much together now [1827].
14. I say my dear Sir, have you not an Idea that there is considerable danger in the present case [1827].
15. I say Captain I have an Idea we have run foul of several things in our passage [1827].
16. I say my clever feller, have you an Idea you can make this thing capable of progression [1827].
17. I have an Idea its ten to one but we are down now &c. [1827].
18. I have an Idea my Lord that nothing but Time or a stone wall will stop them &c. [1827].
19. I say Bob you addent an Idea I could ride so well ad you [N.D.].
20. My high Tom, I have an Idea we shall soon be off, &c. [N.D.].
21. I ave an Idea I am down now Tom [N.D.].
22. I say Joe you addent no Idea it was so deep, ad you, &c. [N.D.].
23. I say my Buck you avent no Idea where the Ounds are, ave you [N.D.].
24. I say my Boy we ave got some Ideas about the Unting now avent we [N.D.].
25. You can have no Idea what a magnificent day I have had [1830].
26. By George Harry, I have an Idea that the thing is not quite so easy as I anticipated.
27. My good fellow, I have an Idea that I shall be right on the top of you [1830].
28. I have an Idea that this is a situation of considerable difficulty [1830].
29. I have an Idea that this is a most important and effective Fall [1830].
30. My dear fellows I should be extremely sorry to speak of any Country with disrespect but I have an Idea that the water here abouts is not exceedingly fragrant [1830].
31. This is just to give you an Idea of a Steeple Chase [1830].
32. I have an Idea that this is our Yeomen Cavalry races [1830].
33. I had not the most distant Idea of Getting in such sport as this [1830].
34. I have a strong Idea we shall hit something this Time [1830].
35. Is that really a Are, &c. [1830].
36. I begin to have an Idea that this Tandem driving is not altogether free from danger [1830].
37. My good people I beg you not to disturb yourselves but have you any Idea which way the Hounds went [1830].
38. My good fellows I have an Idea that this sort of Gate was made for only one at a time to go through [1830].
39. I have an Idea that this Fence is either too High or that my Horse is too Short [1830].
40. I have no Idea what could induce me to follow you over this d . . . d rotten Bridge [1830].
41. I have an Idea I shall win now if I can but carry in my weight [1830].
42. I positively have no Idea what I am to do in this case &c. [1830].

REMARKS.—*First issued in upright folio. A fire consumed part of the stock, and the plates were reissued in oblong folio. These latter are inferior. A reprint was issued in 1900.*

37 ALKEN (H.)

Illustrations to Popular Songs, BY Henry Alken (rule)
"Every man shall sing
The merry songs of peace to all his neighbours"
Shakespeare (rule)

London: Published By Thomas M'Lean, Repository of Wit and Humour No. 26, Haymarket. 1822

COLLATION.—Title as above (v. blank) + Address 1 leaf (v. blank) + 43 coloured plates all marked, H. Alken del London: Published by Thomas McLean Repository of Wit and Humour 26 Haymarket 1822.

1. (Pictured Title)   So fill your Glasses, be this the toast given
         Here's England for ever, the land boys we live in.
2. I am the boy for bewitching them &c.
3. While happy in my native land &c.
4. Sure such a pair were never seen &c.
5. He was famed for deeds of arms &c.
6. With — mixture without Measure &c.
7. Deserted by the waning Moon &c.
8. Go breeze that sweeps the orange grove &c.
9. What beau was armed completer &c.
10. No more I'll court the town bred fair &c.
11. Whats this dull Town to me &c.
12. Music hath power to melt the Soul &c.
13. A Blessing unknown to Ambition and Pride &c.
14. 'Tis he my William come from Sea &c.
15. Far removed from Noise and Smoke &c.
16. My love she is so pretty &c.
17. Ye Gentlemen of England That live at home at ease &c.
18. Turn away those eyes of love &c.
19. How sweet to be as on we rush &c.
20. The bright sunny morning bids the huntsman prepare &c.
21. I saw that form in youthful trim &c.
22. Ye gentle gulls that fan the air &c.
23. The hounds are uncoupled see yonder they fly &c.
24. That loves a tyrant I can prove &c.
25. O would twere my lot &c.
26. The steed with impatience Reviews the far plain &c.
27. True sportsmen are we for the game once in view &c.
28. A southerly Wind and stormy sky &c.
29. The Sportsmen all rode at a desperate rate &c.
30. When jealous out of Season &c.
31. No joys can delight like the sports of the field &c.
32. When in death I shall calm recline &c.
33. Bright chanticleer proclaims the dawn &c.
34. Arise brother sportsmen the landscape survey &c.
35. A fig for the cares of this whirligig world &c.
36. A Highland lad my love was born &c.
37. Mary dear Mary list awake &c.
38. Every pulse every pulse along my veins &c.
39. Throwing off dull Melancholy &c.
40. In sportive mood the fickle god &c.
41. Bewitching Fashion with what power Despotic doth thou rule &c.
42. Ye little loves that round her wait &c.
43. Since the first dawn of reason &c.

Alken's Illustrations to Popular Songs (*contd.*)

Issued in boards, half roan.   The leaf of address is frequently missing.   First issued in 1822, *reissued* 1823, 1825, 1826, 1831.

38 ALKEN (H.)

Indispensible Accomplishments; or Hints to City Gentlemen London Edw. Orme

Oblong Folio.   1824

A series of 4 plates dated 1815, the wrapper dated 1824.

How to purchase a Horse.	Standing it Miserable.
Going Full Speed.	How to come it awkwardly.

39 ALKEN (H.)

Involuntary Thoughts.   A Series of 8 plates, each plate marked Hy. Alken Delt. London Published by Thos. McLean Repository of Wit & Humour 26 Haymarket 1824

1. Involuntary Thoughts May temptation never conquer virtue &c.
2.   ,,   ,,   Involuntary Bondage &c.
3.   ,,   ,,   Wanted an Housekeeper to a Single Gentleman &c.
4.   ,,   ,,   A Man of some Weight in the Parish &c.
5.   ,,   ,,   More Friends, and less need of them &c.
6.   ,,   ,,   A Water Party very Dry &c.
7.   ,,   ,,   May we never want a Friend and a Bottle to give him &c.
8.   ,,   ,,   May we never feel want or want feeling &c.

Eight prints as above in the British Museum (Print Room c 166 b 37).   M'Lean's advertisement of this work in A Touch at the Fine Arts calls for 6 plates only.   Issued in buff paper wrappers with printed title at 12s.

40 ALKEN (H.)

Moments of Fancy and Whim by Henry Alken (rule).   We rather fancy than Know (rule) London: Published by Thomas M'Lean, Repository of Wit and Humour No. 26 Haymarket   1823

A series of 14 plates all marked, Moments of Fancy Hy. Alken Delt., and all bearing M'Lean's imprint, London: Published by Thos. M'Lean Repository of Wit and Humour 26 Haymarket 1822.

A Phaeton and Four.	Who would bear the many shocks that flesh is
Not a bit of Fancy.	heir to.
Real English Fancy.	How dangerous it is, that this man goes loose.
A Fancy Man.	No fancy for a waggon.
Past Consideration.	Playing at Soldiers.
Got an Engagement.	As the thing used to be done.
There is a pleasure in being mad.	Good for neither one or the other.
A Day Nurse.	

Size of engraved surface 13½ × 9½ *inches.*   Issued in two parts in printed paper wrappers.

41 ALKEN (H.)

The National Sports of Great Britain (rule) BY Henry Alken (rule) With Descriptions, in English and French (2 line rule) London: Published by Thomas McLean, 26, Haymarket. Printed by W. Lewis, Finch Lane, Cornhill (short rule).

Folio.   1821

COLLATION.—Title (v. Title in French) + Preface in English 2 pp. + Preface in French 2 pp. + Contents 1 p. (v. Contents in French) + 50 leaves of text (with English on one side and French on other) + Frontispiece + 50 coloured plates.

A COMPOSITE FRONTISPIECE—British Sports (followed by a large vignette consisting of a Huntsman and Sportsman holding up a tableau of 12 small sporting pictures, dogs and dead game in the foreground) by Henry Alken. London Published by Thomas McLean, Haymarket 1821.

50 plates marked, H. Alken delt. I. Clark sculpt. and bearing McLean's imprint dated Jany. 1 1820.

1. Hawking.	26. Pheasant Shooting.
2. The Arabian.	27. Snipe Shooting.
3. Racing from Newmarket Heath.	28. Water Spaniels.
4. Racing.	29. Water Hen Shooting.
5. Racing.	30. Wild Fowl Shooting.
6. The Hunter.	31. Sledging Working up to a Wake.
7. Stag Hounds.	32. Flacker Shooting.
8. Stag Hunting.	33. Bittern Shooting.
9. Fox Hounds.	34. Pigeon Match.
10. Beagles.	35. Pike Fishing.
11. Earth Stopper.	36. Fishing in a Punt.
12. Fox Hunting, going into Cover.	37. Salmon Fishing.
13. Fox Hunting, Breaking Cover.	38. A Prize Fight.
14. Fox Hunting (Hounds in full cry).	39. Cock Fighting Plate I.
15. Fox Hunting the Death.	40. Cock Fighting Plate II.
16. Fox Hunting Digging out.	41. Bull Baiting.
17. Sporting Meeting in the Highlands.	42. Bull Baiting.
18. Coursing.	43. Bear Baiting.
19. Coursing (Death of the Hare).	44. Terriers.
20. Hackney.	45. Crab.
21. Pointers.	46. A Match at a Badger.
22. Setters.	47. Drawing the Badger.
23. Spaniels.	48. Badger Catching.
24. Grouse Shooting.	49. Spearing the Otter.
25. Partridge Shooting.	50. Owling.

ISSUES.—1st Issue.—*As above, except that the frontispiece is dated* 1820. *Extremely Rare.* 2nd Issue.—*Frontispiece dated* 1821.

REMARKS.—*Alken's most important work. The book, though not yet rare in its second state, always commands a high figure, owing to the beauty and size of the plates. Numerous copies have been broken up, and the plates framed separately, and the tendency is for the work to become scarcer and scarcer. It must always form the cornerstone of any Alken collection.*

42 ALKEN (H.)

The National Sports of Great Britain (rule) By Henry Alken (rule) With Descriptions in English and French. (thick and thin rule) London: Printed for Thomas M'Lean, 26

Alken's National Sports of Great Britain (*contd.*)

Haymarket; at the Columbian Press, by Howlett and Brimmer, 10, Frith Street, Soho (short rule)

Folio.   1823

COLLATION.—As in first edition with the exception of the titles, of which there are two, one in English and one in French, the reverse of each title being blank.   The imprint on the plates still remains Jan. 1 1820.

REPRINTS.—Reprinted in 1903 and 1904.

43 ALKEN (H.)

The National Sports of Great Britain, By Henry Alken.   Fifty Engravings with Descriptions.   London: Printed for Thomas M'Lean, Haymarket; by Howlett and Brimmer, 10 Frith Street, Soho

Royal Octavo.   1825

COLLATION.—Title as above (v. blank) + Preface 2 ll. + List of Plates 1 p. (v. blank) + 50 ll. of Text + 50 coloured plates.

Each plate bears publisher's imprint and date 1824.

1. Frontispiece Fox Hunter's Toast.
2. Race Horse.
3. Racing . . . Training.
4. Racing . . . Saddling.
5. Racing . . . Preparing to Start.
6. Racing . . . Off.
7. Racing . . . Doing their best.
8. Racing . . . Going to weigh.
9. Hunter.
10. Running into a Stag.
11. Earth Stopper.
12. Fox Hunting . . . Going to Cover.
13. Fox Hunting . . . Breaking Cover . . . Tally Ho!
14. Fox Hunting . . . Gone away . . . Forward.
15. Fox Hunting . . . Check.
16. Fox .Hunting . . . Leap . . . Swishing at a Rasper.
17. Fox Hunting, Death . . . Who: Whoop.
18. Running into a Fox.
19. Digging out.
20. Coursing.   Going out.
21. Coursing . . . Finding Soho.
22. Coursing   Hilloo!   Hilloo!
23. Coursing   Picking up.
24. Coursing   Dead, Dead.
25. Coursing   Going Home.
26. Shooting   Going out.
27. Pointers.
28. Setters.
29. Grouse Shooting.
30. Partridge Shooting.
31. Pheasant Shooting.
32. Fowl Shooting.
33. Snipe Shooting.
34. Bittern Shooting.
35. Bank Shooting for Fowl.
36. Punting for Fowl.
37. Sledging for Fowl.
38. Poachers.
39. Ferreting Rabbits.
40. Running a Badger to Bay.
41. Otter Hunting.
42. Hunting the Martin.
43. Anglers.
44. Fly Fishing.
45. Prize Fight.
46. Dog Fight.
47. Cock Fighting.
48. Bull Baiting.
49. Bear Baiting.
50. Badger Baiting.

Published at 3 guineas.   The plates are different from the folio edition.

44 ALKEN (H.)

Qualified Horses and Unqualified Riders, or the Reverse of Sporting Phrases; from the work entitled Indispensible Accomplishments . . . By Ben Tally-Ho, an occasional

Alken's Qualified Horses and Unqualified Riders (*contd.*)

visitor in Leicestershire.   London: Published 1st Septr. 1815 by S. and J. Fuller, 34 Rathbone Place.

Oblong Folio.   1815

COLLATION.—Title as above (v. blank) + 7 coloured plates all bearing Fuller's imprint as on title.

1. Going along a slapping pace, for the same reason, that a Criminal goes to Gaol, and at the end of your career; the only difference is that you finish yours with Honour and the acclamation of your friends.
2. Topping a flight of Rails and coming into the next Field (but not so well) if you have the slightest regard for your neck it would be better to make this the last stage.
3. Charging an Ox fence, with good Success.
4. Got in and getting out very clever.
5. Facing a Brook verifying the old Adage, look before you leap.
6. Swishing at a Rasper, from your own timidity, and mismanagement cause the horse to swerve and at last to Bolt through the only bad place in the Fence, leaving you behind in the elegant attitude of a Spread Eagle.
7. Returning Home in Triumph.   He disclaim'd a Slothful Easy Life; so he took to Hunting.

Size of engraved plate $10\frac{1}{2} \times 7\frac{1}{2}$ *inches.*
Issued in dark buff printed wrappers.   Reissued 1821.

REMARKS.—*The first of Alken's coloured books.*

45 ALKEN (H.)

Rudiments for Drawing the Horse, sketched from Nature, and Drawn on Stone, By H. Alken. (thick and thin rule) London: Published by S. & S. Fuller, at the Temple of Fancy, 34 Rathbone Place, and to be had of all Book and Print Sellers in the United Kingdom.   Printed by L. Harrison, 373 Strand (rule) 1822

Oblong Quarto.

COLLATION.—Title as above (v. blank) + 23 coloured lithograph plates by H. Alken. Printed by C. Hullmandel, and bearing Fuller's imprint.

46 ALKEN (H.)

Scenes in the Life of Master George.   London Published by Thos. McLean: Repository of Wit and Humour 26 Haymarket   1823

A series of 12 plates each marked, Hy. Alken Delt., and bearing McLean's imprint as above.

1. Setting Dogs to Fight.   "There Master George I thought you wou'd get it."
2. Fishing.   "Take care George don't pull at him."
3. Rat Hunting, with a visit from Dominie "O master George is this your Latin Lesson!"
4. A Turn Up with the Lads of the Village.   "Ah Master George you won't find this so easy a job."
5. Sparrow Catching.   "Master George take care of the Rats."
6. Giving the Village Donkeys a Treat.   "My Dear George you will be kill'd I must run and tell Papa."
7. Bull Baiting.   "If you go so near Master George he will pink you."
8. Bear Baiting.   "Now Master George—let go fair."
9. Cock Fighting.   "Now Master George what do you think of the black breasted red."
10. Badger Baiting.   "Why—Master George, do you expect that little thing to draw the Badger?"
11. Bringing up to the Bar.   "That Seat will do well Master George."
12. Morning Ride.   "Master George showing off in Hyde Park."

47 ALKEN (H.)

Shakespeare's Seven Ages of Man.   McLean   1824

A series of 7 plates.   Signed Henry Alken + quotation from Shakespeare 1 leaf.

The Infant.
The School Boy.
The Lover.
The Soldier.

The Justice.
The Sixth Age.
Last Scene of All.

48 ALKEN (H.)

The Seven Ages of the Horse

Oblong Folio.   London 1825

At first the foal.
Then the Colt.
The Horse Race.
The Hunter.

The Harness Horse.
The Post Horse.
Last Scene of all.

49 ALKEN (H.)

Shooting, or One Day's Sport of Three real good One's, However ignorant of Sporting Rules.   By Henry Alken.   London: Published by Thomas M'Lean, Repository of Wit and Humour, 26 Haymarket

Oblong Folio.   1823

A series of 6 plates, each marked, "One Day's Sport of Three real good Ones." Hy. Alken Delt.   London Published by Thos. McLean Repository of Wit & Humour, 26 Haymarket. 1823.

1. "Turning off."
2. "1st Shot at Game . . . no luck."
3. "Sport,—and something like Sport;—The Johnny Raws coming down."
4. "A regular Set too—Tipping the Johnny Raws a few London tactics."
5. "Numbers will beat Science—the Corinthians bearing the brunt."
6. "The Corinthians making it up . . . by showing the Johnny Raws—how to Grog it."

50 ALKEN (H.)

Some do, and some do not; It is all a notion.

Oblong Folio.   (1821)

COLLATION.—1 leaf of text signed Ben Tally-Ho and 7 plates, each plate with imprint, London: Pub. Jany. 1st 1821 by S. & J. Fuller, at their Sporting Gallery, 34 Rathbone Place.

1. Getting into a difficulty.
2. Getting over a difficulty.
3. Getting a Fall.
4. Getting a Dive.

5. Getting into a Bog.
6. Getting dead Beat.
7. Getting home.

The above titles are at the top of the plates respectively.   Each plate in addition bears a more or less lengthy inscription below the engraving further elaborating the above titles.

Size of engraved surface 10¼ × 7¼ *inches.*

Issued in paper covers with printed title on wrapper.

51 ALKEN (H.)

Specimens of Riding, near London, etc., Drawn from Life, by Henry Alken.   London: Published by Thomas M'Lean, Repository of Wit and Humour, No. 26, Haymarket.

Oblong Folio.   1821

COLLATION.—Printed title as above (v. blank) + 18 plates.   Each plate bears M'Lean's imprint and date.

1. One of the comforts of riding in company   H. Alken 1821.
2. Symptoms of Things going down hill   H. Alken 1821.
3. The pleasure of riding in Company.   One would stop if the other Could   H. Alken 1821.
4. Preparing for the Easter Hunt (I shall be over Jack)   H. Alken 1821.
5. The Consequences of having plenty of company on the Road.   H. Alken 1821.
6. A thing of the last consequence   H. Alken 1821.
7. Delighted   S. Alken del et sc.   Augt. 1 1821.
8. Perfectly Satisfied   S. Alken del et sc.   Augt. 1 1821.
9. Dissatisfied   S. Alken del et sc.   Augt. 1 1821.
10. Surprised   S. Alken del et sc.   Augt. 1 1821.
11. Displeased   S. Alken del et sc.   Augt. 1 1821.
12. Terrified   S. Alken del et sc.   Augt. 1 1821.
13. Taste—View near Knigtsbridge   Drawn and Engraved by S. Alken   Septr. 1 1821.
14. Lords—View in Hyde Park   Oct. 1 1821.
15. Yeomanry of England paying a visit   H. Alken del et sc.   1821.
16. Fancy—View near Grays Inn Road   Drawn and Engraved by H. Alken   Septr. 1 1821.
17. Folly—View near Acton   Drawn and Engraved by H. Alken   Septr. 1 1821.
18. Knights—View in the City Road   Oct. 1 1821.

Size of engraved surface 8½ × 6½ inches.

52 ALKEN (H.)

Specimens of Riding near London, Drawn from Life by Henry Alken (rule) London: Published by Thomas M'Lean, Repository of Wit and Humour, 26, Haymarket   1823
The Second Edition, Collation as above, except for variation in title.   Issued in boards.

53 ALKEN (H.)

Sporting Discoveries

Oblong Folio.   (1818)

A series of 7 plates.

A Simple Discovery.   A Painful Discovery.
A Fatal Discovery.   A Troublesome Discovery.
A Trifling Discovery.   A Curious Discovery.
A Common Discovery.

54 ALKEN (H.)

Sporting Notions   (1831–33)
A collection of 36 coloured soft ground etchings and aquatints, each plate headed Notions, and marked, Hy. Alken Delt., and bearing Mclean's imprint.

1. All he is fit for Sir, now is to be cut up.   I have a Notion that he cant be more cut up than myself.
2. I have a Notion that the Brute is going to make the best of his way out and leave me to shift for myself.

Alken's Sporting Notions (*contd.*)

3. I had not the most distant Notion that my Horse was going to stop.
4. I had a Notion that Timber jumping was quite an easy thing.
5. I begin to have a Notion that my Horse is dead.
6. I have a Notion that this is what is called a Bog.
7. I have a Notion this may be called "Riding to the Hounds at a Smashing rate."
8. This gives me a Notion its better to "Look before you Leap."
9. I have a Notion you must either pull him over or persuade him to pull you back again.
10. I have a Notion this Bridge will aBridge my Sport.
11. I had no Notion of the Comforts of Hunting by Water.
12. My good fellows have you any Notion where you can get a Saw.
13. My dear fellows I have a Notion that I am committing some sort of Trespass here.
14. My Notion is we shall get him up pretty shortly, whats your Notion.
15. Its my Notion that this is the only way to get her along.
16. I have a Notion that my Horse looks like 40 Guineas in the Pound.
17. Hav'nt you a Notion that this is the best mode of conveyance over a Brook?
18. I have a Notion that I don't look like Mazeppa.
19. Hallo you ditchers why the devil did you not sing out? you have no Notion what injury you may do my Horse.
20. I have a Notion however hard work it is—that this is the only way to get my Lame Horse Home.
21. I say my fine fellow if you don't pull back, Dam-me I'll make ye—I've a Notion you will frighten my Hunter.
22. I had a Notion that there was room for two to go through at a time.
23. I have a Notion that Ducrow could not excell this.
24. I have a Notion that even Chiffney could not do the thing better.
25. I have a Notion that anything is acceptable in a hot day after a hard chase.
26. I have a Notion that you are going the wrong way, don't you see your party out yonder.
27. I have a Notion that Ive made a Bull.
28. I have a Notion you've made a damn dear shot.
29. I have a Notion he's pinn'd him—he's a regular good un.
30. Woo— Woo— I have a Notion that I shall lose him or break my neck.
31. I have a strong Notion that this is a Coal hole.
32. A Gad I had no Notion that picking up a Fox was such sharp work.
33. Well I have a very strong Notion I should not like Stag Hunting.
34. I have a Notion that I am not quite up to this riding in Surry.
35. I have a Notion that this is about the hardest mouthed Horse in England.
36. I now have a Notion that you should always "Look before you Leap."

55 ALKEN (H.)

A Steeplechase   1827

A series of 6 coloured etchings each headed "A Steeplechase" and each marked, H. Alken del. et sc., and with imprint Pubd. Jany. 1 1827 by S. & J. Fuller 34 Rathbone Place London.

1. The Start—off they go with white for choice.
2. Getting over an Old blind roadway and doing it well—even betting.
3. A Slap at a Stone enclosure—five to four on White.
4. Crossing a Deep ravine dangerous to pass with 6 to 2 on White.
5. Covering a Strong Bullock fence down for a hundred without any odds on White.
6. The Winner, and to such Wondrous doing brought his horse—Hamlet.

Size of engraved surface $10\frac{1}{2} \times 7\frac{1}{2}$ *inches.*

56 ALKEN (H.)

The Stable, The Road, the Park, the Field.   London, M. and N. Hanhart.

Oblong Folio.   1854

Alken's The Stable (*contd.*)

A series of 6 plates, each with several views.

The Olden Time.	Sporting Ponies.
Changing Horses.	Dressing.
Smart Turn Out.	The Park.

57 ALKEN (Henry)

Symptoms of Being Amused (coloured vignette of 6 persons looking at an album) by Hy. Alken Vol. I London.   Published by Thos. McLean: Repository of Wit and Humour, 26, Haymarket.

Oblong Folio.   1822

COLLATION.—Title as above (v. blank) + 41 coloured plates (42 with title).

All plates marked, H. Alken del et sc., and all bearing McLean's imprint.   Each plate contains several designs.

1. Fit for the home station &c.	22. Of Delight &c.
2. of being up with adown prospect &c.	23. of a Spree &c.
3. of Tragedy &c.	24. of Patience &c.
4. of the Managers judgement &c.	25. of how do you do &c.
5. of learning to do the things genteel &c.	26. of none of your stuff &c.
6. of Full Pay &c.	27. of being wanted.
7. of promising a vote &c.	28. of doing the Outside edge &c.
8. of Sporting Friends likely—to go together &c.	29. of Notice to quit &c.
9. of to be sold &c.	30. of backing Gas &c.
10. of a doze after dinner &c.	31. of entering Quod &c.
11. of a great one &c.	32. not fond of Harness &c.
12. of Com'ing from the Hunt &c.	33. of fine feelings &c.
13. of Watching &c.	34. of unwelcome Guests &c.
14. of you slut let us hear all about it &c.	35. of being bang up &c.
15. of a Rout &c.	36. of doubtful Amusement—or Craneing &c.
16. of being very Windy &c.	37. of a few neat ones going to a Mill &c.
17. of a Wild One tamed &c.	38. of being married &c.
18. of did not know the house had Stopped Payment &c.	39. of not being both of the same mind &c.
19. of—Cant wait &c.	40. of catch my horse &c.
20. of a View on Bagshot Heath 1st Sept. &c.	41. of takin' Lessons &c.
21. of being drawn &c.	42. [Title].

Published in 7 numbers and on completion in 1 vol. boards for 4 guineas.   Although Vol. I appears on the title page, no other volume was completed; a second was commenced, but only reached 18 plates.   These latter are extremely rare.   They bear imprint, London Published by Thomas McLean Repository of Wit & Humour 26 Haymarket 1824, and all marked, Symptoms as follows.

1. of Doubtful Amusement—or Craneing &c.	10. of Drawing a Horse & Gig &c.
2. of Sporting friends likely—to go together &c.	11. of Drawing a Countryman &c.
3. of Tragedy &c.	12. of Drawing a Horse &c.
4. of Promising Vote &c.	13. of being a man of Family &c.
5. of a View of Bagshot Heath 1st Sept. &c.	14. of Coming out &c.
6. of How do you do &c.	15. of an Engagement for the Day &c.
7. of Drawing Blood &c.	16. of being perfectly quiet to Ride &c.
8. of Drawing the Long Bow.	17. of being determined to do the thing.
9. of Drawing Room.	18. of an awkward subject &c.

58 ALKEN (H.)

A Touch at the Fine Arts: illustrated by Twelve Plates, with descriptions, by Henry Alken. (thick and thin rule) London: Published by Thomas M'Lean, Repository of Wit and Humour, No. 26, Haymarket (short rule)

Royal Octavo. 1824

COLLATION.—Half title—A Touch at the Fine Arts (v. blank) + Title as above (v. blank) + Preface 1 p. (v. blank) + 12 plates, each plate with 1 leaf of text + 1 leaf of advertisement.

Each plate is marked, Hy. Alken Delt. London Published by Thos. McLean Repository of Wit and Humour, 26 Haymarket 1824.

1. A Touch at the Fine Arts—An Imposing Effect.
2.   ,,   ,,   ,, —Unpleasant in Effect—but the keeping is good.
3.   ,,   ,,   ,, —A Moving Effect—the Execution Rapid.
4.   ,,   ,,   ,, —A Striking Effect—The handling by no means good, or pleasant to the eye.
5.   ,,   ,,   ,, —(Frontispiece) The Subject far from good, but Rich.
6.   ,,   ,,   ,, —A Forcible Effect.
7.   ,,   ,,   ,, —A Sudden Effect.
8.   ,,   ,,   ,, —A surprising Effect—but no Execution.
9.   ,,   ,,   ,, —A very Warm Effect.
10.   ,,   ,,   ,, —A Powerful Effect—but the Subject rather hurried.
11.   ,,   ,,   ,, —A spirited Effect—but no order kept in the grouping of the Figures.
12.   ,,   ,,   ,, —A very Brilliant Effect.

Published in pink boards at one guinea.

59 ALKEN (H.)

Tutors Assistant, containing a Variety of Amusing Scenes, by Henry Alken 1823

A series of 6 plates, all marked, Hy. Alken delt. London Published by Thos. McLean: Repository of Wit and Humour, 26 Haymarket 1823.

1. A Diphthong is the meeting of Two Vowels U and I perhaps &c.
2. Letters are divided into Vowels and Consonants &c.
3. The feminine gender Signifies Animals of the female kind &c.
4. The Glittering Prospect charms my eyes &c.
5. A Verb Neuter expresses neither action nor passion &c.
6. Imperative Mood, or do you die &c.

Published at 12s. in grey paper printed wrappers.
See also under Annals of Sporting, Apperley, Egan, Sporting Repository and Surtees.

Analysis of the Hunting Field 1846. See under Surtees (R.).

60 ANGAS (G. F.)

The Kafirs Illustrated in a Series of Drawings taken among the Amazulu, Amaponda, and Amakosa Tribes: also, Portraits of the Hottentot, Malay Fingo, and other Races inhabiting Southern Africa: together with Sketches of Landscape scenery in the Zulu Country, Natal, and the Cape Colony. By George French Angas, Author of "South Australia Illustrated"; "The New Zealanders Illustrated"; "Savage Life and Scenes"; "Pomara, a Tale of Real Life"; "A Ramble in Malta and Sicily, etc." (8 line verse by Pringle) London: Published by J. Hogarth, 5 Haymarket (rule)

Angas's Kafirs Illustrated (*contd.*)

Folio. 1849

COLLATION.—Title as above (v. London: Printed by G. Barclay, Castle St. Leicester Sq.) + Dedication to Maj. Gen. Sir Harry Smith 1 p. (v. blank) + List of Illustrations 1 p. (v. blank) + Introduction 2 pp. (v–vi) + General Remarks 2 pp. (vii–viii) + pp. 9–52 + frontispiece + 30 coloured lithograph plates.

Frontispiece Portrait of George French Angas.

1. Cape Town, from the Camps Bay Road George French Angas del. J. Needham lithog.
2. Hadji Hasan Nudin Ibanu Abdallah or Karel; Nazea a Malay Woman in her walking costume From Nature and on Stone by George French Angas. M. & N. Hanhart Lith. Printers.
3. [Wynberg] George French Angas delt. J. Needham Lithogr. M. & N. Hanhart Lith. Printers.
4. [Malay Creole Boy: Malay Boy of Cape Town] George French Angas delt. et lithog. M. & N. Hanhart Lith. Printers.
5. Hottentot Holland and Somerset West. George French Angas del. J. Needham Lithogr. Printed by Charles Lovell.
6. The Paarl. George French Angas del. J. Needham Lithogr. Printed by Charles Lovell.
7. Hottentot Herd Boys (Genadendal) From Nature and on stone by George French Angas. M. & N. Hanhart Lith. Printers.
8. [Hottentot Herdsman, Genadendal An old Hottentot Woman aged 97 and half cast children Genadendal] George French Angas del. et lithog. M. & N. Hanhart Lith Printers.
9. [Genadendal] George French Angas delt. J. Needham Lithog. M. & N. Hanhart Lith. Printers.
10. Bariaan' Kloof "The Glen of the Baboons" near Genadendal. George French Angas Del. J. Needham Lithogr.
[11]. [Umpanda the King of the Amazulu] George French Angas del. et lithog. M. & N. Hanhart Lith. Printers.
12. [Panda reviewing his Troops at Nonduengu] George French Angas Del. J. Needham Lithogr.
13. [Utimuni Nephew of Chaka] George French Angas Del. et Lithog. M. & N. Hanhart Lith. Printers.
14. Zulu Hunting Dance near the Engooi Mountains. George French Angas del et. litho. M. & N. Hanhart Lith. Printers.
15. [Young Zulus in dancing costume] From Nature and on Stone by George French Angas. M. & N. Hanhart Lith. Printers.
16. [Kraal on the Umgani Zulu Cattle & Sheep] George French Angas del. et lithog. M. & N. Hanhart Lith Printers.
17. [Zulu Boys in dancing dress] George French Angas del. et lithog. M. & N. Hanhart Lith. Printers.
18. Mouth of the Umvoti, on Indian Ocean. George French Angas Del. J. Needham Lithog. Printed by Charles Lovel.
19. [Nc'Pae a Young Zulu in Gala Dress. Two of King Pandas Dancing Girls] George French Angas del. et lithog. M. & N. Hanhart Lith. Printers.
20. Zulu Soldiers of King Panda's Army From Nature and on stone by George French Angas. M. & N. Hanhart Lith. Printers.
21. [Zulu Kraal at Umlazi with huts and Screens] George French Angas del. et lithog. M. & N. Hanhart Lith. Printers.
22. On the Umnonoti River Natal George French Angas del. J. Needham lithog. Printed by Charles Lovell.
23. Zulu Blacksmiths at Work George French Angas del et lithog. M. & N. Hanhart Lith. Printers.
24. Charley a Half Caste Kafir Boy George French Angas delt. A Laby lith.
25. Inanda Kraal Natal George French Angas del. J. Needham lithog. Printed by Charles Lovell.
26. Gudu's Kraal at the Tugala Women making beer George French Angas del. et lithog. M. & N. Hanhart lithog. Printers.
27. Zulu Kraal near Umlazi Natal George French Angas del. J. Needham lithog. Printed by Charles Lovell.
28. [Durban Port Natal from Berea] George French Angas delt. J. Needham lithog. M. & N. Hanhart Lith. Printers.
29. Tragelaphus Angasii (Gray) the New Antelope from St. Lucia Bay George French Angas del. B. W. Hawkins lithog. M. & N. Hanhart Lith. Printers.
30. New and Remarkable Species of Lepidoptera from Natal and the Zulu Country George French Angas del. W. Wing lithog. Printed by Hullmandel & Walton.

Angas's Kafirs Illustrated (*contd.*)

The three large works by George French Angas, the "Kaffirs," New Zealanders and South Australia are amongst the most important of the illustrated travel books of their period, and have greatly appreciated in value in the last few years. Of the three works the "Kaffirs" is the most uncommon.

61 ANGAS (George French)

The New Zealanders Illustrated: By George French Angas, author of "South Australia Illustrated," "Savage Life and Scenes," "A Ramble in Sicily and Malta," etc. (rule) 4 line verse (rule) London: Thomas M'Lean, No. 26 Haymarket.

Folio.   1847

COLLATION.—Coloured picture Title + Printed Title as above (v. blank) + Engrd. Dedication 1 p. (v. blank) + Preface 1 p. (v. blank) + Subscribers 2 pp. (iii–iv) + General Remarks on New Zealanders 3 leaves (unpaged) + 60 coloured plates each with 1 leaf of text.

Each plate marked, George French Angas (i.e. delt.). Plates 31, 33–35, 37, 39–44, 46, 47, 54, 55 and 60 also lithographed by him.

Coloured Title, The New Zealanders, Illustrated by George French Angas (Natives, idol, canoe, pigs, &c.) W. Hawkins. Printed at 70 St. Martins Lane London Published for the Proprietor by Thomas McLean 26 Haymarket 1846.

1. Honi Heki and Patuone (W. Hawkins).
2. Taranaki or Mount Egmont War Canoe (Early Morning) (J. W. Giles Lithog.).
3. Ngeungeu and her son James Maxwell (W. Hawkins).
4. Rangihaeatas Celebrated House on the Island of Mana called "Kai Tangata" (Eat Man).
5. Te Moanaroa (Stephen) Waingaroa Te Awaitaia (William Naylor) (W. Hawkins).
6. Scene in a New Zealand Forest near Porirua (J. W. Giles).
7. Nga Toenga Daughter of the Barrier Island Chief (W. Hawkins).
8. Volcano of Tongariro with Motupoi Pah from Roto-Aire Lake (J. W. Giles).
9. E. Wai and Kahoki Nieces of Rauparaka (W. Hawkins).
10. Monument to Tewhereo's Favorite Daughter at Raroera Pah near Otawhao (J. W. Giles).
11. Hongi Hongi (W. Hawkins).
12. Roperta of Kawhia George Thoms a Half Caste Boy Nephew of Rauparaha (J. W. Giles).
13. E. Rua, E. Pari, and E. Hoki, Women of Ngatitoa Tribe Cook's Straits (Louisa Hawkins).
14. A Woman and her sons of Nga Ti Toa Tribe Porirua Cooks Straits (W. Hawkins).
15. Tu Kaitote, the Pah of Te Whero Whero, on the Waikato Taupiri Mountain in the Distance (J. W. Giles).
16. Te Mutu, Chief of the Shutai, with his sons Patuoni and Te Kuri Hokianga (F. W. Giles).
17. Nene or Tamita Waka Chief of Hokianga (J. W. Giles).
18. Te Henheu's Old Pah of Waitahanui at Taupo Lake (J. W. Giles).
19. Na Horua or Tom Street (Elder Brother of Rauparaha) at Kahotea near Porirua E. Wai His Wife Tuarau or Kopai his son (W. Hawkins).
20. E. Pori, E. Rangi Wawa (W. Hawkins).
21. House of Hiwikau, mother of Te Heuneu and Falls of Ko Waihi, at Te Rapa, Taupo Lake (J. W. Giles).
22. Children on the Banks of the Waipa   Children at the Boiling Springs near Taupo Lake.
23. Tomb of Huriwenua, a late chief of the Nga Ti Toa Tribe Queen Charlotte Sound (J. W. Giles).
24. Rangitakina A Chief of the Bay of Plenty on the East Coast (W. Hawkins).
25. Maketu House Otawhao Pah built by Puatia to commemorate the taking of Maketu (J. W. Giles).
26. E. Tohi A Young Woman of Barrier Island (W. Hawkins).
27. Mungakahu Chief of Motupoi and his Wife Ko Mari (J. W. Giles).
28. The Volcanic Region of Pumice Hills looking towards Tongariro and the Ruapahu (J. W. Giles).
29. Horomona Maruhau or Blind Solomon (W. Hawkins).

Angas's New Zealanders (*contd.*)

30. Whatas or Patukas (Storehouses for Food) (J. W. Giles).
31. A. Girl at Pipitea Pah, a Boy of Te Aro, E. Rangi and E. Tohi, Girls of Port Nicholson with Kiko an old woman of Tiakiwai.
32. Motupoi Pah and Roto-Aire Lake Tongariro in the Distance (J. W. Giles).
33. Poahu and E. Koti Two Lads of Poverty Bay, Children of Te Pakaru the Principal Chief of Kaiohia.
34. Tara of Irirangi Principal Chief of the Nga Ti Tai Tribe.
35. Paratene Maioha a chief of Waingaroa wearing the Parawai or Dogs Skin Robe.
36. A Feast at Mata-Ta, on the East Coast Mt. Edgcumbe in the Distance Throwing the Spear the Mode of Salutation. A Party of Visitors arriving (J. W. Giles).
37. To Ngaporutu and his wife Rihe at Wakatumutu Ngawhea of Te Mahoa a Chief of the Ngatiamania-poto Tribe & Nga Miho wife of Rangituataia.
38. Entrance to a House at Raroera Pah Waipa (J. W. Giles).
39. Native Ornaments &c.
40. A Group at the Aro Pah Port Nicholson.
41. Te Ohu, a Heathen Priest of the Ngatimaniapoto Tribe Ahuahu, Ko Tauwaki a chief of the Tukanu Ko Teonionga a boy of Te Rapa Taupo Lake.
42. Ornamental Canoe Heads, Paddles &c.
43. Te Maru, a Boy of Koruakopopo, on the Waikato, Te Amotutu, a Young Chief of the Nga-ti-pou Tribe, Ko Tariu, a chief of Taupo and his principal wife E. Proi.
44. Te Werowero or Potatau the Principal Chief of all Waikato Te Waro Principal Chief of the Nga Ti Apakura Tribe Te Pakaru principal Chief of the Nga Te Maniapoto Tribe.
45. Weeping over a deceased chief (J. W. Giles).
46. Ornamental Carvings in Wood.
47. Ko Nga Waka Te Karaka (or Clark) The Christian Chief of the Nga ti Waoroa Tribe Waikato and Wakauenuku his Attendant Boy.
48. Taupo Pah (J. W. Giles).
49. Typical Portraits of New Zealanders (J. W. Giles).
50. Native Tombs (J. W. Giles).
51. Muriwhenua, Kahawai (J. W. Giles).
52. A Tangi or Meeting of Friends Mount Egmont in the Distance (J. W. Giles).
53. Native Swing, War Dance before the Pah or Oinemutu near Roturua Lake (J. W. Giles).
54. Toea, daughter of Te Awaitaia chief of Waingaroa with an attendant Boy carrying water.
55. Implements and Domestic Economy.
56. Te Heuheu and Hiwikaw Taupo Te Kawaw and his nephew Orakai (J. W. Giles).
57. Rangihaeata's Pah with the Island of Mana, and the Opposite Shores of Cooks Straits (J. W. Giles).
58. Weapons and Implements of War Warriors preparing for a Fight (J. W. Giles).
59. Domestic Sketches (J. W. Giles).
60. A Tiki, at Raroera Pah.

62 ANGAS (George French)

South Australia Illustrated: By George French Angas, Author of "The New Zealanders Illustrated," "Savage Life and Scenes," "A Ramble in Malta and Sicily," etc. (rule) 11 lines of verse (rule) London: Thomas M'Lean, No. 26 Haymarket,

Folio. 1847

COLLATION.—Engraved title depicting native family Kangaroo's &c. W. Hawkins delt. et lith. Printed at 10 St. Martins Lane. London Published for the Proprietor by Thomas McLean 26, Haymarket. 1846 (v. blank) + Printed title as above (v. blank) + Engraved Dedication 1 p. (v. blank) + List of Subscribers 2 pp. (iii–iv) + Preface 1 p. + General Remarks 3 pp. + 60 plates, each plate with 1 leaf of text.

Each plate marked, George French Angas (i.e. Delt.) (except plates 41 and 54 by T. S. Gill, being views of Adelaide). Plates 55 and 54 are lithographed by him. All the other

Angas's South Australia (*contd.*)

plates lithographed by J. W. Giles, except 8, 11, 18 and 24, which are lithographed by W. Hawkins, and 37, 48 and 50 by W. Wing.

1. The City of Adelaide from the Torrens near the Reed Beds.
2. Grass Trees at Yankalilla with the Red Kangaroo (Macropus Laniger Group).
3. The River Murray above Moorundi.
4. Crater of Mount Schanck.
5. Portraits of the Aboriginal Inhabitants.
6. Native Weapons and Implements.
7. Port Adelaide.
8. Portraits of the Aboriginal Inhabitants.
9. Scene on the Coorung near Lake Albert with the Halmaturus Greyii a new Species of Kangaroo.
10. View from Mount Lofty, looking over the plains of Adelaide, the Port and St. Vincents Gulf in the Distance.
11. Portraits of the Aboriginal Inhabitants.
12. Klemsic a Village of German Settlers near Adelaide.
13. Port Lincoln, looking across Boston Bay towards Spencers Gulf, Stanford Hill and Thistle Island in the Distance.
14. Lynedoch Valley looking towards the Barossa Range.
15. The Palti Dance.   The Kuri Dance.   (2 views on 1 plate.)
16. Encounter Bay.
17. Mount Gambier, and one of its volcanic lakes (after sunset).
18. Portraits of the Aboriginal Inhabitants.
19. Kangaroo Hunting near Port Lincoln Albert Peak in the Distance.
20. Waungerri Lake and the Marble Range Westward of Port Lincoln.
21. Coast Scene near Rapid Bay Sunset, Natives Fishing with Nets.
22. Portraits of the Aboriginal Inhabitants.
23. Lower Falls of Glen Stuart on the Moriatta Rivulet in the Hills near Adelaide.
24. Portraits of the Aboriginal Inhabitants in their various dances.
25. The River Murray near Lake Alexandrina.
26. Old Gum Tree on the Gawler.
27. The Aboriginal Inhabitants [Implements] [2 leaves of text].
28. Angaston.   Evening.
29. Entrance to the Gorge at Yankalilla,—Messrs. Arthur's Sheep Station, with one of the Volcanic Wells Mount Schank in the distance—Early Morning, together on 1 plate.
30. The Aboriginal Inhabitants [Implements Domestic Economy].
31. The Kapunda Copper Mine.
32. Native Dwellings   I Hut of the Milmendura Tribe on the Koorung   II Native Encampment near Lake Albert   III Winter Huts on the Lake   IV Bark Hut near the River Light.
33. Currakalinga looking over St. Vincents Gulf.
34. The Devil's Punch Bowl near Mt. Schank.
35. Typical Portraits of the Aborigines.
36. The Aboriginal Inhabitants   I An old man and girl in the shores of the Coorung   II Native Encampment at Portland Bay "Cold Morning" and his Family.
37. South Australian Lepidoptera.
38. Rivoli Bay Before Sunrise.   Penguin Island off Rivoli Bay, 2 views on 1 plate.
39. Rapid Bay Encampment of Yankallilla Blacks.
40. Native Tombs and Modes of Disposing of their Dead.
41. Adelaide, Hindley Street from the corner of King William St.
42. Portraits of the Aboriginal Inhabitants.
43. Sea Mouth of the Murray.
44. Lake Albert.
45. Cape Jervis.
46. Interior of Mount Gambier.
47. The Aboriginal Inhabitants.
48. Entomology.
49. Yattagolinga.
50. Entomology (Coleoptera).

Angas's South Australia (*contd.*)

51. The Aboriginal Inhabitants Implements and Utensils.
52. The Golwa with part of Hindmarsh Island Mt. Barker and Mt. Magnificent in the Distance (Evening).
53. Views from Hall's Gulley looking over Angas Park the Belvedere Range in the Distance, On the Barossa Surveys looking North towards German Pass, 2 views on 1 plate.
54. The departure of Captn. Sturt August 1844.
55. South Australian Botany Native Flowers.
56. Encampment of Native Women near Cape Jervis, Natives of Encounter Bay making cord for fishing nets, in a hut formed of the ribs of a whale.
57. Falls of Glen Stuart.
58. From the Barossa looking over part of Angas Park Gawler Plains in the Distance, North Bend of the River Gawler, together on 1 plate.
59. Tyilkilli A Young Man of the Parnkallah Tribe Port Lincoln, Mintalta a Man of Coffins Bay.
60. Bethany a Village of German Settlers at the Foot of the Barossa Hills.

Issued in 10 parts, at 1 guinea per part, lettered South Australia Illustrated by George French Angas, with same Illustration as Frontispiece with advertisement of Angas's New Zealanders on back cover.

63 ANGAS (George French)

South Australia.

COLLATION OF THE PARTS.—Ten parts numbered part I(–10). Price to subscribers £1 1s. Issued in paper covers with cloth backstrip. On each part, the front page of wrapper bears a replica of the pictorial title, in sepia, page 2 of wrapper is blank, page 3 bears Dedication to Queen Adelaide, page 4 bears advertisement of Angas's New Zealanders.

Part 1. Lithographed pictorial title + printed title + Engraved Dedication + List of Subscribers 1 leaf + Preface 1 p. + General Remarks 3 pp. + Plates 1–6, each with leaf of text and a blank sheet to face plate.
Part 2. Plates 7–12 each with leaf of text.
,, 3. ,, 13–18 ,, ,, ,, ,,
,, 4. ,, 19–24 ,, ,, ,, ,, plate 23 misnumbered 22.
,, 5. ,, 25–30 ,, ,, ,, ,, plate 27 has two leaves of text.
,, 6. ,, 31–36 ,, ,, ,, ,,
,, 7. ,, 37–42 ,, ,, ,, ,, 4to insert slip advertising Highland Shepherds Home.
,, 8. ,, 43–48 ,, ,, ,, ,,
,, 9. ,, 49–54 ,, ,, ,, ,,
,, 10. ,, 55–60 ,, ,, ,, ,,

Parts 1–2 dated 1846. Parts 3–10 dated 1847.

Angelo (H.) Hungarian and Highland Broadsword. See under Rowlandson.

64 ANNALS OF SPORTING

The Annals of Sporting and Fancy Gazette; a Magazine, Entirely appropriated to Sporting Subjects and Fancy Pursuits; Containing every Thing worthy of Remarks on

Hunting	Cocking,	Cricket,
Shooting,	Pugilism,	Billiards,
Coursing,	Wrestling,	Rowing,
Racing,	Single Stick,	Sailing,
Fishing,	Pedestrianism,	&c. &c.

Accompanied with Striking Representations of the Various Subjects (rule) Vol. I January

Annals of Sporting (*contd.*)

to June, 1822. (rule) London: Printed for Sherwood, Neely and Jones Paternoster Row (rule)

13 vols.   Octavo.   1822(–8)

COLLATION VOL. I.—Jan.–June 1822.   Half-title "The Annals of Sporting and Fancy Gazette" 1 p. (v. blank) + Title as above (v. blank) + pp. 1–444 (including index 8 pp.) + 12 plates.

All plates throughout the series are uncoloured unless the contrary is stated.

In Vol. I each plate bears imprint, Published by Sherwood, Neely and Jones [and date].

1. Front (composite) consisting of a large centre vignette of a lady and gentleman taking tea, surrounded by 15 small vignettes.   Jan. 1 1822 (coloured).
2. p.   9. Grouse shooting.   Drawn by S. Alkin.   Feb. 1 1822 (coloured).
3. p. 28. To Daniel Haigh Esqr. and the Gentlemen Subscribers of the Surrey Hunt.   Portrait of one of their Members.   Jany 1 1822 (coloured).
4. p. 75. Race Horses Exercising.   Drawn by S. Alkin.   Feb. 1 1822 (coloured).
5. p. 144. . . . View of Breaking Cover Engraved by Sutherland from a Painting by S. Alkin.   March 1 1822 (coloured).
6. p. 159. Rattle and Clinker, the Half bred Dog and Terrier Bitch.   Engraved by Percy Roberts from a Painting by S. Alkin.   March 1 1822 (coloured).
7. p. 213. Piper, a celebrated Greyhound, Engraved by Sutherland from a Painting by S. Alkin.   April 1822 (coloured).
8. p. 278. Jack Spigot (the Winner of the Doncaster St. Leger (1821)   Engraved by Sutherland from a Painting by Mr. J. F. Herring.   April 1 1822 (coloured).
9. p. 285. Filho da Puta.   Engraved by Sutherland from a Painting by Mr. J. F. Herring,   May 1st 1822 (coloured).
10. p. 303. Race Horses (Plate 3) Mounting.   Drawn by S. Alkin.   May 1st 1822 (coloured).
11. p. 361. Race Horses Winning.   Drawn by S. Alkin.   June 1st 1822 (coloured).
12. p. 370. Cock Fighting.   Setting to.   Drawn by S. Alkin.   June 1st 1822 (coloured).
and 47 woodcuts in the text.

VOL. II.—July–Dec. 1822.   Title + Preface 2 pp. (iii–iv) + pp. 1–434 (including 10 pp. index).   A starred leaf 321*–322*, "Pheasant Shooting," is inserted before p. 321 and p. 216 (in some copies misprinted p. 144) + Errata to Vols. I and II 1 p. (v. Marchant, Printer, Ingram Court, London) + 12 plates.

Each plate bears imprint, "Published by Sherwood Neely and Jones" (and date).

13. p.   9. Gudgeon Raking.   Drawn and Engraved by D. T. Egerton.   July 1st 1822 (coloured).
14. p. 24. North West View of the Stable, lately erected by J. R. Scott Esq. Cheltenham.   Drawn and Engraved by D. T. Egerton   July 1st 1822 (coloured).
15. p. 74. Terms commonly made use of to denote the external parts of the Horse (outline engraving).
16. p. 116. A Visit to the Fives Court.   Designed and Etched by J. R. Cruikshank.   Augt. 1st 1822 (folding coloured plate).
17. p. 145. Duck Shooting.   Engraved by Sutherland from a Drawing by S. Alkin.   Sep. 2nd 1822 (coloured).
18. p. 150. Interior of the Stables lately erected by J. R. Scott Esqr. Cheltenham.   Drawn and Engraved by D. T. Egerton.   Agut. 1st 1822 (coloured).
19. p. 225. Partridge Shooting.   Engraved by Sutherland from a Drawing by S. Alkin.   Octr. 1 1822 (coloured).
20. p. 235. Pigeon Shooting.   Engraved by Sutherland from a Drawing by S. Alkin.   Novr. 1st 1822 (coloured).
21. p. 290. Sportsmen Refreshing   Drawn by S. Alkin.   Octr. 1 1822 (coloured).
22. p. 305. North American Deer.   Drawn and Engraved by D. T. Egerton.   Novr. 1 1822 (coloured).
23. p. 321. * Pheasant Shooting.   Engraved by Sutherland from a Drawing by Alkin   Decr. 1 1822 (coloured).
24. p. 362. Theodore [Racehorse].   Engraved by J. Webb from a Painting by Mr. J. F. Herring.   Decr. 2 1822.
and 15 woodcut illustrations in the text.

Annals of Sporting (*contd.*)

VOL. III.—Jan.–June 1823. Half-title + Title + Directions to Binder 1 p. (v. List of Prints from the Sporting Magazine) + pp. 1–440 (including 8 pp. index) + 12 plates. Between pp. 302–3 is a folded sheet, "Cockfighters Shorthand Exemplified" [p. 382 is misprinted p. 182].

The Imprint on the title and plates is changed to Sherwood Jones & Co. 1823, except plates 26 and 36, which maintain Sherwood, Neely and Jones 1821.

25.   Full Cry. Engraved by Sutherland from a Drawing by S. Alkin. Jan. 1 1823 (coloured).

26. p. 44. Tom Hickman. Drawn by G. Sharples Engd. by Percy Roberts. April 1 1821.

27. p. 73. Fan. Engraved by J. Webb from a Painting by Himself. Feby. 1 1823 (coloured).

28. p. 92. Near side view of a Horse's Bones. Neele & Son fc. (folding coloured plate).

29. p. 146. Unkenneling. Engraved by Sutherland from a Drawing by Alkin. Feb. 1 1823 (coloured).

30. p. 169. Skaiting (*sic*) Match at St. Ives. March 1 1823 (coloured).

31. p. 217. Ferreting Rabbits. Engraved by Sutherland from a Drawing by S. Alkin. March 1 1823 (coloured).

32. p. 291. Colonel Thornton. May 1 1823.

33. p. 322. Stag at Bay. Engraved by J. Gleadah from a Drawing by S. Alkin. April 1 1823 (coloured).

34. p. 385. Drawing a Badger. Engraved by J. Gleadah from a Drawing by S. Alkin. June 1 1823 (coloured).

35. p. 397. Magistrate [Racehorse]. Engraved by Sutherland from a Painting by Mr. J. F. Herring. May 1 1823 (coloured).

36. p. 411. Tom Spring. Drawn by G. Sharples Engd. by Percy Roberts. April 1 1821.
and 24 woodcut illustrations in the text.

VOL. IV.—July–Dec. 1823. Half-title + Title + pp. 1–436 (including 8 pp. index) + 12 plates with imprint Sherwood Jones & Co. [and date].

37. p.   3. Race Horses—Saddling. Engraved by Sutherland from a Drawing by S. Alkin. July 1 1823 (coloured).

38. p. 31. Otter Hunting Engraved by Sutherland from a Drawing by S. Alkin. July 1 1823 (coloured).

39. p. 74. Race Horses—Preparing for Second Heat. Engraved by Sutherland from a Drawing by S. Alkin. Augt. 1 1823 (coloured).

40. p. 92. Duck Hunting. Engraved by Percy Roberts from a Drawing by S. Alkin. Augt. 1 1823 (coloured).

41. p. 146. Hunting for Moor Game. Engraved by Thos. Landseer from a Painting by Reinagle. Sep. 1 1823.

42. p. 175. Blacklock [Racehorse]. Engraved by Sutherland from a Painting by Mr. J. F. Herring. Augt. 1 1823 (coloured).

43. p. 220. Toko. Engraved by T. Landseer from a Sketch by his Brother Edwin. Oct. 1 1823.

44. p. 249. Hare Hunting. Engraved by Percy Roberts from a Drawing by Alken. Oct. 1 1823 (coloured).

45. p. 292. Down Charge. Engraved by T. Landseer from a Sketch by his Brother Edwin. Nov. 1 1823.

46. p. 363. Pheasant Shooting with Springers. Engd. by T. Landseer from a Sketch by his Brother Edwin. Nov. 1 1823. Another issue of plate has the word Engraved spelt in full.

47. p. 385. Coursing. Engraved by Sutherland from a Drawing by S. Alkin. Nov. 1 1823 (coloured).

48. p. 389. Rat Hunting. Engraved by Roberts from a Drawing by S. Alkin. Decr. 1 1823.
and 17 woodcut illustrations in the text.

VOL. V.—Jan.–June 1824. Half-title + Title + pp. 1–440 (including 8 pp. index) + slip "Directions to Binder" + 12 plates with imprint as before + Turf Herald 1824 pp. 1–16.

49. p.   4. Brutus [Bull Terrier] Painted by E. Landseer and Engraved by T. Landseer Jan. 1 1824.

50. p. 22. Topthorn [Hunter] Engraved by S. Barenger from a Painting by his Brother Jan 1. 1824.

50a. p. 33. [Gymnastics] No title or imprint Outline engraving of 6 figures.

51. p. 83. Barefoot (Winner of St. Leger) Engraved by H. R. Cook from a Painting by Mr. Herring April 1 1824.

52. p. 88. Foxes. Engraved by Thos. Landseer from a Drawing by his Brother Edwin Feby. 2 1824.

53. p. 108. Terriers and Pole Cat P. Reinagle R.A. Pinxit J. Scott Junr. Sculpt. Feb. 2nd 1824.

Annals of Sporting (*contd.*)

54. p. 178. Nelson, a Setter,   Engraved by H. C. Cook from a Painting by Martin T. Ward   March 1 1824.
55. p. 188. Neptune [Newfoundland Dog]   Engraved by T. Landseer from a Drawing by his Brother Edwin   March 1 1824.
56. p. 247. Marengo [Napoleon's Charger]   Engraved by S. Barenger from a Painting by his Brother   April 1 1824.
57. p. 311. Thos. Cribb   Engd. by Percy Roberts from a Painting by Sharples   May 1 1824.
58. p. 337. A Hackney and Springer.   Engraved by J. Phelps from a Painting by Clowes   May 1 1824.
59. p. 372. Fox Hounds of the Hatfield Hunt.   Ellinor, Cottager, Strider, Rachell, Adamant.   Engraved by Thos. Landseer from a Painting by his Brother Edwin   June 1 1824.
60. p. 395. Stag and Hind.   A Cooper R. A. Pinkt.   J. Scott Junr. Sct.   June 1 1824.
and 12 woodcut illustrations in the text.

VOL. VI.—July–Dec. 1824.   Half-title + Title [the following names are added to the imprint Lloyd & Son, J. M. Richardson, Sheardown & Son, Wolstenholm, Wrightson, Grapel, Williams, Matchett & Stevenson, Lasbury, Ingaltoy, Rogers, Brodie & Co. Edwards & Savage, R. Millikin, C. Le Grange, C. Smith & Co. and Carey and Lea of Philadelphia].

The imprints on the plates remain, Published by Sherwood Jones & Co. [and date] + pp. 1–387 (including Index 7 pp.) p. 388 (blank) + Turf Herald or Annual Racing Calendar 1824 pp. 17–136 + Directions to Binder + 8 leaves of Advertisement at end [p. 75 misprinted p. 57].

61. p.   3. Portrait of a Cross of the Dog and Fox   Engraved by T. Landseer from a Sketch by his Brother Edwin   July 1 1824.
62. p.   28. Plan and Survey of Ascot Race Course by W. Kemp.   Davies sculpt.   July 1824 (coloured).
63. p.   68. Fox of Spitzbergen   Engraved by W. R. Smith from a Painting by A. Cooper R.A.   Augt. 2 1824.
64. p.   89. Plan and Survey of Pontefract Race Course by W. Kemp.   Davies sc.
65. p. 132. Going out.   Engraved by J. Scott from a Painting by W. Walter.
66. p. 156. Plan and Survey of Doncaster Race Course by Wm. Kemp.   Davies sculpt. (coloured).
67. p. 157. Front View of the Grand Stand at Doncaster 1824 J. G. Weightman delt.   Benjn. Davies sculpt.   Sept. 1824 (coloured).
68. p. 197. Dogs Setting a Hare.   Engraved by T. Landseer from a Drawing by his Brother Edwin   Oct. 1 1824.
69. p. 259. Vixen, a Thorough bred Scotch Terrier   Engd. by T. Landseer from a Painting by his Brother   Nov. 1 1824.
70. p. 298. Plan and Survey of Stamford Race Course by Wm. Kemp.   Davies sc. (coloured).
71. p. 323. Jerry—winner of the St. Leger.   Engraved by W. R. Smith from an Original Painting by Mr. Herring   Decr. 1 1824.
and 8 woodcut illustrations in the text.

VOL. VII.—Jan.–June 1825.   Engraved title "Annals of Sporting: A Magazine entirely appropriated to Field Amusements" the preceding lettering within woodcut border of foxes' heads, deer's head, fowling pieces, boxing gloves, foils &c. (v. blank) + Printed title as in Vol. VI. + pp. 1–376 (including index 8 pp.) + Directions to Binder, on slip at end + Turf Herald for 1824 pp. 137–154 + Turf Guide for 1825 pp. 155–192 + 12 plates, with imprint as before, except 77 and 81 where Jones's name is omitted.

72. p.   6. Alpine Mastiff.   Engd. by T. Landseer from a Drawing by his Brother   Jan. 1 1825.
73. p.   23. Snipe Shooting.   Engraved by Percy Roberts from a Painting by Mr. N. Fielding   Jan. 1 1825.
74. p.   66. Mahomed the Palmerston Arabian   G. H. Laporte Pinxt.   M. S. Barenger sculpt.   Feb. 1 1825.
75. p. 101. Disputing the Prize [Newfoundland Puppies]   J. M. Ward Pinxit.   J. Scott Junr.   Sculpt.   February 1st 1825.
76. p. 131. Cedric.   J. Rogers del.   M. S. Barenger sculpt.   March 1 1825.
77. p. 196. Wanton, Theodore and Mayday contending for the Gold Tureen, at Leeds June 24 1824.   Engraved by Smith from a Painting by Mr. Herring   April 2 1825.

Annals of Sporting (*contd.*)

78. p. 230. Don [A Pointer]   No Artist Given   March 2 1825.
79. p. 262. Proctor.   Study of a Bloodhound's Head   Engd. By T. Landseer from a Painting by his Brother Edwin   May 2 1825.
80. p. 274. Plan and Survey of the York Race Course by Wm. Kemp.   Davies sc. (coloured).
81. p. 308. The Poacher [Fox]   Engd. by T. Landseer from a Drawing by his Brother Edwin   Augst. 1 1825.
82. p. 340. Covey of Partridges   J. Elmer pinx   J. Scott Junr. Sct.   March 1st 1825.
83. p. 346. Fly [Greyhound]   Engd. by J. Scott Junr. from a Painting by Mr. Herring   June 1 1825.
     and 11 woodcut illustrations in the text.

VOL. VIII.—July–Dec. 1825.   Woodcut title as in Vol. VII + Printed title + pp. 1–400 (including 8 pp. of index) + Turf Herald for 1825 pp. 1–148 + Directions to Binder on slip at end + 12 plates, with imprints Sherwood & Co., Jones's name being omitted except in plates 85, 89 and 94.

84. p. 26. Lady Juliana Berners in her Costume as Prioress of Sopewell.   Drawn from an Antique by Brooke   July 1 1825.   Engraved by Percy Roberts.
85. p. 36. Red Deer.   Engd. by J. Scott from a Painting by Newton Fielding   June 1 1825.
86. p. 65. Black Game Killed in Scotland 1824   Engd. by S. Godden from a Drawing by N. Fielding   August 1 1825.
87. p. 71. Figaro [Racehorse]   Engraved by Scott from a Painting by Herring   July 1 1825.
88. p. 134. Sprite, Study of a Pony's Head   Engd. by J. Scott Junr. from a Painting by G. H. Laporte   Septr. 1 1825.
89. p. 156. Plan and Survey of Egham Race Course by Wm. Kemp.   Davies sculpt. (coloured).
90. p. 174. Doncaster Gold Cup for 1825.
91. p. 199. Pointers   Engd. by J. Scott Jun. from a Painting by J. F. Lewis   Oct. 1 1825.
92. p. 270. Wild Ducks   Engd. by Roberts from a Painting by Newton Fielding   Nov. 1 1825 (coloured).
93. p. 298. Memmon—winner of the St. Leger 1825   Engd. by J. Scott Junr. from a Painting by G. F. Herring   Novr. 1 1825.   Another issue of this plate bears the word Memmon only without the words winner of the St. Leger.
94. p. 352. Bob a favourite Terrier   Engraved by T. Landseer from a Painting by his Brother Edwin   Novr. 1 1825.
95. p. 360. Middleton—winner of the Derby 1825   Engd. by Thos. Landseer from a Painting by R. B. Davis   Dec. 1825.
     and 8 woodcut illustrations in the text.

VOL. IX.—Jan.–June 1826.   Woodcut title + Printed title + pp. 1–400 (including 8 pp. index) + Turf Guide for 1826 pp. 1–40 + Directions to Binder 1 p. + 12 plates, with imprints of Sherwood & Co.

96. p. 19. Fox Hunting (Plate 1)   Hour of Meeting   Engd. by Sutherland from a Painting by R. B. Davis   Jany. 2 1826 (coloured).
97. p. 35. Whisker [Racehorse]   Engd. by Scott from a Painting by Herring   Jan. 2 1826.
98. p. 38. [Gymnastics]   6 figures, no title or imprint.
99. p. 73. Fox Hunting (Plate 2)   Broke Cover—Settling to the Scent   Engd. by Sutherland from a Painting by R. B. Davis   Feby. 1 1826 (coloured).
100. p. 105. Fight between "Jacco Maccacco" a celebrated Monkey and Mr. Thos. Cribbs well known bitch "Puss"   Etch'd by T. Landseer from a sketch at the time by himself   Feb. 1 1826.
101. p. 166. Fighting Horses   Engd. by Scott from a Painting by J. F. Herring   March 1 1826.
102. p. 206. Fox Hunting (Plate 3)   The Chase—Full Cry   Engd. by Sutherland from a Painting by R. B. Davis   April 1 1826 (coloured).
103. p. 241. Lottery [Racehorse]   Engd. by Scott from a Painting by J. F. Herring   April 1 1826.
104. p. 270. Fox Hunting (Plate 4)   Gone to Earth.   Engd. by Sutherland from a Painting by R. B. Davis   June 1 1826 (coloured).
105. p. 286. Richard Davis [Huntsman to George III]   Engraved by P. Roberts   May 1 1826.
106. p. 324. Falling Pheasant   Engd. by J. Scott Junr. from a Painting by M. T. Ward   May 1 1826.
107. p. 357. Tickler a Celebrated Hunter, and Five Stag Hounds of the Westacre Hunt   Engd. by Scott from a Painting by Scraggs   June 1 1826.
     and 14 woodcut illustrations in the text.

Annals of Sporting (*contd.*)

VOL. X.—July–Dec. 1826.   Woodcut title + Printed title + pp. 1–380 (including 8 pp. index) + Turf Herald for 1826 pp. 1–132 + 12 plates [The List of Plates is at the foot of the index] with imprints as before.

108. p. 28. Earl of Egremont   Engd. by Percy Roberts from a Painting by Phillips   July 1 1826.
109. p. 44. Tawpy [Racehorse]   Engd. by Scott from an Original Drawing   July 1826.
110. p. 72. [Gymnastics] folding plate.
111. p. 83. The Promenade at Cowes, with Portraits of Noble Commanders and members of the Royal Yacht Club   Drawn and Engraved by Robt. Cruikshank   Augt. 1 1826 (coloured).
112. p. 105. Mandane [Brood Mare] Engd. by P. Roberts from a Painting by J. F. Herring   Augt. 1 1826.
113. p. 160. New Betting Rooms Doncaster (whole page woodcut).
114. p. 162. The Doncaster Gold Cup for 1826 (whole page woodcut).
115. p. 213. Pheasants Basking   Engd. by J. Westley from a Painting by J. Howitt   Oct. 1 1826.
116. p. 214. His Royal Highness the Duke of York   Engraved by Percy Roberts   Oct. 1 1826.
117. p. 272. Beech—A Bull Bitch   Engd. by H. R. Cook from an Original Painting by Wolstoneholme Junr.   Nov. 1 1826.
118. p. 279. Steeple Chace   Engd. by Hawksworth, from a Sketch by J. D. Paul Esqre.   Novr. 30 1826.
119. p. 337. Pincher [Terrier]   Nov. 30 1826.
and 9 woodcut illustrations in the text.

VOL. XI.—Jan.–June 1827.   Woodcut title + Printed title + pp. 1–368 (including 8 pp. index) [The List of Plates at foot of index] + Turf Herald 1826 pp. 133–156 + Turf Guide pp. 157–204 + Turf Herald for 1827 pp. 1–24 + 12 plates with imprints as before.

120. p. 17. Harlequin [Hunter]   Engd. by Scott from a Painting by G. H. Laporte   Jan. 1 1827.
121. p. 60. A favourite Spaniel   Engraved by J. Westley   Jany. 1 1827.
122. p. 73. Bedlamite [Racehorse]   Engd. by Scott from a Painting by J. F. Herring   Feby. 1 1827.
123. p. 85. German Deer   Engraved by Westley from a Painting by J. E. Redinger   Feby. 1 1827.
124. p. 132. T. F. Salter Esqr. [Author of Anglers Guide &c.]   Wageman del.   T. Woolnoth Sc. March 1 1827.
125. p. 143. "The bright eyed Perch, with fins of Tyrian dye" (whole page woodcut no imprint).
126. p. 180. Partridges   Engd. by J. Westley from a drawing by Howitt   April 1 1827.
127. p. 203. Salmon Trout   J. Scott Junr. Sct.   April 1 1827.
128. p. 273. Map of the Race Courses in England carefully corrected to the present time by John Frost May 1 1827 (folding).
129. p. 277. Chateau Margaux [Racehorse]   Engd. by Percy Roberts from a Sketch by J. H. Laporte June 1 1827.
130. p. 326. Flanders Fireaway [Trotter]   Painted by Scrags   Engd. by Westley   May 1 1827.
131. p. 328. The Sly Intruder Thos. Landseer 1827   June 1 1827.
and 20 woodcut illustrations in the text.

VOL. XII.—July–Dec. 1827.   Woodcut title + Printed title + pp. 1–352 (including 8 pp. index) + Turf Herald for 1827 pp. 1–154 + Turf Guide for 1828, pp. 155–196 + 13 plates with imprints as before.

132. p. 14. Too Hot to Hold   Etched by T. Landseer from a Sketch by Himself   July 1 1827.
133. p. 16. The Chavolant or Kite Carriage   Engraved by Percy Roberts.
134. p. 61. White Grouse or Ptarmigan Engd. by J. Westley from a Drawing by Fielding Aug. 1 1827.
135. p. 81. Fleur de Lis [Racehorse]   Engraved by J. Westley from a Painting by J. F. Herring   Augt. 1 1827.
136. p. 133. Pewets or Lapwings   Engd. by J. Westley from a drawing by Fielding   Sept. 1 1827.
137. p. 146. Grafton [Port. of Duke of]   Engd. by Percy Roberts from an original Picture   Sept. 1 1827.
138. p. 159. The Doncaster Gold Cup for 1827 (whole page woodcut no imprint).
139. p. 195. Rivers [Port. of Lord]   Engraved by Percy Roberts from an original Picture   Oct. 1 1827.
140. p. 202. Fallow Deer   Engd. by J. Westley from a Painting by J. E. Ridinger   Oct. 1 1827.
141. p. 254. Sam, a celebrated Pointer   Engd. by T. Landseer from a Painting by Herring   Nov. 1 1827.
142. p. 265. The Chase is over   Engd. by P. Roberts from a Painting by John Wooton   November 1827.

Annals of Sporting (*contd.*)

143. p. 317. Wild Boar   Engd. by J. Westley from a Painting by J. E. Ridinger   Dec. 1 1827.
144. p. 323. Little Billy a Celebrated Bull Dog   Drawn and Engraved by Thomas Landseer   Decr. 1 1827.

and 12 woodcut illustrations in the text.

VOL. XIII.—Jan.-May 1828.   Woodcut title + Printed title + pp. 1–356 (including index 6 pp.) + 9 plates [p. 97 misprinted p. 79, pp. 241–290 omitted] + Turf Herald for 1828 8 pp.

145. p.   7. Bloodhounds   Engraved by James Westley, from an Original Drawing by Howitt   Jan. 1 1828.
146. p.   82. Red Deer   Engraved by Mr. T. Landseer, from a Painting by Mr. R. Hills   Feb. 1 1828.
147. p.   92. The Old Coaster   Engraved by James Westley from a Painting by J. Bailey   Feb. 1 1828.
148. p. 131. Mameluke [Derby Winner]   Engraved by J. Westley from a Painting by J. F. Herring   March 1 1828.
149. p. 153. Mr. John Jackson [Boxer]   Percy Roberts sc.
150. p. 191. Colonel Joliffe   Engraved by Percy Roberts   April 1 1828.
151. p. 209. Black Cap [Harrier]   Engd. by T. Landseer from a Painting by G. H. Lapore   April 1 1828.
152. p. 318. The Courser   Engd. by James Westley from a Painting by G. H. Laporte   May 1 1828.
153. p. 322. Jack Randall [Boxer]   Drawn by Sharples   Engraved by Hopwood   May 1 1828.

and 17 woodcut illustrations in the text.

Most sets that occur for sale finish as above with May number. Subscribers had dwindled and it was decided to stop publication. One more number was however issued, namely, for June, after which the enterprise was abandoned. This June number is extremely rare.

JUNE NUMBER.—*pp. 357–418 and 2 plates, p. 358 Hunting and p. 375 A Mare by Soreheels.*

RÉSUMÉ.—*13 vols. with 153 plates or 155 plates with the June Number, containing 50 coloured plates of which 24 are by Samuel Alken, 4 by Herring, 4 by Egerton, 4 by R. B. Davis, 3 unsigned and one each by Newton Fielding, J. Webb, J. R. and R. Cruikshank, and Weightman, and 6 coloured plans of racecourses by Kemp. Four of the plates are whole page woodcuts, and there are in addition 214 woodcuts in the text.*

NOTE.—*The Turf Herald and Turf Guide are not necessarily bound up as above, being divided among various vols. at the binder's convenience and sometimes separately on their own. Turf Herald and Turf Guide (1824) pp. 1–192, (1825) pp. 1–148, (1826) pp. 1–204, (1827) pp. 1–196, (1828) 8 pp.*

Issued in 78 parts.

65 APPERLEY (Charles James)

The Life of a Sportsman. By Nimrod: with Thirty Six Coloured Illustrations, By Henry Alken (rule) London: Rudolph Ackermann, Eclipse Sporting Gallery, 191, Regent Street (rule)

Royal Octavo.   1842

COLLATION.—Title as above (v. Wright & Co., Printers, 76 Fleet St.) + Preface 2 ll. (iii–vi) + Contents 1 p. (v. List of Illustrations) + pp. 1–402 + 5 ll. of Advertisements (1 of works by Nimrod, and 4 of other publications by Ackermann, these last 4 paged 1–8) + 36 coloured plates including Frontispiece and Engraved title.

Each plate (with exception of 1st and 9th) is marked, Drawn and Etched by H. Alken, and each plate bears imprint, London Pubd. by R. Ackermann, at his Eclipse Sporting Gallery, 191 Regent Street 1842.

Apperley's Life of A Sportsman (*contd.*)

1. Frontispiece Amstead Abbey.
2.   Engraved Composite Title—The Life of a Sportsman by Nimrod surrounded by 8 small vignettes.
3. p. 13. "Yoicks! Tally Ho!—Look out for the Pastry!" [mounted].
4. p. 14. "Never Mind 'em,—They wont hurt" [mounted].
5. p. 18. "He'll Leather Two such chaps as that!" [mounted].
6. p. 27. Bagging the Badger.
7. p. 38. "You are worth double what I gave for you."
8. p. 43. "He's Heart of Oak!"
9. p. 49. "Dick Knight" from a picture by B. Marshall, J. Harris sc.
10. p. 50. "His Reverence swims like a cork!"
11. p. 55. "Who—whoop!—Ive done it" [mounted].
12. p. 56. Hunting the Marten Cat.
13. p. 59. The Otter Hunt.
14. p. 61. "What's the Price of the Young Nag, Miller?"
15. p. 64. The Shallows below the Mill.
16. p. 76. "The Prince of Wales" Birmingham Coach of the Olden Time.
17. p. 81. "H for Windsor! Go along Bob"
18. p. 98. Bibury Meeting in its Palmy Days. A scene on Burford Race Course.
19. p. 119. " All Captain Askham's Sir!"
20. p. 122. "He is among the Dead!"
21. p. 149. Frank Raby "Flapper Shooting" on the Great Lake in the Park.
22. p. 153. "Mr. Ridgway's Good Health—Now!"
23. p. 174. "Soho!"
24. p. 196. "Follow my Leader."
25. p. 200. A Meet with His Grace the Duke of Rutland.
26. p. 226. A Night Scene with Sir Thomas Mostyn.
27. p. 230. "Not Handels sweet music more pleases the ear
          Than that of the hounds in full cry."
28. p. 261. The Check.
29. p. 294. The Four in Hand.
30. p. 302. The Three Teams.
31. p. 326. The Race for the Welter Stakes.
32. p. 336. "Fox Hunting for Ever."
33. p. 348. The Shooting Drag a le Tandem.
          [*The Second Issue of this plate is lettered " The Tandem" only.*]
34. p. 354. Mr. Musters hunted by his hounds.
35. p. 400. Our Hero's first run with his own hounds.
36. p. 402. The Master of the Raby Hunt—"One Cheer More."

ISSUES.—First issue of the first edition as above, with four plates mounted, with titles beneath them. In a later variation the plates are mounted but bear no titles, and in still later issues are unmounted. Issued in blue cloth with gilt vignettes on spine and upper cover, gilt edges, yellow endpapers, at 2 guineas.

Second Issue of first edition published in red cloth.

REMARKS.—Considered by many to be the premier coloured plate sporting book in the 19th century, by others as sharing this honour with Jorrocks's Jaunts.

Reprinted in 1874, with 2 extra coloured plates " The First Step to the Coach Box" and " The debut or first attempt at the Brush" and again in 1914.

66 APPERLEY (Charles James)

Memoirs of the Life of the late John Mytton, Esq., of Halston, Shropshire; M.P. for Shrewsbury; High Sheriff for the Counties of Salop and Merioneth, and Major in the

Apperley's Life of Mytton 1835 (*contd.*)

North Shropshire Yeomanry Cavalry. With Notices of his Hunting, Shooting, Driving, Racing, and Extravagant Exploits, by Nimrod. (rule) With Numerous Illustrations by Alken (rule) Reprinted from the New Sporting Magazine (thin and thick rule) London: Rudolph Ackermann, Eclipse Sporting Gallery and New Sporting Magazine Office, 191 Regent Street (rule).

Octavo. 1835

COLLATION.—Title as above (v. note "These Memoirs appeared originally in the New Sporting Magazine" &c. Printed by W. Spiers, 399 Oxford Street, London) & Contents pp. iii–iv + Preface 1 leaf + pp. 1–110 + 12 coloured plates.

Each plate marked, Drawn & Etched by H. Alken Aquat. by E. Duncan Pubd. Augt. 1, 1835 by R. Ackermann at the New Sporting Magazine Office 191 Regent Street.

1. Front. The "Meet," with Lord Derby's Staghounds.	7. p. 16. The Oaks filly.
2. p. 11. Mytton shooting in Winter.	8. p. 17. Blood and the Bull Dog.
3. p. 12. Mytton Wild Duck Shooting.	9. p. 18. Mytton masters the savage dog.
4. p. 14. What! never upset in a gig?	10. p. 24. Light come Light go.
5. p. 15. "Stand and deliver."	11. p. 47. Mytton on Baronet clears nine yards of water.
6. *ibd.* A New hunter—Tallyho! Tallyho!	12. p. 76. Damn this hiccup.

FIRST EDITION.—Issued in brown cloth with blind line panels lettered in gilt in centre " The Life of John Mytton Esq. by Nimrod" within gilt frame, back cover blind line panels only, brown endpapers.

NOTE.—Though containing only 12 plates, this first edition is more rare, and valued higher than the second edition which contains 18 plates. Three plates of this first edition, namely 2, 8 and 9, did not appear in the second edition. A most valuable and important book for the sporting life of the period, aptly described by Newton as " a biography of a real man that reads like a work of fiction."

67 APPERLEY (Charles James)

Memoirs of the Life of John Mytton, Esqre. of Halston, [Coat of Arms] Shropshire, Formerly M.P. for Shrewsbury, High Sheriff for the Counties of Salop and Merioneth, and Major of the North Shropshire Yeomen Cavalry: with Notices of his Hunting, Shooting, Driving, Racing, Eccentric, and Extravagant Exploits. By Nimrod. With Numerous Illustrations, by H. Alken and T. J. Rawlins. Here "after Life's fitful fever he sleeps well" (vignette) Second Edition. Reprinted (with considerable Additions) from the New Sporting Magazine (2-line rule) London Rudolph Ackermann, Eclipse Sporting Gallery and N. S. M. Office, 191, Regent Street.

Octavo. 1837

COLLATION.—Engraved title as above (v. blank) + Printed title (v. London: Walter Spiers, Printer, 399, Oxford Street) + Preface 2 ll. (iii-v, p. vi blank) + Contents 2 ll. (vii-ix p. x blank) + List of Plates 1 p. (v. blank) + pp. 1–206 + imprint 1 p. London Walter Spiers, Printer, 399 Oxford Street (v. blank) + 8 numbered pp. of advertisements by Ackermann + 18 coloured plates.

The plates bear imprints Pubd. Jany. 1, 1837, by R. Ackermann at the New Sporting Magazine Office, 191, Regent Street.

Apperley's Life of Mytton 1837 *(contd.)*

1. (or p. 188) Front. "Well done, Neck or Nothing; you are not a bad one to breed from." Drawn and Etched by T. J. Rawlins and H. Alken. Aquat. by H. Alken.
2. p. 6. A nick, or the nearest way home. (With the back View of Halston House) Drawn and Etched by H. Alken and T. J. Rawlins. Aquat. by E. Duncan.
3. p. 17. Mytton wild duck shooting. Drawn and Etched by H. Alken. Aquat. by E. Duncan.
4. p. 21. What! never upset in a gig? Drawn and Etched by H. Alken. Aquat. by E. Duncan.
5. p. 22. "I wonder whether he is a good timber jumper!" Drawn and Etched by H. Alken and T. J. Rawlins Aquat. by E. Duncan.
6. p. 25. The "Meet," with Lord Derby's Stag Hounds. Drawn and Etched by H. Alken. Aquat. by E. Duncan.
7. p. 26. "Stand and deliver" Drawn and Etched by H. Alken Aquat. by E. Duncan.
8. p. 27. A new hunter. Tally ho! Tally ho! Drawn and Etched by H. Alken Aquat. by E. Duncan.
9. p. 30. The Oaks filly. Drawn and Etched by H. Alken. Aquat. by E. Duncan.
10. p. 42. "Light come, light go." Drawn and Etched by H. Alken. Aquat. by E. Duncan.
11. p. 82. Mytton on Baronet clears nine yards of water. Drawn and Etched by H. Alken Aquat. by E. Duncan.
12. p. 127. "D—n this hiccup!" Drawn and Etched by H. Alken Aquat. by E. Duncan.
13. p. 186. A h-ll of a row in a hell—Mytton shows fight. Drawn and Etched by J. T. *(sic)* Rawlins and H. Alken. Engd. by E. Duncan.
14. p. 188. Mytton swims the Severn at Uppington Ferry "He that calls himself a Sportsman, let him follow me." Drawn and Etched by T. J. Rawlins Aquat. by E. Duncan.
15. p. 190. How to cross a country comfortably after dinner. Drawn and Etched by T. J. Rawlins and H. Alken Aquat. by E. Duncan.
16. p. 197. Heron Shooting—"A cooler, after a big drink." Drawn and Etched by T. J. Rawlins and H. Alken Aquat. by E. Duncan.
17. p. 201. "A Squire-trap, by Jove," cries Mytton, "a little more and I should have done it." Drawn and Etched by T. J. Rawlins and H. Alken.
18. p. 201. Now for the honour of Shropshire. The Shavington day—a trial of rival packs, and consequently rival horsemen. Drawn and Etched by T. J. Rawlins and H. Alken Aquat. by E. Duncan.

NOTE.—This second edition contains 6 extra plates, and 3 new plates replace 3 of the old plates of the first edition, making 9 new plates in all.

ISSUES.—First issued as above in dark green cloth with design in gilt on upper cover of hunting and fishing implements on a stand enclosing the words, Life and Death of John Mytton Esqr. R. Ackermann 191 Regent Street, lower cover plain, back strip bearing words Life & Death of John Mytton Esqr. (with dog above and hare below in gilt) and dated at foot in gilt 1847. Second issue has no date at foot of spine.

A later variant has plate 1 Aquatinted by E. Duncan, plate 9, filly spelt filley, and plates 17 and 18 printed for pp. 158 and 159. Yet another variant has plates 17 and 18 marked on the plates as p. 81, plate 17 being without artist or engraver.

68 APPERLEY (Charles James)

Life of Mytton, Third Edition.

Octavo.   1851

COLLATION.—Engraved title as in previous edition, but Second Edition changed to Third Edition and the imprint altered to London. Rudolph Ackermann, Eclipse Sporting and Military Gallery, 191, Regent Street 1851 (v. blank) + Printed title as in Second Edition but differently set up and the lower part changed to—Third Edition, with a Brief Memoir of

Apperley's Life of Mytton (*contd.*)

Nimrod, by the Author of "Handley Cross." (rule) London: Rudolph Ackermann, Eclipse Sporting Gallery, 191 Regent Street. (short rule) 1851 (v. London: Printed by G. Barclay, Castle St. Leicester Sq.) + Preface 2 ll. + Contents 3 pp. (vii–ix) p. x List of Plates + Text pp. 1–218 + Advertisements 4 leaves + 18 coloured plates.

The plates are the same as in the Second Edition, but as they are placed at different pages, the titles are given below in brief for ease in collation.

1. Front. Well done, Neck or Nothing.
2. p. 31. Mytton wild duck shooting.
3. p. 35. What! never upset in a gig?
4. p. 36. "I wonder whether he is a good Timber jumper?"
5. p. 39. The "Meet," with Lord Derby's Stag Hounds.
6. p. 40. Stand and deliver.
7. p. 41. A new hunter—Tally-ho! Tallyho!
8. p. 44. The Oaks filly.
9. p. 56. "Light come, light go."
10. p. 96. Mytton on Baronet clears nine yards of water.
11. p. 134. A nick, or the nearest way home.
12. p. 143. A h-ll of a row in a hell.
13. p. 147. Mytton swims the Severn at Uppington Ferry.
14. p. 149. How to cross a Country comfortably after Dinner.
15. p. 155. Heron Shooting.
16. p. 158. "A Squire-trap, by Jove," cries Mytton.
17. p. 159. Now for the honour of Shropshire.
18. p. 168. "D—n this hiccup."

ISSUES.—First Issue of Third Edition. The engraved title is dated 1850, the printed title 1851 and all the plates bear imprint, Pubd. Novr. 1 1850, by R. Ackermann, at his Eclipse Sporting Gallery, 191 Regent St.

Second Issue of Third Edition. The Engraved title dated 1850, printed title 1851, and all the plates dated 1851.

Third Issue of Third Edition. Both the engraved and the printed title dated 1851, and all the plates dated 1851.

REMARKS.—This Third Edition is a desirable item to add to any collection as it is the first to contain the Life of Nimrod. Published at 25s., "handsomely bound in cloth." Issued in green cloth with design in gilt on upper cover, repeated in blind on lower. Lettered on spine Life and Death of Mytton, with hound above and hare below. The 1850 issue bears Ackermann's name at foot, the 1851 issue does not.

A Fourth Edition was published in 1869, and a Fifth in 1870 and another edition in 1877.

Ask Mamma or the Richest Commoner in England 1858. See under Surtees (R.).

69 ASHMORE

Views in Scotland.

A series of 20 plates each marked, Ashmore delt. Jukes sculpt. Published as the Act directs, by R. Morrison & Son. Perth. Dec. 1793.

1. Lancarty near Perth.
2. Argarton.
3. St. Fillian's Chapel and Pool.
4. Loch Dochart Castle.
5. View of the River Bran, from Ossians Hall, near Dunkild.
6. Tunderagh Castle.
7. Loch Lomon.

Ashmore's Views in Scotland (*contd.*)

8. View from Rest and be Thankfull.
9. Dunglass Castle.
10. Hayfield.
11. Finlarig Castle.
12. Dumbarton Castle.
13. Moncrief House.
14. Fraoch Elan Castle, Loch Awe.

15. Dall—Mally.
16. Bridge at Ben More.
17. Loch Rest in Glencoe.
18. Seat of the Chieftain of Clan Macfarlane.
19. Head of Loch Fyne.
20. Kilchurn Castle, Loch Awe.

70 ASPIN (J.)

The Naval and Military Exploits which have distinguished the Reign of George the Third Accurately described, and methodically arranged (rule) By Jehoshaphat Aspin (rule) embellished with numerous coloured plates (rule) London: Printed for Samuel Leigh, 18 Strand, by W. Clowes, Northumberland Court (rule)

Octavo.   1820

COLLATION.—Title as above (v. blank) + Advertisement pp. iii–vi + Contents pp. vii–viii + Embellishments 1 leaf + pp. 1–784 (including index) + Front and 33 plates.

1. Frontispiece. A Review.
2. p. 100. Bunker's Hill.
3. p. 328. Ld Rodneys Victory.
4. p. 432. Seringapatam.
5. p. 433. Tippo Saib.
6. p. 434. Death of Wang.
7. p. 442. Lincelles.
8. p. 456. Ld Howe's Victory.
9. p. 470. Ld Nelson boarding St. Joseph.
10. p. 476. Ld Duncan's Victory.
11. p. 481. Battle of the Nile.
12. p. 482. Defeat of the French in Ireland.
13. p. 486. St. Jean D'Acre.
14. p. 503. Victory at Copenhagen.
15. p. 508. Death of Abercrombie.
16. p. 549. Ld Nelson Trafalgar.
17. p. 556. Sr R. Strahan's Victory.

18. p. 580. Alexandria.
19. p. 590. Vimiera.
20. p. 598. Death of Moore.
21. p. 610. Oporto.
22. p. 612. Talavera.
23. p. 621. Busaco.
24. p. 629. Albuera.
25. p. 648. Cuidad Rodrigo.
26. p. 650. Badajoz.
27. p. 653. Salamanca.
28. p. 674. San Sebastiano.
29. p. 694. Toulouse.
30. p. 708. Waterloo.
31. p. 715. Bonaparte on the Northumberland.
32. p. 740. Boarding the Chesapeake.
33. p. 763. Storming of Algiers.
34. p. 765. Slaves delivd. Algiers.

Two extra plates are frequently found bound up with above uniform with the rest of the series, viz.

> *p. 665 Vittoria*
> *p. 677 Pampeluna*

The book is complete however without them.   The illustrations are all circular, about 2½ inches in diameter, and most delicately engraved.

71 ATKINSON (J. A.)

A Picturesque Representation of the Naval, Military, and Miscellaneous Costumes of Great Britain, in Thirty-Three Coloured Plates (thick and thin rule) By John Augustus Atkinson (thin and thick rule) With a Descriptive Essay on the Subject of each plate in English and French (rule) London: William Miller, Albemarle Street   1807

Atkinson's Picturesque Representation of Naval and Military Costumes (*contd.*)

COLLATION.—Half-title + Title as above (v. blank) + Dedication to Alexander I of Russia 1 leaf + same in French 1 leaf + Prospectus 1 page (v. blank) + same in French + 33 coloured plates printed on bistre paper each with a leaf of text (one side English other French).

Each plate bears imprint, "London Published Jan. 1, 1807, by William Miller 49 Albemarle Street & James Walker No. 8 Conway Street, Fitzroy Square" and "Drawn & Etched by J. A. Atkinson."

1. Foot Guards.	12. Getting up a Kedge Anchor.	23. Men of War getting under Way.
2. Baggage Wagon.	13. Artillery on a March.	24. Sailors.
3. Post Captain.	14. Launching a Dover Cutter.	25. Rigged Lighter.
4. Highlanders.	15. Dover Pilot Boat.	26. Gravesend Boat.
5. Cottage Girl.	16. Heaving the Lead.	27. Ale House door.
6. Hackney Coach.	17. Sand Boy.	28. Skaiting (*sic*).
7. Barrow Women.	18. Lifeguards.	29. Watermen.
8. Troops Watering Horses.	19. Light Dragoons.	30. Riflemen.
9. Green Cart.	20. Mail Coach.	31. Soldiers Drilling.
10. Artillery Men.	21. Tandem.	32. Farriers Shed.
11. The Fishermen.	22. Husbandmen.	33. Carriers Wagon.

NOTE.—A very fine and rare book that has not been sufficiently appreciated, according to Hardie one of the most charming books on costume. It was originally intended to issue the work in 3 volumes, a variant titlepage bearing the words Vol. I before the imprint. No more were however published.

72 ATKINSON (J. A.) and J. WALKER

A Picturesque Representation of the Manners Customs and Amusements of the Russians, in one hundred coloured plates; with an accurate explanation of each plate in English and French. In Three Volumes (thick and thin rule) By John Augustus Atkinson, and James Walker (thin and thick rule) Vol. I [II, III] London: (thin and thick rule) Printed by W. Bulmer and Co. Cleveland-Row, for the Proprietors; and Sold by Them, at No. 8, Conway-Street, Fitzroy-Square; Messrs. Boydell, Shakspeare Gallery, Pall Mall and No. 90 Cheapside; Mr. Alici, St. Petersburg: and Messrs. Riss and Saucet, Moscow.

Folio.   1803[-4]

COLLATION VOL. I.—Half-title "A Picturesque Representation of the Manners, Customs, and Amusements of the Russians" (v. blank) + Title as above (v. blank) + Dedication to Alexander I 1 p. (v. blank) + Preface 2 pp. + Dedication in French 1 p. (v. blank) + Preface in French 2 pp. + List of Plates 1 p. (v. blank) + 33 coloured plates each with 1 leaf of text (descriptions in French and English).

Each plate is marked, "Drawn & Etched by John Augustus Atkinson Published as the Act Directs May 1st 1803 by J. A. Atkinson and Jas. Walker No. 8, Conway Street, Fitzroy Square, and Messrs. John & Josiah Boydell, Pall Mall & Cheapside London [for vol. II the date is changed to Feby. 1 1804 and Vol. III July 2 1804].

1. Voizok.	7. Baschkirs.	11. Winter Kibitka.
2. Svai.	8. Lapland Sledge.	12. Babki.
3. Pleasure Barges.	9. Summer Kibitka with a Courier.	13. Corn Barks.
4. Droshka.		14. Cozacks.
5. Finland Sledge.	10. Market of Frozen Provisions.	15. Horn Musick.
6. Ochta Milkwomen.		16. Cozack Dance.

Atkinson's Customs of Russians (*contd.*)

17. Sledge.
18. Fetching Water and Rinsing Cloaths.
19. Ice Cutters.
20. Carriage on Sledges.
21. Russian Peasant.
22. Charcoal Bark.
23. Bathing Horses.
24. Gypsies.
25. A Kaback.
26. Peasant Girl.
27. Winter Carriers.
28. Village Council.
29. Finland Beggar.
30. Katcheli.
31. Galiotes.
32. Summer Carriers.
33. Izba.

VOL. II.—Half-title as before + Title as before (but dated 1804) + List of Plates 1 p. (v. blank) + 34 coloured plates each with leaf of text and imprints as in Vol. I (but dated Feby. 1 1804).

34. Pilgrims.
35. Ukrain Drover.
36. Zibitenshik.
37. Children going down an Ice Hill.
38. Lighters.
39. Government Bark.
40. Russ Soldier.
41. Finn Girl Going to Market.
42. Ice Hills.
43. Hussars.
44. Summer Fishery.
45. Finland Wood Barks.
46. Winter Fishery (misprinted Summer Fishery).
47. Ladoga Fishing Boats.
48. Common Travelling Sledge.
49. A Merchants Wife.
50. Russ Merchant.
51. Rafts of Timber.
52. Finland Horse.
53. Jumping on a Board.
54. Cozack Officer.
55. Court Caleche.
56. Yaeger.
57. Skittles.
58. Public Festival.
59. Hay Carts.
60. Monks.
61. Peasant Woman & Child.
62. Baba or Old Woman.
63. Boutoushniki.
64. Stone Carriage.
65. Finland Carts.
66. Sailors.
67. Tartar Camp.

VOL. III.—Half-title as before + Title as in Vol. II + List of Plates 1 p. (v. blank) + 33 coloured plates, each with a leaf of text and imprints as in Vol. I (but date July 2 1804).

68. Tartars Catching Horses.
69. The Plough.
70. Smolenski Carts.
71. Russian Woman in her Winter Dress.
72. Hot Bath.
73. The Wolf Hunt.
74. Boxing.
75. Cooper.
76. Kalatchnik.
77. Race Course.
78. Ogorodnick.
79. Dvornick.
80. Lotka.
81. Village Amusement.
82. Wrestling.
83. The Swing.
84. Fish Barks.
85. Golubtza.
86. Baptism.
87. A Russian Village.
88. Marriage.
89. Burial.
90. Metropolite.
91. Russian Priests.
92. Wood Barks.
93. Farm Yard.
94. Sorting and drying Hemp.
95. Polish Dance.
96. Finn bringing live fish to Market.
97. Consecration of the Waters.
98. Trotting Horse.
99. Nuns.
100. Noble Tcherkesseian.

Second Edition 1812.

Atkinson (J. A.).   See also under Beresford (J.).

73 ATKINSON (J.)

Sketches in Afghanistan by James Atkinson, Esq. (on large vignette "Beloochees in the Boland Pass" Louis Haghe delt.), Lond: Published July 1st. 1842 by Henty Graves & Company, Printsellers to Her Majesty and H.R.H. Prince Albert, 6 Pall Mall, and J. W. Allen & Co., Leadenhall Street, Day and Haghe, Lithrs., to the Queen.

Folio.   1842

COLLATION.—Title as above (v. blank) + Dedication 1 p. (v. blank) + Description of plates 2 pp.

Scene on the River Sutledge, near Pauk—Puttun in the Punjaub.
The Town of Roree and the Fortress off Bukker, on the Indus.

Atkinson's Afghanistan (*contd.*)

The Encampment at Dadur with the Entrance to the Bolan Pass.
View of the Mountain Baba-Naunee, called Kutl-Gahor.
Entrance to the Bolan Pass from Dadur.
The Wild Pass of Siri Kajoor.
The Opening into the Narrow Pass above Siri Bolan.
The Approach to the Fortress of Kwettah.
Entrance into Kojak Pass from Parush.
The Troops emerging from the Narrow Part of the Defile.
Descent through the Koojah Pass.
The Second Descent through the Koojah Pass.
The Third Descent of the Koojah Pass.
The City of Candahar.
The Fortress and Citadel of Ghuznee and the two Minars.
The Valley of Maidan.
The Village of Urghundee.
Surrender of Dost Mohommed Khan, to Sir William Hay Macnachten, Bart. at the Entrance into Caubul
    from Killa—Kazee.
The Main Street in the Bazaar at Caubul in the Fruit Season.
The Bulla Hissar and City of Caubul, from the Upper Part of the Citadel.
Caubul from a Burying Ground on the Mountain Ridge, North East of the City.
The Durbah—Khaneh of Shah Shoojah-ool-Moolk, at Caubul.
The Avenue at Baber's Tomb.
The Tomb of the Emperor Baber.
Caubul Costumes.

Ayton (Richard). Voyage round Great Britain 1814–1825. See under Daniell (William).

74 BAKER (J.)

Atlas of English Towns, The Engravings partly provided by the inhabitants London. C. Whittingham.

COLLATION.—Title + pp. 3–10 + Engraved title, Home Beauties + pp. 3–70 + 18 plates, mostly by J. Wright (including the engraved title). The Views include Rochester, Canterbury, Margate, Broadstairs, Ramsgate, Dover, Southend, Walmer Castle, Royal Artillery Barracks, &c.

75 BAKEWELL (R.)

Travels, comprising observations made during a residence in the Tarentaise, and various parts of the Grecian and Pennine Alps, and in Switzerland and Auvergne, in the years 1820, 1821, 1822. (rule) Illustrated by Coloured Engravings, and numerous wood-cuts, from original drawings and sections. (rule) By R. Bakewell, Esq. (rule) 2 line quote Ovid. (rule) In Two Volumes. Vol. I [II]. London: Printed for Longman, Hurst, Rees, Orme and Brown, Paternoster Row.

2 vol. Octavo. 1823

COLLATION VOL. I.—Title as above (v. London Printed by A. & R. Spottiswoode, New Street Square) + Preface 3–8 + Contents 9–11 + Explanation of Plates & Cuts 13–16 + pp. 1–381 + coloured aquatints.

Bakewell's Travels (*contd.*)

1. Front.   Chateau Duing and the Dent D'Alençon on the Lake of Annecy.
2. p.   14.   The Gibbon Horn near L'Hopital, Valley of the Iserc.
3. p. 253. Baths of Brida in the Tarantaise.

VOL. II.—Title + Contents iii–vii + pp. 1–447 (including index).

4. Front.   Aguille de Dru—Chamouny.

Each plate marked, R. Bakewell, delt. *J. Clark, sculpt.* *London Published by Longman, Hurst, Rees, Orme and Brown.* 1823.

76 BARKER (B.)

The Fine Arts. (rule) Forty-Eight Aquatint Colored Engravings, by Theodore Fielding, from a work containing forty-eight subjects of Landscape Scenery, principally views in and near Bath. (rule) Painted in oil, by Benjamin Barker. (rule) Published by subscription in 1824. (rule) Clark, Printer, Bath. (rule).

Oblong Quarto.   1824

COLLATION.—Title as above (v. blank) + 48 coloured plates.

1. The Village of Wick, near Bath.
2. Scene above Wick Rocks.
3. Scene near Midford.
4. Composition.
5. Scene from Claverton Down.
6. Hampton Cliffs, near Bath.
7. Scene near Bathford.
8. Composition.
9. Scene from Leighwood, near Bristol.
10. Claverton, near Bath.
11. Wick Rocks, near Bath.
12. The Village of Oldlands, near Bath.
13. Stoke, near Bath.
14. Valies-Vale, near Frome.
15. Wick, below the Rocks.
16. Wick, below the Rocks.
17. Hampton Cliffs.
18. Wick Rocks.
19. Wick, below the Rocks.
20. Freshford, near Bath.
21. Hampton Cliffs.
22. Wick, below the Rocks.
23. Valies-Vale, near Frome.
24. Cottage, near Chippenham.
25. Scene near Midford, near Bath.
26. Weston, near Bath.
27. Scene on the Bath Canal.
28. Castle-combe, near Bath.
29. Castle-combe, near Bath.
30. Wick, below the Rocks.
31. Wick, near Bath.
32. Wick, near Bath.
33. Scene on the Bath Canal.
34. Cottage at Chippenham.
35. Cottages at Chippenham.
36. Freshford, near Bath.
37. Hampton Cliffe, near Bath.
38. Cottage, near Chippenham.
39. Oldlands, near Bath.
40. Wick, below the Rocks.
41. Scene near the Old Bridge, Bath.
42. Hampton Cliffs, near Bath.
43. Cottage near Bradford.
44. Scene near Chepstow.
45. Cottage near Chippenham.
46. Castlecombe, near Bath.
47. Cottages at Chippenham.
48. Cottages at Chippenham.

77 BARKER (B.)

Also issued as follows:

The Fine Arts. (rule) Twenty Aquatint Colored (*sic*) Engravings by Theodore Fielding, from a work containing Forty [eight, deleted] subjects of Landscape Scenery, principally views in and near Bath. (rule) Painted in oil, by Benjamin Barker (rule)

Barker's Fine Arts (*contd.*)

Published by Subscription in 1824. (rule) A. E. Binns, Printer, Bath. (rule) (Price 5 guineas)

78 BARKER (B.)

The Fine Arts. (rule) Ten Aquatint Colored Engravings by Theodore Fielding, from a work containing forty eight subjects of Landscape Scenery, principally views in and near Bath (rule) Painted in Oil by Benjamin Barker (rule) Published by subscription in 1824 (rule) A. E. Binns Printer Bath. (rule)

Oblong Quarto.

COLLATION.—Title as above (v. blank) + 10 coloured plates.

No. 1. Village of Wick near Bath.	No. 7. Wick Rocks near Bath [a different view from No. 2].
No. 2. Wick Rocks, near Bath.	
No. 3. Wick, near Bath.	No. 8. Scene from Claverton Down.
No. 4. Hampton Cliffs, near Bath.	No. 9. Cottage near Bradford.
No. 5. Castle-Combe, near Bath.	No. 10. Cottage near Chippenham.
No. 6. Scene at Midford near Bath.	

Issued on buff mounts, titled by means of small printed slips.

79 BARKER (Benjamin)

Benjamin Barker's English Landscape Scenery a Series of Forty Eight aquatint Engravings by Theodore Fielding. From original paintings in Oil by the late B. Barker, Esq. Bath: W. Everett, Pulteney Bridge   1843

COLLATION.—Title as above (v. Bath printed by Wood & Sons, Parsonage Lane) + Dedication to Sir W. S. R. Cockburn 1 page (v. blank) + Memoir of the Artist 3 pages signed E. M [angin] + 48 coloured plates.

1. At Hampton near Bath.	18. Freshford.
2. Claverton.	19. Composition.
3. Western.	20. Cottages at Castle Combe.
4. On the Bath Canal.	21–22. Castle Combe near Bath.
5. Hampton Cliffs.	23. Village of Oldlands near Bath.
6. Near Bathford.	24. Stoke near Bath.
7. Near Hampton Cliffs.	25. Wick.
8. Claverton Downs.	26–27. Village of Wick.
9. Oldlands.	28–29. Wick Rocks.
10. Near the Old Bridge Bath.	30. Above the Rocks.
11. Hampton Cliffs near Bath.	31–36. Below the Rocks.
12. On the Canal.	37–38. Valies Vale near Frome.
13. Hampton Cliffs.	39. Near Chepstow.
14. Hampton Cliffs.	40. Cottages near Bradford Wilts.
15. At Midford.	41. From Leighwood near Bristol.
16. Midford Castle.	42–48. Cottages near Chippenham.
17. At Freshford.	

80 BARRINGTON (George)

The History of New South Wales, including Botany Bay, Port Jackson, Parramatta, (*sic*) Sydney, and all its Dependencies, from the Original Discovery of the Island, with

Barrington's History of New South Wales (*contd.*)
the Customs and Manners of the Natives, and an account of The English Colony, from its Foundation, to the Present Time, by George Barrington, Superintendant of the Convicts. Enriched with Beautiful Coloured Prints (coloured vignette of a Black Swan. Woodthorpe, sculpt.) London: Printed for M. Jones, No. 1. Paternoster Row.

Octavo.   1802

COLLATION.—Engraved title as above (v. blank) + sub-title "The History of New South Wales" (double rule) By George Barrington, Officer of The Peace at Paramatta (double rule) Price 14s. 6d. in Boards (v. printed by W. Flint. Old Bailey, London) + Contents 20 leaves (a–e 4 in 4's) + Dedication 1 leaf + Preface 1 leaf + Introduction 1 leaf + pp. 7–505 + coloured plates.

Each plate marked, V. Woodthorpe sculpt. and with imprint, Published (date) By M. Jones, Paternoster Row.

1. Front.   Sydney.   Dec. 24th 1802.
2. p.   9. A Male and Female Native.   Nov. 1st 1802.
3. p.   13. Manhood.   Dec. 17th 1802.
4. p.   27. Burning the Dead.   Dec. 3rd 1802.
5. p.   35. Courtship.   Nov. 13th 1802 (no engraver given).
6. p.   46. A Native Family.   Feb. 1st 1803 (no engraver given).
7. p.   47. Town and Cove of Sydney.   Mar. 18th 1803.
8. p.   56. Garden Island.   Mar. 5th 1803.
9. p. 104. East View of Sydney.   Feb. 5th 1803.
10. p. 104. Entrance of Paramatta River.   Mar. 25th 1803.
11. p. 124. South View of Sydney.   Mar. 1st 1803.
12. p. 429. A Native Dog.   Nov. 6th 1802.
13. p. 431. Kangaroo.   Dec. 13th 1802.
14. p. 435. Black Cockatoo.   Nov. 13th 1802.
15. *ibd.*   Bird of Paradise.   Dec. 24 1802.
16. p. 439. Hornbill.   Nov. 26th 1802.
17. p. 441. Mountain Eagle.   Nov. 7th 1802 (no engraver given).
18. p. 443. Emu.   Dec. 31st 1802.
19. p. 449. Blue Snake   Black and White Snake.   Dec. 31st 1802.
20. p. 457. Botany [5 plants].   Jan. 21st 1803 (no engraver given).
21. p. 474. Pinchgut Island.   Mar. 11th 1803.
    p. 503. Full page woodcut   View of the New Church at Paramatta.

This is the second issue of the first edition. The first issue is the same as above but has an extra leaf at end (List of Plates) and 14 coloured plates only (Nos. 6, 7, 8, 9, 10, 11 and 21 not being included).

81 BARRINGTON

The History of New South Wales, including Botany Bay, Port Jackson, Parramatta, Sydney, and all its Dependencies, from the Original Discovery of the Island, with the Customs and Manners of the Natives, and an Account of the English Colony from its Foundation, to the Present Time, by George Barrington: superintendant of the Convicts. Enriched with beautiful Coloured Prints (coloured vignette of Black Swan) London: Printed for M. Jones No. 5 Newgate Street, and Sherwood, Neely & Jones. Paternoster Row.

Octavo.   1810

Barrington's History of New South Wales (*contd.*)

COLLATION.—Engraved title as above (v. blank) + Preface to the Second Edition 1 leaf + Preface to the Reader 1 leaf + Two Letters 1 leaf + Dedication 1 leaf + Preface to the First Edition 1 leaf + Introduction 1 leaf + pp. 7–503 + Supplement pp. 504–544 + index 2 leaves + 16 plates. Each plate marked, Woodthorpe sculpt. and bears imprint, Published by M. Jones, Paternoster Row. [date]

1. Front. Town and Cove of Sydney. Mar. 18th 1803.
2. p. 9. A Male and Female Native. Nov. 1st 1802.
3. p. 13. Manhood. Dec. 17th 1802.
4. p. 16. A Native Family. Feb. 1st 1803 (no engraver given).
5. p. 26. Burning the Dead. Dec. 3rd 1802.
6. p. 35. Courtship. Nov. 13th 1802 (no engraver given).
7. p. 429. A Native Dog. Nov. 6th 1802.
8. p. 431. Kangaroo. Dec. 13th 1802.
9. p. 434. Camelopad Spotted Hyena (no engraver given).
10. p. 435. Bird of Paradise. Dec. 24th 1802.
11. p. 437. Black Cockatoo. Nov. 13th 1802.
12. p. 439. Horn bill. Nov. 26th 1802.
13. p. 441. Mountain Eagle. Nov. 7th 1802 (no engraver given).
14. p. 443. Emu. Dec. 31st 1802.
15. p. 449. Blue Snake Black and White Snake. Dec. 31st 1802.
16. p. 456. Botany [5 plants]. Jan. 21st 1803 (no engraver given).
 p. 503. Full page woodcut of Church at Paramatta.

The Illustrations of this edition Printed from the same plates, are greatly inferior to those of the First Edition. They are also less in number. It is necessary for collectors to have this edition, however, for the sake of the text, which is enlarged. The leaf "Preface to the second edition" is not in all copies and as this leaf bears the date 1811 it is possible that there are two issues of this edition, with or without this leaf.

82 BARRINGTON (G.)

An Account of a Voyage to New South Wales, By George Barrington, Superintendant of the Convicts, to which is prefixed a Detail of His Life, Trials, Speeches, etc. etc. Enriched with Beautiful Coloured Prints (coloured vignette of Native Fishing) London: Printed for M. Jones, No 1. Paternoster Row.

Octavo.   1803

COLLATION.—Engraved title as above (v. blank) + Preface 3 pp. + Introduction 3 pp. + Two Letters 1 leaf + pp. 1–467 + index 5 pp. + Portrait + Folding map + 10 coloured plates. Each plate bears imprint, Published by M. Jones, Paternoster Row and date.

83 BARRINGTON (G.)

An Account of a Voyage to New South Wales, by George Barrington, Superintendant of the Convicts, to which is prefixed a Detail of His Life, Trials, Speeches, etc, etc. Enriched with beautiful Coloured Prints. (coloured Vignette of a Native Fishing) London: Printed for M. Jones, No. 5 Newgate Street, and Sherwood, Neely, and Jones, Paternoster Row.

Octavo.   1810.

Barrington's Voyage to New South Wales (*contd.*)

COLLATION.—Engraved title as above (v. blank) + Preface (pp. iii–iv) + pp. 1–472 + index 2 leaves + Portrait + map + 9 coloured plates.

Each plate bears imprint, Published [date] by M. Jones, Paternoster Row.

1. Front. George Barrington, Late Officer of the Peace at Paramatta. Engraved from a Miniature Picture in the Possession of Mrs. Crane. Mar. 25th 1803.
2. p. 89. Ceremony of Ducking and Shaving. May 1st 1810.
3. p. 121. A Plan of New South Wales. Apr. 2nd 1803.
4. p. 125. The Peak of Teneriffe. Feb. 20th 1803.
5. p. 145. The Cape of Good Hope. Mar. 19th 1803.
6. p. 467. Sydney. Dec. 24th 1802.
7. p. 468. South View of Sydney. Mar. 1st 1803.
8. p. 470. East View of Sydney. Feb. 5th 1803.
9. p. 472. Entrance of Paramatta River. Mar. 25th 1803.
10. *ibd.* Pinchgut Island. Mar. 11th 1803.
11. *ibd.* Garden Island. Mar. 5th 1803.

84 BARROW (John)

Travels in China, containing descriptions, observations, and comparisons, made and collected in the course of a short residence at the imperial palace of Yuen-Min-Yuen, and on a subsequent journey through the country from Pekin to Canton in which it is attempted to appreciate the rank that this extraordinary empire may be considered to hold in the scale of civilized nations. "Non cuivis homini contingit adire corinthum." It is the lot of few to go to Pekin (swelled rule) By John Barrow, Esq. late private secretary to the Earl of Macartney, and one of his suite as ambassador from the King of Great Britain to the Emperor of China (swelled rule) Illustrated with several Engravings. London: Printed by A. Strahan, Printers-Street, for T. Cadell and W. Davies, in the Strand.

Quarto. 1804

COLLATION.—Title as above (v. blank) + Dedication to Macartney 1 p. (v. blank) + Contents 6 pp. (v–x) + List of Plates and Errata 1 p. (v. advertisement) + pp. 1–632 (including index) + 5 coloured plates and 3 uncoloured.

Each plate bears imprint of Cadell and Davies, each coloured plate is engraved by T. Medland after W. Alexander (with 2 exceptions noted below); each plain plate is engraved by Neale.

1. Front. Portrait of Van-ta-gin.
2. p. 37. A Foreign Trader. A Rice Mill (together on 1 plate).
3. p. 50. A Chinese, A Hottentot [the latter after S. Daniell, together on 1 plate].
4. p. 128. View in the Eastern side of the Imperial Park at Gehol. Drawn by W. Alexander from a Sketch by Captn. Parish, Roy. Artily.
   p. 302. Sketches of Chinese Artillery (uncoloured) folding plate.
   p. 314. Chinese Musical Instruments (uncoloured) folding plate.
   p. 338. Construction of the Arch of a Chinese Bridge (uncoloured).
5. p. 545. A Village and Cottagers, Dwelling of a Mandarin or Officer of State (together on 1 plate).

Second Edition 1806.

85 BARROW (John)

Travels into the Interior of Southern Africa in which are described the Character and the Condition of the Dutch Colonists of the Cape of Good Hope and of the Several

Barrow's Travels in Southern Africa (*contd.*)

Tribes of Natives beyond its Limits: the Natural History of such subjects as occurred in the animal, mineral, and vegetable kingdoms: and the geography of the Southern extremity of Africa comprehending also a Topographical and Statistical Sketch of the Cape Colony with an Inquiry into its importance as a naval and military station as a commercial emporium; and as a Territorial Possession (swelled rule) By John Barrow, Esq. F.R.S. author of "Travels in China" (swelled rule) "Africa semper aliquid novi offert" (swelled rule) In Two Volumes Vol. I [Vol. II] The Second Edition, with additions and alterations. Illustrated with several engravings, and charts. London: Printed for T. Cadell and W. Davies, in the Strand

2 vols.   Quarto.   1806

COLLATION VOL. I.—[No half-title] Title as above (v. Strahan and Preston New Street Square) + Dedication to Lord Melville 1 p. (v. blank) + Preface pp. v–xvi + Contents of First Volume 1 p. (v. blank) + pp. 1–427 + 8 coloured plates.

Each plate marked, S. Daniell delt.   T. Medland sculpt.   Published Feby. 14 1806 by Messrs. Cadell & Davies Strand London [plate 6 dated June 4 1806.]

1. p. 31. A Boor's wife taking her coffee.
2. p. 66. Broad tailed Sheep of Southern Africa.
3. p. 108. A Hottentot.
4. p. 132. Passing a Kloof.
5. p. 167. Kaffer Woman.
6. p. 217. The Gnoo.
7. p. 237. A Bosjesman in Armour.
8. p. 348. The African Rhinoceros.

VOL. II.—Half-title "Travels into the Interior of Southern Africa" Vol. II (v. Strahan and Preston New Street Square London) + Title as before (v. blank) + Contents to Second Volume 1 p. (v. blank) + pp. 1–372 (including index) + Directions for placing the plates [in both vols.] 1 p. (v. blank) + 9 maps and charts.

1. face title. General Chart of the Colony of the Cape of Good Hope (folding).
2. p. 223. Military Plan of the Cape Peninsula by Lt. Col. Bridges.
3. p. 274. Chart of Table Bay 1786 (folding).
4. p. 277. False Bay with soundings 1797 by Rear Adml. Pringle (folding).
5. p. 280. Coast of Africa from Table Bay to Saldanha Bay (folding).
6. p. 285. Mossel Bay by Lt. McPherson (folding).
7. p. 287. Chart of the Knysna by J. Callender (folding).
8. p. 288. Plettenbergs Bay Lt. McPherson (folding).
9. p. 290. Algoa Bay (folding).

Second and Best Edition (*The First Edition of* 1801–4 *does not contain any of the coloured plates*).

86 BARROW (John)

A Voyage to Cochin China, in the years 1792 and 1793: containing a general view of the valuable productions and the political importance of this flourishing kingdom; and also of such European Settlements as were visited on the voyage: with sketches of the Manners, character, and condition of their several inhabitants.   To which is annexed An Account of a Journey made in the years 1801 and 1802 to the residence of the chief of the Booshuana Nation, being the remotest point in the interior of Southern Africa to which Europeans have hitherto penetrated.   The Facts and descriptions taken from a manuscript journal with a chart of the route (swelled rule) By John Barrow, Esq. F.R.S. author of "Travels in Southern Africa," and "Travels in China." (swelled rule) 3 line latin quotation (swelled rule) Illustrated and Embellished with several engravings by

Barrow's Voyage to Cochin China (*contd.*)

Medland, coloured after the original drawings by Mr. Alexander and Mr. Daniell London: Printed for T. Cadell and W. Davies in the Strand

Quarto.   1806

COLLATION.—Title as above (v. Strahan & Preston New Street Square, London) + Dedication to Sir George Staunton 1 p. (v. blank) + Preface pp. v–xi (p. xii blank) + Contents pp. xiii–xviii + Directions for placing the plates 1 p. (v. blank) + pp. 1–447 (including index) + 2 charts + 19 plates.

Each plate bears imprint "Published June 4 1806 by Messrs. Cadell and Davies Strand London" and words Engraved by T. Medland (the first plate marked, T. Medland Engraver to His Royal Highness the Prince of Wales).

1. p.   5. Funchall   S. Daniell delt.
2. p.   8. Chamber of Skulls in the Franciscan Convent   Drawn by S. Daniell.
3. p. 32. View of Santa Cruz [Teneriffe]   Drawn by W. Alexander.
4. p. 65. Porto Praya in the Island of St. Jago   Drawn by W. Alexander.
5. p. 80. Arcos de Carioco, or Grand Aqueduct in Rio de Janeiro   Drawn by W. Alexander.
6. p. 135. Sketch of the Town and Harbour of Rio de Janeiro (folding).
7. *ibd.*   View of the land round the harbour of Rio de Janeiro (folding) no artist given.
8. p. 162. Javanese and wounded shark   Drawn by W. Alexander.
9. p. 164. Tomb of Colonel Cathcart in the Fort of Anjorie   Drawn by W. Alexander.
10. p. 176. The Calvinistic Church in Batavia   Drawn by W. Alexander.
11. p. 185. The Mangoostan   Drawn by W. Alexander.
12. p. 186. The Rambootan [no artist given] a fruit of the Poolasang.
13. p. 284. Cochin chinese Soldier   Drawn by W. Alexander.
14. p. 296. Scene in a Cochin chinese Opera   Drawn by W. Alexander.
15. p. 309. A Group of Cochin chinese   Drawn by W. Alexander.
16. p. 320. Cochin Chinese Shipping on the River Taifo   Drawn by W. Alexander.
17. p. 328. An Offering of First Fruits to the God Fo   Drawn by W. Alexander.
18. p. 361. A Chart of the Southern Extremity of Africa.
19. p. 373. An African Woman [Kora Hottentot]   Drawn by S. Daniell.
20. p. 392. Booshuana Village   Drawn by W. Alexander from a sketch by S. Daniell.
21. p. 394. Bushooana Man and Woman   Drawn by W. Alexander from a sketch by S. Daniell.

87 BELLASIS (G. H.)

Views of Saint Helena. (thick and thin rule) By George Hutchins Bellasis, Esq. (thin and thick rule) London: (thin and thick rule) Printed by John Tayler, Rathbone Place.   The Plates printed by W. B. M'Queen, 72, Newman Street

Oblong Folio.   1815

COLLATION.—Title as above (v. blank) + Dedication to Duke of Wellington 1 p. (v. blank) + List of Subscribers 2 ll. + Introduction 1 leaf + 6 coloured aquatint plates each with 1 leaf of text.

Each plate marked, "Drawn by George Hutchins Bellasis Esqr.   Engraved by Robt. Havell 3, Chapel St. Tottenham Court Road."   The plates numbered and bearing in the bottom right-hand corner, London Published Novr. 1 1815 by G. H. Bellasis Esqr.

1. St. Helena taken from the Sea.
2. The Roads St. Helena.
3. Scene taken from the Castle Terrace.
4. Plantation House, the Country Residence of the Governor.
5. The Friar Rock in Friars Valley.
6. The Column Lot, Fairy Land, Sandy Bay.

Issued in brown paper wrappers with printed side label within Etruscan border.

88 BERESFORD (James)

The Miseries of Human Life; or the Groans of Samuel Sensitive, and Timothy Testy; with a few supplementary sighs from Mrs Testy. (rule) In Twelve Dialogues as overheard by James Beresford, Fellow of Merton College, Oxford. (rule) The Seventh Edition. London: Printed for William Miller, Albemarle Street, By J. Ballantyne & Co. Edinburgh.

2 vols. Octavo. 1807

COLLATION VOL. I.—Title as above (v. blank) + Dedication, To the Miserable, 2 pp. (5–6) + Contents 2 pp. (7–8) + pp. 1–337 + Advertisement of Vol. II, one leaf + Coloured folding front of the four Characters, with 1 leaf of Text "The Miseries of Human Life" + folding coloured title to the plates "Sixteen Scenes taken from The Miseries of Human Life, By one of the Wretched" (coloured vignette with quotation from Pope). London: Published by Wm. Miller, Albemarle Street. March 1st 1807. + 8 coloured folding plates, each plate marked with plate number, page number, and misery number, at head. Drawn and Etched by John Augustus Atkinson. Published March 1st 1807 by William Miller, Albemarle Street. The 8 plates to text are at pp. 32, 46, 68, 122, 112 [plate 5 misprinted plate 6, at p. 142], 172, 231, 288.

VOL. II.—Title "The Miseries of Human Life, or the Last Groans of Timothy Testy and Samuel Sensitive" . . . In Nine Additional Dialogues (v. blank) + Contents 2 pp. (5–6) + pp. 1–292 + 6 leaves Advertisements by Miller + Folding front. Miseries Personified, J. Beresford Invt. and del. Edward Scriven Fect. (uncoloured) + Leaf of text, The Miseries of Human Life, + 8 coloured plates as in Vol. I. at pp. 17, 46, 49, 159, 169, 214, 232 and 279 + p. 160 folding playbill, At the Theatre Royal, The Tempest etc. p. 214 folding leaf of description to extra long folding plate. The plates bear no titles. There are woodcuts in text.

Each volume issued in Boards at 8s.

Atkinsons plates were also issued separately in boards at 12s.

89 BERESFORD (James)

Sixteen Scenes taken from The Miseries of Human Life, by one of the Wretched. "He best can Paint them, who has felt them Most." Pope. (circular coloured vignette) London: Published by Wm. Miller. Albemarle Street. March 1st. 1807

COLLATION.—Title as above (v. blank) + 16 plates, each marked, Drawn and Etched by John Augustus Atkinson. Published March 1st. 1807. by William Miller, Albemarle Street. The plates do not bear titles, but each plate is accompanied by 1 leaf of text.

1. (Miseries of the Country. Attempting to spring over a five barred gate.)
2. (Miseries of Games, Sports etc. Seeing the boy who is next above you flogged.)
3. (Miseries of London. Walking briskly forwards while you are looking backwards.)
4. (Miseries of Stage Coaches. Stopping at Inn where Passengers are to sup.)
5. (Miseries of Social Life. Miscarriage of a Letter arrival at Night.)
6. (Miseries of Reading and Writing. Reading a Comedy aloud.)
7. (Miseries Domestic. The Handle of the tea urn coming off in the servant's hand.)
8. (Miseries Miscellaneous. The first or prelusive squall of a fractious brat.)
9. (Miseries of Watering Places. Ploughing knee deep in sand, shells, or pebbles.)
10. (Miseries of Fashionable Life. Crawling down to breakfast room.)
11. (Miseries of Fashionable Life. Going to the Exhibition at so exquisately late an hour.)
12. (Miseries of London. The theatres.)

Beresford's Miseries of Human Life (*contd.*)

13. (Miseries of Travelling.   Sleeping overnight at a sordid Inn.)
14. (Miseries of the Table.   Slipping your knife suddenly and violently, off a bone.)   This plate is folding.
15. (Miseries Domestic.   Pulling at crammed up drawer.)
16. (Miseries Miscellanious.   Handing a Lady out of a Boat.)

Issued in boards with printed paper label.   Text by James Beresford.

Blackmantle (Bernard).   See under Westmacot (C. M.).

90 BLAGDON (F. W.)

Authentic Memoirs of the late George Morland, with remarks on his abilities and progress as an artist: in which are interspersed a variety of anecdotes never before published; together with a Facsimile of his writing, specimens of his hieroglyphical sketches, &c. &c.   The whole collected from numerous manuscript communications. (thick and thin rule) By Francis William Blagdon, Esq. (thin and thick rule) Embellished with Engravings (swelled rule) (4 lines verse by Dryden) (short thick and thin rule) London Printed for Edward Orme New Bond Street, By Barnard and Sultzer, Water Lane, Fleet Street (short rule)

Oblong folio.   1806

COLLATION.—Title as above (v. blank) + Text pp. 3–15 (p. 16 blank) + 20 plates as under.

(1.) George Morland   From an Original Drawing in the possession of John Graham Esqr.   To whom this engraving is respectfully inscribed by his obliged hble. Servt. Edwd. Orme.   Published Jany. 1805 by Edward Orme His Majesty's Printseller 59 Bond Street Lond. (uncoloured).

(2.) Ass and Pigs   T. Vivares sct.   Published and Sold by Edwd. Orme 59 New Bond Street July 1 1804 (uncoloured).

(3.) Conversation.   Published and Sold by Edwd. Orme 59 New Bond Street July 1 1804 (uncoloured).

(4.) (Four small groups on 1 plate sheep, cows, horses, donkeys)   Sold and Pubd. Jany. 1 1793 by D. Orme and Co. at the Morland Gallery No. 14 Old Bond Street London.   Republished by Orme Conduit Street Jany. 1 1799 (uncoloured).

(5.) (Water Mill)
(Two children picking Flowers)   T. Vivares sct.
     The Two drawings on 1 sheet, each with the same imprint Sold & Published as the Act directs Septr. 1802 by Edwd. Orme 59 New Bond Street, London (uncoloured).

(6.) (Stable &c.)   Sold and Pubd. Jany. 1 1793 by D. Orme & Co. at the Morland Gallery No. 14 Old Bond Street London.   Republished by Orme Conduit Street Jany. 1 1799 (uncoloured).

(7.) An Ass Race.   Painted by G. Morland   Engrav'd by W. Ward London   Pubd Novr. 20 1789 by P. Cornman and republished 1805 by Edwd. Orme 59 Bond Str. (coloured).

(8.) A Mad Bull.   Painted by G. Morland   Aquatint by R. Dodd London   Pubd. Nov. 20 1789 by P. Cornman and Republished 1805 by Edwd. Orme 59 Bond Street (coloured).

(9.) (Rustic Scene Cottage & Cart) G. Morland 1792   Sold & Pubd. Jany. 1 1793 by D. Orme & Co. at the Morland Gallery No. 14 Old Bond Street London.   Republished by Orme Conduit Street Jany. 1 1799 (uncoloured).

(10.) (Rustic Bridge &c.)   Sold & Published Jany. 1794 by D. Orme & Co. at the Morland Gallery No. 14 Old Bond Street, London, Republished by Orme Conduit Street Jany. 1 1799 (uncoloured).

(11.) (Haymakers by Stile)   Sold and Published Jany. 1 1794 by Danl. Orme & Co. No. 14 Old Bond Street London.   Republished by Orme Conduit Street Jany. 1 1799 (uncoloured).

(12.) (White Pony and Figures in Rain).
(Rustic Scene, women two men & stile)   T.V.
     The two drawings on 1 sheet each with same imprint   Sold and Published June 4th 1804 by Edwd. Orme His Majesty's Printseller 59 New Bond Street London (uncoloured).

(13.) The Frighten'd Horse.   Painted by G. Morland   Engraved by E. Bell.   Sold & Published Jany. 1 1804 by Edward Orme His Majesty's Printseller 59 New Bond Street London (coloured).

Blagdon's Memoirs of George Morland (*contd.*)

(14.) (Washing) Republished by Orme Conduit Street Jany. 1 1799 Sold and Published May 1 1793 by D. Orme & Co. at the Morland Gallery 14 Old Bond Street (uncoloured).

(15.) (Alehouse seat) Republished by Orme Conduit Street Jany. 1 1799 Sold and Published, May 1 1793 by D. Orme & Co. at the Morland Gallery 14 Old Bond Street (uncoloured).

(16.) (Horse Drinking) Republished by Orme Conduit Street Jany. 1 1799 Sold & Published May 1 1793 by D. Orme & Co. at the Morland Gallery 14 Old Bond Street (coloured).

(17.) (Horse & Ostler) Republished by Orme Conduit Street Jany. 1 1799 Sold & Published May 1 1793 by D. Orme & Co. at the Morland Gallery 14 Old Bond Street (coloured).

(18.) Morlands Ass. Malgo sculp. Published 1804 by Edwd. Orme 59 New Bond Street London (uncoloured).

(19.) The Rustic Hovel. Painted by G. Morland Engraved by E. Bell Sold & Published Jany. 1 1804 by Edwd. Orme His Majesty's Print-seller 59 New Bond Street London (coloured).

(20.) The Cottage Sty. Painted by G. Morland Engraved by E. Bell Sold & Published Jany. 1 1804 by Edwd. Orme His Majesty's Printseller 59 New Bond Street London (coloured).

+3 small drawings reproduced in the text.

The above collation taken from the copy in the British Museum the paper watermarked Whatman 1803.

Another copy in the Library of the Victoria and Albert Museum, also in oblong folio 1806, has the same text. The plates have been abstracted and placed separately in the Print Room and as they are laid down and mounted it is not always possible to see the imprint or the watermarks.

It contains 21 plates in all, and has all those plates in the British Museum copy except numbers 4, 7 and 13. The double plates are separated and the two undermentioned are not in the B.M. copy:—

(Seven studies on 1 plate (man with whip &c.))

(Three studies on 1 plate (cart, wheelbarrow, man and boy.))

Both are uncoloured. Plates 9 and 11, which in the B.M. copy are uncoloured, are coloured in the V. & A. copy.

Blagdon's Memoirs of George Morland is an extremely rare book and I have had great difficulty in tracing copies to compare. From the above two examples it would appear that the plates were not uniformly selected for this edition.

In 1824, however, there was a definite uniform edition with 20 plates all coloured. The title page is still dated 1806 and the plates still bear their original imprints, but the watermark is J. Whatman Turkey Mills 1824.

91 This issue is as follows:

Oblong Folio.   1806 (1824)

(1.) George Morland.	(11.) (Rustic Scene Cottage & Cart.)
(2.) A Mad Bull.	(12.) (Rustic Bridge &c.)
(3.) The Cottage Sty.	(13.) (Horse & Ostler.)
(4.) Conversation.	(14.) (Pony & Figures in Rain.)
(5.) (rustic Scene Two women two men & stile) T.V.	(15.) (The Rustic Hovel.)
(6.) (Washing.)	(16.) (Horse Drinking.)
(7.) (Stable &c.)	(17.) (Alehouse seat.)
(8.) Morlands Ass.	(18.) (Two children picking flowers.)
(9.) Ass & Pigs.	(19.) (Haymakers by stile.)
(10.) (Water Mill.)	(20.) An Ass Race.

+3 small drawings reproduced in the text.

92 *Another issue Upright Folio.*   1806 (1824)

This issue has the same coloured plates as the preceding but the printed text is changed. It

Blagdon's Memoirs of George Morland (*contd.*)

consists of printed title as before (still dated 1806), Text pp. 3–12 + 20 coloured plates + 1 uncoloured facsimile plate. The facsimile plate contains a drawing of a pig &c. with an example of Morland's handwriting; in the other issue this was included in the text. The surrounding paragraphs of text are omitted.

93 BLAGDON (Francis William)

A Brief History of Ancient and Modern India, from the Earliest Periods of Antiquity, to the Termination of the Late Mahratta War. By Francis William Blagdon, Esquire. (rule) 2 line quote from Cicero (rule) London: (thin and thick rule) Published by Edward Orme, Printseller to His Majesty, and the Royal Family, New Bond Street

Folio.   1805

COLLATION.—Engraved title dated 1805 (v. blank) + Printed title as above (v. blank) + Preface 1 p. (v. Description of Front and Description of Portraits of Native Judges) + "A Brief History" pp. 1–22 + 2 coloured plates.

1. Front. The Palace of the late Nabob of Arcot, Colonel Ward, Pinxt. W. Orme Delt. Edward Orme Excut. J. C. Stadler, Aquaforte. Published and Sold Jan. 1st 1803, by Edward Orme Printsellers to His Majesty and the Royal Family, 59 New Bond Street, London.

2. p. 22. The Native Judges and Officers of the Court of the Recorder Bombay. Interpreter, Judge of the Hindoo Law, Hindoo Officer, Officer to the Mooremen, Judge of the Mahomedan Law, Havralder. The Drawings taken from the Life, By desire of Sir William Syer Kt. the first Recorder and now in possession of Lady Syer. Published and Sold, Jan. 1st 1805, by Edwd Orme, His Majesty's Printseller, 59 Bond Street, London.

+ New engraved and coloured Title " '24 Views in Hindostan' Drawn by William Orme, from the Original Pictures, Printed by Mr. Daniell, and Colonel Ward etc. Edward Orme delt. Vivares sculpt. Sold and Published as the Act directs, by Edward Orme, Printseller in Ordinary to the King and Royal Family, No. 59, the corner of Brook Street in Bond Street, London where may be had all British Engravings, wholesale and for Exportation " (v. blank) + Printed Title "Appendix" etc. 1 p. (v. blank) + Description of plates 4 pp. + coloured plates.

Each plate bears Orme's imprint and date.

1. A View from the King's Barracks, Fort St. George. Colonel Ward Pinxt. Edward Orme Excud. Harraden Aquatinta. March 1st 1804.
2. A. View of Part of St Thome Street, Fort St George. Colonel Ward Delt. Edward Orme Excudit. H. Merke Aquatinta. June 4th 1804.
3. A View in the North Street of Fort St George. Colonel Ward Pinxt. Edward Orme Excudit. Harraden Aquaforta. Jan 1st 1805.
4. Fort Square, from the South Side of the Parade, Fort St George. Colonel Ward Pinxt. Edward Orme Excut. J. C. Stadler sculpt. Jan 1st 1805.
5. A View within the Walls of a Pagoda, Madras. Colonel Ward Pinxt. Edward Orme Excudit. H. Merke Aquatinta. March 1st 1804.
5. South East View of the Rock of Tritchinopoly. Colonel Ward Delt. Edward Orme Excudit. H. Merke Aquatinta. Sept 1st 1804.
6. A Choultry or Place of Worship, Carved out of the top of the Rock of Tritchinopoly, in high repute, by the Malabars. Colonel Ward Pinx. Wm. Orme Delin. Edward Orme Excudit. J. C. Stadler Aquatinta Jan. 1st 1802.
7. A View of Ossoore. Daniell Pinxt. Edward Orme Excudit. J. C. Stadler Aquatinta. July 30th 1804.
8. Thebet Mountains. Daniell Pinxt. E. Orme Excudit. H. Merke Aquatinta Jan. 1 1804.
9. West Gate of Firoz Shah's Cotillah, Delhi. Daniell Pinxt. Wm. Orme Delin. Edward Orme Excudit. Fellows Aquatinta. Jan 1 1802.
10. Anchshur, A Vakeels Castle, in the Teritory of Bengal. Colonel Ward Pinxt. Wm. Orme Delin. Edward Orme Excudit. J. C. Stadler Aquatinta. Jan 1 1802.

Blagdon's Brief History of Ancient and Modern India (*contd.*)

11. A Pagoda. Daniell Pinxt. Edward Orme Excudit. J. C. Stadler Aquatinta. 1804.
12. A Hindoo Place of Worship. Daniell Pinxt. Edward Orme Excudit J. C. Stadler Aquatinta. July 30 1804.
13. Dalmow, on the Ganges. Daniell Pinxt. Edward Orme Excudit. J. C. Stadler Aquatinta. July 30 1804.
14. Fortress of Gwallior, taken by General Popham in 1780. Edward Orme Excudit. June 4 1804.
15. The Old Court House Calcutta Colonel Ward Pinxt. Edward Orme Excut. Harraden Aquaforta. Jan 1 1805.
16. The Bridge at Juonpore, Bengal. Daniell Delt. Edward Orme Excudit. H. Merke Aquatinta. July 21 1804.
17. Distant View of Mootee Thurna, a Waterfall in the Rajemahl Hills, Bengal. Daniell Pinxt. Wm. Orme Delin. Edward Orme Excudit. Fellows Aquatinta. Jan. 1802.
18. Multura Fort. Colonel Ward Pinxt. W. Orme Delin. Edward Orme Excut. Jan 1 1803.
19. The Tomb of a Moorish Lady, Bengal. Daniell Pinxt. W. Orme Delin. Edward Orme Excut J. C. Stadler Aquaforte. Jan 1 1803.
20. The Burial Place of a Peer Zada, Anopther. Colonel Ward Pinxt. W. Orme Delt. Edward Orme Excut. Jan 1 1803.
21. Felicity Hall, late the Residence of the Honourable David Anstruther, near Moorshedabad, Bengal. Daniell Pinxt. Edward Orme Excut. Harraden Aquatinta. March 1 1804.
22. Kuttull Minor, Delhi. Jan 1 1805.

Hunter's Views in Mysore are frequently found bound up with this work.

94 [BLAGDON (F. W.)]

An Historical Memento representing the Different Scenes of Public Rejoicing, which took place the First of August in St. James's and Hyde Parks, London in celebration of the Glorious Peace of 1814 and of the Centenary of the Accession of the Illustrious House of Brunswick to the Throne of these Kingdoms. London: Edited Published and Sold by Edward Orme Publisher to His Majesty, and His Royal Highness the Prince Regent, Bond Street, Corner of Brook Street.

Quarto.   1814

COLLATION.—Half-title "An Historical Memento &c. &c. (v. blank) + Title as above (v. blank) + Introduction (by F. W. Blagdon) and Text pp. 5–64 + 6 coloured aquatint plates.
Each plate bears "J. H. Clark Del" "M. Dubourg Sculpt." and the imprint, "Published & Sold Augt. 12th 1814 by Edwd. Orme, Publisher to his Majesty and H.R.H. the Prince Regent Bond Street (corner of Brook Str) London."

1. The Tower & Preparation of the Fireworks, with the Balloon in the Park   Aug 1st 1814.
2. The Fleet on the Serpentine River Commemoration of the Battle of the Nile, Augt. 1st 1814.
3. The View of the Fair in Hyde Park   Augt. 1st 1814.
4. The Chinese Bridge Illuminated On the Night of the Celebration of the Peace 1814.
5. The Chinese Bridge and Pagoda Erected in the Park in commemoration of the Glorious Peace of 1814.
6. The Revolving Temple of Concord Illuminated as Erected in the Park, in celebration of the glorious Peace of 1814.

95 BOWDICH (T. E.)

Mission from Cape Coast Castle to Ashantee, with a Statistical Account of that Kingdom, and Geographical Notices of other parts of the Interior of Africa (thick and thin rule) By T. Edward Bowdich Esq. Conductor (thin and thick rule) (Quotation) London: (thin and thick rule) John Murray, Albemarle Street

Quarto.   1819

Bowdich's Ashantee (*contd.*)

COLLATION.—Half-title (thick and thin rule) Mission to Ashantee (thin and thick rule) 1 p. (v. blank) + Title as above (v. London Printed by W. Bulmer and Co. Cleveland Row, St James's) + Introduction 1 lf. (pp. v–vi) + Contents 1 leaf (vii–viii) + Directions for placing the plates 1 p. (v. Glossary) + sub-title 1 p. (v. blank) + pp. 3–512 (including Appendix) + 3 maps, 10 coloured illustrations on 7 plates and 3 leaves of music.

Each coloured plate marked, Drawn by T. E. Bowdich Esq. and with imprint, Published Decr. 2 1818 by John Murray Albemarle Street.

Front.		Map shewing the Discoveries and Improvements in the Geography of Western Africa resulting from the Mission to Ashantee.
1.	p. 32.	Captain in his War Dress No. 1.
	p. 128.	Arabic Circular (folding).
	p. 211.	Map from Dapper (Besin to Congo).
2.	p. 275.	The First Day of the Yam Custom. Engraved by R. Havell & Son (folding).
3–4.	p. 307.	The Oldest House in Coomasaee No. 3 Part of the Quarters of the Mission No. 4 (2 views on 1 plate).
5–6.	ibd.	Odumata's Sleeping Room No. 5 Inner Square of Apookoos House No. 6 (2 views on 1 plate).
7–8.	p. 308.	Part of a Piazza in the Palace No. 7 ditto No. 8 (2 views on 1 plate).
9.	ibd.	Part of Adoom Street No. 9 (folding).
10.	ibd.	The King's Sleeping Room No. 10.
	p. 323.	Iconographical Sketch of Coomassie.
	p. 364.	The Oldest Ashantee and Warsaw Air (4 engraved pp. of music).
	p. 449.	Empoongwa Song (1 leaf of music).

96 BOWYER (R.)

The Triumphs of Europe, in the Campaigns of the years 1812, 1813, 1814 commemorated by a Series of Twelve Views of Moscow, the Kremlin, Leipsic, Dresden, Berlin, Frankfort on the Maine, Amsterdam, the Hague, Hamburgh &c. &c. &c. (rule) from Original Drawings in the Collection of His Imperial Majesty the Emperor of Russia, and from other authentic sources (rule) to which is prefixed, a concise History of those important events (rule) London: Printed by T. Bensley, Bolt Court, Fleet Street, for R. Bowyer, Marlborough Place, Pall Mall.

Folio.   1814

COLLATION.—Title as above (v. blank) + pp. 3–27 (p. 28 blank) followed by 8 unnumbered leaves of text + 11 plates.

1. Moscow (folding) Published by R. Bowyer Pall Mall 1814 6 pp. text.					
2. The Kremlin Moscow	,,	,,	,,	,,	
3. Dantzic	,,	,,	,,	,, 1	,,
4. Berlin	,,	,,	,,	,, 1	,,
5. Leipsic	,,	,,	,,	,, 2	,,
6. Amsterdam	,,	,,	,,	,, 1	,,
7. Rosiere	,,	,,	,,	,, 1	,,
8. Frankfort	,,	,,	,,	,, 1	,,
9. Dresden	,,	,,	,,	,, 1	,,
10. Hamburgh	,,	,,	,,	,, 1	,,
11. View of the Hague	,,	,,	,,	,, 1	,,

Evidently a popular work it was issued the following year (though with the same title still dated 1814) with 5 extra plates, Map exhibiting the retreat of the French Army from Moscow to Paris,

Bowyer's Events in Europe (*contd.*)

Grand Entry of the Allied Sovereigns into Leipsic (dated 1815), View of the Grimma Suburb Leipzic (dated 1815), Precipitate flight of the French through Leipsic (dated 1815), and Porto Ferrajo, portrait of Napoleon and map of Elba together on 1 plate (dated 1815).

97 BOWYER (R.)

An Illustrated Record of Important Events in the Annals of Europe during the years 1812, 1813, 1814, & 1815. Comprising a Series of Views of Paris, Moscow, the Kremlin, Dresden, Berlin, The Battles of Leipsic etc. etc. etc. (rule) Together with a History of those Momentous Transactions (rule) London: Printed by T. Bensley, Bolt Court, Fleet Street, for R. Bowyer, Marlborough Place, Pall Mall. (rule)

Folio.   1815

COLLATION.—Title as above (v. blank) + Concise History pp. 3–60 + Appendix 2 unnumbered leaves + Memoir of Alexander I + pp. 61–76.

Each plate bears Bowyers imprint and date.

p. 61. Medallion Portraits of Leaders.	[1815]
p. 76. Facsimile Autographs.	[1815]
1. Moscow folding plate. 6 pp. text unnumbered.	[1814]
2. The Kremlin Moscow.	[1814]
Map exhibiting Retreat of French Army from Moscow to Paris.	[1815]
3. Smolensko. 4 pp. text.	[1814]
4. Dantzic. 1 p. text.	[1814]
5. Berlin. 1 p. text.	[1814]
6. Hamburgh. 1 p. text.	[1814]
7. View at the Hague. 1 p. text.	[1814]
8. Frankfort. 1 p. text.	[1814]
9. Dresden. 1 p. text.	[1814]
10. Amsterdam. 1 p. text.	[1814]
11. Rosiere. 1 p. text.	[1814]
12. Entrance into Hanau over the Kinzig Bridge. 2 pp. text.	[1814]
13. Grand Entrance of the Allied Sovereigns into Paris on 31 March 1814. 2 pp. text.	[1815]
14. Ceremony of Te Deum by the Allied Armies on the Square of Louis XV at Paris the 10th April 1814 (folding).	[1815]
15. Leipsiz. 2 pp. text.	[1814]
16. Precipitate Flight of the French through Leipsic pursued by the Allied Armies 19th October 1813 (folding).	[1815]
17. Grand Entry of the Allied Sovereigns into Leipsic 19th October 1813 (folding). 3 pp. text.	[1815]
18. View of the Grimma Suburb Leipsic.	[1815]
19. Map of Elba, Port. of Napoleon & View of Porto Ferrajo on 1 plate with 1 page of text.	[1815]

+ Biographical Notices of Sovereigns, Warriors & Statesmen &c. pp. 1–10 with 2 plates uncoloured.

Portraits of the British & their Allies.	[1816]
The Royal Family of France, Family of Bonaparte, French Generals &c.	[1816]

This work was sometimes bound up with "Campaign of Waterloo": see following item.

In an accompanying slip Directions to the Binder is written "In the early Part of the Work a few copies of the First Part were sent out with Title of Triumphs of Europe the binder is to take notice that the proper title is The Illustrated Record, and the other is to be cancelled."

However some copies exist with both titles bound in. A further series of 4 plates exists by Capt.

Bowyer's Illustrated Record (*contd.*)

Weir, engraved by Jukes, as follows: Porto Ferrajo from the Sea, Porto Ferrajo from within the Bay, West side of Porto Ferrajo, and East side of the Bay and Watering Place Porto Ferrajo. Sometimes bound up with the above.

98 BOWYER (R.)

The Campaign of Waterloo, illustrated with Engravings of Les Quatre Bras, La Belle Alliance, Hougoumont, La Haye Sainte, and Other principal scenes of Action; including a Correct Military Plan, together with a Grand View of the Battle on a large scale. To which is prefixed a History of the Campaign, compiled from official documents and other authentic sources. (swelled rule) London: Printed by T. Bensley and Son, Bolt Court, Fleet Street, for Robert Bowyer, No. 80, Marlborough Place, Pall Mall (rule)

Folio.   1816

COLLATION.—Title as above (v. blank) + Campaign of Waterloo &c. &c. pp. 1–34 with map and 4 coloured aquatints.

Each plate marked "Published by R. Bowyer Pall Mall 1816."

1. p. 16. View from Mont St. Jean of the Battle of Waterloo at the commencement of the grand Charge made on the French about 7 o'clock in the Evening of the 18th June 1815 (folding).
    p. 31. A Plan of the Glorious Battle of Waterloo Davies sculpt. Compton Str. Brunswk. Square.
2. *ibd.* Les Quatre Bras, looking towards Waterloo ⎫ together on 1 plate.
    La Belle Alliance looking towards Genappe ⎭
3. p. 32. Hougoumont looking towards Waterloo ⎫ together on 1 plate.
    La Haye Sainte, looking towards Waterloo ⎭
4. p. 33. Waterloo Conveying the French Cannon from the Field of Battle, on the 24th of July 1815. followed by "Biographical Notices of the Sovereigns, Warriors and Statesmen" &c.
    pp. 1–10 . . . Appendix 4 pp. (unnumbered) with 2 plates uncoloured.
    p. 1. Portraits of the British and their Allies (48 small oval portraits on 1 plate).
    p. 5. The Royal Family of France, The Family of Bonaparte French Generals Statesmen &c. (50 small oval portraits on 1 plate).

Complete in itself and issued as a separate publication, but sometimes bound up with the Illustrated Record.

Printings of the Three works continued for several years, and care should be taken to see that watermarks are prior to date of publication.

99 BOWYER (R.)

An Impartial Historical Narrative of those Momentous Events which have taken place in this country during the period from the year 1816 to 1823 Illustrated with Engravings By the First Artists (rule) London Printed by Thomas Bensley, Crane Court, Fleet Street, for Robert Bowyer, 74 Pall Mall.

Folio.   1823

COLLATION.—Title (v. blank) + pp. 1–56 + Key and 7 plates. Each plate bears Bowyer's imprint and date.

Front.   Key to the different plates.
1. p. 8. Medallions of H.R.H. the Princess Charlotte & Queen Caroline Wyatt's Cenotaph to memory of former. T. Stothard Esq. R.A. & I. Stephanoff delt. G. Murray & W. Morrison sculpt. (1822).

Bowyer's Momentous Events (*contd.*)

2. p. 23. Arrival at Brandenburgh House of the Watermen &c. with an address to the Queen 3rd October 1820. Dubourg sculpt. 1 Octr. 1821 (coloured).
3. p. 26. View of the Interior of the House of Lords during the important investigation in 1821 Painted by J. Stephanoff Engraved by John George Murray June 1 1823.
4. p. 40. Facsimiles of Autographs of the Royal Family &c. Augt. 1 1822.
5. *ibd.* Autographs of those Peers who voted during the investigation of the charges against Queen Caroline 1 Augt. 1822.
6. *ibd.* The Queen returning from the House of Lords Dubourg sculpt. 1 Octr. 1821 (coloured).
7. p. 145. The Coronation of His Majesty George the Fourth. Stephanoff Pinxt. Dubourg Sculpt. June 4 1822 (coloured).

100 BOWYER (R.)

A Selection of Fac-Similes of Water-Colour Drawings, from the Works of the most distinguished British Artists (rule) London: Published by R. Bowyer, the Proprietor, No. 74, Pall-Mall; Printed by T. Bensley, Crane Court, Fleet Street. (thin rule).

Folio. 1825

COLLATION.—Title as above (v. blank) + 12 coloured plates with 9 leaves of text. Each plate marked, Pub. by R. Bowyer, Pall Mall, 1825.

1. Fountain of the Stone Cross at Rouen S. Prout delt.
2. Driving Cattle to Market R. Hills delint.
3. Cattle &c. at Willans Farm R. Hills delint.
4. Robin Hood's Bay F. Nicholson delt.
5. Fountains Abbey Yorkshire I (*sic*) Smith delt.
6. Juvenile Shrimpers—Deal W. Collins R.A.
7. Shipwreck on the Black Rocks, near Scarborough F. Nicholson delt.
8. Le Place de la Pucelle (Rouen) S. Prout delt.
9. The Dropping Well at Knaresborough F. Nicholson delt.
10. Ghent with the Cathedral &c. S. Prout delt.
11. Group of Donkies and Rustic Children R. Hill delint.
12. South Entrance to the Cathedral of Rouen S. Prout delt.

Issued in blue grey boards with paper label. In the first state the plates are without titles.
101 *Reissued in 1828 by R. Bowyer & M. Parkes with 10 leaves of Text and 6 additional plates, as follows: Teignmouth, Devon, J. M. W. Turner; Bala Lake, N. Wales, G. F. Robson; Fishing Boats off Hastings, Copley Fielding; View on the Sands at Ryde, Copley Fielding; Caernarvon Castle, J. Glover; Fort Rouge, Calais, C. Stanfield.*

102 BOYDELL (J. and J.)

An History of the River Thames Vol. I [II] London (thin and thick rule) Printed by W. Bulmer and Co. for John and Josiah Boydell.

2 vols. Folio. 1794[-6]

COLLATION VOL. I.—Title as above (v. blank) + Dedication to the Rt. Honble. Horace, Earl of Orford, by the Publishers (v. blank) + Preface 6 pp. (ix–xiv) + Table 1 p. (v. blank) + List of Plates in Vol. I 1 p. (v. blank) + pp. 1–312 + plan and 46 plates.

The plates are marked, J. Farrington R.A. delt. J. C. Stadler sculpt. Published [date] by J. & J. Boydell Shakespeare Gallery Pall Mall & No. 90 Cheapside London.

Boydell's History of Thames (*contd.*)

Plan of the course of the River Thames, from its Source to the Sea; engraved for Boydells Rivers by John Cooke of Hendon. [Folded, p. 1.]

1. p.   2. Thames Head   June 1 1793.
2. p.   4. Bridge in Kemble Meadow   June 1 1793.
3. p.   6. Ewen Mill   June 1 1793.
4. p. 34. Cirencester   June 1 1793.
5. p. 38. Cricklade   June 1 1793.
6. p. 48. Junction of the Thames and Canal near Lechlade   June 1 1793.
7. p. 52. Buscot Park   June 1 1793.
8. p. 66. Stanton Harcourt   June 1 1793.
9. p. 76. Langley Ware   June 1 1793.
10. p. 86. [View of] Blenheim   June 1 1793.
11. p. 88. ditto.   June 1 1793.
12. p. 90. View of Blenheim   June 1 1793.
13. p. 118. [View of] Oxford   June 1 1793.
14. p. 120. View of High Street, in Oxford   June 1 1793.
15. p. 170. View in Broad Street, in Oxford   June 1 1793.
16. p. 182. View from Nuneham towards Oxford   June 1 1793.
17. p. 188. View of Carfax & Abingdon, from Whiteheads Oak   June 1 1793.
18. p. 190. View of Nuneham, from the Wood   June 1 1793.
19. p. 206. View of Abingdon, from Nuneham Park   June 1 1793.
20. p. 220. Wallingford   June 1 1793.
21. p. 226. Streatley and Goring.   June 1 1793.
22. p. 228. View towards Bassilden, from Steatley Hill   June 1 1793.
23. p. 230. Whitchurch   June 1 1793.
24. p. 232. Hardwick and Maple-Durham   June 1 1793.
25. p. 234. Pangborn and Whichurch, from Purley   June 1 1793.
26. p. 236. View of Reading from Caversham   June 1 1793.
27. p. 252. Henley   June 1 1793.
28. p. 254. Scene at Park Place including the Druids' Temple   June 1 1793.
   [on text p. 256]   The Mask of the Tame on the Central Arch of Henley Bridge executed by the
   Honble. Mrs. Damer.   J. Parker sc.   [This does not appear on the text of L.P. and early copies.]
29. p. 258. Fawley Court and Henley   June 1 1793.
30. p. 262. Culham Court   June 1 1793.
31. p. 264. The Windings of the Thames below Culham   June 1 1793.
32. p. 266. Temple & Harleford   June 1 1793.
33. p. 268. Bisham Abbey   June 1 1793.
34. p. 270. Court Garden, and Great Marlow   June 1 1793.
35. p. 272. Great Marlow   June 1 1793.
36. p. 274. Hedsor Lodge, looking towards Maidenhead   June 1 1793.
37. p. 278. Cliefden   June 1 1793.
38. p. 282. View of Windsor from Clewer   June 1 1793.
39. p. 284. Windsor Bridge   June 1 1793.
40. p. 290. Windsor and Eaton   June 1 1793.
41. p. 292. Eaton   June 1 1793.
42. p. 294. View of Windsor Castle from Coopers Hill   June 1 1793.
43. p. 300. View of Chertsey Bridge from Wooburn Farm   June 1 1793.
44. p. 304. View of Walton Bridge from Oatlands   June 1 1793.
45. p. 306. The Late Mr Garrick's Villa   June 1 1793.
46. p. 308. Hampton Court   June 1 1793.

VOL. II.—Title as before (dated 1796) + List of Plates in Second Volume 1 p. (v. blank) + Table 1 p. (v. blank) + pp. 1–294 + 30 plates.

47. p.   2. Strawberry Hill   June 1 1793.
48. p.   4. Pope's House   June 1 1795.
49. p.   8. View of Richmond Hill from Twickenham   June 1 1795.

Boydell's History of Thames (*contd.*)

50. p. 24. [View] from Richmond Hill, up the River   June 1 1793.
51. p. 26. [View] from Richmond Hill, down the River   June 1 1793.
52. p. 28. Richmond   June 1 1793.
53. p. 30. View of Sion House, from Kew Gardens   June 1 1795.
54. p. 70. Putney Bridge   June 1 1793.
55. p. 86. Battersea, Chelsea, and London from Mr. Rucker's Villa   June 1 1795.
56. p. 100. View of Chelsea & Battersea from East Wandsworth   June 1 1795.
57. p. 110. View up the River from Milbank   June 1 1793.
58. p. 112. View of Lambeth from Millbank   June 1 1795.
59. p. 158. View of London from Lambeth (folded)   June 1 1795.
60. p. 170. View of Black Friars Bridge from Somerset Place   June 1 1795.
61. p. 180. View of Somerset Place, the Adelphi &c. from the Temple garden   June 1 1795.
62. p. 226. London Bridge   June 1 1795.
63. p. 236. The Tower   June 1 1795.
64. p. 242. View of Greenwich from Deptford Yard   June 1 1795.
65. p. 244. View of Greenwich, and down the River   June 1 1795.
66. p. 246. View of London from Greenwich Park (folded)   June 1 1796.
67. p. 248. View of Greenwich, & up the River   June 1 1795.
68. p. 254. Woolwich   June 1 1795.
69. p. 260. View of Purfleet, Erith, and Long Reach   June 1 1795.
70. p. 266. Gravesend   June 1 1795.
71. p. 270. Penshurst   June 1 1795.
72. p. 274. Tunbridge Castle   June 1 1795.
73. p. 276. Maidstone   June 1 1795.
74. p. 284. Rochester Bridge and Castle   June 1 1795.
75. p. 286. Rochester and Chatham (folded)   June 1 1795.
76. p. 290. View from Upnor towards Sheerness   June 1 1795.

There were early and late issues of this popular work the text of which is by William Combe. First issues have double titles, and these early impressions within aquatint borders are infinitely superior to later pulls. Poor and mediocre copies are relatively common, the work is almost invariably stained with offsets, and even the text is frequently spotted. Large-paper copies are the best, and fine, clean, and perfect copies are really rare, some part of the preliminary leaves are often missing. They should be as follows:

VOL. I.—General Title " An History of the Principal Rivers of Great Britain" Vol. I London (thin and thick rule) Printed by W. Bulmer and Co. Shakespeare Printing Office for John and Josiah Boydell; from the Type of W. Martin 1794 + Particular Title "History of the River Thames &c." + Dedication to George III 1 p. (v. blank) + Table 1 p. (v. blank) + List of Plates vol. I 1 p. (v. blank) + Preface 6 pp. A separate pull of the engraving "The Mask of the Tame" is used as a frontispiece.

VOL. II.—General Title as before + Particular Title + Dedication to Earl of Orford 1 p. (v. blank) + Table 1 p. (v. blank) + List of Plates to Vol. II 1 p. (v. blank).

Issued in boards with printed label on side and spine at £10. 10s. In some copies the map is divided into two, and bound half in each volume (from source to Barnes, and Barnes to sea). The finest copy I have seen is in the possession of Harvey Frost Esq., it measures 17¼ × 12½ inches.

The work was reissued in 1831–4.

103 BOYDELL

Boydell's Picturesque Scenery of Norway: with the Principal Towns from the Naze, by the Route of Christiania, to the Magnificent Pass of the Swinesund; from Original

Boydell's Norway (*contd.*)

Drawings made on the spot, and engraved by John William Edy. With Remarks and Observations made in a Tour through the country, and revised and corrected by William Tooke, F.R.S. member of the Imperial Academy of Sciences, and of the Economical Society at St. Petersburgh (rule). In two volumes Vol. I [II] (rule) London: Published by Hurst, Robinson, and Co. Cheapside: Late Boydell and Co. (short rule)

2 vols. Folio.   1820

COLLATION VOL. I.—Half-title "Boydell's Picturesque Scenery of Norway" (v. London Printed by Thomas Davison, Whitefriars) + Title as above (v. blank) + pp. i–xlv (xlvi blank) + sub-title, Description of the Picturesque Scenery of Norway 1 p. (v. blank) + Index to the Plates 2 pp. + Index Norsk 2 pp. + 31 plates each with 1 leaf of Text (unless otherwise stated). The plates bear no artist's or engraver's name. The first 10 are unnumbered, but 11 to 80 are numbered in the centre. On the left of each plate is the title in English, on the right the title in Norse. Each plate bears imprint, pub. [date] by Boydell & Co. 90 Cheapside London.

1. A View near the Naze   Septr. 2 1811.
2. Heliesund Harbour   Septr. 2 1811.
3. The Islands of Hellisöe & Heliesund Septr. 2 1811.
4. A View between the Islands of Heliesund & Hellisoe Sept. 2 1811.
5. Rocks in Heliesund   Sept. 2 1811.
6. A Bold romantic Scene in Heliesund   Sept. 2 1811.
7. A pass in Heliesund between the Rocks Sept. 2 1811.
8. A Valley in Heliesund   Sept. 2 1811.
9. View of the Chrystal Rocks   Sept. 2 1811.
10. The City of Christiansand   Sept. 2 1811.
11. View in Torresdales River   May 2 1812.
12. Saw Mills at Tved   May 2 1812.
13. Vale of Landvig   May 2 1812.
14. Landvig Lake   May 2 1812.
15. Lake Sinli   May 2 1812.

16. View on Lake Sinli   May 2 1812.
17. Rör Vand near Arendal (4 pp. of text) May 2 1812.
18. Arendal with Töyöen   May 2 1812.
19. Arendal from Tromöe (10 pp. of text) May 2 1812.
20. View of the River Nid   July 1 1812.
21. Rock near Lundy   22 May 1813.
22. Town of Öster Rüsöer   22 May 1813.
23. View near Öster Rüsöer (4 pp. of text) 22nd May 1813.
24. Porter   22nd May 1813.
25. View near Krageröe   22nd May 1813.
26. Town of Krageröe   22nd May 1813.
27. Isle of Gomöe   22nd May 1813.
28. Rock near Krageröe   22nd May 1813.
29. Waller Ferry   22nd May 1813.
30. Road near Waller   22nd May 1813.
31. Brekke   July 31 1813.

VOL. II.—Title as before (v. blank) + plates 32–80 each with 1 leaf of text.

32. Bamble Church   July 31 1813.
33. Town of Brevig   July 31 1813.
34. Brevig from Skeen Firth   July 31 1813.
35. Town of Porsground   July 31 1813.
36. Town of Skeen   July 31 1813.
37. Distant View of Skeen   July 31 1813.
38. A romantic bridge near Skeen.   July 31 1813.
39. A Scene in Longsound Firth   July 31 1813.
40. The ferry at Helgeraae   July 31 1813.
41. Lake Lenongen   May 2 1814.
42. Lake Lenongen [a different view]   May 2 1814.
43. Lake Tanum   May 2 1814.
44. Town of Laurvig   May 2 1814.
45. Town of Holmstrand   May 2 1814.
46. Dram Bay   May 2 1814.
47. Ulivold.   The Seat of John Collett Esqr. May 2 1814.

48. View from Holman   May 2 1814.
49. City of Christiania   May 2 1814.
50. Harbour of Christiania   May 2 1814.
51. Great Church at Christiania   May 1 1815.
52. Christiania Bridge   May 2 1815.
53. Castle of Aggerhus   May 1 1815.
54. View from Egeberg   May 1 1815.
55. View from Egeberg [a different view]   May 1 1815.
56. Alum Mine at Egeberg   May 1 1815.
57. Haoe fall   May 1 1815.
58. Town of Drobak   May 1 1815.
59. Soleberg fall   May 1 1815.
60. Town of Aasgaarstrand   May 1 1815.
61. Larkoul   July 1 1815.
62. Larkoul & Slettery   July 1 1815.
63. Remarkable Stone in Larkoul   July 1 1815.
64. Burial Ground at Larkoul   July 1 1815.

Boydell's Norway (*contd.*)

65. Fortifications at Larkoul July 1 1815.	73. Fredericks-hald Aug. 1 1817.
66. Town of Mos July 1 1815.	74. Leer Foss near Drontheim Aug. 1 1815.
67. Mos above the Bridge July 1 1815.	75. Town of Christiansund Aug. 1 1817.
68. Honble. B. Anker's House at Mos July 1 1815.	76. City of Bergen Aug. 1 1817.
	77. North Bergen. Aug. 1 1817.
69. Van Soe near Mos July 1 1815.	78. Town of Molde Aug. 1 1817.
70. View near Dillengen July 1 1815.	79. Svinesund Ferry, Norwegian Side Aug. 1 1817.
71. Dram Aug. 1 1817.	
72. City of Drontheim Aug. 1 1817.	80. Svinesund Ferry Swedish Side Aug. 1 1817.

The most important English colour plate book on Norway.   Size uncut $19\frac{5}{8} \times 13\frac{3}{8}$ *inches.*

Boydell (J) See also under Repton and Webber.

104 BOYS (T. S.)

Original Views of London as it is. (rule) Drawn from Nature expressly for this Work and Lithographed by Thomas Shotter Boys. Exhibiting its Principal Streets and Characteristic Accessories, Public Buildings in Connexion with the Leading Thoroughfares, &c. &c. &c. With Historical and Descriptive Notices of the Views by Charles Ollier (rule) London: Published by Thomas Boys, Printseller to the Royal Family, 11 Golden Square, Regent Street (rule)

Folio.   1842

COLLATION.—Printed title as above (v. blank) + Dedication to Rt. Hon. Lord Francis Egerton 1 p. (v. blank) + 26 coloured lithographs each with 1 leaf of text (in English and French) including frontispiece.

1. Front. Doorway, Temple Church (bearing on right hand wall "London as it is drawn and lithographed by Thos. Shotter Boys 90 Great Portland St. Printed by C. Hullmandel London Published by T. Boys, 11, Golden Square").
2. Mansion House, Cheapside &c.   T. Shotter Boys del. et lith.
3. The Tower and Mint from Great Tower Hill   T. S. Boys del et lith.
4. The Custom House   T. S. Boys del et lithog.
5. London Bridge &c. from Southwark Bridge   T. S. Boys del et lithog.
6. London from Greenwich   T. S. Boys del et lithog.
7. Blackfriars, from Southwark Bridge.   T. S. Boys del et lithog.
8. Westminster from Waterloo Bridge   T. S. Boys del et lithog.
9. Westminster Abbey Hospital &c.   T. S. Boys del et lith.
10. Board of Trade, Whitehall &c. from Downing Street.   T. S. Boys del et lith.
11. Buckingham Palace from St. James's Park   T. S. Boys del et lith.
12. N. Front to James's Palace, from Cleveland Row   T. S. Boys del et lith.
13. The Club Houses &c. Pall Mall   T. Shotter Boys del et lith.
14. The Horse Guards &c. from St. James's Park   T. Shotter Boys de et lith.
15. Hyde Park Corner.   T. S. Boys del et lith.
16. Hyde Park near Grosvenor Gate   T. S. Boys del et lith.
17. Piccadilly looking towards the City   T. S. Boys del et lith.
18. Regent Street looking towards the Quadrant   T. S. Boys del et lithog.
19. Regent Street looking towards the Duke of York's column   T. S. Boys del et lithog.
20. Entry to the Strand from Charing Cross.   T. S. Boys del et lith.
21. The Strand   T. S. Boys del et lith.
22. Temple Bar, from the Strand   T. S. Boys del et lith.
23. St. Dunstans &c. Fleet Street   T. S. Boys del. et lith.
24. St. Paul's from Ludgate Hill   T. S. Boys del et lithog.
25. Guidhall   T. S. Boys del et lithog.
26. The Bank looking towards Mansion House   T. S. Boys del et lithog.

Boys' London (contd.)

Issued in 3 forms. Plain, coloured and mounted on thick cards. The last form which may be called the de luxe edition is the rarest and finest. Boys himself is said to have coloured six of them. They were issued in a Roxburghe portfolio with a leather title piece on the side, with accompanying text in wrappers. The finest of the lithograph books on London.

105 BOYS (T. S.)

Picturesque Architecture in Paris, Ghent, Antwerp Rouen &c. drawn from nature on stone by Thomas Shotter Boys [preceding lettering on the wall of Rue de la Licorne] London Published 1839, by Thomas Boys, Printseller to the Royal Family, 11, Golden Square Regent St. Printed entirely in Colours by G. Hullmandel London.

Folio.   1839

COLLATION.—Title as above (v. blank) + Dedication 1 p. (v. blank) + 25 plates + 1 leaf of Text.

 1. Vignette Title. Rue de la Licorne.
 2. Fish Market Antwerp.
    Hospice des Vieillards Gand.
 3. Belfry Gand.
 4. Byloke Ghent.
 5. Tour de Remy Dieppe.
 6. L'Hotel de Ville, Arras.
 7. Laon [Cathedral].
 8. Rue de Rivage, Abbeville.
 9. St. Laurent Rouen.
10. Rue de la Grosse Horloge, Rouen.
11. L'Abbaye de Saint Amand Rouen.
12. Hotel de Cluny Paris.
13. Hotel Cluny Paris.
14. Hotel de Sens Paris.
15. [Church of] St Severin, Paris.
16. Porte Rouge, Notre Dame, Paris.
    Doorway of Hotel, Rue des Marmousets, Paris.
17. La Sainte Chapelle Paris.
18. [Rue] Notre Dame Paris.
19. [Church of] St Etienne du Mont Paris.
20. St Etienne du Mont and the Pantheon Paris.
21. Pavillon de Flore, Tuileries.
22. Hotel de la Tremouille Rue des Bourdonnois Paris.
    Vielle Rue, du Temple Paris.
23. La Chapelle de L'Institute Paris.
24. Notre Dame Paris from the Quai St. Bernard.
25. S. Porch of Chartres Cathedral.
26. St. André Chartres.

106 BRADFORD (Rev. W.)

Sketches of the Country, Character, and Costume in Portugal and Spain, made during the campaign, and on the route of the British Army, in 1808 and 1809. Engraved and Coloured from the Drawings by the Rev. William Bradford, A.B. of St. John's College, Oxford, Chaplain of Brigade to the Expedition. With incidental Illustration and appropriate descriptions, of each subject. (rule) London: Printed for John Booth, Duke Street, Portland Place, by William Savage, Bedford Bury, Covent Garden (rule)

Folio.   1809

COLLATION.—Title as above (v. blank) + 40 plates each with leaf of text.

1. p. 1. Creek of Maceria.
2. p. 2. A Car of Portuguese Estramadura.
3. p. 3. Torres Vedras from the North West.
4. p. 4. Peasant of Torres Vedras.
5. p. 5. Cintra.
6. p. 6. Cintra from the Lisbon Road.
7. p. 7. Franciscans.

Bradford's Portugal (*contd.*)

8. p. 8. Lisbon & Aqueduct of Alcantara.
9. p. 9. Aqueduct of Alcantara.
10. p. 10. A Portuguese Gentleman.
11. p. 11. Female of Lisbon in her Walking Dress (of the Middle Class).
12. p. 12. Pass in the Mountains between Nisa and Villa Velha.
13. p. 13. A Peasant Boy of Nisa.
14. p. 14. Peasant in a Straw Coat.
15. p. 15. View on the Tagus near Villa Velha.
16. p. 16. Girl of Guada.
17. p. 17. Bishop of Guada.
18. p. 18. Peasant of the Corregimiento of Salamanca.
      Peasant of the Corregimiento of Salamanca [different plate].
19. p. 19. Armed Peasant of the Ciudad Rodrigo Militia.
20. p. 20. The Boleras Dance.
21. p. 21. Salamanca.
22. p. 22. A Doctor of Salamanca.
23. p. 23. A Student of the Irish College, Salamanca.
24. p. 24. Interior of the Cathedral Salamanca.
25. p. 25. A Spanish Lady with her attendant Going to Mass.
26. p. 26. An infant Capuchin.
27. p. 27. Interior of the Dominican Church Salamanca.
28. p. 28. Servant Girls of Salamanca.
29. p. 29. Aliejos—a Town in the Plains of Leon.
30. p. 30. Spanish Courier.
31. p. 31. Peasants of the Corregimiento of Toro.
32. p. 32. Toro
33. p. 33. Shepherds of the Plains of Leon.
34. p. 34. Castle of Benevente.
35. p. 35. Pass of Manzanal.
36. p. 36. Villa Franca.
37. p. 37. Pass near Villa Franca.
38. *ibd.*   View near Villa Franca.
39. p. 38. View between Constantin & Nogales.

+List of Plates 1 p. (v. blank). + Fresh Title "Sketches of the Military Costume of Spain and Portugal" 1810 (v. blank) + Text pp. 1-8 + 13 coloured plates.

1. Spanish Military Costume   Light Infantry—
   Artillery.
2. Spanish Infantry.
3. Spanish Grenadiers.
4. Spanish Light Horse.
5. Spanish Heavy Horse.
6. Portuguese Military Costume.
7. Lisbon Police Guard. Armed Peasant of
   Algarva.
8. Novion, or Lisbon Police Cavalry.
9. Portuguese Regiment of Alcantara.
10. Portuguese Legion of Alorgna.
11. Portuguese Marine.
12. A Private of French Infantry.
13. A French Dragoon.

107 BRADFORD (Rev. W.)

Sketches of the Country, Character, and Costume, in Portugal and Spain, made during the campaign, and on the route of the British Army, in 1808 and 1809, engraved and coloured from the drawings by the Rev. William Bradford, A.B. of St John's College, Oxford, Chaplain of Brigade to the Expedition. With incidental illustration, and appropriate descriptions, of each subject. (line) London: Printed for John Booth, Duke Street, Portland Place, by William Savage, Bedford Bury, Covent Garden. (small rule).

Folio.   1810

Bradford's Portugal (*contd.*)

COLLATION.—Title as above (v. blank) + List of Plates 1 leaf (v. blank) + 40 plates, each plate with a leaf of text + 2nd title + 8 pp. of text + 13 plates.

All plates marked, Rev Mr. Bradford, Delt. I. Clark sculpt. with the exception of plate 9, where the artist's name is not given.

Front. The Monument erected at Corunna by the Spaniards to the memory of Sir John Moore, K.B. & etc. Published by John Booth, Duke Street, Portland Place. Jan. 6th 1810.

1. Creek of Maceira.	19. Armed Peasant of Ciudad Rodrigo Militia.
2. A Car of Portuguese Estremadura.	20. The Boleras Dance.
3. Torres Vedras from the North West.	21. Salamanca.
4. Peasant of Torres Vedras.	22. Doctor of Salamanca.
5. Cintra.	23. Student Irish College Salamanca.
6. Cintra from the Lisbon Road.	24. Interior of Cathedral.
7. Franciscans.	25. Spanish Lady with her attendant.
8. Lisbon and Aqueduct of Alcantara.	26. Infant Capuchin.
9. Aqueduct of Alcantara.	27. Interior Dominican Church Salamanca.
10. A Portuguese Gentleman.	28. Servant Girls of Salamanca.
11. Female of Lisbon in her walking dress (Middle Class).	29. Aliejos Town Plains of Leon
12. Pass in the Mountains between Nisa and Villa Velha.	30. Spanish Courier.
	31. Peasants Corregimiento of Toro.
13. A Peasant Boy of Nisa.	32. Toro.
14. Peasant in Straw Coat.	33. Shepherds Plains of Leon.
15. View of the Tagus, near Villa Velha.	34. Castle of Benevente.
16. Girl of Guarda.	35. Pass of Manzanal.
17. Bishop of Guarda.	36. Villa Franca.
18. Peasant of the Corregimiento of Salamanca.	37. Pass near Villa Franca.
ibd. Peasant of the Corregimiento of Salamanca.	38. View near Villa Franca.
	39. View between Constantin and Nogales.

Followed by fresh title "Sketches of Military Costume in Spain and Portugal," intended as Supplement to the Rev. Mr Bradford's Sketches of the Country, Costume and Character in Portugal and Spain. . . . John Booth 1810 (v. blank) + 8 pages of text + 13 plates.

1. Spanish Military Costume.	8. Novion or Lisbon Police Cavalry.
2. Spanish Grenadiers.	9. Portuguese Legion of Algorna.
3. Spanish Infantry.	10. Portuguese Regiment of Alcantara.
4. Spanish Light Horse.	11. Portuguese Marine.
5. Spanish Heavy Horse.	12. Private French Infantry.
6. Portuguese Military Costume.	13. French Dragoon.
7. Lisbon Police Guard, Armed peasant Algarva.	

Published in 24 parts, paper wrappers at 10s. 6d. each, large paper at 16s. and on completion, issued bound with printed label on front cover, within an ornamental border, at £8 8s. and large paper £11.

108 *Reissued 1812 with title in English and French (the English part the same as in 1810 edition). The imprint changed to, London; Printed for John Booth, Duke Street, Portland Place. By B. R. Howlett 49 Brewer Street, Golden Square 1812.*

Text in English and French (38 ll.). The plates are as in preceding edition.

109 *Another issue ND (1813). Imprint altered to, London; Printed for John Booth, Duke Street, Portland Place, by Howlett and Brimmer, Frith Street, Soho Square.*

110 *Another issue 1823. Imprint changed to, London; Printed for Thomas M'Lean, Haymarket, by Howlett and Brimmer, Frith Street, Soho Square, 1823.*

III. The British Dance of Death, exemplified by a series of Engravings, from Drawings by Van Assen; with Explanatory and Moral Essays (vignette of skull etc.) London Printed by and for Hodgson and Co. 10 Newgate Street.

Octavo.

COLLATION.—Title as above within engraved border of skulls (v. blank) + Preface (pp. iii–iv) + Text pp. 1–72 + 19 coloured plates.

1. Front. [Death with globe in centre, 2 small vignettes above and two below.]   Robt Cruikshank fecit. Published by Hodgson & Co. 10 Newgate Street.
2. p. 1. Death and Infancy.
3. p. 5. Death and Juvenile Piety.
4. p. 9. Death and the Student.
5. p. 13. Death and the Sempstress.   J. Gleadah sct.
6. p. 17. Death and the Musical Student.
7. p. 21. Death and the Dancer.   J. Gleadah sct.
8. p. 25. Death and the Female Student.
9. p. 29. Death and the Lovers.   J. Gleadah sculpt.
10. p. 33. Death and the Industrious Wife.
11. p. 37. Death and the Warrior.
12. p. 41. Death and the Pugilists.
13. p. 45. Death and the Glutton.
14. p. 49. Death and the Drunkard.
15. p. 53. Death and the Watchman.   J. Gleadah sculpt.
16. p. 57. Death and the Fishwoman.   J. Gleadah sculpt.
17. p. 61. Death and the Physician.
18. p. 65. Death and the Miser.
19. p. 69. Death and Old Age.   J. Gleadah sct.

All the plates bear Hodgson's imprint.

112 The British Military Library; or Journal: comprehending complete body of military Knowledge; and consisting of original communications: with selections from the most approved and respectable Foreign Military Publications (thick and thin rule) quotation (thin and thick rule) Vol I (thick and thin rule) London: Printed for R. Phillips, by J. Rider, No. 36 Little Britain   Published by J. Carpenter & Co. Booksellers to His Royal Highness Field Marshall the Duke of York, Old Bond Street; by H. D. Symonds Paternoster Row, and by H Colbert Dublin 1799

2 vols.   Quarto.   1799–[1801]

COLLATION VOL. I.—Title as above (v. blank) + Preface pp. iii–iv + Text pp. 1–496 (misprinted 196) + Index and D. to Binder 2 leaves + 13 coloured plates.

1. Front.   Military Portraits of the King the Prince of Wales, and the Duke of York.   C. Tomkins sculpt.
   p.   1. Sheet Music   The Field of Honour.
2. p. 10. First Regiment Life Guards.
   p. 26. German Pike Exercise &c.
   p. 40. Map County Mayo &c.
   ibd.   Sheet Music.   Field of Mars.
   p. 52. Mining.
3. p. 73. Foot Guards.
   p. 80. Map of Egypt.
   ibd.   Sheet Music.   The Flying Camp.
   p. 106. Map of Malta.

British Military Vol. I (*contd.*)

4. p. 114. Royal Horse Guards [Blues].
   p. 124. Map. Seat of War in Italy.
   ibd. Sheet Music. British Valour.
   p. 135. Plan of Menin.
5. p. 150. Second Regiment Life Guards.
   p. 164. Sheet Music. No title.
   p. 170. Plan Battle Prague.
6. p. 193. Royal Artillery.
   p. 205. Sheet Music. The Soldiers Joy.
   p. 232. Plan action near Meer.
   p. 240. Plan of engagement at Quiberon.
7. p. 240. First (or Royal) Regiment of Foot.
   p. 244. Music. The Triumph.
   p. 246. Plan Freyburg.
8. p. 273. First (or the Kings) Regiment of Dragoon Guards.
   p. 285. Sheet Music. Flying Colours.
   p. 287. Battle of Leuthen plan.
9. p. 318. Second (or the Queens) Regiment of Dragoon Guards.
   p. 323. Seat of War in Germany Map.
   p. 324. Sheet Music. The General.
   p. 331. Plan of Quarters Paderborn.
10. p. 356. Third (or The Prince of Wales's) Regt. of Dragoon Guards.
    p. 365. Sheet Music. The Expedition.
    p. 372. Plan of a Fortified Cordon.
11. p. 399. Second (or the Queen's) Regiment of Foot.
    p. 408. Map of Hindostan.
    ibd. Sheet Music. No title.
    p. 424. Plan of Fort Querqueville.
12. p. 437. Third Regiment of Foot [Buffs].
13. p. 480. Second (or Royal N. British) Regt. of Dragoons.
    p. 480. Plan of Review Hyde Park.

VOL. II.—Title dated 1801 + Preface to Second Volume pp. iii–iv + Text pp. 1–604 + Index and D. to Binder 4 leaves + 16 coloured plates.

    p. 24. (2) Sheets Music. The Commander in Chief.
14. p. 29. Fourth Regiment of Foot.
    p. 37. Seat of War in Holland.
    p. 43. Plan Chambery Gozo.
    p. 64. Map of the West Indies.
15. p. 75. Fourth (or Royal Irish) Dragoon Guards.
16. p. 81. Sword at Recover (5th Regt. of Foot).
    p. 86. Sketch of Part of North Holland Battle 19th Oct.
    p. 88. Sketch of Battle of 2nd Oct. 1799.
    p. 114. Plan Mantua.
17. p. 138. [Uniform of the Rothsay and Caithness Fencibles].
    p. 144. Map Part N. Holland Battle 19th Sept–6 Oct.
    p. 167. Plan fortified Castle. Plan of Seringapatam.
    p. 176. Sketch Action 24 April 1794 Villers en Couche.
18. p. 187. Fifth Regiment of Dragoon Guards.
    p. 210. Circular Redoubt.
    p. 216. Best mode of defending villages.
19. p. 219. The Marching Salute (6th Regt. of Foot).
20. p. 225. Fifth (or Royal Irish) Dragoons.
    p. 234. Sketch of Actions near Lille.
    p. 248. Plan of Polygon & its Profiles.
    p. 257. Plan Town of Coni.

British Military Vol. II (*contd.*)

p. 262. On the Construction of Mines.
21. p. 279. Seventh Regiment of Dragoon Guards.
p. 296. Entrenched Army. Entrenched Camp.
22. p. 315. Passing in Review. Quick Time (7th Regt. of Foot, Royal Fusileers).
23. p. 324. Advancing to the Charge. The First (or Royal) Regt. of Dragoons.
p. 328. Battles of Jemappes.
p. 358. Outworks of Fortress.
24. p. 376. An officer standing at ease—Seventeenth Regt. of Foot.
p. 406. The March of Lord Moira's Army.
25. p. 410. 33d Regt. of Foot. 56th Regt. Foot. 50th Regt. Foot.
p. 423. Star Redoubts. Tetes de Pont.
26. p. 440. The 10th (or the Prince of Wales's own) Regiment of Light Dragoons, and the 8th (or Kings Royal Irish) Regt. of Light Dragoons.
p. 464. Sheet Music. No title.
p. 465. Field Fortification.
p. 468. Field Fortification.
27. p. 474. The 7th (or the Queens own) Regt. of Light Dragoons and The 16th (or the Queens) Regt. of Light Dragoons.
p. 481. Plan Strassburg.
28. p. 520. Highland Infantry. 76th & 42nd.
29. p. 564. An Officer in Colonel Coote Manninghams Corps of Riflemen and An Officer of Marines.
p. 568. Military Utensils, Manoeuvre Light Infantry, General Plan (together on 1 sheet).
p. 592. Plan Gibraltar, Light Infantry Manoeuvres.
p. 600. Map of United States.

113 BRITTON (J.)

The History and Description, with Graphic Illustrations, of Cassiobury Park, Hertfordshire: the Seat of the Earl of Essex (rule) By John Britton, F.S.A. Honorary Member of the Institute of British Architects, and of other English and Foreign Societies, Author of the Architectural and Cathedral Antiquities, etc. (vignette Entrance Lodge R. W. Billings, Delt. J. Wright, sculpt.) (rule) London: Published by the Author, Burton Street. (rule)

Octavo.   1837

COLLATION.—Title as above (v. Note of No. of copies issued and Whittingham's imprint) + Dedication 1 p. (v. blank) + Preface pp. 5–6 + Contents 1 p. (v. List of Subscribers) + pp. 9–32.

Face Title Portrait of George, Earl of Essex, by Turner after Hoppner Feb. 1st 1812.
p. 9. George Viscount Malden and Lady Elizabeth Capel by Turner after Reynolds. Jul. 14th 1817.
p. 32. Ground Plan of Cassiobury House, Hertfordshire (uncoloured) + 20 Coloured plates (mostly without titles) + 12 Plate outlines.

Issued plain and coloured. Only 20 large-paper copies and 150 small-paper copies were issued. The Plates by J. M. W. Turner, Pugin and Eldridge were aquatinted by R. Havell.

114 BROUGHTON (T. D.)

Letters written in a Mahratta Camp during the year 1809, descriptive of the Character, Manners, Domestic Habits, and Religious Ceremonies, of the Mahrattas, With Ten Coloured Engravings, from drawings by a native artist. (thick and thin rule) By Thomas Duer Broughton, Esq. Late Commander of the Resident's Escort, at the Court

Broughton's Mahratta Camp (*contd.*)

of Scindia.   (thin and thick rule) London: Printed for John Murray, 50 Albemarle Street (rule)

Quarto.   1813

COLLATION.—Half-title "Letters written in a Mahratta Camp, during the year 1809." (v. blank) + Title as above (v. blank) + Dedication 1 leaf + Contents 5 leaves + pp. 1–358 + D. to Binder 1 leaf + 10 coloured plates.   Each with imprint, Published April 5th, 1813, by J. Murray, Albemarle Street.

1. Front. A Bazar in Seendhiya's Camp.   Drawn and Etched from the original by J. A. Atkinson.
2. p. 49. A Mahratta Surdar entertaining Brahmins.   Etched by T. Baxter, from the original drawing by Deen Alee.
3. p. 72. The Procession of the Taziya.   Etched by J. A. Atkinson from the original drawing by Deen Alee.
4. p. 91. Playing the Hohlee.   Etched by T. Baxter, from the original drawing by Deen Alee.
5. p. 102. A Mahratta Pandit and his Family.   Etched by T. Baxter, from the original drawing by Deen Alee.
6. p. 129. A Muhunt and Gosaeens.   Etched by J. A. Atkinson, from the original drawing by Deen Alee.
7. p. 137. A Meena of Jajurh.   Etched by T. Baxter, from the original drawing by Deen Alee.
8. p. 192. A Girl dancing the Kuharwa.   Etched by J. A. Atkinson, from the original drawing by Deen Alee.
9. p. 219. An Ukhara, with a view of the British Resident's Camp.   Etched by Moses from the original drawing by Deen Alee.
10. p. 258. The Junumushtoomee.   Drawn and Etched from the original by J. A. Atkinson.

115 BROWNE (Hablot Knight)

Hunting Bits by "Phiz."   London: Chapman and Hall, 193, Piccadilly.

Oblong Folio.   [1862]

COLLATION.—Title as above (v. blank) + List of plates 1 p. (v. blank) + 12 plates. 12 coloured lithographs, all bearing Chapman and Hall's imprint and H. K. Browne Delt. et Lith.   M. & N. Hanhart Impt.

1. After you, m'am!
2. The Train's a coming.
3. Hare Hunt Extraordinary.
4. Pounded.
5. Rather too Bad.
6. Bellows to mend.
7. Look before you Leap.
8. Running the Rail.
9. Taking a good line of country.
10. Surrey H'ills.
11. Very fond of the Sport.
12. Something like a finish.

116 BURCHELL (W. J.)

Travels in the interior of Southern Africa, by William J. Burchell, Esq. (rule) Volume I [II] (rule) With an entirely new map, and numerous engravings. (rule) London: Printed for Longman, Hurst, Rees, Orme, and Brown, Paternoster Row.

2 vols.   Quarto.   1822 [Vol. II 1824]

COLLATION VOL. I.—Half-title "Travels in the interior of Southern Africa" Vol. I (v. London: Printed by A. & R. Spottiswoode, New-Street-Square) + Title as above (v. blank) + Preface pp. v–viii + Contents 1 p. + List of Plates + Vignettes 2 pp. + 1 blank page + pp. 1–582 + half page Errata Slip + 1 large folding map + 10 coloured plates + 50 vignettes in text.

Each plate is marked, Engraved after the original Drawing made by W. J. Burchell Esq. [date] London Published by Longman & Co. August 1, 1821.

Burchell's Travels in Southern Africa (*contd.*)

1. p. 25. A view of Cape Town, Table Bay, and Tygerberg 26 December 1810 (folding).
2. p. 167. Portrait of Speelman, a Hottentot 21 Sep. 1814.
3. p. 178. Crossing the Berg River 23 June 1811.
4. p. 282. Caravan of Waggons assembled at Zak river on the borders of the Country of the Bushmen 3 Sep. 1811 (folding).
5. p. 294. The Rock Fountain, in the Country of the Bushmen 9 September 1811.
6. p. 316. Scene on the river Gariep 16 September 1811.
7. p. 325. A Hottentot Kraal on the banks of the Gariep 17 Sept 1811.
8. p. 360. A View of Klaarwater, looking towards the North-east 5 June 1811 (folding).
9. p. 459. Portrait of a Bushman, playing on the Gorah 17 Nov 1811.
10. p. 490. Portrait of a Kora 10 Decemb 1811.
    p. 582. Map "The Extratropical Part of Southern Africa, constructed by William J. Burchell Esq. &c. large folding sheet.

VOL. II.—Half-title, Title as before [Green's name added to imprint and date altered to 1824] (v. blank) + Contents 1 p. + List of Plates and Vignettes 2 pp. + Errata 1 p. + pp. 1–648 (including General Index) + Hints on Emigration to the Cape of Good Hope 4 pp. + 10 coloured plates + 46 woodcuts.

Each plate marked, "Published by Longman & Co. May 1 1823 Engraved & coloured after the original Drawing made by W. J. Burchell Esq".

1. p. 44. A Natural Obelisk in the Country of the Bushmen.
2. p. 133. Descending from the Snow Mountains.
3. p. 160. Portrait of Juli, a faithful Hottentot.
4. p. 198. View of a Bushman Kraal (folding).
5. p. 362. View on entering the Town of Litakun.
6. p. 464. A View in the Town of Litakun (folding).
7. p. 484. Portrait of a Massisān.
8. p. 494. Portrait of Mahutu.
9. p. 515. Section and Plan of a Bachapin House.
10. p. 561. Portrait of Chaasi, a Bachapin.

Published in boards with printed labels.

The Errata slip is frequently missing, as is also the half-title to Vol. II. This half-title has often passed unnoticed as there is nothing to indicate its presence, but I have seen it in a fine copy in boards (11¼ × 8¾ inches) in the possession of Messrs. Francis Edwards.

117 BURKILL (J.)

The Pictorial Beauties of Mona a selection of Drawings from the Romantic Scenery of the Isle of Man by J. Burkill Esqre. Author of "Bolton Illustrated" the "Abbeys & Monasteries" &c. &c. (vignette of Manx arms, with list of plates either side). Dedicated by Permission to his Excellency the Lieutenant Governor of the Island (2 line rule) First Series (2 line rule) Lithographed by Day & Son, Lithographers to the Queen, Gate Street London 1857. Published J. Mylrea July 1st 1857 Douglas.

Folio.

COLLATION.—Title as above (v. blank) + 6 lithograph plates, each marked, J. Burkill Del- J. Needham Lith. Published by J. Mylrea, July 1st 1857 Douglas.

1. Douglas Town, Bay, and Harbour.
2. Peel Castle (Summer Time).
3. Peel Castle (stormy).
4. Laxey Village and Bay.
5. Castletown.
6. Ramsay Town, Bay, and Harbour.

Issued in blue cloth lettered in gilt with Royal Arms.

Burkill's Scenery of the Isle of Man (*contd.*)

There are two issues of the title page. In the above copy Mylrea's imprint is in small type below the date. In the other issue Mylrea's imprint is set in large type.

118 BURNEY (F.)

Evelina: or the History of a Young Lady's Introduction to the World. (thick and thin rule) By Miss Burney. (think and thick rule) A New Edition, embellished with engravings. (swelled rule) London: Published by Edward Mason, Creed Lane, Ludgate Street. (rule)

Octavo. 1821

COLLATION.—Engraved title + Printed title as above. (v. blank) + Recommendations of this work 1 p. (v. blank) + pp. 5–522 + 6 coloured plates [pp. 41–48 repeated]

1. Front. Engraved Title lettered, "Evelina or the History of a Young Lady's Introduction to the World," surrounded by small vignette.
2. p. 25. Evelina, Mrs Mirvan and Maria, Shopping.
3. p. 69. The Captain attacking Madame Duval.
4. p. 101. Evelina, Visit to the Opera with the Branghtons. W. Heath delt.
5. p. 179. The Captain hunting Madame Duval in the Ditch.
6. p. 277. Madame Duval Dancing a Minuet, at the Hampstead Assembly. W. Heath delt.
7. p. 515. Evelina, Mr Lovel and the Monkey. W. Heath delt.

119 BURNEY (F.)

Evelina: or Female Life in London: being the History of a Young Lady's Introduction to Fashionable Life, and the Gay Scene of the Metropolis; displaying a Highly Humorous, Satirical, and Entertaining Description of Fashionable Characters, Manners, and Amusements, in the Higher Circles of Metropolitan Society. (rule) Embellished and Illustrated with a series of Humorous colored (*sic*) Engravings, by the First Artists. (rule) London: Published by Jones and Co., Warwick Square; (2 line rule)

Octavo. 1822

COLLATION.—Title as above (v. Printed by T. Hamblin, Garlick Hill, Thames Street.) + Recommendations of this work 1 p. (v. blank) + Text pp. 5–522 (pp. 41–48 are repeated) + 7 coloured plates, each with imprint, Published by Jones & Co., [and date].

1. Front. Lettered Evelina, or the History of a Young Lady's Introduction to the World, with vignette scenes surrounding it.
2. p. 24. Evelina, Mrs Mirvan and Maria, Shopping.
3. p. 68. The Captain attacking Madame Duval.
4. p. 100. Evelina's Visit to the Opera with the Branghtons. W. Heath, Delt. Feb. 16 1822.
5. p. 178. The Captain hunting Madam Duval in the Ditch. Mar 9th 1822.
6. p. 277. Madame Duval Dancing a Minuet at the Hampstead Assembly. W. Heath, Delt.,
7. p. 514. Evelina, Mr Lovel and the Monkey. W. Heath, Delt., Jan 20th 1822.

Burton's Adventures of John Newcome in the Navy 1818. See under Rowlandson (T.).

120 BURY (T. T.)

Coloured Views on the Liverpool and Manchester Railway, with plates of the Coaches, Machines, &c. from Drawings made on the spot by Mr. T. T. Bury. With Descriptive Particulars, serving as a guide to Travellers on the Railway (rule) London: Published by

Bury's Railways (*contd.*)

R. Ackermann, 96, Strand, and sold by R. Ackermann Jun. 191 Regent Street: Printsellers in Ordinary to his Majesty.

Quarto.   1831

COLLATION.—Title as above (v. blank) + Text pp. 1–8 + 13 plates.   Each plate marked, T. T. Bury delt., the first 7 plates bearing imprint London Pubd. by R. Ackermann 96 Strand 1831.

1. The Tunnel   H. Pyall sculpt.
2. Entrance of the Railway at Edge Hill Liverpool   H. Pyall sculpt.
3. Excavation of Olive Mount 4 miles from Liverpool   H. Pyall sculpt.
4. Viaduct across the Sankey Valley   H. Pyall sculpt.
5. View of the Railway across Chat Moss   H. Pyall sculpt.
6. Entrance into Manchester across Water Street   H. Pyall sculpt.
7. Coaches &c.   Employed on the Railway   H. Pyall sculpt.
8. Railway Office Liverpool   S. G. Hughes sculpt.
9. Warehouses &c. at the end of the Tunnel towards Wapping   S. G. Hughes sculpt.
10. Moorish Arch looking from the Tunnel   S. G. Hughes sculpt.
11. Near Liverpool looking towards Manchester   H. Pyall sculpt.
12. Rainhill Bridge   H. Pyall sculpt.
13. Taking in Water at Parkside   H. Pyall sculpt.

Copies occur with 2 extra folding coloured aquatint plates by I. Shaw, engraved by S. G. Hughes viz. "A Train of First and Second Class Carriages with the Mail" and "Train of Waggons with Goods, Cattle &c."

121   *A later edition with the plates re-engraved was issued in 1833.   This may have a further additional plate "Bridge on the line of the St. Helen's and Runcorn Gap Railway."*

122 BURY (T. T.)

Six Coloured Views of the London and Birmingham Railway, from drawings made on The Line with the Sanction of the Company.   By Mr. T. T. Bury. (rule) Part I. (rule) London: Published by Ackermann and Co., 96, Strand, and to be had of R. Ackermann, 191, Regent Street; Printsellers by Appointment to her Majesty, and her Royal Highness the Duchess of Kent.   Price Twelve Shillings

Quarto.   1837

COLLATION.—Title as above (v. blank) + 6 coloured aquatint plates.

Each plate numbered and headed London and Birmingham Railway, and with imprint, London Published September 18th 1837 by Ackermann & Co. 96 Strand.   All plates marked, T. T. Bury delt.

Plate 1. The Station at Euston Square.   J. Harris sculpt.
  ,,   2. View taken from under the Hampstead Bridge.   C. Hunt sculpt.
  ,,   3. View taken from the Bridge over the Canal, Camden Town.   N. Fielding sculpt.
  ,,   4. Viaduct at Watford.   J. Harris sculpt.
  ,,   5. Entrance to the Tunnel at Watford.   N. Fielding sculpt.
  ,,   6. Bridge over the Canal near Kings-Langley.   J. Harris sculpt.

Issued in buff wrappers repeating the printed title on p. 1, Ackermann's Advts. p. 2, surmounted by Royal arms p. 3, ditto p. 4, Railroad Views &c.

One of the rarest of English colour plate books.

123 BUSBY (T. L.)

Costume of the Lower Orders of London. (rule) Painted and Engraved from Nature, by T. L. Busby. (rule) London: Published for T. L. Busby, by Messrs. Baldwin and Co.,

Busby's Costume of London (*contd.*)

Paternoster-Row; At the Artist's Depository, 21, Charlotte-Street, Fitzroy-Square; (one door above Goodge-Street) and to be had of all the Booksellers and Printsellers in the United Kingdom

Quarto. [1820]

COLLATION.—Title as above (v. Printed by W. Clowes, Northumberland-court, Strand.) + Introduction 2 pp. (iii–iv) + 24 coloured plates each marked (with the exception of the frontispiece), Drawn & Engd. by T. L. Busby Pubd. [date] for T. L. Busby by Messrs. Baldwin & Co., Paternoster Row, & at the Artists Depository 21, Charlotte St., Fitzroy Square. Each plate has 1 page of text with the exception of plate 6 "Draymen" which has 2 pages of text.

1. Frontispiece or Engraved Title consisting of a sandwich man bearing a placard on his back "Costume of the Lower Orders of London." Designed & Engrav'd from Nature by T. L. Busby, a similar placard in French in his hand.
2. Billy Waters [the Dancing Fiddler] Novr. 1 1819.
3. Jemmy Lovel [the Tinker] Novr. 1 1819.
4. Mechanical Fiddler Novr. 1 1819.
5. Owen Clancey [the Frostbitten Sailor] Jany. 1 1820.
6. Draymen Feby. 15 1820.
7. Bell Ringer [Joseph Hill] Feby. 15 1820.
8. Fish Woman Feby. 15 1820.
9. Milk Girl Jany. 1 1820.
10. Mat Man [Thomas Musto] Jany. 1 1820.
11. Fortune Teller Jany. 1 1820.
12. Pedlar Feby. 15 1820.
13. Rabbit Man March 15th 1820.
14. Water Cresses March 15th 1820.
15. Apple Boy March 15th 1820.
16. Watchman March 15th 1820.
17. Mayday May 15th 1820.
18. Shoe Black May 15th 1820.
19. Match Girl May 15th 1820.
20. Dustman May 15th 1820.
21. Fireman March 15th 1820.
22. Chimney Sweepers Aug. 1 1820.
23. Postman July 1st 1820.
24. Pieman Augt. 15th 1820.

The plates being unnumbered are not necessarily in the above order. There are two issues of this work, the first issue being as above but the imprint being London: Published by Baldwin, Cradock and Joy Paternoster Row. Plate 10 Mat man is spelt with a double tt Matt Man, and plate 11 Fortune Teller is not marked, Drawn and Engraved by T. L. Busby.

124 BUSBY (T. L.)

Dedicated, by most gracious permission, to His Majesty. (decorated rule) Civil and Military Costume of the City of London. (rule) Painted and Engraved by Thomas Lord Busby. (rule) London: Published by Robert Jennings, 2 Poultry; and at The Artist's Depository and Circulating Library, 21, Charlotte-Street, Fitzroy-Square. 1824. (rule) John Nichols and Son, Parliament-Street

Folio. [1824–5]

COLLATION.—Title as above (v. blank) + Dedication to George IV 1 p. (v. blank) + a coloured plate.

1. Lord Mayor Sir Wm. Curtis Bart. M.P. Painted & Engraved by T. L. Busby—Pub 1823, at the Artists Depository 21, Charlotte Street, Fitzroy Square (4 pp. of text) slip note announcing Mr. Busby's indisposition + Title as before + 1 coloured plate.
2. Alderman W. Heygate Esqr. M.P. Portrait Painted by A. Wivell & the Costume by T. L. Busby—Eng. by T. L. Busby. Pubd. 1825, at the Artists Depository 21, Charlotte Street, Fitzroy Sqe. (2 pp. text). Title as before (but dated 1825) + 1 coloured plate.
3. Recorder Sir John Silvester Bart. Painted & Engraved by T. L. Busby (1 page of text v. blank) Title as before (but dated 1825) + 1 coloured plate.

Busby's Costume of London (*contd.*)

4. Common Councilman W. J. Reeves Esqr. Painted & Engraved by T. L. Busby—Pubd. 1825 at the Artists Depository 21, Charlotte Street, Fitzroy Square (1 page of text).

The intention of this work was to publish 1 number a month in double-elephant Quarto (consisting of 1 portrait with letterpress) for 12s. Nineteen portraits were planned but only the above number issued in this form. The British Museum copy from which the above collation is taken has the leaf of prospectus laid in in front of title.

125 BUSBY (T. L.)

The Fishing Costume and Local Scenery of Hartlepool, in the County of Durham. (rule) Painted and Engraved from Nature, By T. L. Busby. (thick and thin rule) London. Printed for J. Nichols and Son, Red Lion Passage, Fleet Street; Colnaghi and Co. Cockspur Street; Rowe and Waller, Fleet Street; T. L. Busby, 21, Charlotte Street, Fitzroy Square; and G. Andrews, Durham

Quarto.   1819

COLLATION.—Title as above (J. Nichols and Son, Printers, Red Lion Passage, Fleet Street, London) + General Account of the Town pp. 1–6 + 6 coloured plates, each marked, T. L. Busby delint. et. Sc. and 1 page of Text bearing short description of each plate.

1. Fishermans Son, of Hartlepool Hartlepool Pier.
2. A Fishermans Daughter, of Hartlepool Rocks from the Pier Hartlepool.
3. Shrimp Seller, of Hartlepool.
4. Lobster Catcher of Hartlepool.
5. Shrimp Catcher of Hartlepool.
6. Fisherman, of Hartlepool.

Busby (T. L.). See also under Leigh Picture of London.

126 BUTLER (Capt. H.)

South African Sketches; illustrative of the Wild Life of a Hunter on the Frontier of the Cape Colony. By Captain H. Butler, 59th Regiment. London: Published by Ackermann and Co., 96 Strand.

Quarto.   1841

COLLATION.—Engraved pictured title + Printed title + pp. 1–15 (p. 16 List of Subjects) + 15 plates containing 31 drawings, 16 of which are in colour. The plates are numbered 1–15.

1. Kat River Bastard and his afterrider.
2. Off saddled, near Death Valley Bontebok Flats.
   Death of a Springbok.
3. The wounded Blesbok.
4. A fog on the Flats.
5. Travellers pointing out the route.
6. Wildebeeste Gnu.
7. Camp at Modder Key (going out in the morning).
8. The Game fleeing before the Hunters.
9. Chase of the Hartebeest.
10. Smoking out the Tiger Klip Plaats R.
11. The Bontebok or Blesbok.
12. The Ostrich near the Klip Plaats River.
13. The Game successfully driven thro' a bend in the Klip Plaats River.
    Bontebok Flats.
14. The Eland blown Tsitse River.
15. The death of the Buffalo.

There are 31 vignettes in all, mostly 2 on each plate, 1 plain and 1 coloured. The above are the titles of the coloured, the rest are in outline only.

Butler (Samuel) Hudibras. See under Clark (I).

Cabinet of the Arts.   See Hodson (T.) and Dougal (I.).

Cambria Depicta.   See under Pugh (E.).

Campaign of Waterloo 1816.   See under Bowyer (R.).

127 CAMPBELL (Rev. John)

Travels in South Africa, undertaken at the Request of the London Missionary Society; being a Narrative of a Second Journey in the Interior of that Country (thick and thin rule) By the Rev. John Campbell. (thin and thick rule) With a map and coloured prints (thin and thick rule) Vol. I [II] (rule) London: Printed for the Society, Published and sold by Francis Westley, 10 Stationers Court, Ludgate Street and sold by Black and Co., Leadenhall Street; Waugh and Innes, Edinburgh. and Chalmers and Collins, Glasgow (rule)

2 vols.   Octavo.   1822

COLLATION VOL. I.—Half-title (v. blank) + Title as above (v. T. C. Hansard, Printer, Peterborough Court, Fleet Street) + Dedication 1 p. (v. blank) + Advt., 1 leaf + Contents (to both vols.) pp. 1–12 + Introduction pp. 1–4 + pp. 5–322 + D., to Binder (to both vols.) 1 p. + 3 pp. Advts., of Publications of Westbury + 1 p. blank (v. Printer's imprint, T. C. Hansard & etc.) + folding map and 8 coloured aquatints.   Each plate is marked, Campbell delt., Clark, sculpt., London Published by F. Westbury, Stationers Court.   1822

  1. Front.   The Author's method of Travelling in the interior of South Africa.
     p.   1.   Folding map South Africa.
  2. p. 222.   The Kings district of the City of Kurreechane, in the Marootzee Country.
  3. p. 244.   Houses and Yard of Sinosee, in Kurreechane.
  4. p. 260.   Mocelway, young King of the Marootzee.
  5. p. 265.   Liqueling, Regent of the Marootzee Nation.
  6. p. 269.   Interior of Sinosee's House, Kurreechane.
  7. p. 276.   [Plate containing, House to protect from Lions, Tammaha House Furnace etc.]
  8. p. 294.   Head of a Unicorn killed near the city of Machow.

VOL. II.—Half-title (v. blank) + Title (v. Hansard's imprint) + pp. 1–384 + 4 coloured aquatint plates.

  9. Front.   Mahootoo Queen of the Lattakoo, in full dress.
10. p. 53.   Burders Place, Near Lattakoo, containing Mission Houses and Church.
11. p. 138.   A Lattakoo Chief and his Wife.
12. p. 201.   Dress worn by females at the annual circumcision feast at Lattakoo, and the Rainmakers wife
        at Kurreechane.

The last 3 leaves in Vol. I (D. to Binder, Advts. and Imprint leaf are frequently missing).

128 CARELESS (John)

The Old English 'Squire.   "A Jovial Gay Fox Hunter, Bold, Frank and Free."   A Poem, In Ten Cantos. (small swelled rule) By John Careless, Esq. (small swelled rule) Illustrated with plates, By One of the Family (rule) London: Printed for Thomas M'Lean, 26, Haymarket, By Howlett and Brimmer, Frith Street, Soho

Octavo.   1821

Careless's Old English 'Squire (*contd.*)

COLLATION.—Half-title "Old English 'Squire" (v. blank) + Title as above (v. blank) + Preface 4 pp. (v–viii) + pp. 1–136 + 24 coloured plates.

Each plate bears a 2 line quotation from text and imprint, Published May 1821 by Thos. McLean, Hay Market.

1. Front. The Old Squire.
2. p. 10. Fetching the Midwife.
3. p. 12. Dressing the Young Squire—who is obstropolous.
4. p. 21. Young Squire gets Ferrul'd for neglecting his Studies.
5. p. 22. Breaking Cover, or Hunting in Hampshire.
6. p. 23. Tries a New Shooting Poney—which wont do.
7. p. 25. Crammed at College by his Tutor for a Degree.
8. p. 37. Gets Cheated by his Miller who grinds Oats for Him.
9. p. 41. Young Squire goes to London and gets his Pockets Eased.
10. p. 47. Takes Lessons in Dancing.
11. p. 50. Sits for His Portrait.
12. p. 67. Goes to the Opera.
13. p. 71. Goes to a picture sale.
14. p. 73. Buys an Historical Picture. St. Anthony preaching to the Fishes.
15. p. 83. Rides Home on a Borrowed Horse.
16. p. 87. Mistakes Mushrooms for Game and Spoils their Shape.
17. p. 89. Meets with a Small Accident.
18. p. 91. His Gun Misses fire—because He Had Forgot to Load It.
19. p. 98. Goes with Some Friends to Shoot Grouse on the Moors.
20. p. 104. Not the Safest Way to Carry Loaded Guns in a Wood.
21. p. 105. Spurs Himself in the Wrong Place.
22. p. 111. Sees a Water Kelpy.
23. p. 132. The Village Schoolmaster—fond of Little Bits.
24. p. 133. A Cheerful Dance.

Issued in boards with printed label on side and spine at £1 11s. 6d. The half-title is frequently missing.

129 CAREY (David)

Life in Paris; comprising the Rambles, Sprees, and Amours, of Dick Wildfire, of Corinthian Celebrity, and his Bang-up Companions, Squire Jenkins and Captain O'Shuffleton; with the Whimsical Adventures of the Halibut Family; including Sketches of a Variety of other Eccentric Characters in the French Metropolis (rule) By David Carey (rule) (woodcut vignette) Embellished with Twenty-One Coloured Plates, representing Scenes from Real Life, designed and engraved by Mr. George Cruikshank. Enriched also with Twenty-Two Engravings on Wood, drawn by the same Artist, and executed by Mr. White (rule) London: Printed for John Fairburn, Broadway, Ludgate Hill; Sold by Sherwood, Neely, and Jones; Longman, Hurst, Rees, Orme, and Brown; and Baldwin, Craddock and Joy; Paternoster-Row, Simpkin and Marshall, Stationers Court, Whittakers Ave Maria-Lane; Humphry, St. James Street and Wilson, Royal Exchange

Octavo.   1822

COLLATION.—Half-title "Life in Paris" (v. Marchant, Printer, Ingram-Court London) + Printed title as above (v. blank) + Preface 2 ll. (v–viii) + Illusts. 4 ll. (ix–xvi) + Contents 4 ll. (xvii–xxiv) + pp. 1–489 + To the Binder 1 p. (v. blank) + 21 coloured plates.

Each plate is marked, "Drawn & Engraved by Mr. George Cruikshank, Published (date) by John Fairburn, Broadway, Ludgate Hill."

Carey's Life in Paris (contd.)

1.   Engraved Title Life in Paris as a base with pediment of Le Jeu, L'Amour, La Politesse, L'Honneur Musique, & Vive la Bagatelle on top.

2. p. 27. Dick Wildfire preparing for a Dash "à la Francoise" Novr. 15th 1822.

3. p. 33. Dick Wildfire and the Captain promenading in the Gardens of the Thuilleries Decr. 1st 1822.

4. p. 90. Dick Wildfire & Squire Jenkins seeing "Real Life" in the Galleries of the Palais Royal April 15th 1822.

5. p. 108. Dick, Jenkins, The Captain, Lady Halibut & Lydia, enjoying a Lounge in the Italian Boulevard Jany. 15th 1822.

6. p. 116. Dick, The Captain and Squire Jenkins, Dining at Very's in the Palais Royal Jany. 1st 1822.

7. p. 122. Dick and his Companions Smashing the Glim, or A Spree by Lamplight Decr. 15th 1822.

8. p. 145. Dick and The Captain paying their Respects to the Fair Limonardière in the Café de Mille Colonnes Feb. 15 1822.

9. p. 147. Dick Wildfire introduced by Captain O'Shuffleton to a Rouge et Noir Table in the Palais Royal March 1 1822.

10. p. 201. Dick and his Valet shewing Fight in a Caveau, or, Low Life in Paris Feb. 1 1822.

11. p. 256. "Life" behind the Curtain, at the Grand Opera, or, Dick and the Squire larking with the Figurants Augt. 1 1822.

12. p. 286. Dick and Squire Jenkins enjoying the Sport at les Combats des Animaux, or The Parisian Duck Lane March 15 1822.

13. p. 305. Dick Wildfire & Jenkins in a Theatrical Pandemonium or the Café de la Paix in all its glory May 15 1822.

14. p. 323. "Life" among the Dead!! or Dick Wildfire, Squire Jenkins and the Halibut Family in the Catacombs May 1 1822.

15. p. 331. "Life" among the Connoisseurs; or, Dick Wildfire & his Friends in the Grand Gallery of the Louvre. June 1 1822.

16. p. 335. Dick Wildfire and Jenkins enjoying a Frolic in the Café d'Enfer or Infernal Cellar Ap. 1 1822.

17. p. 384. "Life" on Tip-Toe, or Dick Wildfire Quadrilling it, at the Saloon de Mars, in Champs Elysee June 13 1822.

18. p. 450. Entre to the Opera; or Dick Wildfire & his Friends going to see "Life" among the Figurantes July 15 1822.

19. p. 452. Morning of the Fete of St. Louis, or Dick & Jenkins, enjoying "Life" in the Elysian Fields Septr. 1 1822.

20. p. 457. Evening of the Fete of St. Louis, or Dick, Jenkins, & the Halibuts witnessing the Canaille in all their glory Sept. 15 1822.

21. p. 471. "Life" in a Billiard Room, or Dick Wildfire & Squire Jenkins "au fait" (awake) to the Parisian Sharpers July 1 1822.

Issued in 21 parts paper wrappers on small and large paper and on completion in buff pictorial boards with the vignette of the title page repeated on the upper cover, 2 woodcuts on back cover and on the spine. This was lettered Demy Edition price £1 1s. Some large-paper copies were, however, issued in plain boards, and these in Cohn's opinion antedate the picture boards. The Leaf of Directions to Binder is frequently missing as was the case in the Suzannet copy in boards ($9\frac{1}{16} \times 5\frac{1}{2}$ins., size of boards $9\frac{5}{16} \times 5\frac{9}{16}$). The letterpress of pp. 143–4 and 335–6 is different in the parts, and cancel leaves were issued at the end of the parts.

A second edition was published in 1828 with Cumberland's imprint.

130 CARPENTER (P.)

Dedicated by Permission to the Calcutta Tent Club. Hog Hunting in Lower Bengal, illustrated by Percy Carpenter (oval vignette "Vultures devouring the Hog," described in the Text to plate 7. E. Walker, lith. Day & Son, Lithrs., to the Queen) London:

Carpenter's Hog Hunting in Lower Bengal (*contd.*)

Published Dec. 2nd 1861 by Day & Son Lithographers to the Queen. W. Thacker & Co., London.   Thacker, Spink & Co., Calcutta.

Folio.   1861

COLLATION.—Title as above + Introduction 1 leaf (v. blank) + 8 plates, each with leaf of text.

Each plate bears imprint, Percy Carpenter, delt.   E. Walker, Lith. Day & Son Lithogrs., to the Queen.   London Published Dec. 2nd 1861, by Day & Son Lithographers to the Queen, W. Thacker & Co., London, and Thacker Spink and Co., Calcutta.

1. The Meet.
2. The Beat.
3. Tally Ho!
4. 1st Spear.

5. The Charge.
6. The Hog at Bay.
7. The Death.
8. Tent Club at Tiffin.

131 CARTWRIGHT (J.)

Selections of the Costume of Albania and Greece with explanatory quotations from the poems of Lord Byron and Gally Knight including a highly finished Portrait of Ali Pacha the whole from original drawings by J. Cartwright, Esq (rule) London: Published by R. Havell, 3 Chaple Street Tottenham Court Road.   1822

COLLATION.—Title as above (v. J. G. Havell Printer Chaple Street Tottenham Court Road) + 12 coloured plates.

(1) Ali Pacha of Jannina.
(2) An Albanian of Jannina.
(3) A Greek Bishop.
(4) Albanian Female.
(5) A Red Shawled Arnaut.
(6) A Parguinote.

(7) A Suliotte in his Shaggy Capote.
(8) A Tartar.
(9) Corfu Costume.
(10) An Albanian.
(11) Lefchimo Costume.
(12) Captain of Suliote Albanians.

All plates engraved by Robert Havell & Son.   Drawn by J. Cartwright with Havell's imprint at foot 1821-2.

132 CARTWRIGHT (J.)

Views in the Ionian Islands.

COLLATION.—Dedication + Title page + 3 ll. descriptive text + 12 coloured aquatint plates.

1. Town, Citadel and Harbour of Corfu, from the Island of Vido.
2. The feast of St Jason and Sosipatros, in the Island of Corfu.
3. The Street of Vasili from the Esplanade in Corfu, with a Procession of St Spiridione.
4. The Ferry of Perama, Entrance to the Southern Passage of Corfu and Homers Island, called the Ship of Ulysees.
5. Santa Maura, from the Upper Acropolis of the Ancient City of Leucadia.
6. Sappho's Leap at Cape Ducato.
7. The Sanita, or Health Office, at Santa Maura.
8. View of the Town and Harbour of Vathi, in Ithaca.
9. View of the Fountain of Arethusa and Rock Corax in Ithaca.
10. Town and Harbour of Argostoli in Cephalonia.
11. The Piazza of St Mark in Zante.
12. The Town and Harbour of Zante.

133 Catherwood (F.)

Views of Ancient Monuments in Central America Chiapas and Yucatan by F. Catherwood, Arch^t.

Folio.

COLLATION.—Title as above in red and gold within broad decorated coloured border +25 coloured lithographs all mounted on thick card. Accompanying text in smaller format, viz. Dedication 1 lf. + Outline map of central America and Yucatan 1 lf. + Introduction pp. 1–10 + Text (to plates) pp. 11–24.

1. [Idol at Copan on stone by A. Picken].
2. [Pyramidal Building and Fragments of Sculpture at Copan on stone by H. Warren].
3. Back of an Idol, at Copan on stone by H. Warren].
4. [Broken Idol at Copan on stone by H. Warren].
5. [Idol and Altar at Copan on stone by W. Parrott].
6. [General View of Palenque on stone by A. Picken].
7. { [Principal Court of the Palace at Palenque on stone by H. Warren.]
 { [Interior of Casa No. III Palenque on stone by H. Warren].
8. [General View of Las Monjas, at Uxmal on stone by H. Warren.]
9. [Ornament over the principal doorway, Casa del Gobernados Uxmal, on stone by W. Parrott.]
10. [Archway: Casa del Gobernados, Uxmal on stone by A. Picken].
11. [Gateway of the great Teocallis, Uxmal on stone by T. S. Boys.]
12. [Ornament over the Gateway of the great Teocallis Uxmal on stone by W. Parrott.]
13. [General View of Uxmal, taken from the Archway of Las Monjas looking south on stone by A. Picken.]
14. [Portion of a Building; Las Monjas, Uxmal on stone by A. Picken.]
15. [Portion of La Casa de Las Monjas, Uxmal on stone by A. Picken.]
16. [General View of Kabah on stone by A. Picken.]
17. [Interior of the principal building at Kabah on stone by A. Picken.]
18. [Well and building at Sabachtsche on stone by H. Warren.]
19. [Gateway at Laborah on stone by J. C. Bourne.]
20. [Well at Bolonchen on stone by H. Warren]
21. [Las Monjas, Chichen-Itza on stone by G. Moore.]
22. [Teocallis, at Chichen-Itza on stone by A. Picken.]
23. [Castle, at Tuloom on stone by A. Picken.]
24. [Temple at Tuloom on stone by W. Parrott.]
25. [Colossal Head at Izamal on stone by H. Warren.]

Usually issued plain, but large-paper copies mounted on thick boards as above were coloured.

134 CATLIN (G.)

Catlin's North American Indian Portfolio. (2 line rule) Hunting Scenes and Amusements of the Rocky Mountains and Prairies of America. (2 line rule). From Drawings and Notes of the Author, made during eight years travel amongst Forty-eight of the Wildest and most remote Tribes of Savages in North America. George Catlin. Egyptian Hall, Piccadilly, London. 1844 C. & J. Adlard, Printers, Bartholomew Close, London.

Folio.

COLLATION.—Title as above (v. blank) + To the Reader 1 leaf + pp. 5–20 + Coloured lithograph plates.

Each plate marked, Catlin, delt. on Stone by McGahey, Day & Haghe, Lithrs., to the Queen. (from Catlins N.A. Indian Collection) (Plates 1 and 14, bear variation, Catlin Del. et lith. Plates 15, 17, 21 and 22, bear variation, Catlin delt. McGahey, lith.).

Catlin's North American Indian (*contd.*)

1. North American Indians.
2. Buffalo Bull Grazing.
3. Wild Horses at Play.
4. Catching the Wild Horse.
5. Buffalo Hunt, Chase.
6. Buffalo Hunt, Chase (different scene).
7. Buffalo Hunt Chase (different scene).
8. Buffalo Dance.
9. Buffalo Hunt Surround.
10. Buffalo Hunt, White Wolves attacking a Buffalo Bull.
11. Buffalo Hunt, Approaching in a Ravine.
12. Buffalo Hunt Chasing Back.
13. Buffalo Hunt under the White Wolf Skin.
14. The Snow Shoe Dance.
15. Buffalo Hunt on Snow Shoes.
16. Wounded Buffalo Bull.
17. Dying Buffalo Bull, in Snow Drift.
18. The Bear Dance.
19. Attacking the Grizzly Bear.
20. Antelope Shooting.
21. Ball Players.
22. Ball—Play Dance.
23. Ball Play.
24. Archery of the Mandans.
25. Wi-Jun-Jon an Assinneboin Chief Going to Washington. [and] Returning to His Home. (2 portraits on 1 plate.)

135 CERVANTES

The Spirit of Cervantes; or, Don Quixote abridged. Being a Selection of the Episodes and Incidents, with a Summary Sketch of the Story, of that popular Romance. (thick and thin rule) In Two Parts, with superior coloured engravings. (thin and thick rule) London: Printed for F. C. & J. Rivington, No. 62, St Paul's Church-Yard, and No. 3, Waterloo Place, Pall Mall (rule)

Octavo. 1820

COLLATION.—Title as above (v. Printed by R. Gilbert, St John's Square) + Preface 2 pp. + pp. 5–8 (Sketch of Cervantes) + Contents pp. IX–XV (p. XVI blank) + pp. 1–310 and 4 coloured plates (after Hayman).

Frontispiece. Examination of Don Quixote's Library.
p. 1. Don Quixote Knighted by the Innkeeper.
p. 105. Dispute between Sancho and the Barber.
p. 201. Sancho as Governor of Barataria.

Don Quixote 1819. See under Clark I.

Chrysal or the Adventures of a Guinea. See under Johnstone (Charles).

136 CHAMBERLAIN (Lieut.)

Views and Costumes of the City and Neighbourhood of Rio de Janeiro, Brazil, from Drawings taken by Lieutenant Chamberlain, Royal Artillery, during the years 1819 and 1820, with Descriptive Explanations. (thick and thin rule) London: Printed for Thomas M'Lean, No. 26 Haymarket, by Howlett and Brimmer, Columbian Press, No. 10 Frith Street, Soho Square.

Folio. 1822

COLLATION.—Title as above + Address 1 p. (v. blank).

1. Approach to Rio de Janeiro from the Westward Sugar Loaf, about four leagues distant. Entrance of Rio de Janeiro, Sugar Loaf, about 2 miles distant. (2 views on 1 long folding plate.)
2. The City of Rio de Janeiro. 4 pp. long folding view.
3. Tijuca Mountains. 1 p. 1 pl.
4. A Market Stall. 2 pp.
5. The Seje or Chege and Cadeira. 1 p. 1 pl.

Chamberlain's Costumes of Brazil (*contd.*)

6. A Brazilian Family. 2 pp. 1 pl.
7. Pretos de Ganho, or Black Porters. 2 pp. 1 pl.
8. Fort Santa Cruz. 2 pp. 1 pl.
9. The Rede or Net. 1 p. 1 pl.
10. Boa Viagem. 1 p. 1 pl.
11. The Slave Market. 1 p. 1 pl.
12. The Waterfall of Tijuca. 1 p. 1 pl.
13. The Lazaretto. 1 p. 1 pl.
14. Largo de Freitas. 1 p. 1 pl.
15. Braganca. 1 p. 1 pl.
16. Na Sa Da Gloria. 1 p. 1 pl.
17. Point of Calhabouca, from the Gloria. 2 pp. long folding plate.
18. Western side of the Harbour of Rio de Janeiro. 3 pp. long folding plate.
19. The Carro or Stone Cart. 1 p. 1 pl.
20. Galley Slaves. 1 p. 1 pl.
21. S.W. View of the City of Rio de Janeiro. 1 p. 1 pl.
22. Pleasuring Carts. 1 p. 1 pl.
23. Eastern side of the Harbour of Rio de Janeiro. 1 p. long folding pl.
24. Funeral of a Negro. 1 p. 1 pl.
25. Troperos or Muleteers. 1 p. 1 pl.
26. The Palace. 1 p. 1 pl.
27. Espirito Santo. 1 p. 1 pl.
28. View near Botafogo Bay. 1 p. 1 pl.
29. Sick Negroes (Sick Slaves). 1 p. 1 pl.
30. View from the Landing place at the Gloria. 1 p. 1 pl.
31. Huma Historia—Gossiping. 1 pl. 1 pl.
32. Botafogo Bay (plate I). 1 p. 1 pl.
33. Botafogo Bay (plate II). 1 p. 1 pl.
34. A Pedlar and his Slave. 1 p. 1 pl.
35. Food for Criminals (Criminals carrying Provisions). 1 p. 1 pl.
36. Largo da Gloria. 1 p. 1 pl.
List of plates (1–36).

Issued in boards with printed title slips: Rio de Janeiro (2 line rule) Views and Costumes of the City and Neighbourhood of Rio de Janeiro By Lieutenant Chamberlain R.A. Containing 36 coloured engravings. Price £6. 6s. extra boards.

A reproduction was issued in Rio de Janeiro (315 de luxe and 1000 ordinary copies) Livraria Kosmos Editoria Erich Eichner & Cia Ltda. The finest English colour plate book on Brazil. Extremely rare.

137 CLARK (I.)

Views in Scotland Drawn on the spot by I. Clark Published by Smith Elder & Co. Cornhill London

Oblong Folio. 1824[-5]

COLLATION.—Title (v. blank) + Index to the engravings 1 p. (v. blank) + 35 coloured aquatints marked Drawn on the spot by I. Clark, all with Smith Elder & Co.'s imprint and the date.

1. The Town of Dumfries. 1824.
2. The Town of Jedburgh. 1825.
3. The Town of Kirkcudbright. 1825.
4. The Town of Melrose. 1825.
5. The City of Edinburgh. 1824.
6. The Town of Linlithgow. 1824.
7. The Town of Peebles. 1825.
8. The Town of Lanark. 1825.
9. The Town of Hamilton. 1825.
10. The City of Glasgow. 1824.
11. The Town of Port-Glasgow. 1825.
12. The Town of Greenock. 1824.
13. The Town of Renfrew. 1824.
14. The Town of Paisley. 1825.
15. The Town of Ayr. 1825.
16. The Town of Dunbarton. 1824.
17. The Town of Falkirk. 1824.
18. The Town of Stirling. 1824.
19. The Town of Cupar. 1824.
20. The Town of St. Andrews. 1824.
21. The Town of Perth. 1824.
22. The Town of Inverary. 1824.
23. The Town of Rothesay. 1824.
24. The Town of Forfar. 1824.
25. The Town of Dundee. 1824.
26. The Town of Montrose. 1824.
27. The Town of Dunkeld. 1824.
28. The City of Aberdeen. 1825.
29. The Town of Peterhead. 1824.
30. The Town of Banff. 1825.
31. The Town of Elgin. 1824.
32. The Town of Inverness. 1823.
33. The Town of Cromarty. 1824.
34. The Town of Dingwall. 1824.
35. Gretna Green.

Plates Nos. 1–4, 7–9, 11, 14, 15, 20, 23, 28, 30, 33 and 35 bear the imprint, " London, Published by Smith Elder & Co. 65 Cornhill," the remainder have imprint " London Published by Smith & Elder, Fenchurch Street." One of the rarest colour plate books.

138 CLARK (J.)

The Amateurs Assistant; or a Series of Instructions in Sketching from Nature, the Application of Perspective, Tinting of Sketches, Drawing in Water-Colours, Transparent Painting, etc., etc., To accompany the subjects which form the Portable Diorama. (thick and thin rule) By John Clark, (thin and thick rule) 2 line quotation from Dr. Johnson (thick and thin rule) London: Printed for Samuel Leigh, 18 Strand.

Quarto.   1826

COLLATION.—Title as above (v. Printed by L. Harrison, 373 Strand) + Directions for displaying the views in the Portable Diorama (v. List of Plates) + Preface V–VI + pp. 1–66 + 2 leaves of Advt., describing Practical Instructions in Landscape-Painting in Water Colours, By John Clark, in 4 parts at 6 guineas, and the Portable Diorama at 3 guineas + 10 plates. The plates are numbered but without titles. Plates 7, 8 and 9 are tinted, plate 10 fully coloured.
Issued in boards with printed vignette label.

139 CLARK (J.)

The Adventures of Gil Blas de Santillane translated from the French of Le Sage, by Tobias Smollett, M.D., embellished with fifteen highly finished engravings, from drawings designed expressly for this edition. (rule) In Three Volumes (rule) Vol. I [II, III] London: (thin and thick rule) Printed from Thomas M'Lean; John Bumpus: W. H. Reid; John Brumby; and Priestly and Weale (rule)

3 vols. Octavo.   1819

COLLATION VOL. I.—Half-title "The Adventures of Gil Blas de Santillane" 1 p. (v. blank) + Title as above (v. Printed by J. Brettell Rupert Street, Haymarket, London) + Authors Declaration 2 pp. + Gil Blas to Reader 2 pp. (vii–viii) + Contents 4 pp. (ix–xii) + pp. 1–384 + 5 coloured plates.

The plates though not signed are by J. Clarke and all bear imprint, Published July 1 1819 by Thos. McLean.

1. Front. Gil Blas and the Panegyrist   Book 1 Chap. 2.
2. p. 114. Gil Blas and the Licenciate   Book 2 Chap. 1.
3. p. 138. Gil Blas and Dr. Cuchillo   Book 2 Chap. 4.
4. p. 160. Gil Blas overtaken by the Barber   Book 2 Chap. 6.
5. p. 270. Gil Bla's interview with Aurora   Book 4 Chap. 2.

VOL. II.—Half-title as before + Title as before + Contents 4 pp. (v–viii) + pp. 1–378 + 5 coloured plates.

6. p. 12. Gil Blas and Don Gonzales   Book 4 Chap. 7.
7. p. 40. Don Alphonso and Seraphina   Book 4 Chap. 10.
8. p. 67. Don Raphael and Farruckhnaz   Book 5 Chap. 1.
9. p. 191. Gil Blas and Sephora   Book 7 Chap. 1.
10. p. 219. Gil Blas and the Archbishop   Book 7 Chap. 4.

VOL. III.—Half-title as before + Title as before + Contents 7 pp. (v–xi) + pp. 1–392 + 5 coloured plates.

11. p. 60. Gil Blas in the Tower of Sigovia   Book 9 Chap. 5.
12. p. 105. Young Scipio as a Mendicant   Book 9 Chap. 10.
13. p. 284. Gil Blas and Dr. Sangrado   Book 11 Chap. 7.
14. p. 285. Gil Blas and Fabricio   Book 11 Chap. 7.
15. p. 325. Gil Blas and Lucretia   Book 12 Chap. 1.

140 CLARK (J.)

Don Quixote de la Mancha. Translated from the original Spanish of Miguel de Cervantes Saavedra, by Charles Jarvis, Esq. embellished with twenty-four highly finished engravings, from drawings designed expressly for this edition (rule) in four volumes (rule) Vol. I [II, III, IV] London: (thin and thick rule) Printed for T. M'Lean, Bookseller and Publisher (rule)

4 vols. Octavo.   1819

COLLATION VOL. I.—Half-title "Don Quixote de la Mancha" (v. blank) + Title as above (v. Printed by J. Brettell, Rupert Street, Haymarket, London) + Translator's Preface pp. v–xxxviii + Supplement to Translator's Preface pp. xxxix–lix (lx blank) + Life of Cervantes pp. lxi–lxix (p. lxx blank) + Author's Preface pp. lxxi–lxxxiii (p. lxxxiv blank) + Contents pp. lxxxv–lxxxviii + pp. 1–376 + 7 coloured plates.

Twenty-four coloured aquatint plates (in the 4 vols.) by J. Clark though not signed by him, each bearing imprint, Published by Thos. McLean Feby., 1819.

1. Frontispiece. Don Quixote dubbed a Knight.
2. p. 84. Don Quixote attacking the Biscainer.
3. p. 154. Don Quixote and Sancho after the meeting with the Yanguesians.
4. p. 200. Don Quixote attacking the flock of sheep.
5. p. 244. Don Quixote attacking the barber.
6. p. 275. Don Quixote stoned by the Gally Slaves.
7. p. 334. Don Quixote's pranks in the sable mountain.

VOL. II.—Half-title as before + Title as before + Contents pp. v–vii (p. viii blank) + pp. 1–403 + 5 coloured plates.

8. Frontispiece. Dispute between Sancho and the Barber.
9. p. 33. Dorothea at the feet of Don Quixote.
10. p. 54. Don Quixote enraged at Sancho's improper language before the princess.
11. p. 148. Don Quixote attacking the Wine-Skins.
12. p. 387. Don Quixote's quarrel with the goat herd.

VOL. III.—Half-title as before + Title as before + Preface to the Reader pp. v–xii + Contents pp. xiii–xvi + pp. 1–370 + 6 coloured plates.

13. Frontispiece Don Quixote attacking the puppets.
14. p. 19. Sancho's visit to Don Quixote opposed.
15. p. 101. Don Quixote mistaking the Peasant Girl for Dulcinea.
16. p. 179. Don Quixote's adventure with the lion.
17. p. 217. Don Quixote and Sancho at the marriage of Camacho.
18. p. 369. Sancho appealing to the Duchess.

VOL. IV.—Half-title as before + Title as before + Contents pp. v–viii + pp. 1–440 + 6 coloured plates.

19. Frontispiece Don Quixote on the wooden Horse.
20. p. 130. Don Quixote instructing Sancho.
21. p. 150. Don Quixote visited by the Old Duenna.
22. p. 181. Teresa Panza receiving the message from the duchess.
23. p. 272. Don Quixote meeting the shepherdesses.
24. p. 351. Don Quixote subdued by the Knight of the White Crescent.

Issued in boards with printed paper labels "Don Quixote" by Jarvis 24 Plates in Four Volumes. Price £2 8s. Harvey Frost's copy measures $8\frac{7}{8} \times 5\frac{1}{2}$ inches.

141 CLARK (J.)

Hudibras, a Poem, by Samuel Butler, with Notes, selected from Grey and other authors: to which are prefixed, A Life of the Author, and a Preliminary Discourse on the Civil War &c. (rule) In Two Volumes (rule) A New Edition, embellished with Engravings (thick and thin rule) Vol. I [II] (thin and thick rule) London: Printed by W. Lewis, 21 Finch-Lane for Thomas M'Lean, Bookseller and Publisher, and may be had of all Booksellers (rule)

2 vols.   Octavo.   1819

COLLATION VOL. I.—Title as above (v. blank) + Advertisement pp. iii–iv + Life of Butler pp. v–xvii + Preliminary Discourses xix–lxxxiv + 1 blank leaf (e4) + pp. 1–444 (including index) + 7 coloured plates.

All plates marked, J. Clark del et sc.   London Published by T. Mclean 1819.

1. Frontispiece. Hudibras Part 2 Canto 1 Line 115 [see also plate 6].
2. p.   98. Hudibras Part 1 Canto 2 Line 82.
3. p. 127. Hudibras Part 1 Canto 2 Line 775.
4. p. 134. Hudibras Part 1 Canto 2 Line 945.
5. p. 142. Hudibras Part 1 Canto 2 Line 1124.
6. p. 292. Hudibras Part 2 Canto 1 Line 115.
7. p. 363. Hudibras Part 2 Canto 2 Line 40.

VOL. II.—Title as before + pp. 3–494 (including index) + 5 coloured plates.

8. Frontispiece. Hudibras Part 2 Canto 3 Line 495.
9. p.   47. Hudibras Part 2 Canto 3 Line 1056.
10. p. 148. Hudibras Part 3 Canto 1 Line 160.
11. p. 207. Hudibras Part 3 Canto 1 Line 1576.
12. p. 413. Hudibras Part 3 Canto 3 Line 675.

Issued in boards with printed label at £1 11s. 6d.   Published the same year as Don Quixote and Gil Blas it is frequently sold with them as a set.

142   *Reissued 1822, with variation in the title page and the advertisement.   The plates are inferior. Collation as above.*

143 CLARK (J. H.)

A Practical Essay on the Art Of Colouring and Painting Landscapes in Water Colours. Accompanied With Ten Engravings, (swelled rule) By John Heaviside Clark, (swelled rule) 1807. London, Printed for and sold by Edward Orme, Bond Street, the Corner of Brook Street, where also are sold, Books of Instructions in every Branch of Drawing, Colours, Drawing Books, and Every Requisite Used in Drawing. Printed by J. Hayes, Dartmouth Street, Westminster.

Folio.   1807

COLLATION.—Title as above (v. blank) + List of Plates 1 p. (v. blank) + Introduction pp. 1–3 + Technical Terms and Elementary Instructions pp. 4–7 (p. 8 blank) + Essay on the Art of Colouring etc. pp. 9–25 (26 blank) + 10 plates.

1. p. 15. [Pencils, diagrams, tints etc.]   J. Clark. sculpt.   Published and sold Jan. 1st. 1807 by Edward Orme 59, Bond Street (coloured).
2. p. 17. Outline to Landscape (uncoloured).

Clark's Practical Essay (*contd.*)

3. p. 17. First Tints in Preparation (sepia).
4. p. 18. Preparation. J. Clark, delt. J. Hamble, sculpt. (sepia). Published by Edward Orme, 59, Bond Street. Sept. 1st, 1806.
5. p. 19. Coloured Landscape. J. Clark, delt. J. Hamble, sculpt. (sepia). Published by Edward Orme, 59, Bond Street. Sept. 1st, 1806.
6. p. 20. Preparation For Sunset (sepia).
7. p. 20. Sunset Subject (coloured).
8. p. 21. Moonlight Subject (coloured).
9. p. 22. Snow Subject (coloured).
10. p. 23. Fire Subject (coloured).

144 CLARK (J. H.)

A Practical Essay on the Art of Colouring and Painting Landscapes in Water Colours, with ten illustrative engravings, by John Heaviside Clark (swelled rule) Second Edition (swelled rule) 1812 London Printed for and sold by Edward Orme, Bond Street, the corner of Brook Street, where are also sold, Books of Instruction in every branch of Drawing Colours, Drawing books, and every Requisite used in Drawing (rule) Printed by J. Hayes, Dartmouth-Street, Westminster.

Quarto.   [1811]

COLLATION.—Title as above (v. blank) + List of Plates 1 p. (v. blank) ⊦ Intro. pp. 1–4 + Technical Terms pp. 5–28 + 2 pp. Advts. + 10 plates.

1. (p. 10). [Pencil Diagrams Tints &c.] J. Clark sculpt. Published & Sold Jany. 1 1807 by Edward Orme 59 Bond Street.
2. (p. 18). Outline to Landscape.
3. (p. 18). First Tints in Preparation.
4. (p. 19). Preparation J. Clark del. J. Humble sculpt. Sept. 1 1806.
5. (p. 20). Coloured Subject, ditto.
6. (p. 21). Sunrise.
7. (p. 22). Sunset Pubd. Sept. 1811 by Edward Orme Bond St. London.
8. (p. 23). Moonlight ditto.
9. (p. 24). Snow J. Clark del. J. Humble sculpt. Sept. 1 1806.
10. (p. 25). Fire Sept. 1811.

145 CLARK (J. H.)

A Practical Illustration of Gilpin's Day, representing the various Effects on Landscape Scenery from Morning till Night, in Thirty Designs from Nature; by the Rev. Wm. Gilpin, A.M. Prebendary of Salisbury, and Vicar of Boldre, near Lymington. With Instructions in, and explanation of, the Improved Method of Colouring, and Painting in Water Colours; by John Heaviside Clark, Author of an Essay on Colouring, and Painting in Water Colours (rule) [5 line quotation from Spencer] (rule) London: Published by Edward Orme, Printseller to His Majesty, Engraver and Publisher, Bond Street, Corner of Brook Street, 1811 Printed by J. Hayes, Dartmouth Street, Westminster.

Quarto.   1811

COLLATION.—Title as above (v. blank) + Dedication 1 p. (v. blank) + Introduction i–viii + sub-title 1 p. (v. Description of plate 1) + 30 coloured plates each plate with 1 page of text except plate 10 which has 2 pp. of text.

Clark's Gilpin's Day (*contd.*)

1. Dawn of Day.	11. Mid Day.	21. Ruddy Sunset.
2. Early Morn.	12. Thunder Storm.	22. Freaky Sunset.
3. Dull Morning.	13. Lightening.	23. Evening Closing In.
4. Sun Rise.	14. Rain.	24. Silent Lightening.
5. Turbid Sunrise.	15. Distant Rainbow.	25. Twilight.
6. Bright Sunrise.	16. Clearing after Rain.	26. Crescent.
7. Cool Morning.	17. Sun set.	27. Full Moon.
8. Cloudy Morning.	18. Sun set preceding a storm.	28. Cloudy Moonlight.
9. Hazy Morn.	19. Calm Sunset.	29. Clear Moonlight.
10. Rainbow.	20. Sultry Sunset.	30. Waning Moon.

146 *Reissued in 1824 with the same plates but the Title altered to read "by the late Rev. Wm Gilpin" and the imprint changed to London Published for the Proprietors by Priestley and Weale No 5 High Street, Bloomsbury; and C. Knight, near the Water Colour Painters Exhibition Rooms, Pall Mall East; and to be had of most Book and Print Sellers, and Dealers in Drawing Materials in the United Kingdom 1824.*

147 CLARK (W.)

Ten Views in the Island of Antigua in which are represented the process of sugar making and the employment of the Negroes, in the Field, Boiling House, and Distillery (rule), from drawings made by William Clark, during a residence of three years in the West Indies, upon the estates of Admiral Tallemach, (rule) London. Published by Thomas Clay, Ludgate-Hill (short rule)

Oblong Folio. 1823

COLLATION.—Title as above (v. blank) and 10 fine aquatint plates each with 1 leaf of text.

1. The Court-House St John's Antigua.
2. Holeing a Cane-Piece on Weatherell's Estate Antigua.
3. Planting the Sugar-Cane on Bodkins Estate Antigua.
4. Cutting the Sugar Cane on Delap's Estate Antigua.
5. A Mill Yard on Gamble's Estate Antigua.
6. Interior of a Boiling House on Delap's Estate Antigua.
7. Exterior of a boiling House on Weatherell's Estate Antigua.
8. Exterior of a Distillery, on Weatherells Estate Antigua.
9. Interior of a Distillery on Delap's Estate Antigua.
10. Shipping Sugar Willoughby Bay Antigua.

Issued in buff paper wrapper, with printed title within Etruscan border. Price £2 2s.

148 [CLOWES (G.)]

A Picturesque Tour by the New Road from Chiavenna over the Splugen, and along the Rhine, to Coira, in the Grisons (rule) (quote from Virgil) (rule) London: Printed for William Cole, 10, Newgate Street (rule)

Quarto. 1826

COLLATION.—Half-title "A Picturesque Tour, etc. etc." (v. Printed by G. H. Davidson, Ireland Yard, Doctors' Commons.) + Title as above (v. blank) + Introduction pp. 5–11 (p. 12

Clowes's Chiavenna (*contd.*)

blank) + Text pp. 13–35 (i.e. 1 leaf of text to each plate, imprint on p. 36) + 13 coloured lithographs.

Each plate marked, G.C. Esq. delt. F. Calvert lithog. London Pub. by W. Cole, 10 Newgate Street, Printed by R. Martin.

1. Front. Embouchure of the Adda into the Lake of Como.
2. p. 13. Chiavenna.
3. p. 15. Cascade below St. Giacomo.
4. p. 17. Church of St. Guglielmo—and part of the Splugen Mountain.
5. p. 19. Madonna di Galivaggio.
6. p. 21. Campo Dolcino.
7. p. 23. Cascade of Pianezza and first Gallery.
8. p. 25. Ascent from Isola with a view of the Second & Wooden Galleries.
9. p. 27. Splugen Village.
10. p. 29. Via Mala.
11. p. 31. Tussis.
12. p. 33. Castle of Ortestein—Valley of the Rhine.
13. p. 35. Coira.

Issued in boards at One Guinea, later increased to two. Label Title " A Picturesque Tour by the New Road from Chiavenna over the Splugen. With Thirteen Views taken on the Spot by G. C. Esq. and lithographed by F. Calvert."

149 COLEBROOK (R. H.)

"Twelve Views of Places in The Kingdom of Mysore, The Country of Tippoo Sultan."

1. "East View of Bangalore."
2. "The Lake of Mooty Tallaow, near Seringapatam."
3. "Prospect of the Country near Mooty Tallaow."
4. "Pagodas at Maugry with a distant view of Sewandroog."
5. "N.W. View of Nandydroog."
6. "North View of Sewandroog shewing the attack in Decr. 1791.
7. "South View of Sewandroog."
8. "S.W. View of Ootra-Durgum."
9. "West View of Rangherry."
10. "The Mausoleum of Hyder Aly Khan at Laulbaug."
11. "East View of Seringapatam."
12. "N.W. View of Seringapatam."

150 [COMBE (W.)]

A History of Madeira. With a Series of Twenty-seven coloured Engravings illustrative of the Costumes, Manners and Occupations of the Inhabitants of that island (coloured vignette) London: Published by R. Ackermann 101 Strand, and sold by all the Booksellers in the United Kingdom

Imperial Octavo.   1821

COLLATION.—Title as above (v. blank) + Preface 2 ll. + pp. 1–118 + Contents 1 leaf (v. London Printed by William Clowes Northumberland Court) + 27 coloured plates.

1. Front. A Prior of the Order of St Francis and a Lay Brother.
2. p. 34. Rural Toil.
3. p. 65. Inside a Cottage.

Combe's History of Madeira (*contd.*)

4. p. 69. Peasants going to Market.
5. p. 71. Manner of Cultivating the Ground.
6. p. 73. A Farmer & his daughter going to town.
7. p. 75. [Female Peasants grinding corn] Rural Occupation.
8. p. 77. Peasants in usual Costume.
9. p. 79. Costume peculiar to some of the Western Inhabitants of the Island.
10. p. 81. Fishermen.
11. p. 83. Country Musicians.
12. p. 87. Manner of drawing Pipes &c. by means of the Sledge.
13. p. 89. An Accident upon the Road.
14. p. 93. A Franciscan Friar collecting donations for his convent.
15. p. 95. A Franciscan Father on a Journey.
16. p. 97. Priests in different attire.
17. *ibd.* Manner of bringing wine to town when clear.
18. p. 99. Lay Sisters of Order of the Lady of Mount Carmel.
19. p. 101. A Nun and her Attendant.
20. p. 103. A Lady & her Servant going to Church.
21. p. 105. Usual mode of travelling in Hammocks.
22. p. 107. Manner of visiting among the Ladies at Funchal.
23. p. 109. Members of the Senate.
24. p. 111. Official dress of the members of the Camera or Senate on the Death of the King and Accession of his Successor.
25. p. 113. An Officer and Private of the Garrison of Funchal.
26. p. 115. Drilling.
27. p. 117. West View of Loo Fort.

Published at 2 guineas in half roan, and later in cloth.

151 [COMBE (W.)]

The Life of Napoleon, A Hudibrastic Poem in Fifteen Cantos by Doctor Syntax, embellished with Thirty Engravings by G. Cruikshank (rule) London: Printed for T. Tegg, 111 Cheapside, Wm. Allason, 31 New Bond Street & J. Dick, Edinburgh

Octavo. 1815

COLLATION.—Titles as above within figured border (v. blank) + pp. 1–260 [p. 83 misprinted 88, p. 109 misprinted 107, p. 121 misprinted 211, p. 187 misprinted 188 (Cohen cites another variation where p. 113 is misprinted 213) and yet another is 253 misprinted 453] with 30 coloured plates including title [There is no printed title or other preliminary matter].

All the plates bear the imprint, London Published by Thomas Tegg No. 111 Cheapside [and dated from Nov. 10, 1814 to Jan. 23 1815].

1. Engraved Title.
2. p. 6. Napoleon dreaming in his cell at the military college.
3. p. 9. Napoleon blowing up his comrades   Nov. 10th 1814.
4. p. 23. Napoleon working the gun at Toulon   Nov. 17 1814.
5. p. 26. Massacre at Toulon   Nov. 17th 1814.
6. p. 37. Marriage to Josephine   Novr. 28th 1814.
7. p. 44. Bridge of Lodi   Nov. 28 1814.
8. p. 58. Seizing the Italian Relics   Dec. 1 1814.
9. p. 62. The Blindfolded Austrian Officer   Dec. 1 1814.
10. p. 77. Massacre in Egypt   Dec. 2 1814.
11. p. 81. Burning the Mosques   Dec. 4 1814.
12. p. 91. Shooting the Prisoners in Egypt   Nov. 29 1814.
13. p. 92. Poisoning the Sick at Jaffa   Nov. 29 1814.

Combe's Life of Napoleon (*contd.*)

14. p. 94. Seige (sic.) of Acre   Dec. 4 1814.
15. p. 96. Flight from Egypt.   Dec. 5 1814.
16. p. 98. Council of Five Hundred   Dec. 13 1814.
17. p. 109. Crossing the Alps   Dec. 13 1814.
18. p. 111. Murder of Dessaix   Dec. 7 1814.
19. p. 135. Murder of Duke D'Enghien   Dec. 7th 1814.
20. p. 142. Crowning himself Emperor of France   Dec. 13, 1814.
21. p. 177. Napoleon & Alexander on the Raft   Dec. 13 1814.
22. p. 208. First Interview with Marie Louisa   Dec. 14 1814.
23. p. 214. Nursing the King of Rome   Dec. 14 1814.
24. p. 227. Burning of Moscow   Jan. 9 1815.
25. p. 228. Retreat from Moscow   Jan. 23 1815.
26. p. 233. Blowing up the Bridge at Liepsic (sic.)   Jan. 6 1815.
27. p. 234. Pursued by Cossacks   Jan. 9 1815.
28. p. 239. The Red Man   Jan. 6 1815.
29. p. 253. Signing his Abdication   Jan. 7 1815.
30. p. 259. Landing in Elba   Jan. 7 1815.

Published in boards with printed label.

152 *Reissued 1817 with inferior impressions of the plates.*

153 [COMBE (W.)]

The Wars of Wellington, a Narrative Poem; in fifteen Cantos. Embellished with Thirty Engravings, coloured from the original paintings, by Heath. (thick and thin rule) By Dr. Syntax. (thin and thick rule) (9 lines of verse) (thick and thin rule) London: Printed by C. Whittingham, Goswell Street, for the Author; and sold by all booksellers in the United Kingdom (short rule)

Quarto.   1819

COLLATION.—Half-title "The Wars of Wellington" (v. blank) + Title as above (v. blank) + Introduction pp. v–vi + Arrangement of plates 1 p. (v. blank) + Text pp. 1–175 (p. 176 blank) + 30 coloured aquatint plates.

Each plate marked, Drawn & Etched by W. Heath.   Aquatinted by J. C. Stadler.   London Published by T. Tegg, 111 Cheapside April 1 1818.

1. p. 5. Battle of Mallavelly.
2. p. 11. Storming of Seringapatam   May 4th 1799.
3. p. 20. Battle of Assye.   Sept 23 1803.
4. p. 21. Battle of Assye.   Septr 23 1802 (sic)   [Rout of the Enemy].
5. p. 39. Battle of Roleia.   Augt. 17th 1812.
6. p. 41. Battle of Vimeira.
7. p. 64. Battle of Oporto.
8. p. 74. Battle of Talavera.
9. p. 89. Battle of Bussaca.
10. p. 100. Battle of Barossa.
11. p. 113. Taking of Ciudad Rodrigo.   Jany 19th 1812.
12. p. 116. Badajos.
13. p. 118. Storming of the Bishops Palace at Badajos.
14. p. 121. Lord Wellington entering Salamanca.
15. p. 121. Battle of Salamanca,   July 22nd 1811.
16. p. 132. Battle of Vittoria,   June 21 1813.
17. p. 140. Storming of St. Sebastian.   Augt 31 1811 (sic).
18. p. 143. Halting in the Pyrenees   July 26, 27, 28th 1813.

Combe's Wars of Wellington (*contd.*)

19. p. 143. Battle of the Pyrenees.
20. p. 145. Battle near the Village Sorausen.
21. p. 146. Battle of the Pyrenees   July 27, 1813   [rout of the French].
22. p. 147. Crossing the Bidassoa   Octr 7th 1813.
23. p. 148. Reconnoitering, after crossing the Bidassoa.
24. p. 154. Battle of Toulouse.
25. p. 157. The Duke of Wellington entering the city of Thoulouse   Octr 1813.
26. p. 163. Signing the Treaty of Peace at Vienna.
27. p. 165. Intelligence of the Battle of Ligny.
28. p. 168. Battle of Waterloo,   June 18th 1815.
29. p. 168. Battle of Waterloo.
30. p. 172. Meeting of Wellington & Blucher, at La Belle Alliance.

154   *Reissued in 1821 with fresh title and 6 plates only.*

COMBE (W.)   *See also under Ackermann's "Histories of Westminster Abbey," "Public Schools," "Cambridge," "Oxford" and "Microcosm of London," and Boydell's "Thames." Also under Rowlandson's "Tours of Dr. Syntax" (and Syntax imitations), "Dance of Death," and "Life, and History of Johnny Quae Genus."*

Commercial Tourist 1822.   See under (Hempel (C. W.).

Comic History of England, ditto Rome.   See under Leech (J.).

155 COMPTON (Thomas)

The Northern Cambrian Mountains, or a Tour through North Wales, describing the Scenery and General Characters of that Romantic Country, and embellished with a series of highly finished coloured Views engraved from original drawings by Thomas Compton, of the Royal Military Academy, Woolwich (thick and thin rule) London: Printed for the Author, by C. Corrall, Charing Cross

Oblong Quarto.   1817

COLLATION.—Title as above (v. blank) + Dedication to the Marquis of Angelsey 1 p. (v. blank) + Preface 2 pp. + 30 coloured plates each with 1 leaf of text.

POINTS.—In the first issue the plates are variously dated from 1 June 1815 to Decr. 31, 1816, and all bear words: Published by T. Compton R.M.A. Woolwich. For description of plates, see *infra*. Copies exist in proof state with artist's and engraver's names given but without the Legends.

COLLATION OF THE PARTS.—Issued in 10 parts, brown paper wrappers each upper cover bearing the Printed title as follows: "No. 1 [&c.] (Price Ten Shillings and Sixpence) of the Scenery of the Northern Cambrian Mountains: The Engravings by John Baily (for Parts 1 and 2, by D. Havell for parts 3–10) from Original Drawings By Thomas Compton, of the Royal Military Academy, Woolwich (thin and thick rule) London: Published by the Proprietors, and sold by Macdonald, Poet's Gallery, 39, Fleet Street, where Subscribers' Names are received: and also by Colnaghi and Co. Cockspur Street; Clay, Ludgate Hill; Orme, New Bond Street; Molteno, 29, Pall Mall; Jenkins, 48, Strand; Lambe, 96 Gracechurch Street: and by Mr. Compton, R. M. Academy, Woolwich.   June 1, 1815 [Part 2 November 30, 1815, Parts 3–10 undated] [the preceding with printed border, below] C. Corrall, Printer, Charing Cross."   The back cover of Part I bears an advertisement, the remaining back covers are blank.   After Part I Colnaghi's and Jenkin's names are omitted from imprint.

Compton's Cambrian Mountains (*contd.*)

The 10 parts each consist of 3 plates, each plate with a leaf of text, each plate bearing in left-hand corner, Drawn by T. Compton, and in the right-hand corner the engravers name (with the exception of Part I where neither artist nor engraver's name is Printed). All bear in centre Pub. [or Published] [date] by T. Compton R.M.A. [or Academy] Woolwich.

Part 1. No. 7. Rhaiadyr Du 1 June 1815.
No. 13. Cwm Maentwrog June 1 1815.
No. 27. Snowdon from Capel Curig 1 June, 1815.
Part 2. No. 1. Pistyll Rhaiadyr Engraved by I. Baily Sepr. 15, 1815.
No. 2. Bala Lake Engraved by I. Baily Sepr. 15, 1815.
No. 3. Bwlch y Groes Engraved by I. Baily Sep. 15, 1815.
Part 3. Slip advertisement stating proprietor's dissatisfaction with their engraver with assurance that from part 4 onwards the plates will be engraved by D. Havell.
No. 4. Pont Fallwyd Engraved by Daniel Havell Feby. 10th, 1816.
No. 5. Cader Idris Engraved by T. Cartwright Jan. 1816.
No. 6. Pen y Cader Engraved by Daniel Havell Feby. 10th 1816.
Part 4. No. 8. Llyn y Cau on Cader Idris Engraved by Daniel Havell April 15th 1816.
No. 9. Abermaw Engraved by Daniel Havell April 15th 1816.
No. 10. Harlech Castle Engraved by Daniel Havell April 15th 1816.
Part 5. No. 11. Rhaiadyr y Mawddach Engraved by Dl. Havell June 1 1816.
No. 12. Pistyll y Cain Engraved by Dl. Havell June 1 1816.
No. 14. Pont Aberglasllyn Engraved by D. Havell June 1 1816.
Part 6. Slip note correcting plates 11 and 12 in preceding part which have been misnumbered and should be transposed.
No. 15. Aberglasllyn Engraved by D. Havell July 1 1816.
No. 17. South View from the Summit of Snowdon. Engraved by D. Havell July 1 1816.
No. 16. Beddgelert Engraved by D. Havell July 1 1816.
Part 7. No. 18. Llyn Gwynant Engraved by D. Havell Septr. 1 1816.
No. 19. Nant Beris Engraved by D. Havell Septr. 1 1816.
No. 20. Snowdon from Nant Lle Engraved by D. Havell Septr. 1 1816.
Part 8. No. 21. Llanberis Lake Engraved by D. Havell Octr. 1 1816.
No. 22. Rhaiadyr Benglog Engraved by D. Havell Octr. 1 1816.
No. 23. Bangor Engraved by D. Havell Octr. 1 1816.
Part 9. No. 24. Caernarvon Engraved by D. Havell Novr. 1 1816.
No. 25. Beaumaris Bay Engraved by D. Havell Novr. 1 1816.
No. 26. Nant Francon Engraved by D. Havell Novr. 1 1816.
Part 10. No. 28. Aberconway Engraved by D. Havell Decr. 1 1816.
No. 29. The Llugwy at Pont Engraved by D. Havell Dec. 31, 1816.
No. 30. The Vale of Llangollen Engraved by D. Havell Decr. 31 1816.

+ Title + Dedication + Preface + small slip Directions to Binder.
Rare. Not cited by Prideaux or Hardie.

156 COMPTON (Thomas)

Northern Cambrian Mountains.

Oblong Quarto. [Second Issue.] 1817[-18]

COLLATION.—Title 1 lf. + Dedication 1 lf. + Preface 1 leaf exactly as in first issue + 30 coloured plates, each plate marked, Drawn by T. Compton and each with leaf of text.

1. Pystyll Rhaiadyr. Engraved by I. Baily.
2. Bala Lake Engraved by I. Baily.
3. Bwlch-y-Groes Engraved by I. Baily.
4. Pont Fallwyd Engraved by Daniel Havell.
5. Cader Idris Engraved by T. Cartwright.
6. Pen y Cader Engraved by Daniel Havell.
7. Rhaiadyr Du (no artist or engraver).
8. Llyn y Cau on Cader Idris Engraved by Daniel Havell.
9. Abermaw Engraved by Daniel Havell.

Compton's Northern Cambrian Mountains (*contd.*)

10. Harlech Castle   Engraved by Daniel Havell.
11. Rhaiadyr y Mawddach   Engraved by Dl. Havell.
12. Pistyll y Cain   Engraved by Dl. Havell.
13. Cwm Maentwrog (no artist or engraver).
14. Pont Aberglasllyn   Engraved by D. Havell.
15. Aberglasllyn   Engraved by D. Havell.
16. Beddgelert   Engraved by D. Havell.
17. South View from Summit of Snowdon   Engraved by D. Havell.
18. Lyn Gwynant   Engraved by D. Havell.
19. Nant Beris   Engraved by D. Havell.
20. Snowdon from Nant Lle   Engraved by D. Havell.
21. Llanberis Lake   Engraved by D. Havell.
22. Rhaiadyr Benglog   Engraved by D. Havell
23. Bangor   Engraved by D. Havell.
24. Caernarvon   Engraved by D. Havell.
25. Beaumaris Bay   Engraved by D. Havell.
26. Nant Francon   Engraved by D. Havell.
27. Snowdon from Capel Curig.
28. Aberconway   Engraved by D. Havell.
29. The Llugwy at Pont y Pair   Engraved by D. Havell.
30. Llangollen   Engraved by D. Havell.

POINTS.—*The above plates are the same as in the first issue with the exception of the imprint in centre which is altered to Pubd. March 2, 1818 by T. Clay 18 Ludgate Hill London.*

It was again reissued in 1820 with a new title as follows:

157 The Northern Cambrian Mountains; or A Tour through North Wales: describing the Scenery and General Characters of that Romantic Country. (thick and thin rule) Embellished with a series of highly finished coloured views, engraved from original drawings, by Messrs Turner R.A.; Compton; Robson; Gaudy, A.R.A.; Nicholson; Girtin; De Wint; Fielding; and Prout; (thick and thin rule) London: Printed for Thomas Clay, No 18, Ludgate Hill; By John Hill, Water Lane, Blackfriars (rule) 1820

COLLATION.—Title as above (v. blank) + Preface 1 lf. + 38 unnumbered leaves of Text and extra plates.   The new plates being as follows:

Conwy Castle.   Drawn by I. Gandy, A.R.A.   Engraved by T. Fielding.   March 1 1820.
Rhaiadyr Y Wennol.   Drawn by F. Nicholson.   Engraved by T. Fielding.   May 1 1820.
Bala Lake.   Drawn by G. F. Robson.   Engraved by T. Fielding.   March 1 1820.
Llangollen Vale.   Drawn by G. F. Robson.   Engraved by T. Fielding.   Mar. 1 1820.
Chirk Castle.   Painted by P. de Wint, from a sketch by T. Girtin.   Engraved by T. Fielding.   May 1 1820.
Denbigh Castle.   Drawn by F. Nicholson.   Engraved by T. Fielding.   May 1 1820.
St. Asaph.   Drawn by C. V. Fielding.   Engraved by T. Fielding.   May 1 1820.
Flint Castle.   Drawn by S. Prout, from a Sketch by Girtin.   Engraved by T. H. Fielding.   July 1 1820.
View near Plynlimmon.   Montgomeryshire.   Drawn by J. M. W. Turner, R.A.   Engraved by T. H. Fielding.   July 1 1820.

158 COPLOW (Billesdon)

Indispensable Accomplishments. (four line verse, "Ev'ry species of ground every Horse does not suit" & etc.) (8½ lines of text signed Billesdon Coplow) Published June 24th, 1811 by H. Humphrey, No. 27 St James's Street. 1811

COLLATION.—Title as above (v. blank) + 6 plates.   Each plate bearing " R. Frankland invt., et fecit, Published June 24th 1811 by H. Humphrey, No. 27 St James's Street."

1. Going along a slapping pace.
2. Topping a flight of Rails, and coming well into the Next Field.
3. Charging an Oxfence.
4. Going in and out clever.
5. Facing a Brook.
6. Swishing at a Rasper.

Issued in wrappers.   Billesdon Coplow pseud. for R. Frankland.

159 COUTS (Joseph)

A Practical Guide for the Tailor's Cutting-Room being a Treatise on Measuring and Cutting clothing in all styles, and for every period of life from childhood to old age By Joseph Couts (rule) with numerous diagrams and pictorial illustrations (rule) Blackie and Son: Queen Street Glasgow; South College Street, Edinburgh; and Warwick Square, London.

Quarto.

COLLATION.—Title as above (v. blank) + Preface 1 lf. + Contents 3 pp. (v–vii) + List of Plates (p. viii) + 27 plates + Introduction pp. 1–4 + Text pp. 5–166 + 18 plates of diagrams (1 repeated starred).   Plates 15–27 of first series are coloured, numbered in top right-hand corner and all bear imprint, Blackie & Son Glasgow, Edinburgh, & London.

15. The Morning Ride (Ladies).
16. One stroke for Life & Victory (Dragoon & Rifleman).
17. The Fancy Dress Ball (Highland Dresses Fancy & Regimental).
18. Page and Tiger.
19. A Friendly Pinch (Footmans Dresses).
20. Important Intelligence (Footmans Dresses).
21. An Arrival (Footmans Dresses).
22. In Attendance (Footman Full dress & Greatcoat).
23. Grooms in Dress & Undress.
24. The Morning of Ascot (Grooms Full Dress).
25. Leaving the Stables (Groom & Coachman).
26. A Departure from Town (Groom & Coachman).
27. Old Whip & Young Spur (Postillion & Coachman in Box coat).

160 COWEN (W.)

Six Views of Woodsome Hall; embellished with Costume Figures of the Olden Time. Drawn and Engraved by W. Cowen.   Dedicated by Permission to the Earl of Dartmouth. (3 line rule) London: Published by W. Cowen, Gibraltar Cottage, Thistle Grove, Old Brompton

Oblong Folio.   **1851**

COLLATION.—Title as above (v. blank) + 6 coloured plates.

1. Woodsome Hall.	4. Front View of Woodsome Hall.
2. The Hall.	5. The Hall.
3. Court Yard.	6. Woodsome Hall.

With imprint, "Printed by Hullmandell & Walton."

161 [COX (David)]

A Series of Progressive Lessons intended to elucidate the Art of Painting in Water Colours: with introductory illustrations on perspective and drawing with pencil (rule) London: Ackermann and Co. 96, Strand

Oblong Quarto.   **1841**

COLLATION.—Title as above (v. blank) + Advt. Introductory Remarks and Sketching pp. 1–24 + 4 further leaves of unpaged text.

Cox's Progressive Lessons (*contd.*)

Plates   1. Figs. 1–4 Perspectives.
    ,,   2. Figs. 5–7 Perspectives.
    ,,   3. Figs. 8–9 Perspectives.
    ,,   [4.] [Cottage Roofs etc.] D. Cox Junr del.   A. Ducote Lithogy 70 St. Martins London.
    ,,   [5.] [Farmhouse and Bridge] ditto.
    ,,   [6.] Beaucliff Abbey. D. Cox Junr delt.
    ,,   [7.] ditto in sepia.
    ,,   [8.] Battle Abbey Sussex.
    ,,   [9, 10 and 11]. the same plate in different stages of colour.
    ,,   [12]. [Goodrich Castle, Herefordshire] (coloured aquatint).
    ,,   [13]. [Moel Shabboa, North Wales].
    ,,   [14]. [Lake Tal y Llyn, North Wales] (coloured aquatint).
    ,,   [15]. [Dutch Boats on the Scheldt, off Antwerp] (coloured aquatint).
    ,,   [16]. [Water Mill near Dolbenmaen, North Wales] (coloured aquatint).
    ,,   [17]. [Scene near Balquidder, North Britain] (coloured aquatint).
    ,,   [18] [Bolton Abbey, Yorkshire] (coloured aquatint).

162 COX (David)

Six Views of the City of Bath: from Drawings made by David Cox Price £1 10s. in colours (thick and thin rule) London: Published by S. & J. Fuller, Temple of Fancy, 34, Rathbone Place; and to be had of Mr. Salmoni, Mr. Fasana, Mr. Upham, and Mr. Gibbons, Bath: Mr. Rees, Bristol; Mr. Bettison, Cheltenham; and by the Booksellers in Town and Country (thick and thin rule)

Oblong Folio.   1820

COLLATION.—Printed label on cover as above and a series of 6 plates, each marked, D. Cox Del. Smart & Sutherland sculpt. London Published Jany. 1st 1820 by S. & J. Fuller 34 Rathbone Place.

1. The Town Hall & Abbey Bath.   4. The Pump Room Bath.
2. The Royal Crescent Bath.   5. Pulteney Street Bath.
3. Lansdown Crescent Bath.   6. Bath from the Beacon Cliffs.

SIZE.—16½ × 12¾ *inches.* *Size of engraved surface average* 11 × 8 *inches.*

163 COX (David)

A Treatise on Landscape Painting and Effect in Water Colours: from the first rudiments to the finished picture: with examples in Outline, Effect, and Colouring (2 line rule) By David Cox. (2 line rule) London: Printed by J. Tyler, Rathbone Place, For S. & J. Fuller, at the Temple of Fancy, Rathbone Place (short 2 line rule)

Oblong Folio.   (1813–)1814

COLLATION.—Title as above (v. blank) + Advertisement 1 p. (v. blank) + 1 p. Dedication + Text pp. 5–32 + 56 plates. The first 24 plates are soft ground etchings, mostly containing several sketches to each plate, the next 16 plates consist of uncoloured aquatint views, and the last 16 plates are coloured aquatints.

Each of the 16 coloured plates is marked, D. Cox del. R. Reeve sc. (with the exception of plate 4 marked R. & D. Havell sc. 7 and 9 bear no engraver's name) and all bear Fuller's imprint with date.

1. View of part of Battle Abbey Sussex Nov. 1st 1813.
2. View in Surry Nov. 1st 1813.

Cox's Treatise on Landscape Painting &c. (*contd.*)

3. Morning.   Composition [the imprint not dated].
4. Mid day View a Cornfield.   Novr. 1st 1813.
5. Evening Windsor Castle   Septr. 1st 1813.
6. A Heath Windy Effect   Septr. 1 1813.
7. Cloudy Effect View of Caernarvon North Wales   Decr. 1 1813.
8. Storm View on the Coast of Hastings   Decr. 1 1813.
9. Afternoon A View in Surry   Feby. 1st 1814.
10. Rain Heath Scene   Decr. 1st 1813.
11. A Calm Hastings Fishing Boats   Feby. 1st 1814.
12. Twilight View of Harlech Castle North Wales   Decr. 1st 1813.
13. Misty Morning Pollard Willows   Jany. 1 1814.
14. Rainbow Effect View on the Thames   Jany. 1 1814.
15. Snow-scene   Feb. 1 1814.
16. Moonlight, View on the Thames near Chertsey   Feb. 14 1814.

Issued in 12 parts each with printed paper wrapper.   It is the best and most important of the early drawing books.

FIRST ISSUE.—Errors in the numbering of the plates.   The first series of plates contain an illustration of Convict Hulks on the Thames.   The first two parts in addition have blank inside wrappers.   The back wrappers bear an address to the Public.   Wrappers dated 1813.

SECOND ISSUE.—The numbering of the plates corrected.   An illustration of Haymaking and Reaping takes the place of the Convict Hulks.   Publishers advertisement takes the place of Address to Public on the Wrappers.

Another edition was published in 1816 and yet another in 1841.

Craig Itinerant Traders of London.   See under Phillips (R.) Modern London.

164 CROKER (J. W.)

[Naval Costume.]

COLLATION.—Text p. 1–11.   Dated Admiralty Office, 1st January, 1825.

1. Admiral of the Fleet.   Full Dress.
2. Admiral of the Fleet.   Undress.
3. Commodore of the first class, Captain of the Fleet, and First Captains of Ships.   Full dress.
4. Captains.   Full Dress.
5. Captains.   Undress.
6. Lieutenants.   Full Dress.
7. Master of the Fleet.
8. Mate.
9. Master of Fleet; Physician; Secretary to Commander in Chief; Secretary to Junior Flag Officers and Commodores not Commanders in Chief.
10. Master; Surgeon; Purser; Midshipman.
11. Buttons.
12. Width of the different Gold Laces of the Naval Uniform.
13. [Hats]   J. Scharf del. et lithog.
14. [Swords]   G. Scharf del. et lithog.
15. Sword belt clasps, Buckels and Swivels.

CRUIKSHANK (George)

See under Carey (D.) Life in Paris 1822 [Combe (W.)] Life of Napoleon 1815.
See under Egan Life in London 1821.
See under Ireland (W. H.) Life of Napoleon Bonaparte.

165 [CRUIKSHANK (I. R.)]

Lessons of Thrift, Published for General Benefit By a Member of the Save-all Club (rule) Aut simul et jucunda et utilia dicere vitae (circular vignette) London. Printed for Thomas Boys, 7 Ludgate Hill (rule)

Octavo.   1820

COLLATION.—Engraved title as above (v. blank) + Preface pp. i–vi + Approbations of the Committee 2 pp. (vii–viii) + Note 1 p. (v. blank) + Save All Club 1 p. (v. blank) + Rules of Club 2 pp. (xiii–xiv) + Contents 2 pp. (xv–xvi) + pp. 1–240 + 12 coloured plates [pp. 39–42, 87–110 and 163–178 omitted].

Each plate is marked, "Designed and Etched by J. R. Cruikshank," and bears imprint, "Published by Thomas Boys Ludgate Hill, London Dec. 1 1819."

1.	p.	20.	Roast and Boiled at Two Pence a Head.	7. p. 132.	Gascon Courage.
2.	p.	30.	The Lord High Chancellor of France.	8. p. 158.	The Pleasures of Angling.
3.	p.	33.	The Physician.	9. p. 160.	Royalty and Courtesy.
4.	p.	72.	The Politicians.	10. p. 184.	Honour and Magnanimity.
5.	p.	116.	Uninvited Guests civilly dismissed.	11. p. 186.	The Gentlemen of the White Goose.
6.	p.	122.	Flint Soup.	12. p. 216.	An Unexpected Welcome.

Issued in boards. Some copies have a leaf of advertisement at end, this is however usually wanting.

166 [CRUIKSHANK (I. R. and WILLIAMS (C.)]

My Cousin in the Army or, Johnny Newcome on the Peace Establishment. (rule) A Poem. (rule) By a Staff Officer. (swelled rule) "Arma Virumquae cano"—Virg. (thin & thick rule) London: Printed for J. Johnston, 98, Cheapside (rule)

Octavo.   1822

COLLATION.—Title as above (London: Shackell and Arrowsmith, Johnson's Court, Fleet Street.) + Dedication 1 p. (v. blank) + pp. 1–316 + 16 coloured plates.

1. Front. My Cousin relating his exploits.
2. p. 30. Johnny Newcome consoled by his brother officers on the prospects of half pay   I. R. Cruikshank del   C. Williams fc.
3. p. 35. Johnny Newcome supposed by the servants to have committed suicide   I. R. Cruikshank del   C. Williams fc.
4. p. 55. Johnny Newcome's First interview with his patron   Williams del et fc.
5. p. 73. Johnny Newcome's unlucky introduction to his Patrons lady   Williams del et fc.
6. p. 95. Johnny and his Man Snub finishing the Night at the Palais Royale.
7. p. 110. Johnny and his Patron under an odd mistake.
8. p. 147. Cousin John in the Cyder Cellar   Drawn & Engraved C. Williams.
9. p. 168. Shewing Cousin John the Lions.
10. p. 174. Cousin John's First Parade in the Cavalry   Drawn & Engraved C. Williams.
11. p. 195. Major Swallows Horse obliges his rider & Cousin John to take a cold Bath.
12. p. 208. Snubb arrives with my Cousin's Stud.
13. p. 234. My Cousin taking lessons in the new School.
14. p. 266. My Cousin cozen'd at the Rouge et Noir.
15. p. 286. My Cousins Patron Poaching.
16. p. 315. My Cousin's Return to his Aunt.

167   *A Second Edition was issued in 1823.*

Cruikshank (I. R.) See also under Egan, Life in London and Tour of Dr. Syntax through London.

168 DANIELL (Samuel)

To Lieutenant General Francis Dundas late Lieut and Acting Governor of the Cape of Good Hope under whose patronage the materials of the present work were collected this first part of African Scenery & Animals is inscribed with the greatest respect By His most obliged and faithful humble servant Samuel Daniell (the preceding on a rock, surrounded by Natives, lions skin, palm &c.).

Large Folio. [1804–5]

COLLATION.—Dedication as above used as title (v. blank) + 15 coloured plates + 5 leaves of Text (descriptions for 3 plates on each leaf of text).

Each plate is numbered and marked, Drawn & Engraved by Samuel Daniell. The first 3 plates bear imprint, London Published as the Act directs [date] by Samuel Daniell No. 32, Clipstone Street Fitzroy Square, the last 12 bear imprint, London Published (date) by Samuel Daniell No. 9 Cleveland Street Fitzroy Sque.

1. A Korah Hottentot Village on the left bank of the Orange River   January 1st 1804.
2. Bush-men Hottentots armed for an Expedition   January 1st 1804.
3. The Gnoo   January 1st 1804.
4. A Kaffer Village   April 15, 1804.
5. Kaffers on a March   April 15, 1804.
6. The Loodoo   April 15 1804.
7. A Boosh-Wannah Hut   June 15 1804.
8. Boosh Wannahs   June 15 1804.
9. The Pallah   June 15 1804.
10. New Theatre, Hottentot Square   November 20 1804.
11. Boors returning from Hunting   November 20 1804.
12. The Hippopotamus   November 20 1804.
13. The Military Station at Algoa Bay   December 20 1804.
14. (4 Heads) Hottentot & Kaffer man & woman   December 20 1804.
15. The Quahkah   December 20 1804.

Followed by second title on reverse of zebra's hide held aloft by 2 vultures, the whole within an oval frame, "To David Davies Esqr. this second part of African Scenery and Animals is most respectfully inscribed from a grateful recollection of his long and valuable friendship by his much obliged and faithful humble servant Samuel Daniell " (v. blank) + 5 leaves of text (each bearing descriptions for 3 plates) + 15 coloured plates.

Each plate is numbered (from 16–30) and each bears imprint, "Drawn Engraved & Published by Samuel Daniell No. 9 Cleveland Street Fitzroy Square London [date]."

16. A Boor's House   July 15 1805.
17. Halt of a Boor's Family   July 15 1805.
18. The Springbok, or Leaping Antelope   July 15 1805.
19. Scene in Sitsikamma   Augt. 15 1805.
20. Korah Hottentots preparing to remove   Augt. 15 1805.
21. The African Hog   Augt. 15 1805.
22. The Town of Leetakoo   Septr. 15 1805.
23. Booshuana Women manufacturing Earthenware   Septr. 15 1805.
24. The Tackhaitse   Septr. 15 1805.
25. Cascade on Sneuwberg   Octr. 15 1805.
26. Bosjesmans Frying Locasts   Octr. 15 1805.
27. The Klip-Springer,   Octr. 15 1805.
28. View of the Lion's Head   Novr. 15 1805.
29. [Four Heads] Bosjesman & Booshuana man & woman   Novr. 15 1805.
30. The African Rhinoceros   Novr. 15 1805.

The finest colour plate book in English on African Life and Scenery.

Daniell's Africa (*contd.*)

169 *Reissued in* 1831 *with text to the plates compressed on to* 4 *leaves, Daniell's imprint removed from the plates which all bear new imprint, London Published* 1831 *by R. Havell* 77 *Oxford Street. This reissue is extremely rare.*

170 DANIELL (Samuel)

A Picturesque Illustration of the Scenery, Animals, and Native Inhabitants, of the Island of Ceylon: in Twelve Plates, Engraved after the Drawings (from Nature) of Samuel Daniell (swelled rule) London: Printed by T. Bensley, Bolt Court, Fleet Street.   Published January 15

Oblong Folio.   1808

COLLATION.—Title as above (v. blank) + 12 coloured aquatint plates each marked Drawn by Samuel Daniell and with imprint, "London, Published [date] by Samuel Daniell No. 9 Cleveland Street, Fitzroy Square" + 4 ll. of text each leaf containing description of 3 plates.

1. Distant View of Trincomale   March 1st 1807.
2. The Spotted Antelope   March 1st 1807.
3. A Maha Modliar and Toddy Gatherer   March 1st 1807.
4. View between Galle & Mattura   June 1st 1807.
5. Wild Boar   June 1st 1807.
6. Water Carrier   June 1st 1807.
7. The Ferry at Caltura   Septr. 1st 1807.
8. The Elk   Septr. 1st 1807.
9. A Gentoo Chitty Man & Woman   Septr. 1st 1807.
10. The Fishing Cove near Columbo   Decr. 1st 1807.
11. The Elephant   Decr. 1st 1807.
12. A Singaleze Man & Woman   Decr. 1st 1807.

A fine work, equal in treatment to African Scenery.

171 *Another edition was published in* 1810.

172 DANIELL (Thomas and William)

Oriental Scenery; or Views of the Architecture, Antiquities, and Landscape Scenery of Hindostan.

Six Parts, Large Folio and Octavo Text.   1795–1808

Each part has Dedication title and following plates.

COLLATION PART I.—24 plates.

1. Eastern Gate of the Jummah Musjed, Delhi.
2. Hindoo Temples at Binrabund, on the river Jumna.
3. North-east View of the Cotsea Bhaug, on the River Jumna Delhi.
4. Ruins at the ancient City of Gour, formerly on the Banks of the River Ganges.
5. Raje Gaut, the principal Road up to Rotas Ghur, Bahar.
6. The Chalees Satoon in the Fort of Allahabad, on the River Jumna.
7. Remains of an ancient Building near Firoz Shah's Cotilla, Delhi.
8. Part of the Palace in the Fort of Allahabad.
9. Gate of the Tomb of the Emperor Akbar, at Secundra, near Agra.
10. Part of the City of Patna, on the River Ganges.
11. An ancient Hindoo Temple in the Fort of Rotas, Bahar.
12. The Mausoleum of Mucdoom Shah Dowlut, at Moneer, on the River Soane.
13. The western Entrance of Shere Shah's Fort, Delhi.

Daniell's Hindostan (*contd.*)

14. Ramnagur, near Bernares, on the River Ganges.
15. The Sacred Tree of the Hindoos at Gya, Bahar.
16. Dusasumade Gaut, at Bernares, on the Ganges.
17. Mausoleum of Sultan Chusero, near Allahabad.
18. The Taje Mahel, at Agra.
19. Hindoo Temples at Agouree, on the River Soane, Bahar.
20. North-west View of Rotas Ghur Bahar.
21. Near Currah, on the River Ganges.
22. Mausoleum of Sultan Purveiz, near Allahabad.
23. The Jummah Musjed, Delhi.
24. Gate leading to a Musjed at Chunar Gur.

PART II.—24 plates.

1. Part of the Esplanade, Calcutta.
2. View on the Chitpore Road, ditto.
3. The Council House, ditto.
4. The Writers Buildings, ditto.
5. Govinda-ram Mittee's Pagoda, ditto.
6. Part of Cheringhee, ditto.
7. South-west View of Fort St. George, Madras.
8. Part of the Black Town, ditto.
9. Government House, Fort St. George, ditto.
10. Armenian Bridge, near St. Thomas's Mount, ditto.
11. The Assembly Rooms on the Race Ground, ditto.
12. Western Entrance of Fort St. George, ditto.
13. Part of the Palace of Madura.
14. View in the Fort, ditto.
15. Interior View of the Palace, ditto.
16. An Hindoo Temple, ditto.
17. Ruins of the Palace at, ditto.
18. Tremal Naig's Choultry, ditto.
19. The Rock of Tritchinopoly, taken on the River Cauvery.
20. Great Pagoda, Tritchinopoly.
21. Tank in the Fort of Tritchinopoly.
22. The Idol call the Great Bull, at Tanjore.
23. South-east View of Tritchinopoly.
24. Great Pagoda, Tanjore.

PART III.—24 plates.

1. Near the Fort of Currah, on the River Ganges.
2. Rotas Ghur, Bahar.
3. Gate of the Loll-Bhaug, at Fyzabad.
4. Mausoleum of the Ranee, Wife of the Emperor Jehangire, near Allahabad.
5. The Punj Mahalla Gate, Lucknow.
6. Mausoleum of Amir Khusero at the ancient City of Delhi.
7. Ruins at Cannouge.
8. The Entrance to the Mausoleums in Sultan Khusero's Garden, near Allahabad.
9. A Mosque at Juanpore.
10. Gate of a Mosque built by Hafez Ramut at Pillibeat.
11. Jag Deo and Warrangur, Hill Forts in the Barramahl.
12. Ryacotta, a Hill Fort in the Barramahl.
13. Verapadroog, a Hill Fort in the Barramahl.
14. Ousoor, ditto, ditto.
15. View of Gyah, an Hindoo Town in Bahar.
16. Palace of Nawaub Suja Dowla, at Lucknow.
17. Lucknow taken from the opposite Bank of the River Goomty.
18. A Baolee, near the Old City of Delhi.
19. View of Delhi, taken near the Mausoleum of the Emperor Humaioon.

Daniell's Hindostan (*contd.*)

20. The Baolee at Ramnagur.
21. View from the Ruins of the Fort of Currah, on the Ganges.
22. View of Mutura, on the River Jumna.
23. Mausoleum of Kausim Solemanee, at Chunar Gur.
24. Mausoleum of Nawaub Assoph Khan, at Raje Mahel.

PART IV.—24 plates.

1. Cape Comorin, taken near Calcad.
2. Waterfall of Puppanassum, in the Tinnevelly District.
3. Waterfall at Courtallum in ditto.
4. Shevagurry, ditto.
5. Cheval-Pettore, ditto.
6. Near Attore, in the Dindigul District.
7. Sankry Droog.
8. Near Bandell, on the River Hoogley.
9. Siccra Gulley, on the Ganges.
10. Ramgur, in the Benares District.
11. Dhuah Koonde, ditto.
12. Cannoge, on the River Ganges.
13. View at Nigeibabad, near the Coaduwar Gaut.
14. Coaduwar Gaut.
15. View in the Coah-nullah.
16. Juganor, in the Mountains of Serinagur.
17. View near Daramundi, in ditto.
18. Near Dusa, ditto.
19. Buddell, opposite Bilcate, ditto.
20. View of the Ramgunga, ditto.
21. View between Natan and Taka-ca-munda, ditto.
22. Between Taka-ca-munda and Serinagur.
23. The Rope Bridge, at ditto.
24. View near the City of Serinagur.

PART V.—A series of Indian Antiquities.   24 plates.

1. Sculptured Rocks at Mauveleporam, on the Coast of Coromandel.
2. The Entrance of an Excavated Hindoo Temple at Mauveleporam.
3. View of an excavated Temple on the Island of Salsette.
4. The Portico of the excavated Temple (No. 3) on the Island of Salsette.
5. An Hindoo Temple at Deo, in Bahar.
6. An Inside View of the preceding Temple (No. 5) at Deo.
7. The Entrance to the Elephanta Cave.
8. Part of the Interior of the Elephanta.
9. South-west View of the Fakeer's Rock in the River Ganges, near Sultaun-gunge.
10. South-east View of the Fakeer's Rock, near Sultaun-gunge.
11. Part of the Kanaree Caves, Salsette.
12. Interior of the excavated Temple (No. 3).
13. The Temple of Mandeswara, near Chaynpore, Bahar.
14. An Antique Reservoir, near Colar, in the Mysore.
15. Exterior of an Edee-gah, near Chaynpore, Bahar.
16. Interior of a Temple, near Muddunpore, ditto.
17. View near Bangalore.
18. Entrance to an Hindoo Temple, near Bangalore.
19. } The Observatory at Delhi.
20. }
21. A Pavilion belonging to an Hindoo Temple.
22. Interior of the Temple of Mandeswara, near Chaynpore, Bahar.
23. A Minar, at Gour.
24. The Cuttub Minar, near Delhi.

Daniell's Hindostan (*contd.*)

PART VI.—Hindoo Excavations in the Mountains of Ellora, near Arungabad in the Decan. 24 plates.

1.
2. } A General View of the Mountain of Ellora.
3.
4. Jagannâthâ Sabhâ.
5. Paraswa Râma Sabhâ.
6. The Entrance of Indra Sabhâ.
7. Indea Sabhâ, looking outwards.
8. Indra Sabhâ.
9. Doomar Leyna.
10. Junwassa; or, the Place of Nuptials.
11. Râmêswara.
12. The Entrance to Kailâsa, the Paradise of the Gods.
13. South-west View of Kailâsa.
14. North-east View of ditto.
15.
16. } The Upper part of ditto.
17. Dasâvatâra.
18.
19. } Râvana.
20. Tîn-Tali.
21. Dô-Tali.
22.
23. } Viswakarmâ.
24. Dehr Warra.

The finest illustrated work ever published on India, originally published at 200 guineas, later increased to £30 unbound per part. Part V was issued in 2 series of 12 plates, and 8 plans were added to Part VI.

173 DANIELL (Thomas and William)

A Picturesque Voyage to India; by the Way of China. (thick and thin rule) By Thomas Daniell R.A. and William Daniell A.R.A. (thin and thick rule) London: Printed for Longman, Hurst, Rees, and Orme, Paternoster-Row; and William Daniell, No. 9, Cleveland Street, Fitzroy Square. By Thomas Davison, Whitefriars (rule)

Small Folio. 1810

COLLATION.—Title as above (v. blank) + Introduction 2 pp. + 50 coloured aquatint plates.

Each plate marked, Drawn & Engraved by Thos & Willm Daniell Published by Messrs. Longman, Hurst, Rees & Orme Paternoster Row [date]. Each plate has 1 leaf of text.

1. Gravesend Jany. 1 1810.
2. Passing Beechy-Head Jany. 1 1810.
3. Madeira Jany. 1 1810.
4. Off Madeira Jany. 1 1810.
5. Crossing the Line Jany. 1 1810.
6. Gale off the Cape of Good Hope Feby. 1 1810.
7. A Man Overboard Jany. 1 1810.
8. Cape of Good Hope Feby. 1 1809.
9. Albatross Feby. 1 1810.
10. Java Head Feby. 1 1810.
11. Malaye Proas & Canoes Feby. 1 1810.
12. Anjere-Point Straits of Sunda March 1 1810.
13. Dutch Residence at Anjere-Point Marh. 1 1810.
14. Watering place Anjere Point April 1 1810.
15. Malays of Java March 1 1810.
16. A Malaye Village March 1 1810.
17. Malaye Proas March 1 1810.
18. Malays of Java Arpil 1 1810.

Daniell's Voyage to India (*contd.*)

19. Cocoa Nut & Betel Trees   April 2 1810.
20. Chinese Trading & Fishing Vessels   May 1st 1810.
21. Macao, China   June 1 1810.
22. Chinese Husbandman   June 1 1810.
23. Hotun, on the Canton River   June 1 1810.
24. Chinese Vessels   June 1 1810.
25. Near Whampoa, China   June 1 1810.
26. Whampoa Pagoda   July 1 1810.
27. Chinese Tomb   July 1 1810.
28. Chinese Gentleman   July 1 1810.
29. Chinese Lady   July 1 1810.
30. Scene on the Canton River   July 1 1810.
31. Hoe Chu Fou Toe a Chinese Fort near Canton   Augst. 1 1810.
32. South West View of Canton   Augst. 1 1810.
33. Chinese Barber   Augst. 1 1810.
34. Chinese Lady   Augst. 1 1810.
35. Chinese of Rank   Augst. 1 1810.
36. Chinese Junks   Septr. 1 1810.

37. Chinese Pavillion   Septr. 1 1810.
38. An Offering to the God of Fire   Septr. 1 1810.
39. View in a Chinese Garden   Septr. 1 1810.
40. A Chinese Military Officer   Sept. 1 1810.
41. Chinese Duck Boat   Octr. 1 1810.
42. Camoens Cave Macao   Octr. 1 1810.
43. Coast of Cochin China   Oct. 1 1810.
44. Pedro Branco, Straits of Malacca   Octr. 1 1810.
45. Cape Ricardo Straits of Malacca   Octr. 1 1810.
46. Fowl Island Bay of Bengal   Novr. 1 1810.
47. Near Gangwaugh Colly, on the River Hoogly   Novr. 1 1810.
48. Near Cucrahattce, on the River Hoogly   Novr. 1 1810.
49. View of Calcutta from the Garden Reach   Novr. 1 1810.
50. Old Fort Gaut Calcutta   Novr. 1 1810.

174 DANIELL (William)

Illustrations of the Island of Staffa, In a Series of Views, accompanied by Topographical and Geological Descriptions (rule) By W. Daniell, A.R.A. (rule) London: Printed by Thomas Davison, Whitefriars, for Longman, Hurst, Rees, Orme and Brown, Paternoster-Row; and William Daniell, No. 9, Cleveland-Street, Fitzroy-Square (short rule)

Oblong Quarto.   1818

COLLATION.—Half-title "Illustrations of the Island of Staffa" (v. blank) + Title as above (v. blank) + pp. 1–11 + 9 coloured aquatints.

Each plate bears at foot, "Drawn & Engraved by Willm. Daniell, Published by Messrs Longman & Co. Paternoster Row & W. Daniell 9, Cleveland Street, Fitzroy Square London [and date]."

1. The Island of Staffa from the East   Octr. 1 1817.
2. Clam-shell Cove, Staffa—Iona in the Distance   June 2 1817.
3. Exterior of Fingal's Cave, Staffa   July 1 1817.
4. Entrance to Fingals Cave Staffa   July 1 1817.
5. In Fingals' Cave Staffa   July 1 1817.
6. Staffa near Fingals Cave   Sepr. 1 1817.
7. The Cormorants Cave—Staffa   Septr. 1 1817.
8. View from the Island of Staffa   Sep. 1 1817.
9. The Island of Staffa from the South West   Octr. 1 1817.

175 DANIELL (William)

To George Dance Esquire R.A.   Architect to the City of London &c.   These Six Views of the Metropolis of the British Empire, are respectfully dedicated by William Daniell London January 1st

Large Oblong Folio.   1805

Daniell's City of London (*contd.*)

COLLATION.—Dedicatory title leaf with lettering as above on a monumental tablet forming part of a large uncoloured engraving containing a composite vignette of London + 6 coloured aquatint plates.

The first plate only bears a title, but all are marked, Drawn Engraved and Published by William Daniell No. 9 Cleveland Street, Fitzroy Square London.

1. London From Greenwich Park Plate I   Augt. 1 1804.
2. London Plate II (Tower & the Pool)   Augt. 1 1804.
3. London Plate III (London Bridge)   June 1 1804.
4. London Plate IV (N. Bank with St Pauls & Blackfriars Bridge)   June 1 1804.
5. London Plate V (Somerset House, before the Embankment)   Jany. 1805.
6. London Plate VI (Westminster Abbey & Bridge)   Jany. 1805.

The complete series of these large views measuring 25 × 16 inches (engraved surface) is rare.
Daniell did a further series of 6 large aquatints of the London Docks, without title, but all bearing his name and imprint.

(1). An Elevated View of the New Docks & Warehouses now constructing on the Isle of Dogs near Limehouse for the reception & accomodation of the Shipping in the West India Trade   Oct. 15 1802.
(2). An Elevated View of the New Dock in Wapping   Jany. 1 1803.
(3). View of London, with the Improvements of its Port   Augt. 15 1803.
(4). Brunswick Dock on the Thames at Blackwall   Octr. 20 1805.
(5). A View of the London Dock   Oct. 1 1808.
(6). A View of the East India Docks   Octr. 20 1805.

176 DANIELL (William)

Views in Bootan; From the Drawings of Samuel Davis, Esq. by William Daniell.

Oblong Folio.

COLLATION.—Printed title as above (v. blank) + Engraved Dedicatory Title, "Views in Bootan, (from the Drawings of Mr Davis), respectfully inscribed to Warren Hastings Esqr. late Governor General of India by Willm. Daniell London June 15 1813 [the above lettering on a rock with mountain scenery] (v. blank) + 6 coloured plates each with 1 leaf of text.

Each plate marked, Drawn by S. Davis Esqr.   Engraved by W. Daniell with imprint, Published by Wm Daniell No. 9 Cleveland Street Fitzroy Square, London [and date].

1. The Palace of the Deib Rajah, at Tassisudon   June 1 1813.
2. View of Choka   June 1 1813.
3. View at Tassisudon   June 1 1813.
4. View on the River Teenchoo   July 25 1813.
5. View between Murichom & Choka   July 25 1813.
6. A Temple of Bode   July 25 1813.

177 DANIELL (William)

A Voyage round Great Britain, undertaken in the summer of the year 1813, and commencing from the Land's-End, Cornwall, by Richard Ayton. With a Series of Views, Illustrative of the Character and Prominent Features of the Coast, Drawn and Engraved by William Daniell, A.R.A. (thick and thin rule) London: Printed for Longman, Hurst, Rees, Orme, and Brown, Paternoster-Row; and William Daniell, No. 9, Cleveland Street, Fitzroy Square (short rule) 1814[-25]

Daniell's Voyage Round Great Britain (*contd.*)

COLLATION VOL. I.—Title as above (v. T. Davison, Lombard-Street, Whitefriars, London) + Engraved Dedication to Rt. Hon. and Hon. the Master and Assistants of the Corporation of Trinity House + Introduction 3 pp. (iii–v, vi blank) + pp. 1–215 (p. 216 blank) + Errata 1 p. (v. blank) + 26 coloured plates, each marked, "Drawn and engraved by Willm. Daniell Published by Messrs. Longman & Co Paternoster Row & W. Daniell 9 Cleveland St. Fitzroy Square London."

1. The Lands-end, Cornwall	Jany. 1 1814
2. The long-ships lighthouse off the lands end Cornwall	Jany. 1 1814
3. The entrance to Portreath, Cornwall	Feby. 1 1814
4. Boscastle Pier on the coast of Cornwall	Feby. 1 1814
5. Hartland pier North Devon	April 1, 1814
6. Clovelly on the Coast of North Devon	April 1, 1814
7. Ilfracomb, on the coast of North Devon	April 1, 1814
8. View of Ilfracombe, from Hilsborough	May 1, 1814
9. Near Combmartin, on the coast of North Devon	June 1, 1814
10. Lynmouth, on the coast of North Devon	June 1, 1814
11. St Donats Glamorganshire	July 1, 1814
12. Britton Ferry Glamorganshire	July 1 1814
13. The Mumbles light-house, in Swansea bay	Augst. 1 1814
14. The Worms-head, in Tenby bay	Augt. 1 1814
15. Tenby, Pembrokeshire	Septr. 1st 1814
16. The Eligug-stack, near St. Gowans-head, Pembrokeshire	Septr. 1st 1814
17. Solva, near St Davids, Pembrokeshire	Octr. 1, 1814
18. View of the entrance to Fishguard, from Goodwych sands	Octr. 1st 1814
19. Goodwych Pier, near Fishguard, Pembrokeshire	Novr. 1, 1814
20. View near Aberystwith, Cardiganshire	Novr. 1 1814
21. Barmouth, Merionethshire	Decr. 1 1814
22. View of Caernarvon Castle, from Anglesea	Decr. 1st 1814
23. The Harbour light-house, Holyhead	Jany. 2 1815
24. Light-house on the South Stack, Holyhead	Jany. 2 1815
25. Part of the South Stack Holyhead	April 1 1815
26. The Rope Bridge, near the Lighthouse, Holyhead	Feby. 2 1815

VOL. II.—Title as before (with addition of Vol. II between two double rules immediately above the imprint, and dated 1815 instead of 1814) + pp. 3–223 (p. 224 List of Plates to Vol. II) + 30 coloured plates, with imprint as before.

27. Black Marble Quarry, near red Wharf bay Anglesea	May 1 1815
28. The entrance to Amlwch harbour Anglesea	Feby. 1 1815
29. Red Wharf Bay Anglesea	April 1 1815
30. Beaumaris Castle Anglesea	March 1 1815
31. View on Puffin Island, near Anglesea	March 1 1815
32. The Bath, built by Lord Penryn, near Bangor N. Wales	May 1 1815
33. Penman-maur, taken from near Aber, N. Wales	June 1 1815
34. View of Conway Castle, Caernarvonshire	June 1 1815
35. The Light house on Point of Air, Flintshire	July 1 1815
36. View near Hoyle-lake Cheshire	July 1 1815
37. The Towns-end Mill Liverpool	Decr. 1 1815
38. Seacombe Ferry, Liverpool	Septr. 1 1815
39. Liverpool, taken from the opposite side of the River	Octr. 1 1815
40. Lancaster Castle	Jany. 1 1816
41. View near Lower Heysham, Lancashire	March 1 1816
42. Distant View of Whitbarrow Scar, Westmoreland	Feby. 1 1816
43. Castle-head Westmoreland	Feby. 1 1816
44. Peel Castle Lancashire	March 1 1816
45. Whitehaven Cumberland	April 1 1816

Daniell's Voyage Round Great Britain (*contd.*)

46.	Harrington near Whitehaven Cumberland	April 1 1816
47.	Mary Port, Cumberland	May 1 1816
48.	Carlaverock Castle, Dumfrieshire	May 1 1816
49.	Kirkudbright	Septr. 1 1816
50.	The Mull of Galloway Wigtonshire	July 1 1816
51.	Port Patrick Wigtonshire	August 1 1816
52.	Cardness Castle, near Gatehouse, Kirkudbrightshire	Augst. 1 1816
53.	Near Carsleith, Galloway	Septr. 1 1816
54.	Wigton, Galloway	June 1 1816
55.	Cree-town Kirkudbrightshire	June 1 1816
56.	Dunsky Castle, near Port Patrick Wigtonshire	July 1 1816

VOL. III.—Title as in Vol. II (changing Vol. II to Vol. III and dated 1818, "Drawn and Engraved by" and "Richard Ayton's" name dropped) Dedication to Walter Scott Esq. 2 pp. + pp. 1–80 + 42 coloured plates, with imprint as before.

57.	The Crag of Ailsa	Decr. 2 1816
58.	Culzean Castle, Ayrshire	Decr. 2 1816
59.	Distant View of Ayr	Decr. 2 1816
60.	Pier at Ardrossan Ayrshire	Jany. 1 1817
61.	The Isle of Arran, taken near Ardrossan	Jany. 1 1817
62.	Ardgowan, Renfrewshire	Jany. 1 1817
63.	Greenock, on the Clyde	Feby. 1 1817
64.	Steam Boat on the Clyde near Dumbarton	Feby. 1 1817
65.	Mount Stuart, Isle of Bute	Feby. 1 1817
66.	Loch Ranza Isle of Arran	April 1 1817
67.	Duntrune Castle, Loch Creran Argylshire	May 1 1817
68.	Soch Swene Argylshire	April 1 1817
69.	Rassella near Kilmartin Loch Creran Argylshire	May 1 1817
70.	On the Isle of Jura	May 1 1817
71.	Inverary Castle Argylshire	May 1 1817
72.	Dunolly Castle, near Oban Argylshire	May 1 1817
73.	Dunstaffnage Castle, Argylshire	June 2 1817
74.	Clam-shell Cave, Staffa Iona in the distance	June 2 1817
75.	Exterior of Fingal's Cave Staffa	July 1 1817
76.	Entrance to Fingal's Cave Staffa	July 1 1817
77.	In Fingal's Cave Staffa	July 1 1817
78.	Staffa near Fingals cave	Sepr. 1 1817
79.	The Cormorant's Cave, Staffa	Septr. 1 1817
80.	View from the Island of Staffa	Sep. 1 1817
81.	The Island of Staffa from the East	Octr. 1 1817
82.	The Island of Staffa, from the South West	Octr. 1 1817
83.	View of Iona, from the N. East	Octr. 1 1817
84.	The Cathedral at Iona	Octr. 1 1817
85.	View of Ben-more from near Ulva house	Novr. 1 1817
86.	Remains of the Chapel &c. on Inch Kenneth	Novr. 1 1817
87.	Gribune-head in Mull	Decr. 1 1817
88.	Loch-na-gael, near Knock on Mull	Decr. 1 1817
89.	Distant View of Cruachan-ben, taken near Arros bridge Isle of Mull	Decr. 1 1817
90.	Arros Castle, Isle of Mull	Feby. 1 1818
91.	Tobermory, on the Isle of Mull	Feby. 2 1818
92.	Mingarry Castle, Argylshire	Feby. 2 1818
93.	Ardnamurchan point Argylshire	March 2 1818
94.	Scoor Eig on the Isle of Eig	April 2 1818
95.	Part of the Isle Rum	April 1 1818
96.	Armidal, the Seat of Lord Macdonald, Isle of Skye	May 1 1818
97.	Iloransay Isle of Skye	May 1 1818
98.	Balmacarro-house Loch-alsh Roshire	May 1 1818

Daniell's Voyage Round Great Britain (*contd.*)

VOL. IV.—Title as in Vol. III (changing Vol. III to Vol. IV and dated 1820) + Dedication to Marchioness of Stafford 1 p. (v. blank) + pp. 1–96 + 42 coloured plates, with imprint as before.

99.	Castle Ellen-Donan	Decr. 1 1818
100.	Loch-Duich Ross-shire	Decr. 1 1818
101.	Ilan-dreoch Glenbeg Invernesshire	Decr. 1 1818
102.	The bay of Barrisdale in Loch Hourne	Jany. 1 1819
103.	Loch Hourne head	Jany. 1 1819
104.	Glen-coe taken near Ballachulish	Jany. 1 1819
105.	Near Kylakin Skye	Feby. 1 1819
106.	Liveras near Broadford, Skye	Feby. 1 1819
107.	Portree on the Isle of Skye	Feby. 1 1819
108.	Glenvargle bridge near Portree Skye	April 1 1819
109.	Duntulm Isle of Skye	April 1 1819
110.	Dunvegan Castle, Isle of Skye	April 1 1819
111.	Dunvegan Castle	May 1 1819
112.	Little Brieshmeal, near Talisker Skye	May 1 1819
113.	Loch Scavig Skye	June 1 1819
114.	Loch Coruisq near Loch Scavig	Augst. 1 1819
115.	The Coolin, taken from Loch Slapin	Augst. 1 1819
116.	From the Isle of Rasay, looking Westward	Augst. 1 1819
117.	Castle Broichin on the Isle of Rassay	Octr. 1 1819
118.	Rowadill in Harris	Octr. 1 1819
119.	Light House on the Isle of Scalpa, Harris	Octr. 1 1819
120.	Part of the Northern face of one of the Shiant Isles	Decr. 1 1819
121.	Near View of one of the Shiant Isles	Decr. 1 1819
122.	Stornaway, on the Isle of Lewis	Decr. 1 1819
123.	Remains of a Temple at Galston Isle of Lewis	Decr. 1 1819
124.	Druidical Stone at Strather near Barvas, Isle of Lewis	Decr. 1 1819
125.	The Gair-loch Ross-shire	Decr. 1 1819
126.	Gair-loch head Ross-shire	Feby. 1 1820
127.	Creen-stone rock, Loch Broom	Jany. 1 1829
128.	Pier at Tanera, Loch Broom	Feby. 1 1820
129.	Ben Sulvhein, from Loch Inver	Feby. 1 1820
130.	View of Cuniag, from Loch Inver	March 1 1820
131.	Unapool in Kyles-cu Assynt	March 1 1820
132.	Rispand Durness	April 1 1820
133.	Entrance to the cave of Smowe	March 1 1820
134.	Whiten-head Loch Eribol	April 1 1820
135.	Bay on Tongue	May 1 1820
136.	Strath-naver Sutherlandshire	May 1 1820
137.	The Clett-rock, Holborn head	May 1 1820
138.	Thurso, from near Holborn head	June 1 1820
139.	Castle Sinclair, Thurso	June 1 1820
140.	Castle Hill near Thurso	June 1 1820

VOL. V.—Title as in Vol. III (changing Vol. III to Vol. V and dated 1821) + Dedication to the King 1 p. (v. blank) + Pp. 1–36 + 42 coloured plates, all marked, "Drawn and Engraved by Willm. Daniell Published by W. Daniell, Cleveland Street, Fitzroy Square London" and dated except plates 142–147 which still bear Longman's imprint.

141.	Moy Castle, Caithness	June 1 1821
142.	The Ferry at Scarskerry, Caithness Drawn and Engraved by Willm. Daniell Published by Messrs. Longmans & Co. Paternoster Row & W. Daniell 9 Cleveland St. Fitzroy Square London	Nov. 1 1820
143.	Near the Berry-head Hoy Orkney	Nov. 1 1820
144.	The Snook Hoy Orkney	Nov. 1st 1820

Daniell's Voyage Round Great Britain (*contd.*)

145. The Old Man of Hoy   Dec. 1 1820
146. Stromness Orkney   Dec. 1 1820
147. Stones of Stennis, Orkney   Decr. 1 1820
148. The Cathedral of St. Magnus Kirkwall Orkney.
149. S.E. View of the Cathedral & Palace, at Kirkwall Orkney.
150. Kirkwall, Orkney, from the Bay.
151. N. West View of the Cathedral Kirkwall.   +
152. Tower of the Bishops Palace, Kirkwall.
153. Remains of the Earls Palace, Kirkwall.
154. Light House on the Start, Isle of Sandy, Orkney.
155. John O'Groats Caithness.
156. Duncansby stacks Caithness.
157. Keiss Castle Caithness.
158. Ackergill Tower, Caithness.
159. Castles Sinclair & Girnigo, Caithness.
160. Wick Caithness.
161. Old Wick Castle, Caithness.
162. The Stack of Hempriggs, Caithness.
163. Scene at Hempriggs, Caithness.
164. Forse Castle Sutherland.
165. Dunbeath Castle, Caithness.
166. Berrydale Caithness.
167. Castle of Berrydale.
168. Helmsdale Sutherlandshire.
169. Dunrobin Castle Sutherlandshire.
170. Dunrobin Castle from the N.E. Sutherlandshire.
171. Dornoch, Sutherlandshire.
172. Bonar Bridge.
173. Cromarty.
174. Pier at Fortrose, Ross-shire.
175. Inverness.
176. Nairn.
177. Obelish at Forres.
178. Nelson's Tower Forres.
179. Brugh-head, Murrayshire.
180. Coxtown Tower, near Elgin.
181. Finlater Castle, Banffshire.
182. Boyne Castle, Banffshire.

VOL. VI.—Title as in Vol. III (changing Vol. III for Vol. VI and dated 1822) + Dedication to the King 1 p. (v. blank) + pp. 1–94 + 42 coloured plates, with imprint as in Vol. V but dated July 1 1822.

183. Duff House Banff.
184. Banff.
185. Frazerburgh Aberdeenshire.
186. Kinnaird Head Aberdeenshire.
187. Peterhead Aberdeenshire.
188. Slanes Castle Aberdeenshire.
189. Bridge of Don Old Aberdeen.
190. Aberdeen.
191. Dunotter Castle Kincardineshire.
192. Montrose Forfarshire.
193. Inverbernie Bridge.
194. Broughty Castle Forfarshire.
195. Dundee Forfarshire.
196. St Andrews Fifeshire.
197. Wemys Castle Fifeshire.
198. Distant View of Edinburgh with Wemys Castle.
199. Edinburgh from the Castle.
200. Edinburgh with part of the North Bridge & Castle.
201. Edinburgh from Calton Hill.
202. Leith.
203. Tantallon Castle Haddingtonshire.
204. The Bass Rock.
205. Dunbar Haddingtonshire.
206. Berwick upon Tweed.
207. Castle on Holy Island Northumberland.
208. Bamborough Castle, Northumberland.
209. North Shields, Northumberland.
210. Tynemouth Northumberland.

Daniell's Voyage Round Great Britain (*contd.*)

211. Sunderland Pier, Durham.
212. Whitby Yorkshire.
213. Whitby Abbey, Yorkshire.
214. Scarborough Yorkshire.
215. Light-house on Flambro' head, Yorkshire.
216. Hull Yorkshire.
217. Boston, Lincolnshire.

218. Yarmouth from Gorlstone.
219. Lowestoft Suffolk.
220. Southwold Suffolk.
221. The Orford Ness Light houses, Suffolk.
222. Harwich Essex.
223. Mistley near Harwich Essex.
224. South End Essex.

VOL. VII.—Title as in Vol. III (changing Vol. III to Vol. VII and dated 1824) + pp. 1–90 + 42 coloured plates all with imprint as before but dated August 1 1823.

225. Sheerness.
226. The Reculvers.
227. Pier at Margate.
228. North Foreland Light House.
229. Broadstairs.
230. Ramsgate.
231. Deal Castle.
232. Walmer Castle.
233. Dover Castle.
234. Dover from Shakespears Cliff.
235. Shakespears Cliff.
236. Folkestone Kent.
237. Hythe.
238. Dungeness Light House.
239. Rye Sussex.
240. Winchelsea.
241. Hastings, from near the White Rock.
242. Hastings from the East Cliff.
243. Near Beachy-head.
244. Brighton.
245. Near Regents Square Brighton.

246. Ovington near Brighton.
247. Shoreham.
248. Pier at Littlehampton.
249. View from the Park Arundel.
250. Bognor.
251. View from Portsdown Hill.
252. West Cowes.
253. Lord Henry Seymours Castle.
254. Mr Nash's Castle.
255. Ryde.
256. Brading Harbour.
257. Shanklin Chine.
258. Freshwater Bay Isle of Wight.
259. Needles Cliff & Needles Isle of Wight.
260. Distant View of the Needles & Hurst Castle.
261. Christchurch.
262. Poole Dorsetshire.
263. Corfe Castle.
264. Swanage.
265. Lulworth Cove.
266. Weymouth.

VOL. VIII.—Title as in Vol. III (changing Vol. III to Vol. VIII and dated 1825) + Dedication to the King 1 p. (v. blank) + pp. 1–65 + 42 coloured plates, each with imprint as before but dated May 20 1825.

267. Light-house Isle of Portland.
268. St Catherine's Chapel, Dorset.
269. Bridport Harbour, Dorset.
270. Lyme Regis, from Charmouth Dorset.
271. Sidmouth Devon.
272. Exmouth Devon.
273. Teignmouth Devon.
274. Babicombe Devon.
275. Torbay Devon.
276. Tor-abbey Devon.
277. Tor-quay Devon.
278. Brixham Torbay Devon.
279. Entrance to Dartmouth Devon.
280. The Junction of the Dart with the Sea.
281. Near Kingswear, on the Dart, Devon.
282. Kingswear Devon.
283. Salcombe Devon.
284. Bovisand near Plymouth.
285. Quay at Straddon point, near Plymouth.
286. The Citadel Plymouth.
287. Catwater Plymouth from the Citadel.

288. Mount Edgecumbe from the Citadel Plymouth.
289. View from Mount Edgecumbe.
290. Hamoaze from Mount Edgecumbe.
291. Port wrinkle, Cornwall.
292. East Looe, Cornwall.
293. Polperro Cornwall.
294. Fowey from Bodenick Cornwall.
295. Fowey Castle Cornwall.
296. Polkerris Cornwall.
297. Mevagissy Cornwall.
298. Mevagissy Cornwall (another view).
299. Gorran Haven Cornwall.
300. Port-looe, Cornwall.
301. Falmouth Cornwall.
302. The Lizzard Light-houses, Cornwall.
303. Mallyan Cove Cornwall.
304. Near Mullyan Cove Cornwall.
305. St Michael's Mount Cornwall.
306. St Michael's mount, Cornwall (another view).
307. Penzance Cornwall.
308. The Land's end Cornwall.

Daniell's Voyage Round Great Britain (*contd.*)

Published at £60. Twenty-five special copies with the plates mounted on cardboard were also published at the same time for 96 guineas. An Index chart to the Voyage was also published at 6s. but is not usually included, the work being complete without it.

A magnificient series of plates, almost all of equal quality. Valuable as a record and exquisite in its presentation. The most important colour plate book on British Topography.

There are reprints of the plates by Nattali & Maurice.

Daniell. See also under Barrow's Cochin China.

178 DANIELL (William)

(Views of Windsor Castle) To His most excellent Majesty the King. These select Views of Windsor Castle and the adjacent scenery, are, with gracious permission dedicated by his Majesty's faithful subject and servant, William Daniell, R.A. London: Published by Mr W. Daniell, 14 Russell Place, Fitzroy Square.

Large Oblong Folio.

COLLATION.—Dedication title as above (v. blank) + 12 coloured aquatint plates, each plate marked, Drawn and Engraved by W. Daniell, R.A. Published by W. Daniell, 14 Russell Place, Fitzroy Square, London.

1. Glen in Windsor Park near Bishopsgate.
2. Windsor Castle from the S. East.*
3. Windsor Castle from near the Brocas Meadow.
4. The Quadrangle Windsor Castle.
5. Eton College.
6. Scene on the Virginia Water.
7. The Long Walk Windsor Park.
8. View from the Round Tower Windsor Castle.*
9. Windsor Castle from the Brocas Meadow.
10. Windsor Castle from Eton.
11. A West View of Windsor Castle.
12. The Royal Lodge Windsor Park.*

I have seen a copy in which the plates marked with asterisk above, have the imprint of Moon Boys & Graves, 6 Pall Mall, added to that of Daniell, and title with these three publishers names added to the imprint.

179 DAVENPORT (W.)

Historical Portraiture of Leading Events in the Life of Ali Pacha, Vizier of Epirus, surnamed the Lion, in a Series of Designs, drawn by W. Davenport, and engraved by G. Hunt, with a Biographical Sketch (thick and thin rule) London: Published by Thomas M'Lean, 26 Haymarket (rule)

Folio.   1823

COLLATION.—Half-title "Ali Pacha" (v. Howlett & Brimmer, Printers, 10 Frith Street, Soho) + Title as above (v. blank) + List of Plates 1 p. (v. blank) + Preface 1 p. (v. blank) + Biographical Sketch pp. 9–30 + Advertisement by M'Lean. 2 pp. + 6 coloured plates.

Each plate bears, "W. Davenport, delt." "G. Hunt Sculpt" "London Published by Thomas M'Lean, 26 Haymarket."   1823

1. Frontispiece. The Youthful Ali Bey, shewn by his mother to the partisans and vassals of his Fathers House.
2. p. 19. Ali Bey discovers the Chest of Treasure near the Ruins of an old monastery in the Mountain.

Davenport's Life of Ali Pacha (*contd.*)

3. p. 24. The Vow of Vengeance made by Ali Pacha and his Sister Chainitza over the Dead Body of their Mother.
4. p. 27. Ali Pacha, giving the Fatal Signal, for the Slaughter of the Gardi Kiotes shut up in the Kahn of Valiare.
5. p. 29. The Delivery of the Broken Ring, to Ali Pacha's Faithful Slave in The Magazine of the Citadel.
6. p. 30. Ali Pacha and his Brave Officers, resisting the Turkish Generals sent with the Death Firman to Demand the Viziers Head.

180 DELAMOTTE (W. A.)

Views of the Colleges, Chapels and Gardens of Oxford. From drawings made expressly for this work, by W. Alfred Delamotte. (above within architectural and heraldic border) W. Gauci, lith., Printed in Colours by Lefevre. London. Published 1842 by Thomas Boys, Printseller to the Royal Family, 11 Golden Square, Regent Street, Designed and Drawn by W. A. Delamotte.

Folio.   1842

    COLLATION.—Title as above + 25 plates marked, W. Gauci, lith., Printed by Lefevre, and all with the exception of Baliol College Garden, marked, W. A. Delamotte, delt.

1. High Street Oxford.
2. Queens College Oxford.
3. Exeter Garden.
4. Oriel College.
5. Magdalen College from the High St.
6. St Mary's Chapel & All Souls College.
7. St Johns Garden front.
8. Radcliff Quadrangle of all Souls College.
9. Baliol College Garden.
10. Baliol College Quadrangle.
11. Merton College front.
12. Merton College from the Fields.
13. New College Chapel.
14. Trinity College from the Gardens.
15. Trinity College Chapel.
16. Corpus College Oxford.
17. Magdalen College Chapel.
18. Lincoln College Oxford.
19. Front of St. Johns College. 1840.
20. Pembroke College from St Aldates Churchyard.
21. Front of Brasenose College.
22. Broad Walk Christ Church Oxford 1841.
23. Wadham College.
24. West Front Christ Church. 1840.
25. Exeter College Front.

181 DIGHTON (R.)

City Characters, Drawn and Etched by Richard Dighton (thick and thin rule) London: Published by Thomas M'Lean, 20 Haymarket.   1824

    COLLATION.—Title (v. blank) + 39 coloured plates, Drawn Etch'd and Published by Richard Dighton.

Doctor Syntax in Paris. See under Rowlandson's Combe Imitation.

182 DODWELL (Edward)

Views in Greece, from Drawings by Edward Dodwell, Esq. F.S.A. etc. (vignette, emblematic, Greece in chains to Turks) Rodwell and Martin, (short rule).   1821

    COLLATION.—Title as above (v. Thomas Davison, Whitefriars) + Note 1 p. (v. blank) + List of plates 1 p. (v. blank) + 30 coloured aquatint plates, by Dodwell and Pomardi, each with 1 leaf of text (in English and French).

Dodwell's Greece (*contd.*)

Each plate is coloured and mounted on card like a drawing, a printed slip on the back of each card giving, the title of the plate, the imprint "London published. . . . By Rodwell and Martin, Bond Street." "Drawn by E. Dodwell" (unless otherwise stated), and the engraver and colourist's name.

1. Port Bathy and Capital of Ithaca. Engraved by F. C. Lewis. Coloured by W. H. Tims. February 1 1820.
2. Dinner at Crisso. Engraved and coloured by T. Fielding. November 1 1819.
3. The Kastalian Spring. Engraved and coloured by R. Havell. February 1 1821.
4. Parnassus. Engraved by T. Medland. Coloured by W. H. Tims. November 1 1819.
5. Ruins of Orchomenos. Drawn by S. Pomardi. Engraved by J. Bailey. Coloured by W. H. Tims. June 1 1819.
6. Katabathron of Lake Kopais. Engraved and coloured by T. Medland. August 1 1820.
7. View of the Parthenon from the Propylaea. Engraved by J. Bailey. Coloured by W. H. Tims. November 1 1819.
8. West Front of the Parthenon. Engraved by Bennett. Coloured by W. H. Tims. August 1 1820.
9. South-west View of the Erechtheion. Engraved and coloured by R. Havell. February 1 1820.
10. Entrance to the Tower of the Winds. Engraved and coloured by T. Fielding. February 1, 1821.
11. Dance of the Derwisches. Engraved and coloured by T. Fielding. February 1, 1820.
12. Bazar of Athens. Engraved and coloured by T. Fielding. February 1, 1820.
13. Entrance to Athens. Engraved and coloured by T. Fielding. November 1, 1819.
14. Temple of Jupiter Olympios and River Ilissos. Drawn by S. Pomardi. Engraved and coloured by T. Medland. September 1 1819.
15. Athens from the foot of Mount Anchesmus. Engraved and coloured by R. Havell. February 1, 1821.
16. South-East View of the Temple of Sunium. Drawn by S. Pomardi. Engraved by F. C. Lewis. Coloured by W. H. Tims. September 1 1819.
17. Temple of Jupiter Panhellenios. Drawn by S. Pomardi. Engraved and coloured by R. Havell. June 1 1819.
18. Interior of the Temple of Jupiter Panhellenios. Engraved by F. C. Lewis. Coloured by W. H. Tims. June 1 1819.
19. Monastery of Phaineromene. Engraved and coloured by R. Havell. September 1 1819.
20. Pass of Thermopylae. Engraved and Coloured by R. Havell. February 1 1821.
21. Village of Portaria. Drawn by S. Pomardi. Engraved by J. Bailey, coloured by W. H. Tims. September 1 1819.
22. The Hyperian Fountain at Pherae. Engraved and coloured by R. Havell. February 1, 1821.
23. Larissa. Drawn by S. Pomardi. Engraved by F. C. Lewis. Coloured by W. H. Tims. June 1 1819.
24. Mount Olympos, as seen between Larissa and Baba. Engraved and Coloured by R. Havell. February 1 1820.
25. Sepulchre of Hassan Baba. Engraved and coloured by R. Havell. November 1 1819.
26. Gate of the Lions at Mycenae. Engraved by J. Bailey. Coloured by W. H. Tims. August 1 1820.
27. Plain of Olympia. Engraved and coloured by J. Bailey. August 1, 1820.
28. Temple of Apollo Epicurius. Engraved by T. Medland. Coloured by W. H. Tims. June 1 1819.
29. Lake of Stymphalos. Engraved and coloured by R. Havell. September 1 1819.
30. Monastery of Megaspella. Drawn by P. Dewint, from a sketch by Dodwell. Engraved and coloured by R. Havell. August 1 1820.

It is interesting to note that in this work the colourist is named for each plate.

183 DODWELL (Edward)

Views in Greece, from Drawings by Edward Dodwell, Esq. F.S.A. etc. (vignette) John Rodwell, London (short rule)

Folio.   1830

COLLATION.—Title as above (v. Thomas Davison, Whitefriars) + Note 1 p. (v. blank) + List of Plates 1 p. (v. blank) + Frontispiece and 30 coloured aquatint plates, each with 1 leaf

Dodwell's Greece (*contd.*)

of text (in English and French). Each plate is marked, London Published by J. Rodwell. 46 New Bond Street.

Front. Festival at Athens. Published October 1830 by J. Rodwell 46 New Bond St.

The plates are the same as in the first edition.

184 DOYLEY (Charles)

The Costume and Customs of Modern India; from a Collection of Drawings by Charles Doyley, Esq. engraved by J. H. Clark and C. Dubourg; with a preface and copious descriptions, by Captain Thomas Williamson. (thin and thick rule) London: Published and Sold by Edward Orme, Bond-Street, Corner of Brook-Street, Printseller and Publisher to His Majesty

Folio. [1813]

COLLATION.—Half title + Title as above (v. W. Lewis Printer, Finch Lane, London) + Preface pp. v–xxiii (p. xxiv blank) + 20 coloured aquatint plates with text.

Each plate marked, Published and Sold by E. Orme March 1st 1813.

1. An European Gentleman with his Moonshee, or Native Professor of Languages 3 pp. text.
2. A Gentleman in his private Office attended by his Duftoree or Native Office Keeper 2 pp. text.
3. A Gentleman in a Public Office attended by the Crannies or Native Clerks 3 pp. text.
4. A Gentleman Dressing attended by his Head Bearer and other Servants 3 pp. text.
5. A Gentleman attended by his Hajaum or Native Barber 3 pp. text.
6. A Gentleman delivering a Letter to a Soontah-Burdar or Silver Baton Bearer 3 pp. text.
7. A Gentleman's Kedmutgars, or Table Servants bringing in Dinner 2 pp. text.
8. An English Family at Table under a Punkah or Fan, kept in motion by a Khelassy 3 pp. text.
9. A Gentleman with his Sircar, or Money Servant 4 pp. text.
10. A Gentleman with his Hookah Burdar or Pipe Bearer 4 pp. text.
11. A Saumpareeah or Snake Catcher exhibiting Snakes before Europeans 3 pp. text.
12. Marquis Wellesley's Dandy, or Boatman, in his Livery 3 pp. text.
13. An European Lady giving Instructions to her Durzee or Native Tailor 3 pp. text.
14. A Dancing Woman of Bengal, exhibiting before an European Family 3 pp. text.
15. A Dancing Woman of Lucknow exhibiting before an European Family 3 pp. text.
16. An European Lady attended by a Servant using a Hand Punkah or Fan 3 pp. text.
17. An European Lady and her Family attended by an Ayah or Nurse 3 pp. text.
18. Kaut Pootlies, or Puppets exhibited by Native Jugglers for the Amusement of European Children 3 pp. text.
19. A Native Gentleman, smoking a Goorgoory or Hookah in his private Apartments, attended by his Dancing Girls 3 pp. text.
20. Marquis Wellesley & his Suite, at the Nabob of Oude's Breakfast Table, viewing an Elephant Fight 3 pp. text.

Another issue with plates bearing watermark 1820.
2nd Edition 1830.

185 DOYLEY (Charles)

The European in India; from a collection of drawings, by Charles Doyley, Esq. engraved by J. H. Clark and C. Dubourg; with a preface and copious descriptions, by Captain Thomas Williamson; accompanied with A Brief History of Ancient and Modern

Doyley's European in India (*contd.*)

India, from the earliest periods of antiquity to the Termination of the late Mahratta War, by F. W. Blagdon, Esq. London: Published and sold by Edward Orme, Bond Street, Corner of Brook Street, Printseller and Publisher to His Majesty and His Royal Highness the Prince Regent; and by Black, Parry, and Co. Booksellers to the Hon. East-India Company, Leadenhall Street. J. F. Dove, Printer, St. John's Square, Smithfield

Quarto. 1813

COLLATION.—Half-title "The European in India; accompanied with A Brief History of Ancient and Modern India, &c. &c. &c." + Title as above (v. blank) + Preface 11 pp. (unpaged 12th blank) + List of Plates 1 p. (v. blank) + 20 plates + sub-title "A Brief History of Ancient and Modern India by F. W. Blagdon, Esq." 1 p. (v. blank) + Address 2 pp. + Text pp. 65–149 + General Index 9 pp. (unpaged).

The 20 plates are the same as in the preceding item (with the exception that the plates themselves do not bear titles). The pages of text are compressed to some of the plates 3, 4, 5, 8, 12, 13, 14, 16, 17, 18 and 20 having only 2 pages of text instead of 3 pages, and plates 9 and 10 having 3 pp. instead of 4 pp. of text.

186 D'OYLY (Sir C.)

Tom Raw, the Griffin: A Burlesque Poem, in Twelve Cantos: illustrated by Twenty-five Engravings, descriptive of the Adventures of a Cadet in the East India Company's Service, from the period of his quitting England to his obtaining a staff situation in India By a Civilian and an Officer on the Bengal Establishment London Printed for R. Ackermann 96 Strand. 1828

Octavo.

COLLATION.—Half-title "Tom Raw, the Griffin A Burlesque Poem," (v. London: Printed by J. Moyes, Took Court, Chancery Lane) + Title as above (v. blank) + Preface 3 leaves (iii–vii) + Index to plates 1 leaf + pp. 1–325 + 25 coloured plates.

1. p. 10. Tom Raw Crossing the Line.
2. p. 15. Tom Raw at Cape of Good Hope.
3. p. 33. Tom Raw presents letters of intro.
4. p. 44. Tom Raw between smoke & fire.
5. p. 74. Tom Raw treats Lucy to a ride.
6. p. 91. Tom Raw rather awkward at the dance.
7. p. 120. Tom Raw sits for his portrait.
8. p. 149. Tom Raw misfortune at ball.
9. p. 172. Tom Raw mistakes a french millener for Hindoo Goddess.
10. p. 182. Tom Raw at Hindoo Entertainment.
11. p. 199. Tom Raw forwarded to headquarters (used as front.)
12. p. 205. Tom Raw rejects embraces nabob of Bengal.
13. p. 214. Tom Raw brought face to face with enemy.
14. p. 215. Tom Raw mounts elephant for first time.
15. p. 228. The Royal Hindoo Hunt.
16. p. 231. The ferocity of the tiger.
17. p. 237. Tom Raw in danger.
18. p. 256. Tom Raw carried up the country.
19. p. 263. Tom Raw gets introduced to his colonel.
20. p. 280. Tom Raw gains the victory.
21. p. 296. Tom Raw in the midst of his difficulties.
22. p. 304. Tom Raw on short commons.

D'Oyly's Tom Raw (*contd.*)

23. p. 307. Tom Raw disappointed at hearing the will read.
24. p. 313. Tom Raw wounded.
25. p. 321. Tom Raw obtains a staff appointment.

187 D'OYLY (Sir C.)

Views of Calcutta and its Environs, by the late Sir Charles D'Oyly Bart. vignette "East Gate—Government House" London Lithographed & Published by Dickinson & Co. 114 New Bond Street

Folio.   1848

COLLATION.—Lithograph title as above (v. blank) + 25 plates. Each plate marked, Sir C. Doyly delt. Dickinson & Co. lith.

1. Government House from St. Andrews Library.
2. View near the Circular Road.
3. Garden Reach.
4. Custom House Wharf.
5. Town and Port of Calcutta.
6. Banyan Tree.
7. Church Entrance to the Dhuram Tolla.
8. Mosque at Borranypore.
9. Procession of the Churruckpooja (folding plate).
10. Office of the Sudder Board of Revenue from Kyd Street.
11. General View of Calcutta from the Entrance to the Water Gate of Fort William.
12. View in Clive Street.
13. View in the Village of Sheebpore.
14. Calcutta from the Old Course.
15. St Pauls Cathedral Calcutta.
16. Menagerie at Baruckpore   } on 1 plate.
    Entrance to Barackpore Park
17. View in the Serampore Road.
18. The Bishops College   } on 1 plate.
    The Mahommedan College
19. Suspension Bridge at Alipore over Tollys Nulla.
20. View of Part of Chowringhee.
21. Statute of the Marquis of Hastings in Tank Square.
22. Hindoo Mut in the Chitpore Bazaar.
23. Esplanade.
24. Hindoo Temple near the Strand Road.
25. Chowrihchee Road from No. 11 Esplanade.

188 DUBOURG (M.)

Views of the Remains of Ancient Buildings in Rome, and its Vicinity. With a descriptive and historical account of each subject. (small swelled rule) By M. Dubourg (rule) 3½ line quote from Petrarch (rule) London: Printed for J. Taylor, Architectural Library, Holborn, by J. Haddon, Castle Street, Finsbury (rule)

Folio.   1844

COLLATION.—Title as above (v. blank) + Introduction 2 pp. + 16 leaves of Text + 26 plates, each marked, Engraved by M. Dubourg, Published as the Act Directs 1820.

Dubourg's Ancient Buildings in Rome (*contd.*)

Plate 1. Grotto of Egeria.
,, 2. Temple of Vesta.
,, 3. Temple of Fortuna Virilio.
,, 4. Temple of Janus Quadrefrons.
,, 5. Temple of Bacchus.
,, 6. Temple of Vesta at Tivoli.
,, 7. Tomb of Cecilia Metella.
,, 8. Temple of Minerva Medica.
,, 9. Temple of the Dea Tussis.
,, 10. The Panthion.
,, 11. Ponte Lucano.
,, 12. The Coliseum.
,, 13. The Coliseum.

Plate 14. Forum of Nerva.
,, 15. Arch of Titus.
,, 16. Temple of Jupiter Tonans.
,, 17. Trajans Column.
,, 18. Arch of Trajan at Benevento.
,, 19. Tomb of Hadrian.
,, 20. Tomb of Caius Cestius.
,, 21. Arch of Septimus Severus.
,, 22. Temple of Pallas.
,, 23. Claudian Aqueduct.
,, 24. Ponte Salaro.
,, 25. Baths of Dioclesian.
,, 26. Arch of Constantine.

189 DULWICH GALLERY

A series of 30 plates without title mounted on cards all marked In the Dulwich Gallery Drawn, engraved and published by R. Cockburn Dulwich   1818

1. The Cascatella and Villa of Maecenas at Tivoli.   R. Wilson.
2. Jacob and Laban.   Claude.
3. A View near Dort.   Albert Cuyp.
4. A Hunting Party.   P. Wouwermans.
5. A Brisk Gale.   W. Vandevelde.
6. The Fountain.   N. Berchem.
7. Celebrated Picture by N. Poussin.
8. The Chaff-Cutter.   D. Teniers.
9. Jacobs Dream.   Rembrandt.
10. A Seaport.   Claude.
11. From the original by Gaspar Poussin.
12. Crossing the Bridge.   A. Pynaker.
13. Jacob and Rachel.   Murillo.
14. A Watermill.   Hobbema.
15. A View near Utrecht.   Albert Cuyp.

16. From the original by Salvatore Rosa.
17. A Calm.   W. Vandevelde.
18. Sunset.   D. Teniers.
19. From the original picture by J. Both.
20. The Embarkation of St. Paula.   Claude.
21. A Waterfall.   Ruysdael.
22. From the original by Salvatore Rosa.
23. Halt of Travellers.   Wouvermans.
24. Fording the Brook.   N. Bercham.
25. From the original by Albert Cuyp.
26. ,, ,, ,, ,, J. Both.
27. ,, ,, ,, ,, Wouwermans.
28. ,, ,, ,, ,, D. Teniers.
29. Evening by Both.
30. The Assumption of the Virgin.   N. Poussin.

190   *Reissued in 1830, the number of plates being increased to 50.*

191 ECKSTEIN (John)

Picturesque Views of the Diamond Rock, taken on the Spot, and Dedicated to Sir Samuel Hood, K.B., Commodore and Commander-in-Chief of His Majesty's Ships and Vessels employed in the Windward and Charibbee Islands &c. &c. &c. By his most obliged and most humble servant John Eckstein London Published Jany. 1st 1805, for the Author, by J. C. Stadler, No. 15 Villiers Street, Strand.

Oblong Folio.   1805

COLLATION.—Title as above, with a stipple portrait of Sir Samuel Hood K.B., at the head of the title + Portraits of the Officers of his Majesty's Ship Centaur &c. J. Eckstein pinxt. W. Reynolds sculpt. [a stipple plate] + 14 coloured aquatints.

Each plate marked J. Eckstein pinxt. J. C. Stadler direxr. London Published for the Author Jany. 1 1805 by J. C. Stadler 15 Villiers Street, Strand.

1. The Tent of the Miners, making the Covered way, with the Curieux Brig, a Prize.
2. The Saw-Pit and the Carpenters Shop.

Eckstein's Diamond Rock (*contd.*)

3. Hammocks in a Fig-Tree, Sailors visiting a Sick Messmate.
4. The passage upon the Rock, with the Mail Coach.
5. The Forge.
6. The Farm, with a View of the Wild Fig-Tree.
7. The Centaur Battery.
8. A Lodgement under the Rock, on the South west side.
9. The Bay towards the Saline Point, with the Centaur and Blenheim firing at Fort St Anne.
10. The Queen's Battery. Seamen hauling up Spars: the Centaur and Blenheim at Anchor on the Diamond Patch.
11. Portland-place, an eminence on the Rock, with the Governors Tent, Painters Tent &c.
12. General View of the Diamond Rock from the N.E. side with the Queens Battery.
13. South East View of the Diamond Rock, with the Cannon being hauled up from the Centaur, by the cable.
14. Sailors hauling the heavy Cannon, on the foot of the Rock in a Surf.

Rare.

192 EDWARDS (Sydenham)

Cynographia Britannica consisting of coloured Engravings of the various Breeds of Dogs existing in Great Britain drawn from the Life, with observations on their properties and uses by Sydenham Edwards; and coloured under his immediate inspection (thick and thin rule) 2½ line quotation (thick and thin rule) London: Printed by C. Whittingham, Dean Street, Fetter Lane, for the Author, Charles Street, Queen's Elm Chelsea and sold by J. White, Fleet Street; J. Robson New Bond Street; H. D. Symonds, Paternoster-Row: L. B. Seeley Ave Maria Lane; T. Curtis St George's Crescent; and A. and J. Arch, Grace-church-Street (swelled rule)

Quarto.   1800

COLLATION.—Title as above (v. blank) + Introduction pp. 3–8 + 36 unpaged leaves of text and 12 coloured plates.

1. The Newfoundland Dog London Pub. by Syd Edwards.
2. The Beagle London Pub. by Syd Edwards   Augt. 1 1800.
3. The Spaniel London Pub. by Syd Edwards   Jany. 1 1800.
4. The Bull-Dog London Pub. by Syd Edwards   Aug. 1 1800.
5. The Terrier London Pub. by Syd Edwards Charles St. Queen's Elm.   Chelsea.
6. The Shepherds Dog and the Cur Pub. Feb. 1802 by Syd. Edwards Charles Street Queens Elm.
7. The Blood Hound London Pub. by Syd Edwards No. 11 Charles Street Queen Elm   Jan. 1 1803.
8. The Dog of New South Wales & the Pomeranian Dog London Pub. by Syd Edwards No. 11 Charles Street Queen Elm   April 1 1803.
9. The Danish Dog Pub. Nov. 30 1803 by Syd Edwards No. 11 Charles Street Queen Elm.
10. The Pointer Pub. Jan. 1 1803 by Syd Edwards No. 11 Charles Street Queens Elm.
11. The Mastiff London Pub. Jany. 1 1805 by Syd Edwards Queens Elm.
12. The Setter London Published Jan. 1 1805 by Syd Edwards No. 11 Charles St.   Queens Elm.

A very rare book.   It originally appeared in 6 parts (all published) in paper wrappers.
The above collation was taken from a copy in the possession of Messrs. Francis Edwards.

193 EDWARDS (Lt. William)

Sketches in Scinde.

Folio.   1846

COLLATION.—Engraved title 1 lf. + Dedication 1 lf. + Plan 1 lf. + List of plates 1 lf. + 10 plates.

Edwards' Scinde (*contd.*)

1. North West Face Fort Hyderabad.
2. Tombs at Truck.
3. Round Tower Fort Hyderabad.
4. From the Top of the Round Tower, Fort Hyderabad.
5. Main Gateway Fort Hyderabad.
6. Main Guard and Government House Fort Hyderabad.
7. Entrance to Town of Shewan and Lal Shah Baz's Tomb.
8. Roree on the Indus.
9. Fortress of Devrah.
10. Southern Entrance to Bejar Khan's Stronghold at Truckee.

Edy (J. W.) Picturesque Scenery of Norway.   See under Boydell.

194 EGAN (Pierce)

Pierce Egan's Anecdotes (original and selected) of The Turf, the Chase, the Ring, and the Stage; the whole forming a Complete Panorama of the Sporting World; uniting with it A Book of Reference and Entertaining Companion to the Lovers of British Sports (line) Embellished with Thirteen coloured Plates, designed from Nature and etched by Theodore Lane (2 line rule) dedicated to Sir Bellingham Graham, Bart (2 line rule) London: Printed for Knight & Lacey, Paternoster Row and Pierce Egan, 113 Strand (short rule)

Octavo.   1827

COLLATION.—Title as above + Dedication to Sir Bellingham Graham Bart. 1 leaf (iii–iv) + Contents and Directions to Binder 2 ll. (v–viii) + pp 1–304 + 13 coloured plates including frontispiece by Theodore Lane.

1. Front. (Composite) depicting Horse race at top Charley Tell-Tale keeping the PP Gents on the broad Grin with his laughable Anecdotes (view of stag hunt below) Des & etch. Theodore Lane.
2. p. 81. The celebrated dog Billy killing 100 Rats at the Westminster Pit Des. & etch. Theodore Lane.
3. p. 101. Fight between the lion Wallace & the dogs Tinker & Ball in factory yard Warwick Des. & etch. Theodore Lane.
4. p. 146. Royal Stand at Ascot Races. H.M. George IV & Duke of York enjoying the Sports of the Turf.
5. p. 150. Interesting interview between Mr Mathews & his Irish theatrical barber Des. & etch. by Theodore Lane.
6. p. 183. A Parish concern or Prominent reasons for Matrimony.
7. p. 188. The Tavern in an Uproar. Mrs. Bonniface showing more pluck than her good Man Des. & etch. by Theodore Lane.
8. p. 201. How to pick up a "Rum One to look at" and a "Good one to go" in Smithfield Des. & etch. Theodore Lane.
9. p. 249. Grand Duke Nicholas witnessing a let go match by dogs at Olivers Game Bull Des. & Etch by Theodore Lane.
10. p. 266. Unparalleled feat of Mons Ducrow in Character of Wild Indian Hunter Des. & etch. by Theodore Lane.
11. p. 293. Grand Rowing Match for Mr. Keans Prize Wherry.
12. p. 297. Canine fanciers trying qualities of dogs at duck hunt Des. & etch. by Theodore Lane.
13. p. 298. Hopping Match Clapham Common Jackson the runner exhibiting his agility.

With the following woodcuts: p. 1 Leaping fence, p. 21 The swell guard, p. 48 Dogfight, p. 63 Boxing bout, p. 72 Thimble rig, p. 94 Poaching, p. 118 Bull Tossing, p. 137 Patient

Egan's Anecdotes of Turf, Chase etc. (*contd.*)

Angler, p. 164 Woolwich Races, p. 184 climbing the pole, p. 208 Picnic, p. 236 Trotting chaise, p. 253 Through the ice, p. 260 Cockshie, p. 291 Elephant, p. 296 Yachts, p. 297 Pigeon shooting, p. 304 Cockfight.

Issued in pictorial boards.

195 EGAN (Pierce)

The Life of an Actor. By Pierce Egan, author of "Life in London," "Tom and Jerry," "A Musical Drama," etc. Dedicated to Edmund Kean, Esq. (woodcut vignette) The Poetical Descriptions by T. Greenwood. Embellished with Twenty-seven Characteristic Scenes Etched by Theodore Lane; enriched also with several original designs on wood, executed by Mr. Thompson (thick and thin rule) London: Printed for C. S. Arnold, Tavistock Street, Covent Garden (rule)

Octavo.   1825

COLLATION.—Title as above (v. C and C Whittingham, College House, Chiswick) + Dedication to Edmund Kean 4 pp. (iii–vi) + Contents 4 pp. (vii–x) + (Illustrations 6 pp. (xi–xvi) + Prologue p. 1–2 + pp. 3–272 + 27 coloured plates. Each plate marked, "Drawn & Engraved by Theodore or Theoe. Lane," "London Published by C. S. Arnold 21 Tavistock Street Covent Garden." [date]

1. Front. ["Drop scene at one view displaying the difficulty of becoming a First Rate Actor"] Dec. 1 1824.
2. p. 41. House of Call for Actors—Proteus visits the Harp Jany. 1 1824.
3. p. 60. The Author's Retreat—Study and Practice: Proteus rehearsing Hamlet before his friend Horatio Quill. March 1 1824.
4. p. 70. Oxberry's Mixture of Harmony and Talent—Kings and Heroes unbending; Authors & Poets regaling March 1 1824.
5. p. 136. The Green Room at Brillant Shore Theatre—Proteus in Hotspur. Sep. 1 1824.
6. p. 141. Suiting the Action to the Word—Interior of a Hedge Ale House Jany. 1st 1824.
7. p. 186. A Beggarly Account of empty Boxes Proteus losing his Benefit May 1 1824.
8. p. 190. Proteus taking a Benefit according to Law Sepr. 1 1824.
9. p. 200. A scene not calculated upon by the Enthusiast of the Stage Sepr. 1 1824.
10. p. 204. The Vicissitudes of an Actor—Proteus "pulling them in" at Bartholomew Fair Feb. 1 1824.
11. p 206. A spirited Scene and full of Characters Proteus and his brother Actors taking refreshments Octr. 1 1824.
12. p. 213. Acting off the Stage. The well-fed Magistrate listening to the request of the half-famished Player to perform in a Barn Jany. 1st 1824.
13. p. 220. One man in his time plays many parts! Shaks. On and Off the Stage. Feby. 1 1824.
14. p. 223. The Flaming Actor: Proteus unexpectedly receiving a New Light upon his studies July 1 1824.
15. p. 224. A Scene full of Effect without the aid of canvas Actors travelling in search of fame April 1 1824.
16. p. 225. A Scene from the Turnpike Gate Proteus defending himself April 1 1824.
17. p. 228. Provincial Actors on their route Scene the Blue Devils May 1 1824.
18. p. 231. Proteus in search of Lodgings? Peregrine displays too much spirit for Ephraim Smooth May 1 1824.
19. p. 232. The Upper Regions in disorder: rapid descent of the Gods & Goddesses July 1 1824.
20. p. 241. Proteus in Love: Nature his Prompter Feby. 1 1824.
21. p. 245. A love scene not to be found in the works of Shakespeare the Elopement July 1 1824.
22. p. 248. A Scene not contemplated by the author of the play The Prompter not at his Post April 1 1824.
23. p. 249. Extraordinary Sale Disposal of Theatrical Property March 1 1824.
24. p. 257. Proteus visiting "Comic Dick" in the Workhouse Oct. 1 1824.

Egan's Life of an Actor (*contd.*)

25. p. 261. Theatrical Fund Dinner held at Free-Masons Tavern Dec. 1 1824.
26. p. 262. The Actors Climax: Proteus Manager of a Theatre Royal 1824.
27. p. 270. Proteus in his managerial capacity conducting the King and his Suite to the Royal Box Decr. 1 1824.

The 9 woodcuts on Title and pp. 36, 40, 63, 103, 113, 189, 227 *and* 272 *were executed by Thompson.*

Issued in wrappers in 9 parts.

A reissue appeared in 1892.

196 EGAN (Pierce)

Life in London; or, the Day and Night Scenes of Jerry Hawthorn, Esq. and his elegant friend Corinthian Tom, accompanied by Bob Logic, the Oxonian, in their Rambles and Sprees through the Metropolis. (rule) By Pierce Egan, Author of Walks through Bath, Sporting Anecdotes, Picture of the Fancy, Boxiana, &c. (rule) Dedicated to His most gracious Majesty King George the Fourth (vignette St Pauls in the background, boxing gloves, mask, fiddle, dice &c.) Embellished with Thirty-Six Scenes from Real Life, Designed and etched by I. R. & G. Cruikshank; and enriched also with numerous original Designs on Wood, by the same Artists. (rule) London: Printed for Sherwood, Neely, and Jones, Paternoster-Row (small rule)

Octavo.   1821

COLLATION.—Half-title "Life in London" (v. Marchant Printer Ingram-Court, Fenchurch-Street) + Title as above (v. blank) + Dedication to George IV 4 pp. (v–viii) + Contents 4 pp. (ix–xii) + Illustrations 4 pp. (xiii–xvi) + pp. 1–376 + 8 pp. advertisements, 36 coloured plates and 21 wood engravings.

All the coloured plates marked, Drawn and Engraved [or Engd.] by I. R. & G. Cruikshank, and all bearing imprint "Pubd. by Sherwood, Neely & Jones" [with date].

1. Front. Composite consisting of 5 vignettes within a Corinthian Column, Tom Jerry and Logic in centre July 15 1821.
    p. 118. The Music of Corinthian Tom's Song 6 folding pages.
2. p. 146. Jerry in Training for a Swell Augt. 31 1820.
3. p. 155. Tom & Jerry Sporting their "bits of Blood" among the Pinks in Rotten Row Decr. 1 1820.
4. p. 173. Tom & Jerry, in the Saloon of Covent-Garden. Novr. 1 1820.
5. p. 179. Tom & Jerry, taking Blue Ruin after the Spell is broke up. Decr. 1 1820.
6. p. 181. Midnight. Tom & Jerry, at a Coffee-Shop near the Olympic Augt. 31 1820.
7. p. 184. Tom & Jerry in Trouble after a Spree. Octr. 1 1820.
8. p. 186. Bow Street Tom & Jerry's sensibility awakened at the pathetic tale of the elegant Cyprian—the feeling Coachman—and the generous Magistrate Novr. 1 1820.
9. p. 192. Tom & Jerry larking at a Masquerade Supper, at the Opera House Octr. 1 1820.
10. p. 217. Art of Self Defence. Tom and Jerry receiving Instructions from Mr. Jackson, at his Rooms, in Bond Street Jany. 1 1821.
11. p. 220. Cribbs' Parlour. Tom introducing Jerry & Logic to the Champion of England Jan. 1 1821.
12. p. 223. Tom & Jerry sporting their blunt on the phenomenon Monkey, Jacco Macacco, at the Westminster Pit Octr. 1 1820.
13. p. 232. Tom getting the best of a Charley Augt. 31 1820.
14. p. 236. A "Look in" at Tattersals'. Tom taking Jerry's Judgement in purchasing a "Prad" Feby. 1 1821.
15. p. 250. An Introduction. Gay Moments of Logic, Jerry, Tom and Corinthian Kate Novr. 1 1820.
16. p. 252. Fencing. Jerry's admiration of Tom in an "Assault" with Mr O'Shaunessy, at the Rooms, in St. James's Str. Feby. 1 1821.
17. p. 256. Tom & Jerry, catching Kate & Sue, on the Sly, having their Fortunes told Decr. 1 1820.

Egan's Life in London (*contd.*)

18. p. 261. The "Ne Plus Ultra" of "life in London"—Kate, Sue, Tom, Jerry, and Logic viewing the Throne-Room, at Carlton Palace   March 1 1821.
19. p. 276. Life in London.   Peep o'day Boys.   A street Row the Author losing his "reader."   Tom and Jerry "showing fight," and Logic floored   Feby. 1 1821.
20. p. 280. Symptoms of the finish of "Some Sorts of Life" in London—Tom, Jerry and Logic, in the Press Yard, at Newgate   April 1821.
21. p. 283. The Royal Exchange—Tom pointing out to Jerry a few of the primest features of Life in London,   April 1821.
22. p. 286. Lowest "Life in London"—Tom, Jerry, and Logic, among the unsophisticated Sons and Daughters of Nature, at "All Max," in the East   May 1 1821.
23. p. 310. Highest Life in London.   Tom & Jerry "Sporting a Toe" among the Corinthians at Almacks in the West   May 1 1821.
24. p. 318. Tom, Jerry and Logic backing Tommy the Sweep, at the Royal Cockpit   April 1821.
25. p. 320. A Game of Whist.   Tom and Jerry among the Swell "Broad Coves"   Jany. 1 1821.
26. p. 322. Tom, Jerry and Logic, in characters at the Grand Carnival   March 1 1821.
27. p. 324. The Green Room at Drury Lane Theatre.   Tom & Jerry introduced to the Characters in Don Giovanni   June 1 1821.
28. p. 329. Tom, Jerry and Logic "tasting" Wine in the Wood, at the London Docks   June 1 1821.
29. p. 331. Outside of the Opera House at Night—Gallantry of Tom and Jerry   June 1 1821.
30. p. 338. Tom, Jerry and Logic, making the most of an Evening at Vauxhall   July 2 1821.
31. p. 341. A Shilling well laid out.   Tom and Jerry at the Exhibition of Pictures at the Royal Academy   July 1 1821.
32. p. 346. Tom and Jerry "Masquerading it" among the Cadgers, in the "Back Slums" in the Holy Land   July 1 1821.
33. p. 348. Tom and Jerry taking the hint at Logic's being blown up at "Point Nonplus" or long "wanted" by John Doe and Richard Roe, and "must come"   March 1 1821.
34. p. 352. A Whistling Shop.   Tom & Jerry visiting Logic "on board the Fleet"   May 1 1821.
35. p. 361. Jerry "beat to a stand still"!   Dr. Please'em's Prescription.   Tom and Logic's Condolence, and the "Slavey's" on the alert   July 1 1821.
36. p. 375. White Horse Cellar, Piccadilly.   Tom and Logic bidding Jerry "goodbye" upon his going into training & his return to Hawthorn Hall   July 1 1821.

Woodcut figures on the title and on pp. 29, 36, 52, 71, 82, 95, 102, 116, 125, 169, 190, 218, 233, 241, 311, 317, 328, 332, 349 and 376.

An enormously popular work "Life in London" was translated into French, and a version prepared and acted on the stage.   Reprinted in 1822, 1823, 1830, 1841 (1870) and 1904.   Numerous imitations soon appeared namely Carey's Life in Paris, Real Life in London, Real Life in Ireland, even Fanny Burney being influenced to entitle the 1822 edition of Evelina as Evelina: or Female Life in London.

ISSUES.—First Issue has no footnote on p. 9, and the first sheet of music is unnumbered.
Second Issue has a footnote on p. 9, and first sheet of music is unnumbered.
Third Issue has the footnote on p. 9, and the first sheet of music is numbered.

As regards the Half-title, in early issues the printer's imprint on the reverse is on the left-hand side of page; in later issues it is on right-hand side.   An unnumbered leaf "To Subscribers" exists, it is rare and usually missing as it forms no part of a signature, and the work is complete without it.

197 Egan (Pierce)

Pierce Egan's Finish to the Adventures of Tom, Jerry, and Logic in their Pursuits through Life in and out of London: Illustrated by the pencil of Mr. Robert Cruikshank, in 36 scenes from Real Life, & enriched with several Designs on Wood by the same artist (2 line rule) Dedicated to his most gracious majesty King George the Fourth (vignette)

Egan's Finish To Tom, Jerry and Logic (*contd.*)

(2 line rule) London Printed by C. Baynes 13, Duke Street, Lincoln's-inn-fields, for G. Virtue 26, Ivy Lane, Paternoster Row; Bath Street, Bristol; and Great Ancoates Street, Manchester (rule)

Octavo.   1830

COLLATION.—Half-title + Title as above (v. blank) + Dedication to George IV pp. iii–iv + Contents pp. v–xii + Illustrations pp. xiii–xvi + pp. 1–368 + 36 coloured plates, and woodcuts in text.

Each plate (except Nos. 13 and 20) marked, Drawn and Engraved by Robert (or Robt.) Cruikshank.

1. Front. Composite. 2 four-stage vignette with death at banquet centre.
2. p. 90. Travellers see strange Things "Logic without his Specs The Mistakes of a Night [&c.]
3. p. 96. Going off in a hurry! but not making a noise in the World Logic's slippery State of Affairs [&c.].
4. p. 102. Hawthorn Hall: Jerry at Home: The Enjoyements of a comfortable fire side [&c.].
5. p. 105. The hounds at a standstill Jerry enticed by the pretty Gypsey Girl to have his fortune told. Logic breaking cover.
6. p. 119. Logic's Upper Story—but no Premises! Jerry's return to the Metropolis. The Young One on the "qui vive" after his Old Pal Bob.
7. p. 125. Strong Symptoms of Water on the Brain: and Logics Spread of no use in the Floating Capital.
8. p. 129. Tom, Jerry, Logic, and the "uncommonly big gentleman" among the "Show Folks," at Bartholomew Fair. One man in his time plays many parts.
9. p. 137. Tom, Jerry, and Logic assisting at the Ceremony of making the uncommonly big gentleman a Buffalo.
10. p. 142. The Duchess of Do-Good's Screen,—an attractive subject to Tom, Logic and Jerry.
11. p. 148. How to Finish a Night to be Up and dressed in the Morning Tom awake Jerry caught napping Logic on the go [&c.].
12. p. 157. Splendid Jem once a dashing hero in the Metropolis recognised by Tom amongst the Convicts in the Dock Yard at Chatham.
13. p. 177. Logic visiting his old acquaintance on board the Fleet accompanied by Tom and Jerry [&c.]
14. p. 183. The Grand Lounge Regent Street to wit Tom and his Party off to the Races [&c.].
15. p. 211. Life en Passant Fancy Dress Ball near Rag Fair: the Sage of the East quite at Home [&c.].
16. p. 215. Jerry Up, but not dressed a miserable brothel his Pal bolted with the toggers [&c.].
17. p. 224. The Burning Shame! Tom and Jerry, laughing at the turn up between the uncommonly big Gentleman and the hero of the Roundy Ken under suspicious circumstances.
18. p. 226. The Money lender the high bred One trying it on to get the best of Old Screw [&c.].
19. p. 249. Corinthian Kate's Residence—Unexpected arrival of Tom!
20. p. 251. Life in the East Tom Jerry & Logic called to the Bar of Benchers. The John Bull Fighter exhibiting his cups.
21. p. 263. Dangerous to be Safe: or the abrupt departure Jane Merrythought at her Wits end Lady Wanton's reputation in Danger and Jerry compelled to retreat.
22. p. 273. Tom, Jerry, Logic and the uncommonly big Gentleman entering into all the sport of the game of Forfeits.
23. p. 276. "A Bit of Good Truth" Tom, Jerry and Logic enjoying the lark song fun and frisk at a Cock and Hen Club.
24. p. 284. An Early Spreee: or an offhand wager [&c.].
25. p. 289. Archery—Tom, Jerry and the Fat Knight trying their skill to hit the Bull's Eye.
26. p. 290. Popular Gardens. Tom, Jerry and Logic laughing at the bustle and alarm occasioned among the visitors by the escape of a Kangaroo.
27. p. 294. One of those afflicting occurrences in Life in London Tom Jerry and Logic arrested in their progress home by the melancholy discovery of Corinthian Kate in the last stage of a Consumption disease & inebriety.
28. p. 305. Life on the Water Symptoms of "Heavy Whet" or a Drap too much [&c.].
29. p. 308. Pigeon Shooting—Tom, Jerry and the Fat Knight engaged in a match.
30. p. 315. Melancholy end of Corinthian Kate! One of those lamentable examples of dissipated Life in London.

Egan's Finish To Tom, Jerry and Logic (*contd.*)

31. p. 328. Banco Regis Tenterden Park Races. Tom, Jerry, Logic and the uncommonly big Gentleman highly entertained on their visit to Splinter with the race for the Cameza Stake the Ladies shift for themselves.
32. p. 331. Adventures at Court. Tom, Jerry and Logic highly amused with the actions of the Deaf & Dumb Man outwitting his Creditors with, the Big Wigs.
33. p. 338. The House of Accommodation in Flames. The inmates put to flight Jerry narrowly escapes with his life but preserves Ellen Prettyflower his paramour from an untimely death.
34. p. 355. Logic's Testament Last Scene of all that ends this strange eventful history. The Oxonians farewell to Tom and Jerry.
35. p. 364. The Death of Corinthian Tom.
36. p. 367. The Wedding Day—all happiness at Hawthorne Hall Jerry and Mary Rosebud united.

First Issue has woodcuts on pp. 7, 40 and 42, and the engraved title page is dated 1829.
Second Issue.—No woodcuts on pp. 40 and 42.

198 EGAN (Imitation of Life in London)

Real Life in London; or, the Rambles and Adventures of Bob Tallyho, Esq. and his cousin, the Hon. Tom. Dashall, &c. through the Metropolis; exhibiting a Living Picture of Fashionable Characters, Manners and Amusements in High and Low Life (short rule) By an Amateur (short rule) Embellished and Illustrated with a Series of Coloured Prints, designed and engraved by Messrs. Alken, Dighton, Brooke, Rowlandson &c. (rule) London: Printed for Jones & Co. Oxford Arms Passage, Warwick Lane

2 vols. Octavo.   1821(–2)

COLLATION VOL. I.—Frontispiece + Engraved title + Printed title as above (v. B. Bensley, Printer, Bolt Court, Fleet Street, London) + Contents 8 pp. (iii–x Directions to Binder also on p. x) + pp. 3–656 (at foot of page B. Bensley Bolt Court Fleet Street) + 19 coloured plates (20 with front.) all bearing imprint London Published by Jones & Co. [and date].

1. Frontispiece—Composite "The Principal Characters presented to Public Exhibition throughout Real Life in London" Designed by H. Alken Esqr. London Published by Jones & Co. Decr. 15 1821.
2. Engraved Title—Real Life [historiated] in London (vignette "View of Regent Street from Waterloo Place" W. Read del et sculpt.) London Published by Jones & Co. May 26 1821.
3. p. 24. Hyde Park. Tom & his Cousin, dashing among the Pinks in Rotten Row. Drawn & Etched by H. Alken Esqr. May 22 1821.
4. p. 68. Epsom Races, Showing Bob how to drive a Tandem Drawn & Etched by H. Alken Esqr. June 1 1821.
5. p. 108. Sparring at the Fives Court Drawn & Etched by H. Alken Esqr. May 1st 1821.
6. p. 112. The Kings Levee. Tom & Bob gratifying their Curiosity at the Expense of their pockets [H Jones del] June 16 1821.
7. p. 200. Drury Lane Theatre Tom & Bob enjoying a Theatrical treat [H. Jones del] August 11 1821.
8. p. 212. The Honble. Tom Dashall, & his Cousin Bob in the Lobby at Drury Lane Theatre May 1 1821.
9. p. 244. Tattersals. Tom and Bob looking out for a good-one, among the deep ones. Drawn & Etched by H. Alken Esqr. Septr. 29 1821.
10. p. 300. A Modern Hell. Bobs first introduction to Gaming. Drawn and Etched by H. Alken Esqr. July 25 1821.
11. p. 368. Exhibition Somerset House Tom & Bob among the Connoisseurs Drawn & Etched by H. Alken Esqr. July 14, 1821.
12. p. 440. Road to a Fight Plate I Drawn and Etched by H. Alken Esqr. Oct. 20 1821.
13. p. 460. Billingsgate Tom and Bob taking a Survey after a Nights Spree Drawn & Etched by H. Alken Esqr. July 1 1821.

Egan's Real Life in London (*contd.*)

14. p. 592. Political Dinner. Tom & Bob taking a lesson on the Constitution & not neglecting their own. [H. Jones del] Sepr. 8th 1821.
15. p. 596. The Country Squire taking a peep at Charley's Theatre Westmr. Drawn & Etched by H. Alken Esqr. May 22 1821.
16. p. 600. Grand Coronation Banquet [in Westminster Hall] July 19th 1821.
17. p. 612. Road to a Fight Plate II Drawn and Etched by H. Alken Esqr. Oct. 27 1821.
18. p. 620. A Private Turn-up in the Drawing Room of a Noble Marquis Drawn & Etched by H. Alken Esqr. July 21 1821.
19. p. 632. Masquerade Tom and Bob keeping it up in real character Drawn & Etched by H. Alken Esqr. Sept. 29 1821.
20. p. 640. [or Vol. II p. 407] St. George's Day, Presentation at the Levee P. Roberts [not included in the List of Plates optional].

VOL. II.—Frontispiece + Engraved title + Printed title "Real Life in London; or, the Further Rambles and Adventures of Bob Tallyho, Esq. and his cousin, the Hon. Tom Dashall, &c. through the Metropolis; Exhibiting a Living Picture of Fashionable Characters, Manners, and Amusements in High and Low Life (rule) by an Amateur (rule) Embellished and Illustrated with a Series of Coloured Prints, Designed and Engraved by Messrs. Heath Alken, Dighton, Brooke, Rowlandson, &c. (rule) Vol. II (rule) London Printed for Jones & Co. 3, Warwick Square 1822 (v. B. Bensley, Bolt Court, Fleet Street)" + Contents 9 pp. (i–ix Directions to Binder also in ix p. x blank) + pp. 3–668 + 13 coloured plates.

20. Frontispiece—Composite, 11 vignettes forming ladder &c.
21. Engraved Title—Real Life in London Vol. II (historiated Letters to word Life) (vignette "View of London from Adelphi Terrace, and the Lord Mayors Show by Water") London Published by Jones & Co. Decr. 15 1821.
22. p. 16. British Museum. Tom and Bob in search of the Antique. April 17 1822.
23. p. 76. Kings Bench: Tom & Bob taking a peep at Real Characters, in the Abbots Priory. Jany 12 1822.
24. p. 100. Tom & Bob, in Masqurade (sic) Blowing a Cloud & taking their heavy wet at the Black diamond Merchants Free & Easy King Charles's Crib Scotland Yard Designed by Mr Heath.
25. p. 204. Blue Ruin. Tom & Bob tasting Thompson's Best April 25th 1822.
26. p. 232. Almacks. Tom & Bob Sporting their figures at a Fancy Dress Ball. W. Heath del 1822 Feby. 9 1822.
27. p. 308. Easter Hunt. Drawn & Etched by H. Alken Esqr. May 1st 1821.
28. p. 313. Tom & Bob among the Coster Mongers at a Donkey Cart race. June 29 1822.
29. p. 388. Tom & Bob taking a Stroll down Drury Lane at five in the morning. March 9 1822.
30. p. 536. Ascot Races. Tom & Bob winning the long odds from a knowing one. Drawn & Etched by H. Alken Esq. June 22 1822.
31. p. 592. Tom & Bob at a real Swell Party. W. Heath del 1822.
32. p. 665. Bull & Mouth Inn Bob bidding adieu to his friends & Life in London Sept. 28 1822. Tom and Bob Catching a Charley Napping H Jones del May 21st 1822 [not included in List of Plates optional].

Originally published in 56 parts, on completion the work was issued in boards. A few large-paper copies were printed on royal paper hot pressed with proof impressions of the plates. Later copies were bound in publisher's cloth with gilt lettering and design on spine.

A book full of contrarities and difficulties for the bibliographer, there being innumerable variations of the plates. I have examined twenty or thirty copies and noted their peculiarities and points. but doubt if I have run them all to earth. The difficulties are further increased by many copies in modern bindings having been completed or made up of different issues giving combinations that are not true variations.

Published red cloth lettered on spine in gilt, Life in London Vol. I [II] gilt arabesque pattern on spine, sides plain.

FIRST EDITION, FIRST ISSUE VOL. I.—Printed title Oxford Arms Passage dated 1821 (v. Bensley's imprint).

Egan's Real Life in London (*contd.*)

p. 24. Plate marked, Drawn & Etched by H. Alken.
p. 108. Lettered "Sparring at Fives Court."
p. 300. Lettered "A Modern Hell Bobs first Introduction to Gaming" July 5 1821.
p. 596. Marked "Drawn & Etched by H. Alken." Westr. [contracted].

VOL. II.—Printed title dated 1822 (v. Bensley's imprint) Frontispiece has at foot a 4-line verse, "Since Life is a Ladder which some have to climb" &c. at foot of left-hand ladder words, "Way up" at foot of right-hand words, "way down."

p. 100. Plate lettered Maquerade.

Second Issue.—Identical with first except for following variations:

Vol. I. p. 24. The plate is marked, Drawn by H. Alken Esqr. W. Read sc.
p. 596. The plate is marked, Drawn by H. Alken Esqr., and Westminster is spelt in full, not contracted.

Third Issue.—The address of the publishers on the printed title is altered to London: Printed for Jones & Co. 3 Warwick Square 1821.

Vol. I. p. 108. The lettering on plate is changed to Fives Court Tom & Bob Studying Real Life among the Millers.

199 *Later Issue 1823.—Title dated 1823, Brooke's name omitted from list of illustrators, and 3-line verse added after names of illustrators. Publishers address Warwick Square Newgate Street.*

Vol. I. p. 300. Lettering of plate changed to A "Modern Hell," or Fashionable Gaming House.
Vol. II. p. 100. In lettering of plate word Masquerade spelt correctly.

200 *Another Issue 1824.—Identical with previous issue except that Titles are dated 1824, and p. 656 Vol. I is marked, End of Vol. I and p. 668 Vol. II, marked The End, both without printer's imprint. Also the frontispiece to Vol. II is without the 4-line verse and "way up" and "way down". Page x of the same volume contains a Note "A Word to the Wise" instead of being blank.*

NOTE.—There are 2 extra plates, "St George's Day, Presentation at the Levee" and Tom and Bob catching a Charley Napping. Though the work is complete without them, it is desirable to have them included. I have seen them in all issues.

REMARKS.—Real Life in London both as regards the text and the plates is an imitation of Egan's Life in London. Though not the equal of the latter it has considerable merit, serves as a foil to its illustrious contemporary and is an interesting and useful guide to the social history of the period.

201 EGAN (Imitation of Life in London)

Real Life in Ireland: or, The Day and Night Scenes, Rovings, Rambles and Sprees, Bulls, Blunders, Bodderation, and Blarney, of Brian Boru Esq. and his elegant friend Sir Shawn O'Dogherty. (rule) Exhibiting a Real Picture of Characters, Manners Etc. in High and Low Life, in Dublin and Various Parts of Ireland. (rule) Embellished with humorous coloured engravings, from Original Designs by the most eminent Artists (thick and thin rule). By a Real Paddy (thin and thick rule) London Printed by B. Bensley Bolt Court Fleet Street. Published by Jones & Co. 3, Warwick Square: and J. L. Marks, Piccadilly; and sold by all booksellers and newsmen in town and country

Octavo. 1821

Egan's Real Life in Ireland (*contd.*)

COLLATION.—Title as above (v. blank) + Word to Wise 1 p. (v. blank) + Contents pp. i–vii + Directions to Binder 1 p. (viii) + pp. 5–296 + Front. and 18 coloured plates, each with Jones's imprint.

Front.   consiting of 10 small vignettes supported by 2 shillelah's Designed by W. Heath.

1. p. 10. Brian Boru Esqr.   Entering Belfast Piloted by Mrs. Peggy O'Shambles   Designed & Etched by H. Alkin (sic) Esqr.

2. p. 46. Brian Boru, Sir Shawn O'Dogherty, Capt. Grammachree & Poll Kettlewell, upset in a jingle. coming from the Black Rock.

3. p. 53. Brian Boru Esqr. & Sir Shawn O'Dogherty, in a Night Row, with the Charleys in Dame St. Drawn & Etched by H. Alken Esqr.

4. p. 64. His Majesty landing on the Pier at Howth.

5. p. 66. Capn. Grammachree playing "Paddy whack" on his wooden-leg-fife, to amuse the Car party on their Journey to meet the King.   Designed & Etched by H. Alken Esqr.

6. p. 89. A Pillar Committee.

7. p. 92. Going to the Levee.

8. p. 95. Procession and Te Deum Chaunt, for Sir Billy Biscuit.   1822.

9. p. 101. Departure of the King & inconsolable Grief of the Hibernians   Marks Fecit.   1821.

10. p. 108. Wetting an Irish Commission   Marks Fecit.   imprint N. D.

11. p. 126. Disagreeable Adventures of Brian Boru & Capn. Grammachree in an Irish whisky Parlour Marks Fecit.   1821.

12. p. 132. Brian Boru Esqr. proclaim'd the winner of the Boat-race for a Cow.   1822.

13. p. 137. The Squire Tumbling over Capn. Gram's Wooden leg in a Snoozing Cellar.   Marks Fecit. 1822.

14. p. 162. A Squall, the Boat Upset.   1822.

15. p. 170. Squire Boru giving Old Tarpaulin a quietus in a Duel.   Marks Fect.   N.D.

16. p. 184. The Tap in Sheriff's Prison.   1822.

17. p. 193. Sheriffs Prison—Introducing Swan the Exciseman.   1822.

18. p. 228. Captn Gram and his Friends having a small taste of a Row at the Theatre.   1822.

Published in 18 parts and in boards, the frontispiece being repeated on the upper cover in black and white. Though not so good it is more rare than Life in London. A Third Edition was printed in 1822, the collation is the same. Another edition 1829.

202 EGAN (P.)

Sporting Anecdotes, Original and Selected; including numerous characteristic portraits of Persons in Every Walk of Life, who have acquired Notoriety from their Achievements on the Turf, at the Table, and in the Diversions of the Field, with Sketches of various Animals of the Chase: To which is added, an account of noted Pedestrians, Trotting Matches, Cricketers, &c. The whole forming a complete Delineation of the Sporting World (2 line rule) By Pierce Egan. A New Edition, considerably enlarged and improved (2 line rule) vignette (2 line rule) London: Printed for Sherwood Jones and Co. Paternoster Row (short rule)

Octavo.   1825

COLLATION.—Title as above (v. Marchant, Printer, Ingram-Court, Fenchurch-Street.) + Dedication 1 lf. (iii–iv) + Advertisement to the present edition 1 p. (v. Critique) + sub-title "Sporting Notions" (v. woodcut of Captain Barclay) + pp. 1–583 (Errata p. 584) + Index pp. 585–592 (Directions for Placing Plates at foot of p. 592) + Books published by Sherwood Jones & Co. 16 pp. + 6 plates.

Each plate bears Sherwood & Jones's imprint and date.

Egan's Sporting Anecdotes (*contd.*)

1. Front. 8 small vignettes on 1 plate of Hunting, Fishing, Racing, Shooting, Archery, Cock fighting, Walking and Boxing J. R. Cruikshank Invt. P. Roberts Fecit Jany. 1 1820 (uncoloured).
2. p. 32. Monday after the "Great St. Leger" or Heroes of the Turf paying & receiving at Tattersalls. Drawn & Engraved by R. Cruikshank March 1 1824 (coloured).
3. p. 132. Colonel Thornton May 1 1823 (uncoloured).
4. p. 186. A Visit to the Fives Court. Engraved for the Annals of Sporting & Fancy Gazette. Designed & Etched by J. R. Cruikshank Augt. 1st 1822 (folding & coloured).
5. p. 380. Rat Hunting. Engraved by Roberts from a Drawing by S. Alkin Decr. 1 1823 (coloured).
6. p. 539. Thos. Cribb Engd. by Percy Roberts from a Painting by R. Sharples May 1 1824.

Issued in boards at 12s. with woodcut of greyhounds and hare on upper cover, wild duck and funeral urn on spine and advertisement of Annals of Sporting, with woodcut of deer on back cover.

203 [EGERTON (D. T.)]

Fashionable Bores or Coolers in High Life by Peter Quiz Published by W. Sams No. 1 St. James's St. London

Oblong Quarto.   1824

COLLATION.—Coloured emblematic title as above depicting a young buck with fools cap knocking out justice, pursuing a will of the wisp tripping over a placard held by death, followed by 13 coloured plates.

1. The Silent Rebuke Designed & Etched by D. T. Egerton.
* (Knocked senseless by 'Knight of the Whip') London Pub. W. Egerton 1824.
2. The Leech. Designed & Etched by D. T. Egerton.
3. The Tables Turn'd Designed & Etched by D. T. Egerton.
4. The Unfortunate Discovery Designed & Etched by D. T. Egerton.
5. The Insolence of Office Designed & Etched by D. T. Egerton.
6. The Trial of Nerves Designed & Etched by D. T. Egerton.
* The Unwelcome Visit Designed & Etched by D. T. Egerton.
* Vis a Vis Designed & Etched by D. T. Egerton.
* The Pressing Invitation Designed & Etched by D. T. Egerton.
* The Disappointment Designed & Etched by D. T. Egerton.
* The Unpleasant Rencontre Designed & Etched by D. T. Egerton.
* The Finishing Bore Designed & Etched by D. T. Egerton.

Issued in boards with a picture on upper cover same as on title, lower cover blank.
Another Issue. Published by McLean.

204 EGERTON (D. T.)

The Necessary Qualifications of a Man of Fashion. (rule) Twelve Plates, designed and etched by D. T. Egerton (rule) "Fashion, in everything, bears sovereign sway." (thick and thin rule) London Published by Thomas M'Lean, Repository of Wit and Humour, 26 Haymarket.

Oblong Folio.   1823

COLLATION.—Title as above (v. blank) + 12 coloured plates marked pl. 1(–12) D. T. Egerton Esq. Del. and imprint, London Published by Thos. (or Thomas) M'Lean, Repository of Wit and Humour, 26 Haymarket. 1823.

Each plate has a single word title at top and an explanatory legend beneath.

Egerton's Man of Fashion (*contd.*)

1. Negligence.
2. Assurance.
3. Confidence.
4. Impudence.
5. Intemperance.
6. Indifference.
7. Unfeelingness.
8. Forgetfulness.
9. Selfishness.
10. Intrigue.
11. Eccentricity.
12. Inconsistency.

There are late issues of the work.   I have seen an example with watermark Turkey Mills 1835.

205 EGERTON (D. T.)

[Views in Mexico.]   1839–40

COLLATION.—A Series of 12 Views issued in half morocco portfolio, mounted on thick cards measuring 23½ × 16¾ inches.

1. Guanaxuato D. T. Egerton 1840.
2. Real del Monte D. T. Egerton 1840.
3. Sn Augustin de la Cuevas D. T. Egerton 1839.
4. Vera Cruz 1840 D. T. Egerton.
5. Plan del Rio la Conducta D. T. Egerton 1840.
6 Mexico D. T. Egerton 1840.
7. Zacatecas D. T. Egerton 1840.
8. Hacienda de Barrera Guanto. D. T. Egerton 1840.
9. Aguas Calientes D. T. Egerton 1840.
10. Guadalaxara [No Artist or date given].
11. Puebla D. T. Egerton 1840.
12. Canon of Sn. Cayetano Mine of Rayas Guanaxuato D. T. Egerton 1840.

This work has greatly increased in value in the last few years and has become rare.

206 E[GERTON] (M.)

Airy Nothings; or Scraps and Naughts, and Odd-cum Shorts; in a circumbendibus Hop, Step, and Jump, by Olio Rigmaroll (2 line short rule) 6 line quote. (2 line short rule) Drawn and written by M. E. Esq.   Engraved by George Hunt London: Published by Pyall and Hunt, 18 Tavistock Street, Covent Garden (rule)

Quarto.   1825

COLLATION.—Title as above (v. Printed by J. Davy, Queen Street, Seven Dials) + 1 p. of verse + pp. 1–73 + 23 coloured plates.

Each plate is marked M.E. in left-hand corner, Engraved by G. Hunt in right-hand corner.

1. p. 2. [Picture of a Traveller seated on his Trunk].
2. p. 4. Street Breakfast.
3. p. 8. Will Hackraw.
4. p. 17. Spreading.
5. p. 18. The Ne Plus Ultra of Bores.
6. p. 28. Love Lane.
7. p. 31. Inn Midnight.
8. p. 39. Scene—Country Fair.
9. p. 41. Washerwomen. Carlton Hill Edinburgh.
10. p. 43. Porter Fishwoman & Journeyman Flesher Auld Reekie.
11. p. 45. Starting of a Stage Coach—Edinburgh.
12. p. 47. A Trip up Loch Lomond.
13. p. 49. Returning from a Trip to Loch Lomond.
14. p. 50. Scene near Glasgow
15. *ibd.* Glasgow.
16. p. 52. Mr Owen's Institution, Near Lanark Quadrille Dancing.
17. p. 53. Laking it Ulswater.
18. p. 57. Steam Packet—Holyhead to Howth.
19. p. 58. Steam Packet—[different View].
20. p. 60. Car Drivers Dublin.
21. p. 61. A Ride up the Phoenix Park, Dublin.
22. p. 62. Costume North Wales.
23. p. 72. A Rigmaroll.

A second edition was published by McLean.

207 EGERTON (M.)

Here and There over the Water: being Cullings in a Trip to the Netherlands (The Field of Battle and Monuments—Waterloo, &c.) By Omnium Gatherum (thick and thin rule)

"The devil on two crutches rid
"Above the steeples of Madrid
"What care I what the devil did!"
"In a sieve I'll thither sail,
"And like a rat without a tail
I'll do—I'll do—I'll do.

Drawn and written by M. E. Engraved by Geo. Hunt. London: Published by Geo. Hunt, 18 Tavistock Street, Covent Garden (small rule) 1825

COLLATION.—Title as above (v. J. Davy, Printer, Queen Street, Seven Dials) + 24 coloured plates Drawn by M E[gerton] G Hunt sculpt. [or Engraved by G. Hunt] + plates as under + 34 pp. text.

Front. [Flying over the Channel].
1. Quay Custom House & Hotel—Ostend.
2. The Purgatory Gate Ostend.
3. Post Office Ostend.
4. [Dandy chimney sweeper & Merry making party].
5. The Great Coach.
6. Trekschott or Barge.
7. Military—Ghent.
8. Diligences.
9. Peasants in the Neighbourhood of Brussels.
10. Market—Brussels.
11. Pavillion of Prince of Orange at Terrevueren.
12. Peasant &c.—near Antwerp.
13. Exchange at Antwerp.
14. A Birds Eye.
15. Palace of Schoonenberg near Brussels.
16. Cottages—Waterloo.
17. [Tomb & Trees].
18. Tombs—Waterloo Church.
19. Church & Village Waterloo.
20. Tombstone Inscriptions (uncoloured).
21. ditto.
22. ditto.
23. ditto.
24. Monuments—Field of Waterloo.
25. Ruins of the Chateau of Goumont.
26. La Belle Alliance.
27. [similar to Frontispiece, returning across the Channel].

208 ELLIS (H.)

Journal of the Proceedings of the Late Embassy to China; comprising a correct narrative of the public transactions of The Embassy, of the voyage to and from China, and of the journey from the mouth of the Pei-Ho, to the return to Canton. Interspersed with Observations upon the face of the country, the policy, moral character, and manners, of the Chinese nation. The whole, illustrated by maps and Drawings. (rule) By Henry Ellis, Third Commissioner of the Embassy. (rule) 3 line quotation from Bacon (thick and thin rule) London Printed for John Murray, Albemarle-Street.

Quarto. 1817

COLLATION.—Title as above (v. T Davison, Lombard-Street, Whitefriars, London) + Advertisement pp. iii–iv + Contents pp. v–vii (p. viii D. to Binder) + pp. 1–526 including Index + Errata 1 lf. + folding map and plates. Each plate marked, Hon. Charles Abbot. delt. J. Clark, sculpt. London Published by J. Murray. Albemarle-street. 1817.

p. 1. Map of Route of British Embassy.
1. p. 90. Summer Palace of the Emperor, opposite the City of Tien-Sing.

Ellis's China (*contd.*)

2. p. 138. Anchorage at Tong Chow.
   p. 292. Map of Route on Yang-Tse-Kiang.
3. p. 296. Temple of Quan-Yin-Mun near Nankin.
4. p. 312. See Lang Shan.
5. p. 328. Gan-Kin Foo, from the West.
6. p. 331. Seoou-Koo-Shan, from the East.
   p. 450. Track of the Alceste.
7. p. 455. View Island of Pulo Leat. M. Brownrigg Esq. Delt. J. Clark. sculpt.

209 ELPHINSTONE (Hon. Mountstuart)

An Account of the Kingdom of Caubul and its Dependencies in Persia, Tartary, and India; comprising a View of the Afghaun Nation, and a History of the Duoraunee Monarchy (thick and thin rule) By the Hon. Mountstuart Elphinstone, of the Honourable East India Company's service; Resident at the Court of Poona; and late envoy to the King of Caubul (thin and thick rule) London: Printed for Longman, Hurst, Rees, Orme, and Brown, Paternoster Row, and J. Murray, Albemarle Street.

Quarto.   1815

COLLATION.—Title as above (v. imprint) + Preface pp. iii–viii + Notice regarding the Map *v–*vii + List of Plates 1 p. + Contents pp. ix–xxi (p. xxii blank) + Errata 1 p. (v. blank) + Introduction 1–82 (pp. 71–72 repeated starred) + pp. 83–675 + 2 Maps + 1 uncoloured and 13 coloured plates. Each plate is marked, Published by Messrs. Longman, Hurst, Rees, Orme and Brown, Paternoster-Row. 1815.

1. face Title. A Map of the Kingdom of Caubul by Lt. John Macartney 5. Regt. Bengal Native Cavalry. folding.
2. face intro. Caubul on a reduced scale, shewing its relative situation to the neighbouring countries.
3. p. 239. Dooraunee Shepherds.
4. p. 316. A Hindkee in the Winter dress of Peshawar.
5. p. 347. An Eusofzye.
6. p. 369. An Afghaun of Damaun.
7. p. 376. Tope of Maunikyaula.
8. p. 406. A Dooraunee Villager with his Arms.
9. p. 414. A Dooraunee Gentleman.
10. p. 434. A Tanjik in the Summer dress of Caubul.
11. p. 443. A Khawtee Ghiljie in his Summer Dress.
12. p. 469. A Khojch of Uzbek Tartary.
13. p. 481. A Man of the Tymunee Eimauk.
14. p. 483. A Hazaurch.
15. p. 518. A Chaous Baushee in his dress of office.
16. p. 519. An Umla Baushee in his dress of office.

210 EMPSON (Charles)

Narratives of South America; illustrating Manners, Customs, and Scenery containing also numerous facts in Natural History, Collected during a four Years' Residence in Tropical Regions. By Charles Empson. London: Printed by A. J. Valpy, Red Lion Court, Fleet Street, and Published for the Author By William Edwards, Ave Maria Lane

Folio.   1836

Empson's South America (*contd.*)

COLLATION.—Title as above (v. blank) + Dedication 1 p. (v. blank) + Note 1 p. (v. blank) + Preface pp. vii–xi + Contents pp. xii–xvi + pp. 1–322 + 14 plates in outline uncoloured.
All the plates bear " From a sketch on the spot by Charles Empson."

1. p. 1. El Cieneca.	8. p. 105. Paladeros.
2. p. 19. South American Cottage.	9. p. 123. El Salto.
3. p. 33. The Rustic Corridor.	10. p. 151. Merida.
4. p. 53. Cocenas.	11. p. 171. Tolyma.
5. p. 79. Honda.	12. p. 189. Pamplona.
6. p. 89. A La Desconoceda.	13. p. 193. The Ravine of the Unburied Dead.
7. p. 91. The Bridge at Marquita.	14. p. 247. River Claro.

A series of the above plates printed in colour in facsimile of Drawings was issued by Ackermann for the above work and is usually to be found bound up with the volume. They were on tinted mounts and bore no lettering.
An additional coloured plate was added viz.:

15. p. 269. Asserador Hewitsonis taken on the road from Caracas to Bogota, and presented to the British Museum   G. B. Sowerby Jun del et sculpt.

ENGELBACH (Lewis)   Naples.   See under Rowlandson (T.).

English Spy (The).   See under [Westmacott (Charles Molloy)].

211 EXCELLMANNS (pseud. W. H. Ireland)

The Eventful Life of Napoleon Bonaparte, Late Emperor of the French By Baron Karlo Excellmanns (rule) Embellished with Twenty-two coloured engravings. In Four Volumes Vol. I [II, III, IV] (woodcut of Eagle) (rule) London: Printed for John Cumberland, 19 Ludgate Hill

4 vols.   Octavo.   1828

COLLATION VOL. I.—Half-title " Life of Napoleon Bonaparte, late emperor of the French, King of Italy, Protector of the Confederation of the Rhine, Mediator of the Confederation of Switzerland &c. &c." (v. blank) + Title as above (v. blank) + Editors Preface 6 ll. (v–xv, xvi blank) + Contents of Vol. I 12 ll. (xvii–xl) + pp. 1–477 + 4 coloured plates.

Front.   Napoleon Bonaparte.
p.   24. Lewis XVI   W. Bromley sculpt.
p.   36. Napoleon working a gun at the siege of Toulon.
p. 348. Lord Nelson.

VOL. II.—Title as before (v. blank) + Contents of Vol. II 4 ll. (v–xii) + pp. 1–556 + 5 coloured plates.

Front.   Napoleon Francis Charles Joseph Duke of Reichstadt.
p. 160. Ali Pacha of Janina.
p. 356. General Bennigsen.   Engraved by Ridley & Blood.
p. 394. Canova.
p. 528. Archduke Charles of Austria.

VOL. III.—Title as before (v. blank) + Contents of Vol. III 5 ll. (v–xiv) + pp. 1–600 + 6 coloured plates.

Excellmanns's Life of Napoleon Bonaparte (*contd.*)

Front. Napoleon's magnanimous behaviour to the Princess of Hartzfeldt.
p. 44. Field Marshal Prince Blucker Engraved by Hopwood from an original painting London Published by G. Virtue 26 Ivy Lane. (Another issue Field Marshal von Blücher late Prince of Wagstadt &c. (no imprint).)
p. 259. Bernadotte, King of Sweden.
p. 276. Maria Louisa Engraved by T. Blood from an original painting.
p. 320. Alexander I Late Emperor of all the Russias.
p. 477. Count Platoff Hetman of the Cossacks.

VOL. IV.—Title as before (v. blank) + Contents of Vol. IV 3 ll. (iii–viii) + List of Embellishments 1 leaf + pp. 1–542 + 7 coloured plates (pp. 110–115 repeated starred).

Front. Napoleon at St. Helena with View of Longwood.
p. 117. Portrait of Louis XVIII late King of France.
p. *ibd.* Charles Maurice Talleyrand Perigord Prince de Benevente.
p. 121. Facsimile of Napoleons Abdication 1814.
p. 292. Triumphal Column erected in La Place Vendome. Paris.
p. 376. His Royal Highness William Prince of Orange Nassau, Sovereign of the United Netherlands.
p. 384. Duke of Wellington (no engr. or artist given).
p. 389. The most noble the Marquis of Anglesey K G &c. &c. Engraved by I. Thomson from an original painting by Sir William Beechey R.A.

The following is included in Directions to Binder "Pages 149–150 in Vol. II are to be cancelled, and the leaf containing the same pages published in No. 46 of the work to be substituted.

Pages 41 and 42, and also pages 115 and 116, in volume the Third, are to be cancelled, and the pages published in No. 76 to be substituted."

Exceedingly rare, with or without the cancel leaves.

Fashion and Folly. See under Sams (W.).

Fashionable Bores. See under [Egerton (D. T.)].

212 FELLOWES (W. D.)

A Visit to the Monastery of La Trappe, in 1817: with Notes taken during a Tour through Le Perche, Normandy, Bretagne, Poitou, Anjou, Le Bocage, Touraine, Orleanois, and the Environs of Paris (swelled rule) by W. D. Fellowes, Esq. (rule) illustrated with numerous coloured engravings, from drawings made on the spot. (rule) London: Printed for William Stockdale, 181, Piccadilly (rule)

Octavo.   1818

COLLATION.—Title as above (v. T. Bensley and Sons, Bolt Court, Fleet Street, London) + List of Plates 1 p. (v. blank) + Preface pp. v–x + Contents pp. xi–xii + pp. 1–188 + 1 vignette 1 plate in outline, 1 etched plate and 12 coloured aquatint views.

Each plate is marked, W. D. Fellowes delt. I. Clark sculpt. Published May 1, 1818, by Wm. Stockdale 187 Piccadilly.

1. p.   8. View of the Monastery of La Trappe.
2. p.   16. Ruins of the Ancient Church of La Trappe.
3. p.   38. Ruins of the Gateway of the ancient Chartreuse.
   p.   75. (Vignette) Les Noyades. [sometimes on India Paper as insert, sometimes as separate illust.].
4. p.   82. Grotto of Héloise at Clisson.
5. p.   83. Tomb of Abelard and Heloise.
6. p.   84. Ruins of Abelard's House.

Fellowes's Monastery of La Trappe (*contd.*)

7. p.   86. Granite Rock in the Garenne.
    p.   88. Le Connetable de Clisson (outline).
8. p.   92. Ruins of Clisson.
9. p.   94. Tour des Pélerins.
10. p.   99. Mill (sic) aux Chévres.
11. p. 124. Tour d'Oúdon on the River Loire.
12. p. 125. View of St. Florent.
    p. 162. Tomb (etching).

213   *SECOND EDITION.—Collation as above with insertion of words, Second Edition, above imprint, printed in 1820. Another Edition issued in 1823. Printed for Thomas M'Lean 26 Haymarket. Collation otherwise as above.*

214 FIELDING (T. H.)

British Castles; or, A compendious History of the Ancient Military Structures of Great Britain. By T. H. Fielding, Esq. Illustrated by Numerous Views of some of the most interesting castles in Great Britain (rule) London: Printed by Howlett and Brimmer, Frith Street, Soho Square   1825

COLLATION.—Half-title + Title as above (v. blank) + Preface 2 pp. (v–vi) + List of Plates 1 p. (v. blank) + Introduction pp. 1–13 + pp. 15–73 + 25 coloured aquatints.

1. front. Arches of Different Periods T. H. Fielding Delt. London Published by Thomas McLean 26 Haymarket 1823.
2. p. 15. Burgh Castle.
3. p. 18. Entrance to Coningsborough Castle.
4. p. 20. Keep of Coningsborough Castle.
5. p. 22. Oven on the Summit of Coningsborough Castle.
6. p. 23. Saxon Chapel in Coningsborough Castle.
7. p. 24. Brougham Castle.
8. p. 27. Saltwood Castle.
9. p. 31. Grosmont Castle.
10. p. 33. Dover Castle.
11. p. 35. Peel Castle Isle of Man.
12. p. 37. Cathedral in Peel Castle.
13. p. 38. Round Tower in Peel Castle.
14. p. 42. Flint Castle.
15. p. 46. Dolwyddelan Castle.
16. p. 49. Barnard Castle (Durham).
17. p. 50. Mortham Tower.
18. p. 52. Thirlwall Castle.
19. p. 54. St. Briavils Castle.
20. p. 56. Beaumaris Castle.
21. p. 57. Interior of the S. Entrance of Beaumaris Castle.
22. p. 60. Keep of Goodrich Castle.
23. p. 63. Branksome Castle.
24. p. 68. Wilton Castle.
25. p. 73. Cambu (Comber Castle).

215 FIELDING (T. H.)

Cumberland, Westmoreland, and Lancashire Illustrated, in a series of Forty-Four Engravings, exhibiting the Scenery of the Lakes, Antiquities, and other picturesque objects. By T. H. Fielding (thick and thin rule) London: Printed for Thomas M'Lean, No. 26, Haymarket, by Howlett and Brimmer, Columbian Press, No. 10, Frith Street, Soho Square

Folio.   1822

COLLATION.—Half-title "Cumberland Westmoreland and Lancashire Illustrated." (v. blank) + Title as above (v. blank) + Address 1 p. (v. blank) + 44 plates each with 1 leaf of text (including the frontispiece) + List 1 p. (v. blank).

Fielding's Cumberland, Westmoreland, and Lancashire (*contd.*)

Each plate marked, T. Fielding delt. London Published by Thomas McLean Haymarket 1822.

1. Naworth Castle.
2. Cromack Water.
3. Green Crag.
4. Penrith.
5. Skiddaw over Derwent Water.
6. Stockgill Force.
7. Brougham Castle.
8. Rydal Water.
9. Kendal Castle.
10. Dungeon Force.
11. Waste Water.
12. View at Ambleside.
13. Ullswater.
14. Egremont Castle. 1821.
15. Ambleside.
16. Laneroost Priory.
17. Nook End Bridge.
18. Blea Tarn.
19. Lowther Castle.
20. The Lakes of Cromack & Buttermere.
21. St Herberts (sic) Island.
22. Blencowe Hall.
23. Red Tarn.
24. Mill at Ambleside.
25. Part of Furness Abbey.
26. Saddleback.
27. Yew Tree at Blelham Tarn.
28. Cockermouth.
29. Rydal Heads 1821.
30. Mayburgh.
31. Carlisle Cathedral.
32. Wyburn Water.
33. Coniston Tell (sic).
34. Monuments in Calder Abbey.
35. Coniston Old Hall.
36. Bowder Stone.
37. Derwent Water.
38. Workington.
39. Elter Water.
40. Dalton.
41. Little Langdale Water.
42. Borrowdale.
43. Loughrigg Tarn.
44. Eagle Crag.

Large and small-paper copies.

216 Another issue with variations of the plates as follows:—

1. Naworth Castle, 2 figs. in foreground & flag on castle.
2. Cromack Water, figs. altered.
3. Green Crag, fig. & cattle added.
4. Penrith, fig. added.
5. Skiddaw over Derwent Water, horse added.
6. Stockgill Force, 2 figs. added.
7. Brougham Castle, 2 figs. added.
8. Rydal Water, 2 figs. added.
9. A view "Windermere Water" takes the place of Kendal Castle.
10. Dungeon Force, goat added.
11. Waste Water, figs. & boats.
12. View at Ambleside, washerwoman inserted.
13. Ullswater, figs. & boats added.
14. Egremont Castle, 2 figs. & dog.
15. Ambleside, fig. altered & 1 added.
16. Laneroost Priory, figs. added.
17. Nook End Bridge, cart & horseman added.
18. Blea Tarn, 2 figs.
19. Lowther Castle, figs. & flag added.
20. The Lakes of Cromack & Buttermere, 3 figs.
21. St Herberts (sic) Island, 3 figs. in foreground.
22. Blencowe Hall, fig. added.
23. Red Tarn, figs. in foreground.
24. Mill at Ambleside, fig. added.
25. Part of Furness Abbey, 2 extra figs. on left.
26. Saddleback, 2 figs. in foreground.
27. Yew Tree at Blelham Tarn, figs. altered.
28. Cockermouth, horseman on bridge.
29. Rydal Heads [1821], 4 figs. in foreground.
30. Mayburgh, 2 figs. & dog.
31. Carlisle Cathedral, fig. & sheep added.
32. Wyburn Water, horseman & sheep added.
33. Coniston Tell (sic), 2 figs.
34. Monuments in Calder Abbey.
35. Coniston Old Hall, sail added to boat & 2 figs.
36. Bowder Stone, figs. altered & cattle added.
37. Derwent Water, 2 figs., yacht & boat inserted.
38. Workington, figs., boats, & flag on castle.
39. Elter Water, 2 figs.
40. Dalton, horse & cart added.
41. Little Langdale Water, 3 figs. & sheep inserted in foreground.
42. Borrowdale, 1 fig. & extra sheep.
43. Loughrigg Tarn, figs. & boats.
44. Eagle Crag, 3 figs. added.

217 FIELDING (C.) (and T. H.)

Picturesque Illustrations of the River Wye, in a Series of Twenty-Eight Views. Engraved from Drawings made by C. Fielding. London: Published by Mr Fielding, 26, Newman Street (short rule).

Folio.   1821

COLLATION.—Title as above (v. blank) + 2nd Title "A Description of the River Wye, by T. H. Fielding." London: Published by the Author, 26, Newman Street 1822 (v. Printed by Howlett & Brimmer, 10, Frith Street Soho.) + Introduction 2 pp. (iv–v) + Text pp. 1–32 + List of Plates 1 p. (v. blank) + 28 coloured plates.

Each plate marked, Drawn by C [or C. V. or Copley] Fielding, Engraved by T. Fielding [with the exception of plate 24 which is engraved by R. Havell].

1. face title. Junction of the Wye and Severn   London Published Jany. 1, 1818 by C. V. Fielding Grafton Street.
2. p.   1. View of Plinlimmon, from near the source of the Wye   Octr. 1, 1818 by C. V. Fielding 26 Newman Street.
3. p.   3. View of the Wye, from Llangerig Church Yard   Octr. 1 1818 by C. V. Fielding 26 Newman Street.
4. p.   4. Nannerth Rocks   Published June 1, 1820 by Copley Fielding 26 Newman Street, London.
5. *ibd.*   View up the Wye from Rhayader   Published Jany. 1st 1820 by Copley Fielding 26 Newman Street London.
6. p.   5. Rhayader Radnorshire   London Published Augst. 1st 1819 by Copley Fielding 26 Newman Street London.
7. p.   7. View of Buallt Brecknockshire   London Published by Copley Fielding 26 Newman Street July 1st 1820.
8. p.   8. Castle and Church of Aberedwy   Published Jan. 1st 1820 by Copley Fielding 26 Newman Street London.
9. p. 10. Hay Brecknockshire   London Published by Copley Fielding 26 Newman Street   Jany. 1st 1820.
10. p. 12. Clifford Castle   Published June 1st 1820 by Copley Fielding 26 Newman Street London.
11. p. 13. Bradwardine Bridge Herefordshire   Published by Mr Fielding 26 Newman Street   March 1st 1820.
12. p. 16. Hereford from Dynedor Hill   London Published Jany. 1st 1820 by Copley Fielding 26 Newman Street.
13. p. 19. Ross from Wilton Bridge Herefordshire   Published by Mr. Fielding 26 Newman Street March 1st 1821.
14. *ibd.*   Wilton Castle Herefordshire   London Published by Copley Fielding 26 Newman Street July 1 1820.
15. p. 20. Goodrich Castle looking down the Wye   London Published Jany. 1818 by C. V. Fielding Grafton Street.
16. p. 21. Goodrich Castle from the Ferry   London Published Augst. 1st 1819 by C. V. Fielding 26 Newman Street.
17. p. 23. The Coldwell Rocks   London Published Octr. 1st 1818 by C. V. Fielding 26 Newman Street.
18. *ibd.*   View down the River at the New Wier   London Published Octr. 1 1818 by C. V. Fielding 26 Newman Street.
19. *ibd.*   The New Wier looking up the River   London Published by C. V. Fielding June 1st 1818 26 Newman Street.
20. p. 24. Monmouth   Published by Mr Fielding 26 Newman Street   March 1st 1821.
21. p. 25. The Monow Bridge Monmouth   Published by C. V. Fielding 26 Newman Street London June 1 1818.
22. *ibd.*   Part of Monmouth Castle   London Published Augst. 1st 1819 by C. V. Fielding 26 Newman Street.
23. p. 26. St Briavels Castle Gloucestershire   London Published by Mr Fielding 26 Newman Street July 1 1821.
24. p. 27. North View of Tintern Abbey   Engraved by R. Havell   London Published Jany. 1 1818 by C. V. Fielding Grafton Street.

Fielding's River Wye (*contd.*)

25. p. 28. Tintern Abbey looking down the Wye   London Published Augst. 1st 1819 by C. V. Fielding 26 Newman Street.
26. p. 29. Piercefield the Seat of N. Wells Esqre.   London Published by C. V. Fielding June 1st 1818 26 Newman Street.
27. p. 31. Chepstow Castle & Bridge looking S.E.   London Published Jany. 1 1818 by C. V. Fielding Grafton Street.
28. p. 32. Town, Castle & Bridge of Chepstow   London Published Jany. 1 1818 by C. V. Fielding Grafton Street.

218 FIELDING (T. H.)

A Picturesque Description of the River Wye, from the source to its junction with the Severn. By T. H. Fielding, Author of "The Theory of Painting," "Synopsis of Perspective," "Treatise on Painting in Oil and Water Colours," &c.; And Teacher of Painting in Water Colours to the Senior Classes at the Hon. East India Company's Military College, Addiscombe (rule) illustrated by numerous coloured views (rule) London: Published by Ackermann & Co., 96, Strand

Quarto.   1841

COLLATION.—Title as above (v. blank) + List of Plates 1 p. (v. blank) + Introduction 2 pp. (iv–v) + Text pp. 1–32 + 12 coloured plates.

1. Face Title. Tintern Abbey.
2. p. 4. View up the Wye, from Rhayader.
3. p. 7. View of Buallt.
4. p. 8. Castle and Church of Aberedwy.
5. p. 10. Hay.
6. p. 13. Bradwardine Bridge.
7. p. 19. Wilton Castle.
8. p. 20. Goodrich Castle, looking down the Wye.
9. p. 24. Monmouth.
10. p. 29. Piercefield.
11. p. 31. Chepstow Castle and Bridge, looking S.E.
12. p. 32. Junction of the Wye and Severn.

The plates in this abridged reissue are greatly inferior to those of the original edition.

219 FIELDING (T. H.) & J. WALTON

A Picturesque Tour of the English Lakes, containing a description of the most Romantic Scenery of Cumberland, Westmoreland, and Lancashire, with accounts of ancient and modern manners and customs, and elucidations of the History and Antiquities of the part of the country &c. &c. (coloured vignette) Illustrated with Forty-Eight Coloured views, Drawn by Messrs. T. H. Fielding, and J. Walton, during a Two years' residence among the lakes (rule) London: Printed for R. Ackermann, 101, Strand (rule)

Quarto.   1821

COLLATION.—Half-title "Tour of the English Lakes" (v. London: Printed by William Clowes, Northumberland-Court.) + Title as above (v. blank) + Preface 2 leaves (pp. iii–vi) + Contents 1 p. (v. Directions for placing the Engravings) + pp. 1–286 + Index pp. 287–288 + 48 coloured plates.

Each plate bears imprint Published [or Pubd.] [date] at R. Ackermann's 101 Strand.

1. Front. Saddleback & St. John's Vale   T. H. Fielding delt.   Jany 1 1821.
2. p. 4. Purple Tarn, top of Saddleback   T. H. Fielding delt.   Feby. 1 1821.
3. p. 11. North West View of Furness Abbey   T. H. Fielding delt.   May 1 1820.
4. p. 23. Coniston Water   J. Walton delt.   May 1 1820.

Fielding's English Lakes (*contd.*)

5. p. 24. Copper Mill, Coniston Fell   J. Fielding delt.   May 1 1820.
6. p. 26. Yewdale Crags   J. Fielding delt.   May 1st 1820.
7. p. 31. Esthwaite Water   T. H. Fielding delt.   June 1 1820.
8. p. 36. Ferry on Windermere   J. Walton delt.   June 1 1820.
9. p. 38. Station on Windermere   J. Walton delt.   June 1 1820.
10. p. 69. Windermere, from above Trout-beck   J. Walton delt.   July 1 1820.
11. p. 70. Low Wood Inn   T. H. Fielding delt.   June 1 1820.
12. p. 72. Windermere from Trout-beck Lane, with Langdale Pikes   T. H. Fielding delt.   July 1 1820.
13. p. 75. Windermere Head   T. H. Fielding delt.   July 1 1820.
14. p. 76. Ambleside   T. H. Fielding delt.   Augt. 1 1820.
15. p. 86. Stockgill Force   J. Walton delt.   Augt. 1 1820.
16. p. 89. Skelwith Force   T. H. Fielding delt.   Augt. 1 1820.
17. p. 91. Stickle Tarn, near the top of Langdale Pikes   T. H. Fielding delt.   July 1 1820.
18. p. 94. Rydal Water   J. Walton delt.   Augt. 1 1820.
19. p. 104. Rydal Water from White Moss   J. Walton delt.   Septr. 1 1820.
20. p. 106. Grasmere Church & Helm Crag   J. Walton delt.   Septr. 1 1820.
21. p. 112. Grasmere   T. H. Fielding delt.   Septr. 1 1820.
22. p. 125. Wyburn Water & Helvellyn T. H. Fielding delt.   Septr. 1 1820.
23. p. 149. Keswick Lake   T. H. Fielding delt.   Octr. 1 1820.
24. p. 169. Lowdore Fall T. H. Fielding delt.   Octr. 1 1820.
25. p. 176. Keswick   W. Westall delt.   Jany. 1 1821.
26. p. 193. Sty Head Tarn, top of Sty Head   T. H. Fielding delt.   Jany. 1 1821.
27. p. 194. Sty Head   T. H. Fielding delt.   Jany 1 1821.
28. p. 196. Wast Water   T. H. Fielding delt.   Decr. 1 1820.
29. p. 200. Calder Abbey   T. H. Fielding delt.   Decr. 1 1820.
30. p. 206. Ennerdale Water   T. H. Fielding delt.   Decr. 1 1820.
31. p. 215. Lowes Water   T. H. Fielding delt.   Novr. 1 1820.
32. p. 219. Cromack Water   T. H. Fielding delt.   Novr. 1 1820.
33. p. 222. Scale Force   T. H. Fielding delt.   Decr. 1 1820.
34. p. 227. Buttermere   J. Walton delt.   Octr. 1 1820.
35. p. 238. Cockermouth Castle   T. H. Fielding delt.   Novr. 1 1820.
36. p. 241. Bassenthwaite Lake   T. H. Fielding delt.   Novr. 1 1820.
37. p. 248. Skiddaw, from the head of Lowdore Fall   J. Walton delt.   Octr. 1 1820.
38. p. 257. Cottages in St. John's Vale   T. H. Fielding delt.   Feby. 1 1821.
39. p. 259. Penrith Castle   T. H. Fielding delt.   Feby. 1 1821.
40. p. 260. Brougham Castle   T. H. Fielding delt.   Feby. 1 1821.
41. p. 263. Haws Water   T. H. Fielding delt.   March 1 1821.
42. p. 271. Ullswater, from Stybarrow Crag   T. H. Fielding delt.   March 1 1821.
43. p. 272. Grisedale Pike   T. H. Fielding delt.   March 1 1821.
44. p. 277. Patterdale Church, Ullswater Head.   J. Walton delt.   March 1 1821.
45. p. 279. Deepdale   T. H. Fielding delt.   April 1 1821.
46. p. 280. Broader Water   J. Walton delt.   April 1 1821.
47. p. 283. Kirkstone Spring   T. H. Fielding delt.   April 1 1821.
48. p. 284. Kirkstone Pass   T. H. Fielding delt.   April 1 1821.

Issued in 12 monthly parts in wrappers and on completion in boards, 750 at £3 13s. 6d. and 100 on large or elephant paper at £6 6s.

Fielding (Theodore).   See also under Barker's English Landscape Scenery.

——— Views near Bath.

220 FINDEN (W. & E.)

Findens' Tableaux of National Character, Beauty, and Costume. In a series of Illustrations, engraved by W. & E. Finden. With Original Tales in Prose and Poetry, written expressly for the work, by the Countess of Blessington, Miss Mitford, L.E.L.,

Findens' National Character (*contd.*)

Mrs S. C. Hall, Allan Cunningham, Barry Cornwall, Leigh Hunt, and others of the most Popular authors of the day. In Two Volumes (rule). Vol. I. (rule) London: Published by J. Hogarth, 5 Haymarket.

2 vols. Small Folio. (1843–60)

COLLATION VOL. I.—Printed title (1 p. v. blank) + Preface 1 p. (v. blank) + Contents 1 p. (v. blank) + pp. 1–96 + 32 coloured plates (including engraved title).

1. Front. Poland.	Drawn by H. Corbauld.	Engraved by E. Finden.
2. Engraved Title. The Dream.	,, J. Browne.	,, Finden.
3. Greece.	,, F. P. Stephanoff.	,, W. Finden.
4. Switzerland.	,, F. Stone.	,, W. Holl.
5. Arabia.	,, Miss F. Corbaux.	,, E. Finden.
6. The Coronation (Siberia).	,, W. Perring.	,, J. Hollis.
7. France.	,, F. P. Stephanoff.	,, T. Woolnoth.
8. Castile.	,, W. Perring.	,, E. Finden.
9. Georgia.	,, T. Uwins, R.A.	,, H. Egleton.
10. The Romaunt of the Page.	,, J. Brown.	,, W. & F. Holl.
11. Spain.	,, W. Perring.	,, F. C. Lewis.
12. Albania.	,, F. Stone.	,, W. Finden.
13. England.	,, F. P. Stephanoff.	,, E. Finden.
14. India.	,, Brown.	,, H. Egleton.
15. The Buccaneer.	,, J. Brown.	,, E. Finden.
16. Turkey.	,, F. Stone.	,, R. A. Artlett.
17. Andalusia.	,, Brown.	,, W. Holl.
18. The Minstrel of Provence.	,, J. Brown.	,, E. Finden.
19. Ceylon.	,, W. Perring.	,, J. Posselwhite 1860.
20. Persia.	,, J. Browne.	,, H. Egleton.
21. Venice.	,, E. P. Stephanoff.	,, W. Holl.
22. The Cartel.	,, W. Perring.	,, E. Scriven.
23. Tyrol.	,, J. Browne.	,, C. E. Wagstaff.
24. Sicily.	,, T. Uwins, A.R.A.	,, W. Finden.
25. Africa.	,, H. Perring.	,, E. Finden.
26. Naples.	,, T. Uwins, A.R.A.	,, W. Holl.
27. Portugal.	,, Mrs Seyfforth.	,, F. Finden.
28. America.	,, W. Perring.	,, W. H. Mote.
29. Egypt.	,, J. Brown.	,, E. Finden.
30. Zulette (Chamonix).	,, ,,	,, W. Finden.
31. Scotland.	,, W. Perring.	,, J. Hall.
32. The Greek Wife.		

VOL. II.—Printed title dated 1843 (v. blank) + Contents 1 p. (v. blank) + pp. 97–209 (210 v. blank) + coloured plates.

33. Front. Florence.	Drawn by F. P. Stephenoff.	Engraved by C. E. Wagstaff.
34. The Treasure of Gomez Arias.	,, J. Brown.	,, W. H. Egleton.
35. The Rescue.	,, ,,	,, J. Brown.
36. The Beacon.	,, ,,	,, Finden.
37. The Death of Luath.	,, ,,	,, J. Hollis.
38. The Sister of Charity.	,, W. Perring.	,, B. Holl.
39. The Escape.	,, J. Browne.	,, M. Gibbs.
40. The Kings Page.	,, ,,	,, Finden.
41. The Warning.	,, ,,	,, B. Holl.
42. The Novice.	,, W. Perring.	,, W. & F. Holl.
43. The Maids Trial.	,, J. Browne.	,, E. Scriven.
44. A Story of the Woods.	,, W. Perring.	,, W. H. Egleton.
45. The Pilgrim.	,, J. Brown.	,, W. H. Mote.
46. The Barons Daughter.	,, ,,	,, S. Freeman.

Findens' National Character (*contd.*)

47. The Woodcutter.	Drawn by J. Brown	Engraved by Finden.
48. Legend of the Brown Rosary.	,, J. Browne.	,, W. & F. Holl.
49. The Roundhead's Daughter.	,, ,,	,, ,,
50. The Harvest Home	,, F. P. Stephanoff.	,, W. Finden.
51. The Dumb Cake.	,, H. Corbould.	,, Finden.
52. Morning, or the Milk Girls.	,, F. P. Stephanoff.	,, E. Finden.
53. The Return from the Fair.	,, ,,	,, E. Scriven.
54. The Stolen Child.	,, ,,	,, W. & F. Holl.
55. The Rustic Toilet.	,, ,,	,, E. Finden.
56. Home.	,, F. P. Stephanoff.	,, W. H. Egleton.
57. The Village Amenuensis.	,, E. C. Wood.	,, W. & C. Holl.
58. The Love Token.	,, H. Corbould.	,, T. Hollis.
59. The Gleaner.	,, F. P. Stephanoff.	,, Penstone.
60. The Abstracted Letter.	,, H. Corbould.	,, E. Finden.
61. The Hop Garden.	,, F. P. Stephanoff.	,, H. C. Austen.

Usually issued in black and white, but some copies were coloured. In this latter state it is rare and fine.

221 FISKE (Mrs.)

Records of Fashion, illustrated with colored (*sic*) Engravings (thick and thin rule) most humbly inscribed to her Royal Highness the Princess Elizabeth (thick and thin rule) London: published under the direction of Mrs. Fiske, 81, New Bond Street; and to be had of Mr Harris, corner of St. Pauls Churchyard; Mr. Goddard, Pall Mall; and of Messrs. Taylor and Hessey, 93, Fleet Street. (short thick and thin rule) Printed by J. Shaw, Fetter Lane.

Quarto. 1808

COLLATION.—Title as above (v. blank) + Dedication to Princess Elizabeth 1 p. (v. blank) + sub-title "Records of Fashion and Court Elegance, 1807 &c." + Address 2 pp. (3–4) + Text pp. 5–129 + Index pp. i–iv (1 p. (v. blank) of correspondence inserted between pp. 88 and 89), p. 123 omitted, (p. 124 taking the recto of the leaf) + 21 coloured costume plates.

    1. Front. Her Royal Highness the Princess Elizabeth in a Dress designed by the Proprietor. W. M. Craig delt. J. Kennerley sc. Drawn & Engraved for Fiskes Records of Fashion & Court Elegance 1807.

    2. p. 9. [Figure I Full Dress].
    3. p. 11. [,, II Full Dress].
    4. p. 25. [,, I Dancing Dress].
    5. p. 27. [,, II Half Dress].
    6. p. 37. [,, I A Close Carriage Dress] W. M. Craig del. J. Kennerley sc.
    7. p. 39. [,, II Walking Dress] W. M. Craig del. J. Kennerley sc.
    8. p. 49. [,, I Walking Full Dress] W. M. Craig del. J. Kennerley sc.
    9. p. 51. [,, II Walking Dress] W. M. Craig del. J. Kennerley sc.
10. p. 61. [,, I Walking Dress July 1807] W. M. Craig del. J. Kennerley sc.
11. p. 63. [,, II A Promenade Dress] W. M. Craig del. J. Kennerley sc.
12. p. 73. [,, I Ball Dress] W. M. Craig del. J. Kennerley sc.
13. p. 75. [,, II A Morning Dress] W. M. Craig del. J. Kennerley sc.
14. p. 85. [,, I A Full Dress] W. M. Craig del. J. Kennerley sc.
15. p. 87. [,, II An Evening Walking Dress] W. M. Craig del. J. Kennerley sc.
16. p. 97. [,, I Walking Dress] No artist or Engraver.
17. p. 99. [,, II Full Dress] W. M. Craig del. J. Kennerley sc.
18. p. 109. [,, I Walking Dress] W. M. Craig del. J. Kennerley sc.

Fiske's Records of Fashion (*contd.*)

19. p. 111. [„ II Full Dress] J. Kennerley sc.
20. p. 124. [„ I Walking Dress] J. Kennerley sc.
21. p. 126. [„ II A Ball Dress] J. Kennerley sc.

222 FITZCLARENCE (Lt. Col.)

Journal of a Route across India, through Egypt, to England, in the latter end of the year 1817, and the beginning of 1818. By Lieutenant Colonel Fitzclarence, London: (thin and thick rule) John Murray, Albemarle Street (rule)

Quarto. 1819

COLLATION.—Half-title "Journal of a Route across India, through Egypt, to England." (reverse London Printed by Thomas Davison, Whitefriars) + title as above (v. blank) + Dedication 1 leaf (v. blank) + Note by author 1 p. (v. blank) + Contents pp. IX–XXIV + D. to Binder 1 p. (v. blank) + Errata 1 p. (v. blank) + pp. 1–502 (pp. 167–8 are repeated starred being extra to sig Y) + printer's imprint (Ss4) recto blank + 10 maps and plans + 9 coloured plates.

Front.   Pettah, The Citadel, and Pettah of Dowlutabad, A Fortress belonging to the Nizam, near Aurungabad. Each plate (coloured) is marked, G. Fitzclarence, delt. Engraved by R. Havell & Son. London. Published April 1819 by John Murray Albemarle Street

2. p. 1. Map of the Seat of War in India (folding).
3. p. 16. Gorkah Soldier.
4. p. 18. Hattrass, the Fort of Diub Ram. 1817.
5. p. 35. Rocket Corps and Dromedary Corps, Bengal Army. 1817.
6. p. 73. Irregular Cavalry Bengal Army. 1817. Rhohilla Horse Skinners Horse.
7. p. 86. Sketch of the Engagement at Jubbulpoor, with extra leaf of explanatory text.
8. p. 120. Plan of the City of Nagpoor, with extra leaf of explanatory text.
9. p. 182. Sketch of the Battle of Meinpoor, with extra leaf of explanatory text.
10. p. 200. Plan of the Grand Temple Keylos.
11. p. 243. The Great Gun at Agra.
12. p. 264. Seapoys of the Bombay, Bengal and Madras Armies.
13. p. 297. Sketch of the Engagements in the Vicinity of Poonah, with extra leaf of explanatory text.
14. p. 365. Map of route of Author from Cosier to Alexandria.
15. p. 425. A Khanga on the River Nile.
16. p. 454. Second Pyramid of Egypt, exterior.
17. p. 456. Second Pyramid of Egypt, interior and sarcophagus.
18. p. 460. Interior of The Chamber cut in the Rock at base of Great Pyramid of Egypt.
19. p. 496. A Sketch of some of the gold ornaments worn by the women of Timbuctoo.

223 FLIGHTS OF FANCIE

Flights of Fancie [a Series of 37 humorous plates all bearing the imprint of S & I Fuller 34 Rathbone Place].

1. [Four damsels as angels one bearing scroll "Flights of Fancie"]
2. If Ladies be but young and fair.
   They have the Gift to know it. April 1 1821.
3. To Sleep, perchance to dream April 1 1821.
4. Note of admiration & Interrogation April 1 1821.
5. Fresh as the Morning Rose when the dew wets its leaves April 1 1821.
6. Full Stop April 1 1821.
7. Parenthesis April 1 1821.
8. The Man who has a tongue I say is no Man
   If with his tongue he cannot win a Woman April 1 1821.

Flights of Fancie (*contd.*)

9. Touch the Bell   April 1 1821.
10. Capers   1st May 1821.
11. Plaster of Paris   1st May 1821.
12. Influence   1st May 1821.
13. Walking over the Course   1st May 1821.
14. Transferring Stock   1st July 1821.
15. Piano Forte   1st May 1821.
16. Turning over a new leaf or Harmony restord   1st May 1821.
17. Still harping upon my daughter   1st May 1821.
18. Dabbling in the Stocks   1st July 1821.
19. Conscience   1st May 1821.
20. Phlebotomists   April 1822.
21. A Flat—a Sharp—& a Natural   1st July 1821.
22. This is the first time of asking   1st July 1821.
23. Picking a Crow   1st July 1821.
24. Cruets   April 1822.
25. Free Mason   1st July 1821.
26. The Pot & the Kettle   Jany. 1st 1823.
27. The Past   Jany. 1st 1823.
28. The Present   Jany. 1st 1823.
29. The Future   Jany. 1st 1823.
30. Etty Molly Gee & Mother Tongue   Jany. 1st 1823.
31. Sympathy.
32. Prejudice   Jany. 1st 1823.
33. Mother Bunch, Jeho-so-fat & Betty Martin   Jany. 1st 1823.
34. Immortality   Jany. 1st 1823.
35. Mirth . . . that wrinkled care derides.
   and laughter holding both his sides   Jany. 1st 1823.
36. Forget & Forgive   Jany. 1st 1823.
37. Ann Chovy & Sally Forth.

224 FOREIGN FIELD SPORTS

Foreign Field Sports, Fisheries, Sporting Anecdotes, &c. &c. from drawings by Messrs. Howitt, Atkinson, Clark, Manskirch, &c. Containing One Hundred Plates. With a Supplement of New South Wales. London: Published and Sold by Edward Orme, Printseller and Publisher to his Majesty, and His R.H. the Prince Regent, Bond Street, Corner of Brook Street. Printed by J. F. Dove, No. 22, St John's Square, Clerkenwell

Quarto.   1814

COLLATION.—Title as above (v. blank) + 100 coloured plates and 79 leaves of unnumbered text.

Each plate bears imprint, Published & Sold [date] by Edwd. Orme, Bond Street, London.

1. Hindoo Elephant Trap   Jany. 1st 1813 (2 pp. text).
2. Hindoo Method of Taming Elephants   Jany. 1st 1813 (1 p. text).
3. German Deer Shooting, Summer.   Manskirch del.   Dubourg sculpt.   Jany. 1st 1813 (1 p. text).
4. Elephant in a Pitfall   Howitt delt.   Howitt & Merke sculpt.   Jany. 1st 1813 (1 p. text).
5. Sailors shooting a wild stag   Jany. 1st 1813 (1 p. text).
6. Hunted Elephant   Howitt delt.   Howitt & Merke sculpt.   Jan. 1 1813 (4 pp. text).
7. The Elephant Killed   Howitt delt.   Howitt & Merke sculpt.   Jany. 1 1813 (2 p. text).
8. African Rhinocerous Hunting   Howitt del.   Dubourg sculpt.   May 1st 1813 (2 pp. text).
9. Anecdote of Hunters & Rhinocerous.   Howitt del.   Merke sculpt.   Jany. 1st 1813 (2 pp. text).
10. Hog Hunters in India Going out No. 1   Howitt del.   Merke sculpt.   Jany. 1st 1813 (3 pp. text).
11. Hog Hunters in India 2.   Howitt del   Merke sculpt.   Jany. 20th 1813 (2 pp. text).

Foreign Field Sports 1814 *(contd.)*

12. Torch Light Fishing in N. America. I. H. Clark delt. Merke sculpt. March 25th 1813 (1 p. text).
13. Hog Hunters in India 3. Howitt del. Merke sculpt. Jany. 20th 1813 (2 pp. text).
14. Hog Hunters in India 4. Howitt del. Merke sculpt. Jany. 1st 1813 (3 pp. text).
15. Siberian Exiles shooting Deer Howitt del. Dubourg sculpt. Sept. 1 1813 (1 p. text).
16. Shooting Anecdote India 1. Howitt del. Merke sculpt. Jany. 1 1813 (2 pp. text).
17. Shooting Anecdote India 2. Howitt del. Merke sculpt. Jany. 1 1813 (1 p. text).
18. A Tartar Catching his horse Atkinson del. M. Dubourg sculpt. Feby. 1st 1813 (1 p. text).
19. Lions waiting for their prey. From a Picture in the collection of J. Palmer Esq. M. Dubourg sculpt. May 1st 1813 (1 p. text).
20. E. India Company's Stud at Chatterpore Howitt del. Dubourg sculpt. March 1st 1813 (3 pp. text).
21. Caffres hunting a Lion Howitt del. Clark & Dubourg sculpt. Jany. 1st 1813 (2 pp. text).
22. Anecdote, Lion & Hottentot Howitt del. Dubourg sculpt. Jany. 1st 1813 (1 p. text).
23. Arabs Hunting Ostriches J. Clark del. Howitt & Dubourg sculpt. Jany. 1st 1813 (2 pp. text).
24. Russian Coursing Atkinson del. Howitt & Merke sculpt. Jany. 1st 1813 (1 p. text).
25. Shooting an African Buffalo Howitt del. M. Dubourg sculpt. October 1 1813 (2 pp. text).
26. Hunting a Zebra Howitt del. Dubourg sculpt. May 1st 1813 (2 pp. text).
27. Arabs hawking antelopes J. Clark del. Howitt & Dubourg sculpt. Jany. 1st 1813 (2 pp. text).
28. Hunting Antelopes with a Panther Jany. 1st 1813 (1 p. text).
29. German Wolf Trap Howitt del. Howitt & Dubourg sculpt. Jany. 1st 1813 (1 p. text).
30. Hunting a Panther Howitt del. M. Dubourg sculpt. May 1st 1813 (2 pp. text).
31. Killing a Shark J. H. Clark del. Dubourg sculpt. March 1st 1813 (2 pp. text).
32. Hunting the Camelopard Howitt del. Dubourg sculpt. June 4th 1813 (2 pp. text).
33. Anecdote Shooting a Porcupine Howitt del. Dubourg sculpt. May 1st 1813 (2 pp. text).
34. Turtle Fishing in the Water J. H. Clark del. Dubourg sculpt. March 1st 1813 (2 pp. text).
35. Turtle Catching on Land J. H. Clark del. Dubourg sculpt. July 1st 1813 (1 p. text).
36. Bird Catching from below J. H. Clark del. Dubourg sculpt. June 4th 1813 (2 pp. text).
37. Bird Catching from above J. H. Clark del. M. Dubourg sculpt. May 1st 1813 (2 pp. text).
38. Mexican Lizard Catcher J. H. Clark del. Dubourg sculpt. July 1st 1813 (2 pp. text).
39. German Manner of netting partridges Manskirch del. Merke sculpt. June 1st 1813 (1 p. text).
40. German Deer Shooting with Decoy Howitt del. Dubourg sculpt. Sepr. 1st 1813 (1 p. text).
41. Shooting a Leopard Howitt delt. Howitt & Merke sculpt. Jany. 1st 1813 (1 p. text).
42. German Deer Shooting, Winter Manskirch del Dubourg sculpt. Jany. 1st 1813 (1 p. text).
43. German Wild Boar Trap Howitt del Dubourg sculpt. Jany. 1st 1813 (1 p. text).
44. Wild Boar Shooting, in Germany Manskirch del Dubourg sculpt. Sepr. 1 1813 (2 pp. text).
45. Wild Boar attacking the Hunters Manskirch del Dubourg sculpt. Sepr. 1 1813 (1 p. text).
46. Wild Boar wounded Manskirch del. M. Dubourg sculpt. May 1st 1813 (1 p. text).
47. Catching the Badger Manskirch del Dubourg sculpt. July 1st 1813 (1 p. text).
48. Hunting the Tiger Cat Howitt del M. Dubourg sculpt. May 1st 1813 (1 p. text).
49. German Fox Trap Howitt del Dubourg sculpt. Septr. 1st 1813 (1 p. text).
50. Shooting the Hyena Howitt del Dubourg sculpt. May 1st 1813 (1 p. text).
51. Battle with Gt. Boa & a Tiger J. H. Clark del Dubourg sculpt. March 1st 1813 (4 pp. text).
52. Anecdote Gt. Boa Serpent & a Bull Howitt del Merke sculpt. Jany. 1 1813 (1 p. text).
53. The Bear Trap Howitt del Howitt & Dubourg sculpt. Jany. 1st 1813 (1 p. text).
54. Shooting Wolves in Winter Manskirch del Dubourg sculpt. March 1st 1813 (2 pp. text).
55. Spanish Bull Fighting No. 1. Feby. 1st 1813 (2 pp. text).
56.   ,,   ,,   ,,   No. 2. Feby. 1st 1813 (1 p. text).
57.   ,,   ,,   ,,   No. 3. Jany. 1st 1813 } 1 p. text. to 2 plates.
58.   ,,   ,,   ,,   No. 4. Feby. 1st 1813 }
59.   ,,   ,,   ,,   No. 5. Feby. 1st 1813 (2 pp. text).
60.   ,,   ,,   ,,   No. 6. Feby. 1st 1813 (1 p. text).
61.   ,,   ,,   ,,   No. 7. Jany. 1st 1813 (1 p. text).
62.   ,,   ,,   ,,   No. 8. Feby. 1st 1813 (1 p. text).
63.   ,,   ,,   ,,   No. 9. Jany. 1st 1813 (1 p. text).
64.   ,,   ,,   ,,   No. 10. Jany. 1st 1813 } 1 p. text to 2 plates.
65.   ,,   ,,   ,,   No. 11. Feby. 1st 1813 }
66.   ,,   ,,   ,,   No. 12. Feby. 1st 1813 (1 p. text).
67. General View of a Spanish Bull Fight Clark del Dubourg sculpt. Jany. 1813 (9 pp. text).

Foreign Field Sports 1814 (*contd.*)

68. Chamois Shooters in the Tyrol   Manskirch del   Dubourg sculpt.   Jany. 1813 (1 p. text).
69. Chamois Shooters Retreat   Howitt del   Dubourg sculpt.   Jany. 1st 1813 (1 p. text).
70. Chamois Shooters ascending the Rocks   Manskirch del   Dubourg sculpt.   June 4 1813 (2 pp. text).
71. American Anecdote Wolves & Boy   Howitt del   Dubourg sculpt.   Jany. 1st 1813. ⎫ (2 pp. text
72. American Anecdote Shooting the Wolves   Howitt del   Howitt & Dubourg sculpt. ⎬ together
   Jany. 1st 1813. ⎭ for 2 plates).
73. North American Bear Hunt   Howitt del   Dubourg sculpt.   Septr. 1st 1813 (1 p. text).
74. Shooting a White Hare at Tornio.   Atkinson del   M. Dubourg sculpt.   Feby. 1st 1813 (2 pp. text).
75. A Trap to shoot the Bear   Howitt del   Howitt & Dubourg sculpt.   Jany. 1st 1813 (1 p. text).
76. Shooting Antelopes India   Howitt del   Dubourg sculpt.   March 1st 1813 (2 pp. text).
77. Kamtschatka Bear Hunting   Clark del   Dubourg sculpt.   1813 (2 pp. text).
78. Finland Bear Hunting   Manskirch del   Dubourg sculpt.   Sepr. 1st 1813 (2 pp. text).
79. Seaman Killing a Polar Bear   Howitt del   Howitt & Dubourg sculpt.   Jany. 1st 1813 (1 p. text).
80. The Eagle & Wolf disputing the prize   Howitt del et sculpt.   Jany. 1st 1813 (1 p. text).
81. Mackerel Fishing   Clark del   M. Dubourg sculpt.   Feb. 1st 1813 (1 p. text).
82. Laplanders Hunting Atkinson del   M. Dubourg sculpt.   Feby. 1st 1813 (2 pp. text).
83. Hunting the Elk   Howitt del   Howitt & Dubourg sculpt.   Jany. 1st 1813 (2 pp. text).
84. South American catching a Bull   Clark del   Dubourg sculpt.   Jany. 1st 1813 (2 pp. text).
85. Pions in S. America catching wild horses.   J. Clark del.   Howitt & Dubourg sculpt.   Jany. 1st 1813
   (1 p. text).
86. Tartars hunting deer   Howitt del.   M. Dubourg sculpt.   May 1st 1813   (1 p. text).
87. Killing seals in a cavern   Howitt del   M. Dubourg sculpt.   May 1st 1813 (1 p. text).
88. German Fox Trap   Manskirch del   Dubourg sculpt.   Jany. 1st 1813 (1 p. text).
89. A Siberian Exile Shooting a Black Fox   Atkinson del   Clark & Dubourg sculpt.   Jany. 1st 1813
   (1 p. text).
90. Russian Winter Fishery   Atkinson del Southerland sculpt.   June 4th 1813 (1 p. text).
91. Mamalukes exercising the spear   J. H. Clark del   M. Dubourg sculpt.   May 1st 1813 (1 p. text).
92. Mamalukes exercising the sabre.   J. H. Clark del   Dubourg sculpt.   May 1st 1813 (2 pp. text).
93. Egyptian Crocodile catching   J. H. Clark del   Dubourg sculpt.   July 1st 1813 (1 p. text).
94. Greenland Seal Catching   J. H. Clark del   M. Dubourg sculpt.   May 1st 1813 (1 p. text).
95. The African Crocodile Hunters   Clark del Dubourg sculpt.   March 1st 1813 (1 p. text).
96. Taking Vipors (sic)   J. H. Clark del   M. Dubourg sculpt.   October 1st 1813 (1 p. text).
97. A Ship's Boat attacking a whale   Clark del   M. Dubourg sculpt.   Feby. 1st 1813 (4 pp. text).
98. Boats approaching a whale   Clark del   M. Dubourg sculpt.   Feby. 1st 1813 (1 p. text).
99. A whale brought alongside a ship   J. H. Clark del   Dubourg sculpt.   March 1st 1813 (2 p. text).
100. Shooting the Harpoon at a whale   J. H. Clark del   Dubourg sculpt.   March 1st 1813 (1 p. text).

+ Fresh title "Field Sports, &c. &c. Of the Native Inhabitants of New South Wales with Ten Plates . . . London: Published and sold by Edward Orme, . . . 1813" (v. blank) + Dedition to Adml. Bligh 1 p. (v. blank) + Sketch of Manners Pursuits &c. of the Natives 4 pp. (unnumbered) + 10 plates.   Each plate marked, J. H. Clark del.   M. Dubourg sculpt. and each bearing imprint Published & Sold October 1st 1813, by Edward Orme, Bond St. London.

1. Repose (2 pp. text).
2. Fishing No. 1 ⎫
3.   „   No. 2 ⎬ (1 p. text).
4. The Dance (1 p. text).
5. Warriors of New S. Wales (1 p. text).
6. Trial (1 p. text).
7. Smoking out the Opossum (1 p. text).
8. Hunting the Kangaroo (1 p. text).
9. Throwing the Spear (1 p. text).
10. Climbing Trees (1 p. text).

   Text by Capt. T. Williamson.

225 FOREIGN FIELD SPORTS

Foreign Field Sports, Fisheries, Sporting Anecdotes, &c. &c. from Drawings by Messrs. Howitt, Atkinson, Clark, Manskirch, &c. with a Supplement of New South Wales.

Foreign Field Sports 1819 *(contd.)*
(rule) Containing One Hundred and Ten Plates (rule) London: Published and Sold by H. R. Young, 56, Paternoster-Row (rule)   1819

COLLATION.—Half-title "Foreign Field Sports, Fisheries, Sporting Anecdotes, &c. &c." (v. blank) + Title as above (v. Printed by J. M'Creery, Black Horse Court, London) + p. 1–170 + Index (List of plates) 2 pp. and 110 coloured plates.

Each plate bears the imprint, "Published and Sold [date] by Edwd. Orme Bond St. London."

1. American Anecdote Wolves and Boy   Howitt del   Dubourg sculpt.   Jan. 1st 1813.
2. American Anecdote Shooting the Wolves   Howitt & Dubourg sculpt.   Jan. 1 1813.
3. E. India Company's Stud at Chatterpore   Howitt del Dubourg sculpt.   March 1 1813.
4. Lions waiting for their prey   From a picture in the collection of J. Palmer Esq.   M. Dubourg sculpt.   May 1 1813.
5. Caffres hunting a Lion   Howitt del   Clark & Dubourg sculpt.   Jan. 1 1813.
6. Anecdote Lion & Hottentot   Howitt del.   Dubourg sculpt.   Jan. 1 1813.
7. Arabs Hunting Ostriches   J. Clark del.   Howitt & Dubourg sculpt.   Jan. 1 1813.
8. Arabs Hawking Antelopes   J. Clark del.   Howitt & Dubourg sculpt.   Jan. 1 1813.
9. Russian Coursing   Atkinson del   Howitt & Merke sculpt.   Jan. 1 1813.
10. Russian Winter Fishery   Atkinson del   Southerland sculpt.   June 4, 1813.
11. Mamelukes exercising the Sabre   J. H. Clark del.   M. Dubourg sculpt.   May 1 1813.
12. Mamelukes exercising the Spear   J. H. Clark del.   M. Dubourg sculpt.   May 1 1813.
13. Hunting a Panther   Howitt del   M. Dubourg sculpt.   May 1 1813.
14. Hunting Antelopes with a Panther   Jan. 1 1813.
15. German Wolf Trap   Howitt del   Howitt & Dubourg sculpt.   Jan. 1 1813.
16. Wild Boar attacking the Hunters   Manskirch del   Dubourg sculpt.   Sep. 1 1813.
17. Wild Boar shooting in Germany   Manskirch del   Dubourg sculpt.   Sep. 1 1813.
18. Wild Boar Wounded   Manskirch del   Dubourg sculpt.   May 1 1813.
19. German Deer Shooting Winter   Manskirch del   Dubourg sculpt.   Jan. 1 1813.
20. German Deer Shooting Summer   Manskirch del   Dubourg sculpt.   Jan. 1 1813.
21. The Bear Trap   Howitt del   Howitt & Dubourg sculpt.   Jan. 1 1813.
22. German Fox Trap   Howitt del   Dubourg sculpt.   Sep. 1 1813.
23. German Wild Boar Trap   Howitt del   Dubourg sculpt.   Jan. 1 1813.
24. Shooting Wolves in Winter   Manskirch del   Dubourg sculpt.   March 1 1813.
25. Catching the Badger   Manskirch del   Dubourg sculpt.   July 1 1813.
26. A Trap to shoot the Bear   Howitt del   Howitt & Dubourg sculpt.   Jan. 1 1813.
27. German Deer Shooting with Decoy   Howitt del   Howitt & Dubourg sculpt.   Sep. 1 1813.
28. German Manner of Netting Partridges   Manskirch del   Merke sculpt.   June 1 1813.
29. Egyptian Crocodile Catching   J. H. Clark del   Dubourg sculpt.   July 1 1813.
30. Turtle Fishing in the Water   J. H. Clark del   Dubourg sculpt.   March 1 1813.
31. Turtle catching on Land   J. H. Clark del   Dubourg sculpt.   July 1 1813.
32. Bird Catching from Below   J. H. Clark del   Dubourg sculpt.   June 4 1813.
33. Bird Catching from Above   J. H. Clark del   Dubourg sculpt.   May 1 1813.
34. Mexican Lizard Catcher   J. H. Clark del   Dubourg sculpt.   July 1 1813.
35. Greenland Seal Catching   J. H. Clark del   Dubourg sculpt.   May 1 1813.
36. Shooting the Harpoon at a Whale   J. H. Clark del   Dubourg sculpt.   March 1 1813.
37. Boats approaching a whale   Clark del   Dubourg sculpt.   Feb. 1 1813.
38. A Whale brought alongside a ship   J. H. Clark del   Dubourg sculpt.   March 1 1813.
39. A Ship's Boat attacking a whale   Clark del   Dubourg sculpt.   Feb. 1 1813.
40. Finland Bear Hunting   Manskirch del   Dubourg sculpt.   Sep. 1 1813.
41. Kamtschatka Bear Hunting   Clark del   Dubourg sculpt.   — 1st 1813.
42. Laplanders Hunting   Atkinson del   Dubourg sculpt.   Feb. 1 1813.
43. Shooting Anecdote India 1.   Howitt del   Merke sculpt.   Jan. 1 1813.
44. Shooting Anecdote India 2.   Howitt del   Merke sculpt.   Jan. 1 1813.
45. A Tartar catching his horse   Atkinson del   Dubourg sculpt.   Feb. 1 1813.
46. Hog Hunters in India Going Out No. 1   Howitt del   Merke sculpt.   Jan. 1 1813.
47. Hog Hunters in India 2   Howitt del   Merke sculpt.   Jan. 20 1813.
48. Hog Hunters in India 3   Howitt del   Merke sculpt.   Jan. 20 1813.
49. Hog Hunters in India 4   Howitt del   Merke sculpt.   Jan. 1 1813.

Foreign Field Sports 1819 (*contd.*)

50. Shooting Antelopes India   Howitt del   Dubourg sculpt.   March 1 1813.
51. Hunting the Elk   Howitt del   Howitt & Dubourg sculpt.   Jan. 1 1813.
52. South American catching a Bull   Clark del   Dubourg sculpt.   Jan. 1 1813.
53. Pions in S. America catching Wild Horses.   J. Clark del   Howitt & Dubourg sculpt.   Jan. 1 1813.
54. Torchlight Fishing in N. America   J. H. Clark del   Merke sculpt.   March 25 1813.
55. Hunting a Zebra   Howitt del   Dubourg sculpt.   May 1 1813.
56. Battle with the Gt. Boa & a Tiger   J. H. Clark del   Dubourg sculpt.   March 1 1813.
57. Chamois Shooters in the Tyrol   Manskirch del   Dubourg sculpt.   Jan. 1813.
58. Chamois Shooters Retreat   Howitt del   Dubourg sculpt.   Jan. 1 1813.
59. Chamois Shooters Ascending the rocks   Manskirch del   Dubourg sculpt.   June 4 1813.
60. Taking Vipors   J. H. Clark del   Dubourg sculpt.   October 1 1813.
61. The African Crocodile Hunters   Clark del   Dubourg sculpt.   March 1 1813.
62. Shooting an African Buffalo   Howitt del   Dubourg sculpt.   October 1 1813.
63. The Eagle & Wolf disputing the Prize   Howitt del et sculpt.   Jan. 1 1813.
64. Seamen killing a Polar Bear   Howitt del   Howitt & Dubourg sculpt.   Jan. 1 1813.
65. Anecdote Gt. Boa Serpent & a Bull   Howitt del.   Merke sculpt.   Jan. 1 1813.
66. Hunted Elephant   Howitt del   Howitt & Merke sculpt.   Jan. 1 1813.
67. The Elephant killed   Howitt del   Howitt & Merke sculpt.   Jan. 1 1813.
68. Hindoo Method of Taming Elephants   Jan. 1 1813.
69. Hindoo Elephant Trap   Jan. 1 1813.
70. Elephant in a Pitfall   Howitt del   Howitt & Merke sculpt.   Jan. 1 1813.
71. Anecdote of Hunters & Rhinoceros   Howitt del Merke sculpt.   Jan. 1 1813.
72. African Rhinoceros Hunting   Howitt del   Dubourg sculpt.   May 1 1813.
73. Hunting the Camelopard   Howitt del   Dubourg sculpt.   June 4 1813.
74. Killing a Shark   J. H. Clark del   Dubourg sculpt.   March 1 1813.
75. Killing Seals in a Cavern   Howitt del   Dubourg sculpt.   May 1 1813.
76. Tartars hunting Deer   Howitt del   Dubourg sculpt.   May 1 1813.
77. Mackerel Fishing   Clark del   Dubourg sculpt.   Feb. 1 1813.
78. Shooting the Hyena   Howitt del   Dubourg sculpt.   May 1 1813.
79. Shooting a white hare at Tornio   Atkinson del   Dubourg sculpt.   Feb. 1 1813.
80. Shooting a Leopard   Howitt del   Howitt & Merke sculpt.   Jan. 1 1813.
81. Hunting the Tiger Cat   Howitt del   Dubourg sculpt.   May 1 1813.
82. Anecdote Shooting a Porcupine   Howitt del   Dubourg sculpt.   May 1 1813.
83. Siberian Exiles shooting Deer   Howitt del   Dubourg sculpt.   Sep. 1 1813.
84. A Siberian Exile shooting a black Fox   Atkinson del   Clark & Dubourg sculpt.   Jan. 1 1813.
85. German Fox Trap   Manskirch del   Dubourg sculpt.   Jan. 1 1813.
86. North American Bear Hunt   Howitt del   Dubourg sculpt.   Sep. 1 1813.
87. Sailors shooting a Wild Stag   Jan. 1 1813.
88. Spanish Bull Fighting No. 1.   Feb. 1 1813.
89.   „   „   „   No. 2.   Feb. 1 1813.
90.   „   „   „   No. 3.   Jan. 1 1813.
91.   „   „   „   No. 4.   Feb. 1 1813.
92.   „   „   „   No. 5.   Feb. 1 1813.
93.   „   „   „   No. 6.   Feb. 1 1813.
94.   „   „   „   No. 7.   Jan. 1 1813.
95.   „   „   „   No. 8.   Feb. 1 1813.
96.   „   „   „   No. 9.   Jan. 1 1813.
97.   „   „   „   No. 10.   Jan. 1 1813.
98.   „   „   „   No. 11.   Feb. 1 1813.
99.   „   „   „   No. 12.   Feb. 1 1813.
100. General View of a Spanish Bull Fight   Clark del   Dubourg sculpt.   Jan. 1 1813.
101. Smoking out the Opossum   J. H. Clark del   Dubourg sculpt.   October 1 1813.
102. Hunting the Kangaroo   J. H. Clark del   Dubourg sculpt.   October 1 1813.
103. Throwing the Spear   J. H. Clark del   Dubourg sculpt.   October 1 1813.
104. Climbing Trees   J. H. Clark del   Dubourg sculpt.   October 1 1813.
105. Fishing No. 1   J. H. Clark del   Dubourg sculpt.   October 1 1813.
106. Fishing No. 2   J. H. Clark del   Dubourg sculpt.   October 1 1813.
107. The Dance   J. H. Clark del   Dubourg sculpt.   October 1 1813.

Foreign Field Sports 1819 (*contd.*)

108. Warriors of New S. Wales   J. H. Clark del   Dubourg sculpt.   October 1 1813.
109. Trial   J. H. Clark del   Dubourg sculpt.   October 1 1813.
110. Repose   J. H. Clark del.   Dubourg sculpt.   October 1 1813.

The Second Edition.

226   *Another issue was published by Orme without date.*

227 FORREST (Lt.-Col.)

A Picturesque Tour along the Rivers Ganges and Jumna, in India: consisting of Twenty-four highly finished and coloured views, a map, and vignettes, from original drawings made on the spot; with Illustrations, Historical and Descriptive. (rule) By Lieutenant Colonel Forrest, late on the staff of His Majesty's service in Bengal [large coloured vignette "Tomb at Jeswuntnagurh on the Jumna River] London Published by R. Ackermann, 101 Strand July 1

Quarto.   1824

COLLATION.—Title as above (v. blank) + Preface 2 pp. (iii–iv) + Directions for placing plates 1 p. (v. blank) + pp. 1–191 + 24 coloured aquatint plates + folding map "Sketch of the Rivers Ganges and Jumna from their mouths to their issue from the Mountains."

Each plate bears imprint, London Published by R. Ackermann 101 Strand and date and the plates are numbered.

1. p. 126. Hindoo Pagodas below Barrackpore on the Ganges   July 1 1824   G. Hunt sculpt.
2. p. 128. Hindoo Village on the Ganges, near Ambooah   July 1 1824   T. Sutherland sculpt.
3. p. 130. Ghaut of Cutwa on the Ganges   G. Hunt sculpt.   July 1 1824.
4. p. 131. Part of the City of Moorshedabad Ancient Capital of Bengal   T. Sutherland sculpt.   July 1 1824.
5. p. 136. Mountains of Rajemahal where they descend to the Ganges   Engraved by T. Sutherland   Augt. 1, 1824.
6. p. 139. The Motee Girna or Fall of Pearls in the Rajemahal Hills.   T. Sutherland sculpt.   Augt. 1 1824.
7. p. 141. The Rocks of Colgong   G Hunt sculpt.   Augt. 1 1824.
8. p. 143. Ancient Tomb at the confluence of the Boglipore Nulla and the Ganges   G. Hunt sculpt.   Augt. 1 1824.
9. p. 145. A Village on the Ganges above Boglipore   T. Sutherland sculpt.   Septr. 1 1824.
10. p. 146. The Fakeer's Rock at Janguira near Sultangunj.   T. Sutherland sculpt.   Septr. 1 1824.
11. p. 148. Village and Pagoda below Patna Azimabad on the Ganges   T. Sutherland sculpt.   Sepr. 1 1824.
12. p. 151. Hindoo Ghaut on the Ganges below Benares   T. Sutherland sculpt.   Septr. 1 1824.
13. p. 152. City of Benares from the Ganges   Engraved by T. Sutherland   Octr. 1 1824.
14. p. 153. Sacred Tank and Pagodas near Benares   T. Sutherland sculpt.   Novr. 1 1824.
15. p. 155. Mahomedan Mosque and Tomb near Benares   T. Sutherland sculpt.   July 1 1824.
16. p. 156. The Indian Fort of Chunargurh on the Ganges   Engraved by T. Sutherland   Octr. 1 1824.
17. p. 157. Raj Ghaut and Fort of Allahabad at the confluence of the Ganges and Jumna Rivers   T. Sutherland sculpt.   Novr. 1 1824.
18. p. 159. Tombs near Etaya in the Doo-ab on the Jumna River   T. Sutherland sculpt.   Novr. 1 1824.
19. p. 161. Surseya Ghaut Khanpore   T. Sutherland sculpt.   Novr. 1 1824.
20. p. 166. City of Lucknow Capital of Province of Oude on the Goomty River   G. Hunt sculpt.   Novr. 1 1824.
21. p. 178. Palace of the King of Delhi taken from the principal mosque   T. Sutherland sculpt.   Decr. 1 1824.
22. p. 179. The Cuttub Minar in the Ruins of Ancient Delhi   T. Sutherland sculpt.   Decr. 1 1824.
23. p. 184. Grand Gateway and Tomb of the Emperor Acber at Secundra   T. Sutherland sculpt.   Decr. 1 1824.
24. p. 186. The Taj Mahal, Tomb of the Emperor Shah Jehan and his Queen   T. Sutherland sculpt.   Decr. 1 1824.
      Coloured vignette as tailpiece to p. 191 Sicre Gully Pass between Bengal and Bahar.

Forrest's Rivers Ganges and Jumna (*contd.*)

Originally issued in 6 monthly parts in wrappers, both small and large paper.

228   *Another edition was published with Title and 6 pp. of Text in Italian, with plates the same as above.*

229 FRANK (W. A.)

Ten Views In the Vicinity of Bristol, drawn from nature and lithographed by Willm. Arnee Frank, Bristol: Published and Sold by the Artist, 5 Easton Buildgs, 7th Mo: 1831 and may be had of all Book and Printsellers.   Frank's Lithy.,

COLLATION.—List of Subscribers 1 leaf + 10 plates.

All plates marked, "Bristol Drawn Lithogd., and Pubd., by W. A. Frank.   1831" (date omitted in some instances).

1. Ashton Court, a Seat of Sir John Smyth, Bart. (from S.E.).
2. The Seat of Sir John Smyth, Bart. (Stapleton).
3. Clifton, Vincent's Rocks etc. (from Leigh Woods, looking up the River).
4. The Hotel at Portishead Point, Erected by the Corporation of Bristol, 1830.   George Dymond, Architect.
5. Snuff Mill on the River Frome (near Stapleton).
6. Blaize Castle.
7. View at Cheddar (near the Entrance of the Cliffs).
8. Nightingale Valley (Leigh Woods).
9. The Seat of Lord de Clifford (Kingsweston).
10. Stoke House (The Seat of the late Duchess of Beaufort).

Issued in pink wrappers bearing title as above.

230 FRANKLAND (R.)

Eight Representations of Shooting, Engraved by Woodman and Turner, from Drawings by Robert Frankland Esq. to whom these plates are most Respectfully Dedicated, by his Very Obedient and Obliged Servant, W. D. Jones.   Cambridge.   Published September 1st, 1813 by W. D. Jones, at His Repository of Arts, Market Hill.

Small Oblong Folio.   1813

COLLATION.—Engraved title as above (v. blank) + 8 coloured aquatint plates, unnumbered and without titles, but each plate bearing imprint, Cambridge Published Aug. 1st 1813 by W. D. Jones.   Repository of Arts, Market Hill.

Issued in paper wrappers with printed label lettered "Shooting."

Frankland.   See also under Billesdon Coplow.

231 GAINSBOROUGH (T.)

A Collection of Prints, Illustrative of English Scenery from the Drawings and Sketches of Thomas Gainsborough, R.A. London.   Engraved by W. F. Wells and J. Laporte, and Published by John and Josiah Boydell.

Folio.   N.D.

COLLATION.—Title + Dedication 1 leaf + 60 Lithographs, many tinted in colours.   The owner of each picture is given, but no titles.

232 GAUCI (M.)

The Costume of the British Navy as ordered by His Royal Highness the Lord High Admiral in 1828 (thick and thin rule) London Printed and Published by Engelmann, Graf, Coindel & Co. Lithographers to H.R.H. the Duke of Clarence, 92 Dean Street, Soho.

1829

COLLATION.—Drawn and lithographed by M. Gauci, published 1828–30.

1. 2nd Class of Petty Officers. Cockswaine. Nov. 1828.
2. 1st Class of Petty Officers. Master at Arms, or Quarter Master. Nov. 1828.
3. 1st Class of Petty Officers. Midshipman. Nov. 1828.
4. Common Sailor. Nov. 1828.
5. Volunteers of the first and second Class. Nov. 1828.
6. Warrant Officers. Boatswain. 1828.
7. A Greenwich Pensioner. Dec. 1828.
8. 1st Class of Petty Officers. Masters Assistant. 1828.
9. Master and Physician. 1828.
10. Purser, Secretary to the Commander in Chief, and Master of the Fleet. 1828.
11. Lieutenant and Clerk. Feb. 1829.
12. Rear Admiral. Feb. 1829.
13. Physician. Feb. 1829.
14. Lord High Admiral and Admiral. Feb. 1829.
15. Vice Admiral. Feb. 1829.
16. Captain. Feb. 1829.
17. Commander. July 1830.
18. Commodore. July, 1830.

Colas (No. 1504) Lists plates 1–12 only. Abbey, Vol. 2, No. 336, Lists 17 plates, the plate of the Physician not being included in his volume.

233 GELL (Sir William)

Views in Barbary, and A Picture of the Dey of Algiers, Taken in 1813 By W. G. Esq. London. Printed for Edward Orme, Publisher to his Majesty, and to His Royal Highness the Prince Regent, Bond Street, Corner of Brook Street; by J. F. Dove, St John's Square, Clerkenwell.

Oblong Folio.   1815

COLLATION.—Title as above + Text pp. 1–9 + 4 coloured aquatints.

Plates lettered, W. G. Esq., delt., Robt. Havell, sculpt., with imprint, Published and Sold, May 1st, 1815, by Edward Orme, Publisher to His Majesty and H.R.H. the Prince Regent, Bond Street, Corner of Brook St, London.

1. The Dey of Algiers seated in state.
2. The City of Algiers from the sea.
3. Country West of Algiers, from the British Consul Generals Garden.
4. East View of the City and Bay of Algiers.

234 GERNING (J. J. von)

A Picturesque Tour along the Rhine, from Mentz to Cologne: with Illustrations of the Scenes of Remarkable Events, and of Popular Traditions. (rule) By Baron J. J. von Gerning (rule) Embellished with Twenty-four highly finished and coloured engravings, from the Drawings of M. Schuetz; and accompanied by a map (rule) Translated from the German

Gerning's Tour along the Rhine (*contd.*)

by John Black (thick and thin rule) London: Published by R. Ackermann, 101, Strand; and sold by the principal booksellers in the United Kingdom. Printed by L. Harrison, 373, Strand (rule).

Quarto.   1820

COLLATION.—Title as above (v. blank) + Dedication to George IV 2 pp. (iii–iv) + List of Subscribers 4 pp. (v–viii) + Preface by the Translator 4 pp. (ix–xii) + Preface of the Author 2 pp. xiii–xiv + Contents 1 p. (v. List of Plates) + pp. 1–178 + 24 coloured plates.

Each plate bears imprint, "London Pubd [date] at 101 Strand for R. Ackermann's Views on the Rhine."

1. p. 27. Mentz, from the Influx of the Maine into the Rhine Schutz delt. T. Sutherland sculpt. Sept. 1 1819.
2. p. 40. Biebrich, the Summer Residence of the Duke of Nassau. Schutz delt. T. Sutherland sculpt. Sept. 1 1819.
3. p. 56. The Johannes Berg Schutz delt. T. Sutherland sculpt. Octor. 1 1819.
4. p. 70. The Town of Bingen Schutz delt. T. Sutherland sculpt. Octor. 1 1819.
5. p. 75. The Mice Tower [no artist given] D. Havell sculpt. Novr. 1 1819.
6. p. 92. The Castle of Furstenberg C. G. Schutz delt. T. Sutherland sculpt. Decr. 1 1819.
7. p. 96. Bacharach Schutz delt. T. Sutherland sculpt. Novr. 1 1819.
8. p. 98. Pfalz Castle and the Town of Laub Drawn by C. G. Schutz Engraved by T. Sutherland Novr. 1 1819.
9. p. 100. The Town of Oberwesel C. G. Schutz delt. T. Sutherland sculpt. Novr. 1 1819.
10. p. 102. Thurnberg G. C. (sic) Schutz delt. T. Sutherland sculpt. Jany. 1 1820.
11. p. 104. Liebenstein C. G. Schutz delt. D. Havell sculpt. Decr. 1 1819.
12. p. 105. Braubach C. G. Schutz delt. T. Sutherland sculpt. Jany. 1 1820.
13. p. 108. The Church of Johannes at the influx of the Lahn C. G. Schutz delt. T. Sutherland sculpt. Decr. 1 1819.
14. p. 109. St. Goarshausen, St. Goar, and Rheinfels C. G. Schutz delt. T. Sutherland sculpt. Decr. 1 1819.
15. p. 110. Salmon Fishery at Lurley C. G. Schutz delt. T. Sutherland sculpt. Jany. 1 1820.
16. p. 111. Bornhofen C. G. Schutz delt. D. Havell sculpt. Jany. 1 1820.
17. p. 112. Boppard C. G. Schutz delt. T. Sutherland sculpt. March 1 1820.
18. p. 117. Coblentz and the Fortress of Ehrenbreitstein G. C. (sic) Schutz delt. Engraved by T. Sutherland Feby. 1 1820.
19. p. 125. Andernach and Neuwied C. G. Schutz delt. T. Sutherland sculpt. Feby. 1 1820.
20. p. 126. Engers and Sayn C. G. Schutz delt. T. Sutherland sculpt. March 1 1820.
21. p. 129. Hammerstein C. G. Schutz delt. T. Sutherland sculpt. Jany. 1 1820.
22. p. 132. The Castles of Drachenfels & Rolandveck C. G. Schutz delt. D. Havell sculpt. March 1 1820.
23. p. 134. Bodesberg and the Seven Hills C. G. Schutz delt. T. Sutherland sculpt. Feby. 1 1820.
24. p. 160. Cologne C. G. Schutz delt. T. Sutherland sculpt. March 1 1820.
    p. 172. Map of the Course of the Rhine from Mentz to Cologne and of the Course of the Maine and the Lahn Surveyed and drawn by C. F. Ulrich Architect Engraved by W. Bartlett (folding).

Issued in 6 monthly parts in paper wrappers. On completion in Elephant quarto for 4 guineas in boards. A few large-paper copies on Atlas quarto were issued at 6 guineas.

In First issues the plates are unnumbered. Second issue has some of the plates with the imprints dated a month later. In still later issues the plates are numbered.

235 GISCARD

Delineations of the most Remarkable Costumes of the different Provinces of Spain, and also of the Military Uniforms, Bull Fights, National Dances, &c of the Spaniards.

Giscard's Costumes of Provinces of Spain (*contd.*)

(rule) **London: Published by Henry Stokes, 9, Lombard-Street; and may be had of all booksellers (rule).**

Quarto. 1823

COLLATION.—Title as above (v. blank) + 40 coloured plates by Giscard including frontispiece.

1. Front. Spanish Costumes.	21. Maragato.
2. Bolero.	22. A fruit woman of Valencia.
3. Fandango.	23. A woman of Yvissa.
4. Matador.	24. Woman of Aragon.
5. Picador.	25. A Country man of Aragon.
6. A Woman of Catalogna.	26. A Gardner (sic) of Valencia.
7. A sailor of Catalogna.	27. A country man of old Castille.
8. A woman of the Mountains.	28. A country woman of old Castille.
9. A Smuggler.	29. A maid of Salamanca.
10. Gipsy Woman.	30. A Shepherd of Leon.
11. Gipsy Man.	31. A woman of Grenada.
12. A Farmers Wife of Murcia.	32. A man of Mayorca.
13. A Carter of Murcia.	33. Capitan General.
14. A Woman of Navara.	34. A woman of Asturias.
15. A Man of Navarra.	35. Guerilla.
16. A Woman of Gallice.	36. A Muleteer of Malaga.
17. A man of Gallice.	37. Horse Artillery.
18. A Woman of Estramadura.	38. Dragoons.
19. A man of Estramadura.	39. Infantry.
20. Pasiega.	40. Hussars.

236 GODDARD and BOOTH

The Military Costume of Europe; exhibited in a series of highly finished Military Figures, in the Uniform of their several corps; with a concise description, and historical anecdotes; forming Memoirs of the Various Armies of the Present Time. (thick and thin rule).   Vol. I (II) (thin and thick rule) Utile Dulce (small swelled rule) London: Published by T. Goddard, Military Library, No. 1, Pall-Mall; and J. Booth, Duke-Street, Portland Place (swelled rule).

2 vols. Folio. 1812–22

COLLATION VOL. I.—Title as above (v. Printed by W. Clowes, Northumberland Court, Strand) + Advertisement 2 pp. + Plates and Contents of Vol. I 2 pp. + 48 plates (plate 9 being repeated), each with one leaf of text, and all bearing imprint, Published by T. Goddard, 1 Pall Mall, and J. Booth, Duke Street, Portland Place.

1. British General Officer.
2. British Officer of Heavy Cavalry.   1st Regt., Life Guards.
3. British Officer of Heavy Cavalry.   2nd Regt., Life Guards.   Feb. 14th.
4. British Officer of Heavy Cavalry of the Royal Regt. of Horse Guards Blue.
5. Officer of the 5th or Princess Charlotte of Wales's Dragoon Guards.
6. General the Most Noble Marquis of Anglesey, G.C.B. Colonel of the 7th Regt. Lt. Dragoons Hussars. Published by I. Booth for the Military Costume of Europe No. 16.   July 28th 1815.
7. British Officer of Hussars of the 10th or Prince of Wales's own Regt.
8. Officer of the 12th or Prince of Wales's Light Dragoons.
9. British Officer of the 13th Regt., of Light Dragoons.
9. (repeated) Officer of the 15th Lt. Dragoons or Duke of Cumberlands Hussars.

Goddard and Booth's Military Costume of Europe (*contd.*)

10. British Officer 17th Regt. Light Dragoons.
11. British Officer of Hussars of the 18th Regt. in Review Order.
12. Royal British Artillery.   1. Officer of Horse Arty.,
          2. Officer of Foot Arty.,
13. British Officer of Grenadiers 1st Regt. of Foot Guards.
14. British Officer of the 2nd or Coldstream Regt. of Foot Guards.
15. Officer of 9th (or Britannia Regt., of Infantry).
16. British Officer 25th Regt., Foot or King's Own Borderers.
17. British Officer 73rd Regiment of Foot.
18. British Officer of Highlanders 79th or Cameronian Regt.,
19. British Officer 87th or Prince of Wales's own Irish Regt.,
20. British Officer 95th Regt., or Rifle Corps.
21. British Officer 97th Regt. or Queens own.
22. British Troops of the Line.   1. A Sergeant of Highland Infantry.
          2. Dragoon of the 1st Regt., or Royals.
          3. Grenadier of the 4th or King's Own Regt of Foot.
23. British Troops of the Line.   1. Trooper of Heavy Horse 2nd Regt. of Life Guards.
          2. Gunner of the Royal Horse Artillery.
          3. Hussar of the 10th or Prince of Wales's own Regt.,
24. Private of the 12th (or Prince of Wales) Royal Regiment of Lancers.
  Private of the 25th Regt., of Foot.
25. British Light Troops.   1. Soldier of the 43rd Regt., Light Infantry.
         2. Dragoon of the 23rd Regt., Light Dragoons.
         3. Rifleman of the 95th Regt.,
26. British Light Troops.   1. A Private of the 18th Hussars.
         2. A Musician of do. in full review order.
27. British Army A Lance Man (or Hulan).
28. Duke of Brunswick Oels' Corps   Officer of Hussars.
29. Duke of Brunswick Oels' Corps   Officer of Infantry.
30. Duke of Brunswick Oels' Corps.   1. Private of Hussars.
         2. do. of Light Infantry.
         3. do. of the Rifle Company.
31. Officer of Greek Light Infantry.
32. Private of Greek Light Infantry.
33. (1) Officer Calabrian Free Corps } 1st Dec. 1813.
  (2) Private   do.   do.   }
34. French General Officers.   1. Marechal de l'Empire, in his Grand Costume and Decoration of the Legion of Honor.   2. General de Brigade in his full Dress and small Decoration of the Legion of Honor.
35. French General of Division Le Comte Le Febure Desnoettes.
36. French Officer of Grenadiers a Cheval of the 26th Regt., of Dragoons.
37. French Officer of Hussars 5th Regt.,
38. French Officer of Grenadiers 94th Regt.,
39. French Officer of Foot Artillery.
40. French Army A.   1. Curassier of the 6th Regt.,
      2. Horse Artillery Man 1st Regt.
      3. Picture of the 2nd or Chamborant Hussars.
41. French Army B.   1. 4th Regt., of Dragoons.
      2. Grenadier of the 94th Regt., of the Line.
42. French Army C.   Light Troops.   1. 27th Regt., Light Infantry.
          2. 5th Regt., of Chasseurs a Cheval.
43. French Army   A Soldier of the Dromedary Corps.
44. Italian General Officer.
45. Italian Officer of Grenadiers 2nd Regt., of Infantry of the Line.
46. Dutch Marshal.
47. Dutch Officer of Light Dragoons 2nd Regt.,

VOL. II.—Title as before but imprint changed to: Published by John Booth, Duke Street,

Goddard and Booth's Military Costume of Europe (*contd.*)

Portland Place. (swelled rule) 1822 (v. blank) + Plates and Contents of Vol. II 2 pp. + 49 plates, each with 1 leaf of Text.

1. Imperial Austrian General.
2. Austrian Officer of Cuirasiers Regt., Prince Charles of Lorraine.
3. Austrian Officer of Dragoons Regt. de Reisky.
4. Austrian Officer of Hussars of Archduke Ferdinand's Regt. (Hungarian).
5. Saxon Officer of Hussars.
6. Austrian Officer of Hulans Regt., Count Meerveldt in full Dress.
7. Austrian Officer of Foot Artillery.
8. Officer of the Archduke Charles's Regt., of Infantry in his undress uniform.
9. Austrian Army A.   1. Cuirassier of Archduke Joseph's Regt.,
      2. Imperial Corps of Artillery.
10. Austrian Army B.   1. Trooper of Archduke Charles's Regt. of Chevaux Legers Light Horse.
      2. Chasseur of the Tyrolese Regt. of Sharpshooters Count Chastellar.
11. Austrian Army C.   1. Grenadier of the Regt. Spleny (Hungarians).
      2. Hussar of the Regt., County Keinmayer.
12. Austrian Army D.   1. A Soldier of the Emperor's Regt.,
      2. A Dragoon of Archduke Charles Regt.,
      3. Hulan of Prince Schwartzen Verg's Regt.,
13. A Prussian General Officer.
14. Prussian Officer of Cuirassiers Regt. von Quitzow.
15. Prussian Officer of Dragoons, Regt. County Hertzberg.
16. Prussian Officer of 2nd Lieb Regt. of Hussars in his full Court Dress.
17. Prussian Officer of Hussars Regt. Rudorf in His full Review Uniform.
18. Prussian Officer of Hussars Regt. Prince of Anhalt Pless.
19. Prussian Officer of Hulans Regt. Towarszsyz.
20. Prussian Officer and Private of Yaeger Guards of General De Yorck.
21. Prussian Officer of Artillery.
22. Prussian Officer of Grenadier Regt. Friskow.
23. Prussian Officer of Light Infantry.
24. Prussian Officer of Regt. Jung Bornstaedt. 1763.
25. Prussian Officer of Cuirassiers   1763.
26. Prussian Officer of Hussars in the year 1763 Regt. Reusch or Todtenkepfe.
27. Prussian Army A.   1. Hussar of the Regt. Reusch or Todtenkepfe.
      2. Fusilier of the Light Infantry Battalion of Le Noble.
28. Prussian Army B.   1. Hussar of the Regt. Prince de Anhalt Pless.
      2. Fusilier of the Light Infantry Battalion of Pellet Silisian Brigade.
29. Prussian Army C.   Troops at Rossbach.   1. Chasseurs of the 3rd Leib Regt.
      2. Grenadier Duke Ferd., of Brunswick.
30. Prussian Army D.   1. Chasseur of the 3rd Leib Regt.
      2. Grenadier of the Regt. Kleist No. 5.
31. Russian Officer of the Noble Guards.
32. Russian Officer of Infantry of the Line Regt. Petersburg Grenadiers Guard.
33. Russian Officer of Hussars Regt., Ysom.
34. Russian Officer of Horse Artillery.
35. Russian Infantry Officer (Regiment Wyborg).
36. Russian Officer of the 12th Regt. of Chasseurs or Light Infantry.
37. Russian Troops.   1. Trooper of Noble Guards.
      2. Serjeant of Horse Artillery.
      3. Private of Infantry (Regt. Wyborg) in Field Dress.
38. A Russian Regular Cossack.
39. Cossacks.   1. Cossack of the Imperial Guards.
      2. Regular Cossack.
      3. Irregular Cossack.
40. Russian Army A.   1. Cossack of the Don.   2. Russian Lt. Infantry 2nd Regt.
41. Swedish Officer of Light Horse Chevaux Legers Finland Regt.,
42. Swedish Officer of Leib Grenadier Regt.

Goddard and Booth's Military Costume of Europe (*contd.*)

43. 1. Danish Officer of Infantry of the Line Norwegian Life Regt.,
    2. Danish Officer of Light Infantry Regt. Jaeger Schleswig.
44. Spanish Officer of Heavy Horse Regt. Carabinieros de la Reyna.
45. Spanish Officer of Hussars Regt., Maria Louisa.
46. Spanish Officer of Artillery.
47. Spanish Officer of Infantry of the Line Regt. Irlanda.
48. Spanish Army A. 1. Canonier Royal Artillery.
                     2. Fusilier of the 1st Regt. Estremadura.
                     3. Dragoon of the Regt. Zamora.
49. Spanish Guerrillas under Colonel Don Julian Sanchez.

237 GOLDICUTT (J.)

Specimens of Ancient Decorations from Pompeii, by John Goldicutt Architect. Author of the Antiquities of Sicily and Member of the Academy of St Luke at Rome (the above lettering on a decorative panel), Drawn by John Goldicutt. Engraved by Edward Finden. London: Published by Rodwell and Martin.

Small Quarto.   1825

COLLATION.—Engraved title as above (v. blank) + 2 pp. of Text + 19 coloured plates of Ceilings, Mosaic Pavements, Sides of Apartments and Fragments.

Goldsmith (Oliver) Vicar of Wakefield.   See under Rowlandson (T.).

Grandmaster or Adventure of Qui Hi.   See under Rowlandson (T.).

Green (J.) Poetical Sketches of Scarborough.   See under Rowlandson (T.).

238 GREEN (William)

(Views of the Lakes.   A Series of 60 tinted aquatint plates without title.)

Plates numbered right-hand top corners 1–60 and each bearing imprint, Published at Ambleside, June 1st, 1815, by Wm. Green.

1. Coniston Water.	18. Brother Water.
2. Coniston Water.	19. Ulls Water from Glencoin.
3. Man Mountain on Coniston Water.	20. Ulls Water taken near Lyulphs Tower.
4. Coniston Water Head.	21. Ulls Water from Low Field.
5. Esthwaite Water.	22. Ulls Water.
6. Stock Gill.	23. Ulls Water from the Purse Bay.
7. Scandale Beck.	24. Scene on the River Lowther.
8. Windermere taken near Low Wood.	25. Haws Water.
9. North End of Curwens Island on Windermere.	26. View down Haws Water from Mardale.
	27. Head of Haws Water.
10. Curwens Island On Windermere from the Station.	28. Rydal Water.
	29. Outlet to Grasmere Lake.
11. Fort of Windermere from the Station.	30. Grasmere.
12. Windermere from Low Wray.	31. Easedale Tarn.
13. Blea Tarn.	32. St Johns Vale.
14. Langdale Head from Wall End.	33. Leaths Water.
15. Elter Water and Windermere.	34. Raven Crag on Leaths Water.
16. Elter Water.	35. Helvellyn from Leaths Water.
17. Loughrigg Tarn.	36. Derwent Water from Castlerrigg.

Green's Views of the Lakes (*contd.*)

37. Derwent Water from Isthmus.
38. Derwent Water from Barrow Common.
39. Saddleback from Derwent Water.
40. Derwent Water from Castle Crag.
41. Derwent Water taken near Sprinkling Tarn.
42. Crosthwaite Church near Keswick.
43. Bassenthwaite Water.
44. Bowder Stone.
45. Stonethwaite Bridge.
46. Eagle Crag.
47. Borrowdale from Greenup Vale.
48. Styhead Tarn.
49. Sprinkling Tarn.
50. Buttermere from Gatergarth Dale.
51. Buttermere and Crummock Water.
52. Crummock Water and Buttermere.
53. Head of Crummock Water.
54. Lows Water.
55. Ennerdale Water.
56. Head of Wast Water from Crook.
57. Screas on Wast Water.
58. Schofell on Wast Water.
59. Yewbarrow from Borrowdale.
60. Wallowbarrow Crag.

William Green also issued a drawing book with 78 plates published at Ambleside in 1809, entitled "Seventy Eight Studies from Nature."

239 GRINDLAY (Capt. Robert Melville)

Scenery, Costumes and Architecture, chiefly on the Western Side of India, By Captn. Robert Melville Grindlay, member of the Royal Asiatic Society and of the Society of Arts &c. [vignette of native woman, coloured] London, Published by R. Ackermann, Strand

2 vols.   Quarto.   1826[–30]

COLLATION VOL. I.—Title as above, Wm. Allsup Scrip. Wandsworth Wm. Alexander sculp. 50 Strand (v. blank) + Introduction 1 p. (v. blank) + Contents 1 p. (v. blank) + Part I pp. 1–12 with 6 coloured plates, Part II sub-title 1 p. (v. blank) + Advertisement Part II, 2 pp. + 7 unnumbered leaves with 6 coloured plates, Part III sub-title (v. blank) + 10 unnumbered leaves with 6 coloured plates.

VOL. II.—Title viz. "Scenery, Costumes and Architecture.   Chiefly on the Western side of India.   By Captain Robert Melville Grindlay M.R.A.S., &c.   Vol. II. [lithograph vignette uncoloured W. Purser delt. from a sketch by Capt. Grindlay.   On Stone by L. Haghe] Published by Smith, Elder and Co. Cornhill.   1830.   Printed by W. Day 17 Gate Street " (v. blank) + sub-title 1 p. (v. blank) + Advertisement 1 p. (v. blank) + Contents 1 p. (v. blank) + 11 unnumbered leaves of Text + 6 coloured plates, Part V sub-title (v. blank) + 13 unnumbered leaves of Text + 6 coloured plates + Part VI sub-title (v. blank) + Advertisement 1 p. (v. blank) + 9 unnumbered leaves of Text + 6 coloured plates.

In all, 36 coloured aquatint plates.   The first 6 plates with imprint, London Pubd. by R. Ackermann, Strand 1826, plates 7 to 12 London Published by R. Ackermann Strand and W. Sams St. James Street 1826, and remainder with imprint of Smith Elder & Co.

1. Scene in Bombay   From a Drawing by Captn. Grindlay   Engd. by R. G. Reeve.   Cold. by J. G. Hogarth.
2. Approach of the Monsoon Bombay Harbour   From a Drawing by W. Westall A.R.A.   Engd. by T. Fielding   Cold. by J. B. Hogarth.
3. The Shaking Minarets at Ahmedabad   Drawn on the spot in 1809 by Captn. Grindlay   Etchd. by G. Hawkins   Engd. by T. Fielding   Cold. by J. B. Hogarth.
4. Ancient Temple at Hulwud   Painted by F. Witherington from a Drawing by Captn. Grindlay   Engraved by G. Hunt   Cold. by J. Hogarth.
5. The Rajah of Cutch with his Vassalls   Drawn by Captn. Grindlay   Engraved by R. G. Reeve.
6. Mountains of Aboo in Guzerat   [Drawn by W. Westall   Engraved by T. Fielding].

Grindlay's India (*contd.*)

7. Scene in Bombay [Drawn by Capt. Grindlay] Engraved by R. G. Reeve.
8. Approach to the Bore Ghaut Drawn by Wm. Westall A.R.A. from a Painting by Lt. Coll. Johnson C.B. Engraved by T. Fielding Colored by J. B. Hogarth.
9. View in the Bore Ghaut Drawn on the spot in 1803 by Wm. Westall A.R.A. Engraved by T. Fielding Colored by J. B. Hogarth.
10. View from the Top of the Bore Ghaut Drawn on the Spot in 1803 by William Westall A.R.A. Engraved by T. Fielding Colored by J. B. Hogarth.
11. Dowlutabad the ancient Deo Gurh Painted by Wm. Daniell Esqr. R.A. from a Drawing by Capt. Grindlay Engraved by R. G. Reeve Colored by J. B. Hogarth.
12. Great Excavated Temple at Ellora Drawn on the spot for the Honble. Lady Hood, by Captn. Grindlay 1813 Etched. by G. Rawle Engd. by G. Hunt Colored by J. B. Hogarth.
13. Preparation for a Suttee, or the Immolation of a Hindoo Widow from a Drawing by Captn. Grindlay Etchd. by J. Willis and H. Melville Engd. by R. G. Reeve.
14. Tombs of the Kings of Golconda Drawn by Capt. Grindlay 1813 Etched by J. Willis Engraved by G. Hunt (no imprint).
15. Hermitage at Kurrungalle in Ceylon From a drawing by Capt. Chas. Auber of the Quarter Mastr. Genls. Depart. Ceylon Drawn by Wm. Westall A.R.A. Engd. by R. G. Reeve.
16. Fortress of Bowrie in Rajpootana From a drawing by Capt. Chas. Auber of the Quarter Mastr. Genls. Depart. Ceylon Drawn by Wm. Westall A.R.A. Engraved by C. Bently.
17. North West View of the Fort of Bombay Drawn by Wm Westall A.R.A. Engraved by R. G. Reeve.
18. Morning View from Colliann near Bombay Painted by Wm. Daniell R.A. from a Drawing by Capt. Grindlay Engraved by R. G. Reeve.
19. The British Residency at Hyderabad Drawn by Captn. Grindlay in 1813 Etchd. by J. Willis Engd. by R. G. Reeve.
20. The Roza at Mehmoodabad in Guzerat or Tomb of the Vizier of Sultan Mehmood Drawn on the spot by Captn. Grindlay Etchd. by J. Willis Engd. by C. Bentley.
21. Fishing Boats in the Monsoon Northern Part of Bombay Harbour from a sketch by Lieutt. Coll. Johnson C.B. Drawn by Clarkson Stanfield Engraved by C. Bentley.
22. View of the Bridge near Baroda in Guzerat from a Drawing by Captn. Grindlay in 1806 Etched by J. Willis & H. Melville Engraved by C. Bentley.
23. The Town and Pass of Boondi in Rajpootana from a Drawing by Captn. Chas. Auber of the Quarter Master Genls. Department Ceylon Drawn by W. Westall Engd. by C. Bentley.
24. View near Tonk in Rajpootana from a Drawing by Captn. Chas. Auber of the Quarter Mastr. Genls. Department Ceylon Drawn by W. Westall Engd. by R. G. Reeve.
25. Interior of the Cave Temple of India Subba at Ellora From a Drawing made on the spot by Captn. Grindlay for the Hon. Mrs. Stewart Mackenzie Drawn by D. Roberts Engd. by H. Pyall.
26. Scene in Kattiawar Travellers and Escort from a Sketch by Capt. Grindlay Drawn by C. Stanfield Engd. by C. Bentley.
27. View in the Island of Ceylon from the Residence of Sir Alexr. Johnston F.R.S. &c. &c. Late President of His Majesty's Council in that Island in 1811 Drawn by Copley Fielding Engd. by R. G. Reeve.
28. Aurungabad From the Ruins of Arungzebe's Palace From a drawing made on the spot by Capt. Grindlay in 1813 for the Hon. Mrs. Stewart Mackenzie Drawn by W. Purcer Engd. by C. F. Hunt.
29. Entrance of the Great Cave Temple of Elephanta near Bombay from a Drawing made on the spot by W. Westall A.R.A. in 1803 Engraved by C. Bentley.
30. Interior of the Great Cave Temple of Elephanta near Bombay From a drawing made on the spot by W. Westall A.R.A. in 1803 Engraved by J. Baily.
31. View of Sassoor in the Deccan From a sketch taken on the Spot by Capt. Grindlay 1813, for the Hon. Mrs. Stewart Mackenzie Drawn by W. Purser Engd. by R. G. Reeve.
32. The Sacred Town and Temple of Dwarka From a sketch by Capt. Grindlay Drawn by W. Purser Engd. by R. G. Reeve.
33. Entrance of the Great Cave Temple of Elephanta near Bombay Drawn on the Spot in 1803, by W. Westall A.R.A. Engd. by S. G. Hughes.
34. The Great Triad in the Cave Temple of Elephanta near Bombay Drawn on the Spot in 1803 by W. Westall A.R.A. Engd. by T. Edge.
35. View of the City and Fortress of Tonk in Rajpootana From a Sketch by Capt. Chas. Auber of the Quarter Mastr. Genls. Departt. Ceylon Engd. by F. C. Hunt.

Grindlay's India (*contd.*)

36. Portico of a Hindoo Temple with other Hindoo and Mahometan Buildings from sketches by Captn. Grindlay   Drawn by D. Roberts   Engd. by R. G. Reeve.

Next to Daniell, the most attractive colour plate book on India.   One of the few books in which the name of the colourist is mentioned, viz. J. B. Hogarth.   I have heard of a variant of plate 14, Tombs of the Kings of Golconda, engraved by Reeve instead of Hunt but have not seen this.

Guide to the Watering Places between Exe and Dart.   See under Noble (W. B.).

240 HAKEWILL (J.)

A Picturesque Tour of the Island of Jamaica, from drawings made in the years 1820 and 1821, by James Hakewill, author of the "Picturesque Tour of Italy" &c. &c. &c. (thick and thin rule) London: Hurst and Robinson, Pall-Mall; E. Lloyd, Harley Street (short rule).

Folio.   1825

COLLATION.—Title as above (v. London: Printed by Cox and Baylis, Great Queen Street, Lincoln's Inn Fields) + Dedication 1 p. (v. blank) + Introduction pp. 3–8 + Historical Sketch of the Island of Jamaica pp. 9–13 (p. 14 blank) + Directions to Binder &c. 1 leaf + 21 coloured plates each with 1 leaf of text.

Each plate marked, Drawn by James Hakewill, Engraved by Sutherland, Clarke or Fielding.

1. Spanish Town.
2. Bridge at Spanish Town.
3. Kingston and Port Royal from Windsor Farm.
4. King-street, Kingston.
5. Waterfall on the Windward Road.
6. Holland Estate, St. Thomas in the East.
7. Golden Vale, Portland.
8. Spring Garden Estate, St. George's.
9. Agualta Vale.
10. Bridge over the White River, St. Mary's.
11. Port Maria.
12. Trinity Estate, St. Mary's.
13. Cardiff Hall.
14. Mount Diablo.
15. Bog Walk.
16. Williamfield, St. Thomas in the Vale.
17. Bryan Castle Estate, Trelawney.
18. Montego Bay, from Reading Hill.
19. Montpelier Estate, St. James's.
20. Rose Hall, St. James's.
21. Whitney Estate, Clarendon.

A charming colour plate book that has become quite scarce and valuable.

241 HALL (Capt. Basil)

Account of a Voyage of Discovery to the West Coast of Corea, and the Great Loo-Choo Island; with an Appendix containing charts, and various hydrographical and scientific notices (rule).   By Captain Basil Hall, Royal Navy, F.R.S.   Lond. & Edin., Member of the Asiatic Society of Calcutta, of the Literary Society of Bombay, and of the Society of Arts and Sciences at Batavia. (rule) and a Vocabulary of the Loo-Choo Language, by H. J. Clifford, Esq., Lieutenant Royal Navy. (thick and thin rule) London: John Murray, Albemarle Street.

Quarto.   1818

COLLATION.—Half-title "Voyage of Discovery to the West Coast of Corea, and the Great Loo-Choo Island" (v. T. Davison Lombard Street, Whitefriars, London) + Title as

Hall's Corea (*contd.*)

above (v. blank) + Dedication 1 p. (v. blank) + Preface 5 pp. (VII–XI) + p. XII blank + Contents 3 pp. (XIII–XV) + Directions for placing plates 1 p. + pp. 1–222 + Appendix pp. 1–CXXX (including sub-title) + Vocabulary Loo Choo Language A–I 4 in 4's (unnumbered pages).

Each coloured plate marked, Engd., by Robt. Havell & Son Published Jan. 1st, 1818 by John Murray, Albemarle Street, London.

1. Front. Sulphur Island. Drawn by Wm. Havell from a Sketch by Capt. Hall.
2. p. 16. Corean Chief and his Secretary. Drawn by Wm. Havell Calcutta, from a Sketch by Mr C. W. Browne, R.N.
3. p. 77. Napakiang. Drawn by Wm. Havell from a Sketch by Capt. Hall.
4. p. 97. Loo Choo Chief and his Two Sons. Drawn by Wm Havell Calcutta, from a Sketch by Mr C. W. Browne, R.N.
5. p. 132. Priest and Gentleman of Loo Choo. Drawn by Wm Havell Calcutta, from a Sketch by Mr C. W. Browne, R.N.
6. p. 176. The Prince of Loo Choo. Drawn by Wm. Havell, Calcutta, from a sketch by Mr C. W. Browne, R.N.
7. p. 196. Scene after the Prince of Loo Choo's Feast. Drawn by Wm. Havell, Calcutta, from a Sketch by Mr C. W. Browne, R.N.
8. p. 215. Gentleman of Loo Choo in his Cload. Drawn by Wm Havell, Calcutta, from a Sketch by Mr C. W. Browne, R.N.
9. p. 222. Bridge at Napaking. Domestic articles etc. (uncoloured).
   p. V   of Appendix. Track of H.M. Sloop Lyra Gulph of Perchelee.
   p. X   „   Track of H.M.S. Alceste and Lyra Sloop, along W. Coast of Corea.
   p. XIX   „   Chart of Great Loo Choo Island.
   p. XXI   „   Napakiang Roads.
   p. XXIV   „   Eye Draught of Port Melville on N.W. Side of Loo Choo.
   p. XXXIII   „   Wollaston's Dip Sector.

242 HALL (Mrs. S. C.)

The Book of Royalty. Characteristics of British Palaces, by Mrs. S. C. Hall. The Drawings by W. Perring and J. Brown. (rule) London: Ackermann and Company (short rule).

Small Folio.   1839

COLLATION.—Pictured lithograph title ("Coronation of Queen Elizabeth") + Printed title as above (v. London Whitehead and Compy. Printers 76 Fleet Street) + Dedication 1 p. (v. blank) + pp. 5–42 + 12 coloured lithograph plates including pictured title. Each plate marked, London Published 27 October 1838 by Ackermann & Co.

Title   The Book of Royalty with full page vignette Coronation of Queen Elizabeth. Printed by C. Hullmandel.
1. (following Dedication) [Queen] Victoria.
2. p. 7. The Fair Forester James the First and his daughter in Greenwich Park.
3. p. 11. The Summons Katherine Queen of England, comes into court.
4. p. 13. The New Beauty The Court of Queen Anne.
5. p. 17. The Heroine of Savoy.
6. p. 19. Charles the First parting from his children.
7. p. 21. The Doomed Princes.
8. p. 25. The King reproved.
9. p. 29. Fair Rosamond at Woodstock.
10. p. 31. The Death of Lady Anne.
11. p. 35. The Chaplet of Honour.
12. p. 37. Mary of Scotland.

243 HAMILTON (Count A.)

Memoirs of Count Grammont, by Count A. Hamilton. Translated from the French, with Notes and Illustrations. (rule) Second Edition, Revised. (rule) In Three Volumes Vol. I. [II, III] (swelled rule) London: Printed by T. Bensley, Bolt Court, for J. White, Fleet Street, Longman, Hurst, Rees and Orme, Paternoster Row; and J. Scott, Strand

3 vols.   Octavo.   1809

COLLATION VOL. I.—Half-title Memoirs of Count Grammont Vol. I (v. blank) + Title as above (v. blank) + List of Plates (in the 3 volumes) 2 pp. + Advertisement to the 4th Edition pp. v–viii + Advertisement to Present Edition pp. ix–xi (p. xii blank) + pp. 1–378 + 13 plates.

1. Front.   Le Ct. Antoine Hamilton.   W. H. Gardiner sc.
2. p.   5.   Philibert Comte de Grammont.
3. p.   7.   Cardinal Richelieu   Van den Bergh sc.
4. p.   51.   Marechal de Turenne   Bocquet sc.
5. p.   58.   Madame Royale, Daughter of Henry IVth of France   Bocquet sc.
6. p.   129.   Le Mareschal de Humieres   Silvester sc.
7. p.   132.   Albert, Prince Aremberg   Birrell sc.
8. p.   158.   Louis XIV   Parker sculpt.
9. p.   171.   Princess of Orange   Bocquet sc.
10. p.   173.   Duke of Ormond   Bocquet sc.
11. p.   182.   Catherine of Braganza   Freeman sc.
12. p.   202.   Mrs. Hyde, Lady Rochester.
13. p.   203.   Jacob Hall, the Rope Dancer   Freeman sc.

VOL. II.—Title as before + pp. 1–304 + 13 plates.

14. Front.   Charles the Second   Bocquet sc.
15. p.   2.   Miss Hamilton Lady Grammont   Wm. Gardiner sc.
16. p.   30.   Duchess of Newcastle   Bocquet sc.
17. p.   36.   Lady Russell   Bocquet sc.
18. p.   86.   Earl of Chesterfield.
19. p.   93.   Duke of York   N. W. Gardiner sc.
20. p.   105.   Lady Southesk   Bocquet sc.
21. p.   112.   Lady Robarts   F. Bartolozzi sculpt.
22. p.   116.   Miss Brooks Lady Whitmore   Bocquet sc.
23. p.   117.   Sr. John Denham   Le Goux sculpt.
24. p.   164.   Miss Brooks Lady Denham   Bocquet sc.
25. p.   209.   Mary Kirk   Bocquet sc.
26. p.   228.   Miss Price   F. Bartolozzi sc.

VOL. III.—Title as before + pp. 1–278 + Index pp. 279–284 + Books Printed for J. White 4 ll. unnumbered + 14 plates.

27. Front.   Miss Bagot.   Bocquet sc.
28. p.   1.   Miss Temple.
29. p.   16.   Sir Charles Lyttelton   P. W. Tomkins sc.
30. p.   52.   Miss Jennings   T. Cheeseman sc.
31. p.   62.   Duchess of Cleveland   Bocquet sc.
32. p.   67.   John, Earl of Rochester.
33. p.   101.   Somer Hill.
34. p.   103.   Prince Rupert   C. Knight sc.
35. p.   104.   Mr. Hughes   Bocquet sc.
36. p.   167.   Thomas Killigrew   Van den Bergh sc.
37. p.   173.   Countess of Shrewsbury.
38. p.   201.   Nell Gwyn   Sheneker sc.
39. p.   203.   Mrs. Davis   Bocquet sc.
40. p.   210.   Miss Stewart, Duchess of Richmond   W. N. Gardiner sc.

Hamilton's Memoirs of Grammont (*contd.*)

Extremely rare in coloured state. The above collation by permission from a copy in the possession of Messrs. Quaritch.

Handley Cross. See under [Surtees (R.)].

244 HARDINGE (C. S.)

Recollections of India. Drawn on Stone by J. D. Harding from the Original Drawings by the Honourable Charles Stewart Hardinge. Part I British India and the Punjab. London; Thomas M'Lean, 26 Haymarket

Folio.   1847

COLLATION PART I.—Title as above (v. blank) + Dedication to Queen 1 p. (v. blank) + Preface 2 pp. + 13 coloured plates each with 1 p. of Text (with exception of plate 9 Entry of Dhulip Sing into Lahore, which has 2 pp. of Text).

1. Portrait of Maharajah Dhulip Sing.
2. Barrackpore.
3. Return from Hog Hunting.
4. Delhi Palace of the King.
5. View from the Palace & Fort at Agra.
6. Jama Musjid Agra.
7. Battle of Firozshuhur.
8. British Outpost in Advance of Rhodawala.
9. Entry of Dhulip Sing into Lahore.
10. Shah Dhera, Tomb of the Emperor Jehangir.
11. Hazari Bagh Lahore.
12. Sikh Soldiers receiving their pay at the Royal Durbar.
13. Rajah Lal Sing.

PART II.—Title as in Part I but changed to Part II, Kashmir and the Alpine Punjab (v. blank) + 13 coloured plates, each with 1 p. of Text (with exception of first Life of Gulab Sing which has 3 pp. of Text).

14. Gulab Singh.
15. Kote Kangra.
16. Rope Bridge across Chunab River.
17. Poormandel.
18. Oodampore.
19. Hill Fort of Gulab Sing.
20. Janu.
21. Bij Beara.
22. Shupayan Fort.
23. City of Kashmir.
24. Hurri Purbut Fort.
25. Wulur Lake.
26. Sheik Iman-ud-din Runjur Sing & Dewan Dina Nath.

245 HARDY (J.)

A Picturesque and Descriptive Tour in the Mountains of the High Pyrenees comprising Twenty-four Views of the most Interesting Scenes, from original drawings taken on the spot; with some account of the bathing establishments in that department of France (rule) By J. Hardy, Esq. (rule) "The palaces of Nature, whose vast walls Have pinnacled in clouds their snowy scalps." Byron. (thick and thin rule) London: Published by R. Ackermann, 101, Strand (rule).

Octavo.   1825

COLLATION.—Title as above (v. Printed by L. Harrison, 373, Strand) + Dedication 1 p. (v. blank) + Preface pp. v–vii (p. viii blank) + pp. 1–84 + map and 24 coloured plates.

1. p. 10. Distant Mountains of the Pyrenees as seen from Villeneuve de Marsan.
2. p. 14. The Chateau of Henri Quatre at Pau.
3. p. 19. The Bridge over the cave at Betharem.

Hardy's Pyrenees (*contd.*)

4. p. 20. The Castle of Lourdes.
5. p. 23. [Casthel Loubon].
6. p. 26. Village of Pierre-Fitte.
7. p. 27. Village of Cauterets.
8. p. 29. Bath of La Ralliere looking towards Cauterets.
9. p. 30. Cascade of Lutour as seen from the Bath of La Ralliere.
10. p. 36. The Castle and part of the Valley of Luz.
11. p. 38. Approach to Saint Sauveur.
12. p. 39. Entrance to Saint Sauveur.
13. p. 40. View from the Promenade at St Sauveur.
14. p. 41. The Defile leading to Gavarnie.
15. p. 43. Bridge of Sia.
16. p. 44. View from the Bridge of Sia.
17. p. 46. Church and Village of Gavarnie.
18. p. 51. Cascades and Circle of Gavarnie.
19. p. 52. Defile near the Bridge of Sia.
20. p. 55. Bareges.
21. p. 65. Cascade of L'Escoubous.
22. p. 67. Cascade & Village of Grip.
23. p. 70. Village of St Marie in the Valley of Campan.
24. p. 77. Priory of St Paul the Pic du Midi in the distance.

There is no list of plates, but the plates are numbered in right-hand corners 1–24.
Plates mounted as drawings.

246 HARRADEN (R.)

Costume of the University of Cambridge (swelled rule) Drawn and Published by R. Harraden, South Side of Great St. Mary's Church, Cambridge. (swelled rule) To be had of Mr. Miller No. 49, Albemarle Street, Piccadilly London

Quarto. [1805]

COLLATION.—Title as above (v. blank) + Publishers note 1 p. (v. blank) + Engraved title with vignette Published Jany. 1805 by R. Harraden Cambridge (v. blank) + pp. 1–22 + 19 plates (1 uncoloured), marked R. Harraden delt.   J. Whesell sculpt.

1. Kings Coll.   Chapel The Public Library & Senate House Cambridge (uncoloured).
2. The Duke of Graftons Gold Prize Medal.
3. Pensioner. ⎫
4. Pensioner of Trin. Coll. ⎬ 1 p. of text.
5. Fellow Commoner ⎫
6. Fellow Commoner of Trin. Coll. ⎬ 1 p. of text.
7. Fellow Commoner Eml. [no artist or engraver].
8. Bachelor of Arts   1 p. of text.
9. Master of Arts   1 p. of text.
10. Doctor of Divinity   1 p. of text.
11. Doctor of Music   1 p. of text [no artist or engraver].
12. Proctor   1 p. of text.
13. A Nobleman or Fellow of Kings College   1 p. of text [no artist or engraver].
14. Nobleman   1 p. of text.
15. Vice Chancellor   1 p. of text.
16. Esquire Beadle   1 p. of text.
17. Sir Willm. Browne's Gold Prize Medal.
18. A Member of the University in the Volunteer Uniform   1 p. of text.   [no artist or Engraver].

Another Edition was issued in 1822.

247 HARRIS (Capt. W. C.)

Portraits of the Game and Wild Animals of Southern Africa Delineated from Life in their Native Haunts By Captain W. Cornwallis Harris Honble. E. I C. Engineers Bombay Drawn on Stone by Frank Howard (col. Vignette view followed by 5 line quote from Virgil) London Published for the Proprietor 1840 Printed by Hullmandel & Walton.

Folio.   1840

COLLATION.—Engraved title as above (v. blank) + Printed title (v. London Green and Martin Printers Bartletts Buildings) + Dedication 1 p. (v. 26 line verse from Pringle) + Introduction 2 pp. (v–vi) + Subscribers 2 leaves + Contents 1 leaf + pp. 1–175 + 30 coloured plates.

1. Catoblepas Gnoo—The Gnoo.
2. Equus Quagga—The Quagga.
3. Gazella Euchore—The Springbok.
4. Catoblepas Gorgon—The Brindled Gnoo.
5. Equus Burchelli—Burchells Zebra.
6. Boselaphus Oreas—The Eland.
7. Acronotus Caama—The Hartebeest.
8. Acronatus hunata—The Sassaybe.
9. Oryx Capensis—The Gemsbok.
10. Struthio Camelus—The Ostrich.
11. Camelopardalis Giraffa—The Giraffe.
12. Hippopotamus Amphibius—The Hippopotamus.
13. Bubalus Caffer—The African Buffalo.
14. Aigscerus Ellipsiprymnus—The Water Buck.
15. Antilope Melampus—The Pallah.
16. Rhinoceros Africanus—The African Rhinoceros.
17. Gazella Pygarga—The Bontebok.
18. Aigocerus Equina—The Roan Antelope.
19. Rhinoceros Simus—The Square Nosed or White Rhinoceros.
20. Strepsiceros Capensis—The Koodoo.
21. Gazella Albifrons—The Blesbok or White-faced Antelope.
22. Elephas Africanus—The African Elephant.
23. Aigocerus Niger—The Sable Antelope.
24. { Equus Montanus—The Modern Zebra. / Oreotragus Saltatrix—The Klipspringer.
25. { Redunca Capreolus—The Rheebok. / Tragulus Rupestris—The Steenbok.
26. { Tragelaphus Sylvatica—The Bushbuck. / Tragulus Melanotis—The Grysbok. / Cephalopus Caerula—The Cerulean Antelope.
27. { Phacochaerus Africanus—The African Boar. / Reduncu Eleotragus—The Reitbok.
28. { Felis Leopardus—The Leopard. / Felis Jubata—The Hunting Pard.
29. Felis Leo—The Lion.
30. { Hyaena Crocuta—The Spotted Hyaena. / Hyaena Fusca—The Fuscous Hyaena. / Hyaena Venatica—The Wild dog.

There are also fine engraved vignettes on pages 4, 8, 12, 16, 21, 27, 32, 36, 41, 48, 56, 63, 70, 75, 80, 85, 90, 95, 101, 107, 114, 123, 130, 135, 142, 155, 162, 170, and 175.

The List of Subscribers is almost always missing. There was a Second issue without Hullmandel & Walton's name on the engraved title, and a further Edition was issued in 1841.

248 HASSELL (J.)

Aqua Pictura. Illustrated by a Series of Original Specimens from the works of Messrs Payne, Munn, Francia, Samuel, Varley, Wheatley RA, Young, Christal, Cartwright, Girtin, Clennell, Cox, Prout, Hills, Dewint, P. J. de Loutherbourg R.A., Turner R.A., Owen and Glover Exhibiting the Works of the most approved modern Water Coloured Draftsmen, with their Style & Method of Touch, engraved and finished in progressive examples. By J. Hassell. Second Edition. London: Printed for the Proprietors, and sold by Hassell & Co. 11, Clement's Inn, Strand; and Sherwood, Neely, & Co. 20, Paternoster-Row. (rule) W. Wilson, Printer, 4, Greville-Street, Hatton-Garden London

Oblong Folio.   [1818]

COLLATION.—Title as above (v. three and a half line note to Subscribers) + Introduction

Hassell's Aqua Pictura (*contd.*)

dated 1813 1 p. (v. blank) + 18 plates (each plate in 4 states making 72 plates in all), each plate is accompanied by 1 leaf of Text, and each plate is marked, London Pub. July 1 1818 by T. McLean.

1. Cadir Idris   From an original drawing by J. Varley in the possession of T. Rickards Esqr.
2. Shaugh Bridge Devon   From an original drawing in the possession of the proprietors of this work (by S. Prout).
3. Westerham Mill Kent   From an original by G. Samuel in the possession of the proprietor of this work.
4. Autumn—Sowing of Grain   From an original drawing by J. M. W. Turner R.A. in the possession of the proprietors of this work.
5. Composition   From an original drawing by P. Dewint, in the possession of the proprietors of this work.
6. [Haymakers].   From an original drawing by F. Wheatley in the possession of the proprietor of this work.
   [Study of a Landscape].   From an original drawing by F. Wheatley, in the possession of the proprietor of this work.   The above two views together on 1 plate.
7. [Cowes Castle I. of Wight].   From an original drawing by P. J. De Loutherbourg in the possession of the proprietors of this work.
8. Dover Castle   From an original drawing by L. Francia   Aquatinta by J. Hassell.
9. [A Breeze].   From an original drawing by J. Cartwright in the possession of the proprietor of this work.
10. Moel y Shaboed, Carnarvonshire   From an original drawing by J. Christal in the possession of the proprietor of this work.
11. A Glostershire team of Oxen   From an original drawing by R. Hill, in the possession of the proprietors of this work.
12. London [from Stockwell]   From an original drawing by D. Cox in the possession of the proprietors of this work.
13. Sportsmen   From an original drawing by Mr. L. Clennell made expressly for this work and in the possession of the proprietors.
14. Fishing Boats in a Breeze   From an original drawing by S. Owen Esqr. in the possession of the proprietors of this work.
15. Lantony Abbey Monmouthshire   From an original drawing by P. S. Munn   Aquatinta by J. Hassell.
16. Tatershall Castle Lincolnshire   From an original drawing in the possession of Wm. Brand Esqr. of Boston [by Girtin].
17. View on the River Wye   Drawn by Payne Aquata.   J. Hassell.
18. Windermere   From an original drawing by J. Glover in the possession of —Shawe Esqr.

Published in monthly parts.   Each plate was issued in etched outline, aquatinted in Indian ink, the same with a yellow tint superimposed, and a fully coloured plate.

The largest of Hassell's publications.

249   *The First Edition undated but plates bearing imprints of 1812 and 1813 has a varying order to the contributing artists, viz. Messrs Payne, Christal, Francia, Havell, Munn, Nash, Clennell, Glover, Varley, Cooper, Prout, Hassell, De Wint, Samuel, Richards, Cox, &c., and imprint is London Printed for the author and sold by Messrs Sherwood Neely and Jones, 20 Paternoster Row; and J. Hassell 11, Clements Inn, Strand (thin and thick rule) W. Wilson, Printer, 4 Greville Street, Hatton Garden London.   The plates are the same except for the imprint.*

250 HASSELL (J.)

Excursions of Pleasure and Sport on the Thames, illustrated in a series of Engravings in Aqua-Tinta, coloured after Nature, Accompanied by a descriptive, and historical account, of every Town, Village, Mansion and the adjacent Country on the banks of that River, the places and periods for enjoying the Sports of Angling, Shooting, Sailing, etc., also a particular account of all the places of Amusement in its Vicinity, and the list of

Hassell's Pleasure and Sport on the Thames (*contd.*)

Inns and Taverns, for the Accommodation of Company. (rule) By J. Hassell. (rule) 4 line quote from Pope. (thick and thin rule) London: Printed for W. Simpkin and R. Marshall, Stationers Hall Court, Ludgate Street (rule).

Small Octavo. 1823

COLLATION.—Title as above (v. blank) + Index i–iii (iv blank) + List of Plates 1 p. (v. blank) + pp. 1–191 + 24 coloured aquatint plates. Each plate bearing, London. Published (date) By Messrs Simpkin and Marshall.

I. Front.	Custom House.	XIII. p. 73. Vauxhall Bridge. 1st Nov. 1822.
II. p. 18. Blackwall.		XIV. p. 80. Battersea Reach. 1st June 1822.
III. p. 25. Erith Reach.		XV. p. 82. Putney (and Bridge) 1st Dec. 1822.
IV. p. 27. Purfleet. 1st Oct. 1822.		
V. p. 29. Green hithe 1st June 1922.		XVI. p. 107. Richmond (Bridge) Surrey.
VI. p. 30. Northfleet Kent.		XVII. p. 118. Twickenham reach 1st Sept. 1822.
VII. p. 32. Gravesend, West Entrance. 1st June 1822.		XVIII. p. 145. London Bridge. 1st Sept. 1822.
VIII p. 47. Windsor Bridge. 1st Jan. 1823.		XIX. p. 178. Windsor (and the Castle) Bucks.
IX. p. 58. Southwark Bridge.		XX. p. 179. Eton College (to face) Bucks.
X. p. 60. Blackfriars Bridge. 1st Sept 1822.		XXI. p. 180. Charter Island. 1st Sept. 1822.
XI. p. 63. Waterloo Bridge 1st June 1822.		XXII. p. 181. Staines Reach.
XII. p. 64. Westminster Bridge 13th Oct. 1822.		XXIII. p. 182. Chertsey Bridge 1st Dec. 1822.
		XXIV. p. 184. Oatlands (from Shepperton) Surrey.

251 HASSELL (J.)

Picturesque Rides and Walks, with Excursions by Water, thirty miles round the British Metropolis: illustrated in a series of engravings, coloured after nature: with an Historical and Topographical Description of the Country with the compass of that circle (rule) By J. Hassell (rule) Vol. I [II] (rule) 6 lines of verse from Goldsmith commencing "Where'er I roam" (rule) London: Printed for J. Hassell, 27, Richard Street, Islington; and sold by all booksellers

2 vols. Duodecimo. 1817 [Vol. II 1818]

COLLATION VOL. I.—Half-title + Title as above (v. W. Flint, Printer, Old Bailey London) + Dedication to Prince Regent 1 leaf + Preface 1 leaf + pp. 1–249 + Directions for placing plates 1 leaf + Index 4 leaves + 60 coloured plates all marked, Drawn & engvd. [or engraved] by J. Hassell.

1. Front. Carshalton Surrey.	15. p. 40. Under Box Hill.
2. p. 1. St. Albans Abbey Herts.	16. p. 44. Thames Ditton Church.
3. p. 2. St. Albans Abbey Herts.	17. p. 47. Ridge Church Herts.
4. p. 5. Gate of Old Verulam Herts.	18. p. 52. Kew Palace Surrey.
5. p. 8. Sopewell Nunnery Herts.	19. p. 62. Brentford Middsx.
6. p. 11. Mickleham Church Surrey.	20. p. 64. Ivy Cottage Middsx.
7. p. 12. Thames Ditton.	21. p. 69. Fairlop Oak Essex.
8. p. 13. Thames Ditton Lady Sullivans Villa.	22. p. 83. North Mims Church Herts.
9. p. 14. Woodlands Surrey.	23. p. 84. South Mims Church Herts.
10. p. 18. Hendon Middsx.	24. p. 87. Old Palace Croydon Surrey.
11. p. 20. Hendon Church Middsx.	25. p. 94. Beddington Church Surrey.
12. p. 23. Croydon Surrey.	26. p. 99. Carshalton Park Surrey.
13. p. 30. Seat of J. Warner Hornsey.	27. p. 116. Mitcham Villa Surrey.
14. p. 38. Esher Church Surrey.	28. p. 118. Mitcham Grove Surrey.

Hassell's Rides and Walks (*contd.*)

29. p. 134. Seat of T. H. Barrett Ewell Surrey.
30. p. 136. Epsom Surrey.
31. p. 138. Pit Place Surrey.
32. p. 141. Durdans near Epsom.
33. p. 142. Woodcote Park Surrey.
34. p. 143. Ashted House Surrey.
35. p. 144. Leatherhead Church Surrey.
36. p. 145. Norbury Park Surrey.
37. p. 147. Leatherhead Surrey.
38. p. 148. Burford Lodge.
39. p. 151. West Clandon Surrey.
40. p. 154. Albury Park Surrey.
41. p. 156. Sheer Surrey.
42. p. 162. Dorking Surrey.
43. p. 164. Denbighs Dorking.
44. p. 183. Highgate Archway.
45. p. 186. Seat of — Anderson Highwood Hill Middsx.
46. p. 188. Totteridge Church Herts.
47. p. 190. East Barnet Herts.
48. p. 191. Bohun Lodge East Barnet.
49. p. 193. East Barnet Church.
50. p. 195. Holland House Crouch End.
51. p. 200. Barnet Herts.
52. p. 203. Hadley Church Middsx.
53. p. 204. Belmont Herts.
54. p. 205. Beach Hill Hadley.
55. p. 234. Belvidere House Kent.
56. p. 235. Annuity Hall Middsx.
57. p. 236. Ember Court Surrey.
58. p. 237. Cottage Mr Coles Thornton Heath.
59. p. 244. Pavillion Hampton Court.
60. p. 245. Kingston.

VOL. II.—Title as before (changing Vol. I to Vol. II and the 5 line quote from Goldsmith to 4 line quote from Pope) (v. W. Flint, Printer, Old Bailey London) + pp. 1–272 + Index 5 ll. + Directions for placing plates 1 leaf + 60 coloured plates.

1. Front. Claremont S. Front Drawn Hassell aqua D. Havell.
2. p. 20. Windsor Berks Drawn Hassell aqua D. Havell.
3. p. 23. Windsor Castle Berks Drawn & Engrd I Hassell.
4. p. 86. Fulham Middsx Drawn Hassell aqua Havell.
5. p. 98. Entrance King Johns Palace Eltham Drawn Hassell aqua Havell.
6. p. 100. Sundridge Park Kent Drawn & Engrd Hassell.
7. p. 105. Foots Cray Kent Drawn Hassell aqua Havell.
8. p. 106. Foots Cray Place Drawn Hassell aqua Havell.
9. p. 107. North Cray Place Drawn Hassell aqua Havell.
10. p. 118. Riverhead Kent Drawn Hassell aqua Havell.
11. p. 125. Westerham Drawn Hassell aqua Havell.
12. p. 126. Squerries near Westerham Drawn Hassell aqua Havell.
13. p. 131. Hever Castle Kent Drawn Hassell aqua Havell.
14. p. 137. Tunbridge Kent Drawn Hassell aqua Havell.
15. p. 162. Romford Essex Drawn Hassell aqua Havell.
16. p. 166. Brentwood Essex Drawn Hassell aqua Havell.
17. p. 168. Abbotswick House Navestock Essex Drawn Hassell aqua Havell.
18. p. 169. Kelvedon Hall Essex Drawn Hassell aqua Havell.
19. p. 170. Myless Ongar Essex Drawn Hassell aqua Havell.
20. p. 172. Ongar Essex Drawn Hassell aqua Havell.
21. p. 173. Park Hall near Epping Drawn Hassell aqua Havell.
22. p. 176. Epping Essex Drawn Hassell aqua Havell.
23. p. 180. Belle Vue House Essex Drawn Hassell aqua Havell.
24. p. 181. Broxbourne Church Herts Drawn & Engrd I Hassell.
25. p. 186. Nasing House Essex Drawn Hassell aqua Havell.
26. p. 188. Nether Hall Essex Drawn Hassell aqua Havell.
27. p. 196. Hoddesden Herts Drawn Hassell aqua Havell.
28. p. 197. Amwell Church Herts Drawn Hassell aqua Havell.
29. p. 198. Amwell Herts Drawn & Engrd Hassell.
30. p. 199. Amwell-bury Herts Drawn Hassell aqua Havell.
31. p. 200. Ware Herts Drawn & Engrd I Hassell.
32. p. 202. Hertford Drawn & Engrd Hassell.
33. p. 204. Hatfield Drawn Hassell aqua Havell.
34. p. 206. Brocket Hall Herts Drawn Hassell aqua Havell.
35. p. 212. Luton Beds Drawn Hassell aqua Havell.
36. p. 214. Font Luton Church Drawn Hassell aqua Havell.

Hassell's Rides and Walks (*contd.*)

37. p. 216. Luton Hoo   Drawn Hassell aqua Havell.
38. p. 222. Beckhampstead Herts   Drawn Hassell aqua Havell.
39. p. 224. Two Waters Herts   Drawn Hassell aqua Havell.
40. *ibd.*   Abbots Langley   Drawn Hassell aqua Havell.
41. p. 225. The Grove Herts   Drawn Hassell aqua Havell.
42. p. 227. Cashioberry   Drawn Hassell aqua Havell.
43. p. 228. Watford Herts   Drawn Hassell aqua Havell.
44. p. 229. Moor Park Herts   Drawn Hassell aqua Havell.
45. p. 233. Rickmansworth Herts   Drawn Hassell aqua Havell.
46. p. 234. Amersham Bucks   Drawn Hassell aqua Havell.
47. p. 236. Beaconsfield Bucks   Drawn Hassell aqua Havell.
48. p. 238. Burnham Bucks   Drawn Hassell aqua Havell.
49. p. 240. Iver Bucks   Drawn Hassell aqua Havell.
50. p. 242. Uxbridge Middsx   Drawn Hassell aqua Havell.
51. p. 250. Hampstead Heath Middsx   Drawn Hassell aqua Havell.
52. p. 256. Park Place Finchley   Drawn Hassell aqua Havell.
53. p. 260. Melrose Hall Surrey   Drawn Hassell aqua Havell.
54. *ibd.*   Seat of J. Turner Ditton Surrey   Drawn & Engrd. I. Hassell.
55. p. 262. Claremont near Esher [different from front.]   Drawn Hassell   Aqua Havell.
56. p. 265. Paines Hill   Drawn Hassell aqua Havell.
57. p. 268. Guildford Surrey   Drawn Hassell aqua Havell.
58. p. 269. Chalford House Guildford   Drawn & Engd Hassell.
59. p. 270. Godalming Surrey   Drawn Hassell aqua Havell.
60. p. 271. St Catherines Chapel Guildford   Drawn & engrd Hassell.

A charming little work, and valuable as a pictorial record.   Issued originally in 24 parts in paper wrappers.

252 HASSELL (J.)

Tour of the Grand Junction, illustrated in a series of engravings; with an Historical and Topographical Description of those parts of the counties of Middlesex, Hertfordshire, Buckinghamshire, Bedfordshire, and Northamptonshire, through which the Canal passes (rule) By J. Hassell (rule).

> **"Thrice happy he, who always can endulge**
> **This pleasing feast of fancy; who, replete**
> **With rich ideas, can arrange their charms**
> **As his own genius prompts—creating thus**
> **A novel whole." Gilpin.**

(rule) London: Printed for J. Hassell, 27, Richard-Street, Islington; and sold by all Booksellers (rule).

Octavo.   1819

COLLATION.—Title as above (v. blank) + Dedication 1 p. (v. blank) + Preface pp. v–viii + pp. 1–417 + Index and List of Plates 2 ll. + 24 plates.

Each plate is marked, Drawn by I. Hassell Pubd. [date] by I. Hassell 27 Richard St Islington.

1. Front   Ashridge, Herts, seat of the Earl of Bridgewater   [1st March 1819].
2. p. 29.   The Vale of King's Langley   [1st July 1819].
3. p. 30.   Kings Langley Lock—Herts   [1st March 1819].
4. p. 42.   Marsworth, from the Reservoirs—Bucks   [1st Aug. 1819].
5. p. 48.   View from Marsworth Village,—Bucks   [1st Oct. 1819].
6. p. 61.   Leighton Beaudesert—Beds   [1st March 1819].

Hassell's Tour of the Grand Junction (*contd.*)

7. p. 63. Three Locks; Stoke Hammond—Bucks [1st June 1819].
8. p. 66. Fenny Stratford—Bucks [1st March 1819].
9. p. 70. Newport Pagnell—Bucks [1st June 1819].
10. p. 73. View at Linford Moyra, near Standon Bury, Bucks [1st Augt. 1819].
11. p. 75. The Aqueduct at Woolverton—Bucks [1st May 1819].
12. p. 79. Stoney Stratford—Bucks [1st June 1819].
13. p. 82. Locks ascending Stoke Bruern Northamptonshire [1st July 1819].
14. p. 84. View from Stoke Bruern Bridge [1st Oct. 1819].
15. p. 86. The entrance into the great Tunnel, from Blisworth Northamptonshire [1st May 1819].
16. p. 92. View from Stow-hill near Upper Heyford, Northamptonshire [1st July 1819].
17. p. 94. Weedon-beck Church & Embankment across the valley [1st July 1819].
18. p. 104. Remains of the Cluniac Priory at Daventry [1st May 1819].
19. p. 106. The large Reservoir at Daventry Northamptonshire [1st July 1819].
20. p. 108. Daventry—Northamptonshire [1st May 1819].
21. p. 110. Head of the Grand Junction Canal with the small Reservoir at Braunston [1st Oct. 1819].
22. p. 116. Locks descending North of the entrance of the Braunston Tunnell [1st Oct. 1819].
23. p. 138. Leighton & part of the Chiltern Hills from Heath, Bedfordshire [1st Aug. 1819].
24. p. 145. Batchworth Mills,—Herts [1st March 1819].

253 HAVELL (R.)

A Series of Picturesque Views of Noblemen's & Gentlemen's Seats, with Historical & Descriptive Accounts of each subject. Engraved in Aquatinta By R. Havell & Son [the preceding lettering in a circle enclosed within an architectural front containing 12 small views] Drawn, & Etched by H. Shaw. Engraved by R. Havell & Son London, Published July 1, 1823 by R. Havell, Chapel Strt. Tottenham Court Road.

Folio.   1823

COLLATION.—Title as above (v. blank) + 20 coloured aquatint plates, each with one leaf of Text, with the exception of Windsor and Blenheim, which have each 2 leaves of Text.

1. Windsor Castle from the Play-Ground of Eton College. Drawn by Wm. Havell Engraved by R. Havell Published Augst. 1 1814 by Messrs. Colnaghi & Co. 23 Cockspur Street London.
2. Park Place near Henley upon Thames the Seat of the Earl of Malmesbury Drawn by Wm. Havell Engraved by R. Havell Published Augst. 1st 1814.
3. Billingbear, Berks, the Seat of the Rt. Honble. Lord Braybrooke Drawn by Wm. Havell Engraved by R. Havell London Published May 1815 for the Proprietor by Messrs. Colnaghi & Co. Cockspur Street & Messrs. Arch Booksellers Cornhill.
4. View of Frogmore House, Windsor Berkshire to Mrs. Mary Anne Nash This plate is respectfully inscribed by the Proprietor, Drawn by T. Hofland Engraved by R. Havell & Son London Published June 1 1812 by R. Havell 3 Chapel Street Tottenham Court Road.
5. Wanstead House, the Seat of William Pole Tylney Long Wellesley Esqr. Drawn by W. Havell Engraved by Robert Havell London Published Augt. 1 1815 for the Proprietors by Colnaghi & Co. Cockspur Street & Messrs. Arch Booksellers Cornhill.
6. Kings Weston, near Bristol The Seat of Lord de Clifford Drawn by C. V. Fielding from a Sketch by F. Mackenzie Engraved by R. Havell & Son London Published May 1 1816 by R. Havell 3 Chapel Street Tottenham Court Road.
7. Cassiobury, Hertfordshire the Seat of the Earl of Essex To Sarah Countess of Essex an Admirer & patron of the Fine Arts this Plate is respectfully inscribed Drawn by J. M. W. Turner Esqr. R A Professor of Perspective in the Royal Academy Engraved by Robt. Havell & Son London Published Decr. 2 1816 by R. Havell 3 Chapel Street Tottenham Court Road.
8. Buckingham House Middlesex a Palace of Her Majesty to Mrs. Watts Russell of Ilam Hall an admirer & patron of the Fine Arts this Plate is inscribed Drawn by J. Burnett Engraved by R. Havell & Son London Published June 2 1817 by R. Havell 3 Chapel Street Tottenham Court Road.

Havell's Noblemen's Seats (*contd.*)

9. Holland House Middlesex the Seat of the Right Honourable Lord Holland To the Right Honourable Eliza Vassall Lady Holland a patron & lover of polite Literature this Plate is respectfully inscribed Drawn by J. C. Smith   Engraved by R. Havell & Son   London Published June 2 1817 by R. Havell No. 3 Chapel Street Tottenham Court Road.

10. Chiswick House Middlesex the Garden or North Front to His Grace the Duke of Devonshire this Plate of his elegant Villa is respectfully inscribed Drawn by C. Fielding from a Sketch by G. Cattermole   Engraved by R. Havell & Son   London Published July 1 1823 by R. Havell 3 Chapel Str. Tottenham Court Road.

11. Sion House   Drawn by W. Havell   Engraved by R. Havell   London Published March 1 1815 for the Proprietors by Messrs. Colnaghi & Co. 23 Cockspur Street & Messrs. Arch Booksellers Cornhill.

12. View of Blenheim Oxfordshire—The Seat of His Grace the Duke of Marlborough to Susan Duchess of Marlborough this Plate is respectfully inscribed by the Publisher   Drawn by C. V. Fielding Engraved by R. Havell & Son   London Published Sept. 1 1817 by R. Havell 3 Chapel Street Tottenham Court Road.

13. View of Blenheim Oxfordshire, the Seat of His Grace the Duke of Marlborough To I. R. Wheeler Esqr. an Admirer & Patron of the Fine Arts of England This Plate is respectfully inscribed by the Publisher   Drawn by C. V. Fielding   Engraved by R. Havell & Son   London Published April 1 1818 by R. Havell 3 Chapel Street Tottenham Court Road.

14. View of Holkham Hall Norfolk the Seat of Thomas William Coke Esqr. M.P. to Mrs. Dawson Turner of Yarmouth this Plate is respectfully inscribed Drawn by Miss Elizabeth Blackwell   Engraved by R. Havell & Son   London Published April 1 1818 by R. Havell 3 Chapel Street Tottenham Court Road.

15. View of Burghley House Northamptonshire, the Seat of the Marquis of Exeter to Lady Sophia Pierrepont This View of Her Paternal Mansion is respectfully inscribed by the Proprietor Drawn by F. Mackenzie   Engraved by R. Havell & Son   London Published June 1 1819 by R. Havell 3 Chapel Street Tottenham Court Road.

16. A View from Richmond Hill   Drawn by W. Havell   Engraved by R. Havell   Published March 1 1815 for the Proprietors by Messrs. Colnaghi & Co. 23 Cockspur Street, London.

17. Corsham House Wiltshire the Seat of Paul Methuen Esqr. M.P. for Wiltshire To Mrs. Methuen of Corsham House this Plate is respectfully inscribed by the Publishers Drawn by C. V. Fielding after a Sketch by J. Britten   Engraved by R. Havell & Son   London Published Decr. 2 1816 by R. Havell 3 Chapel Street, Tottenham Court Road.

18. Fonthill Abbey Wiltshire View from the South to William Beckford Esqr. the founder of this splendid Mansion the present plate is inscribed Drawn by H. Gartineau from a Sketch by T. Higham Engraved by Havell & Son   London Published July 1 1823 by R. Havell 3 Chapel St. Tottenham Court Road.

19. Longleat, Wiltshire the Seat of the Marquis of Bath   Drawn by C. V. Fielding from a Sketch by F. Mackenzie   Engraved by R. Havell & Son   London Published May 1 1816 by R. Havell 3 Chapel Street Tottenham Court Road.

20. View of the Pantheon &c. Stourhead Gardens Wiltshire Seat of Sir Richard Colt Hoare Bart.   To whom this plate is respectfully inscribed by the Publishers   Drawn by F. Nicholson   Engraved by R. Havell & Son   London Published Sept. 1 1817 by R. Havell 3 Chapel Street Tottenham Court Road.

The plate of Sion House exists in two states with 5, or 7 horses, in the background.   The largest of Havell's publications and rare.

254 HAVELL (R.)

The Tour, or Select Views on the Southern Coast, etc etc, by R. Havell, 1827. (above lettering printed on a representation of the Logan Stone) London.   Published by Smith Elder & Co.   65 Cornhill, and Havell & Son, 29 Warman Street, Oxford Street.

Oblong Octavo.   1827

COLLATION.—Title as above (v. blank).

I. Margate.	III. Broadstairs.
II. 7 Small Views (North Foreland Light-house etc.).	IV. Ramsgate.
	V. 3 Views (Pegwell etc.).

Havell's Views on the Southern Coast (*contd.*)

VI. Dover.
VII. 3 Views (Sandgate etc.).
VIII. Hastings.
IX. 4 Views (Ramsgate pier etc.).
X. Brighton.
XI. 3 Views (Portsmouth Harbour etc.).
XII. Worthing.
XIII. 4 Views (Portsea Castle etc.).
XIV. Portsmouth.
XV. 2 Views Cowes and Ride (sic).
XVI. Plymouth.

XVII. 3 Views (Mewstone etc.).
XVIII. 2 Views (folding) Mount Edgcumbe and Plymouth.
XIX. 3 Views (Weymouth etc.).
XX. Falmouth.
XXI. 4 Views (Penryn etc.).
XXII. Penzance.
XXIII. 3 Views (Pendennis etc.).
XXIV. Liverpool.
XXV. 4 Views (Bristol Channel etc.).

Issued pictorial boards.

255 HAVELL (W.)

A Series of Picturesque Views of the River Thames London Published May 1812 by R. Havell No. 3 Chapel Street Tottenham Court Road.

Folio.   1812

Engraved title and 12 coloured aquatint plates by R. Havell, all dated 1811.

(Title) Source of the Thames.
1. Oxford from the Banks of the Isis.
2. Abingdon Bridge and Church.
3. Wallingford Castle.
4. View of the Thames at Streatley.
5. Caversham Bridge, near Reading.
6. An Island on the Thames, near Park Place, Oxfordshire.

7. The Weir, from Marlow Bridge.
8. Clifden Spring and Woods, near Maidenhead.
9. View of Taplow, from Maidenhead Bridge.
10. Windsor Castle.
11. Datchet Ferry, near Windsor.
12. Staines Church.

A reissue published August 1st 1818 by Thomas McLean.

Hawbuck Grange 1847. See under Surtees (R.).

256 HAWKER (Lt. Col. P.)

Instructions to Young Sportsmen in all that relates to Guns and Shooting. By Lt. Col. P. Hawker. (rule) Third Edition, considerably enlarged and improved; with ten explanatory plates. (rule) London: Printed for Longman, Hurst, Rees, Orme, Brown, and Green.

Octavo.   1824

COLLATION.—Half-title "Instructions to Young Sportsmen" (v. blank) + Title as above (v. London: Printed by Charles Wood, Poppins Court, Fleet Street.) + Preface pp. v–x + Note 1 p. (v. blank) + Contents pp. xiii–xx (p. xx misprinted p. xii) + List of Plates 1 leaf (pp. xxi–xxii) + pp. 1–470 + 10 plates.

Each plate marked, London Published by Longman & Co. July 1824.

1. front.   Commencement of a Cripple chace, after firing 2 lbs of Shot into a skein of Brent Geese, & two Wild Swans.   Invented and Sketched by P. Hawker (coloured).
2. p.   33. Gun Breechings   Drawn by P. Hawker Esqr.   Engraved by Wilson Lowry.
3. p. 255. Check Collar for breaking pointers &c.   Ovendens sculp^t P. H. Esqr delt.
4. p. 327. Hampshire Coast Punt, Stanchion Gun &c.   P. H. Esqr delt   Ovendens sculp^t.
5. p. 332. Mud-Launchers, on the oozes, off Lymington, shoving their Punts up to Widgeon.   Thornton pinx^t.   Inv^d & Sketched by P. Hawker.   Stadler sculp^t. (coloured).
6. p. 334. Poole Canoe, Mudboards &c.   Drawn by P. Hawker Esqr Engraved by Wilson Lowry.

Hawker's Young Sportsmen (*contd.*)

7. p. 343. Approaching Wild Fowl, preparative to the flowing tide. Jackson pinx^t. Inv^d & Sketched by P. Hawker. Stadler sculp^t (coloured).
8. p. 384. Carriage for using a stanchion-gun on land. Inv^d & Drawn by P. Hawker Esqr. Ovendens sculp^t.
9. p. 394. Hut Shooting on the French system. Designed & Painted by P. Hawker. Eng^d by J. Scott Junr & W. H. Timms (coloured).
10. p. 402. Carriage to convey a shooting-canoe over land. P. H. Esq delt. Ovendens sculp^t.

This Third Edition was the first to have several coloured plates.

257 HEATH (W.)

The Life of a Soldier; a Narrative and Descriptive Poem with Eighteen Engravings, by William Heath. (rule) London: Printed for William Sams, Bookseller to His Royal Highness the Duke of York, Royal Library, 1, St. James's-Street (rule).

Royal Octavo. 1823

COLLATION.—Half-title "The Life of a Soldier," a Poem; with Plates by W. Heath. (v. blank) + Title as above (v. London Printed by William Clowes, Northumberland-court.) + Dedication 1 p. (v. blank) + Advertisement 1 p. (v. blank) + Errata slip + Text pp. 1–150 + 18 plates.

The plates bear no titles and appear as front and at pp. 1, 8, 12, 14, 16, 18, 44, 48, 65, 85, 106, 108, 111, 137, 140, ibd. 141.

Each plate bears imprint, London Pub. by W. Sams 1823.

Issued in pink boards with design on upper and lower cover. A leaf of advertisements of Sams publications may be found at the end.

258 HEIDELOFF (N.)

Gallery of Fashion

9 vols. Quarto. 1794–1802

COLLATION.—Each Volume contains an engraved and coloured pictorial title page with lettering Gallery of Fashion, Vol. I, 1794 [to Vol. IX 1802] (v. blank) + 12 monthly sub-titles (April to March for each year) + 12 leaves of Text + 24 coloured plates [except Vol. II, which has 25 plates, there being 3 plates to January 1796].

In addition Vol. I has leaf of advertisement after title and 3 pp. of subscribers (2 pp. English 1 p. Foreign).

Vol. II has leaf of advertisement and additional subscribers 2 pp.

Vol. III has 1 p. of advertisement (v. blank) and additional subscribers 2 pp.

Vol. IV has 1 p of additional subscribers (v. blank).

Vol. VI has 2 pp. of additional subscribers.

The imprint on the title of Vol. I. reads, Published as the Act directs April 1 1794 by N. Heideloff No. 9 Southampton St. Covt. Garden. The imprint on Vol. II is changed to Published as the Act directs April 1 1795 by N. Heideloff at the Gallery of Fashion Office No. 90 Wardour Street. This imprint is repeated with the exception of the change in date up to and including Vol. VI. In Vol. VII the address is changed to Gallery of Fashion Office No. 7 John Street, Oxford Road, and the address is finally changed in Vol. IX to No. 7 Bath Place New Road Fitzroy Square.

Heideloff's Costume (*contd.*)

The monthly sub-titles are lettered " Galley of Fashion month of (name of the month and year)"
the versos being blank. From the month of Sept. 1799 (Vol. VI) onwards the following imprint is
added, London: Printed by W. Bulmer and Co. Russell-Court, Cleveland-Row, St. James's: for
N. Heidleoff, John-Street Oxford-Road.

RÉSUMÉ.—217 coloured plates. The plates bear no titles but each figure is numbered, there
being from one to 2, 3, or 4 figures to a plate. These figures are numbered from 1 to 362.

Issued at 3 guineas per volume to subscribers to Vol. I or 7s. 6d. per number to non-subscribers.
Vol. II was issued at 3 guineas to subscribers and 4 guineas to non-subscribers.

Extremely rare in complete state. The above collation taken with permission from a fine copy
in the possession of Messrs. Batsford measuring $11\frac{3}{8} \times 9\frac{1}{4}$ inches. Copies exist with an additional
2 leaves of Text in English and German, and I have seen a copy with 2 plates of Gentlemen's
costumes. Heideloff's Gallery of Fashion is one of the most beautiful books on costume ever pub-
lished, certainly the finest example of coloured aquatint as applied to fashion plates.

259 [HEMPEL (Charles William)]

The Commercial Tourist; or, Gentleman Traveller. A Satirical Poem in Four Cantos; Embellished with Coloured Engravings. (thick and thin rule) "Let the galled jade wince" Shakespeare (thick and thin rule) The Second Edition, greatly enlarged (thick and thin rule) London: Sold by G. & W. B. Whittaker, Ave-Maria-Lane

Octavo.   1822

COLLATION.—Title as above (v. Polyblank printer Truro) Proem 1 leaf (v. blank) sub-title "The Commercial Tourist; or, Gentleman Traveller" 1 leaf (v. Argument) + pp. 3–140 + 5 coloured plates by I. R. Cruikshank.

1. Front.   General.   Sporting accessories &c. chaise, dog, monkey, &c.   Drawn & Engraved by I. R Cruikshank.
2. p.   13.   This Ham depend on it, thoul't not take hence   I. R. Cruikshank fecit.
3. p.   41.   Then mounts his gig impatient of delay   I. R. Cruikshank fecit.
4. p.   75.   Let her at once attend in nature's plan
                  Twas ne'er designed the business of man.
5. p.   107.   Thus rescued from assassins I appear.

First Illustrated Edition.

Here and There over the Water.   See under Egerton.

260 HERING (George E.)

The Mountains and Lakes of Switzerland, the Tyrol, and Italy. from Drawings made during a tour through those countries, by George E. Hering. With descriptive letter-press. (rule) London: M. A. Natalli, 23 Bedford Street, Covent Garden.

Quarto.   1847

COLLATION.—Title as above (v. blank) + List of Plates 1 p. (v. blank) + 20 coloured lithographs (including front. and dedication).   Engraved title, "The Mountains and the Lakes. Sketches in Switzerland, the Tyrol and Italy," by George E. Hering, with vignette view below Pass Gerlos, Tyrol (and imprint) London: Published by Messrs Ackermann & Co. 96 Strand, and Mr G. E. Hering, 4 Southampton St, Fitzroy Square.

Hering's Switzerland (*condt.*)

Dedication. Vignette Sketch of the Lake of Orta.
1. Konig See, Bavarian Tyrol.
2. Fügin, Ziller Thal, Tyrol.
3. The River Salza near Pass Lueg Tyrol.
4. Convent near Schwatz, Tyrol.
5. Morning on the Traun See, Tyrol.
6. Lake of Hallstadt, Tyrol.
7. From the Cemetery at Thun.
8. Castle of Monspunnen and Jungtfrau, near Interlachen.
9. Chillon, Lake of Geneva.
10. Sion, Canton Vallais.
11. Near Viesch, in the Ober Vallais.
12. Pass of the Grimsel.
13. Locano, Lago Maggiore.
14. Isola de San Giulio, Lago d'Orta.
15. Gandria, Lago di Lugano.
16. Nesso Lago de Como.
17. Bellagio, Lago di Como.
18. Lago di Garda.

Each plate (with exception of Dedication) marked, G. E. H. Dell, and each with 1 page of text, including a leaf of text for the frontispiece and dedication.

261 HERRING (J. F.)

Portraits of the Winning Horses of the Great St. Leger Stakes, at Doncaster from the year 1815 to the present year inclusive (uncoloured vignette) (rule) London: Published by S. & J. Fuller at their Sporting-Gallery, 34 Rathbone-Place (rule) Printed by L. Harrison 5, Prince's Street, Leicester Square

Folio. [1829]

COLLATION.—Title as above (v. blank) + Text of Winners 1 p. (v. blank) + 15 coloured aquatint plates, each with 1 leaf of text.

Each plate has extensive text beneath the engraving giving the name, and particulars of the Winner. The plates are marked, Painted by Mr Herring Doncaster, the first 11 Engraved by Mr. Sutherland, the last 4 Engraved by G. Reeve.

First Series.
(1) Filho da Puta 1815.
(2) The Duchess 1816.
(3) Ebor 1817.
(4) Reveller 1818.
(5) Antonio 1819.
(6) St Patrick 1820.
(7) Jack Spigot 1821.
(8) Theodore 1822.
(9) Barefoot 1823.
(10) Jerry 1824.
(11) Memnon 1825.
(12) Tarrare 1826.
(13) Matilda 1827.

Second Series
(14) The Colonel 1828.
(15) Rowton 1829.

Plates 1–10 were originally issued by Sheardown and Son Doncaster in 1824. Three years later, in 1827, they were transferred to Messrs. Fuller, who issued them in book form; the dates 1815–24 were left on the title though 3 new plates were added, one for each year. Later a title was added as above, and an additional plate added to each year up till 1843, when a new edition was published with the portraits divided into 2 series. The "Derby" winners were added though not mentioned in the title.

In the original Sheardown issue plate 12, "Tarrare," was by Sutherland after D. Dalby. Subscribers' copies of Fuller's publication bear a Minerva head stamped on each plate. There are 4 issues: (1) India Proofs with letters in black; (2) Proofs in black on hand-made Whatman, with letters; (3) India Proofs with letters, coloured; (4) Coloured on Whatman paper.

Second Series (contd.)
(16) Birmingham 1830 (Reeve).
(17) Chorister 1831 (C. Hunt).
(18) Margrave 1832 (C. Hunt).
(19) Rockingham 1833 (C. Hunt).
(20) Touchstone 1834 (R. W. Smart & C. Hunt).
(21) The Queen of Trumps 1835 (C. Hunt).
(22) Elis 1836 (C. Hunt).

Herring's Winners St. Leger (*contd.*)

(23) Mango 1837 (C. Hunt).

Additional St. Leger Winners
(24) Don John 1838 (C. Hunt).
(25) Charles XII 1839 (C. Hunt).
(26) Launcelot 1840 (C. Hunt).
(27) Satirist 1841.
(28) Blue Bonnet 1842.
(29) Nutwith 1843 (C. Hunt).

Derby Winners
(30) Mameluke 1827 (R. G. Reeve).
(31) Cadland 1828 (R. G. Reeve).
(32) Frederick 1829 (R. G. Reeve).

(33) Priam 1830 (R. G. Reeve).
(34) Spaniel 1831 (C. Hunt).
(35) St Giles 1832 (C. Hunt).
(36) Dangerous 1833 (C. Hunt).
(37) Plenipotentiary 1834 (Smart & Hunt).
(38) Mundig 1835 (C. Hunt).
(39) Bay Middleton 1836 (C. Hunt).
(40) Phosphorus 1837 (C. Hunt).
(41) Amato 1838 (C. Hunt).
(42) Bloomsbury 1839 (C. Hunt).
(43) Little Wonder 1840 (C. Hunt).
(44) Coronation 1841 (C. Hunt).
(45) Attila 1842.
(46) Cotherstone 1843 (C. Hunt).

Extremely rare.

Hillingdon Hall 1888. See under Surtees (R.).

Historic Military and Naval Anecdotes (1818). See under Orme (E.).

Historical Memento 1814. See under Blagdon (F. W.).

History of Johnny Quae Genus 1822. See under Rowlandson (T.).

History of Madeira 1821. See under [Combe (W.)].

History (An) of the River Thames. See Boydell (J.).

History of the University of Dublin. See under Taylor.

262 Historical Sketch of Moscow: illustrated by Twelve Views of different parts of that imperial city, the Kremlin, &c. (rule) London: Published by R. Ackermann, Repository of Arts, 101 Strand. Harrison and Leigh, Printers, 373 Strand (rule).

Quarto. 1813

COLLATION.—Title as above (v. blank) + Introduction 1 p. (v. blank) + Text pp. 1–27 (p. 28 blank) + 12 coloured aquatint plates.

Each plate is numbered and bears imprint, Publish'd 1 Jany. 1813 at R. Ackermann's Repository of Arts 101 Strand London.

1. View of the Entrance into Moscow, from Volodemer.
2. View of the City of Moscow, from the Banks of the Mosqua, & near the convent of Spasna Novoi.
3. View of the Great Square, with the Shops at Moscow.
4. View of Moscow, taken from the Imperial Palace.
5. View of the Palace of Petrovski.
6. View of Moscow taken from the Balcony of the Imperial Palace.
7. View of the Imperial Palace of the Kremlin at Moscow.
8. View of the Ice Hills, during the Carnival, at Moscow.
9. Walls of the Kremlin, extending to the Round Tower.
10. View of the Stone Bridge, & the Environs of Moscow.
11. View of the Old Wooden Theatre at Moscow.
12. View of the Holy Gate, & part of the Environs of Moscow.

Issued in boards with printed label, price £2 2s. coloured—plain £1 11s. 6d.

263 HODGES (W.)

Select Views in India drawn on the Spot, in the years 1780, 1781, 1782 and 1783 and executed in aquatinta, by William Hodges, R.A.   London Volume the First

Folio.   (1785–1788)

COLLATION VOL. I.—Title as above with French Translation on left-hand side (v. blank) + Dedication 1 p. (v. blank) + List of Plates 1 p. (v. blank) + Map of the River Ganges, Jumna, Goomty & Gogra + 24 plates.

Each plate marked, "Drawn on the Spot & Engraved by W. Hodges," the first 4 bearing imprint, "Pub as the Act directs 20 May 1785," plates 5–24, "Published [date] by J. Wells No. 22 Charing Cross."

1. A View of part of the City of Oud (1 p. of text).
2. A View of the So West Side, of Chunar Gur } 1 p. of text.
3. A View of the North End of Chunar Gur }
4. A View of the Gate of the Caravan Serai, at Raje Mahel (1 p. of text).
5. A View of the Fort of Gwalior, from the N.W.   April 1st 1786 } a leaf of text.
6. A View of the South Side of the Fort of Gwalior   April 1st 1786 }
7. A View of the Ruins of a Palace at Gazipoor on the River Ganges   4th Octr. 1785 } 1 p. of text.
8. A View of the Tombs at Gazipoor   6th Octr. 1785 }
9. A View of part of the Fort of Lutteefpoor   7th Oct. 1785 } 1 p. of text.
10. A View of the Fort of Bidjegur   May 29th 1786 }
11. A View of the Ruins of part of the Palace and Mosque at Futtypoor Sicri   4th Octr. 1785 } 1 p. of text.
12. A View of the Mosque at Futtipoor Sicri   May 1st 1786 }
13. A View of the Musjid, i.e. Tomb of Iionpoor   Sepr. 15th 1786 } 1 leaf of text.
14. View of Farmyard in Kingdom of Bengal   Augst. 1st 1786 }
15. A View of a Mosque at Rajemahel   Sepr. 15 1786 (1 p. of text).
16. A View of the Fort of Agra on the River Jumna   Augst. 1st 1786 (1 p. of text).
17. A View of a Mosque Mounheer   Decr. 20 1786 } 1 p. of text.
18. A View of the Mosque at Mounheer, from the S.E.   Jany. 1st 1787 }
19. A View of a Mosque, at Chunar Gur   Decr. 20th 1786 (1 p. of text).
20. A View of the Fort of Allahabad   Jany. 1st 1787 (1 p. of text).
21. A View of part of the City of Benares, upon the Ganges   Feby. 24th 1787 } 1 p. of text.
22. A View of the Bridge, over Oodooanulla   Feby. 24th 1787 }
23. A View of the Pagodas at Deogur   March 25th 1787 } 1 p. of text.
24. A View of the Great Pagoda at Tanjore   March 25th 1787 }

VOL. II.—Title as before + List of Plates to Vol. II 1 p. (v. blank) + 24 plates, Imprint as before for plates 25 to 28, for plates 29 to 48 altered to Published [date] by J. Grives 103 Strand.

25. A View of a Hill Village in the District of Bangelepoor   20th June 1787 (1 p. of text).
26. A View of the Gaut at Etarva, on the Banks of the River Jumna   20th May 1787 } 1 p. of text.
27. A View of the Ravines at Etarva   20th May 1787 }
28. A View of Chinsura the Dutch Settlement in Bengal   20th June 1787 }
29. A View of the Fort of Mongheer, upon the Banks of the River Ganges   15th Augst. 1787 } 1 p. of text.
30. The East End of the Fort of Mongheer   1st Septr. 1787 }
31. A Mosque at Gazipoor   1st Septr. 1787 } 1 p. of text.
32. A View of an Insulated Rock, in the River Ganges at Iangerah   15 August. 1787 }
33. A View of the Fort of Jionpoor upon the Banks of the River Goomty   5th Novr. 1787 } 1 p. of text.
34. A View of the Bridge at Jionpoor over the River Goomty   20th Octr. 1787 }
35. A View of part of the Ruins of the City of Agra   20th Octr. 1787 } 1 p. of text.
36. A View of a Mausoleum at Etmadpoor   5th Novr. 1787 }
37. A View of part of the Palace of the late Nabob Suja ul Dowla at Fizabad   14th Dec. 1787 } 1 p. of text.
38. Another View of the same }

Hodges's India (*contd.*)

39. A View of part of the Tomb of the Emperor Akbar at Secundrii   23rd Jany. 1788 } 1 p. of text.
40. A View of Tombs of Secundrii near Agra   23rd Jany. 1788
41. A View of the Cuttera built by Jaffier Cawn at Muxadavad   1st March 1788 } 1 p. of text.
42. A View of Firozeabad   17th March 1788
43. A View of Shekoabad   17th March 1788 } 1 p. text.
44. A View of the Fort of Peteter   1st March 1788
45. A View of the City of Benares   27th April 1788 } 1 p. of text.
46. A View of the Pass of Sicrii Gully   27th April 1788
47. A View of the Jungle Ferry   27th April 1788 } 1 p. of text.
48. A View of a Hindoo Monument   27th April 1788

264   *There is another issue of this work with one general title [French Text above English Text] with the same lettering but with the imprint, London Printed for the Author; and sold by J. Edwards, No. 78 Pall Mall 1 leaf of dedication and 1 leaf of Contents (i.e. List of Plates) to both volumes. The plates with their imprints are exactly the same, but there are a greater number of leaves of text: where 1 leaf of text serves for 3 plates in the above, this other issue has 3 leaves of text.*

265 HODGES (W. P.)

(Beaufort Hunt) A Series of Eight Plates of Fox Hunting from the Original Drawings by W. P. Hodges, Esqr. and Engraved by Mr. Henry Alken.   Dedicated by special permission to his Grace the Duke of Beaufort K.G. London Published by Thos. McLean 26 Haymarket Aug.   **1833**

Engraved coloured front. with fox mask + Title as above + 1 leaf of Dedication dated Augt. 1833 + 8 aquatints in colour each dated July 1st 1833.

1. Going out of Kennel.
2. Coursers tying up their Dogs.
3. The Chase.
4. Hold Hard.
5. Finding (in a bog).
6. Crossing the River Avon.
7. The Death and Treeing.
8. The Return Home.

A supplementary plate was published Nov. 1 1834 viz.

9. Consequences.
10. [The coloured frontispiece].

Issued in pink paper wrappers with inscription and vignette as on frontispiece.   Size 20½ × 12⅜ inches, watermark 1832.

Extremely rare.

266 HODSON (T.) and DOUGALL (I.)

The Cabinet of the Arts, being a new and universal drawing book, forming a complete system of Drawing, Painting in all its branches, Etching, Engraving, Perspective, Projection and Surveying with all their various and appendant parts; containing the whole theory and practice of the Fine Arts in general from the first elements to the most finished principles, displaying in the most familiar manner the whole Rudiments of Imitation, Design, Disposition, Invention and Deception; illustrated with upwards of sixty Elegant Engravings to which is added an appendix containing several curious and useful miscellaneous articles by T. Hodson and I. Dougall, author of the accomplished Tutor London.   Published by T. Ostall Ave Maria Lane

Quarto.   1805

Hodson and Dougall's Cabinet of the Arts (*contd.*)

COLLATION.—Engraved title (v. blank) + Preface 2 ll. + Contents 2 ll. + Text pp. 1–367 + 67 plates.

267 It was reissued in 2 vols. in 1821, London Published by R. Ackermann, the title being slightly changed to read . . . "Illustrated with one hundred and thirty Engravings" . . . "Second Edition with additions" . . .

VOL. I.—Title + Preface 2 ll. + Text pp. 1–384 + Index 2 ll. + Front.

VOL. II.—129 plates (94–98 are coloured aquatint views 105–113 shells and 114–130 flowers and fruit).

The coloured topographical views are:

Bridge at Oakhampton.
View on Windermere.   Craig delt.   Mackenzie sc.
View on the Lea.
Hauling on Shore.
At Deal.

I have seen another copy where the shell plates are numbered 97 to 105 and the flower plates 106 to 122.   These are coloured.

268 HOFLAND (T. C. and Mrs.)

A Descriptive Account of the Mansion and Gardens of White Knights, a seat of His Grace the Duke of Marlborough.   By Mrs. Hofland (thick and thin rule) Illustrated with Twenty-Three Engravings, from pictures taken on the spot by T. C. Hofland (thick and thin rule) 2 line quote Thomson (thin and thick rule) London: Printed for His Grace the Duke of Marlborough, by W. Wilson, Greville-Street, Hatton-Garden.

Folio.   [1819]

COLLATION.—Half-title "White Knights" (v. blank) + Title as above (v. blank) + Dedication 1 p. (v. blank) + sub-title "Introduction" 1 p. (v. blank) + Text of Introduction pp. 1–14 + sub-title "Historical Account of White Knights" 1 p. (v. blank) + pp. 17–151 + Imprint 1 leaf + 23 plates, 8 being coloured aquatints.

Each coloured plate marked, T. C. Hofland pinkt.   Each uncoloured etching marked, T. C. Hofland delt.

1. p.   22. The Gothic Chapel.   T. Medland sculpt. (coloured).
2. p.   28. View of White Knights from the Woods   T. Medland sculpt. (coloured).
3. p.   32. A Scene from the North Front of White Knights.   T. C. Lewis sculpt. (coloured).
4. p.   52. [Gothic Bower]   Etched by R. Peake.
5. p.   62. [Striped Garden]   Etched by L. Byrne.
6. p.   70. View of White Knights from the New Gardens   Etched by L. Byrne.
7. *ibd.*   [Diamond Seat]   Etched by S. Rawle.
8. p.   72. [Round Seat]   Etched by S. Rawle.
9. p.   74. [Cedar Seat]   Etched by C. Heath.
10. p.   78. [Fishing Seat]   Etched by L. Byrne.
11. *ibd.*   View of White Knights from the New Gardens   Etched by L. Byrne [a different view of 6].
12. p.   80. [Three Arched Seat]   Etchd by L. Byrne.
13. *ibd.*   [View of the House &c.]   Etched by L. Byrne.
14. p.   90. [The Seat]   Etched by L. Byrne.
15. p.   92. [The Bower]   Etched by L. Byrne.
16. p.   94. [A Seat]   Etched by L. Byrne.
17. p.   96. [Pavilion]   Etched by L. Byrne.

Hofland's White Knights (*contd.*)

18. p. 98. The Rustic Bridge (coloured).
19. p. 100. The Grotto (coloured).
20. *ibd.* The Spring (coloured).
21. p. 102. The Spring [a different View] I. C. Stadler sculpt. (coloured).
22. *ibd.* The Spring Cottage (coloured).
23. p. 110. [New Fishing Seat] Etched by C. Heath.

SIZE.—17¼ × 13 *inches for largest-paper copies uncut. Extremely rare in this state.*

269 HONAN (Michael Burke)

The Andalusian Sketch Book: Edited by Michael Burke Honan, Esq., author of "The Court and Camp of Don Carlos," Second Edition, London: John Macrone, St James's Square (rule).

Quarto. 1837

COLLATION.—Title as above (v. London; Printed by W. Clowes & Sons, Stamford Street) + Advertisement 1 p. (v. blank) + Preface pp. iii–v (p. vi blank) + Contents pp. vii–viii + pp. 1–160 + Verse 1 p. (v. imprint) + 12 coloured lithograph plates.

Each plate is marked, M. Gauci Lithog., Printed by C. Hullmandel, J se I Becquer Sevilla, Io Pinto London: John Macrone, St. James Sq., 1836.

1. (front.) The Matador
2. p.   1. Dona Mariana Quintana.
3. p. 13. The Bandit.
4. p. 25. The Bandit.
5. p. 63. The Andalusian Maid.
6. p. 71. The Andalusian Peasant.
7. p. 83. The Bethrothed.
8. p. 93. Going to the Feria.
9. p. 109. The Contrabandist.
10. p. 127. La Hermosa Rafaella.
11. p. 139. Matilda Diez.
12. p. 161. La Rosa.

270 HONEYSUCKLE (F.)

The Elegancies of Fashion, and General Remembrancer of Taste and Manners; or impartial record of Painting, Music, Elegant Literature, the Theatre, Costume, and Arts conducive to the Ornament or Amusement of Polished Life (rule) By Florio Honeysuckle (rule) (quotations from Ovid, Terence and Shakespeare, 4 lines) (rule) Vol. I London: (thin and thick rule) Printed for W. N. Gardiner, Pall Mall

Small Quarto. 1804

COLLATION.—Title as above (v. Printed by W. Bulmer and Co. Cleveland Row) + pp. 1–102 and 24 coloured plates.

All published. Issued in monthly parts with 4 plates to each part, this magazine had a brief existence, only 6 numbers, from March to August, appearing. The plates consist of full-length costumes and ladies' headdresses.

Rare. The above collation taken by permission from a copy in the possession of Messrs. Batsford.

271 HORNBROOK (T. L.)

Twelve Views in the Basque Provinces illustrating several of the actions in which the British Legion was engaged with Carlist Troops, 12 fine coloured plates, each marked, Drawn

Hornbrook's Basque Provinces (*contd.*)

on the Spot by T. L. Hornbrook, Marine Painter to H.R.H. the Duchess of Kent.   Day & Haghe Lithrs., to the Queen, with 1 leaf of text being list of plates.

1. San Sebastian, from the Convent of St Francisco, Shewing the Pontoon Bridge, and the commencement of the New Wooden Bridge across the River Uremea.   May 1836 (on stone by A. Picken).
2. View of the Passages, and Fort Hay.
3. View of French Passages Spain.
4. Ernani from the Plateau at the Venta of Oriamendi, Shewing the attack of the Carlists on the Position held by Genl. Evans, on the 16th March 1837, and the last position of the Royal British Marines.
5. Ernami from the Astigaraga Road.
6. Attack on the fort of Irun, 16th May 1837 by the Troops under the Command of Genl. Evans.
7. Attack on the Town of Irun by the combined forces of the British Legion and Christenoes, 17th May 1837, with a distant view of Fontarabia to the left, and the Village of Andage to the Right.
8. Behobia Gate of Irun with the Royal Irish storming.   May 17th 1837.
9. Exterior of the Fontarabia Gate of Irun.   Fixing the Petard and shewing the window where it was first entered.   17th May 1837.
10. Interior of the Fontarabia Gate at Irun, just prior to the entrance of the British Legion.   May 17th 1837.
11. Fuentarabia, from the River Bidassoa.   (J. Brandard, lith.)
12. The Principal Street of Fuentarabia (on stone by A. Picken).

A rare book.

272 HOWITT (S.)

The British Sportsman, by Samuel Howitt, containing Seventy plates (thick and thin rule) A New Edition (thin and thick rule) 1812 London: Published and Sold by Edward Orme, Printseller, &c. to the King, Bond Street, Corner of Brook Street.

Quarto.   1812

COLLATION.—Printed title as above (v. blank) + 72 coloured etchings, including the frontispiece.

Each plate is marked, Howitt in. et f. and bears imprint, Republished by Edwd. Orme Bond St. 1812.

1. Front—Composite—A sylvan glade with victims of the chase against a tomb bearing inscription The British Sportsman. Lettered below To every British Sportsman, and Lover of the Arts is most respectfully dedicated the following work.	13. The Stag-Hound.	34. Hare Hunting P 4.
	14. Fox Hunting P 1.	35. Hare Sitting.
	15. Fox Hunting P 2.	36. Hare running.
	16. Fox Hunting P 3.	37. Hares feeding.
	17. Fox Hunting P 3 (sic).	38. The Greyhound.
	18. Fox Hunting P 5.	39. The Pointer.
	19. Fox Hunting P 6.	40. The Badger.
	20. Bitch Fox & Cubs.	41. The Otter-Hound.
	21. The Hunted Fox.	42. Mares & Foals.
	22. The Fox-Hound.	43. Duck Hawking.
2. Stag Hunting P 1.	23. The Hunter.	44. Pike Fishing.
3. Stag Hunting P 2.	24. The Fox.	45. Fly Fishing.
4. Stag Hunting P 3.	25. Harriers.	46. Minnow Fishing.
5. Stag Hunting P 4.	26. The Racing Stallion.	47. Worm Fishing.
6. Hind & Calf.	27. Racing P 1.	48. The Terrier.
7. The Roe-buck.	28. Racing P 2.	49. The Rabbit.
8. Male Red Deer.	29. Racing P 3.	50. Spaniels.
9. Does & Fawns.	30. Racing P 4.	51. The Otter.
10. Male Fallow-Deer.	31. Hare Hunting P 1.	52. Otter Hunting P 1.
11. Toiling a Buck.	32. Hare Hunting No. 1.	53. Otter Hunting.
12. Shooting a Buck.	33. Hare Hunting P 2.	54. Bat Fowling.

Howitt's British Sportsman (*contd.*)

55. Shooting Poney.
56. Coursing P 1.
57. Coursing P 2.
58. Coursing P 3.
59. The Lurcher.
60. Coursing P 4.

61. Pheasant Shooting.
62. Pheasant Hawking.
63. Snipe Shooting.
64. Woodcock Shooting.
65. The Water Spaniel.
66. Duck Shooting.

67. Partridge Shooting.
68. The Setter.
69. Partridge Hawking.
70. Patridge Netting.
71. Heron Hawking.
72. Grouse Shooting.

Usually found uncoloured. The first issue was in 1800.

273 HOWITT (S.)

Orme's Collection of British Field Sports Illustrated in Twenty beautifully coloured Engravings, from Designs by S. Howitt. Published Jany. 1807 by Edwd. Orme, 59, Bond Street the corner of Brook Street. London

Oblong Folio. 1807[–8]

COLLATION.—Engraved title with lettering as above + 20 aquatint plates + List of Plates with vignette.

Each plate is numbered in arabic numerals (except 18, which bears no number, and plate 8, which is in roman numeral). The title is in English on the left-hand side, and in French on the right-hand side of each plate, and all are marked, Edwd. Orme excudit, and bear imprint Published & Sold [date] by Edwd. Orme Printseller to the King, Engraver and Publisher, Bond Street corner of Brook Street London. [in plates 6 and 8 the imprint is shortened to Published & Sold [date] by Edwd. Orme 59 Bond Street London].

Engraved title with 20 small oval vignettes of sporting scenes, gun, game, and hounds, the whole joined together with vine festoons.

1. Shooters going out in a morning. Saml. Howitt del. Clark & Merke sculp. March 25 1808.
2. Horse Racing [printed overslip for word racing]. Samuel Howitt del. J. Godby & H. Merke sculpt. Jany. 1 1807.
3. Fox Hunting. Saml. Howitt del. Vivares & Merke sculpt. Decr. 1st 1807.
4. Fox Hunting 2nd. Saml. Howit (sic) del. Vivares & Merke sculpt. Jany. 20 1808.
5. Stag Hunting 1. Saml. Howitt del. J. Godby & H. Merke sculpt. March 1 1807.
6. Stag Hunting 2. Saml. Howitt delin. J. Godby & H. Merke sculpt. Feby. 1 1807.
7. Hare Hunting 1. Saml. Howitt del. J. Godby & H. Merke sculpt. March 1st 1807.
8. Hare Hunting 2nd. Samuel Howitt del J. Godby & H. Merke sculp. Jany. 1 1807.
9. Coursing 1. [Lettered by printed overslip] Samuel Howett (sic) J. Godby & H. Merke sculpt. Jany. 1 1807.
10. Woodcock Shooting. Saml. Howitt del. J. Godby & H. Merke sculpt. Septr. 1st 1807.
11. Pheasant Shooting I. Sam. Howitt del. J. Clark & H. Merke sculpt. June 1st 1807.
12. Pheasant Shooting II. Saml. Howitt del. W. M. Craig & H. Merke sculpt. July 1st 1807.
13. Partridge Shooting I. Saml. Howitt del. J. Clark & H. Merke sculpt. June 1st 1807.
14. Patridge Shooting II. Saml. Howitt del. J. Godby & H. Merke sculpt. July 1st 1807.
15. Grouse Shooting. Saml. Howett (sic) del. J. Godby & H. Merke sculp. May 1st 1807.
16. Snipe Shooting. Saml. Howitt del. J. Godby & H. Merke sculp. Augst. 1 1807.
17. Rabbit Shooting. Saml. Howitt del. J. Godby & H. Merke sculp. Augst. 1 1807.
18. Duck Shooting Saml. Howitt del. J. Godby & H. Merke sculp. April 1 1807.
19. Hare Shooting Saml. Howitt del. J. Godby & H. Merke sculp. Sepr. 1 1807.
20. Fox Hunting No. 3 Saml. Howitt del Godby & Merke sculpt. March 25 1808.

List of Plates (in English and French) with large coloured vignette of a hare below, Drawn by S. Howett (sic) Etch'd by J. Swain Pub. March 9 1808 by Edwd. Orme, Bond Street, London (v. blank).

Issued in 9 parts in blue paper wrappers, and on completion in boards (22½ × 18½ inches) as above.

Howitt's British Field Sports (*contd.*)

Size of plate 17½ × 13¾ *inches. The Suzannet Copy measured* 22½ × 18¼ *inches. Siltzer cites plate* 11 *as being by Godby and Merke. Suzannet copy and British Museum copy are as above. A magnificent work, the most valuable English colour plate book on Sport.*

Howitt (S.) See also under Ackermann's Repository and Foreign Field Sports.

274 HULLEY (T.)

Six Views of Cheltenham from drawings made by Mr. T. Hulley (line) Price, in Colours, £1 1s. (line) London: Published at R. Ackermann's, 101, Strand; and to be had of all the Book and Print-Sellers in the United Kingdom (small line) 1813

COLLATION.—Title on buff coloured wrapper as above, no text, each plate marked, "London, Pubd. 1 June 1813 at R. Ackermann's Repository of Arts, 101 Strand."

1. Old Wells & Pump Room, Cheltenham, T. Hulley del H. Merke aquat.
2. Well Walk Cheltenham T. Hulley del H. Merke aquat.
3. Montpellier Pump Room Cheltenham T. Hulley del J. Bluck aquat.
4. The Assembly Room Cheltenham T. Hulley del H. Merke aquat.
5. The Crescent Cheltenham T. Hulley del J. Bluck aquat.
6. Hygeia House Cheltenham T. Hulley del H. Merke aquat.

Impartial Historical Narrative of Momentous Events. See under (Bowyer (R.)).

275 HUNTER (James)

Picturesque Scenery in the Kingdom of Mysore, from Forty Drawings taken on the spot by James Hunter, Lieutenant in the Royal Artillery; serving in a detachment from that corps under Marquis Cornwallis, in the war with Tippoo Sultan. (thin and thick rule) Engraved under the direction of Edward Orme, and published by him in Bond Street, London; (thin and thick rule) Printed by W. Bulmer and Co. Cleveland Row, St James's.

Oblong Folio. 1805

COLLATION.—Title as above (v. blank) + Dedication to H.R.H. Princess Elizabeth 1 p. (v. blank) + Index (List of Plates) 1 p. (v. blank) + 41 coloured plates (numbered throughout). Each plate marked, "Lieut. James Hunter, delin." [del. or pinxt.] "Sold and published [date] by Edwd Orme, His Majesty's Printseller, 59 New Bond Street, London." (slight variation to first plate as follows):

1. Tippoo Sultan. From an original Picture in the possession of the Marquis Wellesley. Engraved by Scott from a Drawing by Edward Orme, His Majesty's Printseller, Bond Street, London.
2. Seringapatam. J. C. Stadler, aquatinta. Jany. 1st 1804.
3. Hyder Ally's Tomb, Seringapatam. H. Merke, aquatinta. Jany. 1st 1804.
4. A Mosque at Seringapatam. H. Merke, aquatinta. Jany. 1st 1804.
5. Music Gallery at the Entrance of the Mosque, Seringapatam. H. Merke aquatinta. Jany. 1st 1804.
6. Garden Gate, Laul Baugh, Seringapatam. H. Merke aquatinta. Jany. 1st 1804.
7. Hyder Ally Khan's Own Family Tomb, at Colar. H. Merke aquatinta. Jany. 1st 1804.
8. East View of Bangalore, with the Cypress Garden from a Pagoda. H. Merke aquatinta. Jany. 1st 1804.
9. North Front of Tippoo's Palace, Bangalore. H. Merke, aquatinta. Jany. 1st 1804.
10. West Front of Tipoo's Palace Bangalore. J. C. Stadler, aquatinta. Jany. 1st, 1804.
11. A Street leading to the Palace of Bangalore. J. C. Stadler aquatinta. Jany. 1804.

Hunter's Kingdom of Mysore (*contd.*)

12. The Square and Entrance into Tippoo's Palace, Bangalore. J. C. Stadler aquatinta. Jany. 1st, 1804.
13. North Entrance of Tippoo's Palace at Bangalore. J. C. Stadler aquatinta. Jany. 1st 1804.
14. The Mysore Gate at Bangalore. J. C. Stadler aquatinta. Jany. 1st, 1804.
15. The North Entrance into the Fort of Bangalore. H. Merke aquatinta. Jany. 1st 1804.
16. The Delhi Gate of Bangalore. H. Merke aquatinta. March 1st 1804.
17. The South Entrance into the Fort of Bangalore. H. Merke aquatinta. March 1st 1804.
18. The Third Delhi Gate of Bangalore. H. Merke aquatinta. Jany. 1st 1804.
19. A Moorish Mosque, at Bangalore. H. Merke aquatinta. Jany. 1st 1804.
20. A View of Mount St Thomas, near Madras. H. Merke aquatinta. June 4th 1804.
21. The Royal Artillery Encampment, Arcot. Harraden Aquatinta. March 1804.
22. A Pagoda at Strupermador. H. Merke aquatinta. June 4th 1804.
23. A Mosque at Strupermador. H. Merke aquatinta. June 4th 1804.
24. A View on the Road at Strupermador. H. Merke aquatinta. June 4th 1804.
25. Overflowing of the Tank, at Strupermador. H. Merke aquatinta. June 4th 1804.
26. A View of Ouscottah, from an Eadgah. Harraden aquatinta. June 4th 1804.
27. Killaders Tomb, Ouscottah. Harraden aquatinta. June 4th 1804.
28. Kistnaghurry. Harraden aquatinta. June 4th 1804.
29. East View of Kistnaghurry. Harraden aquatinta. June 4th 1804.
30. N. W. Angle of Osar. Harraden aquatinta. June 4th 1804.
31. S. E. Angle of Osar. Harraden aquatinta. Augt. 1st 1804.
32. North View of Shole Ghurry. Harraden aquatinta. Jany. 1st 1805.
33. East View of Shole Ghurry, from the Camp at Arnee. June 4th 1804.
34. Ourry Durgam. The Head of the Pass into the Barrah Mauhl. Harraden Aquatinta. Jany. 1st 1805.
35. A View in the Barrah Mauhl. Harraden aquatinta. June 4th 1804.
36. A View from the Royal Artillery Encampment, Conjeveram. H. Merke aquatinta. Jany. 1st 1805.
37. A View from the Royal Artillery Encampment Conditore. Harraden aquatinta. Septr. 1804.
38. A View of Ootra Droog. Harraden aquatinta. Jany. 1st 1805.
39. Nabobs Choultry and Tank, at Conjeveram. Harraden aquatinta Septr. 1804.
40. A House at Bankipore, the Residence of Wm. Hunter Esqr. H. Merke aquatinta. June 4th 1804.
41. Commillah, Late the Residence of John Buller Esqr. H. Merke aquatinta. Jany. 1st 1805.

276 HUNTER (William)

Travels through France, Turkey, and Hungary to Vienna in 1792. To which are added Several Tours in Hungary in 1799 and 1800. In a series of Letters to his sister in England. By William Hunter Esq. of the Inner Temple (2 line rule) Third Edition (2 line rule). In Two Volumes. Vol. I [II] London: Printed for J. White, Fleet Street, by T. Bensley, Bolt Court.

2 vols. Royal Octavo. 1803

COLLATION VOL. I.—Title as above (v. blank) + Advertisement to First Edition pp. iii–iv + Advertisement to Second Edition pp. v–xii + Advertisement to Third Edition p. xiii (p. xiv blank) + Itinerary pp. xv–xxvii (p. xviii blank) + Contents pp. xxix–xxxix + pp. 1–412 + Map + 6 coloured stipple costume plates.

VOL. II.—Title (v. blank) + Contents pp. iii–xix + pp. 1–486 + 6 coloured stipple costume plates.

The plates which are beautifully executed, printed in colours are without titles, artist or engravers' name.

277 IBBETSON, LAPORTE and HASSELL

A Picturesque Guide to Bath, Bristol Hot Wells, the River Avon, and the adjacent country: Illustrated with a set of views, taken in the Summer of 1792. By Messrs

Ibbetson, Laporte and Hassell's Guid to Bath (*contd.*)

Ibbetson, Laporte, and J. Hassell, and engraved in aquatinta. (thick and thin rule) London: Printed for Hookham and Carpenter, Bond Street. (short rule) 1793.

Quarto.

COLLATION.—Half-title + Title as above (v. blank) + List of plates and Errata + pp. 1– 266 + 16 coloured plates.   Plates 1, 6, 9, 12, 13, 15 and 16, are marked, Drawn and Engraved by J. Hassell, the remainder of the plates, the landscape drawn and engraved by Hassell, and the Figure, by Ibbetson, except Plate 8 which is by Laporte, and Plate 14, Drawn and Etched by J. Ibbetson, aquatinta by J. Hassell.

   I. Front. Inside view of Tintern Abbey, looking towards the East Window.
   II. p. 123. Waterfall behind the Turnpike, at Midford.
   III. p. 142. Bath, from the private road leading to Prior Park.
   IV. p. 172. View of the Passage House at the Rownham Ferry, on the River Avon, looking towards Bristol.
   V. p. 174. View of the Rivers Avon and Severn, from the road leading from Clifton to Durdham Down.
   VI. p. 176. Front View of Bristol Hot Wells, and St Vincents' Rocks.
   VII. p. 183. A Back View of the Hot Wells House, on the River Avon.
   VIII. p. 184. View of the River Avon from the Stone Quarries, looking towards Bristol.
   IX. p. 186. Wallis's Wall and Rocks and Cook's Folly, from the Path near the New Hot Wells House.
   X. p. 188. View from Wallis's Rocks on the River Avon, looking towards Bristol.
   XI. p. 225. View on the Severn from the New Passage House in Glostershire, with the Ferry Boat preparing to Depart at low water.
   XII. p. 226. View of the Entrance of the River Wye, from a fishermans cottage, below the New passage House on the Severn.
   XIII. p. 241. View of the Bridge and Entrance to the Town of Usk, from the Road leading to Caerlon.
   XIV. p. 247. View of the Castle Rock from the landing Place on the Flat Holmes.
   XV. p. 258. View of Chepstow Castle, and part of the Town of Piercefield.
   XVI. p. 262. View of Cook's Folly, and the Rivers Avon and Severn, from Durdham Down.

278 IRELAND (W. H.)

Life of Napoleon Bonaparte, late Emperor of the French, King of Italy, Protector of the Confederation of the Rhine, Mediator of the Confederation of Switzerland, &c. &c. (rule) Edited by W. H. Ireland member of the Atheneum of Sciences and Arts at Paris (rule) Embellished with accurate views of his Battles &c. &c. &c. Engraved by G. Cruikshank from the original Designs of Vernet, Denon &c. executed, at Paris, by Duplesis Berteaux (rule) "Great men choose greater Sins . . . Ambition's Mine!" . . . Shakespeare (rule) Vol. I [II III] London: Printed and Published by John Fairburn, Broadway, Ludgate Hill: sold by Longman, Hurst, Rees, Orme, Brown, and Green, and Baldwin, Cradock, and Joy, Paternoster Row; Simpkin and Marshall, Stationers Court; Whittakers, Ave-Maria Lane; Humphrey, St. James's Street; and Wilson Royal Exchange (rule).

4 vols. Octavo.   1823 [–27]

COLLATION VOL. I.—Half-title (v. blank) + Title as above (v. blank) + Editor's Preface pp. v–xv signed W. H. Ireland, dated London 22nd October 1823 (p. xvi blank) + Contents pp. xvii–xl + pp. 1–477 [at foot of p. 477 J. Fairburn, Printer, Broadway, Ludgate Hill] + 8 coloured plates.

Each plate in Vols I, II and III marked, Engraved by Mr George Cruikshank Published [date] by John Fairburn, Broadway, Ludgate Hill.

Ireland's Napoleon (*contd.*)

1. Front. Napoleon Bonaparte on his celebrated white charger from the original drawn from Nature by C. Vernet for the splendid French work entitled "Campaigns in Italy" Nov. 7 1823.
2. p. 65. Napoleon at the sanguinary Battle on the Bridge of Lodi from the original design of C. Vernet executed at Paris by I. Duplessi Bertaux May 10 1823.
3. p. 117. Napoleon & Massena defeating the Austrian Army at the terrible battle of Roveredo from the original design of C. Vernet executed at Paris by I. Dulpessi Bertaux August 1 1823.
4. p. 129. Napoleon & Augereau in the heat of the tremendous battle of St George from the the original design of C. Vernet executed in Paris by I. Duplessi Bertaux June 2, 1823.
5. p. 151. Napoleon forcing the passage of the Bridge of Arcola from the original design of C. Vernet executed at Paris by I. Duplessi Bertaux April 2 1823.
6. p. 225. Napoleon at the passage and battle of the River Tagliamento from the original design of C. Vernet executed at Paris by I. Duplessi Bertaux Septr. 11, 1823.
7. p. 333. Napoleon defeating the Mamelukes, at the battle of the Pyramids, near Cairo from the design of Swebach originally Published at Paris and dedicated to the Grand Army Oct. 7 1823.
8. p. 444. Napoleon & Kleber, defeating the Mamelukes at the Battle of Mount Thabor from the original design of Swebach, Published at Paris. March 1 1824.

VOL. II.—Half-title (v. Marchant, Printer, Ingram Court, Fenchurch Street) + Title (dated 1825 v. blank) and Preface Address pp. i–viii + Contents pp. v–xii + pp. 1–556 + Directions to Binder for Vols. I and II + 8 coloured plates.

9. Front. Napoleon when First Consul, & Madame Josephine (His first Wife) in the garden at Malmaison from the Original Portraits executed by Isabey Miniature Painter to Napoleon Nov. 26 1824.
10. p. 149. Napoleon defeating the Turkish Pacha, at the Battle of Aboukir from the original design of M. Denon executed at Paris by I. Duplessi Bertaux September 22 1824.
11. p. 151. The attack and capture of Naples, by the French, after a most obstinate resistance from the original design of C. Vernet executed at Paris by I. Duplessi Bertaux Dec. 27, 1823.
12. p. 275. Napoleon and his Army, effecting the wonderful Passage of the Alps, at Mount St. Bernard from the original design of C. Vernet executed at Paris by I. Duplessi Bertaux July 1 1823.
13. p. 301. Napoleon's decisive victory over the Austrians, at the battle of Marengo from the original design of C. Vernet executed at Paris by I. Duplessi Bertaux Augt. 14 1824.
14. p. 515. Napoleon receiving the sword of general Mack, on the capitulation of Ulm from the original design of Swebach, Published at Paris Dec. 29 1824.
15. p. 539. Napoleon's Bivouac on the Night preceeding the memorable battle of Austerlitz from the original French Print, published at Paris May 1 1824.
16. p. 543. Napoleon receiving from General Rapp the Austrian Standard, surrendered at Austerlitz from the original French print taken from the celebrated Painting of Girard July 1 1824.

VOL. III.—Half-title + Title (1827 v. blank) + To the Reader pp. iii–iv + Contents of Vol. III pp. v–xiv + pp. 1–600 [pp. 110–115 repeated starred] + 6 coloured plates.

17. Front. Napoleon the Great in his Coronation Robes from the original Painting of Gerard October 13, 1826.
18. p. 41. Napoleon's Entrance into the City of Berlin from the original design of Swebach Published at Paris August 27 1825.
19. p. 53. Napoleon defeating the Prussian Army at the Battle of Eylau from the Original design of Swebach, Published at Paris June 6, 1825.
20. p. 61. Napoleon, & the Emperor Alexander, upon the Raft, on the Nieman, after the treaty of Tilsit from the original of Swebach Published at Paris March 19, 1825.
21. p. 447. Napoleon witnessing the conflagration (sic) of Moscow, from the Palace of the Kremlin. Designed & Engraved by Mr. George Cruikshank Jany. 20 1826.
22. p. 485. Napoleon's Retreat from Moscow from the original German print of C. Beyer May 27 1826.

VOL. IV.—Engraved title (v. blank) + Contents of Vol. IV pp. iii–viii + List of Embellishments 2 pp. (ix–x) + pp. 1–542.

The imprint on title and plates 23, 24 and 26 changed to Published [date] by John Cumberland 19 Ludgate Hill.

Ireland's Napoleon (*contd.*)

23. Front. Napoleon Francis Charles Joseph, Duke of Reichstadt, formerly King of Rome Drawn by Mr. G. Cruikshank and Engraved by Mr. C. Taylor Mr. G. Cruikshank and Mr. R. G. Reeve Jan. 1 1828 (uncoloured).

24. p. 3. Maria Louisa, Arch-Duchess of Austria, Empress of France. Engraved by Mr. C. Taylor and Mr. G. Cruikshank from an original drawing by M. Prudon, and aquatinted by Mr. Mr. R. G. Reeve Nov. 1 1827 (uncoloured).

25. p. 41. Portraits of Napoleons Marshalls and Generals Plate I Engraved from accurate likenesses executed at Paris by the most celebrated artists Published March 17 1827 (uncoloured).

26. p. 261. Napoleon's Arrival at the Tuilleries on his return from Elba.

27. p. 389. Napoleon terminating his Military Carreer (sic) at the memorable Battle of Waterloo Engraved by Mr. George Cruikshank from the original of I. Duplessi Bertaux executed at Paris Oct. 21 1825.

Issued in 64 parts, Parts 1–48 (i.e. Vols. I to III) being published by Fairburn. The publication was then taken over by Cumberland, who issued 16 more parts and published the work in 4 volumes in 1828 in green cloth with printed labels. Cumberland's issue has 4 engraved titlepages with following vignette coats of arms, Vol. I Imperial Arms, Vol. II Arms of Maria Louisa, Vol. III Arms of Napoleon Francis Charles Joseph King of Rome, Vol. IV The Star of the Order of the Legion of Honour. The preface is also differently set up and extends to xvi pages. The text of this work is the same as that for Excellman's History of Napoleon. There is however a difference in the text of first volume. In Excellman the summary headings of the chapters are contracted in small type. In Ireland the headings are in large type spread out occupying the whole or more than the whole of a page.

Mr. Harvey Frost's copy, which is uncut, measures 9⅝ × 6⅛ inches. There are cancel pages 41–42 and 115–116, Vol. III. Copies showing imprints throughout are uncommon, some at least being almost invariably cut into. First issues are distinguished by Fairburn's imprint on all the coloured plates except plate 26. There was no printed title to Vol. 4 in the first issue.

Second issue by Cumberland also has Fairburn's imprint on plates.

279 JACOB (W.)

Travels in the South of Spain, in Letters written AD 1809 and 1810 (thick and thin rule) By William Jacob, Esq. MP. F.R.S. (thin and thick rule) London: Printed for J. Johnson and Co. St Pauls Church-yard, and W. Miller, Albermarle Street; (sic) By John Nichols and Son, Red Lion Passage, Fleet Street.

Quarto.   1811

COLLATION.—Half-title "Travels in the South of Spain" (v. blank) + Title as above (v. blank) + Preface pp. v–vii (p. viii blank) + Contents pp. ix–xiii (p. xiv blank) + Directions to Binder, 1 p. (v. Errata) + pp. 1–407 + Appendix pp. 1–30 + Index 7 pp. + Map and 12 plates.

Front.   Cadiz according to the Plan of Torfini (folding with perspective view below).

1. p. 80. La Lonja Seville.
2. p. 95. Inquisition formerly Jesuits College in Seville (uncoloured etching).
3. p. 122. Cathedral Seville.
4. p. 125. Roman Ruins Alcala.
5. p. 191. Carthusian Convent near Xeres.

6. p. 192. Calvario at Xexes.
7. p. 226. Custom House Malaga.
8. p. 227. Cathedral Malaga.
9. p. 282. Alhambra in Granada.
10. p. 284. Palace of Charles V. in the Alhambra Granada (folding).
11. p. 332. Bridge at Ronda.
12. p. 352. Gibraltar.

Issued in boards.

280 JAMES (Capt.)

The Military Costume of India in an Exemplification of the Manual and Platoon Exercises for the use of the Native Troops and the British Army in General, by Capn. James, 67 Regt., (the above surrounded by military trophies, flags, cannon etc.,) London: Printed and Published by T. Goddard, Military Library, No. 1 Pall Mall.

Quarto.   1813

COLLATION.—Title as above (v. blank) + Preface pp. i–iv + Introduction pp. v–viii + 35 coloured plates (without titles, but numbered throughout 1–35), each marked, Published by T. Goddard, 1, Pall Mall, 1813, Sawyer & Sons, and each with 1 leaf of text (with the exception of Plate I, "Three British Officers," used as a frontispiece. The remainder of the plates are of native infantry.

Issued on super royal paper in octavo, at £2 2s., and on imperial quarto, at £3 3s.

281 (JENKINS (J.))

The Martial Achievements of Great Britain and Her Allies from 1799 to 1815 (vignette) London: Printed for Js. Jenkins, No. 48, Strand, By L. Harrison & J. C. Leigh, 373 Strand.

Quarto.   [1814–15]

COLLATION.—Title as above (v. blank) + Dedication to Duke of Wellington 2 pp. + Engraved dedication with coloured coat of arms 1 p. (v. blank) + Description of vignette title 1 p. (v. blank) + Introduction 4 pp. (v–viii) + Contents (i.e. List of Illustrations) 2 pp. + List of Subscribers + 52 coloured plates and 60 unnumbered ll. of Text.

1. Frontispiece Lettered Martial Achievements Vol. I with vignette W. Heath del. Aquatinted by Sutherland London Published Dec. 1 1814.
2. Storming of Seringapatam May 4th 1799 W. Heath Delt. T. Sutherland sculpt. Dec. 1 1815.
3. Defence of the Breach at St. Jean D'Acre, May 8th 1799 W. Heath delt. T. Sutherland sculpt. Novr. 1 1815.
4. Landing of the British Troops in Egypt March 8 1801 W. Heath Del. Aquatinted by Sutherland Jany. 2 1815.
5. Death of Sir Ralph Abercromby March 21 1801 W. Heath Del. Aquatinted by Sutherland Jany. 1 1815.
6. The Battle of Maida July 4th 1806 W. Heath delt. T. Sutherland aquat. April 1 1815.
7. Storming of Montevideo Feby. 3rd 1807 W. Heath delt. T. Sutherland sculpt. Septr. 1 1815.
8. Battle of Roleia Augt. 17th 1808 W. Heath delt. T. Sutherland aquat. May 1 1815.
9. Battle of Vimiera Augt. 21st 1808 W. Heath delt. D. Havell aquat. May 1 1815.
10. Battle of Corunna Jany. 17th 1809 W. Heath delt. M. Dubourg aquat. Jany. 1 1815.
11. Death of Sir John Moore Jany. 17 1809 W. Heath Delt. Aquatinted by Sutherland Jany. 2 1817.
12. Battle of Grigo May 11th 1809 W. Heath delt. D. Havell sculpt. Novr. 1 1815.
13. Battle of Salamonda May 16th 1809 W. Heath delt. T. Sutherland sculpt. Augt. 1 1815.
14. Battle of Talavera July 28th 1809 W. Heath delt. T. Sutherland sculpt. June 1 1815.
15. Battle of Busaco Septr. 27th 1810 W. Heath delt. T. Sutherland sculpt. June 1 1815.
16. Battle of Barrosa March 5th 1811 W. Heath delt. Etched by Clarke Dubourg aquat. March 1 1815.
17. Battle of Pombal—March 12th 1811 W. Heath delt. T. Sutherland sculpt. Octr. 1 1815.
18. Defeat of a French Division before Badajos W. Heath delt. J. Hill sculpt. Augt. 1 1815.
19. Battle of Fuentes d'Onoro May 5th 1811 W. Heath delt. T. Sutherland sculpt. Septr. 1 1815.
20. Battle of Albuera May 16th 1811 W. Heath delt. T. Sutherland sculpt. Oct. 1 1815.
21. Marshal Beresford disarming a Polish Lancer, at the Battle of Albuera—May 16th 1811 W. Heath delt. T. Sutherland sculpt. Oct. 1 1815.
22. Siege of Badajoz June 11 W. Heath delt. T. Sutherland aquat. Feby. 1 1815.

Jenkins's Martial Achievements (*contd.*)

23. Storming of Ciudad Rodrigo Jany. 19th 1813   W. Heath delt.   T. Sutherland aquat.   May 1st 1815.
24. Gen. Sir Thomas Picton storming the Moorish Castle of Badajos March 31 1812   W. Heath delt.   T. Sutherland aquat. April 1 1815.
25. Battle of Salamanca July 22nd 1812   W. Heath delt.   M. Dubourg aquat.   Jany. 1 1815.
26. Battle of Seville Augt. 27th 1812   W. Heath delt.   T. Sutherland sculpt.   Augt. 1 1815.
27. Burning of Moscow Septr. 1812   W. Heath delt.   T. Sutherland aquat.   March 1 1815.
28. Flight of Bonaparte from the Battle of Krasnoi   W. Heath delt.   T. Sutherland aquat.   April 1 1815.
29. Bonaparte's Flight in Disguise from Russia 1811.   W. Heath Del.   Aquatinted by Sutherland March 1st 1814.
30. Battle of Castalla, April 13th 1813   W. Heath delt.   T. Sutherland sculpt.   July 1 1815.
31. Entrance of Lord Wellington into Salamanca, at the head of a Regiment of Hussars May 20th 1813. W. Heath delt.   M. Dubourg aquat.   June 1 1815.
32. Battle of Morales June 2nd 1813   W. Heath delt.   T. Sutherland sculpt.   Septr. 1 1815.
33. Battle of Vittoria June 21 1813   W. Heath Del.   Etched by I. Clark Aquatinted by M. Dubourg Dec. 1 1814.
34. Battle of Vittoria, Bringing in the Prisoners   W. Heath Del.   Etched by I. Clark   Aquatinted by M. Dubourg   Dec. 1 1814.
35. Siege of St. Sebastian July 1813   W. Heath Del.   T. Sutherland aquat.   April 1 1815.
36. Battle of the Pyrenees July 28th 1813   W. Heath delt.   T. Sutherland sculpt.   July 1 1815.
37. The Storming of St. Sebastian Augt. 31st 1813   W. Heath delt.   T. Sutherland   Novr. 1 1815.
38. Death of Moreau before Dresden Augt. 1813   W. Heath delt.   T. Sutherland aquat.   May 1 1815.
39. Battle of the Bidassoa—Oct. 9th 1813   W. Heath delt.   D. Havell sculpt.   Novr. 1 1815.
40. Battle of Leipsic Octr. 19th 1813   W. Heath delt.   Etched by Clark   M. Dubourg aquat.   Jany. 1 1815.
41. Meeting of the Emperors of Russia & Austria, King of Prussia, & Crown Prince of Sweden in the Great Square of Leipzig Oct. 18th 1813   W. Heath delt.   T. Sutherland aquat.   Feby. 1 1815.
42. Blowing up of the Bridge at Elster   W. Heath Del.   Aquatinted by Sutherland   Dec. 1 1814.
43. Battle of Nivelle Nov. 10th 1813   W. Heath delt.   T. Sutherland sculpt.   Septr. 1 1815.
44. Battle of St. Jean de Luz Dec. 10th 1813   W. Heath delt.   T. Sutherland sculpt.   Augt. 1 1815.
45. Attack on the Road to Bayonne Decr. 13th 1813   W. Heath delt.   T. Sutherland aquat.   March 1 1815.
46. Battle of Orthes Feby. 27th 1814   W. Heath delt.   D. Havell sculpt.   May 1st 1815.
47. Entrance of the Allies into Paris March 31st 1814   W. Heath delt.   T. Sutherland sculpt.   June 1 1815.
48. Battle of Toulouse April 10th 1814   W. Heath delt.   T. Sutherland aquat.   March 1 1815.
49. The Sortie from Bayonne at 3 in the Morning on the 14th April 1814   W. Heath delt.   T. Sutherland sculpt.   Octr. 1 1815.
50. Battle of Quatre Bras June 16th 1815   W. Heath delt.   T. Sutherland sculpt.   Decr. 1 1815.
51. The Centre of the British Army in Action at the Battle of Waterloo June 18th 1815   W. Heath delt. T. Sutherland sculpt.   Dec. 1 1815.
52. The Left Wing of the British Army in Action, at the Battle of Waterloo June 18th 1815   W. Heath delt.   T. Sutherland sculpt.   Decr. 1 1815.

Issued on both small and large paper, and with the plates on India paper.   There are late issues of the plates, which should be examined to see that the watermarks are pre-publication, as the plates were reprinted without any alteration in imprints certainly up till 1835.   Some copies have in addition to the above plates, a portrait of the Duke of Wellington, copies are complete without it.   Large-paper copies exist with the plates in three states.

282 (JENKINS (J.))

The Naval Achievements of Great Britain, From the Year 1793 to 1817 (vignette "view of Castle with Neptune & Britannia") London Printed for J. Jenkins No. 48, Strand, By L. Harrison, 373, Strand.   W. Bartlett Sculpt.

Quarto.   [1816–17]

Jenkins's Naval Achievements (*contd.*)

COLLATION.—Title as above (v. blank) + List of Plates 2 pp. + Introduction 6 pp. (iii–viii) + Dedication to Earl of St Vincent 2 pp. + List of Subscribers + 74 unpaged leaves + 55 coloured plates + 1 uncoloured plate, plan Bombardment of Algiers and plan Battle of Trafalgar.

Each plate marked, "London Pub. [date] at 48 Strand for J. Jenkin's Naval Achievements."

1. View of Gibraltar   Painted by Whitecombe T. Sutherland sculpt.   March 1 1816.
2. Capture of La Cleopatre June 18th 1793   Painted by T. Whitcombe   T. Sutherland sculpt.   April 1 1816.
3. Capture of La Reunion Octr. 21st 1793   Painted by T. Whitcombe   J. Jeakes sculpt.   April 1 1816.
4. Destruction of the French Fleet at Toulon, Dec. 18th 1793   Painted by T. Whitcombe   T. Sutherland sculpt.   April 1 1816.
5. Capture of La Pomone L'Engageante & La Babet April 23rd 1794   Painted by T. Whitcombe   Engraved by T. Sutherland   July 1 1816.
6. Capture of the Castor May 29th 1794   Painted by T. Whitcombe   T. Sutherland sculpt.   June 1 1816.
7. Lord Howe in the Queen Charlotte, Breaking the Enemy's Line. May 29th 1794   Painted by Whitcombe T. Sutherland sculpt.   March 1 1816.
8. Lord Howe's Victory June 1st 1794   Painted by Whitcombe Sutherland sculpt.   April 1 1816.
9. Capture of La Pique Jany. 5th 1795   Painted by Whitcombe   Engraved by Sutherland   Septr. 1 1816.
10. Lord Hotham's Action, March 14th 1795   Painted by Whitcombe   Engraved by T. Sutherland   Septr. 1 1816.
11. Capture of La Gliore, April 10th 1795   Painted by T. Whitcombe   T. Sutherland sculpt.   June 1 1816.
12. Capture of La Prevoyante and La Raison May 17th 1795   Painted by T. Whitcombe   T. Sutherland sculpt.   June 1 1816.
13. Lord Bridport's Action off Port L'Orient June 23rd 1795   Painted by T. Whitcombe   Bailey sculpt.   May 1 1816.
14. Capture of La Minerve June 24th 1795   Painted by Whitcombe   T. Sutherland sculpt.   May 1 1816.
15. Capture of the Mahonesa Octr. 13th 1796 Painted by Whitcombe   Engraved by Sutherland   Novr. 1 1816.
16. Capture of La Prosperine June 13th 1796   Painted by Whitcombe   J. Jeakes sculpt.   May 1 1816.
17. Capture of La Tribune June 8th 1796   Painted by Whitcombe   Engraved by T. Sutherland   Feby. 1 1817.
18. Capture of Le Desius Novr. 1796   Painted by Whitcombe   Engraved by T. Sutherland   Septr. 1 1816.
19. Battle of Cape St. Vincent Feby. 14th 1797   Painted by Whitcombe   Engraved by J. Baily   July 1 1816.
20. Capture of L'Hercule April 20th 1797   Painted by Whitcombe   Engraved by Sutherland   Septr. 1 1816.
21. Action off Camperdown Octr. 11th 1797   Painted by Whitcombe   Engraved by T. Sutherland   June 1 1817.
22. Capture of La Nereide Decr. 21st 1797   Painted by T. Whitcombe   T. Sutherland sculpt.   May 1 1816.
23. Capture of La Confiante May 31st 1798   Painted by T. Whitcombe   Engraved by T. Sutherland   Augt. 1 1816.
24. Capture of the Dorethea July 15th 1798   Painted by T. Whitcombe   Engraved by T. Sutherland   Nov. 1 1816.
25. Capture of the Liguria Augt. 7th 1798   Painted by T. Whitcombe   T. Sutherland sculpt.   July 1 1816.
26. Battle of the Nile Augt. 1st 1798   Painted by T. Whitcombe   T. Sutherland sculpt.   March 1 1816.
27. Battle of the Nile (Plate II) Augt. 1st 1798   Painted by T. Whitcombe   Engraved by Bailey   April 1 1816.
28. Capture of La Loire Octr. 18th 1798   Painted by T. Whitcombe   T. Sutherland sculpt.   Octr. 1 1816.
29. Capture of L'Immortalité Octr. 20th 1798   Painted by T. Whitcombe   Engraved by T. Sutherland   Novr. 1 1816.

Jenkins's Naval Achievements (*contd.*)

30. Capture of the Furie & Waakzamheid Octr. 23rd 1798 Painted by T. Whitcombe Engraved by T. Sutherland Octr. 1 1816.

31. Capture of La Forte Feby. 28th 1799 Painted by T. Whitcombe Engraved by T. Sutherland Feby. 1 1816.

32. Capture of La Vestale Augt. 20th 1799 Painted by T. Whitcombe Engraved by T. Sutherland Augt. 1 1816.

33. Cutting out the Hermione from the Harbour of Porto Cavallo Oct. 25th 1799 Painted by T. Whitcombe Engraved by T. Sutherland Octr. 1 1816.

34. Capture of La Desirée July 7th 1800 Painted by Whitcombe Sutherland sculpt. Novr. 1 1816.

35. Capture of La Vengeance Augt. 21st 1800 Painted by Whitcombe Engraved by Sutherland Decr. 1 1816.

36. Destruction of the Danish Fleet before Copenhagen April 2nd 1801 Painted by Whitcombe Bailey sculpt. June 1 1816.

37. Destruction of the Danish Fleet before Copenhagen (plate II) Painted by Whitcombe Engraved by T. Sutherland Octr. 1 1816.

38. Battle off Cabaretta Point July 12th 1801 Painted by Whitcombe T. Sutherland sculpt. March 1 1816.

39. Capture of La Chiffone Augt. 19th 1801 Painted by Whitcombe Engraved by Sutherland Decr. 1 1816.

40. Capture & Destruction of Four Spanish Frigates Octr. 5th 1804 Painted by Pocock Engraved by T. Sutherland March 1 1817.

41. Sir Robt. Calders Action July 22nd 1805 Painted by T. Whitcombe Engraved by T. Sutherland March 1 1817.

42. Commencement of the Battle of Trafalgar Octr. 21st 1805 Painted by T. Whitcombe Engraved by T. Sutherland March 1 1816.

43. Battle of Trafalgar (Plate II) Painted by T. Whitcombe Sutherland sculpt. March 1 1816.

44. Battle of Trafalgar (Plate III) Painted by Whitcombe Engraved by Sutherland March 1 1817.

45. Sir Richard Strachan's Action Novr. 4th 1805 Painted by T. Whitcombe Engraved by J. Jeakes Septr. 1 1816.

46. Sir J. T. Duckworths Action off St. Domingo Feby. 6th 1806 Painted by T. Whitcombe Engraved by T. Sutherland Feby. 1 1817.

47. Capture of the Maria Riggersbergen Oct. 18th 1806 Painted by T. Whitcomb Engraved by T. Sutherland Jany. 1 1817.

48. Capture of the Badere Zaffer July 6th 1808 Painted by Whitcombe Engraved by T. Sutherland Decr. 1 1816.

49. Destruction of the French Fleet in Basque Roads April 12th 1809 Painted by T. Whitcombe Engraved by T. Sutherland Feby. 1 1817.

50. Capture of Le Sparviere May 3, 1810 Painted by T. Whitcombe Engraved by J. Baily Augt. 1 1816.

51. Capture of the Island of Banda Augt. 9th 1810 Painted by T. Whitcombe Engraved by T. Sutherland Jany. 1 1817.

52. Capture of the Chesapeake June 1st 1813 Painted by T. Whitcombe Engraved by Bailey Jany 1 1817.

53. Capture of the Argus, Augt. 14th 1813 Drawn by I. Whitcombe Engraved by T. Sutherland. Feb. 1 1817.

54. Capture of La Clorinde Feby. 26th 1814 Painted by T. Whitcombe T. Sutherland sculpt. March 1 1817.

55. Bombardment of Algiers Augt. 27th 1816 Painted by T. Whitcombe Engraved by T. Sutherland March 1 1817.

RÉSUMÉ.—*56 plates, including title,* 54 *being by T. Whitcombe, engraved by Sutherland* (45), *Bailey* (6) *and Jeakes* (3), *and* 1 *by Pocock engraved by Sutherland. The title exists in two states with the vignette uncoloured or coloured.*

As in the " Martial Achievements " there are late issues of the plates which must be examined to see that the watermarks are pre-publication. Some copies of this work have one or two additional plates, namely portraits of Nelson and Lord St Vincent. The work is complete without them.

Jenkins's Naval Achievements (*contd.*)

Copies were issued with the plates on India paper and also in etched outline. Some large-paper copies have the plates in three states. More sought after than the Martial Achievements, it is becoming uncommon.

283 JOHNSON (Charles)

Chrysal; or the Adventures of a Guinea: By an Adept. (short rule) A New Edition, to which is now prefixed a sketch of the author's life (rule) Embellished with Plates (rule) (4 line quotation from Shakespeare) (rule) In Three Volumes Vol. I [II, III] (rule) London: Printed for Hector M'Lean, 113, Strand, By Howlett and Brimmer, Frith Street, Soho Square

3 vols. Octavo.   1821

COLLATION VOL. I.—Half-title "Chrysal; or the Adventures of a Guinea" (v. blank) + Title as above (v. blank) + Sketch of the Author's Life 4 pp. (v–viii) + Preface pp. 1–12 + pp. 13–319 + 5 coloured plates.

1. Frontispiece. Adventures of a Guinea   The Adept entranced by the Apparation of Chrysal in his Laboratory   Drawn by Burney   Engraved by Maddocks   Published by Hector McLean 113 Strand.
2. p.   41. Adventure of a Guinea   The distressed situation of Amelia   Drawn by E. F. Burney   W. Read sc.
3. p.   43. Adventures of a Guinea   Traffic visited in his Dungeon by the Gaoler   W. Read sc.
4. p. 126. Adventures of a Guinea   The Author in his Study   W. Read sc.
5. p. 306. Adventures of a Guinea   The insolence of the Baliff to the Young Lord   Drawn by E. F. Burney   W. Read sc.

VOL. II.—Half-title as before + Title as before + pp. 1–321 + 5 coloured plates.

6. Frontispiece. Adventures of a Guinea   The joyful meeting of Olivia and her Father   W. Read sc.
7. p.   95. Adventures of a Guinea   The massacre of the Bulgarian Family   Drawn by E. F. Burney   W. Read Sc.
8. p. 121. Adventures of a Guinea   The King of Bulgaria's Soliloquy upon a Guinea   W. Read sc.
9. p. 140. Adventures of a Guinea   The bounty of the King of Bulgaria to the vanquished foe   Drawn by T. Mawson   W. Read sc.
10. p. 189. Adventures of a Guinea   The Kitchen Maid's daughter confessing her guilt   Drawn by R. Corbould   W. Read sc.

VOL. III.—Half-title as before + Title as before + pp. 1–326 + Books printed for M'Lean 2 pp. + 5 coloured plates.

11. Frontispiece. Adventures of a Guinea   The European Lady discovered in the Woods   Drawn by J. Burney   W. Read sc.
12. p.   23. Adventures of a Guinea   Weighty reasons for continuing the Embargo   Drawn by R. Corbould   W. Read sc.
13. p.   40. Adventures of a Guinea [no other title]   W. Read sc.
14. p. 150. Adventures of a Guinea   The poor Beau at his toilet   W. Read sc.
15. p. 229. Adventures of a Guinea   The Authors humanity   W. Read sc.

FIRST AND BEST EDITION.—*A few copies were printed on large paper.*
The "best scandalous chronical of the day," the supposedly fictitious characters being taken from prominent men of the time. A key to their identity is to be found in Davis's Olio, one of the criticised being General Wolfe. "We may safely rank Johnstone as a prose Juvenal," Sir Walter Scott. Halkett and Laing ascribe the book to C. Johnston, Prideaux to Johnstone, and B. P. C. and B. A. R. to Johnson.
An inferior edition was published in duodecimo the following year. This had only 12 plates.

284 JOHNSON (Lt. Col., J.)

A Journey from India to England, through Persia, Georgia, Russia, Poland, and Prussia, in the year 1817. (thick and thin rule) By Lieut. Col. John Johnson, C.B. (thin and thick rule). Illustrated with engravings. (swelled rule) London: Printed for Longman, Hurst, Rees, Orme and Brown, Paternoster Row.

Quarto.   1818

COLLATION.—Title as above (v. Printed by A. Strahan, Printers Street, London) +Preface pp. iii–iv+Contents pp. v–x+List of Plates 1 p. (v. Errata)+pp. 1–376+13 plates, 5 of which are coloured aquatints. Each plate is marked, Drawn by Lt. Coll. J. Johnson. Engraved by T. Fielding, except plate 9, which bears imprint of Longman, Hurst Rees, Orme and Brown.

1. Front. Khoords (coloured).
2. p. 22. An Arab Bagpiper and Soldier.
3. p. 31. Naptha Springs near Danlky (uncoloured).
4. p. 43. Fallen Statute in the Cave at Shapour (uncoloured).
5. p. 47. Kauzeroon (uncoloured).
6. p. 59. Hafiz and Saahi from Paintings at their Tombs (uncoloured).
7. p. 80. Illyauts (coloured).
8. p. 109. Two Ladies of the Court of Shah Abbas (coloured).
9. p. 113. Plan of Shah Abbas's Humauns. Engraved by Sidy Hall (uncoloured). May 20th.
10. p. 133. Kohrord (uncoloured).
11. p. 146. Tomb of Fatima (uncoloured).
12. p. 176. Persian Husbandmen (coloured).
13. p. 232. Mount Ararat (uncoloured).

285 JOHNSON (J.)

Views in the West Indies: Engraved from Drawings taken recently in the Islands: With letterpress Explanations made from Actual Observation London Published by Messrs. Underwood Fleet Street

Oblong Folio.   1827

COLLATION PART I.—4 plates each marked, Drawn by J. Johnson London Published [date] by T. & G. Underwood Fleet Street.
Each plate has 1 leaf of text.

1. View of Saint John's Harbour Antigua From Friar's Hill   Feby. 1 1827.
2. View in Old North Sound Antigua   February 1 1827.
3. English Harbour Antigua from Great George Fort Monks Hill   Engraved by T. Fielding   1 May 1827.
4. View in Tortola from Ruthy Hill   Engraved by T. Fielding   1st May 1827.

PART II.—4 plates, each marked, Drawn by J. Johnson, Engraved by T. Fielding London Published [date] by T. & G. Underwood Fleet Street.
Each plate has 1 leaf of Text.

5. Kingstown, Saint Vincent From Sion Hill   1st May 1827.
6. Calliaqua, Saint Vincent From the Villa Estate   1st May 1827.
7. View of the Souffriere Mountain Saint Vincent From the Wallibou Estate   Feb. 1 1827.
8. View in the Island of Saint Christopher In the Parish of Nicola Town   Feb. 1 1827.

PART III.—Map and 3 plates, each plate marked, Drawn by Johnson London Published [date] by Smith & Elder Cornhill.

Johnson's West Indies (*contd.*)

9. Map of Antigua.   List of Estates in the Island 1829 1 page (v. List of Governors).
10. Saint John's Antigua From Otto's   Engraved by C. Bentley   March 1 1829.
11. Saint John's Harbour Antigua From the Southward and Eastward   Engraved by C. Bentley   July 1st 1829.
12. View near St. John's Antigua from Gambles   Engraved by G. Reeve   July 1st 1829.

Rare.   The finest colour plate book on these islands.   The above collation taken from a copy in the possession of Messrs. Francis Edwards in original buff printed wrappers measuring 24¾ × 19¼ inches.   The engraved surface of plates measures 16½ × 10½ inches.

286 JOHNSTON (Robert)

Travels through Part of the Russian Empire and the Country of Poland; along the Southern Shores of the Baltic. By Robert Johnston A.M. (line) Illustrated with Maps and Numerous Coloured Plates (rule) Dedicated, by Permission to His Royal Highness the Prince Regent (double rule) London: Printed for J. J. Stockdale, No. 41, Pall Mall (short Line).

Quarto.   1815

COLLATION.—Half-title + Title as above (v. London Printed by Cox and Baylis, Great Queen Street, Lincoln's-Inn-Fields) + Dedication 1 p. (v. blank) + Contents 3 pp. (v–vii) + Errata 1 p. + Preface 14 pp. (i–xiv) + List of Plates 1 p. + sub-title "Travels through Part of Russia, Poland &c. &c. &c." (v. blank) + pp. 17–460 + 2 Maps, 1 uncoloured and 20 coloured plates.

All the plates, with the exception of No. 16, marked, R. Johnston delt. and all bearing imprint, Pub. [date] by J. J. Stockdale 41 Pall Mall.

1. (front).   Flying Mountain   C. Williams sculp.   17 June 1815.
2. (p.   18).   Copenhagen   H. Dawe sculp.   1 June 1815.
   p.   23.   Map of the North West Part of Europe.
3. (p.   25).   Hamburg   C. J. Canton sculp.   13 June 1815.
4. (p.   37).   Stralsund   F. C. Lewis sculp.   12 June 1815.
5. (p.   48).   Monastery of Oliva   F. C. Lewis   1 June 1815.
6. (p.   61).   Frauensberg   F. C. Lewis sculp.   12 June 1815.
7. (p.   69).   Tilsit   H. Dawe sculp.   1 June 1815.
   p.   79.   Map of the North West Part of Russia.
8. (p.   91).   Cronstadt Boatmen   J. Gleadah sculp.   1 June 1815.
9. (p. 101).   Casan Church   J. Gledah. sculp.   5th July 1815.
10. (p. 107).   Hermitage   H. Dawe sculp.   16 June 1815.
11. (p. 148).   Igiora a Village near St Petersburg   F. C. Lewis sculp.   1 June 1815.
12. (p. 204).   Bronnitzi   C. Williams sculp.   23 June 1815.
13. (p. 222).   Females in the Govt. of Novogorod   C. J. Canton sculp.   12 June 1815.
14. (p. 238).   A Russian Village near Moscow   J. Gleadah sculp.   1 June 1815.
15. (p. 256).   Moscow   J. Hill sculpsit   1 June 1815.
16. (p. 273).   Kremlin   T. Cartwright sculp.   21 June 1815.
17. (p. 336).   Borodino   C. Williams   19 June 1815.
18. (p. 365).   Smolensko   J. Hill sculpsit   1 June 1815.
19. (p. 378).   Lithuanian Jewess   H. Dawe sculpt.   11 June 1815.
20. (p. 384).   Borisoff   H. Dawe sculpt.   1 June 1815.
    p. 444.   Uncoloured full page woodcut depicting various ploughs &c. used in Russia, Poland, Lithuania.

Jorrock's Jaunts and Jollities.   See under Surtees (R.).

287 KENRICK (T.)

The British Stage and Literary Cabinet (thick and thin rule) By Thomas Kenrick (thin and thick rule) eight line verse Kelly's Thespis (vignette Shakespeare) Vol. I [–VI] London: Printed by F. Marshall, Kenton Street, Brunswick Square. Published for the proprietors; by J. Chappell, Royal Exchange (swelled rule)

5 vols. (Vol. 6 unfinished)   Octavo.   1817[–22]

COLLATION VOL. I.—Title as above (v. blank) + Address 2 pp. (iii–iv) + Text pp. 1–300 (including index) + 12 plates (plate 8 by R, plates 9 and 10 by I.R., plate 7 unsigned, the rest by George Cruikshank).

1. p.	1.	Mrs Davenport as Miss von Frump (coloured)	January 1817
2. p.	25.	Mr Young as Leontius (uncoloured)	February ,,
3. p.	49.	Mr Liston as Domine Sampson (coloured)	March ,,
4. p.	74.	Mr Oxberry as Justice Greedy (coloured)	April ,,
5. p.	97.	Miss Booth as Little Pickle (coloured)	May ,,
6. p.	121.	Mrs Liston as Dollalolla (coloured)	June ,,
7. p.	145.	Miss Kelly as Carlos (coloured)	July ,,
8. p.	169.	Mr Matthews as Scout (coloured)	August ,,
9. p.	193.	Mr Tokely as Peter Pastoral (coloured)	Sept. ,,
10. p.	217.	Mr Fawcett as Hardy (coloured)	Oct. ,,
11. p.	241.	Mr Munden as Kit Sly (coloured)	Nov. ,,
12. p.	265.	Mr Braham as Don Alphonso (coloured)	Dec. ,,

VOL. II.—Title as before + Address 2 pp. (iii–iv) + Text pp. 1–300 (including index) + 12 coloured plates all by G. Cruikshank (except plate 24 by I.R., engraved by G.).

13. p.	1.	Miss Clara Fisher as Lord Flimnap (coloured)	January 1818
14. p.	25.	Signor Naldi as Figaro (coloured)	Feb. ,,
15. p.	49.	Mr Chas. Kemble as Giraldi Fazio (coloured)	March ,,
16. p.	73.	Mr Macready as Rob Roy Macgregor (coloured)	April ,,
17. p.	97.	Mr Kean as Barabas (coloured)	May ,,
18. p.	121.	Mr Jones as Mathew Sharpset (coloured)	June ,,
19. p.	145.	Mr Farley as Grindoff (coloured)	July ,,
20. p.	191.	Mr Terry as Mr Precise (coloured)	August ,,
21. p.	193.	Mr Russell as Sparkish (coloured)	Sept. ,,
22. p.	217.	Mrs Gibbs as Cowslip (coloured)	Octr. ,,
23. p.	241.	Miss Brunton as Lydia Languish (coloured)	Novr. ,,
24. p.	265.	Mr Farren as Sir Anthony Absolute (coloured)	Dec. ,,

VOL. III.—Title as before + Address 1 p. (v. corrigenda) + pp. 1–292 (including index) + 9 uncoloured plates.

25. p.	1.	Miss Foote as Ulrica	Jan. 1819
26. p.	33.	Miss Stephens as Diana Vernon	Feb. ,,
27. p.	65.	Mrs T. Hill as Hypolita	March ,,
28. p.	97.	Mr Matthews as the Diligentine Personae I. R. Cruikshank	April ,,
29. p.	129.	Mr Knight as Tim J. B. Cruikshank	May ,,
30. p.	161.	Miss Taylor as Jeanie Deans	June ,,
31. p.	193.	Miss Kelly as Lauretta	July ,,
32. p.	225.	Mrs Siddons as Lady Randolph I. R. Cruikshank	August ,,
33. p.	257.	Mr Yates as Iago J. W. Childe	Sept. ,,

VOL. IV.—Title as before + Address 2 pp. (iii–iv) + Text pp. 1–360 (pp. 213–220 repeated) (including index) + 16 plates (5 of which are in colour).

34. p.	1.	Mr Emery as Dandie Dimmont (coloured) I.R.C. fecit	Oct. 1819
35. p.	25.	Mr Dowton as Balthazar (coloured) I.R.C. fecit	Nov. ,,

Kenrick's British Stage (contd.)

36. p.	49.	Mr Elliston as Richmond (coloured) I.R.C. fecit	Dec. 1819
37. *ibd.*		Mr Elliston (portrait uncoloured).	
38. p.	73.	Mr Wilkinson as Roger Sieveskall I.R.C. fecit	Jan. 1820
39. p.	105.	Mr Young as Rolla (coloured) F. Crawley	Feb. ,,
40. p.	129.	Miss O'Neill as Juliet (uncoloured)	March ,,
41. p.	153.	Mr Matthews at his At Home of 1820 (uncoloured)	April ,,
42. p.	173.	Mrs Jordan (uncoloured)	May ,,
43. p.	197.	Mr Kean as Lear (uncoloured)	June ,,
44. p.	221.	Mr H. Johnston (uncoloured)	July ,,
45. p.	237.	Mrs W. S. Chatterley as Marguerite (uncoloured)	August ,,
46. p.	261.	Mr Stephen Kemble (uncoloured)	Sept. ,,
47. p.	285.	Mrs H. Johnston (uncoloured)	Oct ,,
48. p.	309.	Mrs Bartley (uncoloured)	Nov ,,
49. p.	333.	Mr T. P. Cooke as Salvador (uncoloured)	Dec ,,

VOL. V.—Title as before dated 1821 + Address 2 pp. + Text pp. 1–420 + Index 2 ll. (pp. 409–412).

50. p.	1.	Madame Vestris as Don Giovanni (coloured) I. R. Cruikshank	Jan. 1821
51. p.	33.	Mr Grimaldi as Clown (coloured) I. R. Cruikshank	Feb. ,,
52. p.	65.	Miss Wilson as Mundane (coloured) I. R. Cruikshank	March ,,
53. p.	97.	Mr Matthews in his At Home of 1821 (coloured) I. R. Cruikshank	April ,,
54. p.	129.	Mr Liston as Lord Grizzle (coloured) P. Roberts	May ,,
55. p.	161.	Miss Stephens as the Second Violetta (coloured) Percy Roberts	June ,,
56. p.	201.	Mr Harley as Laporello (coloured) I. R. Cruikshank	July ,,
57. p.	241.	Mr Mackay as Bailie Nicol Jarvis (coloured) J. Brooks	August ,,
58. p.	242.	New Theatre Haymarket (coloured).	
59. p.	279.	Portrait from "The Steel Glass."	
60. p.	281.	Mrs Bland as Madge (coloured) Brooks	Sept. ,,
61. p.	321.	Mrs Egerton as Justice Woodcock (coloured) Brooks	Oct. ,,
62. p.	337.	New Haymarket Theatre (coloured).	
63. p.	361.	Mr Munden (coloured)	Nov. ,,
64. p.	393.	Mr Liston as Dominie Sampson	Dec. ,,

VOL. VI.—No title, January & February only when "British Stage" ceased publication pp. 1–88.

65. p.	1.	Mr W. Farren as Sir Fretful Plagiary (uncoloured)	Jan. 1822
66. p.		The Globe & Bear Garden Theatres (uncoloured lithograph)	Feb. ,,

Issued in 62 parts. Six reprints of plays were advertised in one of the parts of which 5 are sometimes found bound up at the end of Vol. VI. The first plate is to be found in two states.

288 KIDD (J. B.)

Illustrations of Jamaica in a Series of Views comprising the Principal Towns Harbours and Scenery. London & Kingston

Large Folio.   1840

50 lithograph plates.   All marked from nature and on stone, by J. B. Kidd, except plate 27 (on stone by J. B. Kidd from a Sketch by his brother William).

1. Plantain Trees.
2. Stewart Town Trelawney.
3. Western Favel Estate Trelawney.
4. Retreat Penn St. Anns.
5. Town of Falmouth Jamaica.

6. The Date Tree.   Sugar Works in distance.
7. Windward Falls nr Kingston.
8. Parade & Upper Part of Kingston from the Church.
9. View on Hope River near Dunsinane.

Kidd's Jamaica (*contd.*)

10. Fort Antonio.
11. Bamboos & Cotton Tree Westmoreland.
12. Rio Bueno.
13. Retirement Estate St James's.
14. Savanah La Mar.
15. Cocoanut Walk on Coast near Runaway Bay.
16. Mountain Cottage Scene.
17. City of Kingston from Commercial Rooms E.
18.   ,,   ,,   ,,   ,,   N.
19.   ,,   ,,   ,,   ,,   S.
20.   ,,   ,,   ,,   ,,   W.
21. Sea side Grape.
22. Lethe Estate on Great River St James's and Harbour.
23. Distant View of the Plains of Westmoreland looking towards Savannah La Mar.
24. Distant View Port Royal & Kingston from a height near the Apostles Battery.
25. Morant Bay.
26. Palm & Banana Trees.
27. Ferry Inn on the road to Spanish Town.
28. Port Royal.
29. Vessels leaving Port Royal.
30. View on Spanish River near Buff Bay.
31. Wild Fig, or Indian God Tree.
32. Town of Bath St. Thomas in the East.
33. St Ann's Bay.
34. The Bog Walk St Thomas in the Vale.
35. Stewart Castle Estate Trelawney.
36. Fern Tree on banks of Rio Grande.
37. Clermont Pen St Marys Anotto Bay in the Distance.
38. Port Maris Cabaretta Is. &c. from Pagee point.
39. Annotto Bay from the Shipping.
40. Belle View Residence near Kingston, Stoney Hill in the Distance.
41. Makaw Trees. St Georges.
42. Ochio Rios Bay St. Anns.
43. Spanish Town from Beacon Hill.
44. Country Residence near Kingston.
45. Lucea from the Coast near Point Estate.
46. Mt. Cabbage Trees. Scene in the Blue Mountains.
47. Kingston Church.
48. Scene at Up Park Camp.
49. Montego Bay from Upton Hill.
50. Black River.

Rare. The finest large scale coloured plates on Jamaica. Plates 1–30, and 33 bear, Printed by W. Clerk or W. Clerk lithog. (except plate 12 which has no imprint). Plates 31, 32 and 34 to 50 bear imprint of Barwick, 2 Shorter's Court, Throgmorton St.

289 KINSEY (Revd. W. M.)

Portugal Illustrated, By the Revd. W. M. Kinsey, B.D. fellow of Trinity College, Oxford, and Chaplain to the Right Hon. Lord Auckland (2 line rule) vignette (arms of Portugal)

Octavo.   1828

COLLATION.—Engraved title as above (v. blank) + Dedication 1 p. (v. blank) + Preface pp. v–xii + Contents xiii–xvii + List of Plates 1 p. (v. Observations) + Text pp. 1–500 + 2 unnumbered leaves + "Second Supplementary Letter" pp. 1–40 + Map + uncoloured plates of views &c. + 9 coloured aquatint plates of Portuguese costume.

1. front.   University of Coimbra.
2. p.   1. Map Portugal.
3. p.   69. Modinhas.
4. p. 122. View of Cintra.
5. p. 154. Plates of Coins.
6. p. 171. View of the Douro.
7. p. 215. Estalagen or Portuguese Inn.
8. p. 224. Aloe in Blossom.
9. p. 234. Travellers in Portugal.
10. p. 255. A Roadside Altar.
11. p. 260. View from fortress of Valenca.
12. p. 271. Night Scene Ponte de Lima.
13. p. 284. Peasant & Family of Minho.
14. p. 312. View across the Douro.
15. p. 350. View down the Douro.
16. p. 408. Castle of Leiria.
17. p. 420. Batalha.

The 9 coloured costume plates bear imprint London Published May 1st 1828 by Messrs Treuttel Wurtz & Co. Soho Square.

1. Senhor P. Mestre Fs. Domingos—Carmelito—Congregado—Mening Orfao.
2. Dominicana—Bernarda Carmelite Nun—Franciscan Nun—Carmelita.

Kinsey's Portugal (*contd.*)

3. Carmelito Descalcado—Carmelite Monk Calcado—Monk of the Franciscan Order—Portuguese Priest Loyo.
4. Female Peasant in the Market Place of Braga—Portuguese Peasant in Holiday Dress—Desembagador or Magistrate—Peasant of Guimaraens.
5. Females of the Better Class in the remote parts of the Minho Province—Females as attired in Portuguese Towns.
6. Female Peasant selling Onions—A Dealer in Honey Cakes—A Peasant in Straw Dress—Lisbon Beggar.
7. A Farmer of the Minho Province—Peasant of the Alentejo—Gallego or Water Carrier of Lisbon—Gallego or Water Carrier of Porto.
8. Peasant selling Ducks at Porto—Fishwoman of Porto—Market Woman of Porto—Fisherman of Ilkaro.
9. Female Peasant of the Tras os Montes—Benta—Frigideira dealer in roasted chestnuts—Beggar Boy.

290 LAMB (Charles)

Felissa; or, the Life and Opinions of a Kitten of Sentiment (rule)

> We'll have our Mottos and Our Chapters too,
> And Brave the thunders of the dread Review,
> Misses no more o'er Misses' woes shall wail,
> But List attentive—to a Kitten's tale.

(thick and thin rule) London: Printed for J. Harris, Corner of St Paul's Churchyard.

1811

COLLATION.—Title as above (v. S. Gosnell, Printer, Little Queen Street, London) + Contents 1 p. (v. blank) + pp. 1–131 + 12 coloured plates.

1. p. 10. Sad Disaster.	7. p. 82. The Poet.
2. p. 23. Departure from the Castle.	8. p. 87. The Alarm.
3. p. 46. Grosvenor Square.	9. p. 93. The Inn.
4. p. 57. The Parsonage House.	10. p. 99. Escape from Drowning.
5. p. 61. Poor Colley.	11. p. 112. Pussy Puzzler.
6. p. 71. The Most Charitable Lady Living.	12. p. 122. Alls well that Ends Well.

291 LANDMANN (George)

Historical, Military, and Picturesque Observations on Portugal, illustrated by seventy-five coloured plates, including authentic plans of the sieges and battles fought in the peninsula during the late war (thick and thin rule) By George Landmann, Lieutenant-Colonel in the Corps of Royal Engineers, the same rank in the Spanish Corps of Engineers, with Brevet Rank of Colonel (thin and thick rule) In Two Volumes (thick and thin rule) Vol. I [II] (thin and thick rule) London (thin and thick rule) Printed for T. Cadell and W. Davies, Strand By W. Bulmer and Co. Cleveland-Row, St James's

2 vols.   Folio.   1818

COLLATION VOL. I.—Half-title "Historical, Military, and Picturesque Observations on Portugal." (v. blank) + Title as above (v. blank) + Dedication to Prince Regent 1 p. (v. blank) + Preface 2 leaves + Directions to Binder 1 leaf + Analytical Summary pp. i–xvi + pp. 1–607 + 20 plates and plans.

1. p. 230. First Degree Torture Inquisition.
2. *ibd.*   Second Degree Torture Inquisition   I. C. Stadler sc.
3. *ibd.*   Third Degree Torture Inquisition.
4. *ibd.*   Fourth Degree Torture Inquisition.

Landmann's Portugal (contd.)

5. p. 454. French Coin General Junot.
6. *ibd.* Spanish Coin.
7. p. 472. Action of Rolica (plan).
8. p. 476. Sketch Action Vimiero (plan).
9. p. 512. Plan action Corunna.
10. p. 529. Plan Battle Talavera.
11. p. 539. Plan Battle Busaco.
12. p. 545. Plan of Tarifa & Island.
13. p. 549. Sketch Action Hill of Barrosa.
14. p. 555. Plan of Badajoz.
15. p. 556. Plan Battle of Albuera.
16. p. 564. Sketch Disposition of Allies Arroyo Molinos.
17. p. 565. Plan Attack Ciudad Rodrigo.
18. p. 572. Plan Battle Arapiles near Salamanca.
19. p. 578. Plan attack city of Burgos.
20. p. 588. Plan Fortress of St Sebastian.

VOL. II.—Half-title as before (v. blank) + Title as before (v. blank) + Contents i–x + Appendix xi–xii + Directions to Binder 1 leaf + pp. 1–293 + 1 blank leaf [sig pp. 4] + sub-title "Documents" 1 leaf [*B] + pp. 3–203 + sub-title "Appendix" + pp. 3–132 + 56 plates.

21. p. 43. Torre Velha de Belem from West   John Jeakes sculpt.
22. p. 48. Palmella, from road leading to Moila   J. C. Stadler sculpt.
23. *ibd.* Town & Harbour of Setubal   C. Landmann delt.   J. C. Stadler sculpt.
24. p. 49. Alcacer do Sal, antiently called Salacia from North   Engraved by J. Hill.
25. *ibd.* Alcacer do Sal from the East   Havell sculpt. (folding).
26. p. 63. Scene on the River Veiras at Mertolla   J. Ogborne sculpt.
27. *ibd.* Mertola from the North   J. C. Stadler sculpt.
28. p. 77. *Faro the Capital of Algarve   G. Landmann delt.   Baily sculpt. (folding).
29. p. 81. Aljustrel from the East   I. Baily sculpt.
30. p. 118. Albofeira from near the road leading to Faro [no engraver given].
31. *ibd.* Albofeira, and the Sea Coast from the East   Engraved by J. Hill.
32. p. 123. Villa Nova de Portimaõ   G. Landmann delt.   J. C. Stadler sculpt.
33. *ibd.* Entrance of the Harbour of Portimaõ   John Jeakes sculpt.
34. p. 124. Silves, the antient capital of Algarve   G. Landmann delt.   J. C. Stadler sculpt.
35. p. 125. Silves from the East   I. Baily sculpt.
36. p. 128. Hot Baths, in the Mountain of Monchique   Hill sculpt.
37. p. 129. Monchique, near Cape San Vicente   J. Baily sculpt.
38. p. 130. Opomar Velho, in the Mountains of Monchique   J. Hill sculpt.
39. p. 134. Sea Coast near Lagos and the Battery called O Pinhaõ   G. Landmann delt.   Baily sculpt.
40. *ibd.* Bay & Harbour of Lagos from O Pinhaõ   Hill sculpt.
41. p. 135. Lagos Bridge Algarve   G. Landmann delt.   J. C. Stadler sculpt.
42. p. 141. Aljezar from the South   J. C. Stadler sculpt.
43. p. 144. Villa Nova de Mil Fontes   J. C. Stadler sculpt.
44. p. 151. Arroyolos antiently called Calentica   G. Landmann delt.   J. C. Stadler sculpt.
45. p. 152. Estremoz, from the Road leading to Elvas.   John Jeakes sculpt.
46. p. 163. *Cintra from the Lisbon Road   Hill sculpt (folding).
47. p. 166. Convent near Cintra on the Highest pinnacle of the rock of Lisboa [no engraver].
48. p. 168. Convent on the highest part of the Rock of Lisboa   J. Baily sc.
49. p. 169. *Cintra from the road leading to Mafra   G. Landmann delt.   J. C. Stadler sculpt. (folding).
50. p. 170. Royal Palace of Mafra   I. Baily sculpt.
51. p. 181. Punhete at the Junction of the river Zezere with the Tejo   I. Baily sculp.
52. p. 194. From the Castle of Abrantes antiently called Tubuci   I. Baily sc.
53. p. 198. Bridge and Ford on the River Niza on the road from Villa Velha to Niza   G. Landmann delt.   J. C. Stadler sculpt.
54. p. 199. Flying Bridge on the Tejo   G. Landmann delt.   J. C. Stadler sculpt.
55. p. 202. Ford on the River Sever between Montalvao in Portugal & Herrera in Spain   G. Landmann delt.   J. C. Stadler sculpt.

Landmann's Portugal (*contd.*)

56. p. 211. Pass in the Mountains near Ladeira [no engraver].
57. p. 213. *Mouth of the Tejo   G. Landmann delt. (folding).
58. *ibd.*   *Lisboa or Lisbon [no artist or engraver given] (folding).
59. *ibd.*   *View up the Tejo   J. C. Stadler sculpt. (folding).
60. *ibd.*   Torres Vedras from the N.   G. Landmann delt.   J. C. Stadler sculpt.
61. p. 228. Sir Arthur Wellesleys Quarters Vimiero   G. Landmann delt.   J. C. Stadler sculpt.
62. p. 228. Vimiero from the road leading to Lorinha   Jn. Jeakes sculpt.
63. p. 240. Leiria, antiently called Collipo   J. Baily sculpt.
64. p. 241. Pombal & Bridge from the S.W.   I. Baily sculpt.
65. p. 247. City of Coimbra . . . from near the Bridge [no engraver].
66. p. 247. *City of Coimbra from the South   G. Landmann delt.   J. C. Stadler sculpt. (folding).
67. p. 254. Bridge of Boats at Porto, on the River Douro   I. Baily sculp.
68. p. 259. *Penafiel de Sousa from the East Entre Douro e Minho   Baily sculp. (folding).
69. p. 261. Amarante on the River Tamega [no engraver].
70. *ibd.*   Amarante and Bridge from the Convent of San Domingo   I. Baily sculp.
71. p. 268. Fountain opposite the Inn at Ponte de Lima   G. Landmann delt.   J. C. Stadler sculpt.
72. *ibd.*   *Ponte de Lima antiently called Forum Limicorum [no engraver given] (folding).
73. p. 271. *Valena do Minho   J. C. Stadler sculpt. (folding).
74. p. 276. City of Tug on the Mino   G. Landmann delt.   J. C. Stadler sculpt.
75. p. 279. Head of the Bay of Vigo   G. Landmann delt.   J. C. Stadler sculpt.
76. *ibd.*   Near San Payo on the road to Redondela looking towards Vigo   G. Landmann del.   J. Ogborne sculp.

Plate 25 is additional, not being given in the List of Plates.   Published in 14 monthly parts at 1 guinea a part.   The most beautiful illustrated English book on Portugal of the period.

292 LATROBE (Rev. C. I.)

Journal of a Visit to South Africa, in 1815, and 1816.   With Some Account of the Missionary Settlements of the United Brethren near the Cape of Good Hope (thick and thin rule) By the Rev. C. I. Latrobe (thin and thick rule) London: Published by L. B. Seeley, 169, Fleet Street, and R. Ackermann, 101, Strand. (short thick and thin rule).

Quarto.   1818

COLLATION.—Title as above (v. blank) + Dedication 1 p. (v. blank) + Preface 3 pp. (v–vii) + Directions to Binder 1 p. (viii) + pp. 1–406 (including index) + Map + 4 plates of panoramas in outline + 12 coloured aquatint plates.

Each coloured plate is marked, Drawn by R. Cocking from a sketch by C. Latrobe (except plates 6 and 8 which are drawn by R. Cocking from a sketch by Mr. Melville).   All Plates bear Ackermann's imprint and date April 1818.

Map to face title " The Southern Division of the Cape of Good Hope Colony (folding).
1. p. 43. Missionary House & Church of Groenekloof.   Cape of Good Hope.   Engraved by Stadler.
2. p. 59. Approach to Gnadenthal Crossing the River Sonderend   Engraved by J. Bluck.
3. p. 64. Interior of the Church at Gnadenthal   D. Havell sculpt.
4. p. 94. General View of the Missionaries' Premises, & Part of the Village of Gnadenthal   Engraved by J. Bluck.
   p. 121. Outline of the Mountains between Gnadenthal & Zwellendam (uncoloured).
5. p. 139. Mossel Bay on the Indian Ocean   D. Havell sculpt.
6. p. 150. Kayman's Gat Plettenberg bay.   Engraved by J. Bluck.
7. p. 152. Trekatackaw in Plettenberg Bay   D. Havell sc.
8. p. 170. The Paerdekop   D. Havell sculpt.
9. p. 188. Encampment at Essenbosch in the District of Uitenhagen   J. Bluck sculpt.
10. p. 271. Interior of the Missionaries' Premises at Gnadenthal   Stadler sculpt.
   p. 293. Outline of Simons Bay, Mountains of Stellenbosch &c. (uncoloured).

Latrobe's South Africa (*contd.*)

11. p. 331. Missionary Settlement at Groenekloof   Stadler sculpt.
    p. 359. Outline of the Environs of the Cape (uncoloured).
12. p. 374. Distant View of Longwood, St. Helena across Devil's Punch Bowl   J. Bluck sculpt.
    p. 385. Outline of Ascension Island (uncoloured).

293 LAURENT (P. E.)

Recollections of a Classical Tour through various parts of Greece, Turkey, and Italy, made in the years 1818 & 1819 (wavy rule). By Peter Edmund Laurent (wavy rule) Illustrated with coloured plates (thick and thin rule) London, Printed for G & W. B. Whittaker, Ave-Maria Lane.

Quarto.   1821

COLLATION.—Title as above (v. Oxford Printed by Munday and Slatter) + Dedication 1 p. (v. blank) + Preface pp. V–VI + Contents pp. VII–XI + Corrigenda 1 p. + pp 1–317 + Index 3 leaves + coloured aquatint plates, each with imprint, Published by G. & W. B. Whittaker. London.

1. Front. Turkish Women Travelling.
2. p. 70. Infy. Officer of Janissaries.   Greek Sailor.
3. p. 91. A Turkish Girl.   Greek Ladies at Constantinople.
   p. 116. Diploma (uncoloured).
4. p. 160. Albanians in the Morea.

294 LEAR (Edward)

Views in Rome and its Environs; Drawn from Nature and on Stone, by Edward Lear. (coloured vignette view of Ostia, Edward Lear, delt. et lit.,)

Folio.   [1841]

COLLATION.—Title as above + 25 coloured plates + 4 pp. (royal octavo of Text and Subscribers).

Each plate marked, Edward Lear, del., et lith.,

1. Ancient Gate of Alatri.	14. Roiate.
2. Braccians.	15. Rome from Monte Pincio.
3. Campagne of Rome from Villa Mattei.	16. Rome from Convent de S.S. Giovanni & Paula.
4. Cervera.	17. Via Porta Pinciana Rome.
5. Civitella de Subiaco.	18. Rome from Via della Porta San Paolo.
6. Collepardo.	19. Rome from above Porta Portese.
7. Frascati.	20. Girano fair of Sant 'Anatolia.
8. Gennazzano.	21. Sanbuci.
9. L'Ariccia.	22. Subiaco.
10. Lake at Nemi.	23. Tivoli.
11. Norba.	24. Tivoli.
12. Olevano.	25. Valmontone.
13. Rocca Giovane.	

295 LEECH (John)

The Comic History of England.   By Gilbert Abbott A'Beckett (vignette "Clio Instructing the Young British Lion In History") With Ten coloured Etchings, and One Hundred

Leech's Comic History of England (*contd.*)
and Twenty Woodcuts By John Leach.   Vol. I [II] Published at the Punch Office, 58, Fleet Street

2 vols. Octavo.   1847 [–8]

COLLATION VOL. I.—Half-title printed in red "The Comic History of England." (v. blank) + Title as above in red and black (v. London: Bradbury and Evans Printers White-friars) + Preface 2 pp. (v–vi) + Contents of Vol. I 2 pp. (vii–viii) + Engravings on Steel 1 p. + Engravings on wood 3 pp. (x–xii) + Text pp. 1–320 + 10 coloured steel engravings.

1. Landing of Julius Caesar front. or p. 1.
2. William inspecting the Volunteers previous to the invasion of England p. 55.
3. Terrific combat between Richard Coeur de Lion and Saladin p. 93.
4. King John Signing Magna Charta p. 111.
5. Edward's Arm in the Hands of his Medical Advisers p. 129.
6. Queen Philippa interceding with Edward III for the Six Burgesses of Calais p. 175.
7. Coronation of Henry the Fourth (from the best Authorities) p. 209.
8. Embarkation of King Henry the Fifth at Southampton A.D. 1415 p. 227.
9. Marriage of Henry the Sixth with Margaret of Anjou p. 265.
10. The Battle of Bosworth Field: A Scene in the Great Drama of History p. 303.

VOL. II.—Half-title printed in red as before + Title as before but dated 1848 + Advertisement to the Second Volume 2 pp. (v–vi) + Contents of Vol. II 2 pp. (vii–viii) + Engravings on Steel 1 p. (v. blank) + Engravings on wood 2 pp. (xi–xii) + pp. 1–304 + 10 coloured steel engravings.

1. Henry VIIIth meeting Francis 1st front. or p. 1.
2. Henry the 8th and his Queen "out a Maying" p. 47.
3. Henry VIII Monk-Hunting p. 69.
4. Queen Elizabeth and Sir Walter Raleigh p. 114.
5. Discovery of Guido Fawkes by Suffolk and Mounteagle p. 133.
6. "Take away that Bauble" Cromwell dissolving the long Parliament p. 188.
7. The Royal Oak. The Pendrill Family have no idea where Charles is!!! p. 212.
8. Evening Party—Time of Charles II p. 227.
9. The Battle of the Boyne p. 258.
10. Georgey Porgey the First going out for a ride in his State coachy Poachy p. 288.

In all 20 coloured plates and 240 woodcut illustrations by John Leech. Issued in 19/20 monthly parts in paper wrappers and on completion in cloth at one guinea. This work is usually listed under A'Beckett, but its value is almost entirely due to Leech. A'Beckett's text is amusing if read in snatches, but 624 pages of unremitting forced wit becomes monotonous, and few would keep the book but for the illustrations. The coloured plates are beautifully rendered, and though the woodcuts do not compare in execution with the etched plates they are as fine in conception, and show infinitely more subtle humour than the text. Among the most popular and best of Leech's work.

The half-titles in first issue must be printed in red.

296 LEECH (John). A'BECKET

Comic History of England.

COLLATION OF PARTS.—Issued in 20 parts (in 19 wrappers, the last two parts issued together) in blue paper wrappers. Lettered on front No. I (XIX–XX) July 1846 to February 1848, Price 1s. The Comic History of England (vignette, Clio instructing the Young British

Leech's Comic History of England (*contd.*)

Lion in History). By Gilbert Abbott A'Beckett. (rule). Illustrated by Leech. (rule). London: Punch Office, 85 Fleet Street, and all Booksellers (all within printed border, below) Bradbury & Evans 1846 (48), Printers, Whitefriars.

Part   I. July 1846. pp. 1–32. Wrappers, p. 2 Contents, p. 3 Work by A'Becket, p. 4 Prospectus of Comic History.

„   II. August 1846. pp. 33–64. Wrappers, p. 2 Contents, p. 3 Advt., Rowlands Kalydor +p. 4 Advt., Burton's Shaves Baths.

„   III. September 1846. pp. 65–96. Wrappers, p. 2 Contents, p. 3 Advt., Rowlands Kalydor +p. 4 Advt., Burton's Shaves Baths. Insert Advt., of Dickens Dombey & Son. (Oliver Twist etc.,)

„   IV. October 1846. pp. 97–128, Wrappers, p. 2 Contents, p. 3 Advt., Rowlands Odonto etc., p. 4 Advt., The Music Book.

„   V. November 1846. pp. 129–160. Wrappers, p. 2 Contents, p. 3 Opinions of Press on Comic History, p. 4 Advt., Rowlands Macassar Oil, 3 inserts. Advts., Dombey 1 lf. Punch 1 small lf. The Music Book 1 lf.

„   VI. December 1846. pp. 161–192. Wrappers, p. 2 Contents, p. 3 Advt., Vanity Fair, p. 4 Advt., Rowlands Macassar Oil etc., 2 inserts, pink slip advt. Battle of Life, Dombey etc. Advt. Punch 1 small lf.,

„   VII. January 1847. pp. 193–224. Wrappers, p. 2 Contents, p. 3 Advt. Music Book etc., p. 4 Adt. Rowlands Macassar Oil. 8 inserts, 4 leaves of pink paper, advertising Vanity Fair, Bechsteins Cage Birds, Works by Dickens, Punch, Daily News etc., +4 leaves of white paper, advertising Chambers Journal (pp. 1–2) and Orr's Publications (pp. 3–8).

„   VIII. February 1847. pp. 225—256 wrappers, p. 2 Contents, p. 3 Advt. Music Book etc. p. 4 Advt. People's Journal etc.

„   IX. March 1847. pp. 257–288. Wrappers, p. 2 Contents, p. 3 Advt. Music Book etc., p. 4 Advt., Dombey etc., 2 leaves insert, Cheap Edition of Dickens Works, with specimen page of Pickwick.

„   X. April 1847. pp. 289–320. Wrappers, p. 2 Contents, p. 3 Advt. The Music Book, p. 4 Advt. Dombey etc.,

„   XI. May 1847. pp. 1–28 +Half-title, printed in red +Title Vol. I +List of Plates & woodcuts 2 ll. +Preface 1 lf. +Contents 1 lf. Wrappers, p. 2 Contents, p. 3 Advt. Elements of Botany etc., p. 4 Advt., Dombey etc.,

„   XII. June 1847. pp. 29–60. Wrappers, p. 2 Contents, p. 3 Advt. Music Book, p. 4 Advt. Works by A'Beckett & Jerrold.

„   XIII. July 1847. pp. 61–92. Wrappers, p. 2 Contents, p. 3 Advt. Music Book, p. 4 Works by A'Beckett, & Vanity Fair.

„   XIV. August 1847. pp. 93–124. Wrappers, p. 2 Contents, p. 3 Advt. Music Book, p. 4 Advt. Works by A'Becket Vanity Fair.

„   XV. September 1847. pp. 125–156. Wrappers, p. 2 Contents, p. 3 Advt. Music Book, p. 4 Advt. Punch and Vanity Fair.

„   XVI. October 1847. pp. 157–188. Wrappers, p. 2 Contents, p. 3 Advt. Lytton's Novels, p. 4 Advt. Punch's Pocket Book etc. 2 ll. insertion Lytton's Works.

„   XVII. November 1847. pp. 189–220. Wrappers, p. 2 Contents, p. 3 Advt. Vanity Fair, p. 4 Punch's Pocket Book etc.

„   XVIII. December 1847. pp. 221–252. Wrappers, p. 2 Contents, p. 3 Advt. Works A'Beckett & Jerrold, p. 4 Punch Almanac 1848.

Parts XIX and XX. February 1848. pp. 253–304 +Half-title, Title, Advt. Contents + Illustrations to Vol. II (6 ll.). Wrappers, p. 2 Contents, p. 3 Advt. The Callantee Show, p. 4 Advt. Vanity Fair. (Price this part 2/-) Each part has 1 coloured plate.

297 LEECH (John)

Comic History of England Undated Edition. The 2 vols. issued in 1 vol. 8vo. red or green cloth with gilt design of Clio instructing the Young British Lion in History on upper cover, gilt back containing 3 figures also taken from Leech's designs, gilt edges.

Leech's Comic History of England (*contd.*)

COLLATION VOL. I.—Half-title printed in black + Title "The Comic History of Eng-land. By Gilbert Abbott A'Beckett (vignette) with twenty coloured etchings, and two hundred woodcuts by John Leech, London: Bradbury, Evans, and Co., 11 Bouverie Street" (v. blank) + Preface 2 pp. + Contents of Vols. I and II 4 pp. + Engravings on Steel 2 pp. + Engravings on Wood 5 pp. (in all pp. i–xviii) + pp. 1–320 + pp. 1–304. The coloured plates are the same as in the first edition.

Reissued 1863; 1881, and an Edition de Luxe undated with the illustrations on China paper.

298 LEECH (John)

The Comic History of Rome By Gilbert Abbot à Beckett. Illustrated by John Leech (within woodcut composition of figures illustrative of the History) Bradbury and Evans, 11, Bouverie Street

Octavo. [1851]

COLLATION.—Half-title "The Comic History of Rome, from the founding of the City to the end of the Commonwealth" (v. blank) + Title as above (v. London: Bradbury and Evans, Printers, Whitefriars) + Preface 2 pp. (v–vi) + Contents 2 pp. (vii–viii) + Engravings on Steel 1 p. (v. blank) + Engravings on wood 2 pp. (xi–xii) + pp. 1–308 + 10 coloured plates.

1. Romulus and Remus discovered by a gentle shepherd p. 1.
2. Tarquinius Superbus makes himself king p. 33.
3. Appius Claudius punished by the People p. 80.
4. The gallant Curtius leaping into the gulf p. 104.
5. Pyrrhus arrives in Italy with his Troupe p. 138.
6. Hannibal, whilst even yet a child, swears eternal hatred to the Romans p. 168.
7. Flaminius restoring liberty to Greece at the Isthonian Games p. 195.
8. The Mother of the Gracchi p. 234.
9. Marius discovered in the Marches at Miturnae p. 261.
10. Cicero denouncing Catiline p. 292.

In all 10 coloured plates and 98 woodcuts in the text. Issued in 9/10 parts in paper wrappers and on completion in green cloth with gilt design on side taken from woodcut on p. 246, gilt lettered on back with 3 figures in gilt, Caius Gracchus at foot copied from woodcut on p. 244 and 2 other figures, Roman eagle and Soldier that do not appear in text.

More rare than the Comic History of England.

A later issue was printed identical with the above but with the addition to the imprint of the words "and Co," Reading Bradbury Evans, and Co. Printers Whitefriars, at foot of pictorial title, verso and foot of p. 308.

299 LEECH (J.)

Mr. Briggs & His Doings. Fishing (vignette, Mr Briggs anxious to become a Complete Angler, studies the "Gentle" Art of Fly Fishing) By John Leech. London: Published by Bradbury and Evans, 11 Bouverie Street, Fleet Street.

Oblong Folio.

COLLATION.—A Series of 12 plates, issued in brown paper covers, without title or text, except title as above, which is printed on page 1 of cover.

1. Mr Briggs contemplates a Days Fishing, and practises with his running tackle.
2. Mr Briggs wont have a man with him, as he thinks he can manage the Punt by himself.

Leech's Mr Briggs and His Doings (*contd.*)

3. Mr Briggs tries for many hours a likely place for Perch.
4. Triumphant Success of Mr Briggs.
5. Mr Briggs is so fortunate as to catch a large Eel.
6. Mr Briggs through the influence of a friend, has a days Spring fishing.
7. Mr Briggs goes out Fly Fishing.
8. Mr Briggs as he appeared from six in the morning until three in the afternoon trying for a Salmon.
9. Mr Briggs having hooked a "Fish" is landed to play it.
10. On arriving at Hells Hole, Mr B. is detained for three quarters of an hour, while the Fish sulks at the bottom.
11. The Fish having refreshed himself, bolts again with Mr B.
12. After a long and exciting struggle, Mr B. is on the point of landing his prize.

300 LEECH (John)

"Young Troublesome" or (coloured vignette, "Here Master Jacky is supposed to have arrived per railway (grown out of all knowledge)") Master Jacky's Holidays (rule). London: Bradbury & Evans, 11 Bouverie Street,

Oblong Folio.

COLLATION.—Half-title "Young Troublesome;" or Master Jacky's Holidays" (v. Persons Represented) + Title as above (v. blank) + 12 coloured plates by Leech (including Title).

1. Title.
2. Here you have him celebrating his arrival, (to the disturbance of Mr Phoenix) with various althletic exercises.
3. Here you have him on a wet day bored to death.   (etc.)
4. Here you have him, in pursuance of a bright thought, playing at cricket in the drawing room.
5. Here Captain Clarence arrives with the Theatre Royal.   (etc.)
6. Here you have Mr Phoenix delivering a lecture on general propriety.   (etc.)
7. Grand evening rehearsal of Miller and his Men.   (etc.)
8. Here you have 'old Bradshaw under the influence of tobacco.   (etc.)
9. Here he bolsters 'old Bradshaw.   (etc.)
10. He embellishes the legs of Ruggles with a burnt stick.   (etc.)
11. Here you have him privileged to leave the dining room with the Ladies.   (etc.)
12. Here you have him presiding over a Juvenile Party at the close of the Holidays.

Leech (John).   See also under Surtees.

301 LEIGH (S.)

Leigh's New Picture of London [&c.] . . . Third Edition London Printed for Samuel Leigh 18 Strand by W. Clowes Northumberland-Court

Duodecimo.   1819

COLLATION.—Title as above + Contents 2 pp. + Preface 4 pp. + pp. 1–510 + General Index 511–524 + Index to Leigh's New Plan of London pp. 1–36 + Works pub. by Leigh 4 ll. This work includes "Costumes of the Lower Orders of the Metropolis" T. L. B(usby), consisting of 24 coloured plates.

1. Newsboy blowing trumpet with title as above.	4. Pedlar.	8. Drayman.
2. Rabbits.	5. Postman.	9. Ballad Singer.
3. Old Clothes.	6. Sweep.	10. Dogs Meat.
	7. Beggar.	11. Scavenger.

Leigh's New Picture of London (*contd.*)

12. Scissors Grinder.	17. Matches.	21. Raree Show.
13. Coal Heaver.	18. Onions.	22. Door Mats.
14. Milk.	19. Kettles to mend.	23. Mackarel.
15. Watchman.	20. Chickens.	24. Waterman.
16. Water Cresses.		

Issued as follows: 6s. bound, 9s. with 108 views inserted, 12s. with 108 views and 24 coloured costume plates as above, and at 15s. with the series of 54 coloured costumes by Rowlandson.

Le Sage Gil Blas 1819. See under Clark (I).

Lessons of Thrift 1820. See under [Cruikshank (I. R.)].

302 LEWIS

Lewis's Sketches of Spain & Spanish Character made during his Tour in that Country in the years 1833-4 (vignette, a scene in the arena Seville) Drawn on Stone from his original Sketches entirely by himself. (two line rule) London Published by F. Moon, Printseller to the King, 20 Threadneedle Street and John F Lewis, 78, Wimpole Street (two line rule) Printed at O. Hullmandel's Lithographic Establishment 49, Gt. Marlborough Street

Folio.   [1836]

COLLATION.—Title as above (v. blank) + Dedication to David Wilkie 1 p. (v. List of Plates) + 25 plates.

1. Front. Peasants dancing the Bolero.	14. Jose Maria, a Brigand.
2. Mendicant Monks receiving alms.	15. Gitanilla Gipsy girls of Ronda.
3. Bull Fighter a Scene in the Arena.	16. Gibraltar Smuggling Feluchos.
4. Plaza de San Francisco Seville.	17. Jewish woman of Gibraltar in Fiesta Dress.
5. Las Dos Hermanos (Spanish Ladies in Maja Dress.	18. Guacin Smugglers coming out of Gibraltar.
6. La Puerta del Sol Madrid.	19. Mosque at Cordova the Cathedral.
7. Contrabandistas Andalucia.	20. Mendicant Monks Granada.
8. Granada Distant View of Sierra Nevada.	21. Cordova Chapel of the Villa Viciosa.
9. Seville Peasant Girl on a mule.	22. Granada Peasants.
10. Ronda Andalusia.	23. El Prior.
11. Muleteers of Ronda, Andalusia.	24. Toledo Sala Capitular.
12. A Convent Door Toledo (San Juan de los Reyes).	25. Interior of a Posada Segovia.
13. A Girl of Seville.	Vignette on Title Mules dragging out dead bull after the combat Seville Arena.

Issued in imperial folio at £4 4s. or with the plates coloured and mounted in imitation of original drawings £10 10s. in portfolio.

Life of Napoleon. See under [Combe (W.)].

Life of a Sportsman. See under [Apperley (C. J.)].

Lory (J.) Picturesque Tour. See under Schoberl (F.).

303 LOUTHERBOURG (P. J. de)

Picturesque Scenery of Great Britain Published by R. Bowyer Historic Gallery Pall Mall

Oblong Folio.   1801

Loutherbourg's Great Britain (*contd.*)

COLLATION.—Engraved title (v. blank) + Text 1 p. (v. blank) + 6 plates engraved by J. C. Stadler after P. J. de Loutherbourg.

1. Ramsgate, in a High Gale.
2. Ramsgate, with a View of the New Light-House.
3. Margate, with the Arrival of the Hoy.
4. Margate, from the Parade.
5. Brighthelmstone, Fisherman Returning.
6. Fisherman going out at Worthing.

Issued in blue paper wrappers.

304 LOUTHERBOURG (P. J. de)

Picturesque Scenery of Great Britain

Oblong Folio. 1808

COLLATION.—Coloured engraved title + leaf of Text + 6 plates, engraved by J. Hill after P. J. de Loutherbourg.

1. Ramsgate, with View of New Lighthouse.
2. Ramsgate in a High Gale.
3. Margate from the Parade.
4. Margate, arrival of the Hoy.
5. Brighthelmstone, Fishermen Returning.
6. Worthing, Fishermen Going Out.

Issued in boards with printed label on side. Size 26 × 20 inches. Size of plates 20 × 13¼ inches. J. and W. Macgavin.

305 LOUTHERBOURG (P. J. de)

The Romantic and Picturesque Scenery of England and Wales, from Drawings made expressly for this undertaking by P. J. de Loutherbourg, Esq. R.A. with Historical and Descriptive Accounts of the several places of which views are given. Engraved by William Pickett, and coloured by John Clark (thin and thick rule) London: Printed for Robert Bowyer, at the Historic Gallery, Pall Mall, by T. Bensley, Bolt Court, Fleet Street

Folio. 1805

COLLATION.—Coloured engraved title. Title as above (v. blank) + Title in French 1 p. (v. blank) + 18 plates, each with 2 leaves of Text (1 English and 1 French). Each plate marked, "From the Original Drawing by P. J. de Loutherbourg R.A. Published by R. Bowyer Historic Gallery Pall Mall Jan. 1 1805."

1. View from Chigwell Row Essex.
2. Storm off Margate.
3. Ramsgate.
4. Ruin at Basingstoke.
5. The Needles Isle of Wight.
6. Gate of Carisbrook Castle.
7. Dudley Castle Gate.
8. Lake of Wyndermere.
9. Brathay Bridge.
10. Peaks Hole Derbyshire.
11. Iron Works, Colebrook Dale.
12. Tintern Abbey.
13. Chepstow Castle.
14. Melen y Nant, near Snowdon.
15. Snowdon.
16. Llyn Ogween.
17. Cataract on the Llugwy.
18. Conway Castle.

Issued in boards. Book Prices Current for 1932 cites an edition of 1803.

306 *Another issue with 18 coloured aquatint plates engraved by W. Pickett coloured by J. Clarke.*

307 LOW (David)

The Breeds of the Domestic Animals of the British Islands; Described by David Low, Esq. F.R.S.E. Professor of Agriculture in the University of Edinburgh; Member of the Royal Academy of Agriculture of Sweden; and of the Royal Economical Society of Saxony; Honorary and Corresponding Member of the Economical Society of Leipsig; Corresponding Member of the Conseil Royal d'Agriculture de France, of the Société Royale et Centrale, etc. and Illustrated with Plates, from Drawings by Mr. W. Nicholson, R.S.A. reduced from a series of Portraits from Life, executed for the Agricultural Museum of the University of Edinburgh, by Mr. W. Shiels. R.S.A. (rule) Part 1. The Horse. (rule) London: Longman, Brown, Green, and Longmans.

4 parts. Folio.   1842

COLLATION PART I.—Half-title "The Breeds of the Domestic Animals of the British Islands." (v. blank) + Title as above (v. blank) + (Text) Part I p. v (vi blank) + Contents of Part I pp. vii–viii + sub-title "Illustrations of the Breeds of the Domestic Animals of the British Islands" (v. blank) + (Text).   The Horse pp. i–xxii + pp. 1–46 + 8 coloured lithographs (as under).   Each plate is marked, Drawn by Mr. Nicholson, R.S.A. from a Painting by Mr. Shiels. R.S.A.   Drawn on Stone, and printed by Fairland (the last 4 plates have in addition Fairlands address.   45 St Johns Square)   Professor Low's Illustrations of the Breeds of the Domestic Animals Published (date) by Longman, Orme, Brown, Green and Longmans, Paternoster Row, London.

Plate   I. p. i. The Arabian Stallion, taken in a skirmish with an Arab Tribe, Brought to England by Sir John McNeill, British Ambassador at the Court of Persia. Published December 1840.
„   II. p. 1. The Race Horse.   Stallion, Vestriss.   11 years old, the property of Mr. Hutchins of Cregane Castle.   By Whalebone out of Verenness, dam of Albert. Published December 1840.
„   III. p. 23. The Old-Irish Hunter.   Gelding 11 years old, the Property of Mr. Seully, Limerick. Bred by Mr. Barny of Sandville, of the Old Merry Andrew Line.   Published December 1840.
„   IV. p. 27. The Connamara Horse.   Gelding 13½ hands high, from the County of Galway, the property of Mr John Bindon Scott of Cahircon.   Published December 1840.
„   V. p. 38. The Old English Black Horse.   Stallion, by Old Blacklegs, from a Mare of the Dishley Breed—Bred by Mr. Broomes at Ormiston, Derby.   Published August 1841.
„   VI. p. 40. The Cleveland Bay.   Stallion by Catfos, the Sire of Bay Chilton:—Dam By Mr. Ayres' Rainbow, Bred by Mr Robertson, of Naperton Holderness.   Published August 1841.
„   VII. p. 42. The Suffolk Punch.   Stallion, rising 7—the property of Mr. Denny Egmoor, Norfolk. Published August 1841.
„ VIII. p. 45. The Clydesdale Breed.   Stallion 7 years old, the property of Mr. Law, Morton, near Edinburgh, with a Zetland Pony, the Property of the Rt. Hon. the Earl of Hopetoun.   Published August 1841.

PART II.—Half-title as before + Title as before (substituting Part II The Ox, for Part I The Horse) + Preface pp. i–iii (iv blank) + (Text) Part II p. v (vi blank) + Contents of Part II pp. vii–viii + List of Paintings . . . in present work 3 ll. (unnumbered) + sub-title 1 p. (v. blank) + Text pp. i–xxii + pp. 1–55 + 22 coloured plates.   Each plate marked, Drawn by Mr. Nicholson R.S.A. from a Painting by Mr. Shiels. R.S.A.   Drawn on Stone and printed by Fairland. Published (date) by Longman, Orme, Brown, Green and Longmans. Paternoster Row, London.

Plate   I. p. 1. Wild or White Forest Breed Cow   8 years old, from Haverford West in the County of Pembroke.   February, 1840.

Low's Domestic Animals of the British Islands (*contd.*)

Plate   II. p. 5. Pembroke Breed. Bull 3 years old bred by Mr. Innes Achland of Boulston:—Cow 5 years old bred by the same Gentleman. February 1840.

„   III. p. 7. West Highland Breed. Bull 4 years old, bred by Colonel McNiel of Barra, by a Bull bred by Mr. Stewart Chesthill. Heifer bred by Mr Campbell of Colis, by a Bull bred by Mr. Campbell. February, 1840.

„   IV. *ibd.* West Highland Breed. Cow, bred by Mr Maxwell of Aross, Mull, by a Dun Bull, bred by Mr. Maxwell:—Young Bull 18 months old, Bred by Mr Campbell of Caolis, by a Black Bull bred by Mr Campbell. February 1840.

„   V. p. 9. Zetland Breed. Cow 5 years old, the property of Mr. Andrew Duncan of Coningsburgh. August 1840.

„   VI. p. 11. Kerry Breed. Cow 6 years old, the property of the Rt. Hon. the Earl of Clare, from a stock selected by the Bishop of Killaloe. August 1840.

„   VII. p. 13. Polled Angus Breed. Bull 4 years old, bred by Mr Hugh Watson Keillor. August, 1840.

„   VIII. p. 15. Galloway Breed. Heifer 3 years old, the property of the Right Honourable the Countess of Selkirk. Bull 4 years old, bred by Mr Marshall. St. Marys Isle, Kircudbrightshire August, 1840.

„   IX. p. 17. The Polled Suffolk Breed. Cow 6 years old, bred by Mr. Richard England, Binham Abbey, from the Stock of Mr. Reeve, Weighton, Norfolk. April, 1841.

„   X. p. 19. The Devon Breed. Bull aged 2 years and 9 months, bred by Mr Denny, Egmoor, County of Norfolk. April, 1841.

„   XI. p. 21. The Sussex Breed. Oxen 6 years old, bred by Mr Pitland, Firle, County of Sussex. April 1841.

„   XII. p. 23. The Glamorgan Breed. Cow 5 years old, bred by Mr. Bradley of Treguff Place, in the County of Glamorgan. April 1841.

„   XIII. p. 25. The Ayrshire Breed. Cow 5 years old the property of Mr. Finlay, Lyonstone, Maybole, Bred in the upper district of Ayrshire. October 1841.

„   XIV. p. 27. The Alderney Breed. Cow and Calf the property of M. Brehaut of Jersey. October 1841.

„   XV. p. 29. The Fifeshire Breed. Cow 6 years old, the property of Mr. B. Ferney of Kilmux, Bred by Mr. Anderson, Kinglassie. October 1841.

„   XVI. p. 31. The Sheeted Breed of Somersetshire. 1 Cow of the Polled Variety, 4 years old, the Property of Mr. John Weir, West Carmel, Somersetshire. 2. Cow of the horned variety 4 years old, from the stock of the late Sir John Phileps, Montacute House. October 1841.

„   XVII. p. 43. The Hereford Breed. Cow bred by the Right Honourable the Earl of Talbot; descended from the Stock of Mr. Tompkins of Kingspion, Hereford. February 1842.

„   XVIII. p. 45. The Long Horned Breed. Bull 4 years old bred by Mr. Wyatt of Hanwell Castle, Oxfordshire, By a bull bred by Mr. Smith of Snidderfield in the County of Warwick. February 1842.

„   XIX. p. 49. The Short Horned Breed. Bull Hecatomb, bred by the Right Honourable Earl Spencer; by Kirby, dam by Monarch, grandam by St Albany etc. February 1842.

„   XX. *ibd.* The Short Horned Breed. Cow Bred by Mr. Hunt, Thornington, by Reformer, dam by Raby, Grandam by Sir Oliver &c. February 1842.

Supplementary Plate I (at end) Wild or White Forest Breed Bull from Chillingham Park, the property of the Right Honourable the Earl of Tankerville April 1842.

Supplementary Plate II (at end). Hereford Breed. Bull bred by the Right Honourable the Earl of Talbot, descended from the stock of Mr Tomkins of Kingspion.

PART III.—Half-title as before + Title as before (substituting Part III The Sheep and The Goat, for Part II The Ox) + (Text) Part III p. v (v. blank) + contents of Part III pp. vii–viii + sub-title (v. blank) + Text pp. 1–72 + sub-title 1 p. (v. blank) + (Text of) The Goat pp. 1–8 + 21 coloured plates.

Each plate is marked, Drawn by Mr Nicholson R.S.A. from a Painting by Mr Shiels. R.S.A. Drawn on Stone and Printed by Fairland, Published (date) by Longman, Orme, Brown, Green and Longmans. Paternoster Row, London.

Low's Domestic Animals of the British Islands (*contd.*)

Plate I. p. 7. Breed of the Zetland and Orkney Islands. Ram 3 years old, of the ancient breed from the Isle of Enhallow. Ewe 3 years old from the Island of Rousay bred by William Traill Esq. of Woodwick. The Lamb, a cross with the pure Cheviot. April 1840.

,, II. p. 9. Breed of the Higher Welsh Mountains. Ewe from the high range of Glamorgan, nort of Neath. Ram of the same race, in a state of improvement, bred by the Right Hon. Viscount Adare M.P. Dunraven Castle, Glamorganshire. Ewe of the same descent, improved, bred by Viscount Adare. April 1840.

,, III. p. 11. Soft-Woolled Sheep of Wales. Ewe, of the soft woolled breed, from the slaty mountains of South Wales. Old Radnor Ewe and Lamb. April 1840.

,, IV. p. 13. Breed of the Wicklow Mountains. Ewe 3 years old, from the higher range of heathy mountains. Ram 3 years old, from the Vale of Glenmalure April 1840.

,, V. p. 15. The Kerry Breed. Wethers, the Property of the Right Honourable the Earl of Clare, Mount Shannon, County of Limerick, selected from the old Mountain Breed of Kerry. October 1840.

,, VI. p. 17. The Forest Breeds of England. 1 Ram of the Exmoor Breed, bred by Mr. Westcott. Hawkhurst Common, Exmoor. 2 Ewe of the same breed. October, 1840.

,, VII. p. 19. The Black Faced Heath Breed. Ewe 3 years old, bred by Mr. Thomas, Robertson, Broomlea, County of Peebles. October, 1840.

,, VIII. p. 23. The Cheviot Breed. Ewe bred by Mr Thomson, Attonburn, County of Roxburgh. October 1840.

,, IX. p. 31. The Old Norfolk Breed. Ewe, 3 years old, the property of Mr Brown, of Norton, descended from the Flock of Mr Turner of Creak. The Lamb, a cross with the Southdown. February 1841.

,, X. p. 33. The Dorset Breed. 1 Ram rising 3 years old, bred by Mr. Millar of Plush, near Dorchester. 2 Ewe rising 3 years old, from the same flock February, 1841.

,, XI. p. 35. The Old Wiltshire Breed. 1. Ram, bred by Mr. Turner, near Hindon, Wiltshire. 2. Ewe from the same Flock. February 1841.

,, XII. p. 37. The Merino Breed. Ram and Ewe, bred by Mr Benett, of Pyr House, Wiltshire. M.P. February, 1841.

,, XIII. p. 47. The Ryeland Breed. Ram and Ewe, from the Stock of the late Mr Tomkins of Kingspion, Herefordshire. June 1841.

,, XIV. p. 49. The South Down Breed Ram, a Four-shear Sheep, bred by Mr. John Ellman Esq. of Glynde in the County of Sussex. June, 1841.

,, XV. *ibd.* The South Down Breed. Ewe and Lamb, bred by Mr. Ellman Esq. Beddingham, from a Ewe bred by the late Mr. Ellman of Glynde. June, 1841.

,, XVI. p. 59. The Old Lincoln Breed. Ram bred by Mr. Jex St Jermains near Lynne, County of Norfolk. June 1841.

,, XVII. p. 61. The Romney Marsh Breed. Ewe in her second fleece, bred by Mr. Bishop of Losenham House, Kent. December, 1841.

,, XVIII. p. 65. The Cotswold Breed. Ewe 8 years old, bred by Mr. Joseph Hewer, Eastlington. Gloucestershire. December, 1841.

,, XIX. p. 67. The New Leicester Breed Ram, a two shear sheep, bred by Mr. Buckley, Normanton Hill, Leicestershire. December, 1841.

,, XX. *ibd.* The New Leicester Breed. Wether, one shear Sheep, bred by Mr Stockes, from the Rams of Mr. Buckley. December, 1841.

Supplementary Plate III. Black Faced Heath Breed Ram 3 years old, bred by Mr Thomas Robertson, Broomlea, County of Peebles. April, 1842.

PART IV.—Half-title as before + Title as before (substituting Part IV. The Hog for Part III. The Sheep and The Goat) + (Text) Part IV p.v (v. blank) + pp. 1–18 + 4 coloured Plates. Each plate is marked, Drawn by Mr Nicholson, R.S.A. from a Painting by Mr Shiels. R.S.A. Drawn on Stone and Printed by Fairland. Published (date) By Longman, Orme, Brown, Green and Longmans. Paternoster Row, London.

Plate I. p. 7. Wild Boar and Sow. Imported from Alentejo in Portugal, and presented to the Earl of Leicester, by His Royal Highness the Duke of Sussex.

Low's Domestic Animals of the British Islands (*contd.*)

Plate II. p. 13. Siamese Breed. Sow 3 years old, imported from Singapore by Messrs. Dugdale, Manchester. The Litter by a half bred Chinese male.

„ III. p. 15. Old English Breed. Old English Sow from the Midland Counties.

„ IV. p. 17. Berkshire Breed. Pig Bred By Mr. Loud Mackstockmill. Warwickshire.

Supplementary Plate IV. Neapolitan Breed. Boar and Sow, the Property of the Right Hon. Earl Spencer, imported from Naples by the Hon. Captain Spencer.

308 LÖWY (Rev. A.)

History of Chivalry and Ancient Armour, with Descriptions of the Feudal System, the usuages of Knighthood, the Tournament, and Trials by Single Combat, Translated from the German of Dr. F. Kottenkamp, By the Rev. A. Löwy. Illustrated with sixty-two coloured engravings of ancient armour and Tournaments London Published by Willis and Sotheran 136, Strand.

Oblong Quarto.   1857

COLLATION.—Title as above + Preface 1 leaf + Contents 1 leaf + List of plates 1 leaf + 28 leaves of Text (enumerated by columns 1–110) + Index 2 ll + 62 numbered coloured plates, many being folding.

309 LUGAR (R.)

Architectural Sketches for Cottages, Rural Dwellings, and Villas, in the Grecian, Gothic and Fancy Styles, with Plans; Suitable to persons of Genteel Life and Moderate Fortune; Preceded by some observations on Scenery and Character, proper for picturesque buildings. By R. Lugar, Architect and Land Surveyor. (thick and thin rule) Elegantly engraved on Thirty Eight Plates (thin and thick rule) London: Printed by T. Bensley, Bolt Court, for J. Taylor, Architectural Library, 59 High Holborn.

Quarto.   1805

COLLATION.—Title as above (v. blank) + Dedication to George Ward 1 p. (v. blank) + Preface 1 p. (v. blank) + pp. 3–27 + 38 plates.

The plates are numbered 1–38 in Roman numerals and all bear Taylor's imprint.

310 LYCETT (J.)

Views in Australia or New South Wales, & Van Diemen's Land delineated, In Fifty Views, with descriptive Letter Press, Dedicated by Permission, to The Right Honble. Earl Bathurst &c. &c. &c. by J. Lycett, Artist to Major General Macquarie, late Governor of these Colonies (coloured vignette, View in Bathurst Plains near Queen Charlotte's Valley) London Published July 1st 1824 by J. Souter 73 St. Paul's Churchyard.

Oblong Folio.   1824

COLLATION.—Engraved title as above (v. blank) + Dedication 1 p. (v. blank) + Advertisement 2 pp. (i–ii) + An Account of the Australian Colonies pp. 1–15 (p. 16 Order of the Plates) + 2 maps + 48 coloured plates [49 with the coloured title-page vignette]. Each plate with 1 leaf of Text.

The plates are marked, J. Lycett Delt et Executa and bear imprint, London Published [date] by J. Soutar 73 St Pauls Church Yard.

Map of New South Wales March 1825.

1. North View of Sidney New South Wales 1825.

Lycett's Australia (*contd.*)

2. Distant View of Sydney, from the Light House at South Head, New South Wales   April 1 1825.
3. The Residence of Edmund Riley Esqr.   Wooloomooloo near Sydney N.S.W.   1 June 1825.
4. Burwood Villa.   New South Wales.   The Property of Alexander Riley Esqr.   May 1 1825.
5. View of Captain Piper's Naval Villa, at Eliza Point near Sidney, New South Wales   May 1 1825.
6. Raby a Farm belonging to Alexander Riley Esqr. New South Wales   May 1 1825.
7. Kissing Point.   New South Wales.   The Property of the late Mr James Squires   1825.
8. View of the Heads at the entrance to Port Jackson New South Wales   Oct. 1 1824.
9. Botany Bay New South Wales   Jan. 1 1825.
10. Parramatta, New South Wales   Sep. 1 1824.
11. View of the Female Orphan School, near Parramatta New South Wales   Jan. 1 1825.
12. The Residence of John McArthur Esqre. near Parramatta New South Wales   April 1 1825.
13. Liverpool, New South Wales   Dec. 1 1824.
14. View of Windsor Upon the River Hawkesbury New South Wales   Nov. 1 1824.
15. View of Wilberforce, on the Banks of the River Hawkesbury New South Wales   Feb. 1 1825.
16. View upon the Napean River at the Cow Pastures New South Wales   Feb. 1 1825.
17. View on the Wingeecarrabee River New South Wales   Dec. 1 1824.
18. View of Lake George New South Wales from the North East   March 1 1825.
19. Newcastle New South Wales   August 2nd 1824.
20. The Sugar Loaf Mountain, Near New Castle New South Wales   Oct. 1 1824.
21. Lake Patterson, near Patterson's Plains Hunters River New South Wales   Sepr. 1st 1824.
22. View of Port Macquarie at the entrance of the River Hastings New South Wales   March 1 1825.
23. Beckett's Fall on the River Apsley New South Wales   1825.
24. Bathurst Cataract on the River Apsley New South Wales   Nov. 1 1824.
    Map of Van Diemens Land   1825.
25. View of Hobart Town, Van Diemen's Land   Oct. 1 1824.
26. Distant View of Hobart Town, Van Diemans land from Blufhead   1825.
27. Roseneath Ferry near Hobart Town Van Diemens Land   Dec. 1 1824.
28. View of Roseneath Ferry (taken from the East Side) Van Diemens Land   March 1 1825.
29. View of the Governors' Retreat New Norfolk Van Diemens Land   Jan. 1 1825.
30. Mount Wellington near Hobart Town Van Dieman's Land   1825.
31. Mount Direction near Hobart Town Van Diemens Land   Nov. 1 1824.
32. Mount Dromedary Van Diemens Land   August 1st 1824.
33. Mount Nelson near Hobart Town from near Mulgrave Battery Van Diemens Land   Feb. 1 1825.
34. View from the Top of Mount Nelson, with Hobart Town in the Distance V.D.L.   1 June 1825.
35. Scene up the River Huon Van Diemens Land   May 1 1825.
36. Ram Head Point Port Davey Van Diemens Land   Nov. 1 1824.
37. Cape Pillar Near the Entrance of the River Derwent Van Diemens Land   Sept. 1 1824.
38. View from near the Top of Constitution Hill Van Diemens Land   Jan. 1 1825.
39. View from the South End of Schouten's Island, Van Diemens Land   1 June 1825.
40. The Table Mountain From the end of Jericho Plains Van Diemens Land   1825.
41. Beaumont's Lake Van Diemans Land   1 June 1825.
42. Salt Pan Plain Van Diemens Land   Octr. 1 1824.
43. The Western or Boundary Lake Van Diemens Land   Decr. 1 1824.
44. View on the Macquarie River Van Diemens Land near the Ford at Argyle Plains   April 1 1825.
45. View upon the South Esk River Van Diemens Land   Feb. 1 1825.
46. View of Tasman's Peak from Macquarie Plains Van Diemens Land   March 1, 1825.
47. Ben Lomond From Arnolds Heights a part of Tasmans Peak Van Diemens Land   Sepr. 1 1824.
48. View on the River Tamar and part of the Asbeston Hills Van Diemens Land   April 1 1825.

The finest colour plate book on Australia. Originally issued in 13 parts. The title and some of the plates were first issued in lithograph. These are extremely rare and a sign of early issue. They were soon replaced by aquatint engravings of the same views with slight alterations.

311 LYON (Capt. G. F.)

A Narrative of Travels in Northern Africa, in the years 1818, 19, and 20; accompanied by Geographical Notices of Soudan, and of the Course of the Niger.   With a Chart of the

Lyon's Travels in Northern Africa (*contd.*)

Routes, and a Variety of Coloured plates, illustrative of the costumes of the several natives of Northern Africa. (rule). By Captain G. F. Lyon, R.N. companion of the late Mr Ritchie. (rule). London: John Murray, Albemarle Street. (short rule).

Quarto.   1821

COLLATION.—Title as above (v. London: Printed by Thomas Davison, Whitefriars) + Dedication 1 p. (v. blank) + Preface 3 pp. (v–vii) + Directions to Binder 1 p. (viii) + Contents 4 pp. (ix–xii) + pp. 1–383 (including index) + Map + 17 coloured lithograph plates. Map face Title. Map of a Route through the Regency of Tripoli and Kingdom of Fezzan (folding).

Each plate is marked, Drawn from Nature, [or from Life] by G. F. Lyon, and bears imprint, London: Published by J. Murray, Albemarle St. Feb 1, 1821 C. Hullmandel's Lithography.

1. p.   7. Costume of Tripoli.   On Stone by M. Gauci.
2. p. 17. Costume of Tripoli.   On Stone by M. Gauci.
3. p. 18. Triumphal Arch Tripoli.   On Stone by G. Harley.
4. p. 46. Arabs Exercising.   On Stone by D. Dighton.
5. p. 67. The Castle of Bonjem.   On Stone by G. Harley.
6. p. 70. A Sand Wind on the Desert.   On Stone by D. Dighton.
7. p. 75. Piper and Dancer Tripoli.   Dancing Woman Sockna.   On Stone by M. Gauci.
8. p. 98. The Castle of Morzouk.   On Stone by D. Dighton.
9. p. 110. Tuarick in a Shirt of Leather.   Tuarick of Aghades.   On Stone by M. Gauci.
10. p. 113. Tuaricks of Ghraat.   On Stone by M. Gauci.
11. p. 161. Costume of Soudan.   On Stone by M. Gauci.
12. p. 182. Negresses of Soudan.   On Stone by M. Gauci.
13. p. 225. Tibboo Woman Full Dress.   On Stone by M. Gauci.
14. p. 235. Tibboo of Gatrone.   On Stone by M. Gauci.
15. p. 293. A Tuarick on his Maherrie.   On Stone by D. Dighton.
16. p. 299. Camel conveying a Bride to her Husband.   On Stone by D. Dighton.
17. p. 325. A Slave Kaffle.   On Stone by D. Dighton.

312 MAASKAMP (E.)

The Costume of the Kingdom of Holland, at the beginning of the Nineteenth Century. (thick and thin rule) London: Printed by J. Barfield, 91, Wardour Street; and Published by Colnaghi and Co. (swelled rule).

Quarto.   1810

COLLATION.—Title as above (v. blank) + Engraved Frontispiece, "La Muse du dessin remet son Ouvrage à Mercure," J. Kuyper, inv. et delin., L. Portman sculp.   Amsterdam 1805. by C. Maaskamp.   London: Published by Colnaghi & Co., Cockspur Street No. 43 + Explanation of Frontispiece 1 leaf + Explanation of the Dresses, Morals, and Customs of Holland 3 pp. + 20 plates, each with 1 or 1½ pp. of Text, the last plate with 2 pp. of Text.

Text to each plate in French and Dutch, and all the plates bear, J. Kuyper derex., L. Portman sculp., and the imprint Amsterdam (date) by E. Maaskamp in de Kalverstraat No. 18 (after plate 12, No. 1) London Published by Colnaghi & Co., Cockspur Street, No. 43 (with the exception of the first plate, that has only the Amsterdam imprint).

1. Une femme bourgeoise et sa Fille allant à l'Englise. 1803.
2. Ecoutez, mon ami! encore un Sou ce sont mes étrennes. 1803.
3. Je vous annonce la mort de. 1803.

Maaskamp's Costume of the Kingdom of Holland (*contd.*)

4. Une pinte, ma fille! pas d'avantage. 1803.
5. Une Mere et sa Fille membres de la Societe des Frères Moraves, a Seist. 1803.
6. C'est un prix fait; il n'y a rien a en rabattre. 1804.
7. Mon homme, comme il faisoit froid au Sermon. C. F. Bounach ad vidum del., 1804.
8. Allons file, file, ma Femme—mes filets sont tout déchirés. 1804.
9. Je ne vous donnerai rien de plus pour les chevrettes; mais avez vous de merlan. G. J. J. van Os ad viv. delin., 1804.
10. Quoi! avec ces beaux habits, vous allez en traineau à Molqueren? G. F. Bounach ad viv. del., 1804.
11. Ah! du beaux frais! eh! bien, Annette, portez le a ma Servante. C. F. van Langenburgh ad viv. del., 1804.
12. Un Paysan et une Paysanne de la Gueldre, revenant de traire les vaches. D. Olsterhoudt ad viv. del., 1804.
13. Allons Jacquette, quand tu auras porté ton beurre et tes Oeufs au Marché, nous irons ensemble nous divertir à la foire. D. de Keyser ad viv. del., 1805.
14. Un Paysan et une Paysanne de Schouwen allant au marché de Zirezee. A. Prince ad viv. del., 1805.
15. Comment, Voisine! vous allez ainsi vous divertir? D. Koning ad viv. del., 1804.
16. Bonjour Jolie Fille! vous allez aussi à Bois le duc? Amersvoort ad viv. del., 1805.
17. La Promenade. C. Overman del., 1807.
18. Chère Marie! voici un bouquet, avec une lettre et une boite toutes remplies de douceurs. C. Overman delin., 1807.
19. Belle Fiancée! Toutes Sortes de prospérité. J. W. Caspari delin., 1807.
20. La Conversation. C. Overman delin., 1807.

313 MACKENZIE (Sir George Steuart)

Travels in the Island of Iceland, during the Summer of the year 1810 (short thin and thick rule). By Sir George Steuart Mackenzie, Baronet, Fellow of the Royal Society of Edinburgh, &c. &c. &c. (thick and thin rule) Edinburgh: Printed by Thomas Allan and Company, for Archibald Constable and Company, Edinburgh; Longman, Hurst, Rees, Orme & Brown; Cadell & Davies; William Miller, and John Murray, London; (rule).

Quarto.   1811

COLLATION.—Half-title "Travels in Iceland" (v. blank) + Title (v. verse from Goldsmith) + Dedication to Frederic, Count Trampe 1 p. (v. blank) + Preface 11 pp. (vii–xvii) xviii blank + Contents 1 p. (v. Errata) + Sub-title "Preliminary Dissertation" 1 p. (v. blank) + pp. 3–483 (484 blank) + Index pp. 485–491 (p. 492 Directions to Binder).

1. p. 82. Reikiavik. Sketched by Sir G. M. Engraved by R. Scott (uncoloured, folding).
2. p. 87. Icelandic Costume. J. Clark direxit (coloured).
3. p. 101. Havnefiord. Sketched by Sir Geo. Mackenzie. J. Clark direxit (coloured).
4. p. 113. Krisuvik & the Sulphur Mountains. Sketched by Sir Geo. Mackenzie. J. Clark direxit (coloured).
5. p. 117. Cauldron of Boiling Mud on the Sulphur Mountains. Sketched by Sir Geo. Mackenzie. J. Clark direxit (coloured).
6. p. 119. Great Jet of Steam, on the Sulphur Mountains. Sketched by Sir Geo. Mackenzie. J. Clark direxit (coloured).
   p. 141. Vignette. Church of Saurbar. Sketched by R. Bright. E. Mitchell sculpt.
   p. 147. Vignette. The Lang Spiel. Engrd., by E. Mitchell.
   p. 166. Vignette. Snuff Box. E. Mitchell sculpt.
   p. 172. Vignette. Snaefell Jokul. Sketched by Mr Holland. E. Mitchell sculpt.
7. p. 174. Natural Arch on the Coast near Stappen. Sketched by Sir G. M. E. Mitchell sculpt.
   p. 175. Vignette. Cave at Stappen. Sketched by R. Bright. E. Mitchell sculpt.
   p. 183. Vignette. Olafsvik. Sketched by Sir G. M. Engrd. by E. Mitchell.
   p. 197. Vignette. Boiling Springs in the River Reikiadalsaa. Sketched by Sir G. M. E. Mitchell sculpt.

Mackenzie's Travels in the Island of Iceland (*contd.*)

p. 201. Vignette. The Tungu Hver and Alternating Geyser. Sketched by Sir G. M. E. Mitchell sculpt.

p. 206. Vignette. Summit of Snaefell Jokul. Sketched by R. Bright. E. Mitchell scu.

p. 212. Vignette. Skalholt. Sketched by R. Bright. E. Mitchell sculpt.

8. p. 215. Map of the Geysers and Neighbouring Springs. Sketched by Sir G. M. Engrd. by E. Mitchell.

p. 217. Vignette. Plan and Section of the bason of the Great Geyser.

9. p. 224. Eruption of the Great Geyser. Sketched by Sir G. M. Engrd., by E. Mitchell.

10. p. 225. New Geyser. Sketched by Sir G. M. Engrd., by E. Mitchell.

p. 229. Vignette. Theory of the Geysers.

p. 245. Vignette. Summit of Hekla as seen from Naifurholt. Sketched by Sir G. M. E. Mitchell sculpt.

p. 254. Vignette. Mount Hekla from the South. Sketched by Sir G. M. E. Mitchell sculpt.

11. p. 255. Eyafialla Jokul from Hliderende. Sketched by H. Holland. J. Clark direxit (coloured).

12. p. 261. Mount Hekla from Odde. Sketched by Sir Geo. Mackenzie. J. Clark direxit (coloured).

13. p. 267. Eyafialla Jokul, Mount Hekla, & the River Elvas, from the Westward. Sketch'd by H. Holland. J. Clark direxit (coloured).

p. 275. Vignette of houses. Sketched by R. Bright. E. Mitchell sculpt.

p. 284. Folding. Population Table.

ibd. Table Political Economy.

p. 337. Folding Table of Imports.

ibd. Table of Exports.

14. p. 377. (Plate of Geological Sections.) Sketched by Sir G. M. E. Mitchell sculpt.

15. p. 469. Plate of Music.

At End. Map of Iceland.

At End. Map of the South West Coast of Iceland by Sir G. S. Mackenzie Bart., F.R.S.E.

314 MACKENZIE (Sir George Steuart)

Travels in the Island of Iceland Second Edition   1812

COLLATION.—Half-title "Travels in Iceland" + Title "Travels in the Island of Iceland, during the Summer of the year 1810." (short thick and thin rule). By Sir George Steuart Mackenzie, Baronet, President of the Physical Class of the Royal Society; Vice President of the Astronomical Institution of Edinburgh &c, &c, &c, (thick and thin rule) Second Edition (thin and thick rule) Edinburgh: Printed for Archibald Constable and Company, Edinburgh; T. Payne; Longman, Hurst, Rees, Orme & Brown; Cadell & Davies; J. Murray; R. Baldwin: C. Law; J. Hatchard; E. Lloyd; W. Lindsell: Cradock & Joy; Gale, Curtis & Fenner; Sharpe & Hailes; and T. Hamilton, London (rule) 1812 (v. verse from Goldsmith, T. Allan and Company, Printers, Edinburgh) + Dedication 1 p. (v. blank) + Preface pp. vii–xv + Contents 1 p. (v. blank) + Advertisement to Second Edition 1 p. (v. blank) + Sub-title "Preliminary Dissertation" 1 p. (v. blank) + pp. 3–484 + Index pp. 485–491 (p. 492 Directions to Binder) + Maps and plates as in 1st Edition.

NOTE.—*This Edition slightly revised and a short account of the Revolution of 1809 added to Appendix.*

315 MALTON (J.)

A Picturesque and Descriptive View of the City of Dublin displayed in a Series of the most Interesting Scenes taken in the Year 1791 By James Malton with a brief authentic History from the earliest accounts to the Present Time Tomkins Scr. Vincent scu.

Oblong Folio.   1794-95

Malton's Picturesque View of Dublin (*contd.*)

COLLATION.—Engraved title as above (v. blank) + Dedication 1 p. (v. blank) + Preface 2 pp. + Brief History of Dublin pp. 1–18 (with 3 plates) + 25 plates each with 1 leaf of Text. Each plate marked, Ja' [or James] Malton del et fecit [or sculpt.].

1. Front. Arms of the City of Dublin.
2. p. 1. A Correct Survey of Dublin as it stood in the year 1610.
3. p. 12. A Correct Survey of the Bay of Dublin.
4. Great Court Yard Dublin Castle.
5. The Parliament House Dublin.
6. Trinity College Dublin.
7. College Library Dublin.
8. Provosts House Dublin.
9. Saint Patricks Cathedral Dublin.
10. West Front of St. Patrick's Cathedral.
11. Royal Exchange Dublin.
12. Custom House Dublin.
13. View of the Law Courts, looking up the Liffey, Dublin.
14. Tholsel Dublin.
15. Old Soldiers Hospital Kilmainham Dublin.
16. Royal Infirmary, Phoenix Park, Dublin.
17. Blue Coat Hospital Dublin.
18. Rotunda & New Rooms Dublin.
19. Lying-in Hospital Dublin.
20. St. Catharine's Church, Thomas Street, Dublin.
21. Marine School, Dublin, looking up the Liffey.
22. Leinster House Dublin.
23. Charlemont House Dublin.
24. Powerscourt House Dublin.
25. View from Capel Street, looking over Essex Bridge Dublin.
26. St. Stephen's Green Dublin.
27. Barracks Dublin.
28. View of Dublin from the Magazine, Phoenix Park.

Outline Key to the last two plates 1 p. (v. blank).

Issued originally in parts from 1792 to 1797 and on completion in book form as above. Usually to be found plain but a few copies exist in colour, in which state it is rare. There are several issues of the plates, the imprints being variously dated 1792–1799.

316 MARCAUD (C.)

To Field Marshall His Royal Highness the Duke of York & Albany, K.G. & G.C.B. Commander in chief &c. &c. &c. These Delineations of the Uniform of the Officers of the British Army are respectfully Dedicated (with His permission) By His Royal Highness' most obliged & obedt. humble Servt. C. Marcaud late of the Quar. Mastr. Genln. Department Horse Guards.

Small Quarto.

COLLATION.—Title Dedication as above (Sidy. Hall sculpt.) + 12 plates containing 146 figures.

1. General Officers.
2. Heavy Cavalry.
3. Dragoons (Hussars & Lancers).
4. Cavalry.
5. Infantry Foot Guards.
6–10. Infantry.
11. Infantry (including Colonial).
12. Royal Artillery.

Markwell (Marmaduke). See under Rowlandson Advice to Sportsmen.

Martial Achievements of Great Britain. See under (Jenkins (J.)).

317 MARTIN (Lieut.)

Operations in the Canton River in April 1847 under the joint command of Major General D'Aigular C.B. and Captain McDougall, of the Royal Navy. (vignette of Bay of

Martin's Operations in the Canton River (*contd.*)

Victoria Hong Kong) from Drawings made on the Spot by Lieut., Martin, 42nd Madras Native Infantry, Acting Engineer. [1847]

Folio.

COLLATION.—Title as above + Dedication, "To the United Services" 1 p. (v. blank) + 2 pp. of Text + List of Plates + 4 plans on 1 sheet (Sketch of the River Chou-Kiang &c.) + 10 coloured plates (including title).

1. Title with View of Bay of Victoria & part of the Military Cantonment.
   Sketch of the River Chou Kiang (Canton River) from Bocca Tigris to Canton.
2. Forts & Batteries of the Bocca Tigris, or First Pass of Canton River. H.M.S. Steamship Vulture &c.
3. Gen. D'Aigular with 18th Royal Irish taking Possession of the Annanchoy Batteries.
4. The Staked Batteries, or Second Pass of the Canton River above Whampoa.
5. Troops attacking Forts Wookongtap & Whampoa Creek.
6. French Folly Fort, within sight of City of Canton.
7. British & Foreign Factories at Canton.
8. The Keep of the French Folly Fort blown up by Royal Sappers & Miners.
9. British Factory at Canton. Troops drawn up to receive Commissioner & Viceroy.
10. The Return to Hong Kong. The Vulture passing the Battery upon Tygris Island.

318 MARVY (L.)

Sketches after English Landscape Painters by L. Marvy. With Short Notices by W. M. Thackeray. London: David Bogue, 86 Fleet Street.

Quarto. [1850]

COLLATION.—Title as above (v. London: Henry Vizetelly, Printer and Engraver, Gough Square, Fleet Street) + Preface (unsigned v. blank) + Contents 1 p. (v. blank) + 20 coloured plates, each signed in right-hand corner, L or Louis Marvy, and in left-hand corner by name of the Artist (no titles given).

The 20 plates are after the following artists.

Sir A. Calcott R.A.	David Cox.	Richard Wilson.
J. M. W. Turner R.A.	T. Gainsborough.	G. Cattermole.
J. Holland.	David Roberts R.A.	F. R. Lee R.A.
R. Redgrave A.R.A.	C. Stanfield R.A.	W. Collins.
E. W. Cooke.	W. J. Muller.	F. Danby A.R.A.
John Constable.	J. D. Harding.	T. Creswick A.R.A.
P. Dewint.	Nasmyth.	

FIRST ISSUE.—Bound in red cloth with gilt lettering within floral design of roses, harebells, &c. gilt back.

319 MARVY (L.)

The Landscape Painters of England: In a Series of steel engravings by L. Marvy. With Short Notices by W. M. Thackeray. London and Glasgow: Richard Griffin and Company, Publishers to the University of Glasgow.

Quarto. [1850]

COLLATION.—Half-title (v. blank) + Title as above (v. Glasgow: Printed by William Mackenzie 45 & 47 Howard Street) + Preface signed W.M.T. 1 p. (v. blank) + Contents 1 p. (v. blank) + 20 coloured plates, each with leaf of text as in preceding item.

Issued in blue cloth, lettering and acorn and foliage design in gilt, blind design in corners, gilt lettering and design on back, yellow ends, gilt edges.

320 MASON (G. H.)

The Costume of China, illustrated by Sixty Engravings: with Explanations in English and French (swelled rule) By George Henry Mason, Esquire, Major of his Majesty's (late) 102d Regiment (thin and thick rule) London: (thin and thick rule) Printed for William Millar, Old Bond Street; By William Blumer and Co. Cleveland-Row St James's

Folio.   1804

COLLATION.—Title as above (v. blank) + Title in French (v. blank) + Preface in English 2 ll. + Preface in French 2 ll. + Table of Contents in English 1 p. (v. ditto in French) + 60 coloured plates each with 1 leaf of Text.

Each plate marked, Pu Qua Canton Delin., Dadley London sculpt. Published May 4 1799 by W. Millar Old Bond Street London.

The plates bear no titles but are as follows:

1. Mandarin.	22. Beggar with Serpent.	42. Porter with Fire wood.
2. Watchman.	23. Traveller.	43. Farrier.
3. Woman making Stockings.	24. Distiller.	44. Serpent Catcher.
4. Money Changer.	25. Fisherman.	45. Miller.
5. Barber.	26. Apothecary.	46. Viper Seller.
6. Bookseller.	27. Labourer.	47. Shoemaker.
7. Frog Catcher.	28. Mender of Porcelain.	48. Cotton Cleaner.
8. Pork Butcher.	29. Bricklayer.	49. Basket Weaver.
9. Bonzee.	30. Carpenter.	50. Fisherman with Scoop.
10. Man with Raree Show.	31. Mandarin in Summer Dress.	51. Cap Maker.
11. Chinese Woman.		52. Female Peasant.
12. Pipe Seller.	32. Stone Hewer.	53. Canister Maker.
13. Tambouriner.	33. Pillow Seller.	54. Boy with Vegetables.
14. Beggar with dog.	34. Flute Seller.	55. Old man polishing Crystals.
15. Arrowmaker.	35. Balancer.	56. Boschee.
16. Porter with Fruit Trees.	36. Man striking gong.	57. Old woman twisting Cotton.
17. Pedlar.	37. Tinker.	
18. Shoemaker.	38. Puppet Show.	58. Soldier.
19. Blacksmith.	39. Fishermonger.	59. Lame Beggar.
20. Lantern Painter.	40. Beggar with Monkey.	60. Lady of Distinction.
21. Woman preparing tea.	41. Woman Embroidering.	

321 MAYER (Luigi)

Views in the Ottoman Dominions, in Europe in Asia, and some of the Mediterranean Islands, from the Original Drawings, taken for Sir Robert Ainslie, by Luigi Mayer, F.A.S. with Descriptions, Historical and Illustrative. (swelled rule) London: Printed by T. Bensley, Bolt Court, Fleet Street, for R. Bowyer, 80 Pall Mall.

Folio.   1810

COLLATION.—Title as above (v. blank) + Dedication 1 p. (v. blank) + List of Plates 1 p. (v. blank) + pp. 1–32 + 71 coloured plates, each with 1 leaf of Text (with exception of plate 55, the text to this being included with text of plate 54). Each plate bears imprint, Published by R. Bowyer, 80 Pall Mall. 1809 (1810 from plate 37 onwards).

I. View of Constantinople (double page folding plate).	IV. Terapia.
	V. Turkish Encampment.
II. Mosque of Sultan Achmet.	VI. Aqueduct near Belgrade.
III. Pera.	VII. Picolo Bent.

Mayer's Views in the Ottoman Dominions, etc. (*contd.*)

VIII. Caravansary at Kustchiuk Czemege.
IX. Ponte Piccolo.
X. Ponte Grande.
XI. Tchiurluk.
XII. Borgas.
XIII. Caravansary at Borgas.
XIV. Kaskerat.
XV. Eski Estamboul.
XVI. Kirkclisia.
XVII. Mount Balkan.
XVIII. Road over the Balkan Mountain.
XIX. Ciala Kavak.
XX. Dance of Bulgarian Peasants.
XXI. View on the Aluta.
XXII. Church and Convent of St Mary.
XXIII. Entrance to the Convent of St Mary.
XXIV. Pitesti.
XXV. Palace at Bucharest.
XXVI. View near Bucharest.
XXVII. Ancient Temples at Agrigentum.
XXVIII. Base of a Colossal Column near Syracuse.
XXIX. Ruins occasioned by the Earthquake at Messina.
XXX. View at Villa Scabrosa.
XXXI. Ancient Bath near the Fountains of the Palici.
XXXII. Ancient Cistern in Val di Hoto.
XXXIII. Crater in the Island of Volcano.
XXXIV. Ancient Temple in the Island of Salina.
XXXV. Island of Stromboli.
XXXVI. Crater in Island of Stromboli.
XXXVII. Fragments at Ephesus.
XXXVIII. Aqueduct near Ephesus.
XXXIX. Stadium at Ephesus.
XL. Theatre at Ephesus.
XLI. Temple of Diana at Ephesus.
XLII. Part of the Grand Gallery of the Temple of Diana.
XLIII. Ruins of the Baths of the Temple of Diana.
XLIV. Port of Latachia.
XLV. Mosque at Latachia.
XLVI. Mosque at Latachia Plate II.
XLVII. Triumphal Arch at Latachia.
XLVIII. Cathedral at Tortosa.
XLIX. View near Tortosa.
L. Fountain of Serpents.
LI. Monument on the Coast of Syria.
LII. Monument on the Coast of Syria Plate II.
LIII. Monument between Tripoli and Tortosa.
LIV. Monuments near Tortosa.
LV. Monuments near Tortosa Plate II.
LVI. The Island of Tortosa.
LVII. Castle in the Island of Tortosa.
LVIII. Ruins of an Ancient Temple in Samos.
LIX. Ruins of the Temple of Juno in Samos.
LX. Western Harbour of the Island of Samos.
LXI. Ancient Aqueduct in Samos.
LXII. Part of Jerusalem.
LXIII. Temple of Solomon.
LXIV. Church of the Holy Sepulchre.
LXV. Chapel of Mount Calvary.
LXVI. Tomb of Jeremiah.
LXVII. Sarcophagus from the Tombs of the Kings.
LXVIII. Bethlehem in Palestine.
LXIX. The Grotto of the Nativity.
LXX. Temple of Jupiter Ammon in Libya.
LXXI. Interior of the Temple of Jupiter Ammon.

322 McIAN (R. R.)

The Clans of The Scottish Highlands, Illustrated By Appropriate Figures, Displaying Their Dress, Tartans, Arms, Armorial Insignia, And Social Occupations, From Original Sketches, By R. R. McIan. With Accompanying Descriptions And Historical Memoranda Of Character, Mode of Life, &c., &c. By James Logan, F.S.A. Sc. Cor. Mem. Soc. Ant. Normandy, &c. Author Of "The Scottish Gael," Introduction to the "Sar Obair Nam Bard Gaelech," Etc. (rule) London: Ackermann and Co. Strand. 1845.

2 vols. Folio.   1845[–7]

COLLATION VOL. I.—Printed title as above (v. blank) + Dedication to Queen (in black and gold, v. blank) + To Highland Society of London 1 p. (v. Printed by Cook and Co. 76 Fleet Street London) + Introduction pp. 1–4 + List of Clans 2 pp. (iv–vi) + Index pp. vii–xii + Text (separately numbered for each clan).

Each plate marked R. R. McIan Pinxit, and bearing Ackermann's imprint.

McIan's Clans of The Scottish Highlands (*contd.*)

Engraved Frontispiece Lettered Vol. I. 1845.

1. Campbell of Breadalbane.	W. Kinnebrook Lith.	(6 pp. text).
2. MacDonnel of Glengarry.	Henning Lith.	(6 pp. ,,).
3. MacGillvray.	W. Kinnebrook Lith.	(4 pp. ,,).
4. Clanranald.	,, ,, ,,	(6 pp. ,,).
5. Chisholm.	,, ,, ,,	(6 pp. ,,).
6. MacNachtan.	,, ,, ,,	(4 pp. ,,).
7. MacKinnon.	W. Bosley Lith.	(6 pp. ,,).
8. Farquharson.	,, ,, ,,	(4 pp. ,,).
9. Menzies.	,, ,, ,,	(4 pp. ,,).
10. MacDuff.	,, ,, ,,	(4 pp. ,,).
11. Gunn.	W. Kinnebrook Lith.	(4 pp. ,,).
12. Robertson.	,, ,, ,,	(4 pp. ,,).
13. Sinclair.	W. Bosley Lith.	(4 pp. ,,).
14. Ross.	H. Aitken Lith.	(4 pp. ,,).
15. Buchanan.	Russell Lith.	(4 pp. ,,).
16. Fraser.	W. Bosley Lith.	(4 pp. ,,).
17. Gordon.	,, ,, ,,	(4 pp. ,,).
18. Drummond.	,, ,, ,,	(6 pp. ,,).
19. MacLean.	,, ,, ,,	(4 pp. ,,).
20. MacKay.	L. Dickinson Lith.	(4 pp. ,,).
21. MacNiel.	,, ,, ,,	(4 pp. ,,).
22. MacKenzie.	,, ,, ,,	(6 pp. ,,).
23. MacGregor.	,, ,, ,,	(6 pp. ,,).
24. Grant.	Louis ,, ,,	(4 pp. ,,).
25. Ferguson.	L. ,, ,,	(4 pp. ,,).
26. Forbes.	,, ,, ,,	(4 pp. ,,).
27. Colquhon.	,, ,, ,,	(4 pp. ,,).
28. MacDugal.	,, ,, ,,	(4 pp. ,,).
29. Matheson.	,, ,, ,,	(4 pp. ,,).
30. Davidson.	,, ,, ,,	(4 pp. ,,).
31. MacFarlan.	,, ,, ,,	(4 pp. ,,).
32. Murray.	,, ,, ,,	(6 pp. ,,).
33. MacDonald of The Isles.	,, ,, ,,	(6 pp. ,,).
34. MacDonald of Glenco.	,, ,, ,,	(6 pp. ,,).
35. Cameron.	,, ,, ,,	(4 pp. ,,).
36. Lamond.	,, ,, ,,	(4 pp. ,,).

VOL. II.—Printed title (Vol. II between rules and dated 1847) + List of Subscribers 1 leaf (iii–iv) + List of Clans, pp. v–vi + Index pp. vii–xiv + 36 plates.

37. Campbell of Argyle.	L. Dickinson Lith.	(6 pp. text).
38. MacLachlan.	,, ,, ,,	(4 pp. ,,).
39. MacNab.	,, ,, ,,	(4 pp. ,,).
40. Graham.	,, ,, ,,	(4 pp. ,,).
41. MacQuarrie.	,, ,, ,,	(4 pp. ,,).
42. Grant of Glenmorrison.	,, ,, ,,	(4 pp. ,,).
43. MacArthur.	,, ,, ,,	(4 pp. ,,).
44. MacAllister.	,, ,, ,,	(4 pp. ,,).
45. Rose.	,, ,, ,,	(4 pp. ,,).
46. Sutherland.	,, ,, ,,	(6 pp. ,,).
47. Cumin.	,, ,, ,,	(4 pp. ,,).
48. MacDonald of Keppach.	,, ,, ,,	(6 pp. ,,).
49. MacBain.	,, ,, ,,	(6 pp. ,,).
50. MacNicol.	,, ,, ,,	(4 pp. ,,).
51. MacLeod.	No artist or lithographer.	(6 pp. ,,).
52. MacIntosh.	L. Dickinson Lith.	(6 pp. ,,).
53. MacCruimin.	No artist or lithographer.	(4 pp. ,,).

McIan's Clans of The Scottish Highlands (*contd.*)

54. MacLaurin.	L. Dickinson Lith.		(6 pp. text).
55. Urquhart.	,,	,, ,,	(4 pp. ,,).
56. Ogilvie.	,,	,, ,,	(4 pp. ,,).
57. MacPhee.	,,	,, ,,	(4 pp. ,,).
58. MacInnes.	,,	,, ,,	(2 pp. ,,).
59. Clan Donchadh, of Mar.	,,	,, ,,	(4 pp. ,,).
60. MacIvor.	,,	,, ,,	(4 pp. ,,).
61. MacRae.	,,	,, ,,	(4 pp. ,,).
62. MacPherson.	,,	,, ,,	(10 pp. ,,).
63. MacColl.	,,	,, ,,	(4 pp. ,,).
64. MacAulay.	,,	,, ,,	(2 pp. ,,).
65. Munro.	,,	,, ,,	(4 pp. ,,).
66. Shaw.	,,	,, ,,	(4 pp. ,,).
67. MacMillan.	,,	,, ,,	(4 pp. ,,).
68. Logan.	,,	,, ,,	(10 pp. ,,).
69. MacIntire.	,,	,, ,,	(4 pp. ,,).
70. MacLennan.	,,	,, ,,	(4 pp. ,,).
71. Ulric.	,,	,, ,,	(4 pp. ,,).
72. Stewart.	,,	,, ,,	(16 pp. ,,).

323 McIAN (R. R.)

The Clans of The Scottish Highlands.

A second edition was issued in 1857 (London Willis and Sotheran) as follows.

VOL. I.—Engraved front + Printed title + Introduction 4 pp. + Note by Ackermann 1 p. + List of Subscribers 2 pp. + List of Clans 2 pp. + Index pp. vii–xii + 36 plates.

VOL. II.—Engraved Front + Printed Title + List of Clans pp. v–vi + Index pp. vii–xiv + 36 plates.

The plates have the same titles as in the first edition but there are some variations. Plate 8 bears no lithographer and plate 11 is by M. & N. Hanhart.

324 MELVILLE (Harden S.)

Sketches in Australia and the adjacent Islands, selected from a number taken during the surveying voyage of H.M.S. "FLY." and "BRAMBLE." under the command of Capt. F. P. Blackwood, R.N. during the years 1842–1846. By Harden S. Melville, Draftsman to the expedition. (rule). Printed and Published by Dickinson & Co. 114 New Bond Street, London.

Oblong Quarto.

COLLATION.—Lithograph title with Vignette view + Printed title as above (v. blank) + Preface 1 p. (v. blank) + 25 coloured lithograph plates.

1. On the Derwent, Hobarton.	10. Wood scene at C. York.
2. Fern Tree Valley, near Hobarton.	11. Ant Hills on Wallis Id.
3. Wombyan Cave.	12. Casuarina Tree.
4. Bush Scene Port Stephens.	13. Natives at Port Essington.
5. Beach at Sandy Cape.	14. Bush scene, Swan River.
6. Part of Encampment at C. Upstart.	15. Natives of Port Philip.
7. Water Gully at C. Upstart.	16. Huts on Mt. Ernest Id.
8. Ravine at Gould Id.	17. Village at Darnley Id.
9. Reef at Low Water, Bird Id.	18. Hut and Natives of Darnley Id.

Melville's Sketches in Australia (*contd.*)

19. Canoe of Darnley Id.
20. Natives of Darnley and Murray Id. dancing.
21. Houses at New Guinea.
22. Malay Village, near Coepany.

23. View of Timor Coepany.
24. Scene near Sourabaya.
25. Street in China.

Memoirs of the Life of John Mytton Esq. See under Apperley (C. J.).

325 MERIGOT (J.)

The Amateur's Portfolio: or the New Drawing Magazine; being a Selection of lessons calculated to make the Art of Drawing Easy, and founded upon the Principles of Geometry and Practical Perspective. (thick and thin rule) (10 line verse quotation Du Fresnoy) (thin and thick rule) By James Merigot, Drawing Master, London, and pupil of the Royal Academy Paris (short thick and thin rule) Vol. I (short thin and thick rule) London: Printed for G. & S. Robinson, Paternoster-Row (short rule).

2 vols. Quarto.   1815[–6]

COLLATION VOL. I—Half-title + Title as above (v. J. Bailey Printer, 13 Rolls Buildings, Fetter Lane) + Dedication 1 p. dated July 1, 1816 (v. blank) + Index 1 p. (v. Direction to Binder) + Introduction pp. i–iii (p. iv blank) + Introductory Observations pp. 5–50 + Progressive lessons pp. 1–32 + Treatise on Perspective pp. 1–16 + following plates.

Front. Viaduct with title beneath bridge. New Drawing Magazine, 1814 (coloured).
1. p. 8. Drawing Instruments (coloured).
2. p. 14. Geometrical Designs.
3. p. 19. Solid Bodies.
4. p. 42. 2 views of House with Towers (coloured).
5. p. 42. Same with castle Towers.
6. p. 44. Two views of Buildings by Water.
7. p. 48. Two Landscape Views (coloured).

2nd Part
8. p. 2. Designs and Angles.
9. p. 2. Buildings and Angles.
10. p. 4. Two Buildings.
11. p. 6. Cottage & Church.
12. p. 10. Six Buildings.
13. p. 10. Cottage outline & finished.
14. p. 12. Six Cottages.
15. p. 12. Two Cottages.
16. p. 12. Two Houses.
17. p. 14. Range of Colours & Church.
18. p. 14. Five Designs.
19. p. 18. Buildings & Abbey.
20. p. 18. Eggs &c.
21. p. 21. Walls & Roofs.
22. p. 22. Colours & Two Skyscapes (coloured).
23. p. 24. Bridges.
24. p. 25. Colours (coloured).
25. p. 28. Lodge &c.
26. p. 30. Two Roses (coloured).
27. p. 30. Two Houses.
28. p. 32. Two Houses.

3rd Part
29. p. 2. Perspective.
30. p. 6. ,,
31. p. 10. ,,
32. p. 14. ,,
33. p. 15. ,,
34. p. 16. Trees.
35. *ibd.* ,,
36. *ibd.* Flowers.
37. *ibd.* Tree.
38. *ibd.* Two Houses.
39. *ibd.* ,, ,,
40. *ibd.* Barns &c.
41. *ibd.* Gateways.
42. *ibd.* Haystacks & Gateway.
43. *ibd.* Cottage & Tree.
44. *ibd.* Barns.
45. *ibd.* 1st View of Langley (coloured).
46. *ibd.* 2nd. View of Langley (coloured).
47. *ibd.* View at Watford (coloured).
48. *ibd.* Castle of Gloom (coloured).
49. *ibd.* View on River Wye (coloured).
50. *ibd.* [ruined castle.]
51. *ibd.* Flower Group.
52. *ibd.* 2 small Flower Groups (foxglove etc.)
53. *ibd.* 2 small Flower Groups (anemone etc.)
54. *ibd.* Flower Group.
55. *ibd.* Iris & Tulip.
56. *ibd.* Shells
57. *ibd.* Flower Group.
58. *ibd.* 6 Flowers.
59. *ibd.* Flower Group.
60. *ibd.* Geranium.
61. *ibd.* Fruit Group.

Merigot's Amateur's Portfolio (*contd.*)

VOL. II.—Title as before but Dedicated, by Permission to the Marchioness of Stafford inserted + Date changed to 1816 + Direction to Binder 1 p. (v. Index) + Introductory Remarks i–iv + Text pp. 1–43 (pp. 17–20 and 21–22 repeated) + Progressive Lessons pp. 1–27 + 1 unnumbered leaf + Perspective pp. 1–16 + 1 leaf Perspective conclusion + following plates.

62.	Front.	Allegorical G. M. Brighty.	93.	p. 26.	Portio (coloured).
63.	p. 37.	Engraving tools &c. (coloured).	94.	*ibd.*	Instruments Engraving.
64.	*ibd.*	Two etchings.	95.	p. 28.	Girl & Pigs (coloured).
			96.	p. 29.	5 columns.

		Part 2			*Part 3*
65.	p. 1.	Ears.			
66.	*ibd.*	Eyes.	97.	p. 2.	Perspective.
67.	p. 2.	Ophelia.	98.	p. 4.	,,
68.	p. 6.	Mouths.	99.	p. 6.	,,
69.	*ibd.*	Noses.	100.	p. 12.	Angles &c.
70.	p. 7.	Knight & lady (coloured).	101.	p. 24.	Design.
71.	p. 9.	Heads.	102.	*ibd.*	Country scene.
71a.	*ibd.*	Hands.	103.	*ibd.*	Church.
72.	*ibd.*	3 Heads.	104.	*ibd.*	Landscape.
73.	*ibd.*	Cordelia.	105.	*ibd.*	Two Houses.
74.	*ibd.*	Arms.	106.	*ibd.*	Grave &c.
75.	*ibd.*	Macbeth.	107.	*ibd.*	Winter Scene (coloured).
76.	p. 14.	Death of Knight (coloured).	108.	*ibd.*	House & Garden (coloured).
77.	*ibd.*	Legs.	109.	*ibd.*	Seascape (coloured).
78.	*ibd.*	Jago.	110.	*ibd.*	Horse browsing &c. (coloured).
79.	p. 16.	Torso.	111.	*ibd.*	Waterfall &c. (coloured).
80.	*ibd.*	Miranda.	112.	*ibd.*	Cows (coloured).
81.	p. 18.	Colours & View (coloured).	113.	*ibd.*	Reaping (coloured).
82.	*ibd.*	Scots costume (coloured).	114.	*ibd.*	Cattle & Sheep (coloured).
83.	*ibd.*	3 figures.	115.	*ibd.*	Night Scene (coloured).
84.	*ibd.*	Falstaff.	116.	*ibd.*	Grape Harvest (coloured).
85.	p. 21.	Antique.	117.	*ibd.*	Group Flowers (coloured).
86.	p. 22.	Bronze (coloured).	118.	*ibd.*	,, ,, ,,
87.	*ibd.*	Etruscan Design (tinted).	119.	*ibd.*	Sweet Peas & Cherry (coloured).
88.	p. 23.	Female figure.	120.	*ibd.*	Shells (coloured).
89.	p. 24.	Portia.	121.	*ibd.*	Flowers in Vase (coloured).
90.	p. 25.	Perspective.	122.	*ibd.*	Flowers.
91.	p. 26.	3 figures.	123.	*ibd.*	Fruit in Basket.
92.	p. 26.	Plaque (tinted).	124.	*ibd.*	Fruit on Dish.

326 MEYRICK (S. R.) and C. H. SMITH

The Costume of the Original Inhabitants of the British Islands, from the Earliest Periods to the Sixth Century; to which is added, that of the Gothic Nations on the Western Coasts of the Baltic, the Ancestors of the Anglo-Saxons and Anglo Danes. (thick and thin rule) By Samuel Rush Meyrick LL.D. and F.S.A. and Charles Hamilton Smith, Esq. (thin and thick rule) [one line quote from Barddas and 1 line quote from Bardic Doctrines] London: (thin and thick rule) Printed by William Bulmer and Co. Shakespear Press, Published by R. Havell, No. 3, Chapel-Street, Tottenham-Court-Road

Folio. 1815

COLLATION.—Half-title + Title as above (v. blank) + Chronological Series of the Plates 1 p. (v. blank) + sub-title 1 p. (v. blank) + pp. 1–59 + Front. + 24 coloured plates.

Each plate is marked, C.H.S. delt. Aquatinted by R. Havell Published June 1 1815 by R. Havell 3 Chapel Street London.

Meyrick's Costume of the British Islands (*contd.*)

Front.	Composite—Druids oak, cromlech, weapons &c.	
1. p. 5.	A Briton of the Interior.	
2. p. 8.	A Belgic Briton and one of the Cassiterides.	
3. p. 16.	A Maaeata and Caledonian.	
4. p. 19.	A Mounted British Warrior.	
5. p. 21.	British Fishing and Husbandry.	
6. p. 22.	Costume of the Druidical Order.	
7. p. 24.	A British Bard and an Ovate.	
8. p. 25.	Bardic Scholars.	
9. p. 27.	Irish Ottamh, and an Heraldic Bard.	
10. p. 28.	An Arch Druid in his Judicial Habit.	
11. p. 30.	Grand Conventional Festival of the Britons.	
12. p. 35.	Boadicea, Queen of the Iceni.	
13. p. 36.	A Romanised Briton and a Feryllt.	
14. p. 37.	Roman British Females.	
15. p. 38.	Roman British Priestesses.	
16. p. 39.	Irish Brehons.	
17. p. 41.	Costume of the Pagan Irish.	
18. p. 43.	Hibernian Male, & Female Costume.	
19. p. 45.	Pabo Post Prydian.	
20. p. 46.	St. Jestin ab Geraint.	
21. p. 50.	Military Costume of the Gothic Nations, on the Western Coasts of the Baltic.	
22. p. 53.	A Drotte and a Fola.	
23. p. 56.	Costume of a Saxon Chief.	
24. p. 57.	Gurm Gamle, King of Denmark and a Danish Youth.	

SECOND EDITION.—Title as before, imprint changed to Printed by Howlett and Brimmer, Columbian Press, No. 10 Frith Street, Soho Square, for T. M'Lean, No. 26 Haymarket, and E. Williams, No. 11 Strand 1821.

327 MEYRICK (S. R.)

Costume of the Original Inhabitants of the British Islands, and adjacent coasts of the Baltic . . . An Improved Edition London Republished by the New Proprietor, J. Dowding, Bookseller, 82, Newgate Street

Folio.   N.D.

COLLATION.—Title (v. blank) + Chronological Series of the Plates 1 p. (v. blank) + 44 unnumbered leaves of text (B–Z1 in 2's) + Front. + 24 coloured plates as in 1815 edn.

The illustrations printed from the same plates are in consequence greatly inferior to those of the preceding edition, aquatinting in many places having worn right away.

328 MIDDLETON (J. J.)

Grecian Remains in Italy, a Description of Cyclopian Walls, and of Roman Antiquities with Topographical and Picturesque Views of Ancient Latium (thick and thin rule) By J. J. Middleton (thick and thin rule) (2 line Greek quotation) London: (thin and thick rule) Printed for Edward Orme, Printseller to His Majesty, Bond Street; By W. Bulmer and Co.   Cleveland-Row St James's

Folio.   1812

COLLATION.—Title as above (v. blank) + pp. 1–50 + 24 plates.   Each plate marked, J. J. Middleton delineavit (Except plates 8 and 9 which are by Phillip Giuntotardi) and marked Dubourg sculpt. (except 7 and 17 which are engraved by Jeakes).

1. p. 1. A View of Rome from Monte Mario (folding).
2. p. 16. View from the summit of Monte Caro (folding).   ⎫ in some copies
3. *ibd.*   Continuation of the View from the summit of Monte Caro (folding). ⎭ together on 1 plate.
4. p. 19. View of the Ancient Tomb near the Scite of Bobilae.

Middleton's Grecian Remains (*contd.*)

5. p. 20. View from the Grotto of the Convent of the Capuchins at Albano.
6. p. 22. Ancient Tomb in the Garden at Palluzuola.
7. p. 24. Albano from the Road to the Lake.
8. p. 25. Lake of Albano 1st View.
9. *ibd.* Lake of Albano 2nd View.
10. *ibd.* Nymphaeum on the Borders of the Lake of Albano.
11. p. 26. Emissary of the Lake of Nemi.
12. p. 27. General View of the Town of Cora.
13. p. 31. Remains of the Temple of Hercules at Cora.
14. p. 33. General View of the Scite of the Ancient City of Norba.
15. p. 34. Interior of the Great Cyclopean Gate of the Citadel of Alatri.
16. p. 37. Ruins of the Temple of Nympha.
17. p. 38. A Cyclopian Gate at Segni.
18. *ibd.* Pointed Cyclopian Gate at Segni.
19. p. 42. Exterior View of the Porta San Pietro at Alatri.
20. p. 44. Exterior of the Great Cyclopian Gate at Norba.
21. p. 46. Exterior of the Great Cyclopian Gate of the Ancient Citadel of the Alatri.
22. p. 47. Small Cyclopian Gate of the Citadel of Alatri.
23. p. 48. Lake of Giuliano.
24. p. 50. Two plates of Sections.

> *A 2nd Edition* 1820.

329 MILES (E.)

An Epitome, Historical and Statistical, descriptive of the Royal Naval Service of England. By E. Miles, with the assistance of Lieutenant Lawford Miles, R.N. Embellished with 8 highly finished coloured engraved Views of Shipping, by W. Knell, besides fourteen coloured illustrations of the Flags, Pendants, and Ensigns, as worn by Her Majesty's Ships and Vessels in Commission. London: Ackermann and Company, 96 Strand.

Octavo.   1841

COLLATION.—Half-title + Title as above + Dedication 1 p. (v. blank) + Note 1 p. (v. blank) + Contents pp. ix–xii + Illustrations 1 p. (v. Errata) + pp. 1–184 + Advertisement by Ackermann 2 pp. "Important Marine Prints" + Advertisements 14 pp. + 8 coloured aquatint plates.

5. Front. A Sloop of War (New Class).   18 Guns as Dido &c.
1. p. 40. A First Rate (New Class) Line of Battle Ship.   110 Guns as the Queen &c.
2. p. 53. A Second Rate (New Class) Line of Battle Ship.   92 Guns as Rodney &c.
3. p. 59. Large Frigate (New Class) of 50 Guns as Vernon &c.
4. p. 61. Frigate (New Class) of 36 guns as Pique &c.
6. p. 70. A Sloop of War Brig (New Class) of 18 Guns as Pilot &c.
7. p. 74. Man of War Schooner (New class) of 6 Guns as Spider &c.
8. p. 76. Man of War Cutter of 10 Guns as Bramble &c.

> *Reissued* 1844 *by M. A. Nattali*, 23 Bedford Street, Covent Garden.

Military Adventures of Johnny Newcome 1815.   See under Rowlandson.

330 MIRROR DE LA MODE

The Mirror de la Mode 1803.   To be continued Monthly Vol. I (thin and thick rule) London: Published by Madame Lanchester, No. 17, New Bond-Street.   Printed by W. Bulmer and Co. Cleveland-Road, St. James's.

Quarto.   1803

Mirror De La Mode (*contd.*)

COLLATION.—Frontispiece "Statute of the Venus de Medicis" + Title as above (v. Description of the Frontispiece) + Dedication pp. 3–6 + pp. 7–100 + 25 coloured plates.

All published. Issued in 12 monthly numbers (Jan.–Dec.) each number containing 2 plates, except Dec. which has 3 plates. The Text is in English, French and Italian. The charming plates all bearing Madame Lanchester's imprint, include, Walking Dress, Evening Dress, Half dress, Full dress, Morning Dress, Ball Dress, undress and Head Ornaments. Rare.

331 MITFORD (J.)

The Adventures of Johnny Newcome in the Navy; A Poem, in Four Cantos (rule) By John Mitford, Esq. R.N. (thick and thin rule) (4 line verse) (thin and thick rule) London: Published by Sherwood, Neely, and Jones, Paternoster Row; J. Johnston, 98, Cheapside; Macredie and Co. Edinburgh; R. Millikin, Dublin; and sold by all Booksellers (short rule).

Octavo.   1819

COLLATION.—Title as above (v. blank) + Dedication 1 p. (v. blank) + To the Reader 3 pp. (v–vii) (p. viii To the Binder) + pp. 1–224 (pp. 187–8 repeated starred, pp. 201–208 omitted) + Notes 34 leaves (unpaged sig A–I2 in 4's) + 20 coloured plates.

1. Front. The Cockpit   William fect.
2. p.   12. Midshipmans' Birth (sic)   Williams sculpt.
3. p.   14. State Cabin—Newcome's Exit after Dinner   C. Williams fect.
4. p.   19. The Quarter Deck before Battle   Williams fecit.
5. p.   23. Newcome capsizing the Admiral   Williams fecit.
6. p.   26. A Cruise in Portsmouth after Game   Williams fecit.
7. p.   36. The Captain in the Nunnery turning the Spit   Williams fecit.
8. p.   48. The Gun Room—Newcome in the Bilboes   Williams fecit.
9. p.   50. Gibralter, Newcome in Disgrace   Williams fecit.
10. p.   51. Market-Day—Gibralter   Williams fecit.
11. p.   61. Gibralter Sally Port News for Newcome   Williams fecit.
12. p.   62. The Navy Tavern Gibralter   Williams fecit.
13. p.   90. Newcome at a Fox Chace   Williams fecit.
14. p. 108. The Parson and his Lass in the Coal Hole   Williams fect.
15. p. 125. The Ward Room Newcome and Capt. Clackit   Williams fect.
16. p. 170. Palermo Pier Newcome Victorious.
17. p. 186. Jamaica—Newcome running from the Black Squadron   C. Williams fecit.
18. p. 188. Barbadoes—Newcome and Mrs. Sambo   C. Williams fct.
19. p. 189. Crossing the Line   Williams fecit.
20. p. 214. Greenwich—Newcome's Farewell to the Navy   C. Williams.

Issued in 8 monthly parts at 2s. 6d. per part and on completion in "one Elegant Volume" royal octavo.

Not to be confused with another book with the same title but illustrated with 16 plates by Rowlandson (see under Rowlandson). In an advertisement in parts of Syntax Tour of London, copies of Newcome's work were offered for sale with the Remark, The Original and Genuine Edition by John Mitford, Esq. of the Royal Navy ... when the former Editions were nearly complete, a work was puffed off under the Title of "The Genuine Edition," which on a comparison, the Public and Naval Gentlemen in particular, will soon perceive was never written by a naval officer.

332 MITFORD (J.)

Johnny Newcome in Navy.   Third Edition

Octavo.   1823

COLLATION.—Title as before with the words, The Third Edition, between rules inserted after the author's name + Dedication 1 leaf + To Reader and Binder 2 ll. + pp. 1–284, including the notes + 20 coloured plates as in the first edition with the exception that the last 2 plates are transferred to pp. 191 and 280 respectively.

333 MOLEVILLE (M. Bertrand de)

The Costume of the Hereditary States of the House of Austria displayed in Fifty Coloured Engravings; with descriptions, and an introduction by M. Bertrand de Moleville (rule) Translated by R. C. Dallas, Esq. London: (thin and thick rule) Printed for William Miller, Old-Bond-Street; by William Bulmer and Co. Cleveland Row, St. James's

Folio.   1804

COLLATION.—Title as above (v. blank) + Title in French 1 p. (v. blank) + Advertisement 2 pp. (i–ii) + Avis 2 pp. (iii–iv) + List of Plates 1 p. (v. Tables des Planches) + 50 coloured aquatint plates each with 1 leaf of Text (in English and French).

Each plate marked, Engraved by Wm. Ellis (except plates 22, 23, 28, 34, 35, 36, 37, 39, 41 and 50 Engraved by Wm. Poole and plates 21 and 29 which bear no engraver).   The plates are numbered and bear Miller's imprint.

1. [Peasant of Upper Austria.]
2. [A Country woman of Upper Austria.]
3. [A Village Girl of Upper Austria.]
4. [A Peasant of Upper Carniola.]
5. [A Peasant of Upper Carniola in Summer Dress.]
6. [A Country woman of Upper Carniola in Summer Dress.]
7. [A Country Girl of Upper Carniola in Holiday Clothes.]
8. [A Peasant of Upper Carniola in Winter Dress.]
9. [A Countrywoman of Upper Carniola in Winter Dress.]
10. [A Tyrolian Hunter.]
11. [A Tyrolian Wrestler.]
12. [A Serving maid of a Inn at Inspruck.]
13. [Peasants of the Neighbourhood of Inspruck.]
14. [A Hungarian Peasant.]
15. [A Hungarian Country woman.]
16. [A Sclavonian Peasant.]
17. [A Sclavonian Country Girl.]
18. [A young Peasant of Egra.]
19. [Woman & Girl of Egra.]
20. [Young Bride of Egra.]
21. [Peasants of Egra Summer Clothes.]
22. [Bohemian Serf.]
23. [Bohemian Woman.]
24. [Peasant of Flipovan.]
25. [Country woman of Flipovan.]
26. [Country women of Hermenstadt.]
27. [Peasant of Hermenstadt.]
28. [Saxon Ladies of Hermenstadt.]
29. [Citizens of Hermenstadt.]
30. [Croatian Women.]
31. [Polish Jew.]
32. [Polish Jewess.]
33. [A Jew of Montgatz.]
34. [A Zouppanese Count.]
35. [A. Zouppanese Countess.]
36. [A Zouppanese & his wife.]
37. [Man & Woman of Risano.]
38. [Greek Priest.]
39. [Serethian.]
40. [Pandoar.]
41. [Moravian Mountaineer.]
42. [Country woman Moravia.]
43. [Peasant Lowlands Moravia.]
44. [Country woman Lowlands Moravia.]
45. [Inhabitant Lowlands Moravia Winter Clothes.]
46. [Country woman Lowlands Moravia Winter Dress.]
47. [Hannachian Woman.]
48. [Russian Peasant.]
49. [Russian Woman.]
50. [Blacksmith Upper Austria.]

There are late reissues with plates bearing watermark of 1820.

334 MOORE (J.)

To the Honorable the Court of Directors of the East India Company. These Eighteen Views Taken at & near Rangoon are respectfully dedicated by Permission by their Gratefull Obedient Humble Servant Joseph Moore Lieut of His Majesty's 89th Regt. (the above lettering on emblematic engraving Drawn by Thos. Stothard R.A. Engraved by R. W. Smart) Published by Thos. Clay 18 Ludgate Hill London

Folio. [1825–6]

COLLATION.—Dedication as above (v. blank) + List of Subscribers 4 leaves (the first having an emblematic engraved heading by J. Bromley after T. Stothard) + 18 coloured plates all marked, Drawn by J. Moore and all with imprint Published [date] by Kingsbury & Co. 6 Leadenhall Strt. and T. Clay 18 Ludgate Hill London.

1. The Harbour of Port Cornwallis, Island of Great Andaman, with the Fleet getting under Weigh for Rangoon   Engraved by G. Hunt.   Octr. 1 1825.
2. View of the landing at Rangoon of part of the Combined Forces from Bengal and Madras, under the Orders of Sir Archd. Campbell, K.C.B. on the 11th of May 1824   Engraved by H. Pyall   Octr. 1 1825.   Kingsbury Perbury & Allen.
3. The Principal approach to the Great Dagon Pagoda at Rangoon   Engraved by T. Fielding   Novr. 9, 1852.
4. View of the Great Dagon Pagoda at Rangoon and Scenery adjacent to the Westward of the Great Road   Engraved by H. Pyall   Novr. 9 1825.
5. Scene upon the Terrace of the Great Pagoda at Rangoon looking towards the North   Engraved by G. Hunt   Octr. 1 1825,
6. The Attack upon the Stockades near Rangoon by Sir Archibald Campbell, K.C.B. on the 28th of May 1824   Engraved by G. Hunt   Novr. 9th 1825.
7. The Gold Temple of the principal Idol Guadma, taken from its front being the Eastern face of the Great Dagon Pagoda at Rangoon   Engraved by G. Hunt   Octr. 1 1825.
8. Inside View of the Gold Temple on the Terrace of the Great Dagon Pagoda at Rangoon   Engraved by G. Hunt   Novr. 9th 1825.
9. Scene from the Upper Terrace of the Great Pagoda at Rangoon, to the South East   Engraved by H. Pyall   Jan. 2, 1826.
10. The Storming of the Lesser Stockade at Kemmendine near Rangoon on the 10th of June 1824   Engraved by G. Hunt   Jan. 2nd 1826.
11. View of the Lake and part of the Eastern Road from Rangoon taken from the Advance of the 7th Madras Native Infantry   Engraved by H. Pyall   Novr. 9th 1825.
12. The Position of part of the Army previous to attacking the Stockades on the 8th of July 1824   Engraved by G. Hunt   Octr. 1 1825.
13. Scene upon the Eastern Road from Rangoon looking towards the South   Engraved by G. Hunt   Novr. 9, 1825.
14. Scene upon the Terrace of the Great Dagon Pagoda at Rangoon taken near the Great Bell   Engraved by G. Hunt   Jany. 2nd 1826.
15. Rangoon.   The Storming of one of the principal Stockades on its inside on the 8th of July 1824   Engraved by G. Hunt   Octr. 1 1825.
16. View of the Great Dagon Pagoda and ajacent (sic) Scenery taken on the Eastern Road from Rangoon   Engraved by T. Fielding   Novr. 9 1825.
17. The Conflagation of Dalla on the Rangon River   Engraved by G. Hunt   Jan. 2 1826.
18. The Attack of the Stockades at Pagoda Point, on the Rangoon River by Sir Archd. Campbell K.C.B. 8th July 1824   Engraved by Reeve Junr. Jan. 2 1826.

Plate 16 exists in 2 states, in First Issue word adjacent spelt ajacent. This is corrected in Second Issue. Some copies have a plan in addition to the plates, and there are likewise 3 leaves of Indian subscribers, but copies are complete without them. Two volumes of text were issued one to the above and one to the following work, but they rarely are present.

The following 6 plates by Capts. Marryat & Thornton are sometimes to be found bound up with Moore's Views. Each of these plates bears imprint, Published Sepr. 12, 1826 by Thos. Clay 18 Ludgate Hill London and each is engraved by H. Pyall.

Moore's Rangoon (*contd.*)

1. The Storming of the Fort of Syriam by a combined force of Sailors and European & Native Troops, on the 5th Augut. 1824   Painted by T. Stothard R.A. from an original sketch by Captn. Marryat R N.
2. The Attack of the Dalla Stockade by the Combined Forces, on the 4th Septr. 1824   Printed by T. Stothard R.A. from an original Sketch by Captn. Marryat R.N.
3. The Attempt of the Birmans to retake the Stockades of Dalla, on the Night of the 6th Septr. 1824   Painted by D. Cox from an Original Sketch by Captn. Marryat R N.
4. One of the Birman Gilt War Boats Captured by Captn. Chads R N in his successful expedition against Tanthabeen Stockade   Painted by T. Stothard R A from an Original Sketch by Captn. Marryat R.N.
5. H.M.S. Lorne H C Cruizer Mercury, Heroine, Carron & Lotus Transports attacking the Stockades at the entrance of Bassein River on the 26th Feby. 1825   Painted by G. Webster from an Original Sketch by Captn. Marryat R N.
6. The Combined Forces under Brigadier Cotton C.B. and Captns. Alexander C.B. & Chads R.N. passing the Fortress of Donabue to effect a junction with Sir Archibald Campbell on the 27th March 1825   Painted by T. Stothard R A from a Sketch by Captn. Thornton R.N.

335 MORISON (D.)

Views of the Ducal Palaces and Hunting Seats of Saxe Coburg and Gotha by Douglas Morison. (this lettering above coloured view "Entrance to the Fortress of Coburg")

Folio.

COLLATION.—10 leaves of Text + 21 coloured plates including title viz., Title as above + Text "Memoirs of the Ancient House of Saxe-Coberg-Gotha 2 pp. + House of Saxe-Weimar 1 p. + Modern House of Saxe-Gotha and House of Saxe-Coburg-Saalfield, now Saxe-Coburg Gotha 3 pp. + pp. 3–10 + Dedication to H.S.H. the Reigning Duke of Saxe Coburg Gotha 1 leaf + Preface 1 leaf.

1. Fortress of Coburg. Gateway.	12. Gotha Friedenstein.
2. „ „ Entrance.	13. „ Friedrichsthal.
3. „ „ Distant View.	14. Reinhardsbrunn Exterior.
4. Palace of Ehrenburg. Exterior.	15. „ Garden View.
5. „ „ „ Giants Hall.	16. „ View from Inselsberg Mountain.
6. Rosenau View from Gardens.	
7. „ ditto.	17. Schloss Friedrichsworthe Garden View.
8. „ View from Terrace.	18. „ „ Terrace.
9. Schloss Callenberg. Exterior.	19. Molsdorf.
10. „ „ Courtyard.	20. The Castle of Tenneberg.
11. „ „ View from the Wood.	21. The Wachsenburg.

Mr. Facey's Romford's Hounds 1865.   See under [Surtees (R.)].

Mr. Sponge's Sporting Tour 1853.   See under [Surtees (R.)].

My Cousin in the Army 1832.   See under [Cruikshank (I. R.)].

336 MUDFORD (William)

An Historical Account of the Campaign in the Netherlands, in 1815, under his grace the Duke of Wellington, and Marshal Prince Blucher, comprising the Battles of Ligny, Quatre Bras, and Waterloo; with a detailed narrative of the political events connected with those memorable conflicts, down to the surrender of Paris, and the departure of

Mudford's Waterloo (*contd.*)

Bonaparte for St. Helena. (rule) Drawn up from the first authorities by William Mudford. (rule) illustrated by numerous public and private official documents, and other papers, hitherto unpublished, communicated by officers of the highest distinction. (rule) Embellished with a series of plates, descriptive of the country between Brussels and Charleroi, from drawings made on the spot, by James Rouse, Esq. also a Plan of the Battles, and a Map, shewing the March of the Allied Armies to Paris (rule) London: Printed for Henry Colburn, Conduit Street, Hanover Square (rule).

Quarto.   1817

COLLATION.—Half-title "Historical Account of the Campaign in the Netherlands, &c. &c." (v. blank) + Frontispiece + Engraved title "An Historical Account of the Battle of Waterloo" [with bust of Wellington at top, British troops representing different sections of the army on either side, military trophies at foot Drawn & Etched by G. Cruickshank Rouse sculp. Published by H. Colburn Conduit Street London 1816] (v. blank) + Printed title as above (v. W. Flint, Printer, Old Bailey London) + Dedication to Duke of Wellington 2 ll. (pp. v–viii) + Preface pp. ix–xiii (p. xiv blank) + Description of Plates pp. xv–xviii + Explanation of figures in plan 1 p. (v. Errata + Directions to Binder) + pp. 1–320 pp. 13–14 are a sub-title "An Historical Account of the Battle of Waterloo" (v. blank) + Appendix pp. 321–362 + Index pp. 363–8 + Map + Plan + 28 plates (31 in all including engraved title).

Each plate with imprint, Published by H. Colburn Conduit Street 1816 (with exception of frontispiece which bears no imprint).

Plate 27. Frontispiece. Waterloo, in Memory of the Heroic Deeds of Shaw of 1st Life Guards. Engraved title.
Plate 30. p. 1. Map from Brussels to Paris (folding).
  ,,   29. p. 1. Plan of the Battles of Ligny, Quatre Bras & Waterloo (folding).
  ,,   28. p. 1. The Battle of Waterloo Delineated under the inspection of Officers who were present at memorable conflict. Drawn & Etched by G. Cruikshank James Rouse sculp. (folding).

The remainder of the plates (1–26) *should be bound at the end of the volume. They bear no titles but are as follows:*

Plate 1. A   The city of Brussels, from the entrance of the Forêt de Soigné, with the Barrier Rouse delin. & sculp.
  ,,   2. B   Entrance to the Forêt de Soigné, where the two roads from Brussels meet Rouse delin. & sculp.
  ,,   3. C   Approach to the village of Waterloo, with the chapel of Waterloo seen in the distance. Rouse delin & sculp.
  ,,   4. D   Chapel of Waterloo Rouse delin. & sculp.
  ,,   5. DD Interior of the Chapel of Waterloo   Rouse delin. & sculp.
  ,,   6. E   Headquarters of the Duke of Wellington in the village of Waterloo Rouse delin. & sculp.
  ,,   7. F   Skirt of the Foret de Soigne, with a distant view of the village of Mont St Jean Rouse delin. & sculp.
  ,,   8. G   Part of the village of Mont St Jean Rouse delin. & sculp.
  ,,   9. H   The farm house of Mont St Jean Rouse delin. & sculp.
  ,,   10. I   View of the cottage of Valette Rouse delin. & sculp.
  ,,   11. J   Chateau of Frischermont Rouse delin & sculp.
  ,,   12. K   The farm of La Haye Sainte Rouse delin. & sculp.
  ,,   13. L   A front view of the farm of La Haye Sainte Rouse delin. & sculp.
  ,,   14. M   La Belle Alliance, the centre of the French position Rouse delin. & sculp.
  ,,   15. N ⎱ Another View of La Belle Alliance Rouse delin. & sculp.
  ,,   16. O ⎰   ,,   ,,   ,,   ,, Rouse delin. & sculp.
  ,,   17. P ⎫ Hougoumont View of wood skirting chateau Rouse delin. & sculp.
  ,,   18. Q ⎬   ,,   Burial ground after battle Rouse delin. & sculp.
  ,,   19. R ⎭   ,,   Interior Rouse delin. & sculp.

Mudford's Waterloo (*contd.*)

Plate 20. S   Observatory Rouse delin. & sculp.

,, 21. T   Village of Genappe Rouse sculp. C. C. Hamilton del.

,, 22. V   Les Quatre Bras Rouse sculp. C. C. Hamilton del.

,, 23. U   Ligny Castle Rouse sculp. C. C. Hamilton del.

,, 24. W   The ruins of the village of Ligny Rouse sculp. C. C. Hamilton del.

,, 25. Y   Flight of Bonaparte from the Field of Waterloo accompanied by his Guide Drawn & Etched G. Cruikshank Rouse sculp.

,, 26.   Portraits of the General Officers 1 The Prince of Orange 2 The Duke of Brunswick 3 The Duke of Wellington 4 Genl. Lord Hill 5 Genl. Sir Thos. Picton 6 Prince Blucher 7 Marquis of Anglesea Drawn & Etched by G. Cruikshank James Rouse sculp.

The frontispiece Shaw of the Life Guards is usually missing, plate 26 Portraits of General Officers taking its place. Plates B, D, DD, and L are to be found mounted.

337 NASH (Joseph)

The Mansions of England in the Olden Time; Four Series.   1839–1849

Folio.

First Series.

The Mansions of England in the Olden Time by Joseph Nash A.D.   1839

COLLATION.—Title as above engraved on portal of East Barham Norfolk + 26 coloured lithographs.

1. Hall-Hatfield Herts.
2. Staircase Hatfield Herts.
3. Ockwells Berks.
4. { Porch Ockwells Berks.
   { Corridor Ockwells Berks.
5. Hall Ockwells Berks.
6. Staircase Wakehurst Sussex.
7. Hall Wakehurst Sussex.
8. Bramshill Hants.
9. Terrace Bramshill.
10. Crewe Hall Cheshire.
11. Southam Glocester.
12. Westwood Worcestershire.
13. Hall Beddington Surrey.
14. Boughton Malherbe Kent.
15. Penshurst Kent.
16. Franks Kent.
17. Holland House Kensington.
18. Holland House Kensington.
19. Sutton Place near Guildford.
20. Lorelly near Guildford.
21. Drawing Room Haddow Derbyshire.
22. Chapel Haddow Derbyshire.
23. Long Gallery Haddow Derbyshire.
24. Dining Room Haddow Derbyshire.
25. Hall Haddow Derbyshire.

Second Series.

The Mansions of England in the Olden Time. By Joseph Nash Second Series

(1840)

COLLATION.—Title as above on Doorway of Coombe Abbey Warwickshire + 25 coloured lithographs + 1 folio leaf of Text (description of plates) and sometimes found inserted 2 leaves Dedication and Prospectus quarto size (also containing description of plates).

1. Hall Audley End Essex.
2. Porch Audley End Essex.
3. Hall Littlewates Wilts.
4. Hall Moat House Ightham Kent.
5. Chapel Moat House Ightham Kent.
6. Hall Bolsover Castle Derbyshire.
7. Drawing Room, Broughton Castle Oxon.
8. Porch Wroxton Abbey Oxon.
9. Hall Wroxton Abbey Oxon.
10. Gallery Hardwicke Hall Derbyshire.
11. Presence Chamber Hardwicke Hall Derbyshire.
12. Grand Staircase Hardwicke Hall Derbyshire.
13. Grand Entrance Hardwicke Hall Derbyshire.
14. Hever Castle Kent.
15. Bay Window Gallery Hever Castle.
16. Sutton Place near Guildford Surrey.
17. Knole Staircase.
18. Knole Brown Gallery.
19. Knole Room leading to Chapel.

Nash's Mansions (*contd.*)

20. Knole Bedchamber.
21. Knole Gallery over the Hall.
22. Knole Cartoon Gallery.
23. Knole Hall.

24. { Stairs to the Terrace Bramshill Hants.
{ Postern Gate Bramshill Hants.
25. Room Postlip Hall, Gloucestershire.

Third Series.

Mansions of England in the Olden Time By Joseph Nash (Third Series)   (1841)

COLLATION.—Title as above on Porch Cranbourne Dorsetshire + 25 coloured lithographs + 1 folio leaf of Text (description of plates).

1. Burleigh Northamptonshire.
2. Burleigh Staircase.
3. Hall Parkam Sussex.
4. Wollaton Nottinghamshire.
5. Wallaton Hall.
6. Gallery Lanhydroc Cornwall.
7. Staircase Aldermaston Berks.
8. Waterstone Dorsetshire.
9. Athelhampton Dorsetshire.
10. Athelhampton Hall.
11. Garden Front Cranbourne.
12. Drawing Room Chastleton Oxon.
13. Gallery in the Hall Hatfield Herts.
14. Gallery Hatfield.
15. Charlcote Warwickshire.
16. Hall Hampton Court Middlesex.
17. Presence Chamber Hampton Court.
18. Drawing Room Dorfold Cheshire.
19. Porch Montacute Somerset.
20. Hall Penshurst Kent.
21. Compton Wyngate Warwickshire.
22. Hall Compton Wyngate.
23. Bramhall Hall Cheshire.
24. Bramhall Bay Window in Hall.
25. Bramhall Drawing Room.

Fourth Series.

The Mansions of England in the Olden Time By Joseph Nash Fourth Series

A.D. 1849

COLLATION.—Title as above on Entrance to the Moat House Ightham Kent + 25 coloured lithographs.

1. Bay Window in the Drawing Room. Lyme Hall Cheshire.
2. Levens Westmoreland.
3. Levens Hall.
4. Levens Dining Room.
5. Levens Drawing Room.
6. Levens Small Drawing Room.
7. Brereton Cheshire.
8. Banqueting Room Bramhall Cheshire.
9. Inlaid Chamber Sizerch Westmoreland.
10. Hall Crewe Hall Cheshire.
11. Drawing Room Ashton Hall Warwickshire.
12. Bingham Melcomb Dorsetshire.
13. Fire Place Kenilworth Warwickshire.
14. Speke Hall Lancashire.
15. Hall Speke Lancashire.
16. Bay Window Hall Speke Lancashire.
17. Fire Place Drawing Room Speke Lancashire.
18. Little Moreton Hall Cheshire.
19. Hall Adlington Cheshire.
20. Hall Milton Abbey Dorsetshire.
21. Borwick Hall Lancashire.
22. Garden Front Speke Lancashire.
23. Gallery Ashton Hall Warwickshire.
24. Carved Parlour Crewe Hall Cheshire.
25. Staircase Aston Hall Warwickshire.

RÉSUMÉ.—*104 plates (incld. titles) London Published by Thomas M'Lean, 26 Haymarket Printed by Moyes & Barclay Castle Street Leicester Square. The plates printed by Hullmandel. There is a dedication leaf with a List of Plates on the reverse to each series but this is not found in all copies. Issued plain and coloured, the coloured copies being issued on stout cardboard mounts in a Roxburghe portfolio with leather title panels. One of the most important of the lithograph books when coloured, there being an enormous difference in value between the two states.*

338 NASH (J.)

The Royal Pavilion at Brighton. Published by the Command of, and dedicated by permission to the King, by His Majesty's dutiful Subject and Servant, John Nash.

Folio. [1826]

COLLATION.—Dedication as above (v. blank) + Index of Subjects 1 p. (v. blank) + 31 plates, 28 being in colour.

1. The Steine Front previous to the Alterations.	17. Music Gallery.
2. The Steine Front as originally designed.	18. Salon.
3. Ground Plan.	19. Banqueting Gallery.
4. Geometrical View of the Steine Front.	20. Banqueting Room.
5. Perspective View of the Steine Front.	21. The King's Bed Room.
6. Centre part of Steine Front.	22. The Private Library.
7. West Front.	23. Gallery on Chamber Floor.
8. Principal Entrance (West Front).	24. The Kitchen.
9. North Front & Principal Entrance.	25. Perspective View of the Stable Building from Pleasure Grounds.
10. Kings Private Apartments.	26. Interior of the Rotunda.
11. Staircases & Octagon Hall.	27. Stables towards Church Street & Riding House.
12. Great Hall.	28. Section through the State Apartments (long folding plate).
13. Small Drawing Room.	
14. Gallery as it was.	
15. Gallery as it now is.	
16. Music or Concert Room.	

All the above plates were printed in outline, except 1, 3, 7, 17, 27, and in addition, 3 further plates were executed in outline, and not done in colour, each plate marked, John Nash Esq. Archt., & Invent., viz.

March 1825. Pavilion Salon. Augt. Pugin delt. Gladwin sculpt.
Dec. 1824. „ Blue Room. A. Pugin delt. T. Kearnan sculpt.
March 1825. „ Yellow Drawing Room. Augt. Pugin delt. C. Moore sculpt.

339 NASH (Joseph)

Views of the Interior and Exterior of Windsor Castle (coloured vignette Royal Entrance to Quadrangle) by Joseph Nash (rule) London: Thomas M'Lean, 26 Haymarket

Folio. 1848

COLLATION.—Title as above (v. blank) + Dedication to Queen Victoria 1 p. (v. blank) + 1 p. of Text (note, the verso blank) + List of Plates 1 p. (v. blank) + 25 plates each with leaf of Text.

1. Lower Ward St George's Chapel & the Round Tower.	13. The South Corridor.
2. The Grand Staircase.	14. Angle of the Corridor.
3. The Guard Chamber.	15. The East Corridor.
4. The Vandyke Room.	16. The Private Chapel.
5. The Rubens Room.	17. South East View of the Castle.
6. The Quadrangle looking East (Moonlight).	18. The White Drawing Room.
7. The Throne Room.	19. The Green Drawing Room.
8. The Waterloo Gallery.	20. The Crimson Drawing Room.
9. St. George's Hall (the Garter Banquet 1844).	21. The Private Dining Room.
10. St George's Hall (the Garter Banquet 1844 the Guests seated).	22. Castle & Terrace Garden.
11. The State Reception Room an Evening Party.	23. The Queens Private Sitting Room.
12. The Quadrangle looking West.	24. The Library.
	25. Interior of St. George's Chapel.

Nash J. See also under Price (L.). Venice.

340 NATTES (J. C.)

Bath, Illustrated by a Series of Views, from the Drawings of John Claude Nattes with Descriptions to each plate (vignette) London: (thin and thick rule) Published by William Miller, Albemarle-Street, and William Sheppard Bristol

Folio.   1806

COLLATION.—Half-title "Bath, illustrated by a Series of Views (thin and thick rule) London (thin and thick rule) Printed by W. Bulmer and Co. Cleveland Row, St James" (v. blank) + Title as above (v. blank) + Preface 3 pp. + List of Plates 1 p. + 28 plates each with a leaf of Text.

Each plate is marked, J. C. Nattes del (plate 9 J. C. Nattes delin) I. Hill Aquatinta (except plates 5, 6, 7 and 14 which are marked, F. C. Lewis Aquatinta) and all plates bear imprint London Published by W. [or William] Miller Albemarle Street and date.

1. A General View of Bath from the Claverton Road   Novr. 1804.
2. View of Cross Bath, Bath Street &c.   Novr. 1804.
3. New Bridge &c.   Novr. 1804.
4. Crescent &c.   Novr. 1804.
5. Milsom Street &c.   April 1st 1805.
6. South Parade.   Nov. 1804.
7. Orange Grove   April 1st 1805.
8. The Pump Room   Novr. 1804.
9. Axford & Paragon Buildings &c.   Novr. 1804.
10. North Parade   Novr. 1804.
11. Bath Wick Ferry &c.   Augst 1805.
12. Interior of the Concert Room   June 1805.
13. Sydney Hotel &c.   Augst. 1805.
14. The Bridges over the Canal in Sidney Gardens   May 1805.
15. Old Bridge   Novr. 1804.
16. Pump Room   Novr. 1804.
17. A General View [of Bath]   June 1805.
18. New Room   Novr. 1805.
19. Inside of Queen's Bath   Novr. 1804.
20. Marlborough St. &c.   Nov. 1805.
21. View of the Town Hall, Market & Abbey Church   Nov. 1804.
22. Interior of the Abbey 1805 [no month].
23. Pultney Bridge &c. &c.   May 1st 1805.
24. Old Ferry &c.   Novr. 1805.
25. Aquaduct Bridge Claverton 1805 [no month].
26. The Crown &c. 1805 [no month].
27. Bradford &c. 1805 [no month].
28. Sydney Gardens 1805 [no month].
Vignette on Title [Kings Bath].
Vignette on p. 56 [View of Pulteney Street].

RÉSUMÉ.—28 *coloured plates,* 24 *being aquatinted by I. Hill and* 4 *by F. C. Lewis, and* 2 *vignettes.*

NOTE.—*Issued in boards with title printed on upper cover and price at foot, namely seven guineas. Size of uncut copy* 19½ + 13⅝ *inches. The half-title is frequently missing. Some copies have the vignettes uncoloured.*

341 NATTES (J. C.)

Nattes "Oxford delineated" plates.   Published 1st Aug. 1805 by J. Cundee.

Folio.   1805

1. Front. Vignette.   "Radcliff Library from Exeter College Terrace"   Nattes delt.   Merigot. sculpt.
2. "Entrance into Oxford from the London Road"   C. A. Pugin delt.   F. C. Lewis sculpt.
3. St Peters in the East.   C. A. Pugin delt.   Merigot. sculpt.
4. Merton Church from The Grove.   C. A. Pugin delt.   Merigot. sculpt.
5. West Entrance into Christ Church College.   Taken from Pembroke Lane.   J. C. Nattes delt.   Merigot sculpt.
6. Vignette.   Merton Tower, taken from Magpie Lane.   Pugin delt.   Merigot. sculpt.

342 NATTES (J. C.)

Versailles, Paris, et Saint Denis; ou Une Suite de Vuës d'apres des desseins par J. C. Nattes, pour servir a l'Illustration de la capitale de France et des Environs.   avec une

Nattes' Paris (*contd.*)

description historique. (thick and thin rule) A Londres: Chez W. Miller, Albemarle Street; J. C. Nattes, No. 23, Welbeck Street, et Chez M. Vandremeni, Michael's Place, Brompton. Imprimé par W. Savage, Bedford Bury

Folio.   [1810]

COLLATION.—Title as above (v. blank) + List of Plates 1 p. (v. blank) + pp. 1–79 (French text) + 40 coloured aquatint plates.

Each plate marked, J. C. Nattes del [or delin] I Hill Aquatinta (with the exception of plate 29 which is marked Cartwright Aquatinta) and each plate bears the imprint Published [date] by W. Miller Albemarle Str.   London & Vandemaire (sic) North End (with the exception of plates 1, 2, 3, 4, 17, 33, 36).

1. Avant Cour Versailles The Entrance   1805.
2. du coté de l'Orangerie Versailles from the Orangerie   1805.
3. Escalier de la Chapelle Versailles Stair-case leading to the Chapel   1806.
4. Chateau du grand Trianon Versailles Chateau of Trianon   1805.
5. Fontaine des lions dans les Jardins du Trianon Grand Trianon Fountain in the Garden   1809.
6. La Tour de Marlborough dans les Jardins de Trianon. Trianon The Tower of Marlborough   1809.
7. Salle à manger du petit Trianon Versailles The eating Room at the little Trianon   April 1 1807.
8. Le Boudoir du petit Trianon Petit Trianon The Boudoir   1809.
9. Pavillion de Lucienne Machine de Marly Versailles The Pavillion of Lucienne Waterworks of Marly   1806.
10. Grande allée du Parc St Cloud Le Pont de Sevres Maison de Lanchera Chateau de Bellevue St. Cloud The great walk of St Cloud The Bridge of Sevres &c. &c. 1809.
11. Pont et machine hydraulique de St. Cloud Partie du chateau de St. Cloud Partie de l'Grande allée du Parc St. Cloud Water Engine St. Cloud   1809.
12. Le Pont de Neuilli &c.   Paris The Bridge of Neuilli &c.   1807.
13. Vue prise dans le Jardin Anglois de Bagatelle Environs of Paris Bridge at Bagatelle   1809.
14. Le Pompe à feu du Gros Caillou Guinguettes des environs de Paris Les Thuilleries Paris Fire Engine &c. &c.   1809.
15. Place et Pont de la Concorde Le Garde Meuble Les Thuilleries Pont La Reunion Paris Square and Bridge of the Concorde The Gard Meuble The Thuilleries The Bridge Reunion   1806.
16. Le Louvre Le Pont Neuf Le College des 4 Nations Le Quai de Voltaire &c.   Paris The Louvre, The Pont Neuf The College of the 4 Nations, Voltaire's Quay &c.   1806.
17. Eglise de St. Germains Paris The Church of St. Germains   1810.
18. La Monnoie Le College des 4 Nations, Le Pont de la Reunion Le Louvre Paris The Mint The College of the 4 Nations The Bridge of Reunion The Louvre   1806.
19. Vue prise sous la derniere arche du Pont St. Michel Le Pont Chatelet Une partie de l'Hotel Dieu Les Tours de Notre Dame &c. &c. Paris From under the Arch of St. Michel's Bridge   1809.
20. Le lavoir de l'hotel dieu Pont de la Tournelle Paris The washing place belonging to the hospital of l'hotel Dieu The Bridge de la Tournelle   1806.
21. Pont de l'hotel Dieu Notre Dame Paris Bridge of the hotel dieu The Church of Notre Dame   1806.
22. Pont de l'hotel dieu dit de St. Charles Petit Pont &c. &c.   Paris Bridge of the Hotel Dieu call'd St. Charles Little Bridge &c. &c.   1806.
23. Vue prise sous une des Arches du Pont Notre Dame Partie de L'Isle St. Louis Le Pont Mairie Partie de l'ancienne Cité Paris From one of the Arches of Notre Dame   1809.
24. Vue prise sous la premiere Arch du Pont de l'Hotel Dieu pres l'Archeveché Le Petit Pont, Partie de l'Hotel Dieu, Lavoir de l'Hotel Dieu Paris View taken under the first Arch of the Bridge of Hotel Dieu The Little Bridge Part of Hotel Dieu   1809.
25. L'isle St. Louis Les Tours de Notre Dame Pont Notre Dame Le Louvre Ports aux Bleds &c. &c. Paris The Island of St. Louis The Towers of the Church of Notre Dame, The Bridge of Notre Dame, The Louvre, The Corn Quay &c.   1806.
26. Vue prise de dessous l'Arche de Givri Le Pont au change les Tours du Palais ou la Reine de France a ete prisonneire L'Horloge du Palais dont la cloche a donne le signal de l'horrible massacre de la St. Barthelemy Le Palais ou la Reine de France a été sugée Quay d'Essais &c.   Paris View drawn from under the Arch of Givry Pont au Change Les Tours du Palais where the Queen of France was

278

Nattes' Paris (*contd.*)

kept Prisoner L'Horloge du Palais, the Bell of which gave the Signal for the horrible Massacre of St. Bartholomew The Palace in which the Queen of France was tried Quay of Essais &c. 1807.

27. Le Pont Marie L'Isle St. Louis et une partie de l'Ancienne Cité Paris The Bridge of Marie The Island of St. Louis and part of the ancient city April 1807.
28. Les bains de Julien Paris Julians Baths 1809.
29. Aqueduc d'Arcueil Arcueil pres Paris Aqueduct at Arcueil Cartwright aquatinta 1806.
30. College de Navarre Etablissement des Freres Piranesi Paris College of Navarre 1809.
31. La Halle aux Bleds Paris Corn Market 1808.
32. Interieur du Chatelet La Morne Partie du Quai de la Féraille Paris Interior of the Chatelet Part of the Quay of Feraille 1809.
33. Le Temple Paris The Temple 1805.
34. Fossés de la Bastille Partie de L'Arsenal La Salpetriere &c. Paris Interior of the Fosses of the Bastille Part of the Arsenal &c. 1809.
35. Moulin a Charenton Paris Mill at Charenton April 1 1807.
36. Le Chateau de Vincenne Paris The Castle of Vincenne 1810.
37. Eglise de St. Denis Paris The Church of St. Denis &c. April 1 1807.
38. Intereur de l'Eglise de St. Denis St. Denis Interior of the church of St. Denis 1806.
39. Tombeau de Turenne Tombeau de St. Denis The Burial place of Turenne &c. &c. 1809.
40. Habitation de Rousseau Montmorancy The Residence of Rousseau 1809.

Naval Achievements of Great Britain. See under Jenkins (J.).

343 NAYLER (Sir G.)

The Coronation of His most Sacred Majesty King George the Fourth solemnized in the Collegiate Church of Saint Peter Westminster upon the Nineteenth Day of July 1821 undertaken by his Majesty's Especial Command, by the late Sir George Nayler Garter Principal King at Arms and since his decease completed from the Official Documents (thin and thick rule) London Published by Henry George Bohn, York Street Convent Garden

Folio.   1837

COLLATION.—Title as above (v. London: R. Clay, Printer, Bread Street Hill, Doctors' Commons) + Dedication to George IV 1 p. (v. blank) + Advertisement 1 p. (v. blank) + Court of Claims pp. i–xlii + Petitions pp. xliii–lvi + Coronation of George IV pp. 1–134 + Index 4 leaves (unnumbered) + List of Plates 1 p. (v. blank) + 45 coloured plates mostly marked, "Published as the Act directs [date] by Sir George Nayler Garter."

1. Vignette Title "His Majesty George the Fourth Proclaimed King. at Carlton House on Monday 31st January 1820, headed by a coloured aquatint of the ceremony at Carlton House C Wild Delint. R. Havell sculpt.
2. His Majesty George the Fourth Proclaimed King at the Royal Exchange London 31st Jan.
3. The Court of Claims in the Painted Chamber of the Palace at Westminster 1821. J. Stephanoff delt. S. W. Reynolds Engraver to the King sculpt. Jany. 1824.
4. Procession of the Dean and Prebendaries of Westminster with the Regalia July 19th 1821 Charles Wild Delt. M. Dubourg scut. Jany. 1824.
5. The King's Herbwoman and her Six Maids Strewing Flowers Miss Fellowes Miss Garth Miss Collier Miss Ramsbottom Miss Hill, Miss Daniel Miss Walker 19th July 1821.
6. A Gentleman of His Majesty's Privy Chamber Sir Frederick G. Fowke Bart 19th July 1821 Stephanoff pinxit H Meyer sculpsit March 1826.
7. The Dean of Westminster in a rich Cope Bringing the Crown from the Altar upon a Cushion of Cloth of Gold 19th July, 1821 John Ireland D.D. F. P. Stephanoff delt. Engd. by Wm. Bond & St. Reynolds Engr. to the King.
8. A Knight Commander of the most Honourable Military Order of the Bath in the Mantle and Habit

Nayler's Coronation of George IV (*contd.*)

of that Order 19th July 1821 Admiral Sir Edward Nagle P. Stephanoff delt. E. Scriven Historical Engraver to His Majesty sculp. Jany. 1826.

9. A Knight Grand Cross, of the most Honourable Military Order of the Bath in the full Habit and Collar of the Order 19th July 1821 Admiral Sir John Borlase Warren Bart P. Stephanoff delt. Engd. by Wm. Bond & Wm. Bennett.

10. Clerk of His Majesty's most Honourable Privy Council in Ordinary 19th July 1821 James Buller Esqre. P. Stephanoff delt. Engd. by S. Reynolds & E. Scriven Engrs. to the King.

11. The Chancellor of His Majesty's Exchequer in his Coronation Dress and Robe of State The Right Hon. Nicholas Vansittart now Baron Bexley P. Stephanoff pinxit Reynolds & Scriven Engravers to His Majesty sculpt.

12. A Member of His Majesty's Most Honourable Privy Council 19th July 1821 The Earl of Yarmouth now Marquess of Hertford.

13. A Knight of the Garter in the Habit and Collar of that Most Noble Order 19th July 1821 The Marquess of Londonderry Jas. Stephanoff delt. Engd. by Wm. Bond & Wm. Bennett.

14. Officer of the Jewel House attendant upon the Vice Chamberlain of his Majestys Household Thomas Baucutt Mash Esq. 19th July 1821 F. Stephanoff pinxt. H. Meyer sculpt. Jany. 1826.

15. The Treasurer of His Majesty's Household bearing the Crimson Bag with the Medals Lord Charles Bentink 19th July 1821 Stephanoff pinxit E. Scriven sculpsit March 1826.

16. The Earl of Lauderdale bearing the Standard of Scotland Lord Beresford bearing the Standard of Ireland Pages Viscount Exmouth Viscount Sidmouth in their Robes of Estate 19th July 1821.

17. The Standard of St. George borne by a Baron in his Coronation Dress and Robes of Estate attended by His Page Lord Hill—Lord Wm. Pitt Lennox 19th July 1821 P. Stephanoff pinxit. H. Meyer sculpst October 1825.

18. A Duke in the Coronation Dress and Robes of Estate 19th July 1821 The Duke of Norfolk P. Stephanoff delt. S. Reynolds Engraver to the King sculpt.

19. The Duke of Montrose in his Robes of Estate The Duke of Argyll in his Robes of Estate the Earl of Westmorland as Lord Privy Seal The Earl of Harrowby as Lord President of Council 19th July 1821.

20. The Lord High Chancellor of Great Britain bearing the Purse with the Great Seal, and attended by a Page 19th July 1821 John Lord Eldon—His Page James Farrer Esqre. Jas. Stephanoff pinxit. Reynolds & Scriven Engravers to His Majesty sculpt.

21. The Lord Archbishop of Canterbury Charles Manners Sutton in his Rochet, Carrying the Coronation Service.

22. The Marquess of Salisbury carrying St. Edward's Staff Lord Calthorpe carrying the Gold Spurs The Marquess of Wellesley carrying the Septre with the Cross 19th July 1821.

23. The Earl of Galloway bearing the Third Sword The Duke of Devonshire bearing Curtana The Duke of Northumberland bearing the Second Sword 19th July 1821.

24. The Lord Mayor of London in his Coronation Robe 19th July 1821 The Rt. Hon. John Thomas Thorpe T. Uwins pinxit H. Meyer sculpst. Jany. 1826.

25. Lord Gwydyr Deputy Lord Great Chamberlain in his Robes of Estate Lord Howard of Effingham Deputy Earl Marshall of England in his Robes of Estate.

26. His Royal Highness Prince Leopold in the full Habit of the Order of the Garter carrying his Baton, as Field Marshall, His train borne by Sir Robert Gardiner K.C.B. 19th July 1821.

27. His Royal Highness the Duke of Clarence (now his most excellent Majesty William IVth) His train borne by Captain Pechell, R.N. 19th July 1821.

28. A Prince of the Blood Royal In the Coronation Dress and Robes of Estate attended by his Trainbearer His Royal Highness the Duke of York—Lieut. Col. H. F. Cookes J. Stephanoff pinxit Reynolds Engraver to His Majesty sculpt.

29. The Duke of Wellington, as High Constable of England.

30. The Duke of Rutland Carrying the Sceptre with the Dove 19th July 1821.

31. The Marquess of Anglesey as Lord High Steward of England Carrying St. Edwards' Crown 19th July 1821.

32. The Duke of Devonshire, Carrying the Orb 19th July 1821.

33. The Bishop of Gloucester carrying the Patina, The Bishop of Ely carrying the Bible The Bishop of Chester carrying the Chalice.

34. (The King in his Royal Robes, wearing a Cap of Estate; His Majesty's Train borne by Eight eldest Sons of Peers, assisted by the Master of the Robes.)

Nayler's Coronation of George IV (*contd.*)

35. The Keeper of His Majesty's Privy Purse The Right Honourable Sir Benjamin Bloomfield 19th July 1821 Stephanoff pinxit Meyer sculpsit.
36. The Lieutenant of the Yeomen of the Guard 19th July 1821 George Colman Esq. Stephanoff pinxit Mayer sculpsit Janry. 1826.
37. Harbinger of the Band of Gentlemen Pensioners 19th July 1821 P. Stephanoff delt. P. W. Tomkins sculpt. Janry. 1826.
38. The King seated in St. Edwards Chair, Crowned by the Archbishop of Canterbury 19th July 1821 Figures by Stephanoff Architecture by Augs. Pugin F. C. Lewis sculpsit Jany. 1824.
39. The Ceremony of the Homage 19th July 1821 Architecture by Augs. Pugin Figures by J. Stephanoff W. Bennett sculpst. Jany. 1824.
40. The Royal Banquet The bringing up of the First Course 19th July 1821 Plate 1st Chas. Wild delt. R. Havell Junr. aquat.
41. The Royal Banquet First Course continued Chas. Wild delt. W. I. Bennett sculpt. Jany. 1824.
42. Explanatory Key to the Grand Historical Print of the Coronation of his most Gracious Majesty King George the Fourth Published by G. Humphrey 27 St. James's Street London Jany. 25th 1822.
43. View of Interior of Westminster Hall as fitted up and prepared for the Banquet B. Winkles Etch (outline only uncoloured).
44. Longitudinal Section of Westminster Hall.
45. Ancient Coronation Chair called St. Edwards, the Chair of State, Litany Chair Fald Stools.

Intended to be issued in 5 parts, the first appeared in 1823, the second in 1827. Sir George Nayler died in 1831 and further work was suspended. Bohn acquired the copperplates and copyright in 1837, and combining them with Whittakers plates "Ceremonial of the Coronation of George IV", produced the above work. It was republished in 1839. Plate 5 of the King's Herbwomen is supposed to be rare, but it has been in all the copies I have examined.

344 NEALE M.D. (A.)

Travels through some parts of Germany, Poland, Moldavia and Turkey. (swelled rule) By Adam Neale, M.D. Late Physician to The British Embassy, at Constantinople, Physician to the Forces, and Member of the Royal College of Physicians of London. (swelled rule) London; Printed for Longman, Hurst, Rees, Orme, and Brown, Paternoster Row, and A. Constable & Co. Edinburgh.

Quarto.   1818

COLLATION.—Title as above (v. imprint) + Preface pp. iii–v (p. vi blank) + Direction to Binder 1 p. (v. Errata) + Contents pp. ix–xiii (xiv blank) + pp. 1–295 + 11 coloured plates, each plate marked A. N. delt. J. Clark. sculpt. Published by Messrs Longman, Hurst, Rees, Orme and Brown, Paternoster Row. 1818.

```
  I. front.       A Greek Reis.
 II. p.  70.      Dresden.
III. p.  71.      Konigstein on the Elbe, Saxony.
 IV. p.  78.      Meissen on the Elbe, from the West.
                       ,,        ,,        ,,       East.
  V. p.  83.      Prague.
 VI. p. 118.      The Wisse-gorod at Prague.   The Bath of Libussa.
                  City of Brinn and Fortress of Spielberg.   Moravia.
VII. p. 152.      River Niester and Ruins of Halitz.
                  English Ambassador's Palace, at Terapia.
VIII. p. 161.     Jassy.
 IX. p. 192.      Agatopoli, a Port in the Black Sea.
  X. p. 193.      Harbour of Incada, Black Sea.
 XI. p. 249.      Greek Barber   Turkish Boatman.
```

345 NEWHOUSE (C. B.)

Scenes on the Road.   Published March 2 by T. McLean, 26 Haymarket

Oblong Folio.   1834-5

All plates marked, C. B. Newhouse, and bear McLean's imprint.

1. The Disappointment.
2. A Frost.
3. Repose in the Mail.
4. An Alarming Reason.
5. A Faithfull Ally.
6. A Signal of Distress.
7. Just in Time.
8. A Lazy Horsekeeper for the Mail.
9. An Affair of Moment.
10. A Lesson for the Horsekeeper.

11. An Insubordinate Gatekeeper.
12. A Passing Remark.
13. Accidents will happen in the Best Appointed Coaches.
14. A Flood Tide Ship Ahoy.
15. A Practical Lesson.
16. An Indiscreet Artist.
17. An Accommodating Fare.
18. A Race Team.

Nos. 1-4, 6 and 11 engraved by R. G. Reeve.

346 NEWHOUSE (C. B.)

The Roadster's Album.   London: Messrs. Fores   Jan. 2nd

Folio.   1845

Composite title.   Small vignettes of coaching scenes with two coachmen and driving paraphernalia at foot (v. blank) and 16 coloured aquatints.

Each plate marked, C. B. Newhouse delt. and each with Fores imprint.

1. Travelling in a Hunting Country—"I hope you are not much hurt, Sir."
2. An Unwelcome Fare—"All that luggage by the Mail, Ma'am, quite impossible."
3. The Drag is broke and we are on the Bank.
4. Is the Bottom pretty sound?
5. A False Start.
6. Taking an Inside Birth (sic) "It strikes me we're going to have some rough weather."
7. "No time to lose, Ma'am; here's the other Coach close behind."
8. "Hold hard! you have forgot the Lady."
9. An Awkward Place in a Frost.
10. I'm afraid we have now got into the Ditch.
11. The Sleepy Gatekeeper.
12. The Old Grey loosed his Trace again.
13. "Quite full, Sir."
14. One Mile from Gretna, our Governor in sight.
15. An Arrival at Gretna—Overtaken by the Guardian.
16. Going to the Moors.

Nimrod.   See under Apperley (C. J.).

347 [NOBLE (W. B.)]

A Guide to the Watering Places, on the Coast, between the Exe and the Dart; including Teignmouth, Dawlish, and Torquay, embellished with a general view of Teignmouth and Dawlish, and the various Seats around Them, With a short Description of the Neighbourhood; to which will be subjoined by special Leave from the Honourable the Board of Ordnance a reduced part of their Grand Map.   Dedicated, by permission, to the Rt. Hon. Lord Viscount Exmouth (thick and thin rule) Teignmouth: Printed and Sold by E. Croydon, Public Library; sold also at Gore's Dawlish and Gilbert's Torquay (short rule).

Octavo.   1817

Noble's Guide to the Watering Places (*contd.*)

COLLATION.—Title as above (v. blank) + Dedication 1 p. (v. blank) + Introduction pp. v–viii + Text (Teignmouth) pp. 1–95 (End of first part) + sub-title "Part the Second Dawlish and its Vicinity" (v. blank) + pp. 1–84 + sub-title "Part the Third Torquay" (v. blank) + pp. 5–72 + Conchology 10 unnumbered leaves + List of Subscribers 4 leaves + folding map + 15 plates.

Front. Map of Teignmouth & its Vicinity. Engrd., J. Smith (folding).
 1. p. 7. View of Teignmouth from the Ness. Noble delt. D. Havell sculpt. (folding).
 2. p. 20. Croydon's Public Library Noble delin. Shary sc.
 3. p. 38. Mrs Kendall's Cottage. W. B. Noble delt. D. Havell sculpt. (folding).
 4. p. 42. The Residence of Mr Tayleur, M.D. W. B. Noble delt. D. Havell sculpt.
 5. *ibd.* Cliffden House W. B. Noble delt J. Shary sculp.
 6. p. 43. Cambrian Cottage. W. B. Noble delt. D. Havell sculpt.
 7. p. 45. Grove Cottage (on printed overslip) W. B. Noble delt D. Havell sculpt.
 8. p. 46. Lindridge W. B. Noble delt. D. Havell sculpt.
 9. *ibd.* Seymour Cottage W. B. Noble delt. J. Shary sculpt.
10. p. 55. Vicars Hill W. B. Noble delt. D. Havell sculpt.
11. p. 59. Ugbrook, the Seat of the Rt. Honble Lord Clifford. W. B. Noble delt D. Havell sculpt.
      18 Howard Street Surrey Street Strand (folding).
12. p. 63. Ingsdon House. W. B. Noble delt. D. Havell sculpt.
13. Front., Part II. View of Dawlish from the West Cliff. Noble delt. Stadler sculp. (folding).
14. p. 13 (Part III). Tor Abbey. W. B. Noble delt. D. Havell sculpt.
15. p. 48 (Part III). Berry Castle near Totnes. W. B. Noble delt. D. Havell sculpt.

348 Another Edition.

Octavo.   1821

COLLATION.—Title as before but reference to Ordnance map deleted and imprint changed to Teignmouth Printed and Sold by E. Croydon, Public Library; also to be had of Knighton and Westcott, Dawlish, and Cole Torquay 1821.

The collation is the same as in the preceding edition except that the folding map is omitted and an extra plate, Trafalgar Cottage, takes its place making 16 plates in all.

349 OLIVER (R. A.)

A Series of Lithographic Drawings, from Sketches in New Zealand, etc. By R. A. Oliver, Commander R.N. Dedicated by Permission to His Royal Highness Prince Albert (flowered rule) Lithographed and published by Dickinson Bros., Publishers to the Queen, 114, New Bond Street.

Folio   1852

COLLATION.—Title as above (v. blank) + 8 coloured Lithographs. Each plate marked Capt. Oliver Delt (except plate 6 R. A. Clive Delt) Dickinson & Co. Lith.

1. Te Rancihaeta New Zealand Chief.
2. A Korero
3. A Tangi (at Motoneka).
4. Falls of the Kiri Kiri.
5. Stranger's House (Houraki Pah).
6. Half Castes Pomare's Pah (Bay of Islands).
7. Puebo. New Caledonia.
8. Harry Bluff. Johnny.

Issued in buff paper wrappers at £2 2s. coloured. Also issued uncoloured.

Oriental Field Sports. See under Williamson.

350 ORLOWSKI (G.)

Russian Cries, in correct Portraiture from Drawings done on the Spot by G. Orlowski (vignette of sledge coloured) and now in the Possession of the Rt. Honble. Lord Kinnaird 1809 Pub^d March 25 & Sold by Edwd Orme Printseller to the King. Engraver and Publisher Bond St. corner of Brook St. London.

Small Folio.

COLLATION.—Engraved title as above (v. blank) + Portrait frontispiece and 16 coloured plates.

1. Front. Alexander, the Great Emperor of all the Russias. Pinchon pinxt in Russia. God-by sculp London.	9. Water carrier.
	10. A Peasant in a Too Loop.
	11. Sailor.
2. Title as above with vignette.	12. Chasseurs Guard.
3. Miasnick or Butchers Meat.	13. Guard at Night.
4. Pasouda Khoroche = Good Turnery Wares.	14. Soldier of the Police.
5. Krass Phoroche or Cran bery liquor good.	15. Foot Guard.
6. Skra Svya = Kavias fresh.	16. Cosach.
7. Kalatche Khorosh = a sort of White Bread.	17. Infantry.
8. Sbiten goriatchi—Tea hot.	18. Body Guard.

Plates 3–10 all marked, G. Orlowski delt. J. Godby sculpt and all with Orme's imprint, March 25 1809.

Plates 11–18 have neither artist's nor engraver's name but all bear an amended imprint, Published and Sold Jany 1 1807 by Edwd Orme Bond Street London.

351 ORME (Edward)

Orme's Graphic History of the Life, Exploits, and Death of Horatio Nelson, [6 lines of Nelson's titles] containing Fifteen Engravings; and intended as an accompaniment to the three celebrated whole sheet plates of His Lordship's splendid victories viz. the Battles of St. Vincent's, the Nile, and Trafalgar, which are explained by references and keys. (thick and thin rule) The Memoirs by Francis William Blagden, Esq. (thin and thick rule) quote from Virgil 6 lines (thick and thin rule) London Printed for, published and sold by Edward Orme, 59, Bond Street, the Corner of Brook Street, and by Longman, Hurst, Rees and Orme, Paternoster Row (swelled rule) J. G. Barnard Printer, 57 Snow Hill

Folio.   1806

COLLATION.—Title as above (v. blank) + Dedication 1 p. (v. blank) + Tribute to Nelson 1 p. (v. blank) + pp. 5–66 + pp. iii–iv + vii–viii + unnumbered leaf + List of Plates 1 p. (v. blank) + Advertisement Orme 1 p. (v. blank).

1. face   Tribute.   Bust of Nelson (uncoloured).
2. p.   6. Young Nelson's attack and chase after a bear.
      p. 19. vignette. Battle of Nile. J. Clark del. Pickett sculp^t.
      p. 25. vignette. Battle of St. Vincent. J. Clark del. Pickett sculp^t.
      p. 26. vignette. Battle of Copenhagen. J. Clark del. Pickett sculp^t.
      p. 31. vignette. Battle of Trafalgar. J. Clark del. Pickett sculp^t.
3. p. 32. Nelson explaining plan of attack previous to Battle of Trafalgar (tinted).
      p. 41. Facsimile of Nelson's handwriting.
      p. 42. Lord Nelson's Funeral Procession by Water, from Greenwich to White-Hall Jany. 8th 1806.

Orme's Nelson (*contd.*)

Taken from Bankside, exhibiting a View of St. Paul's, London Bridge &c. Turner pinx^t. J. Clarke & H. Merke sculp. (Orme's imprint in centre.) folding coloured aquatint.

*p. 45. The Shallop which brought Body of Nelson (coloured).

*p. 48. Funeral Procession passing through Temple Bar (partly coloured, folding).

p. 49. The Funeral Procession of Lord Nelson Jany. 9th 1806. Wm. Craig del. J. Godby sculp^t. Edwd. Orme excu^t. (coloured, folding).

p. 54. The Ceremony of Lord Nelson's Interment in St. Paul's Cathedral Jany. 9th 1806. Drawn by William Orme from a Sketch made on the spot by the Rev Holt Waring. J. Clark & J. Hamble sculp^t. (folding coloured aquatint).

*p. 56. Coffin (coloured).

p. 62. vignette. Procession, Greenwich Hospital.

ibd. Ode Heny James Pye within border of flags.

p. 66. Proclamation of Nelson to inhabitants of ex Venetian Islands.

p. iv. Key to picture of Battle St. Vincent.

p. viii. Key to picture of Battle Nile.

Key to picture of Death of Nelson.

Issued in boards with printed title label of Funeral Car at 2 gns. Those marked * not in List of Plates. Another issue undated.

352 ORME (EDWARD)

Historic, Military, and Naval Anecdotes, of Personal Valour, Bravery, and Particular Incidents which occurred to the armies of Great Britain and her Allies, in the last long-contested war, terminating with the Battle of Waterloo (rule) Under the Patronage of, and Dedicated with Permission to his Royal Highness the Commander-in-Chief (rule) London: Edited and Published by, and engraved under the direction of, Edward Orme, Publisher to his Majesty, and to his Royal Highness the Prince-Regent, Bond Street, Corner of Brook-Street

Quarto.   [1818]

COLLATION.—Title as above (v. blank) + List of Subscribers 2 pp. + Address 1 p. (v. blank) + pp. 3–98 + 40 coloured plates.

All the plates bear Orme's imprint, address and date (with slight variations in imprint).

1. Frontispiece Bivouac in the Pyrenees The Night before the Battle J. A. Atkinson del Fry & Sutherland sculpt. June 4th 1815.

2. p. 4. British Sailors boarding a Man of War J. A. Atkinson del Fry & Sutherland sculpt. June 4th 1815.

3. p. 7. A British Soldier taking two French Officers at the Battle of the Pyrenees J. A. Atkinson del M. Dubourg sculp. Septr. 1 1815.

4. p. 8. Marshal Beresford engaged with the Polish Lancer, at the Battle of Albuera 1811 Manskirch delt M. Dubourg sculpt. Augt. 20 1815.

5. p. 15. The Battle of Waterloo decided by the Duke of Wellington heading a charge upon the French Imperial Guards June 18th 1815 J. A. Atkinson del. M. Dubourg sculpt. Septr. 1 1815.

6. p. 17. The Marquis of Anglesea wounded whilst heading a charge of heavy Cavalry at the close of the Battle of Waterloo June 18th 1815 J. A. Atkinson del. M. Dubourg sculpt. Sepr. 1 1815.

7. p. 19. Prince Blucher under his horse at the Battle of Waterloo at the time the French Cavalry were making the charge over him J. A. Atkinson del. M. Dubourg sculpt. Augt. 20 1815.

8. p. 21. The Prince of Orange at the Battle of Waterloo distributing, at the moment, to the brave Troops the orders he then wore J. A. Atkinson delt. M. Dubourg sculpt. Augt. 20 1815.

9. p. 25. The boasted crossing of the Nieman At the opening of the Campaign in 1812 by N. Bonaparte From a drawing by an officer Clark & Dubourg sculpt. Jan. 1st 1816.

Orme's Military and Naval Anecdotes (*contd.*)

10. p. 28. Napoleon's Flight across the Rhine near the City of Mentz, pursued by the Allies 1812 Manskirch del. Clark & Dubourg sculpt. Jany. 1 1816.

11. p. 30. Russian Loyalty and Heroism. Anecdote of the Russian Peasant of Smolensk, who being forced by the French cooly chopped off his hand rather than serve Bonaparte on his march towards Moscow. I. A. Atkinson del. Clark & Dubourg sculp. Jany. 1 1816.

12. p. 32. Anecdote of the Bravery of the Scotch Piper of the 11th Highland Regiment, at the Battle of Vimiera Manskirch del. Clark & Dubourg sculp. Jany. 1 1816.

13. p. 33. Sailors at Prayers on board Lord Nelson's ship after the Battle of the Nile J. A. Atkinson del. Clark & Dubourg sculpt. April 1st 1816.

14. p. 35. The Grand Te Deum on the Field of Battle near Toplitz attended by the Allied Sovereigns & Troops 1813 Clark del. from a sketch on the spot M. Dubourg sculpt. April 1 1816.

15. p. 37. French Troops retreating through and plundering a village Clark del. from a sketch on the spot Dubourg sculpt. April 1st 1816.

16. p. 38. The Tyrolese Patriots Men & Women storming the fortress of Kuffstein with their Wooden Guns Manskirch del. Clark & Dubourg sculpt. April 1st 1816.

17. p. 41. The Allied Army crossing the Rhine to invade France 1813 I. H. Clark del. from a sketch by an Officer M. Dubourg sculpt. July 1 1816.

18. p. 42. Wellington & Blucher meeting by accident at the close of the Battle of Waterloo J. A. Atkinson del. M. Dubourg sculpt. June 4th 1816.

19. p. 44. French Cuirassiers in the battle of Waterloo charged and defeated by the Highlanders & Scotch Greys J. A. Atkinson del. M. Dubourg sculpt. June 4th 1816.

20. p. 47. Boarding and Taking the American Ship Chesapeake by the Officers & Crew of H.M. Ship Shannon Commanded by Capt. Broke June 1813. Heath delt. M. Dubourg sculpt. July 1 1816.

21. p. 49. A true Picture of a Field of Battle Manskirch del. M. Dubourg sc. Jany. 1 1817.

22. p. 52. Two French Officers taken by a Sergeant of the 18th Hussars, at the battle of Albuera W. Heath del. M. Dubourg sculpt. Jany. 1 1817.

23. p. 54. Death of Major Genl. Sir Wm. Ponsonby Manskirch del. M. Dubourg sculpt. Jany. 1st 1817.

24. p. 56. Death of Sir Thomas Picton J. A. Atkinson del. M. Dubourg sculpt. Jany. 1st 1817.

25. p. 59. Review of the British Troops at Montmartre, near Paris By the Duke of Wellington 21st October 1815 G. Scharf del. M. Dubourg sculpt. March 25th 1817.

26. p. 60. Encampment of the British Army, in the Bois de Boulogne, 1815 Manskirch del. M. Dubourg sculpt. March 25th 1817.

27. p. 62. Anecdote of the Battle of Trafalgar W. Heath del. M. Dubourg sculpt. Augt. 1 1817.

28. p. 64. The Death of the Duke of Brunswick June 15th 1815 Manskirch del. M. Dubourg sculpt. June 1st 1817.

29. p. 67. The Cockpit, Battle of the Nile Heath del. M. Dubourg sc. June 4th 1817.

30. p. 71. The French Conscripts J. A. Atkinson del. M. Dubourg sculpt. June 4th 1817.

31. p. 73. The Horse Guards at the Battle of Waterloo, One of the officers having killed a French Colonel cuts off his Epaulette in triumph Heath del. M. Dubourg sc. June 4th 1817.

32. p. 75. Head Quarters Waterloo 1815 Manskirch del. M. Dubourg sculpt. March 25th 1817.

33. p. 77. Taking a French Eagle at Barrossa Deigton del. Dubourg sculpt. March 1st 1818.

34. p. 79. The Buffs at the Battle of Albuera Manskirch del. Dubourg sculpt. March 1st 1818.

35. p. 81. Capture of General Paget, 1812 Atkinson del. Dubourg sculpt. Augt. 1st 1817.

36. p. 83. Landing Troops J. A. Atkinson del. M. Dubourg sculpt. Augt. 1 1817.

37. p. 87. The Duke of Wellington & his Staff crossing the Bidossa & entering France 1813 Rigaud pinxt. Dubourg sc. Augt. 1 1818.

38. p. 93. Entrance of the Allies into Paris Clark & Dubourg sc. Augt. 1 1818.

39. p. 95. The Allies before Dantzig in Winter Clark delt. Dubourg sculpt. Decr. 1 1818.

40. p. 97. A Corporal of the 13th Dragoons Killing a French Colonel Dighton del. M. Dubourg sculpt. Decr. 1 1818.

353 *Another issue identical with the above with the exception that the 2 rules are deleted from the title, and that it is dated at foot 1819. This issue contains 98 pp. of text but the last 4 unnumbered. Historic, Military and Naval Anecdotes is sometimes sold with Naval and Martial Achievements published by Jenkins as a 3 volume series.*

354 ORME (E.)

Italian Scenery; representing the Manners, Customs, and Amusements of the different states of Italy; containing Thirty-two Coloured Engravings by James Godby, from original drawings by P. van Lerberghi (decorative rule) The Narrative by M. Buonaiuti (swelled rule) London: Printed for Published and Sold by Edward Orme, Bond Street, the corner of Brook Street, sold also by Longman, Hurst, Rees and Orme, Paternoster Row (small rule) 1806 J. C. Barnard Printer, 57 Snow Hill.

Folio.

COLLATION.—Title as above (v. blank) + Preface 1 p. (v. blank) + Index 1 p. (v. blank) + Text pp. 1–74 (in English and French) + 32 coloured plates.

1. Front. Lazzaronis.	16. p. 33. Street Singers.
2. p. 3. Dance of Lazzaroni Children.	17. p. 35. The Protestant Church Yard at Rome.
3. p. 5. Napolitans eating Macaroni.	18. p. 39. A Fountain near Rome.
4. p. 7. The Fishmonger.	19. p. 41. A Capuchin Friar.
5. p. 9. A Calessino or Hackney Chaise.	20. p. 43. A Direction Post on the Highway near Rome.
6. p. 11. Dance of the Tarantella.	
7. p. 13. Playing at the Ring.	21. p. 47. The Confession.
8. p. 15. Washing Place at Torre del Greco.	22. p. 49. A Vintage.
9. p. 17. Country Eating House.	23. p. 51. The Temple of Hercules.
10. p. 19. An Hermitage.	24. p. 55. A Play with the Fingers called Mora.
11. p. 23. The Fauntain of Capua.	25. p. 59. A Piedmontese Dance.
12. p. 25. Interior of a House at Fondi.	26. p. 61. A Fountain at Masso.
13. p. 27. A Roman Family and the Temple of Minerva Medica.	27. p. 63. A Tinker.
	28. p. 65. The Catechism.
14. p. 29. The Fishmarket at Rome and Octavia's Portico.	29. p. 67. The Miners.
	30. p. 69. A Country Inn.
15. p. 31. Playing at Bomble Puppy and the Temple of Vesta.	31. p. 71. The Young Savoyards Departure.
	32. p. 73. The Young Savoyards Return.

355 ORME (Edward)

A Picture of St. Petersburgh, represented in a collection of Twenty interesting Views of the City, the Sledges, and the People. Taken on the spot at the Twelve different months of the year: and accompanied with an Historical and Descriptive Account. London: (thin and thick rule) Printed for Edward Orme, Publisher to His Majesty, and to His Royal Highness the Prince Regent, Bond Street, Corner of Brook Street; By J. F. Dove, St John's Square, Clerkenwell

Folio.   1815

COLLATION.—Title as above (v. blank) + pp. 1–34 + pp. iii–iv + 20 plates (the text is in English and French).

All plates are marked "Drawn by Mornay [except 15, 16 and 18 which are marked Mornay Del] Clark & Dubourg sculp.," and all bear imprint London Published & Sold April 28, 1815 by Edwd. Orme Publisher to his Majesty & H.R.H. the Prince Regent Bond Street Corner of Brook Street.

1. View of the Imperial Bank and the Shops at St. Petersburgh.
2. View of the Marble Palace in the Grand Millione St. Petersburgh.
3. View of the Square and the Grand Theatre at St. Petersburgh.
4. View of the Parade & the Imperial Palace at St. Petersburgh.

Orme's St. Petersburgh (*contd.*)

5. View of the Place of Peter the Great and the Senate House at St. Petersburgh.
6. View of the Neva the Harbour and the Exchange at St. Petersburgh.
7. View of the Canal of the Moika, the Bridge & the Police Establishment.
8. View of the Centre of the Great Bridge of the Neva and of St. Petersburgh.
9. View of the Champ de Mars & the Summer Garden at St. Petersburgh.
10. View of the Square of Kassan and the Cathedral at St. Petersburgh.
11. View of the Canal of Fontanka and the Barracks at St. Petersburgh.
12. View of the Arsenal and the Foundry at St. Petersburgh.
13. The Stand of the Hackney Coachman.
14. Russian Females entering a Sledge.
15. The Russian Sledge or Public Carriage.
16. The Sledge of a Russian Citizen.
17. Public Vehicles for Summer.
18. The Russian Country Carriage.
19. The Winter Russian Travelling Carriage.
20. A Russian Courrier Conveying Dispatches.

Engraved Frontispiece bearing Title and Russian Eagle.

Published in boards, with the frontispiece repeated as a shield on the upper cover, at six guineas coloured (size 13½ × 19⅜ inches).

Orme. See also under Blagdon, Howitt, Middleton and Williamson.

356 OUSELEY (William Gore)

Views in South America, from original Drawings made in Brazil, the River Plate, the Parana, &c. By William Gore Ouseley Esqr. late her Majesty's Minister Plentipotentiary to the States of La Plata and formerly Charge d'Affaires at the Court of Brazil (swelled rule). London: Thomas McLean, 26, Haymarket Lithographed and Printed at 70, St Martins Lane.

Folio. [1852]

COLLATION.—Title as above (v. blank) + Dedication 1 p. (v. List of Plates) + 25 plates + 1 plan + 1 full page vignette.

Each plate is marked, W. Gore Ouseley del J. Needham lith Printed at 70 St Martins Lane (with the exception of plate 23 which is marked, M. Ouseley del and plate 25 which bears no artists name).

Serra de Estrella (vignette).
1. Fort Loureiro, near Funchal Madeira.
2. Hotel formerly a convent, Teneriffe.
3. Near Bahia [Fort St. Antonio Entrance of Harbour].
4. Victoria Hill and Cemetery Harbour of Bahia.
5. Harbour of Bahia.
6. Ruined Chapel of S. Gonsalvo (Bahia).
7. Ruined Chapel of San Gonsalvo Rio Vermelho Bahia [interior].
8. Entrance of Harbour of Rio de Janeiro & Sugar Loaf Rock.
9. Chapel & Fortaleza of Boa Viagem Rio Janeiro. (sic)
10. Grotto in the Bay of Jurujube, Harbour of Rio de Janeiro.
11. Corcovado Mountain from Praia Grande Rio de Janeiro.
12. Convent near Rio de Janeiro [Convent de N.S. da Penha].
13. Aqueduct & Convent of Sta. Teresa Rio de Janeiro [Matacavallos Street].
14. Church of Nossa Senora da Gloria & Aqueduct Rio de Janeiro.
15. Mangueiras suburbs of Rio de Janeiro (for some years occupied by the British Legation).

Ouseley's South America (*contd.*)

16. Entrance of Harbour from Larangeiras Rio de Janeiro.
17. The Sugar Loaf Rock—Rio de Janeiro.
18. Botafogo Bay, suburbs of Rio de Janeiro.
19. Serra dos Orcaos Cabeca do Fraile.
20. The Waterfall of Itamaraty Distant two days journey from Rio de Janeiro.
21. Monte Video, from the Cemetery.
22. Quinta occupied by Mr. W. Gore Ouseley while her Majesty's Minister at Buenos Aires.
23. The Capital of Buenos Ayres from the English Ministers Garden [M. Ouseley del.].
24. Govt. House & Capitania del. Puerto Corrientes (on the Parana).
25. Corrientes—on the Parana [no artist given].
   Plan of Obligado showing the position of the ships at 12 h 30 m when all had reached their stations.

357 PALLAS (P. S.)

Travels through the Southern Provinces of the Russian Empire in the years 1793 and 1794 (rule) Translated from the German of P. S. Pallas, Counsellor of State to his Imperial Majesty of all the Russias, Knight, &c. (rule) In Two Volumes. Vol. I [II] with many coloured vignettes, plates, and maps. London: Printed by A. Strahan, Printers-Street, for T. N. Longman and O. Rees, Paternoster-Row; T. Cadell Jun. and W. Davies, Strand; and J. Murray and S. Highley, Fleet Street

2 vols.   Quarto.   1802–3

COLLATION VOL. I.—Title as above (v. blank) + Author's Preface 2 pp. (iii–iv) + Translator's Preface 3 pp. (v–vii) p. viii blank + Explanation of Plates and Vignettes in First Volume 6 pp. (ix–xiv) + Explanation of the Vignettes and Notice Respecting Maps 3 pp. (xv–xvii) + Table of Contents 6 pp. (xviii–xxiii) + p. xxiv Errata + sub-title "Travels into the Southern Provinces of the Russian Empire in the years 1793 and 1794" (v. blank) + pp. 3–541 + Index pp. 543–552 + 25 coloured plates.

	p. 3.	Vignette A Winter Landscape Geissler d. et f.
1.	p. 48.	Domestic Cat, arms of the Town of Mokshan &c. G. Geissler del. et fec.
2.	p. 74.	Representation of Strelnie Gory or sandy rocks bank of Volga Geissler d. et. fec. (folding).
	p. 88.	Vignette View of Birch Forest Geissler d. et. f.
	p. 89.	Pillar of Horses skulls Geissler d. et f.
3.	p. 99.	View of the Colony of Sarepta, on the banks of the Sarpa G. Geissler del. et fec. (folding).
	p. 107.	Profiles Mongolian Girl &c. G. fec.
4.	p. 117.	Common Kalmuk and Kalmuk Priest G. Geissler del. et fec.
5.	*ibd.*	A Kalmuk housewife and Girl G. Geissler d. et fec.
6.	p. 172.	Rural Encampment of the Kundure Tartars G. Geissler del. et fec.
7.	p. 174.	Woman and girl of Kundure Tartars G. Geissler del et fec.
8.	p. 254.	Idolatrous shrine Astrakhan G. f. (uncoloured).
9.	p. 257.	Indians engaged in solemn prayer Nach des Natur gezeichnet von G. Geissler gestochen von C. Schule Leipzig 1798 (uncoloured).
	p. 279.	Taking pheasants by means of gins Kuma and Kuban Geissler d. et f.
10.	p. 298.	Turcoman with bow, quiver and whip G. Geissler del. et fec.
11.	p. 312.	Plan of Greater or Upper Madshary.
12.	p. 328.	S.W. View of Four Tartar Chapels Great Madshary Geissler del. et fec (folding).
13.	p. 329.	Separate representation of second structure of preceding Geissler del et fec.
	p. 338.	Vignette Sepulchral Chapel Mahometans Great Madshary Geissler del. et fec.
	p. 339.	Vignette Circassian Tombs belong family Prince Dshambulat Geissler d. et f.
14.	p. 336.	Plan, Elevation, and Section of Tartar Chapel Masslof-Kuut Drawn on the spot by Alexr. Digby Architect Engraved by T. Medland (folding, uncoloured).
15.	p. 340.	Georgiesk and Part Mount Caucasus G. Geissler del. et fec. (folding).

Pallas's Russian Empire (*contd.*)

16. p. 347. Map Well of Alexander &c. (folding).
17. p. 358. Mount Metshuka   G. Geissler del. et fec.
    p. 380. Planimetrical delineation Mount Burg-ussan Grundling sculp.
    p. 381. Sepulchral Monument of Circassian princely family   V.S. del.   G. fec.
18. p. 399. Circassian of Distinction and Princess   G. Geissler del. et fec.
19. p. 400. Circassian Prince and Nobleman   G. Geissler del. et fec.
20. p. 401. Circassian Nobleman in full accoutrement   G. Geissler del. et fec.
21. p. 412. Delineation of the principal races of Circassian and Abassian horses.
22. p. 436. Two Ingushians   G. Geissler del. et fec.
    p. 444. Circassian and Ingushian Beehive.
    p. 445. Four Male and Two female stone statues Geissler d. et f.
23. p. 484. View of Fortress and Roads of Taganrog.
24. p. 488. Lady of distinction among Nagays, Princess Nagays, Female slave.
    p. 508. Vignette   Armenian Windmill   Geissler d. et f.
    p. 509. Vignette   Strata granite &c.   G d et f.
25. p. 534. Matron of Kozaks and girl of Tsherkask   G. Geissler del. et fec.
    p. 541. Vignette   Strata Granite &c.   G. f.

VOL. II.—Title as in Vol. I (changing date to 1803) (v. blank) + Dedication 1 p. (v. blank) + Dedication continued 3 pp. v–vii (p. viii blank) + Author's Preface 3 pp. (ix–xi) p. xii blank + Explanation of Plates 6 pp. (xiii–xviii) + Explanation of Vignettes 2 pp. (xix–xx) + Contents 10 pp. (xxi–xxx) + Errata 1 p. (v. blank) + sub-title "Travels into the Southern Provinces of the Russian Empire in the years 1793 and 1794" (v. blank) + pp. 3–510 + Index pp. 511–523.

    p.   3. Vignette   Prospect of Mount Tshatyrdag   Geissler delt.
26. p.   7. View of the Gate of Perekop   Geissler delt (folding).   Medland sculp.
    p. 24. [—cited as p. 69 in list of vignettes].
27. p. 27. Town of Bakhtshisarai   Geissler delt.   Medland sculp. (folding).
28. p. 38. Prospect of Eski-Yourt   Geissler delt.   Medland sculp. (folding).
29. p. 45. View of the Port & Town of Akhtiar   Geissler delt.   Medland sculp. (folding).
    p. 55. Inscription (vignette heading) not included in list of vignettes.
30. p. 74. Ancient coins and inscriptions (uncoloured, folding).
    p. 75. Inscription in white marble [cited as p. 74 in list of vignettes] (uncoloured).
    p. 82. Chapel hewn in rock Inkerman [cited as p. 85 in list of vignettes] (uncoloured).
31. p. 84. View of the Monastic Cells at Inkerman   Geissler delt.   Medland sculp. (folding).
    p. 90. View of Monastery of St George [cited as p. 91 in list of vignettes].
32. p. 91. Prospect of the Greek Monastery of St George   Geissler delt.   Medland sculp. (folding).
    p. 95. Mountains of calcareous rock.
33. p. 100. View of the Valley & Village of Tshorguna   Geissler delt.   Medland sculp. (folding).
34. p. 115. Genoese Fortress of Soldaya or Sudagh   Geissler delt.   Medland sculp. (folding).
    p. 120. Vignette   Fortress of Yoursuf [p. 176 in list of vignettes].
35. p. 131. Prospect beyond the Harbour of Balaklava   Geissler delt.   Medland sculp. (folding).
36. *ibd.*   A common Arnaut and his wife   Geissler delt.   Medland sculp.
37. p. 148. Valley of Simäus   Geissler delt.   Medland sculp.
    p. 161. Vignette   Plough and Sledge [cited as p. 159].
    p. 185. Marble inscription Isle of Taman [cited p. 301].
38. p. 208. Eastern Part of the Town of Kerassubasar   Geissler delt.   Medland sculp. (folding).
39. p. 219. Accumulated Rocks of Taraktash   Geissler delt.   Medland sculp. (folding).
    p. 244. Antique Greek Tomb Ovidiopol.
40. p. 267. Ruinous Town of Theodosia, or Kaffa   Geissler delt.   Medland sculp. (folding).
41. p. 283. Inscriptions on Stone Crim Tartary   Geissler delt.   Medland sculp. (folding, uncoloured).
42. *ibd.*   ditto Bas-reliefs.
    p. 316. Vignette   2 sculptured heads [cited as p. 308].
    p. 318. Vignette plan of muddy volcano I. of Taman.
43. p. 341. Common Tartars   Geissler delt.   Medland sculp.
    p. 342. Vignette   Tartar mode of threshing [cited as p. 393].
44. p. 345. Tartar Nobles.
45. p. 346. Dress of Females of Crim Tartary   Geissler delt.   Medland sc.

Pallas's Russian Empire (*contd.*)

46. p. 346. Two Tartar Mountaineers   Geissler delt.   Medland sculpt.
47. p. 348. Tartar & Nagay Musician   Geissler delt.   Medland sculpt.
48. p. 452. Crimean Camel   Geissler delt.   Medland sculp.
49. p. 455. Crimean Sheep   Geissler delt.   Medland sculp.
50. p. 455. A lamb of the same breed   Geissler delt.   Medland sculp.
51. p. 455. Peasant and Girl of Russia Minor   Geissler delt.   Medland sculp.
   p. 510. Vignette View of Bronnitza.
         3 Maps (1) Map of the Steppe between Lower Volga & the Don   J. Russell sculpt.
             (2) Map of Country between Black & Caspian Seas 2 sheets   J. Russell sculpt.
             (3) Special Map of the Isle of Taman   J. Russell sculpt.

Published £3 3s. in boards.   A few copies were done on fine royal paper £4 4s. boards with proof impressions of the plates.   An extremely charming colour plate book that has not so far been much appreciated, fetching only a small price.   It deserves a place in every colour plate collection for its numerous attractive coloured vignettes, an unusual feature.   The plates themselves are also interesting technically, various forms of engraving being employed.

358   *2nd Edition* 1812.

359   PAPWORTH (J. B.)

Rural Residences, consisting of a Series of Designs for Cottages, Decorated Cottages, Small Villas, and other Ornamental Buildings, accompanied by Hints on Situation, Construction, Arrangement and Decoration, in the Theory & Practice of Rural Architecture; interspersed with Some Observations on Landscape Gardening: By John. B. Papworth, Architect, Author of Essay on the Dry Rot, &c. &c. (thick and thin rule) London: Printed for R. Ackermann, 101 Strand, by J. Diggins, 14, St Ann's Lane (short thick and thin rule).

Imperial Octavo.   1818

COLLATION.—Half-title " Designs for Rural Residences &c. &c." (v. blank) + Title as above (v. blank) + Introduction 2 ll. (pp. v–viii) + pp. 9–106 + Index 2 pp. (107–8) + Index to plates 1 p. (v. Printed by J. Diggins, St Ann's Lane, London) + 27 coloured plates.

All the plates numbered and marked, Pubd. at R. Ackermann's Repository of Arts 101 Strand June 1818 and initialed J. B. P.

1. Frontispiece. A Bath.	15. p. 61. A Villa.	
2. p. 9. Four Cottages.	16. p. 65. A Villa.	
3. p. 13. A Cottage.	17. p. 69. A Villa.	
4. p. 17. Steward's Cottage.	18. p. 73. Plan of a Cottage Ornée.	
5. p. 21. A Bailiff's Cottage.	19. p. 77. Park Lodge & Entrance.	
6. p. 25. Gothic Cottage.	20. p. 81. A Park Entrance.	
7. p. 29. Cottage Ornée.	21. p. 85. A Gothic Conservatory.	
8. p. 33. Cottage Ornée.	22. p. 89. A Dairy.	
9. p. 37. A Gothic Cottage.	23. p. 93. Fishing Lodge.	
10. p. 41. A Cottage Orné.	24. p. 97. An Ice House.	
11. p. 45. A Vicarage House.	25. p. 101. Garden Seats.	
12. p. 49. A Cottage Orné.	26. p. 103. A Verandah.	
13. p. 53. Cottage Ornée.	27. p. 105. A Domestic Chapel.	
14. p. 57. A Cottage Orné.		

Published in boards at £1 11s. 6d., this work was originally issued in Ackermanns Repository 1816 and 1817.

360   Papworth Rural Residences 2nd Edition.

Octavo.   1832

Papworth's Rural Residences (*contd.*)

COLLATION.—The Second Edition is the same as the first, with the addition of the words "Second Edition" between rules before the imprint, the latter being changed to, London. Printed for R. Ackermann 96 Strand, by Sedding and Turtle. The plates are the same except for the change of date to 1832.

361 PAPWORTH (J. B.)

Select Views of London: with Historical and Descriptive Sketches of some of the most interesting of its public Buildings. Compiled and arranged by John B. Papworth, Architect, Author of an Essay on the Dry Rot, &c. &c. (thick and thin rule) London: Printed for R. Ackermann, 101, Strand, by J. Diggins, St Ann's Lane. (thick and thin rule).

Imperial Octavo.   1816

COLLATION.—Title as above (v. blank) + Introduction 4 pp. + Contents 2 pp. + Text pp. 1–159 + 76 coloured aquatint plates.

1. St James's Palace p. 1.
2. Carleton House p. 6.
3. Carlton House (folding) *ibd.*
4. The Staircase at Carlton House (folding) p. 8.
5. The Conservatory at Carlton House (folding) p. 10.
6. Warwick House The residence of Her Royal highness Princess Charlotte of Wales p. 12.
7. View of the Temple of Concord in the Green Park (folding) A. Pugin delt. J. C. Stadler aquat. p. 13.
8. View of the Bridge & Pagoda St James's Park A Pugin delt. J. R. Hamble aquat. (folding) p. 13.
9. The Bason in the Green Park St James's p. 16.
10. St. Stephen's Chapel & Speaker's House from Westminster Bridge p. 18.
11. Westminster Abbey & St. Margarets p. 21.
12. St. John's Church Westminster from the river p. 24.
13. St. Martin's in the Fields p. 25
14. St. Clement Danes p. 30.
15. St. James Square p. 34.
16. North Side of Grosvenor Square p. 36.
17. Berkeley Square p. 38.
18. Lansdowne House, Berkeley Square p. 39.
19. Portman Square North Side p. 41.
20. Manchester Square North Side p. 43.
21. Cavendish Square, North Side p. 45.
22. George Street Hanover Sqre. p. 47.
23. Soho Square p. 49.
24. Leicester Square from Leicester Place p. 52.
25. Lincoln Inn Fields coming in from Gt. Queen Street p. 55.
26. Queen Square p. 56.
27. New Drury Lane Theatre p. 58.
28. Theatre Royal Covent Garden from Bow Street p. 61.
29. Saloon to the Private Boxes Covent Garden Theatre p. 68.
30. Montague House—now the British Museum p. 70.
31. British Museum New Building p. 73.
32. Somerset House and the New Church; Strand taken from the Morning Post Office p. 82.
33. The Hall at the Royal Academy Somerset House p. 84.
34. Russell Institution Great Coram Street p. 86.
35. The Pantheon p. 85.
36. Bullock's Museum 22, Piccadilly p. 89.
37. Bullock's Museum Piccadilly (exterior) *ibd.*
38. The Banqueting House p. 91.
39. Whitehall Chapel p. 91.

Papworth's Views of London (*contd.*)

40. Whitehall Yard (from the Street opposite the Horse Guards) p. 96.
41. A View of Whitehall & the Horse Guards p. 97.
42. Charing Cross looking up the Strand p. 98.
43. Buckingham Stairs Water Gate, from the River p. 101.
44. Royal Menagerie Exeter 'Change, Strand p. 103.
45. Portland Place p. 104.
46. Tyburn Turnpike p. 106.
47. Oxford Street & Entrance into Stratford Place p. 106.
48. View of Piccadilly from Hyde Park Corner Turnpike p. 108.
49. Tottenham Court Road Turnpike & St James's Chapel p. 110.
50. View of Cornhill, Lombard Street & Mansion House p. 111.
51. Guildhall p. 112.
52. Bank of England from Lothbury p. 115.
53. South View of the Bank p. 115.
54. Interior View of the Bank p. 116.
55. Royal Exchange p. 117.
56. A North View of the India House Leadenhall Street p. 119.
57. St. Paul's Cathedral West Front p. 121.
58. St. Stephen's Church Walbrook p. 125.
59. Christ Church-Spitalfields p. 127.
60. St. Leonard Shoreditch p. 178.
61. View of St. Dunstan's Church Fleet Street p. 130.
62. Town Hall Southwark p. 134.
63. The Hall of the Auction Mart p. 135.
64. Auction Mart Coffee Room p. 135.
65. The London Commercial Sale Rooms Mark Lane p. 137.
66. Cheapside p. 139.
67. Mercers Hall p. 141.
68. Ironmonger Hall p. 142.
69. Bridge Street Blackfriars p. 143.
70. Blackfriars Bridge from the Strand Bridge p. 144.
71. View of London Bridge p. 146.
72. The New Custom House p. 149.
73. The Monument p. 153.
74. Lunatic Hospital of St. Luke's p. 154.
75. The Old Bailey p. 155.
76. Cold Bath Fields Prison p. 158.

Published in paper boards with yellow printed label at £3 13s. 6d. This work is a re-issue in separate form from Ackermann Repository 1810–15.

The text is by Papworth

---

362 Paris and Dover; or, To and Fro; a Picturesque excursion: being a Birds Eye Notion of a few "Men and Things" by Roger Book'em (thin and thick rule) 2 line verse (rule) London: Published by H. Fores, 16 Panton Street, Haymarket, and sold by all the principal Book and Print sellers in Town and Country. J. Wilson, Printer, 6 George Court, Piccadilly (rule)

Small Quarto.   1821

COLLATION.—Printed title as above (v. blank) + 48 plates each with 1 leaf Text, except front.

Frontispiece.	Calais Pier, and Custom House.	Diligence.
From Dover.	Gates of Calais.	Conductor and Postillion.
To Calais.	Office of Passports Calais.	Peasants.
The Cabin.	Kingston Hotel Calais.	Inn (Sign of Frederick Great).

Paris and Dover (*contd.*)

Plowing.
Royal Mail.
Street Paris.
Streets.
Streets.
Passage.
Italian Boulevards.
Cemetery of Pere la Chaise.
Cemetery of Pere la Chaise.
Italian Boulevards.
Palais Royal.
La Morgue.

Gens D'Armes (foot).
Gens D'Armes (mounted).
Cabriolets.
Garde du Corps.
Grenadiers of the Royal Guard.
Eau Sucree.
Cuirassiers of the Royal Guard.
Cuckoos.
Blanchesseuses.
Infantry of Line.
National Guard.
Cent Suisses.

Gondola.
Jardin des Plantes.
Champs Elysees.
Tivoli Gardens.
From Paris.
To Calais.
Embarkation Calais Pier.
Dover Beach.
Custom House Dover.
From Dover.
To London.
Roger.

363 PAUL (I. D.)

A Trip to Melton Mowbray. From Drawings by I. D. Paul, Esq. London: Published for the Proprietor, by S. & I. Fuller, at their Sporting Gallery, Temple of Fancy, 34 Rathbone Place 1822

  1. Solvitar acris hyems—it thaws—we must be off to Melton.
  2. Go! I fancy he can! Milton loquitar upon my soul a lie! Shakespeare
  3. Doing a bit of City.
  4. All the world's a stage (Bull and Mouth Inn).
  5. At his head a grass green turf and at his heels a stone.
  6. These come hopping.
  7. Non effectives;—Nec possum dicere quare.
  8. Frogs and Cranes—shewing a friend the short way to cover.
  9. My soul's on fire, and eager for the field.
10. A Struggle for a start.
11. Candedates for Brooke's—nunc est bibendum.
12. Gens humana ruit O'Crus—O Brachia! (a check).
13. Death and the Doctors.
14. Dulce domum,—jamdudum animus est in patinis, exeunt in fumo.

364 PAUL (I. D.)

Leicester Hunt [1825]

A Struggle for the Start.
The First Ten Minutes, Shaking of the Cocktails.

Symptons of a Skurry in a Perry Country
The Death

365 PAYNE (W.)

Picturesque Views in Devonshire, Cornwall, &c. (thin rule) London: Printed by Howlett and Brimmer, 10, Frith Street, Soho 1826

COLLATION.—Title as above (v. blank) + List of Plates 1 p. (v. blank) + 16 aquatint plates, each with leaf of text.

Mostly marked, London Published August. 6 1803 by John P. Thompson Gt. Newport Street (Nos. 13, 14 and 16 vary, see below).

  1. View on the River Usk, Monmouthshire.
  2. Ivy Bridge Devon.

Payne's Picturesque Views (*contd.*)

3. View near Plymouth W. Payne del. Pickett sculp.
4. View in Glamorganshire.
5. Stoke Church Mount Edgecumbe (W. Payne on View).
6. View on the Tamar Cornwall.
7. Thaugh Bridge Devon.
8. Milford Haven (W. Payne on View).
9. Mill Bay.
10. Mount Edgecumbe.
11. View Cornwall.
12. View at Mount Edgecumbe.
13. View in Cornwall W. Payne del. Pickett sculp. London Pub. Jany. 1 1797 by John P. Thompson Gt. Newport Street.
14. View on River Wye W. Payne del. Pickett sculp. London Pub. Jany. 1 1797 by John P. Thompson Gt. Newport Street.
15. Bickley Devon (W. Payne on View).
16. Brent Church Devon W. Payne del. Pickett sculp. London Pub. Jany. 1 1797 by John P. Thompson Gt. Newport Street.

Uncommon.

366 PHILLIPS (G. F.)

Principles of Effect and Colour, as applicable to Landscape Painting; illustrated by Examples for the Amateur and Professional Student in Art. By G. F. Phillips, member of the New Society of Water-Colour Painters. (swelled rule) 1 Line quotation (swelled rule) London: F. G. Harding, 24 Cornhill.

Oblong Quarto.   1833

COLLATION.—Title as above (v. J. & C. Adlard, Printers, Bartholomew Close) + Preface 1 p. (v. blank) + pp. 5–28.

p. 13. Diagrams of Colour.
p. 21. plate 1. Mill (uncoloured).
p. 22.   „   2. Lane (uncoloured).
p. 23.   „   3. Canal (coloured).
p. 24.   „   4. Coast Scene (coloured).
p. 25.   „   5. Morning (coloured).
p. 26.   „   6. River Scene, Noon (coloured).
p. 27.   „   7. Old Fortress and Dyke (coloured).
Front.   „   8. Coast Scene sunlight (coloured).

2nd Edition 1838.

367 PHILLIPS (G. F.)

Principles of Effect and Colour as Applicable to Landscape Painting. Illustrated by Examples for the Amateur and Professional in Art. By G. F. Phillips, Member of the New Society of Painters in Water Colours. (rule) "It is by attention to principles that lessons become instructive"—Dr. Price. (rule) The Third Edition, Considerably enlarged, with descriptions of the tints made use of in each subject. London: Darton and Clark, Holborn Hill.

Oblong Octavo.   1839

Phillips's Principles of Effect and Colour (*contd.*)

COLLATION.—Vignette title (v. blank) + Title as above (v. blank) + Preface pp. ii–iv + Principles of Effect and Colour etc. On Effect. pp. 6–12 + Explanation of Diagrams pp. 13–14 + On Colour pp. 15–19 (20 Blank) + Description of Plates pp. 21–30 + Advertisements 2 pp.

Each plate bears the imprint; London, Published by Darton and Clark, Holborn Hill.

```
1. Facing p. 21.   Mill (sepia).
2.   ,,   p. 22.   Lane Scene.  Evening (sepia).
3.   ,,   p. 23.   Canal (coloured).
4.   ,,   p. 24.   Coast Scene (coloured).
5.   ,,   p. 25.   Morning (coloured).
6.   ,,   p. 26.   River Scene.  Noon (coloured).
7.   ,,   p. 27.   Old Fortress and Dyke, Twilight (coloured).
8. Frontispiece.   Coast Scene.  Sunlight (coloured).
9. Vignette Title. Stormy Weather At Sea (coloured).
Colour diagram.   Facing p. 13.
```

368 *In another issue both the titles and the plates bear imprint, London B. B. King Monument Yard London.*

369 PHILLIPS (J.)

Mexico Illustrated, with Descriptive Letterpress, in English and Spanish, by John Phillips (two line rule) Order of the Plates 1. Title, near Vera Cruz. 2. Campeachy. 3. Vera Cruz. 4. Jalapa. 5. Orizaba. 6. Plains of Perote. 7. Puebla. 8. Rio Frio. 9. Popocatepetl. 10. Mexico. 11. Cathedral of Mexico. 12. Interior of Cathedral. 13. Church of Santo Domingo, (dividing line) 14. Convent of La Merced. 15. The Passes. 16. Chapultepec. 17. Man's Hand Mountain. 18. San Agustin de las Cuevas. 19. Real del Monte. 20. Church of Zimapan. 21. Mountains in El. Doctor. 22. Lagos. 23. Zacateus. 24. San Luis Potosi. 25. Pass in the Sierra Madre. 26. Matamoras (rule) Published by E. Atchley, Library of Fine Arts, 106, Great Russell Street, Bedford Square, London

Folio.   1848

COLLATION.—Title as above (v. blank) followed by 25 leaves of Text (1 leaf to each plate except title) + 26 plates as given in the title each plate bearing, Day & Son Lithrs. to the Queen.

The title that has fuller lettering is as follows: "Mexico Illustrated in Twenty-six Drawings." By John Phillips and A. Rider with descriptive Letterpress in English and Spanish (View "Near Vera Cruz") Lithographed by Messrs. Riders & Walker. Published by E. Atchley Library of Fine Arts, 106 Gt. Russell St., Bedford Sqre., London Day & Son Lithrs. to the Queen.

Plate 3 bears Alfred Rider in left-hand corner, Plate 12 bears lettering "Cathedral de Mejico," Plate 13 St Domingo (only), Plate 14 "Convent de Merced," Plate 17 the lettering is "Near Caneles—Madre Monte" (instead of Man's Hand Mountain), Plate 18 San Augustin (only), Plate 19 bears John Phillips in left-hand corner, Plate 20 Zimapan (only), Plate 21 El Doctor (only), Plate 23 Zacatecas (spelt correctly), Plate 25 Pass in the Sierra Madre-near Monterey.

Edition de Luxe. Issued in half morocco portfolio, the illustrations are on thick cards. The ordinary issue was uncoloured and smaller in size.

370 PHILLIPS (R., publisher)

Modern London: being the History and Present State of the British Metropolis London Printed for Richard Phillips

Quarto.   1805

COLLATION.—Title (v. blank) + Advertisement 2 ll. + Contents 1 lf. + pp. 1–501 with map and 22 plates followed by "Description of the Plates, representing the Itinerant Traders of London in their ordinary costume; with notices of the remarkable places given in the background." 31 plates each with 1 leaf of Text (the text to the first plate being on the reverse of the title).

1. Baking or Boiling Apples—Stratford Place.	17. Lavendar—Temple Bar.
2. Band Boxes—Tabarts Juvenile Library.	18. Mackerel—Billingsgate.
3. Baskets—Whitfield's Tabernacle.	19. Matches—The Mansion House.
4. Bellows to mend (Part of Smithfield).	20. Milk Below—Cavendish Square.
5. Brick Dust—Portman Square.	21. New Potatoes—Middlesex Hospital.
6. Buy a Bill of the Play—Theatre Drury Lane.	22. Old Clothes—Fitzroy Square.
7. Cat's & Dog's Meat!—Bethlem Hospital.	23. A Poor Sweep, Sir—Blackfryars Bridge.
8. Chairs to mend—Soho Square.	24. Rabbits—Portland Place.
9. Cherries—St. Jame's Place.	25. Rhubarb—Russell Square.
10. Door Mats—Charing Cross.	26. Sand O! St. Giles Church.
11. Dust O! New Church Strand.	27. A Showman—Hyde Park Corner.
12. Green Hasteds! Newgate.	28. Slippers—Somerset House.
13. Hair Brooms—Shoreditch Church.	29. Sweep Soot O—Foundling Hospital.
14. Hot Loaves—St. Martins Church.	30. Strawberries—Covent Garden.
15. Hot spiced Gingerbread—Pantheon.	31. Water Cresses—Hanover Square.
16. Knives to Grind—Whitehall.	

followed by an Appendix pp. 537–564 + Index pp. 565–571 + List of Copperplates 2 pp. + Books published by Phillips 3 pp. (unnumbered).

ISSUES.—*There are 6 issues of the coloured plates.*

1st Issue.—*Double framed borders, sepia washed, quarto. Title of the trader and name of the locality within the outer border Imprint below the outer border "Craig del. Published (on various dates—April 25th, July 7th, August 7th and August 25th 1804) by Richard Phillips, 71, St. Paul's Church Yard." Size of engraved surface $3\frac{7}{8} \times 2\frac{11}{16}$. Whatman paper dated 1803 and 1804. No plate mark shown for the reason that the plate was larger than the paper used (11 × 8 inches) Printed in black and coloured. Issued as a separate publication.*

2nd Issue.—*As in the 1st issue except that the inner and outer borders are aquatinted. No plate mark. The plate was larger than the paper used, 11 × 8. Quarto.*

3rd Issue.—*Double framed borders not washed, quarto. Title of Trader within the outer border, and name of locality within the inner border. Imprint below the inner border, "Pub. by R. Phillips" 1804. Size of engraved surface 4 × 2¾ inches. Laid paper Printed in brown from copper plates $5\frac{9}{16} \times 4\frac{1}{4}$ inches and coloured. Issued as separate plates*

4th Issue.—*Single framed border not washed, quarto. Title of Trader printed below the border and name of locality within. No imprint. The plate employed for this variation has been cut down to the size of the original outer border of Nos. 1, 2 and 3. Size of engraved surface $3\frac{7}{8} \times 2\frac{11}{16}$ inches, John Hall's paper dated 1805 and 1808. Printed from the copper plates which had been cut down to 5 × 4⅛ inches for Phillips London 1804. The plates being pulled on 1805 and 1808 paper suggest that the addition of the 31 plates was an afterthought. Printed in black and coloured.*

5th Issue.—*Single framed border not washed. Quarto. The plates are the same as No. 4 except that they are pulled on Whatman paper dated 1812 for Phillips London 1804.*

Phillips's Modern London (*contd.*)

6th Issue.—Single framed borders not washed, octavo. Title of Trader outside and name of locality inside the border. No imprint. Size of engraved surface 4 × 2¾ inches. Thin wove paper Printed in black and not coloured from copper plates 5¹¹⁄₁₆ × 4¼ inches. Issued as separate plates.

I am indebted for the above particulars to the kindness of C. W. F. Goss, Esq., Chief Librarian of the Bishopsgate Institute.

371 PICKEN (A.)

Madeira Illustrated 1840 By Andw. Picken (vignette of Machico) London Printed and Published at Day & Haghe's, Lithrs to the Queen, 17, Gate St., Lincoln's Inn Fields October

Folio. 1840

COLLATION.—Title as above + Dedication to Mrs. J. D. Webster Gordon (v. List of Subscribers) + Map "Island of Madeira for Pickens Madeira Illustrated Novr. 1840" + pp. 1–4 (Historical Sketch) + pp. 1–21 + 8 coloured lithographs and uncoloured lithograph at end "Point St. Lourenço."

1. Funchal from the Bay p. 1.
2. Funchal from Saõ Lazaro p. 3.
3. Funchal from the East p. 5.
4. Canera de Lobos The Sea Wolf's Den p. 7.
5. Curral (The Nuns Fold) p. 9.
6. Ravine of St. Jorge p. 11.
7. Penha D'Aguia (The Eagle's Rock) from near the Portella p. 13.
8. O Rabaçal p. 15.

All bearing in the left-hand corner From Nature and on Stone by A. Picken, and in right-hand corner, Day & Haghe Lithrs. to the Queen.

The imprint at bottom of p. 21 of text reads, T. C. Savill Printer, 107 St Martin's Lane. Edited by Dr. James Macaulay M.A.

372 PICKEN (A.)

Madeira Illustrated. Second Edition

Folio. 1842

COLLATION.—There are two issues of the Second Edition, either with the word Second Edition printed immediately over the imprint on the title page and the date altered to 1842, or without the words Second Edition and just the date altered to 1842. Otherwise they are identical and their collation is the same as for the first edition but they contain one or two minor differences. The text is slightly differently set up, 11 more names are added to List of Subscribers (4 at end of first column commencing Hon Miss E Skeffington, 3 at end second column and 4 at end of third column ending William Gordon Esq, 2 copies) p. 21 has a note added at end of text and the imprint is changed to "Printed for Day & Haghe, Lithographers to the Queen 17 Gate Street, Lincoln's Inn Fields by E. Lowe, Playhouse Yard, Blackfriars."

Published at £2 2s. plain and £4 4s. coloured. Colouring varies considerably some being fully coloured, some being only partly coloured.

Picture of St Petersburgh 1815. See under Orme (Edward).

373 PICTURESQUE

A Picturesque Description of North Wales: embellished with Twenty Select Views from Nature (2 line rule, thin and thick) **London: Published by Thomas M'Lean, 26 Haymarket, Printed at the Columbian Press, By Howlett and Brimmer, 10, Frith-Street, Soho** (small rule).

Oblong Quarto. 1823

COLLATION.—Half-title "Views in North Wales (v. blank) + Title as above (v. blank) + Preface 1 p. (v. blank) + List of Plates 1 p. (v. blank) + 20 coloured aquatints. Each with 1 p. of Text.

Each plate, marked London Published by Thomas McLean, Haymarket 1822.

1. Flint Castle.	11. Llyn-y-Dinas, near Bedgellert.
2. Vale of Clywdd.	12. River Glass Llyn.
3. View on River Dee.	13. Mountain of Cnight.
4. View on River Conway.	14. Head of Vale of Festiniog.
5. Conway Castle.	15. Rhaiadr-y-Mawddach.
6. Caernarvon Castle.	16. Dolgetty Bridge.
7. Dolbadron Castle.	17. Bala Lake.
8. Llanberris Lake & Dolbadron Castle.	18. Tal-y-Llyn.
9. Moel Shabod, near Capel Curig.	19. West Tower Goodrich Castle.
10. View in Nant Gwynant.	20. Interior of Goodrich Castle.

374 Picturesque Representations of the Dress and Manners of the English. Illustrated in Fifty Coloured Engravings, with descriptions London: (thin and thick rule) **Printed for John Murray, Albemarle Street, by W. Bulmer and Co. Cleveland-Row.**

Octavo. 1814

COLLATION.—Title as above (v. blank) and List of Plates 1 p. (v. blank) + 50 plates each with 1 leaf of Text, and bearing words England Plate 1 (2 &c.) and imprint, Published Jan. 7 1813 by J. Murray, Albemarle Street.

1. Sovereign.	18. Sailor.	35. Baron.
2. Farmers Boy.	19. Match Girl.	36. Blue Coat Boy.
3. Waterman to Coach Stand.	20. Herald.	37. Gipsey.
4. Yeoman of Guard.	21. Chimney Sweep.	38. Dragoon.
5. Schrimper.	22. Barrow Woman.	39. Baker.
6. Peer in his Robes.	23. Lord Mayor.	40. Alderman.
7. Dustman.	24. Postman.	41. Serjeant Trumpeter.
8. Hastings Fisherman.	25. Lady in Summer Dress.	42. Hussar.
9. Fireman.	26. Highland Shepherd.	43. Private 42 Regt.
10. Judge.	27. Rifleman.	44. Market Woman.
11. Billingsgate Fishwoman.	28. Watchman.	45. Grenadier 1st Guards.
12. Greenwich Pensioner.	29. General Officer.	46. Beadle of Church.
13. Bishop.	30. Dairy Maid.	47. Welsh Woman.
14. Chelsea Pensioner.	31. Drayman.	48. Newsman.
15. Milk-maid.	32. Speaker (H. of C.).	49. Officer R.H.A.
16. Drover.	33. Butchers Boy.	50. Private Life Guards.
17. Knight of the Garter.	34. Admiral.	

NOTE.—The above and the four following works, which complete the series, were also issued with M'Lean or Goodwin's imprint. M'Lean's printer was Howlett and Brimmer, and Goodwin's W. Lewis. Also published in Large paper with plates in two states, plain and coloured.

Picturesque (*contd.*)

375 Picturesque Representations of the Dress and Manners of the Austrians Illustrated in fifty coloured engravings with descriptions (rule) by William Alexander (thin and thick rule) London Printed for John Murray, Albemarle-Street, by W. Bulmer and Co. Cleveland Row.

Octavo. 1814

COLLATION.—Title as above (v. blank) + List of Plates 2 pp. (unnumbered) + Introduction pp. i–xv + 50 coloured plates, each plate with 1 leaf of Text.

The plates bear no titles but are marked, Austria Plate 1 (2 &c.), and bear Murray's imprint June 1, 1813.

376 Picturesque Representations of the Dress and Manners of the Chinese. Illustrated in fifty coloured engravings with descriptions (rule) By William Alexander (thin and thick rule) London Printed for John Murray, Albemarle-Street, by W. Bulmer and Co. Cleveland Row.

Octavo. 1814

COLLATION.—Title as above (v. blank) + List of Plates 2 pp. (unnumbered) + 50 coloured plates, each with 1 leaf of Text. Plates marked China Plate 1 (2 &c.) and bear Murray's imprint 1814.

377 Picturesque Representations of the Dress and Manners of the Russians Illustrated in Sixty Four coloured engravings with descriptions. London: (thin and thick rule) Printed for John Murray, Albemarle-Street, by W. Bulmer and Co. Cleveland Row.

Octavo. 1814

COLLATION.—Title (v. blank) + Dedication 1 p. (v. blank) + Preface pp. iii–iv + Contents 2 pp (unnumbered) + 64 coloured plates, each with 1 leaf of Text. The plates bear no titles but are marked Russian Plate 1 (2 &c.) no imprint.

378 Picturesque Representations of the Dress and Manners of the Turks. Illustrated in Sixty Coloured Engravings with descriptions London: Printed for John Murray, Albemarle-Street, by W. Bulmer and Co. Cleveland Row.

Octavo. 1814

COLLATION.—Title (v. blank) + Preface i–iv + Contents 2 pp. (unnumbered) + 60 plates, each with 1 leaf of Text. The plates bear no titles but are marked, Turkey Plate 1 (2 &c.). No imprint.

379 Picturesque Tour from Geneva to Milan, by way of the Simplon: illustrated with Thirty Six coloured Views of the most striking scenes and of the principal works belonging to the new road constructed over that Mountain, engraved from designs by J. & J. Lory, of Neufchatel; and accompanied with particulars historical and descriptive by Frederic Schoberl (thick and thin rule) London: Published by R. Ackermann, at his

Picturesque (*contd.*)

Repository of Arts, and sold by All the Booksellers in the United Kingdom (decorative rule).

Octavo. 1820

COLLATION.—Title as above (v. Printed by J. Diggens, St Ann's Lane London) + Preface 3 ll. + Text pp. 1–136 + List of Plates 2 unnumbered pages + Folding map and 36 coloured aquatint plates.

Each plate bears R. Ackermann's imprint.

Face title   Plan of the Road of the Simplon.
  1. p.   1. View of Geneva.
  2. p. 18. View on the Banks of the Lake of Geneva near St Gingouph.
  3. p. 20. View of the Extremity of the Lake of Geneva.
  4. p. 26. View of the Bridge of St Maurice.
  5. p. 40. Waterfall of Pissevache.
  6. p. 42. West View of Sion.
  7. p. 50. East View of Sion.
  8. p. 51. View of Brieg.
  9. p. 61. View of The Gallery & Bridge of the Ganther.
 10. p. 67. View from the Entrance of the Gallery of Schalbet.
 11. p. 68. View of the Gallery of Schalbet from Italian Side.
 12. p. 70. View of the Gallery of the Glaciers.
 13. p. 72. View of the Site of the Monastery of the Simplon & of Mount Rosa.
 14. p. 74. View of the Village of Simplon.
 15. p. 76. View of the Exterior of the Gallery of Algaby.
 16. p. 78. View of the Interior of the Gallery of Algaby.
 17. p. 80. Alto Bridge.
 18. p. 82. View of the New Road near the Grand Gallery.
 19. p. 84. View of the Interior of the Grand Gallery.
 20. p. 86. View of the End of the Grand Gallery towards Italy.
 21. p. 88. A View near Gondo.
 22. p. 91. View of the Gallery of Issel.
 23. p. 93. Entrance of the Valley of Dovedro.
 24. p. 95. View of the Bridge over the Cherasca.
 25. p. 97. View of the Entrance of the Last Gallery.
 26. p. 99. View of the Bridge of Crevola and the Valley of the Domo D'ossola.
 27. p. 105. Bridge of Crevola.
 28. p. 107. Villa.
 29. p. 109. View of the Bridge of Baveno, & of the Madre Islands.
 30. p. 112. View of the Lago Maggiore and the Boromeo Islands.
 31. p. 117. View of the Beautiful Island.
 32. p. 118. View from Stresa of the Beautiful Island.
 33. p. 121. View of Arona.
 34. p. 125. View of Sesto.
 35. p. 127. View of Pliniana, on the Lake of Como.
 36. p. 131. View of Milan.

380 PINKERTON (Robert)

Russia: or, Miscellaneous Observations on the Past and Present State of that Country and its Inhabitants. Compiled from Notes made on the Spot, during travels, at different times, in the service of the Bible Society, and a Residence of many years in that Country, by Robert Pinkerton, D.D. Author of "The Present State of the Greek Church in Russia," and Foreign Agent to the British and Foreign Bible Society. (two line rule) London: Seeley & Sons, 169, Fleet Street, Hatchard & Son Piccadilly.

Octavo. 1833

Pinkerton's Russia (*contd.*)

COLLATION.—Half-title "Russia" (v. blank) + Title as above (v. Printed by R. Watts, Crown Court, Temple Bar) + Preface 2 pp. + Contents 6 pp. + pp. 1–486 + List of Engravings 1 p.

1. p.   25. Hawker of Sacred Pictures or Ikons.
2. p.   35. Merchants Wife, or Kuptschiha in her Every Day—Dress.
3. p.   70. The Mushroom Gatherer.
4. p.   73. The Izbitentschik, Carpenter and Milkmaid.
5. p.   75. A National Dance.
6. p. 276. The Moujick and Family.
7. p. 295. Svaika, a Favourite Game of the Moujicks.
8. p. 302. Village Amusements of the Russians.

Plain or Ringlets 1860.   See under [Surtees (R)].

381 POCOCK (Lieut. W. Innes)

Five Views of the Island of St. Helena, from Drawings taken on the Spot: to which is added A Concise Account of the Island (thick and thin rule).   By Lieut. W. Innes Pocock, R.N. (thin and thick rule) London: Printed by D. N. Shury, Berwick Street, Soho: And Published by S. & J. Fuller, at the Temple of Fancy, Rathbone Place (small rule).
Folio.   1815

COLLATION.—Title as above (v. blank) + pp. 1–12 + List of Subscribers 1 leaf + 5 coloured plates.

Each plate marked, Drawn by Lieut. W. J. Pocock R N T. Sutherland Sculpt.   London, Published 1st Septr. 1815 for the Proprietor, by S. & J. Fuller 34 Rathbone Place.

1. General View of St. Helena (folding).
2. View of High Knowle, & Waterfall at head of James Valley.
3. View from Diana's Seat looking to the Northward.
4. View from Diana's Peak looking Southward towards Sandy Bay.
5. View of the High Knowle & Ruperts Hill, looking Northward.

A later edition was issued in 1845.

Poetical Magazine.   See under Rowlandson (T.).

382 PORTER (Robert Ker)

Travelling Sketches in Russia and Sweden, during the Years 1805, 1806, 1807, 1808 (rule) By Robert Ker Porter (rule) In Two Volumes Vol. I [II] (rule) London: Printed for Richard Phillips, Bridge-Street, Blackfriars.   By T. Gillet, Crown-Court, Fleet Street (short rule).
2 vols.   Quarto.   1809

COLLATION VOL. I.—Title as above (v. blank) + Preface 4 pp. (iii–vi) + Contents 5 pp. (mispaged as follows vii, viii, iii, iv, v) + List of Plates 1 p. (vi) + pp. 1–303 + 28 plates.

All the plates marked, R. K. Porter delt.   P. A. Hubert direxit, J. C. Stadler sculpt. and all bearing imprint, Pub Jany. 2 1809 by R. Phillips, Bridge Street London.

1. (p.   4). A View of Elsineur Castle from Hamlets Garden.
2. (p. 19). View from the English Quay at St. Petersburg.

Porter's Travelling Sketches in Russia (*contd.*)

3. (*ibd.*) The Stone Theatre at St. Petersburg.
4. (p. 31). The Place of St. Isaac.
5. (p. 106). Monks of St. Basil (coloured).
6. (*ibd.*) Nuns of St. Basil (coloured).
7. (p. 109). Russian Boors in their Winter Sledge (coloured).
8. (*ibd.*) A Hackney Sledge (coloured).
9. (p. 112). A Russian Tradesman (coloured).
10. (*ibd.*) A Travelling Russian Boor (coloured).
11. (p. 117). A Gentleman in his Winter Walking Dress (coloured).
12. (p. 144). A Russian Nurse (coloured).
13. (p. 161). A Regular Cossac (coloured).
14. (p. 164). An Uralsky Cossac (coloured).
15. (*ibd.*) An Officer of the Donsky Cossacs (coloured).
16. (p. 170). An Officer of the Imperial Foot Guards (coloured).
17. (*ibd.*) A Soldier of the Imperial Foot Guards (coloured).
18. (p. 185). The Inside of a Russian Post House (coloured and folding).
19. (p. 198). A View of Moscow.
20. (p. 228). A Russian Tradesman's Wife in her Gala Dress (coloured).
21. (*ibd.*) A Russian Tradesman's Wife in her Summer Dress (coloured).
22. (p. 238). View of the Monastery of Divitchy.
23. (p. 289). An Archimandrite in his ordinary habit (coloured).
24. (p. 290). The Monastery of Voskrashensky.
25. (p. 291). Nicons Hermitage.
26. (p. 295). A Russian Peasant in his Summer Dress (coloured).
27. (*ibd.*) A Russian Peasant in her Summer Dress (coloured).
28. (p. 303). A Bohemian or Gypsey (coloured).

VOL. II. Half-title + Title as before + Contents 4 pp. (v–viii) + pp. 1–260 + Index pp. 261–296 + 13 plates.

29. (p. 58). A Baskhir Trooper (coloured).
30. (p. 59). The Chief of the Bashkirs (coloured).
31. (p. 60). Kirghises (coloured).
32. (p. 63). A Kalmuc Horseman (coloured).
33. (p. 79). A Peasant of Finland in his Winter Dress (coloured).
34. (p. 118). The Palace at Stockholm.
35. (p. 163). Gustavas Vasa.
36. (p. 173). A Mine.
37. (p. 201). The retreat of Gustavus Vasa.
38. (p. 206). A Dalecarlion Peasant (coloured).
39. (p. 207). A Dalecarlion Female Peasant (coloured).
40. (p. 252). The Falls of Inthatta.
41. (*ibd.*) Swedish Washerwomen (coloured and folding).

383 Travelling Sketches in Russia and Sweden. Second Edition 1813

COLLATION.—Title " Travelling Sketches in Russia and Sweden during the years 1805, 1806, 1807, 1808 " (thick and thin rule) By Robert Ker Porter (thin and thick rule) The Second Edition, with Forty-one Plates. In Two Volumes, Vol. I (II) (rule) London: Printed for John Stockdale, Piccadilly 1813 (v. Strahan and Preston Printers Street London) + Preface 4 pp. (iii–vi) + Contents 5 pp. (vii–xi) + List of Plates (p. xii) + pp. 1–303 + 28 plates as in 1st Edition, Vol. II, Half-title " Travelling Sketches in Russia and Sweden Vol. II " (v. Strahan & Preston Printers Street London) + Title as in Vol. I + Contents 4 pp. (v–viii) + pp. 1–296 including Index + 13 plates as in 1st Edition.

384 PORTER (Robert Ker)

Travels in Georgia, Persia, Armenia, Ancient Babylonia, etc. etc. during the years 1817, 1818, 1819, and 1820. (thick and thin rule). By Sir Robert Ker Porter. (thin and thick rule). With numerous engravings of portraits, costumes, antiquities etc. (rule). In Two Volumes. Vol. I [II] (rule) London: Printed for Longman, Hurst, Rees, Orme, and Brown, Paternoster Row.

Quarto. 1821

COLLATION VOL. I.—Title as above (v. London Printed by A. & R. Spottiswoode, New-Street Square) + Dedication 1 leaf + Preface 4 leaves (pp. v–xi, p. xii blank) + List of Monarchs pp. xiii–xx + Contents pp. xxi–xxiii (p. xxiv blank) + Text pp. 1–720.

Front. Fettch Ali Shah, King of Persia, after a sketch from Life by Sir Robert Ker Porter. W. T. Fry sculpt. (in 3 states, 1 plain and 2 coloured).

Folding map p. i + 1 unnumbered plate p. vi of Preface, 1 diagram p. 76 + 58 plates numbered, of which 4 are coloured as under.

p. 232. A Persian Lady. Sir Robert Porter J. Clark sculpt.
p. 448. A Persian Khan. Sir Robert Porter J. Clark sculpt.
p. 454. A Persian Woman Enveloped in Her Chadre Sir Robert Porter. J. Clark, scuplt.
p. 460. A Wild Ass. Sir Robert Porter. J. Clark, scuplt.

VOL. II.—Title as before + To Reader 1 leaf + Contents of 2nd Volume 2 leaves + List of Plates 1 p. (v. Errata) + pp. 1–869 (including Index) + Front. Abbas Mirze, Prince Royal of Persia (in 3 states, as in Vol. I) + plates 59–87 + Folding map p. 808 and 1 col. plate p. 581 A Soldier of the European Organization in the Service of Abbas Mirza.

385 PRICE (Lake) and Richard FORD

Tauromachio, or the Bull-Fights of Spain, illustrated by Twenty-Six Plates, representing the most Remarkable Incidents and Scenes in the arenas of Madrid, Seville, and Cadiz the whole drawn and lithographed from studies made expressly for the work, By Lake Price: with Preliminary Explanations By Richard Ford. (rule) J. Hogarth, 5 Haymarket, London.

Folio. 1852

COLLATION.—Printed Title as above (v blank) + Dedication 1 leaf (v blank) + Preface 1 leaf (v blank) + text pp. 7–16 + Engraved pictured title (Office for the Sale of Tickets) + 25 lithograph plates.

1. The Bulls in the Corral of the Plaza.
2. Mules of the Plaza de Toros.
3. Matadors.
4. The Plaza de Torros of Madrid.
5. Entry of the Toreros in Procession.
6. The Alguazil delivering the Keys of the Toril.
7. Picador challenging the Bull.
8. The Dogs.
9. Bull charging a Picador.
10. The Bull tossing the Picador and Horse.
11. The Bull following up the charge.
12. The Picador dismounted.
13. The Picador in danger.
14. Chulos playing the Bull.
15. The Bull leaping the Barriers.
16. The Banderillas.
17. The Cachetero.
18. The Leap or Salta Tras Cuernos.
19. La Suerte de la Capa.
20. Banderillas de Fuego.
21. The Plaza of Seville.
22. The Matador.
23. The Death of the Bull.
24. Mules dragging out the Bull.
25. Toreros reposing between the Bulls.

Issued plain and coloured. Special copies on cards in portfolio.

386 PUGH (E.)

Cambria Depicta: a Tour through North Wales, illustrated with Picturesque Views. (swelled rule) By a Native Artist (swelled rule) (quote 4 lines) (double rule) London: Printed by W. Clowes Northumberland Court; for E. Williams, Bookseller to the Duke and Duchess of York. No 11 Strand (rule).

Quarto.   1816

COLLATION.—Title (v. blank) + Preface pp. iii–viii + Contents pp. ix–xii + List of Plates 2 ll. + Text pp. 1–476 + Advertisements 2 ll. + 71 coloured plates.

1. Frontispiece. Unsigned, undated.
2. View near the Loggerheads. T. Cartwright. 15 April 1813.
3. The Estuaries of the Dee & Mersey. T. Cartwright. 15 Mch 1814.
4. Moel Famma. T. Cartwright. 15 Dec 1813.
5. Conway Castle. T. Cartwright. 15 Jan 1815.
6. Pont-y-Cammau. T. Cartwright. 15 Apr 1815.
7. An Overshot Mill near Caer Hun. T. Cartwright. 15 Mch 1814.
8. Princess Joan's Coffin Lid. T. Cartwright. 15 Nov. 1814.
9. Bishop's Throne Anglesey. T. Cartwright. 15 July 1813.
10. Shane Bwt. R. Havell. 15 Feb. 1815.
11. Paris Mines in the Year 1800. I. Havell. 15 Jan 1814.
12. Paris Mines in 1804. T. Cartwright. 15 June 1813.
13. The Skerries Lighthouse. I. Havell. 25 April 1814.
14. Holyhead Wake. R. Havell. 15 Feb 1815.
15. Cavernous Rocks near Holyhead. I. Havell. 15 Nov 1813.
16. Rocks near Holyhead. T. Cartwright. 15 July 1813.
17. Emma Dolben. R. Havell. 15 Feb 1815.
18. Cadnant. T. Cartwright. 15 May 1813.
19. The Bed of the Tudors. T. Cartwright. 15 July 1814.
20. The Infant Hercules. T. Cartwright. 15 Feb 1815.
21. Ogwen Bank. I. Havell. 15 Nov 1814.
22. Nant Francon. T. Cartwright. 30 June 1813.
23. Rhaiadr-Wenol. I. Havell. 15 April 1814.
24. N. East View of Snowdon. I. Havell. 15 Nov 1813.
25. Bethgelert Church. T. Cartwright. 15 July 1814.
26. A Cromlech at Ystim Cegid. T. Cartwright. 15 May 1814.
27. The Cnucht. T. Cartwright. 15 Oct 1813.
28. A Fall of Rocks. T. Cartwright. 15 July 1814.
29. Cwm Llyn Llydaw & Cwm Llyn Glas. T. Cartwright. 30 Jun 1813.
30. View in Nant Nanhwynen. I. Havell. 15 Nov 1813.
31. Hugh Llwyd's Pulpit. I. Havell. 15 Jan 1814.
32. Vale of Festiniog. I. Hassel. 15 April 1813.
33. The Sources of the Dee. T. Cartwright. 15 May 1814.
34. The Great Peat Mountain. T. Cartwright. 15 Mch 1814.
35. A Visit to Cader Idris. T. Cartwright. 15 Nov 1814.
36. View between Barmouth & Dolgelly. Unsigned. 15 Apr 1813.
37. Cader Idris from Barmouth Heights. I. Havell. 15 Nov 1813.
38. Mary Thomas the Fasting Woman. R. Havell. 25 Feb 1815.
39. Cader Idris and Craig-y-Derin. T. Cartwright. 15 Dec 1813.
40. Glyndwr's Parliament House. T. Cartwright. 15 Sep 1814.
41. Darran Rhos y Gareg. T. Cartwright. 15 Oct 1813.
42. Breddyn Mountains from Powis Castle Grounds. I. Havell. 15 April 1814.
43. Plinlimmon Mountain. I. Hassel. 15 April 1813.
44. The Source of the Severn. T. Cartwright. 15 Jun 1814.
45. On the Severn a few miles from Llanidloes. T. Cartwright. 15 March 1814.
46. View on the Virnwy Dolanag. I. Havell. 15 Jan 1814.
47. Donalog Bridge. T. Cartwright. 15 April 1813.

Pugh's Cambria Depicta (*contd.*)

48. The Monuments of Jorwerth Drwn Dwn and St. Melangell.   T. Cartwright.   15 Nov 1814.
49. Moel Ddu Fawr.   T. Cartwright.   15 July 1813.
50. Carreg Diddos.   I. Havell.   15 Nov 1814.
51. On the Streamlet Crossing Llangollen.   Unsigned.   15 April 1813.
52. Llangollen.   T. Cartwright.   15 April 1813.
53. Llangollen.   T. Cartwright.   15 Jan 1815.
54. Pont Cysyllty Aqueduct.   I. Havell.   15 Nov 1814.
55. Nant-Y Bela.   T. Cartwright.   15 May 1813.
56. Nant-Y Ffridd Fall.   T. Bonnor.   15 July 1813.
57. Kate of Cymmau's Cottage.   T. Cartwright.   15 Sep 1814.
58. Caergwrle Castle.   T. Cartwright.   15 May 1814.
59. The Gates of Leeswood.   T. Cartwright.   15 Aug 1814.
60. The Vale of Mold.   T. Cartwright.   15 Oct 1813.
61. Hallelujah Monument.   T. Cartwright.   15 May 1814.
62. St. Winefird's Well.   I. Havell.   15 Nov 1814.
63. Clwyddian Hills from Newmarket.   I. Havell.   15 Jan 1814.
64. View near Dyserth.   T. Cartwright.   15 July 1813.
65. View on the Elwy.   T. Cartwright.   15 Oct 1813.
66. Bella, the Fortune Teller.   T. Cartwright.   15 Feb 1815.
67. Byrn Bella, or Mrs Piozzi's House.   T. Cartwright.   15 June 1814.
68. The Perilous Situation of Robert Roberts.   T. Cartwright.   15 Aug 1814.
69. Leolinus Magnus's Coffin.   T. Cartwright.   15 Nov 1814.
70. Eyarth Rocks.   I. Havell.   15 April 1814.
71. View on the Clwyd near Eyarth.   T. Cartwright.   15 Jun 1813.

387 PYNE (J. B.)

The English Lake District, by J. B. Pyne. (large circular coloured vignette of Dungeon Gill Force) Published by Thos. Agnew & Sons, 1853.   W. Gauci lith., Hanhart impt.,

6 Large Portfolios.   1853

COLLATION.—Title as above + 1 leaf of Text, "Dungeon Gill Force" + Introduction pp. i–vi + 24 coloured lithographs, each with one leaf of Text.

1. Langdale Pikes.	13. Bassenthwaite Lake Vale & Village.
2. Buttermere.	14. Grassmere from Loughrigg Fell.
3. Windermere from Orrest Head.	15. Brothers Water.
4. Druidical Circle near Keswick.	16. Ulleswater.
5. Lowes Water.	17. Rydal Water.
6. Coniston Water and Coniston Old Man.	18. Skiddaw.
7. Vale of Keswick Bassenthwaite Lake and River Greeta.	19. Windermere after the Regatta.
8. Hawes Water and Watergill Force.	20. Derwent Water.
9. Ennerdale Lake.	21. Thirlemere or Wytheburn.
10. Windermere Waterhead.	22. Derwent River & Barrowdale.
11. Lake Windermere.	23. Vales of Ennerdale & Buttermere.
12. Wastwater.	24. Crummoch Water.

Parts 1, 2 and 3, issued at £12 12s.   Parts 4, 5 and 6, issued at £12 12s.

388 PYNE (W. H.)

The Costume of Great Britain (thin and thick rule) Designed, Engraved and written by W. H. Pyne (coloured vignette of Beefeaters) London: (thin and thick rule) Published by William Miller, Albemarle-Street

Folio.   1808

Pyne's Costume of Great Britain (*contd.*)

COLLATION.—Half-title "The Costume of Great Britain (thick and thin rule) Price Nine Guineas Boards (thin and thick rule) The Letter Press by W. Bulmer and Co. Cleveland Row" (v. blank) + Title as above (v. blank) + Publisher's Preface 3 pp. (i–iii) + Table of Contents 1 p. + 60 coloured plates each with 1 leaf of Text. Each plate bears imprint, "Published by William Miller Albemarle Street Jany. 1 1805."

1. Pottery.	21. Alderman.	40. The Grass Roller.
2. Tanning.	22. Bishop.	41. General.
3. Yeoman of the King's Body Guard.	23. Doctor of Civil Law.	42. Fishermen.
	24. Milk Woman.	43. Bill Sticker.
4. Fireman.	25. Fishermen.	44. Lord Mayor's Barge.
5. Woman Selling Salop.	26. Knight of the Garter.	45. The Round about.
6. Herald.	27. Waterman to a Coach Stand.	46. Baron.
7. Chelsea Pensioner.		47. Baker.
8. Wardmote Inquest.	28. Dustman.	48. Worsted Winder.
9. Welsh Peasants Washing.	29. Lamp Lighter.	49. Highland Shepherd.
10. A Country Fair.	30. The Pillory.	50. Prison Ships.
11. The Halfpenny Showman.	31. Guy Fawkes.	51. Lord Mayor's State Coach.
12. Brewers.	32. Admiral.	52. Smithfield Drove.
13. Woman Churning Butter.	33. Rabbit Woman.	53. Dragoon.
14. Coal Heavers.	34. Judge.	54. Royal Mail.
15. Beadle of the Church.	35. Barges.	55. Life Boat.
16. Lord Mayor.	36. Speaker of the House of Commons.	56. Royal State Carriage.
17. Serjeant Trumpeter.		57. Lottery Wheel.
18. Slaughterman.	37. Peer of the Realm.	58. Butcher.
19. Brick Maker.	38. Waggon.	59. Shrimper.
20. Knife Grinder.	39. Watering Cart.	60. Highland Piper.

The plates themselves do not actually bear titles, the above are taken from the accompanying leaves of text. It will be seen that they vary slightly from the Table of Contents.

Issued in 3 states, with uncoloured background, with partially coloured backgrounds and fully coloured backgrounds, the last state being the most desirable.

The first edition was issued in 1804.

389 PYNE (W. H.)

The History of the Royal Residences of Windsor Castle, St. James's Palace, Carlton House, Kensington Palace, Hampton Court, Buckingham House, and Frogmore. By W. H. Pyne. Illustrated by One Hundred Highly finished and coloured Engravings, Fac-similies of original drawings by the most eminent artists. In Three Volumes. Vol. I [II III] (thick and thin rule) London: Printed for A Dry, 36 Upper Charlotte Street, Fitzroy-Square; and sold by the principal booksellers in the United Kingdom. L. Harrison, Printer, 373 Strand (rule).

3 vols. Quarto. 1819

COLLATION.—Title as above (v. blank) + Dedication to the Queen 1 p. (v. blank) + Advertisement 2 pp. (i–ii) + sub-title "The History of the Royal Palace of Windsor Castle" 1 p. (v. blank) + pp. 1–188 + 25 coloured plates.

Each plate bears imprint of Pyne or Dry with date of issue.

1. Front. North Front of Windsor Castle G. Samuel delt. T. Sutherland sculpt. Feb. 1 1819.
2. p. 14. Ancient Kitchen Windsor Castle Drawn by I. P. Stephanoff Engraved by W. I. Bennett Feb. 1 1818.

Pyne's Royal Residences (*contd.*)

3. p. 35. Ancient Bell Tower Windsor Castle   R. Cattermole delt.   R. Reeve sculpt.   Agut. 1 1818.
4. p. 83. The Upper Ward Windsor Castle   C. Wild delt.   T. Sutherland sculpt.   April 1 1819.
5. p. 87. Staircase Windsor Castle   C. Wild delt.   W. I Bennett sculpt.   April 1 1818.
6. p. 88. Queens Guard Chamber Windsor Castle   Drawn by C. Wild   Engraved by T. Sutherland Feb. 1 1817.
7. p. 90. The Queens Presence Chamber Windsor Castle   Drawn by C. Wild   Engraved by J. Bennett   April 1 1817.
8. p. 93. Queens Audience Chamber Windsor Castle   Drawn by C. Wild   Engraved by W. J. Bennett Feb. 1 1818.
9. p. 99. Ball Room Windsor Castle   Drawn by C. Wild   Engraved by Sutherland   Feb. 1 1817.
10. p. 106. The Queens Drawing Room Windsor Castle   Drawn by C. Wild   Engraved by T. Sutherland   Aug. 1 1816.
11. p. 116. Queens State Bedchamber Windsor Castle   J. Stephanoff delt.   J. Baily sculpt.   April 1 1818.
12. p. 135. The Kings Closet Windsor Castle   Drawn by C. Wild   Engraved by W. I. Bennett   Oct. 1 1816.
13. p. 147. The Kings Dressing Room Windsor Castle   Drawn by C. Wild   Engraved by W. I. Bennett Oct. 1 1816.
14. p. 152. The Kings Old State Bedchamber Windsor Castle   Drawn by C. Wild   Engraved by T. Sutherland June 4 1816.
15. p. 155. The Kings Drawing Room Windsor Castle   J. Stephanoff delt.   T. Sutherland sculpt. Decr. 1 1817.
16. p. 161. Queen Ann's Bed Windsor Castle   Drawn by C. Wild   Engraved by T. Sutherland   April 1 1816.
17. p. 166. The Kings Audience Chamber Windsor Castle   C. Wild delt.   T. Sutherland sculpt. Feb. 1 1818.
18. p. 170. Kings Presence Chamber Windsor Castle   J. Stephanoff delt.   W. J. Bennett sculpt. April 1 1818.
19. p. 172. Kings Guard Chamber Windsor Castle   C. Wild delt.   T. Sutherland sculpt.   Feb. 1 1818.
20. p. 176. St. Georges Hall Windsor Castle   Drawn by C. Wild   Engraved by W. J. Bennett   Dec. 1 1816.
21. p. 179. The Royal Chapel Windsor Castle   C. Wild delt.   T. Sutherland sculpt.   June 1 1818.
22. p. 182. Choir of St. Georges Chapel Windsor Castle   C. Wild delt.   T. Sutherland sculpt.   Dec. 1 1818.
23. p. 183. St. Georges Chapel from the Altar Windsor Castle   C. Wild delt.   T. Sutherland sculpt. June 1 1819.
24. p. 187. Ancient Staircase (Round Tower) Windsor Castle   J. Stephanoff delt.   R. Reeve sculpt. Dec. 1 1818.
25. p. 188. Old Guard Chamber Round Tower Windsor Castle   Drawn by James Stephanoff   Engraved by T. Sutherland Feb. 1 1818.

+ sub-title "The History of the Queens House of Frogmore" 1 p. (v. blank) + pp. 1–21 with 6 coloured plates.

26. front. Frogmore C. Wild delt.   W. J. Bennett sculpt.   Aug. 1 1819.
27. p. 3. The Dining Room Frogmore C. Wild delt.   T. Sutherland sculpt.   April 1 1817.
28. p. 8. The Queens Library Frogmore   C. Wild delt.   W. J. Bennett sculpt.   Octr. 1 1817.
29. p. 13. The Green Pavillon Frogmore   C. Wild delt.   D. Havell sculp.   June 1 1817.
30. p. 17. The Japan Room Frogmore   C. Wild delt.   R. Reeve sculp.   June 1 1819.
31. p. 21. Green Closet Frogmore   C. Wild delt.   W. J. Bennett sculp.   June 1 1819.
Vignette tailpiece on p. 31 "The Queens Hermitage."

VOL. II.—Title as before (v. blank) + Dedication to the Prince of Wales 1 p. (v. blank) + sub-title "The History of the Royal Palace of Hampton Court" 1 p. (v. blank) + pp. 1–88 + 13 coloured plates.

32. front. Hampton Court Palace   W. Westall A.R.A. delt.   R. Reeve sculpt.   July 1 1819.
33. p. 3. The Chapel Hampton Court   C. Wild delt.   T. Sutherland sculpt.   July 1 1819.

Pyne's Royal Residences (*contd.*)

34. p.   19. Banqueting Hall Hampton Court   R. Cattermole delt.   R. Reeve sculpt.   May 1 1819.
35. p.   31. Quadrangle Hampton Court   W. Westall A.R.A. delt.   T. Sutherland sculpt.   June 1 1819.
36. p.   32. Grand Stair Case Hampton Court   R. Cattermole delt.   D. Havell sculpt.   Augt. 1 1817.
37. *ibd.*   Gothic Hall Hampton Court   C. Wild delt.   W. I. Bennett sculpt.   Sepr. 1 1819.
38. p.   33. Guard Chamber Hampton Court   J. Stephanoff delt.   R. Reeve sculpt.   Feb. 1 1819.
39. p.   41. The Throne Room Hampton Court   J. Stephanoff delt.   R. Reeve sculpt.   Decr. 1 1818.
40. p.   44. Second Presence Chamber Hampton Court   J. Stephanoff delt.   R. Reeve sculpt.   June 1 1819.
41. p.   58. Kings Writing Closet Hampton Court   R. Cattermolle (sic) pint.   R. Reeve sculpt.   Feb. 1 1819.
42. p.   63. Queen Mary's State Bedchamber Hampton Court   Drawn by R. Cattermole   Engraved by Havell   June 4th 1816.
43. p.   68. The Ball Room Hampton Court   R. Cattermolle delt.   R. Reeve sculpt.   Aug. 1 1818.
44. p.   77. Cartoon Gallery Hampton Court   J. Stephanoff delt.   W. J. Bennett sculpt.   Sep. 1 1819.

+sub-title "The History of the Royal Palace of Buckingham House" 1 p. (v. blank) + pp. 1–28 +11 coloured plates.

45. p.   1. Buckingham House   W. Westall A.R.A. delt.   T. Sutherland sculpt.   Augt. 1819.
46. p.   5. Staircase Buckingham House   Drawn by J. Stephanoff   Engraved by W. J. Bennett   Feby. 1 1818.
47. p.   7. Stair Case Buckingham House   Drawn by R. Cattermole   Engraved by W. I. Bennett   Octr. 1 1817.
48. p.   9. The Kings Library Buckingham House.   J. P. Stephanoff delt.   J. Baily   Decr. 1 1817.
49. p.   13. The Saloon Buckingham House   J. Stephanoff delt.   W. J. Bennett sculpt.   Octr. 1 1818.
50. p.   14. Drawing Room Buckingham House   Drawn by I. Stephanoff   Engraved by T. Sutherland   Feb. 1 1817.
51. p.   15. Second Drawing Room Buckingham House.   J. P. Stephanoff delt.   T. Sutherland sculpt.   June 1 1818.
52. p.   18. The Blue Velvet Room Buckingham House   C. Wild delt.   D. Havell sculpt.   Aug. 1 1817.
53. p.   19. The Green Closet Buckingham House   J. Stephanoff delt.   D. Havell sculpt.   March 1 1819.
54. p.   21. The Queens Breakfast Room Buckingham House   Drawn by I Stephanoff   Engraved by D. Havell   Feby. 1 1817.
55. p.   26. The Kings Library Buckingham House Plate II   J. Stephanoff delt.   R. Reeves sculpt.   Feb. 1 1818.

+sub-title "The History of the Royal Palace of Kensington" 1 p. (v. blank) + pp. 1–88 + 12 coloured plates.

56. front.   Kensington Palace   W. Westall A R A delt.   R. Reeve sculpt.   May 1 1819.
57. p.   29. The Great Staircase Kensington Palace   C. Wild delt.   R. Reeve sculpt.   April 1 1819.
58. p.   33. Presence Chamber Kensington Palace   Drawn by I. P. Stephanoff   Engraved by D. Havell   Dec. 1 1816.
59. p.   46. Queen Caroline's Drawing Room Kensington Palace   Drawn by C. Wild   Engraved by T. Sutherland   Aug. 1 1816.
60. p.   53. The Admirals Gallery Kensington Palace   J. Stephanoff delt.   D. Havel sculpt.   April 1 1817.
61. p.   56. Old Dining Room Kensington Palace   J. Stephanoff delt.   T. Sutherland sculpt.   Octr. 1 1818.
62. p.   63. The Queens Closet Kensington Palace   J. Stephanoff delt.   W. J. Bennett sculpt.   Decr. 1 1817.
63. p.   67. The Queens Gallery Kensington Palace   J. Stephanoff delt.   T. Sutherland sculpt.   Sep. 1 1819.
64. p.   72. The Cupola Room Kensington Palace   Drawn by R. Cattermole   Engraved by T. Sutherland   April 1 1817.
65. p.   74. The Kings Great Drawing Room Kensington Palace   Drawn by C. Wild   Engraved by W. J. Bennett   Feb. 1 1816.

Pyne's Royal Residences (*contd.*)

66. p. 78. The Kings Gallery Kensington Palace   Drawn by C. Wild   Engraved by T. Sutherland   Oct. 1 1816.

67. p. 83. The Queens Bed Chamber Kensington Palace   R. Cattermolle delt.   W. J. Bennett sculpt.   Aug. 1 1818.

68. p. 85. The Kings Closet Kensington Palace   J. Stephanoff delt.   R. Reeve sculpt.   March 1 1819.

VOL. III.—Title as before (v. blank) + Dedication to H.R.H. Prince Frederick Duke of York 1 p. (v. blank) + sub-title "The History of the Royal Palace of St James's" 1 p. (v. blank) + pp. 1–80 + 10 coloured plates.

69. front.   St. James's Palace   C. Wild delt.   R. Reeve sculpt.   July 1 1819.

70. p.   9. Guard Chamber St. James's   C. Wild delt.   R. Reeve sculpt.   June 1 1818.

71. p. 10. The Kings Presence Chamber St. James's   Drawn by C. Wild   Engraved by T. Sutherland   April 1 1816.

72. p. 15. The Queen's Levee Room St. James's   Drawn by C. Wild   Engraved by W. I. Bennett   Aug. 1 1816.

73. p. 33. Old Bed Chamber St. James's In which was born the son of James II   C. Wild delt.   R. Reeve sculp. Septr 1 1819.

74. p. 39. The German Chapel St. James's Palace   C. Wild delt.   Engraved by D. L. Havell   Augt. 1 1816.

75. p. 43. Kitchen St. James's Palace   J. Stephanoff delt.   W. J. Bennett sculpt.   April 1 1819.

76. p. 60. The Queen's Library St. James's   C. Wild delt.   R. Reeve sculpt.   June 1 1819.

+ sub-title "The History of the Royal Residence of Carlton House" 1 p. (v. blank) + pp. 1–92 + 24 coloured plates.

77. p.   1. Carlton House South Front   W. Westall A.R.A. delt.   R. Reeve sculpt.   April 1 1819.

78.   Carlton House North Front   W. Westall A.R.A. delt.   R. Reeve sculpt.   April 1 1819.

79. p. 13. The Hall of Entrance Carlton House   C. Wild delt.   R. Reeve sculpt.   March 1 1819.

80. p. 15. The Vestibule Carlton House   C. Wild delt.   R. Reeve sculpt.   April 1 1819.

81. p. 16. Grand Stair-case Carlton House   C. Wild delt.   J. Reeve sculpt.   [not dated].

82. *ibd.*   Gallery of the Staircase Carlton House   C. Wild delt.   T. Sutherland sculpt.   May 1 1819

83. p. 17. The West Ante Room Carlton House   C. Wild delt.   R. Reeve sculpt.   April 1 1819.

84. p. 20. Crimson Drawing Room Carlton House   Drawn by C. Wild   Engraved by Sutherland   Oct. 1 1816.

85. p. 24. The Circular Room Carlton House   Drawn by C. Wild   Engraved by T. Sutherland   June 1 1817.

86. p. 25. The Throne Room Carlton House   C. Wild delt.   T. Sutherland sculpt.   Oct. 1 1818.

87. p. 28. Ante Chamber leading to the Throne Room Carlton House   Drawn by C. Wild   Engraved by T. Sutherland   Dec. 1 1816.

88. p. 31. The Rose Satin Drawing Room Carlton House   C. Wild delt.   D. Havell sculpt.   Dec. 1 1817.

89. p. 32. Rose Satin Drawing Room (Second View) Carlton House   C. Wild delt.   R. Reeve sculpt.   Dec. 1 1818.

90. p. 40. Ante Room Carlton House   Drawn by C. Wild   Engraved by T. Sutherland   Oct. 1 1817.

91. p. 43. Ante Room (Looking North) Carlton House   C. Wild delt.   W. J. Bennett sculpt.   Oct 1 1818.

92. p. 45. The Blue Velvet Room Carlton House   Drawn by C. Wild   Engraved by D. Havell   Oct. 1 1816.

93. p. 48. The Blue Velvet Closet Carlton House   C. Wild delt.   R. Reeve sculpt.   Aug. 1 1818.

94. p. 52. The Lower Vestibule Carlton House   C. Wild delt.   R. Reeve sculpt.   April 1 1819.

95. p. 58. The Golden Drawing Room Carlton House   Drawn by C. Wild   Engraved by T. Sutherland   June 1 1817.

96. p. 60. The Alcove Golden Drawing Room Carlton House   C. Wild delt.   W. J. Bennett sc.   June 1 1817.

97. p. 63. Gothic Dining Room Carlton House   Drawn by C. Wild   Engraved by T. Sutherland   Augt. 1 1817.

98. p. 80. Dining Room Carlton House   Drawn by C. Wild   Engraved by T. Sutherland   Octr. 1 1817.

Pyne's Royal Residences (*contd.*)

99. p. 84. The Conservatory Carlton House   C. Wild delt.   T. Sutherland sculpt.   Aug. 1 1817.
100. p. 88. Conservatory (Second View) Carlton House   C. Wild delt.   R. Reeve sculpt.   March 1 1819.

+ List of Portraits in the Royal Collections described in this work pp. 1–13 (14 blank) + List of Plates to the 3 vols. 2 pp.

Issued in 25 parts in printed wrappers on large and small paper.   Watermarks must be pre-publication.

390 QUEBEC

The Quebec Volunteers (vignette—Palace Gate "Roll drums, merrily—march away") Quebec.   Printed and Published by Peregrine Pouchbelt and Roderick Ramrod, No. 32 Carronade Square

Quarto.   1839

COLLATION.—Title as above (v. blank) + 10 coloured lithograph plates.

1. Quebec Volunteer Cavalry.
2. Quebec Royal Engineer Rifles 1st and 2nd Companies.
3. Royal Quebec Volunteer Artillery.
4. Quebec Loyal Artificers or Faugh a Ballagh 1839.
5. The Sailors Compy. or "Queen's Pets."
6. The Queen's Own (Light Infantry) of Quebec 1839.
7. Queen's Volunteers.
8. Quebec Light Infantry 1st Company 1839.
9. The Highland Company.
10. Quebec Light Infantry.

Very rare.   The above collation by permission of Messrs. Robson.

Quiz.   The Grand Master or Adventures of Qui Hi.   See under Rowlandson (T.).

391 RAFFLES (T. S.)

The History of Java.   By Thomas Stamford Raffles, Esq. Late Lieut-Governor of that Island and its Dependencies, F.R.S. and A.S. Member of the Asiatic Society at Calcutta, Honorary Member of the Literary Society at Bombay, and late President of the Society of Arts and Sciences at Batavia. (waved rule) In Two Volumes (waved rule) with a Map and Plates. (rule) Vol. I [II] (thick and thin rule) London: Printed for Black, Parbury, and Allen, Booksellers to the Hon East-India Company, Leadenhall Street; and John Murray, Albemarle Street (short rule).

2 vols.   Quarto.   1817

COLLATION VOL. I.—Title as above (v. Printed by Cox and Bayliss Great Queen Street, Lincoln's Inn Fields) + Dedication to Prince Regent 3 pp. (v–vii) p. viii blank + pp. ix–xiii p. xiv blank + Contents Vol. I pp. xv–xvi + List of Plates Vol. I 1 p. (v. blank) + Introduction pp. xix–xlviii + pp. 1–479 + 2 Maps + 28 plates.

Each plate bears imprint, "London Published by Black, Parbury & Allen, Leadenhall Street 1817."

1. Front.   Raden Rana Dipura.
   p. 62. Folding statistical table.
2. p. 84. A Javan of the lower class (coloured).
3. p. 86. A Javan Woman of the lower class (coloured).

Raffles's History of Java (*contd.*)

4. p. 88. A Javan Chief in his ordinary dress (coloured).
5. p. 90. A Javan in the War dress (coloured).
6. p. 92. A Javan in the Court Dress (coloured).
7. p. 94. A Madurese of the rank of Mantri (coloured).
8. p. 112. Implements of Husbandry.
9. p. 168. (Stamps used in making the Batck Cloths &c.).
10. p. 174. Carpenters Tools.
11. p. 296. Javan Weapons 1. Plate of Krises.
12. *ibd.*   „   „   2. Varieties of Javan Kris.
13. *ibd.*   „   „   3. Javan Weapons.
14. *ibd.*   „   „   4. Javan Weapons.
15. *ibd.*   „   „   5. Javan Weapons & Standards.
16. *ibd.*   The Mangkara-bahia.
    p. 306. Folding table of Revenues.
17. p. 318. A Penganten Wadon or Bride (coloured).
18. p. 320. A Penganten Lanang or Bridegroom (coloured).
19. p. 336. Topeng or Masks Wayang or Senic Shadows.
20. p. 342. A Ronggeng or dancing Girl (coloured).
21. p. 360. Ancient forms of the Javan Alphabet.
22. *ibd.*   Aksara Jawa, or Letters of the Javan Alphabet (printed).
23. p. 368. Specimen of an Inscription in the ancient Deranagari.
24. p. 370. A Table of the Dera nagari Consonants.
    p. 412. Sketch of the Situation of the Different Countries referred to in the Brata Yud'ha (map).
25. p. 470. Musical Instruments Gamelan Salindro.
26. *ibd.*   Javan Music.
27. p. 474. Fac-simile of Signs representing the Pascar or Market Days.
28. p. 478. Fac-simile of the Signs of the Zodiac as represented in the Cheribon MS.
    At end Folding Map of Java engraved by Walker.

VOL. II.—Title as before + Contents to Vol. II 2 pp. (v–vi) + List of Plates in Vol. II 2 pp (vii–viii) + p. 1–288 + 2 leaves unpaged + Appendix pp. i–cclx + Advertisement 1 leaf + 37 plates.

29. front. Bitara Gana or Ganesa.
30. p.   1. S. E. View of the Palace at Kulasan near Brambanan   Engraved by J. Walker.
    p.   1. Vignette   S.W. View of the principal Temple at Suku   Engraved by J. Walker.
    p. 11. Vignette   N.E. View of the Principal Temple at Jongrangan 1815   Engraved by J. Mitan.
31. p. 12. From Subjects in Stone found in the central districts of Java.
    p. 16. Vignette   One of the small Temples at Chandi Sewu 1815   Engraved by J. Walker.
32. p. 16. One of the smaller Temples at Brambanan in its present state.
33. p. 18. One of the smaller Temples at Brambanan restored to its original state.
34. *ibd.*   The large Temple at Brambanan.
35. *ibd.*   The large Temple at Brambanan restored (folding).
    p. 20. Vignette   The Principal Temple at Chandi Sewu 1815   Engraved by J. Mitan.
36. p. 32. One of the Temples on the Mountain Dieng or Prahu.
37. *ibd.*   One of the Temples on the Mountain Dieng or Prahu restored to its original state.
38. p. 42. From Subjects in Stone found near Singa Sari in the district of Malang.
39. p. 44. From Subjects in stone.
40. p. 46. From the ruins at Suku near the Mountain Lawu.
    p. 51. Vignette Western front of the larger Temple at Jabang near Probolingo 1815   Engraved by J. Mitan.
41. p. 52. A Stone Pillar called Tugu.
    p. 54. Vignette   One of the Gateways at Majapahit   Engraved by J. Walker.
42. *ibd.*   Durga called Lava Jong grang by the Modern Javans.
43. *ibd.*   From a Subject in Stone near Singa Sari.
43a. *ibd.*   From Subjects in Stone found near Brambanan.
44. *ibd.*   From Subjects in Stone collected in different parts of Java.
45. *ibd.*   From Subjects in stone collected by the Chinese and deposited in their Temple of Worship near Batavia.

Raffles's History of Java (*contd.*)

46. p. 54. From Subjects in Stone found in the vicinity of Bovo Bodo in Kedu.
47. p. 56. From Casts in Metal found near Brambanan.
48. *ibd.* From Casts in Copper &c. found in the District of Kedu.
49. *ibd.* From Casts in Metal found in Kedu.
50. *ibd.* From Casts in Metal found near the ruins at Brambanan.
51. *ibd.* From Casts in Metal found in Kedu.
52. *ibd.* From Casts in Copper found in the vicinity of the Mountain Dieng.
53. *ibd.* From Casts in Metal found in the vicinity of the Mountain Dieng.
54. *ibd.* From Casts in Metal found in the vicinity of the Mountain Dieng.
55. *ibd.* Zodiacal Cup in Copper.
56. *ibd.* From Casts in Brass &c. found in the district of Kedu.
57. p. 58. Fac simile reduced from the original Inscription on a stone called Batu tulis.
58. *ibd.* Fac simile (reduced) of an ancient inscription on stone at Kwali in Cheribon.
59. *ibd.* Fac simile of an Inscription on Stone found in Pakalongan.
60. *ibd.* Specimen of the Kawi character &c.
61. *ibd.* Facsimile (reduced) of an ancient inscription at Suku.
62. p. 60. Ancient Coins with their supposed dates.
   p. 63. Vignette The smaller Temple at Jabung near Probolingo.
   p. 134. Vignette Remains of a Gateway at Majapahit.
   p. 240. Vignette (on blank page) Temple near Kulasan North Face 1815 Engraved by J. Mitan.
63. p. clxxxviii. Ugi or Mengkasar Alphabet.
64. p. ccxxxvi. A Papuan or Native of New Guinea 10 years old (coloured).

392 RALFE (J.)

The Naval Chronology of Great Britain; or an Historical Account of Naval and Maritime Events, from the Commencement of the War in 1803, to the End of the Year 1816: also, Particulars of the most important Courts-Martial, Votes of Parliament, Lists of Flag-Officers in Commission, and of promotions for each year: The Whole forming a complete Naval History of the above Period. Illustrated with numerous engravings. (short thick and thin rule) By Mr. J. Ralfe, (thin and thick rule) In Three Volumes. Vol. I (rule) London: Published by Whitmore and Fenn, Charing-Cross; and sold by the principal booksellers in the United Kingdom. Printed by L. Harrison, 373, Strand (short rule).

3 vols. Octavo.   1820

COLLATION VOL. I.—Title as above (v. blank) + Dedication 2 pp. (iii–iv) + List of Subscribers 2 pp. (v–vi) + Preface 4 pp. (vii–x) + List of Plates to the 3 volumes 2 pp. unnumbered + pp. 1–288 + plates 1–19.

All plates marked, Painted by T. Whitcombe [or Whitcombe without initial] Engraved by T. Sutherland unless otherwise stated.

1. Front. His Royal Highness the Prince Regent. Drawn by H. Bone Esq. R.A. Engraved by R. Cooper.
2. p. 49. Sir Sidney Smith's squadron engaging an enemy's flotilla May 16th 1804. From a Drawing by Sir W. Parker Bart.
3. p. 56. Sir Graham Moore's Action, Octr. 5th 1804 From a plan by Sir J. Gore. Engraved by D. Havell.
4. p. 57. Sir Graham Moore's Action off Cape St Mary, Octr 5th 1804 From a Sketch by Sir J. Gore.
5. p. 76. Defeat of Adml. Linois by Commodore Dance, Feby 15th 1804. From a Drawing by Mr. W. Daniel under the direction of Sir N. Dance.
6. p. 81. Defence of the Centurion in Vizagapatam Road Septr 18th 1804. From a Plan by Captn Sir James Lind.
7. p. 126. Sir Robert Calder's Action, July 22nd 1805. From a plan by Sir R. Calder, in the possession of Mr Whitcomb.

Ralfe's Naval Chronology of Great Britain (*contd.*)

8. p. 126. Situation of the hostile Squadrons on the morning of the 23rd July 1805. From a plan by Robt. Calder, in the possession of Mr Anderson.

9. p. 129. Capture of La Didon, Augt. 10th 1805 From a Drawing executed under the direction of Captn. T. Baker.

10. *ibd.* Capture of La Didon, Augt. 10th 1805 From a Drawing in the possession of Captn. Baker.

11. p. 130. Battle of Trafalgar From a Plan by Sir E. Harvey.

12. p. 131. Situation of the Temeraire at half past 3 p.m. October 21st 1805 From a painting in the possession of Sir E. Harvey Engraved by J. Baily.

13. p. 131. Situation of the Bellerophon, at the moment of the death of her gallant commander Captn Cooke October 1st 1805 From a Painting in the possession of C Cooke Esq Painted by T. Whitcombe Engraved by T. Sutherland.

14. p. 141. The Santa Margaretta, Captn Wilson Rathbone & The Phoenix, Captn T. Baker, engaging four French sail of the line previous to the coming of the squadron under the command of Commodre Sir R. J. Strachan From a Drawing in the possession of Captn Rathbone Engraved by F. C. Lewis.

15. p. 142. Sir Richard Strachan's Action Nov 5th 1805 From a Drawing in the possession of Sir R. Strahan Painted by Whitcomb Engraved by T. Sutherland.

16. p. 245. Capture of La Gueriere—July 19th 1806 From a plan by Sir T. Lavril Painted by T. Whitcomb Engraved by T. Sutherland.

17. p. 253. The Sirius, Captn Prowse engaging a French Squadron off the mouth of the Tiber April 17th 1806. From a painting in the possession of Captn Prowse Whitcomb pixnt. T. Sutherland sculpt.

18. p. 267. Capture of the Pomana. From a Drawing by Sir C. Brisbane Painted by Whitcombe Engraved by T. Sutherland.

19. p. 271. Capture of the Maria Riggersbergen, Octr 18th 1806 From a sketch by Captn Rainier Painted by Whitcomb Engraved by Bailey.

VOL. II.—Title as before (v. blank) + pp. 1–284 + plates 20–34.

20. Front. [Design for a Monument to commemorate the Services of the British Navy] J. T. Mackenzie delt F. C. Lewis sculpt.

21. p. 3. Loss of the Blanche March 4th 1807 From a Plan by Sir T. Lavril Painted by T. Whitcombe Engraved by T. Sutherland.

22. p. 28. The squadron under the command of Sir J. T. Duckworth forcing the narrow channel of the Dardenelles February 19th 1807 From a Drawing by Sir W. Parker Bart. Painted by T. Whitcombe Engraved by T. Sutherland.

23. p. 29. Destruction of the Turkish Fleet Feby 19th 1807 From a Plan by Capt Mowbray Painted by T. Whitcombe Engraved by T. Sutherland.

24. p. 44. Capture of Curacoa From a Drawing by Sir C. Brisbane Painted by T. Whitcombe Engraved by J. Bailey.

25. p. 79. Capture of La Thetis Novr 10th 1808 From a Sketch by Captn. W. Hill Painted by Whitcombe Engraved by T. Sutherland.

26. p. 87. The Implacable, Captn T. B. Martin, engaging the Sewolad Augt. 26th 1808 From a Drawing in the possession of Sir T. Byam Martin Painted by Whitcombe Engraved by Baily.

27. p. 88. Burning of the Sewolod Augt. 27th 1808 Painted by T. Whitcombe Engraved by T. Sutherland.

28. p. 123. The Theseus Captn. J. Beresford, leading the British squadron of 4 sail of the line, near the Isle of Grouais, in the face of the Brest fleet of 8 sail of the line, obliging them to haul their wind and preventing their joining the l'Orient squadron then laying ready to put to sea Feb 24th 1809 From a Sketch by Sir J. Beresford Engraved by F. C. Lewis.

29. p. 124. The Squadron under the command of Rear Adml. Stopford engaging three French frigates. From a plan by Sir H. Hotham Painted by T. Whitcombe Engraved by T. Sutherland.

30. p. 126. Capture of Le Nieman April 6th 1809 From a Sketch by Captn W. Hill Painted by Whitcombe Engraved by Sutherland.

31. p. 226. The Prometheus & Melpomene standing into the Gulph of Riga, to meet the boats of the British squadron, and prizes cut out during the night August 1809 From a Drawing by Mr Hood Midn. of the Melpomene Painted by Whitcombe Engrav'd by Havell.

Ralfe's Naval Chronology of Great Britain (*contd.*)

32. p. 230. Capture of the Var, Feby 15th 1809   From a sketch by Sir James Brisbane   Painted by Whitcomb   Engraved by Sutherland.
33. p. 247. Capture of La Furieuse Augt. 6th 1809.   From a plan by Captn. Mounsey   Painted by Whitcombe   Engraved by T. Sutherland.
34. *ibd.*   Capture of Furieuse Augt. 6th 1809   From a plan by Captn. Mounsey   Painted by Whitcombe   Engraved by T. Sutherland.

VOL. III.—Title as before (v. blank) + pp. 1–313 (p. 314 Errata) + Index pp. 315–318 + plates 35–60.

35. Front   [Design for a Mausoleum to the Fallen]   F. Mackenzie delt.   T. Sutherland sculpt.
36. p. 37. The Spartan, Captn. J. Brenton, engaging a French Squadron in the Bay of Naples May 3 1810   From a drawing by Sir J. Brenton in the Bay of Naples   Painted by Whitcombe   Engraved by Bailey.
37. p. 38. Capture of Le Sparviere May 3rd 1810   From a drawing by Sir J. Brenton   Painted by Whitcombe   Engraved by T. Sutherland.
38. p. 65. Capture of the Island of Banda Augt. 9th 1810   From a plan by Sir C. Cole   Painted by T. Whitcombe   Engraved by T. Sutherland.
39. p. 99. The Rinaldo, Captn. J. Anderson engaging four privateers   From a sketch by Captn. Anderson   Painted by Whitcombe   Engraved by W. Bailey.
40. p. 108. Representation of the gallant attack made by the Rinaldo, Captn. Anderson, and the Redpole, Captn. C. Campbell, on a Division of the Enemy's flotilla, in Boulogne Bay Septr. 3rd 1811   From a Sketch by W. A. Armstrong, Master of the Rinaldo   Engraved by Sutherland.
41. p. 111. Capture of the Ville de Lyons, Septr. 21st 1811   From a Plan by Mr. Armstrong Master of the Rinaldo   Painted by T. Whitcombe   Engraved by T. Sutherland.
42. p. 124. Sir W. Hoste's Action off Lissa, March 13th 1811   From a Sketch by Lieut. the Hon W. Waldegrave   Engraved by W. J. Bennett.
43. p. 134. The Imperieuse engaging a Battery & Gun-Boats, Octr. 11th   From a drawing by Mr Hood   Painted by T. Whitcombe   Engraved by T. Sutherland.
44. p. 135. Capture of the Pomone   Painted by T. Whitcombe   Engraved by T. Sutherland.
45. p. 140. Commencement of Captn. Schomberg's Action off Madagascar May 26th 1811   From a drawing by Mr Beechey   Painted by T. Whitcombe   Engraved by T. Sutherland.
46. *ibd.*   The Squadrons becalmed   From a drawing by Mr Beechey   Painted by Whitcombe   Engraved by W. Bailey.
47. p. 141. The Action renewed by Night   From a Drawing by Mr Beechey   Painted by T. Whitcombe   Engraved by I. Bailey.
48. p. 143. Surrender of Tamatave   From a drawing by Mr. Beechey   Painted by T. Whitcombe   Engraved by T. Sutherland.
49. p. 165. The Northumberland, Captn. Hotham engaging Two French frigates   From a painting in the possession of Sir H. Hotham   Painted by T. Whitcombe   Engraved by T. Sutherland.
50. p. 166. Destruction of the French Frigates L'Arianne & L'Andromache   From a painting in the possession of Sir H. Hotham   Painted by T. Whitcombe   Engraved by Sutherland.
51. p. 173. Capture of the Rivoli Feby 22nd 1812   From a sketch by Captn. J. W. Andrew   Engraved by T. Sutherland.
52. p. 177. The Leviathan, Imperieuse, Curacao and Eclair attacking two Towns on the Coast of Genoa June 27th 1812   From a Drawing by Mr Hood   Painted by Whitcombe   Engraved by T. Sutherland.
53. p. 194. Capture of the Argus, August 14th 1813   From a painting in the possession of Captn. Maples   Painted by Whitcombe   Engraved by T. Sutherland.
54. p. 195. Destruction of the Flibustier, Octr. 13th 1813   From a sketch by Captn. Scriven   Painted by T. Whitcombe   Engraved by W. Bailey.
55. p. 199. Capture of the Island of Ponza, Feby 26th 1813   From a Plan by Captn. Mounsey   Painted by T. Whitcombe   Engraved by T. Sutherland.
56. p. 210. Capture of the Chesapeake, June 1st 1813   Executed under the direction of Captn. Sir P. B. V. Broke Bart.   Painted by T. Whitcombe   Engraved by W. I. Bennett.
57. p. 303. Bombardment of Algiers   From a plan by Sir J. Brisbane   Painted by T. Whitcombe   Engraved by Bailey.

Ralfe's Naval Chronology of Great Britain (*contd.*)

58. p. 311. The Imperieuse & Thames attacking a Castle and Gunboats Novr 2nd 1811   From a drawing by Mr Hood of the Imperieuse Painted by T. Whitcombe Engraved by T. Sutherland.

59. p. 312. The Imperieuse & Cephalus engaging an enemy's squadron in sight of the Town of Naples From a drawing by Mr Hood Painted by T. Whitcombe Engraved by T. Sutherland.

60. p. 313. The squadron under the command of Sir J. Brisbane attacking Fort Maurigio From a Sketch by Sir J Brisbane Painted by T. Whitcombe Engraved by T. Sutherland.

Issued in 12 Parts, brown buff wrappers, plain and in colours.   Genuine coloured copies are rare.

393 RAWSTORNE (Lawrence)

Gamonia: or, the Art of Preserving Game; and an improved method of making Plantations and Covers, explained and illustrated.   By Lawrence Rawstorne, Esq. with fifteen coloured drawings by J. T. Rawlins, taken on the spot. (thin rule) London: Published for the Proprietor, by Rudolph Ackermann, Eclipse Sporting Gallery, 191 Regent Street (short rule).

Octavo.   1837

COLLATION.—Half-title "Gamonia: or, the Art of Preserving Game" + Title as above (v. London: Walter Spiers, Printer, 399 Oxford St) + Dedication to Edward Earl of Derby dated Penwortham, Oct. 17th 1837 2 ll. + Description of Plates 1 leaf + Preface 2 leaves + sub-title "Gamonia Part I" 1 leaf + pp. 17–208 small errata slip (7 lines) pasted on last leaf + 15 coloured plates.

Each plate marked, T. J. Rawlins del & sc.

1. Front. Part 1. Penwortham, with the commencement of battue A good beginning makes a good ending A. W. Reeve Aq.
2. p. 17. Tulketh Hall & Town of Preston Old Sporting School J. H. Banks aq.
3. p. 18. Vale of Ribble New Sporting School J. H. Banks aq.
4. p. 111. Front Part II Penwortham with conclusion of battue Alls well that ends well J. H. Banks aq.
5. p. 161. Castle Hill Sharp's the word quick the motion J. H. Banks aq.
6. p. 175. The Lower Ridding More haste the worst speed J. H. Banks aq.
7. p. 179. Penwortham Church Slow & Sure (in the old style) J. H. Banks aq.
8. p. 180. The Round Wood No stolen goods, Honesty's the best policy J. H. Banks aq.
9. p. 182. Blashaw Dam Fair play's a jewel J. H. Banks aq.
10. p. 184. Crow Wood The misfortune of being under the mark H. Guest aq.
11. p. 186. Hangman's Bank Bird in the Hand's worth two in the Bush H. Guest aq.
12. p. 189. West End of the Four Acre Gay deceivers or more keen than sure A. W. Reeve aq.
13. p. 191. Howick, from Blashaw Wood The Destructives or killing no Murder J. H. Banks aq.
14. p. 193. East End of Four Acre The Destructives or three good things better than one J. H. Banks aq.
15. p. 194. Penwortham Muff a favorite Retriever H. Paprill aq.

Published at one guinea.   Issued by publisher in green morocco binding with gilt borders and gilt edges.

394 RAYE (Charles)

A Picturesque Tour through the Isle of Wight By Charles Raye Esq.   Illustrated by numerous views, London Printed for the Proprietor, By Howlett and Brimmer, Firth Street Soho.

Oblong Quarto.   1825

Raye's Isle of Wight (*contd.*)

COLLATION.—Map of the Isle of Wight by George Brannon + Title as above (v. blank) + List of Plates 1 leaf + Introduction 1 leaf + 24 coloured plates with a leaf of text to each plate.

1. Front. View. I. of Wight from Portsmouth.
2. Village of Carisbrook.
3. Distant View Carisbrook Castle.
4. Entrance Carisbrook Castle.
5. The Needles from Chale Bay.
6. Rocks in Chale Bay.
7. Niton.
8. Sandrock near Niton.
9. Black Gang Chine.
10. View from Opening Black Gang Chine.
11. Church of St Lawrence.
12. Undercliff near Mirables.
13. Bonnchurch.
14. View near Luccombe.
15. Ventnor Cove.
16. Dunnose.
17. View at Shanklin.
18. Shanklin Church.
19. Shanklin Chine.
20. Culver Cliff, from Sandham Bay.
21. Distant View of Culver Cliff, taken from Shanklin.
22. Cowes Castle.
23. View near Ryde.
24. Freshwater Gate.

Real Life in Ireland. See under Egan Imitation.

Real Life in London. See under Egan Imitation.

395 Records of the Royal Military Academy, Woolwich. Printed at the Royal Artillery Institution. Published by Parker, Furnival and Parker, Military Library, Whitehall, London.

Folio. 1851

COLLATION.—Emblematic lithograph title, with Lettering as above (v. blank) + Dedication 1 p. (v. blank) + Introduction 2 pp. + List of Appointments 4 pp. + pp. 1–152 + Description of Plates 1 p. (v. blank) + 9 lithograph plates, the first four being coloured.

1. The Cadet Barracks in the Arsenal (coloured).
2. Interior of a Barrack Room at the R.M.A. (coloured).
3. Uniforms at various periods (coloured).
4. Uniforms at various periods (coloured).
   Each of the above plates marked, Printed in Colors by Standridge & Co. Old Jewry.
5. Triumphs.
6. North Window.
7. South Window.
8. East Window.
9. West Window.

396 REPTON (H.)

Designs for the Pavilion at Brighton. Humbly inscribed to His Royal Highness the Prince of Wales. (swelled rule) By H. Repton Esq. with the assistance of his Sons, John Adey Repton, F.S.A. and G. S. Repton, Architects. (swelled rule) London: Printed for J. C. Stadler, No 15, Villiers Street, Strand; and sold by Boydell and Co. Cheapside; Longman, Hurst, Rees, and Orme, Paternoster Row; White, Fleet Street; Cadell and Davies, Strand; Payne and Mackinlay, Strand; Payne, 86, Pall Mall; Millar, Albemarle Street; and Taylor, Holborn 1808 (small swelled rule) The Letter Press by T. Bensley, Bolt Court, Fleet Street.

Folio. 1808

Repton's Pavilion at Brighton (*contd.*)

COLLATION.—Title as above (v. blank) + Dedication 1 p. (v. blank) + Preface Observations pp. i–x + Text pp. 1–41 + 8 plates and 12 vignettes.

Each plate is marked, H. Repton Esq delt. J. C. Stadler sculpt and dated May 1 1808.

1. p.   1. Composite plate Flora cherishing Winter &c (coloured, also exists in uncoloured state) with movable overslip.
2. p.   4. General ground plan (coloured).
    p.   7. View of the Stable Front seen from the Garden (coloured) with movable overslip.
    p. 11. View from the Dome with movable overslip.
    p. 13. Vignette headpiece [a Residence overlooking river].
    p. 23. Vignette headpiece Principles of Pressure.
    p. 24. Vignette tailpiece [Colonade].
    p. 25. Vignette tailpiece [buttress].
    p. 28. Vignette tailpiece [Rocky Island].
    p. 31. Vignette tailpiece Specimens of Columns.
3. p. 33. West Front of the Pavillion.
    p. 35. Vignette headpiece [Dining Room].
    p. 38. Vignette tailpiece [Indian Architecture details].
4. p. 38. The General View from the Pavillon [double page folding plate with 2 movable overslips. coloured].
    p. 39. Vignette headpiece [West Corridor] (coloured).
5. *ibd.*   Design for an Orangerie (coloured) with 2 movable overslips.
6. *ibd.*   The Pheasantry (coloured).
    p. 41. Vignette tailpiece View from the Proposed Private Apartment (coloured) with movable overslip,
7. *ibd.*   West Front of the Pavillon towards the Garden (coloured) with movable overslip.
8. *ibd.*   North Front towards the Parade (long folding plate) (coloured) with movable overslip.

Issued in boards with printed label on upper cover, size 15 × 21½ inches.

397   *Another issue undated, with title as above, except that thick and thin rules take the place of the swelled rules, there being no date on the title, and the printers being Howlett and Brimmer, Columbian Press, Frith Street, Soho Square, instead of Bensley. Otherwise the Collation is the same. A variant title page gives the initials only of Repton's sons.*

398 REPTON (H. and J. Adey)

Fragments on the Theory and Practice of Landscape Gardening. Including some remarks on Grecian and Gothic Architecture, collected from various manuscripts, in the possession of the different noblemen and gentlemen, for whose use they were originally written; the whole tending to establish fixed principles in the respective arts. (thick and thin rule) By H Repton Esq. assisted by his son, J. Adey Repton, F.A.S. (thin and thick rule) London: Printed by T. Bensley and son, Bolt Court, Fleet Street, for J. Taylor, at the Architectural Library, High Holborn.

Quarto.   1816

COLLATION.—Half-title + Title as above (v. blank) + Dedication to Prince Regent 1 p. (v. blank) + Preface 1 leaf (vii–viii) + Table of Contents 2 leaves (ix–xii) + pp. 1–238 + List of Plates and Errata 1 p. (v. T. Bensley & Son Bolt Court Fleet Street, London) + 42 plates.

Each plate bears imprint, London Published by J. Taylor Feb 1 1816.

    p.   1. Emblematic woodcut vignette.
1. p.   2. Characters of houses (6 specimens).
2. p.   4. Grecian Gothic (2 views on 1 plate).

Repton's Fragments (*contd.*)

3. p.   6. Fence near the house.
   p.   12. Gardens of Cobham Hall Kent (plan with text).
4. p.   12. Entrance and North Front of Cobham Hall, Kent.   Earl Darnley.
5. p.   14. The Cottage of Apsley Wood belonging to the Duke of Bedford.
   p.   18. Gothic Window exterior (vignette tailpiece).
6. p.   20. A Design to exemplify irregularity of outline in castle gothic (coloured).
7. p.   22. South Front of Harleston Park, Northamptonshire, R. Andrew Esq (coloured, with overslip).
8. p.   28. Blenden Hall, Kent. J. Smith Esqr. (2 views on 1 plate).
9. p.   30. Barningham Norfolk J. T. Mott Esq (with overslip).
10. p.   32. Barningham Hall, Norfolk, J. T. Mott Esq (view & plan on 1 plate).
11. *ibd.*   Window at Barningham (coloured).
12. p.   36. Example of outline in castle gothic (view & plan).
13. p.   48. Beaudesert, Staffordshire, Marquis of Anglesea (coloured, with overslip).
14. p.   50. Colours (2 small views & examples of colour).
15. p.   58. Interiors (2 views on 1 plate, coloured).
   p.   64. Lodge at Wingerworth (vignette tailpiece with overslip).
16. p.   64. Wingerworth, Derbyshire, Sir W. Hunloke Bart (with overslip).
   p.   67. Effect of Single Trees (vignette tailpiece).
17. p.   76. A common improved in Yorkshire (coloured, with overslip).
18. p.   82. Belt at Ealing Park.
19. p.   84. Lord Sidmouth's in Richmond Park (coloured, with overslip).
20. p.   90. Sections of a Garden near Oporto.
21. p.   92. Entrance to Uppark, Sr. H. Featherstone Bart (with overslip).
22. p. 100. Sunshine after Rain (coloured).
23. p. 104. View from the South Front of Frome House Dorset N. Gould Esqr. (coloured with overslip).
24. p. 114. Design alluded to in Fragment xxiii.
25. p. 122. General View of Longleate from the Prospect Hill; shewing the water as it has been finished, and the surface lowered, to raise the house (folding coloured plate).
26. p. 126. The Vinery (coloured).
27. p. 128. Fragment xxv A Plan explained (coloured).
28. p. 136. View as proposed to be altered, from the portico of a villa near London (coloured with overslip).
29. p. 140. The Rosary at Ashridge (coloured).
30. *ibd.*   Arrangement proposed for the Gardens at Ashridge Herts.
31. *ibd.*   Design for a Conduit, proposed at Ashridge, with a distant view of the Rosary and Monks Garden (coloured).
32. p. 146. Fences called invisible (2 views on 1 plate).
   p. 160. Viaduct (vignette tailpiece).
33. p. 164. Approach to Woburn Abbey, before it was altered.
34. *ibd.*   Approach to Woburn Abbey as it has been altered.
35. p. 168. At Woburn Abbey (Garden Door).
36. *ibd.*   Forcing Garden in Winter (coloured).
   p. 183. Luxury of Gardens (vignette tailpiece).
   p. 184. Park Keepers Lodge Cobham (vignette headpiece).
   p. 187. The School house at Longnor, Shropshire (vign. tailpiece).
   p. 188. Water Fences (vignette headpiece with overslip).
37. p. 194. Improvements (2 views on 1 plate).
38. p. 194. General View of Sheringham Bower Norfolk Abbot Upcher Esq (coloured & folding plate with overslip).
39. p. 212. Sherringham Bower (view with overslip & plan).
40. *ibd.*   General View of the South and East Fronts of the Cottage at Endsleigh, Devonshire— Dutchess of Bedford (folding plate coloured, with overslip).
   p. 221. Endsleigh Cottage on the Tamar (vignette tailpiece).
41. p. 227. The Work House (coloured).
42. p. 236. View from my own cottage in Essex (coloured with overslip).

Issued in boards with printed label on spine (size $11\frac{1}{2} \times 14\frac{3}{8}$ inches).

399 REPTON (H.)

Observations on the Theory and Practice of Landscape Gardening. Including some Remarks on Grecian and Gothic Architecture, collected from Various Manuscripts, in the Possession of the Different Noblemen and Gentlemen, for whose use they were originally written; the whole tending to establish fixed principles in the respective arts (thick and thin rule) By H. Repton, Esq (thin and thick rule) London: Printed by T. Bensley, Bolt Court, for J. Taylor, at the Architectural Library, High Holborn.

Quarto.   1803

COLLATION.—Title as above (v. blank) + Dedication to the King 1 p. (v. blank) + Advertisement pp. 5–8 (vignette foot p. 8) + Preface pp. 9–14 + List of Places pp. 15–16 + pp. 1–222 + Index and List of Plates 2 pp. + 28 plates including portrait.

The plates bear imprint, London Published [date] by J. Taylor, High Holborn.

1. front.   Humphry Repton   S. Shelley del   W. Holl fecit   June 4th 1802.
2. p.   9.   View from the Fort, near Bristol (overslip showing part of the town) coloured   4 June 1802.
3. p.   14.   Wentworth Yorkshire (overslip showing sand deer workmen &c.) coloured   4 June 1802.
4. p.   28.   Morning tinted   4 June 1802.
5. *ibd.*   Evening tinted   4th June 1802.
6. p.   34.   West Wycombe, Buckinghamshire (overslip of trees cattle &c) coloured   Augt. 1 1802.
7. p.   40.   Water at Wentworth Yorkshire (overslip showing meadow &c) coloured   Augt. 1 1802.
8. p.   48.   Artificial Scenery, Natural Scenery   4th June 1802 uncoloured.
9. p.   51.   Browsing Line (2 views lower with overslip showing trees thinned out), uncoloured   4 June 1802.
10. p.   64.   View from the House at Shardeloes (overslip showing trees altered), coloured   4 June 1802.
11. p.   67.   Map of Bulstrode uncoloured   4 June 1802.
12. p.   94.   Farm and Park uncoloured   June 4 1802.
13. p.   102.   Flower Garden Valley-Field coloured   4 June 1802.
14. p.   106.   Pavillion & Green House for a Gothic Mansion tinted   4th June 1802.
15. p.   112.   Example of Row of Trees uncoloured (overslip of trees)   4 June 1802.
16. p.   133.   Burley, Rutlandshire (overslip of terrace garden) coloured   June 4 1802.
   p.   145.   View on text of Entrance to Blaize Castle (overslip with trees & wooden gate), uncoloured.
   p.   155.   Cottage at Blaize Castle (overslip showing trees only), uncoloured.
17. p.   162.   A Cottage altered, in Langley Park (overslip of cottage) coloured   4 June 1802.
18. p.   171.   Houses of various Dates uncoloured   June 4 1802.
19. p.   179.   Michel Grove, Sussex (overslip showing roadway horses &c.), uncoloured   June 4 1802.
20. p.   182.   Example of a plan for an extended front, uncoloured   Augt. 1 1802.
21. p.   186.   Villa at Brenbry Hill (and plan) uncoloured   4 June 1802.
22. p.   188.   Corsham House uncoloured   4 June 1802.
23. p.   192.   Port Eliot St. Germains (overslip showing different building) coloured.
24. p.   200.   Ashton Court (double page folding plate), tinted   4 June 1802.
25. p.   203.   Map of Bayham coloured.   4th June 1802.
26. p.   208.   General View of Bayham (long folding plate with overslip showing meadow in place of water), coloured   4 June 1802.
27. p.   209.   Plan of Bayham uncoloured.   Augt. 7 1802.
28. p.   212.   Hall for a Gothic Mansion   J. Adey Repton inv et delint.   S. Porter sculpt. (uncoloured line engraving).   June th (sic) 4 1802.

Issued in pink boards with Etruscan Key pattern design on Sides, white back with paper label (size 11½ × 14¼ inches).

Second Edition 1805.

400 REPTON (H.)

Sketches and Hints on Landscape Gardening. Collected from Designs and Observations now in the Possession of the Different Noblemen and Gentlemen, for whose use

Repton's Sketches (*contd.*)

they were originally made. The whole tending to establish Fixed Principles in the Art of Laying out Ground (thick and thin rule) By H. Repton, Esq. (thin and thick rule) London (thin and thick rule) Printed by W. Bulmer and Co Shakespeare Printing Office, and sold by J. and J. Boydell, Shakespeare Gallery; and by G. Nicol, Bookseller to His Majesty, Pall Mall.

Oblong Folio.   1794

COLLATION.—Half-title "Sketches and Hints on Landscape Gardening" (v. blank) + Title as above (v. blank) + Dedication to the King 2 pp. (v–vi) + Contents 1 p. (v. blank + Advertisement 2 pp. (ix–x) + Catalogue 2 pp. (xi–xii) + Introduction 4 pp. (xiii–xvi) + pp. 1–83 (p. 84 blank) + Explanation of plates 1 p. (v. blank) + 16 plates by Repton without imprint, artist's or engraver's name.

1. p. 3. Scene garden Bransbury (overslip of fence and 3 figures) coloured.
2. p. 4. Rivenhall Place (2 overslips showing house partly in red brick) coloured.
3. p. 10. Wembly (2 page folding plate with 2 overslips one from each side depicting red house with flat roof) coloured.
4. p. 12. West Front of Welbeck (overslip with red tiled roof), coloured.
5. p. 15. View of Water at Welbeck (small overslip), uncoloured.
6. p. 16. The Gate used at Welbeck uncoloured.
7. p. 18. Two Ideal Houses (2 circular views each with a small overslip) uncoloured.
8. p. 23. Avenue at Langley Park (1 overslip showing tree plantation) uncoloured.
9. p. 24. View from Hanslope Park (1 overslip showing avenue of trees) uncoloured.
10. p. 26. Sections of ground uncoloured.
11. p. 30. View water & large oaks Welbeck (2 page folding plate with 1 central overslip showing house with red roof) coloured.
12. p. 32. View from the house at Tatton (2 page folding plate, 2 overslips one from each side depicting sheep behind railing) coloured.
13. p. 40. Entrance grounds Castle Hill (1 overslip showing grass foreground) coloured.
14. p. 42. View from the tower at Wembly (2 page folding plate 2 overslips one from each side showing trees with red house) coloured.
15. p. 46. View from the House at Lathom (1 overslip showing stone walls & water) coloured.
16. p. 52. Entrance into Tatton Park (1 overslip showing village street) coloured.

401 ROBERTS (David)

The Holy Land, Syria, Idumea, Arabia, Egypt & Nubia from drawings made on the spot by David Roberts R.A. with historical descriptions by the Revd. George Croly LL.D. lithographed by Louis Haghe. Vol. I (coloured vignette entrance to the Holy Sepulchre) London F. G. Moon 20 Threadneedle Street, Publisher in Ordinary to Her Majesty.

3 vols. Folio.   1842

COLLATION VOL. I.—Front. + Engraved title as above (v. blank) + Dedication to Queen 1 p. (v. blank) + List of Subscribers 2 leaves + Notice of Mr. Robert's Journey in the East 1 leaf + Armorial Ensign of Jerusalem 1 leaf + Israel pp. 1–30 + 42 coloured lithograph plates (43 including title) each with 1 p. of Text.

Front. David Roberts R A   Drawn on Stone from Life by C. Baugniet   London 1844 Day & Haghe Lithrs. to the Queen uncoloured.
1. Engraved Title as above.
2. Gate of Damascus Jerusalem   April 4 1839.
3. Greek Church of the Holy Sepul. Jerusalem   April 11 1839.

Roberts' Holy Land (*contd.*)

4. Tomb of St James Valley of Jehosophat   April 1830.
5. Jerusalem [, from the Road leading to Bethany]   April 9 1839.
6. Entrance to the Tombs of the Kings Jerusalem.
7. Mosque of Omar shewing the Site of the Temple.
8. Tomb of Zechariah Valley of Jehosophat.
9. [Jerusalem from the South] David Roberts   April 12 1839.
10. Church of the Holy Sepulchre Jerusalem.
11. [The Pool of Bethesda]   David Roberts.
12. Citadel of Jerusalem without the Walls.
13. Shrine of the Holy Sepulchre   April 10 1839   David Roberts.
14. Golden Gate of the Temple Shewing part of the ancient walls.
15. [Church of the Purification] Jerusalem   April 5th 1839.
16. Fountain of Siloam Valley of Jehosophat.
17. Jerusalem from the Mount of Olives   April 8th 1839.
18. The Stone of Unction Holy Sepulchre   D. Roberts   March 30th 1839.
19. Crypt of the Holy Sepulchre Jerusalem (Chapel of St Helena).
20. Fountain of Job Valley of Hinnom.
21. [Jerusalem from the North] Jerusalem   April 1839.
22. Lower Pool of Siloam Valley of Jehosophat.
23. Citadel of Jerusalem [Entrance]   April 19 1841.
24. Absaloms Pillar Valley of Jehosophat.
25. [Calvary] Jerusalem   April 10 1839.
26. Mount Tabor from the Plain of Esdraelon   April 19 1839.
27. Nazareth (General View)   April 28th 1839.
28. Fountain of the Virgin Nazareth   April 21st 1879   David Roberts R A.
29. Convent of the Terra Santa Nazareth   April 21st 1839.
30. [Shrine of the Annunciation Nazareth]   April 20th 1839   David Roberts R A.
31. Chapel of the Annunciation Nazareth   April 28th 1839.
32. Fountain at Cana   April 21st 1839.
33. Site of Cana of Galilee   April 21st 1839.
34. Town of Tibarias, (sic) looking towards Lebanon   David Roberts R A.
35. Sea of Galilee or Genezareth looking towards Bashan   April 21st 1839.
36. Tabarius (sic) from the Walls Saffet in the Distance   April 22nd 1839   David Roberts R A.
37. City of Tiberias on the Sea of Galilee   April 22nd 1839 [looking towards Hermon].
38. Tomb of Joseph at Shechem   David Roberts R A 1839.
39. Jacobs Well at Sheckem   April 17th 1839.
40. Entrance to Nablous   April 17th 1839.
41. Nablous ancient Shechem   April 17th 1839.
42. Ruins of the Church of St John Sabaste   David Roberts 1839.
43. Sebaste ancient Samara   April 17th 1839.

VOL. II.—Title as before but dated 1843 and the coloured vignette, changed to Baalbec from the Fountain May 7th 1839 + Leaf of Text containing descriptions of vignettes on titles of Vols. 2 and 3 (v. List of Subjects) + 1 leaf of text Bethlehem + 42 coloured lithographs (43 including title) each with 1 p. of Text.

44. Title as above.
45. Encampment of Pilgrims Jericho   April 1st 1839.
46. Descent upon the Valley of the Jordan.
47. Banks of the Jordan   April 2nd 1839.
48. Jericho   April 3rd 1839.
49. The Dead Sea looking towards Moab   April 4th 1839   David Roberts R A.
50. Convent of St. Saba   April 4th 1839   David Roberts R A.
51. Chapel of the Convent of St Saba   April 5th 1839   D Roberts R A.
52. Convent of St Saba [Wilderness of Engedi]   April 1839.
53. Beit Jebrin   March 7th 1839.
54. Hebron   March 18th 1839   David Roberts R A.
55. Semua [Ruins]   March 16th 1839   David Roberts R A.

Roberts' Holy Land (*contd.*)

56. Askelon   D Roberts R A.
57. Ashdod   March 24th 1839   David Roberts R A.
58. Gaza   March 21st 1839   David Roberts R A.
59. Christian Church of St George at Lud ancient Lydda   March 29 1839   David Roberts R A.
60. Jaffa ancient Joppa   April 16th 1839   David Roberts R A [looking south]
61. Jaffa   March 26th 1839   David Roberts R A [looking North]
62. Caiphas looking towards Mount Carmel   April 24th 1839.
63. Ramla ancient Arimathea   March 27th 1839   David Roberts R A.
64. St Jean d'Acre   April 24th 1839 [from Land].
65. St Jean d'Acre   April 25th 1839   David Roberts R A [from Sea].
66. Ras el Abiad coast of Syria   April 26th 1839.
67. Port of Tyre   April 27th 1839   David Roberts R A.
68. Tsur ancient Tyre   April 27th 1839   David Roberts R A.
69. Ruins called Om El Hamed near Tyre   April 25th 1839   David Roberts R A.
70. Tsur ancient Tyre from the Isthmus   April 27th 1839   David Roberts.
71. Sarepta   April 27th 1839   David Roberts R A.
72. Sarda ancient Sidon   April 28th 1839   David Roberts R A.
73. Sidon   April 28th 1839   David Roberts R A [from the North].
74. Sidon looking towards Lebanon.
75. Citadel of Sidon   April 28th 1839   David Roberts R A.
76. [Baalbec]   David Roberts R A.
77. Jenin ancient Jezreel   April 17th 1839   David Roberts R A.
78. Baalbec [Remains of Western Portico].
79. Lesser Temple of Baalbec   May 5th 1839 looking towards Mount Lebanon   David Roberts R A.
80. Baalbec [The Doorway]   May 7th 1839   David Roberts R A.
81. Circular Temple at Baalbec   May 7 1839   David Roberts R A.
82. Ruins of the Eastern Portico of the Temple of Baalbec   May 6th 1839   David Roberts R A.
83. Shrine of the Nativity Bethlehem   April 6th 1839.
84. Bethlehem   April 6th 1839.
85. Bethany   April 1st 1839   David Roberts R A.
86. Chancel of the Church of St Helena   D. Roberts R A.

VOL. III.—Title as before but dated 1849 and coloured vignette changed to Excavated Temple at Petra called El Khasneh or the Treasury David Roberts R.A. L. Haghe lith. (v. blank) + leaf of Text Idumea 1 leaf + 36 coloured lithographs each (37 including title) with 1 p. of Text.

87. Title as above.
88. Arabs of the Tribe of the Benisaid   Feby 17th 1839.
89. El Deir Petra   March 8th 1839   David Roberts.
90. Mount Seir Wady el Ghor   March 4th 1839   David Roberts R A.   [Encampment of the Alloeen.]
*91. Petra   March 7th 1839   [El Khasne.]
92. Approach to Petra An Ancient Watch tower commanding the Valley of El Ghor   Feb 5th 1839.
93. Temple called El Khasne Petra   March 7th 1839   David Robers R A.   Louis Haghe Lith.
94. Triumphal Arch across the Ravine leading to Petra   David Roberts R A.
95. Petra [Eastern End of the Valley]   March 8th 1839   David Roberts.
96. Tomb of Aaron Summit of Mount Hor   March 11th 1839   David Roberts R A.   Louis Haghe lith.
97. Entrance to Petra [The Theatre]   March 10th 1839   David Roberts.
98. Gebil Hor   March 5th 1839   David Roberts R A.
99. Remains of a Triumphal Arch at Petra   March 8th 1839   David Roberts   L. Haghe lith.
100. Conference [of Arabs] at Wady Moosa, Petra   March 6th 1839   David Roberts.
101. Lower end of the valley showing the Acropolis Petra   March 9th 1839.
102. Excavated Mansions of Petra.   Petra March 7th 1839.
103. [The Ravine] Petra   March 10th 1839   David Roberts.
104. Sepulchral Monuments Petra   March 9th 1839   David Roberts R A.
105. Petra looking South   March 9th 1839   David Roberts.

* Plate 91 not included in list of plates.

Roberts' Holy Land (*contd.*)

106. Fortress of Akabah Arabia Petra   Feb 28th 1839   David Roberts R A.
107. Island of Graia Gulf of Akabah Petraea   Feb 27th 1839   David Roberts R A.
108. The Convent of St. Catherine Mount Sinai   Feb 21st 1839   David Roberts R A.
109. Encampment of the Aulad Sa'id Mount Sinai   Feb 18th 1839   David Roberts R A.
110. Rock of Moses Wady-el-Leja Mount Horeb   Feb 22nd 1839   David Roberts R A.
111. Chapel of the Convent of St Catherine on Mount Sinai   Feby 21st 1839 [interior]   David Roberts R A.
112. Christian & Mahomedan Chapels on the Summit of Sinai   Feby 20th 1839   David Roberts R A.
113. Ascent of the Lower Range of Sinai   Febuary 18th 1839   David Roberts R A.
114. Ascent to the Summit of Sinai   Feb 20th 1839   David Roberts R A.
115. The Convent of St Catherine Mount Sinai looking Towards the Plain of the Encampment   Feb 21 1839   David Roberts R A.
116. Chapel of Elija on Mount Horeb   Feb. 20th 1839   David Roberts R A.
117. Convent of St Catherine with Mount Horeb   Feb 11th 1839   David Roberts R A.
118. Temple on Gebel Garabe called Surabit el Khadim   Feb 17th 1839   David Roberts R A.
119. [Principal court of the convent of St Catherine]   David Roberts R A.
120. Wells of Moses Wilderness of Tyn   February 12th 1839   David Roberts R A.
121. Approach to Mount Sinai Wady Barah   Feby 17th 1839   David Roberts R A.
122. Quay at Suez   February 11th 1839   David Roberts R A.
123. Suez [General View]   Febry 11th 1839.
   Map to illustrate the Route of David Roberts Esq R A in the Holy Land Petrea & Syria.

Usually sold with the following as a 6 volume work.

402 ROBERTS (David)

Egypt & Nubia, from drawings made on the spot by David Roberts, R.A., with historical descriptions by William Brockedon, R.F.S., Lithographed by Louis Haghe (swelled rule) large coloured vignette Entrance to the Great Temple of Aboo Simble, Nubia. David Roberts, R.A., L. Haghe lith. London, F. G. Moon, 20 Threadneedle Street, Publisher in Ordinary to her Majesty.

3 vols.   Folio.   1846

COLLATION.—Lithograph title as above + Dedication to Louis Philippe 1 p. (v. blank) + Egypt an Introduction pp. 1–8 + 1 p. of Descriptive Text of vignette title (v. blank) + 42 coloured plates (43 including title).   The plates are marked, David Roberts, R.A., L Haghe Lith, and each has 1 p. of Text.

1. Front. View under the Grand Portico Philae [the text to this on verso of last leaf].
2. Engraved Title as above.
3. Pyramids of Gerzeh, from the Nile.
4. View on the Nile looking towards The Pyramids of Dashour and Taccara.
5. Pompey's Pillar Alexandria.
6. Kom Ombo   Novr 21st 1838.
7. Temple at Tafa in Nubia   Nov 16th 1838.
8. The Great Temple of Aboo simble, Nubia [Colossal Figures].
9. Excavated Temple of Gyrshe—Nubia.
10. Portico of the Temple of Edfou—Upper Egypt   Novr 23rd 1838.
11. Statues of Memnon Thebes   Decr 4th 1838.
12. Thebes   Decr 4th 1838 [Colossal Statutes of Amunoph III].
13. Sanctuary of the Temple of Aboo-Simbel Nubia.
14. Interior of the Temple of Aboo Simbel   Novr 9th 1838 Nubia.
15. Ruins of Luxor, from the South West.
16. General View of the Ruins of Luxor from the Nile   1838.
17. The Great Sphinx, Pyramids of Gerzeh [side view].
18. The Great Sphinx, Pyramids of Girzeh   July 17th 1839.

Roberts' Egypt (*contd.*)

19. Dakke in Nubia   Nov 14th 1836.
20. Thebes Great Hall at Karnac   Nov 28, 1838.
21. Obelisk at Alexandria commonly called Cleopatra's needle.
22. Luxor   Decr 1st 1838 [Obelisk].
23. Wady Maharraka Nubia   Nov 14th 1838.
24. Temple at Esneh   Nov 25th 1838.
25. Temple of Wady Kardassy in Nubia.
26. General View of the Island of Philae Nubia   Nov 18th 1838.
27. Abyssinian Slaves resting at Korti Nubia.
28. Portico of the Temple of Kalabshe.
29. At Luxor, Thebes, Upper Egypt.
30. Libyan Chain of Mountains from the Temple of Luxor.
31. Approach of the Temple of Wady Saboua—Nubia.
32. View from under the Portico of Temple of Edfou—Upper Egypt.
33. One of two Colossal Statues of Rameses II Entrance to the Temple of Luxor.
34. Temple of Edfou—Ancient Appolinopolis Upper Egypt.
35. Dendera   Decr. 1838 [Gateway].
36. Dendera   Decr 7th 1838 [Portico of the Temple].
37. Siout—Upper Egypt.
37. *Ruins of Karnack [General View].
38. Nubian Women at Kortie, on the Nile.
39. Grand Portico of the Temple of Philae—Nubia.
40. Entrance to the Caves of Beni Hassan.
41. Grand Approach to the Temple of Philae—Nubia.
42. Temple of Wady Saboua, Nubia.

VOL. II.—Title with lettering as before but with vignette changed to "Great Gateway, leading to the Temple of Karnac—Thebes," and dated 1849 + 1 p. of Text descriptive of title vignette (v. List of Subjects in Vol. I and Vol. II) + 42 plates and map (43 including title). Page of text to each plate.

1. Front. Elevation of the Great Temple of Aboosimble Nubia [text on verso of last leaf].
2. Vignette   Title as above.
3. Group of Nubians—Wady Kardassy.
4. Fragments of the Great Colossi at the Memnorium—Thebes.
5. Fortress of Ibrim—Nubia.
6. Approach to The Fortress of Ibrim Nubia.
7. Colossus in front of Temple of Wady Saboua—Nubia.
8. Ruins of the Memnorium Thebes   Decr 5th 1838.
9. A Persian Wheel, used in raising the Water from the Nile.
10. Entrance of the Temple of Amun—Thebes.
11. Island of Philoe, on the Nile—Nubia [Sunset].
12. Hager Setsilis.
13. Part of the Hall of Columns at Karnack—Thebes.
14. Karnack   Novr 27, 1838 [View looking across the Hall of Columns].
15. Ruins—Temple of the Island of Biggeh—Nubia.
16. Karnac,   Novr 29th 1838 [The Dromos or First Court].
17. Remains of the Temple of Medamout, near Thebes.
18. Medinet Abou Thebes   Decr 5th 1832 [Ruins of Christian Church].
19. Temple of Amdda of Hassaya in Nubia.
20. Medint About, Thebes   Decr 8th 1838.
21. Temple of Dandour—Nubia.
22. The Hypaethral Temple at Philae called the Bed of Pharoah.
23. Temple of Isis on the roof of the great Temple of Dendera.
24. Pyramids of Geezeh.
25. Lateral View of the Temple called the Typhonaem at Dendera.
26. View from under the Portico of the Temple of Dendera.

* Not included in List of Plates.

Roberts' Egypt (*contd.*)

27. Ruins of The Temple of Kardeseh, Nubia.
28. General View of Essouan and The Island of Elephantine.
29. Obelisk of Heliopolis 1839.
30. Karnac, Nov 29th 1838 [Oblique View of the Hall of Columns].
31. Temple at Wady Dabod, Nubia.
32. Karnak [General View looking towards Baban-el-Molook].
33. Dayr el Medineh—Thebes [View from under the Portico].
34. Entrance to the Tombs of the Kings of Thebes—Bab-el-Malouk.
35. Excavated Temples of Aboosimble Nubia.
36. Statues of Memnon at Thebes, during the Inundation.
37. Wady Dabod Nubia   Novr 16th 1638.
38. Grand Entrance to the Temple of Luxor.
39. Temple of Kalabshee—Nubia   Novr 1838.
40. Edfou   Nov 24th 1838 [Facade of the Pronaos].
41. Hermont   Novr 26th 1838   Ancient Hermontin.
42. Kom Ombo   Novr 21 1838.
43. Philae   Novr 18, 1838 [The Island of, looking down Nile].
   Map to illustrate Sketches of David Roberts Esq R.A. in Egypt and Nubia   1849.

VOL. III.—Title with lettering as in Vol. I but vignette changed to "Street Scene in Cairo" and dated 1849 + 1 p. of Text describing the front. (v. text to vignette title and List of Plates) + 37 plates (38 including title).

1. Front.   Interview with the Viceroy of Egypt at His palace, at Alexandria   May 12th 1839.
2. Vignette   Title.
3. Gate of Victory and Minaret of the Mosque El Hakim.
4. Alexandria [approach to].
5. Gate of the Medwaleys—Cairo.
6. Minarets and Grand Entrance of the Metwaleys at Cairo.
7. Ruined Mosques in the Desert West of the Citadel.
8. Mosque of Sultan Hassan Cairo.
9. One of the Tombs of the Khalifs Cairo.
10. Bazaar of the Silk Mercers Cairo.
11. Tombs of The Caliphs—Cairo.
12. Tombs of the Khalifs Cairo [Mosque of the Sultan Kait bey].
13. The Minaret of the Mosque El Rhamree.
14. Cairo looking West.
15. The Holy Tree Metereah.
16. The Entrance to the Citadel of Cairo.
17. Tombs of the Caliphs Cairo Mosque of Ayed Bey.
18. Bazaar of the Coppersmiths Cairo.
19. Minaret of the principal Mosque Siout Upper Egypt.
20. Interior of the Mosque of the Metwaleys.
21. Tombs of the Memlooks Cairo [with an Arab Funeral].
22. Grand Entrance to the Mosque of the Sultan Hassan.
23. Cairo [The Aqueduct of the Nile from the Is. of Rhoda].
24. Mosque El Mooristan Cairo.
25. Bullack Cairo [Principal Mosque].
26. Cairo from the Gate of Citizeneb looking towards the Desert of Suez.
27. In the Slave Market at Cairo.
28. Approach of the Simoon Desert of Gizeh.
29. The Nileometer Island of Rhoda.
30. View of the Nile Ferry to Gizeh.
31. The Letter Writer Cairo.
32. Modern Mansion shewing the arabesque architecture of Cairo.
33. Tombs of the Memlooks, Cairo.
34. The Citadel of Cairo Residence of Mehemet Ali.

Roberts' Egypt (*contd.*)

35. The Coffee Shop.
36. Interior of the Mosque of The Sultan El Ghoree.
37. Dancing Girls at Cairo.
38. Mosque of the Sultan Hassan from the Great Square of the Rumeyleh.

403 ROBERTS (Peter)

The Cambrian Popular Antiquities; or, an Account of some Traditions, Customs, and Superstitions, of Wales with Observations as to their origin, &c. &c. (swelled rule) Illustrated with copper-plates. Coloured from Nature (thick and thin rule) By Peter Roberts, A.M., Rector of Llanarmon, Vicar of Madeley, and author of Collectanea Cambrica, etc (thin and thick rule) London: Printed for E. Williams, Bookseller to the Duke and Duchess of York, No. 11, Strand (swelled rule).

Octavo.   1815

COLLATION.—Half-title + Title as above (v. Printed by W. Clowes, Northumberland Court, Strand) + Dedication to Rev. David Hughes 1 p. (v. blank) + Index 2 pp. + Preface 2 pp. + Introduction pp. 1–3 (p. 4 blank) + pp. 5–353 (p. 354 List of Plates).

1. p. 123. Fives Playing   I Havell sculp.
2. p. 125. Easter Monday   J. Havell sculpt.   Published 15 July 1814 by E. Williams Strand.
3. p. 159. The Bidder   J. Havell sculpt.   Published 15 July 1814 by E. Williams Strand.
4. p. 164. Singing to the harp & dancing   I. Havell sculpt.   Published 15 August 1814 by E. Williams Strand.
5. p. 163. The Quintain   I. Havell sculpt.
6. p. 175. The Funeral   I. Havell sculpt.   Published 15 August 1814 by E. Williams Strand.
7. p. 203. The Fairies   I. Havell sculpt.
   p. 212. Plan of City of Troy.
8. p. 301. The Bow of War or Peace   I Havell sculpt.   Published 15 August 1814 by E. Williams Strand.
9. p. 311. Ancient Method of Reaping   I. Havell sculpt.   Published 30th Septr. 1814 by E. Williams Strand.

404 ROBERTSON (David)

A Tour through the Isle of Man: To which is subjoined a Review of the Manks History. (2 line rule) By David Robertson Esq. (2 line rule) London: Printed for the Author, by E. Hodson, Bell Yard Temple Bar. Sold by Mr Payne, Mews Gate; Messrs Egertons, Whitehall; Whites, Fleet Street, and Deighton, Holborn. (thin and thick rule).

Octavo.   1794

COLLATION.—Title as above (v. blank) + Dedication 1 p. (v. blank) + 2 leaves + Contents 2 leaves + pp. 1–235 + 8 coloured aquatint plates.

1. p. 7. Douglas Pier.
2. p. 47. Rushen Abbey.
3. p. 51. Abbey Bridge.
4. p. 64. Castle Rushen.

5. p. 85. Tynwald Hill.
6. p. 89. Pecle Castle.
7. p. 92. St. Patricks Church.
8. p. 93. St Germains Cathedral.

Generally issued plain, but large-paper copies issued printed in 4 colours, blue, green, sepia and red-brown.

405 ROBSON (G. F.)

Scenery of the Grampian Mountains; Illustrated by Forty-One Plates, representing the principal Hills from such points as display their picturesque features, diversified by Lakes and Rivers: with an Explanatory page affixed to each plate, giving an account of those objects of natural curiosity and historical interest, with which the district abounds, by George Fennell Robson, Member of the Society of Painters in Oil and Water Colours, London. The Engravings executed by Henry Morton, and coloured from original drawings made on the spot, by the author. (thin and thick rule) London: Published by Longman, Hurst, Rees, Orme, and Brown, Paternoster Ros. (short rule).

Folio.   1819

COLLATION.—Title as above (v. blank) + Dedication 1 p. (v. blank) + List of Subscribers 1 p. (v. blank) + Preface 1 p. (v. blank) + Folding Map + 41 coloured aquatint plates, each with 1 p. of Text.

1. View from Stirling.
2. Ben Lomond (from road of N. side Loch Ard).
3. Loch Lomond.
4. Ben Lomond (from the west).
5. Ben Lomond (from road opposite Macfarlane's Island).
6. Glen Falloch.
7. Ben Lomond (from Strath Gartney).
8. Ben Venue (from E. end of Loch Achray).
9. Ben Venue (from upper end of Loch Achray).
10. Ben Venue (part of E. end of Loch Katerine).
11. The west end of Loch Katerine.
12. Ben Ledi.
13. Glen Finglass.
14. View from the Vicinity of Crief.
15. Ben Vorlich.
16. Ben More (from between Glen Ogil and Killin).
17. Ben More (from N. side of Glen Dochart).
18. Ben Lawers (from above Killin).
19. Ben Lawers (from S. banks of Loch Tay).
20. View of Loch Tay.
21. Shichallien.
22. Loch Tumel.
23. Dunkeld.
24. View of the River Tay.
25. Ben Vracky (from outlet of Loch Tumel).
26. Ben Vracky (from West of Blair Atholl)
27. Ben-y-Gloe (and pass of Killicrankie).
28. Ben-y-Gloe (and vicinity of Blair Atholl).
29. Ben-y-Gloe (from head of Glen Tilt).
30. View from the Vicinity of Ballater.
31. Lochan-y-Gar (from N. banks of Dee).
32. Lochan-y-Gar (and vicinity of Invercauld).
33. Ben-y-Bourd.
34. Ben-Na-Muich-Duidh.
35. Loch Avon.
36. Ben-Na-Muich Duidh (from South of Dee).
37. Brairiach and Carn Toul.
38. Ben Vrotan.
39. Carn Gorm (from Abernethy).
40. Carn Gorm (from North side Lochan Eilan).
41. Ben Nevis.

+ Index (i.e. List of Plates + 1 p. (v. blank)).

406 ROWLANDSON (Thomas)

The Adventures of Johnny Newcome in the Navy; A Poem, in Four Cantos: with plates by Rowlandson, from the Author's designs (swelled rule) By Alfred Burton (swelled rule) "Dulce bellum inexpertis." (thick and thin rule) London: Published by W. Simpkin and R. Marshall, Stationers'-Court, Ludgate-Street. (rule).

Octavo.   1818

COLLATION.—Title as above (v. W. Wilson, Printer, 4, Greville-Street, Hatton Garden, London) + Advertisement 1 p. (v. blank) + pp. 1–259 (p. 260 Errata) + 16 coloured plates.

1. Front. Leaving-Home Rowlandson, delt. W. Read sculpt.
2. p. 26. Sheerness Boat.
3. p. 36. The Admiral has made it Sun set, Sir! Drawn & Etched by Rowlandson W. Read sculpt.
4. p. 42. Turning in—and out again Rowlandson delt. W. Read sculpt.
5. p. 52. Sea-Sick Rowlandson delt. W. Read sculpt.

Rowlandson's Johnny Newcome (*contd.*)

6. p. 55. Sent to hear the Dog-Fish Bark   Rowlandson delt.   W. Read sculpt.
7. p. 57. The Captain's going out of the Ship—Gentlemen!   Drawn and Etched by Rowlandson.
8. p. 72. Seized up in the Rigging   W. Read sculpt.
9. p. 77. Cobbed—Watch!   Watch   Rowlandson delt.   W. Read sculpt.
10. p. 117. Crossing the Line   W. Read sculpt.
11. p. 160. Plymouth-Playhouse   Rowlandson delt.   W. Read sculpt.
12. p. 166. Going to Ivy-Bridge   Rowlandson delt.   W. Read sculpt.
13. p. 173. In the Grocer's Shop Rowlandson delt.   W. Read sculpt.
14. p. 192. Johnny and Maria   Rowlandson delt.   W. Read sculpt.
15. p. 240. Mast-headed   Rowlandson delt.   W. Read sculpt.
16. p. 241. A-Sleep at the Mast-head   W. Read sculpt.

Not to be confused with another work published the following year with exactly the same title, but illustrated with 20 coloured plates by Williams.   See under Mitford (J.).

407 ROWLANDSON (T.)

Advice to Sportsmen, Rural or Metropolitan, Noviciates or Grown Persons; with Anecdotes of the most renowned shots of the day: Exemplified from Life.   Including Recommendatory Hints in the choice of Guns, Dogs, and Sporting Paraphernalia: Also, Characters, Costume, and Correspondence. (thick and thin rule) Selected from the Original Notes, &c. of Marmaduke Markwell, Esq. (rule) Thou shalt not Kill—Exodus. A bold Pheasantry, a country's pride, when once destroyed, can never be supplied. Goldsmith (two line rule) London: Published by Thomas Tegg, 111, Cheapside.   Printed by Heney & Haddon, Tabernacle Walk.

Duodecimo.   1809

COLLATION.—Half-title "Advice to Sportsmen Rural or Metropolitan" (v. blank) + Title as above (v. blank) + Dedication to Sir William Curtis 1 p. (v. blank) + Preface 4 pp. (v–viii) + Directions to place the Plates 1 p. (v. blank) + pp. 1–132 + 16 plates.

1. Front. The Cockneys first attempt at shooting flying   Rowlandson inv.
2. p.   1. Rat Hunting   Rowlandson inv.
3. p.   6. How to Moist your Neck   Rowlandson inv.
4. p.   13. Night   Rowlandson inv.
5. p.   22. Noon   Rowlandson inv.
6. p.   29. Morning   Rowlandson 1809.
7. p.   32. The dangerous consequences of Sporting   Rowlandson inv.
8. p.   44. Miss Spitfires encounter   Rowlandson inv.
9. p.   55. The advantage of coupling Sporting dogs   Rowlandson inv.
10. p.   61. Finishing a Gamekeeper   Rowlandson inv.
11. p.   90. How to come in at the Death   Rowlandson inv.
12. p.   98. How to cool your Courage   Rowlandson inv.
13. p. 107. A Duck Hunt in Bartholemew Lane   Rowlandson inv.
14. p. 118. Neck or Nothing   Rowlandson inv.
15. p. 123. A shooting parson or pot-hunter   Rowlandson inv.
16. p. 129. Evening   Rowlandson inv.

408 ROWLANDSON

Comforts of Bath

Oblong Folio.

A Series of 12 plates each lettered Comforts of Bath Pl. 1 (–12) and each with imprints, Pubd. June 6th 1798 by S. W. Fores No. 50 Piccadilly corner of Sackville Street.

Rowlandson's Comforts of Bath (*contd.*)

Each plate marked, Rowlandson fecit bottom right-hand corner, except plates 2, 4, 6, 7 and 12 which are unsigned.

One of the rarest of Rowlandson items. The Abbey copy varies; Nos. 5, 6, 8, 9, 11 and 12 being unsigned.

409 ROWLANDSON (T.)

Cries of London. A Series of 8 plates, each plate marked, Cries of London. No. 1(–8) Rowlandson Delin. Merke Sculp. London published (date) 1799 at R. Ackermann's, 101 Strand.

Folio.   1799

1. Buy a Trap, a Rat Trap, buy my Trap. Jan. 1st.
2. Buy my Goose, my Fat Goose. Jan. 1st.
3. Last dying Speech and Confession. Feb. 20th.
4. Do You Want Any Brick-dust. Feb. 20th.
5. Water Cresses, Come Buy my Water Cresses. Mar. 1st.
6. All a growing, a growing, heres Flowers for your Gardens. Mar. 1st.
7. Old Cloaths, any Old Cloaths. May 4th.
8. Hot Cross Bunns, Two a penny Bunns. May 4th.

There are later issues of the plates bearing water marks 1806 and 1816.

410 ROWLANDSON (T.)

The Dance of Life, A Poem, by the author of "Doctor Syntax"; illustrated with coloured Engravings, by Thomas Rowlandson. (6 line quotation from Horace) London: Published by R. Ackermann, Repository of Arts, 101, Strand.   1817

COLLATION.—Coloured Frontispiece [The Dance of Life vignettes on scroll, 12 figures scrutinising it, including Father Time] Engraved Title ["The Dance of Life A Poem", vignette of woman surrounded by 6 children, 6 line quotation from Horace Published Dec. 1 1817 at R. Ackermann's Repository of Arts, No. 101, Strand.] Printed title as above (v. blank) +Advertisement 1 leaf (i–ii) + Index to Plates 1 leaf (i–ii) + pp. 1–285 + Advertisement (announcement of a forthcoming but unspecified publication of Rowlandson's, Unpaged) 1 leaf + 26 coloured plates (including Frontispiece and Engraved Title).

Each plate bears Ackermann's imprint and date.

1.		Frontispiece as described above	Decr 1 1817
2.		Engraved Title ditto	Decr 1 1817
3. p.	26.	The Dance of Life Begins with all its charms In the fond dangling of the Nurse's arms	May 1 1817
4. p.	89.	The tender Nurse's care is now resign'd To the first grave instructor of the mind	May 1 1817
5. p.	95.	The Stern Preceptor, with his threat'ning Nod, Calls in the Correction of the Rod.	July 1 1817
6. p.	110.	Wine makes the Head to Ach: but will the Art Of the grave, solemn Lecture reach the Heart?	June 1 1817
7. p.	150.	To part with thee, my Boy, how great the Pain! How great the Joy, to see thee once again.	June 1 1817
8. p.	178.	'Tis hop'd 'midst foreign Scenes some Power he'll find To mend his Manners, & improve his Mind	June 1 1817

Rowlandson's Dance of Life (*contd.*)

9.	p. 180.	He pays his lively Court, as 'tis the Ton, To the fat Princess of the Milles Colonnes	July 1 1817
10.	p. 194.	The widow's Mother hastens forth to meet Her Son, Sir Henry, to his ancient Seat	July 1 1817
11.	p. 212.	The Hounds the flying Stag pursue; But Dian does the Hunting rue	Septr 1, 1817
12.	p. 220.	As the first step in Follys wanton waste He pulls his Mansion down, to shew his Taste	July 1 1817
13.	p. 224.	Of Four in hand he joins the vulgar Rage: Wields the long whip and overturns a stage	Augt 1 1817
14.	p. 228.	The Mask that scene of wanton Folly May convert Mirth to Melancholy	Octr 1 1817
15.	p. 230.	By Gamblers link'd in Folly's Noose Play ill or well, he's sure to lose	August 1 1817
16.	p. 231.	The Victim of the Betting-Post: His Bets as soon as made, are lost	Augt 1 1817
17.	p. 236.	For such a mild, and placid Dear, He pays two Thousand Pounds a year	Septr 1 1817
18.	p. 239.	For my own good, and your's I'm bent, My worthy friends towards Parliament	Novr 1 1817
19.	p. 246.	In his oppress'd and adverse Hour Virtue resumes its former Power	Octr 1 1817
20.	p. 262.	The wild Exuberance of Joy May Reason's sober Power destroy	Dec 1 1817
21.	p. 271.	Sweet is the voice whose Powers can move, And call the vagrant Heart to love	Septr 1 1817
22.	p. 273.	Blest Hymen, whose propitious Hour Restores to Virtue all its Power	Novr 1 1817
23.	p. 277.	Rural Sports are better far Than all his former pleasures were	Novr 1 1817
24.	p. 278.	To sooth the Rigour of the Laws Let Beauty plead the Culprit's Cause	Octr 1 1817
25.	p. 282.	By Piety's due Rites 'tis given To hold communion with Heaven	Decr 1 1817
26.	p. 285.	Here Virtue views, with smiling Pride, The Blessings of her Fire-side	Decr 1, 1817

Published originally in 8 monthly numbers, and on completion issued in boards at 21s.

I have seen copies in original boards with 4 leaves of Advertisement at end, containing notifications of Ackermann's publications, but as the first book is stated to be "Second Tour of Doctor Syntax" this day published [the date of publication was 1820] and the Third Tour is advertised as forthcoming, the two copies I have seen in this state must either have been bound in boards from the original sheets or parts three years after publication, or these advertisements were inserted at a later date and do not form an integral part of the book. The Dance of Life was issued as a companion volume to the English Dance of Death, and the three volumes are frequently sold together. The text is by William Combe.

411 Rowlandson (T.)

The English Dance of Death, from the designs of Thomas Rowlandson, with metrical illustrations, by the author of "Doctor Syntax."

Pallida Mors aquo pulsat pede pauperum tabernas
Regumque turres   Hor. Lib. 1 od. 4

Rowlandson's Dance of Death (*contd.*)

—With equal Pace, impartial Fate
Knocks at the Palace, as the Cottage Gate

Vol. I [II] London: Printed by J. Diggins, St. Ann's Lane; Published at R. Ackermann's Repository of Arts, 101, Strand; and to be had of All the Book and Print-sellers in the United Kingdom.

2 vols.   Octavo.   1815[–1816]

COLLATION VOL. I.—Frontispiece + Engraved title + Printed title as above (v. blank) Advertisement pp. iii–vii (viii blank) + Index to First Volume 2 ll. + pp. 1–295 [p. 296 blank save for imprint, J. Diggins, Printer, St. Ann's Lane, London] + 36 coloured plates.

Front. [Death Crowned, with Dart, Sitting on World etc.]

Engraved Title. "The English Dance of Death" [vignette of skeletons dancing in churchyard Quotation from Horace as on printed title] Vol. I London, Published March 1 1816 by R. Ackermann 101 Strand.

1. p.   1. Time and Death their Thoughts impart
        On works of Learning and of Art
2. p. 15. Fungus at length contrives to get
        Death's Dart into his Cabinet
3. p. 23. Such mortal Sport the Chase attends
        At Breck-Neck Hill the Hunting Ends
4. p. 29. Not all the Statesmen's power of art
        Can turn aside Deaths certain Dart
5. p. 37. His blood is stopp'd in evry vein
        He ne'er will eat or drink again
6. p. 47. The Dangers of the Ocean o'er
        Death wrecks the Sailors on the Shore
7. p. 57. Her Tongue, and Temper to subdue
        Can only be perform'd by you
8. p. 68. What, do these sav'ry Meats delight you?
        Be gone, and stay, till I invite you
9. p. 73. I list you, and you'll soon be found
        One of my Regiment, under Ground
10. p. 77. Be not alarm'd—I'm only come
        To choose a Wife, and light her Home
11. p. 85. I have a secret Art, to cure
        Each Malady, which Men endure
12. p. 97. Drunk and Alive, the Man was thine
        But drunk and dead, why:—he is mine
13. p. 106. When the old Fool has drank his Wine
        And gone to rest—I will be thine
14. p. 119. Yes, Nimrod, you may look aghast:
        I have unkennell'd you, at last.
15. p. 121. No scene so blest in Virtue's Eyes
        As when the man of Virtue dies
16. p. 129. Nature and Truth are not at strife
        Death draws his Pictures after life
17. p. 137. On that illumin'd Roll of Fame
        Death waits to write your Lordship's Name
18. p. 147. The Catchpole need not fear a jail
        The Undertaker is his Bail
19. p. 157. Insure his Life—But, to your Sorrow
        You'll pay a good, round Sum, tomorrow
20. p. 168. Death with his Dart, proceeds to flog
        Th' astonish'd flogging Pedagogue
21. p. 175. I'll lead you to the splendid Croud
        But your next Dress will be a Shroud

Rowlandson's Dance of Death (*contd.*)

22. p. 181. On with you dead; and I'll contrive
    To bury this old Fool-alive
23. p. 185. The Doctor's sick'ning Toil to close,
    "Recipe Coffin" is the Dose
24. p. 190. Such is the Power, and such the Strife
    That ends the Masquerade of Life
25. p. 205. How vain are all your Triumphs past
    For this Set-To will be your last
26. p. 217. As it appears, though dead so long,
    Each skull is found to have a Tongue
27. p. 229. What watchfull Care the Portal keeps
    A Porter He, who never sleeps
28. p. 238. Behold the Signal of Old Time
    That bids you close your Pantomime
29. p. 245. This is very break-neck Heat
    And 'Squire Jockey you are beat
30. p. 253. Some find their Death by Sword & Bullet
    And some by Fluids, down the Gullet
31. p. 258. Whene'er Death plays, He's sure to win
    He'll take each knowing Gamester in
32. p. 264. Such is, alas, the common Story
    Of Blood and Wounds of Death and Glory
33. p. 272. Plutus commands; and to the Arms
    Of doting Age, she yields her Charms
34. p. 283. On the frail Ice the whirring slate
    Becomes an Instrument of Fate
35. p. 285. Here Honour, as it is the Mode
    To Death Consigns the Weighty Load
36. p. 291. Though I may yield my forfeit Breath
    The Word of Life defies thee, Death

VOL. II.—Title as before but dated 1816 (v. blank) + Index to Second Volume 2 ll. + pp. 1–299 + 36 coloured plates.

37. p.   1. Death smiles, and seems his Dart to hide
    When he beholds the Suicide
38. p. 18. Have Patience, Death, nor be so cruel
    To spoil the Sick man's Water-Gruel
39. p. 33. Death rocks the Cradle, Life is O'er
    The infant sleeps, to wake no more
40. p. 38. Why, I was looking at the Bear
    But what strange Planet see I there?
41. p. 43. The Doctors say, that you're my Booty
    Come, Sir, for I must do my Duty
42. p. 49. Death can contrive to strike his Blows
    By over-turns, and over throws
43. p. 62. Another whiff and all is o'er
    And Gaffer Goodman is no more
44. p. 70. O, the unconscionable Brute
    To murder—for a little Fruit
45. p. 79. The fatal Pilot graps the Helm
    And Steers the Crew to Pluto's Realm
46. p. 87. No one but me shall set my Clock
    He set it—and behold the shock
47. p. 95. 'Twere well to spare me two or three
    Out of your num'rous Family
48. p. 101. In this World all our Comfort's o'er
    So let us find it at Deaths Door

Rowlandson's Dance of Death (*contd.*)

49. p. 106. Let him go on with all his Rigs
We're safe—He'll only burn his Pigs
50. p. 116. Old Dad at length is grown so kind
He dies, and leaves his Wealth behind
51. p. 126. Love, spread your Wings, I'll not outstrip 'em
Though Deaths behind, He will not clip 'em
52. p. 137. By Gar, that horrid, strange Buffoon
Cannot keep Time to any Tune
53. p. 144. Thus, it appears, a Pond of Water
May prove an Instrument of Slaughter
54. p. 152. Thou slave to ev'ry gorging Glutton
I'll spit thee, like a Leg of Mutton
55. p. 158. Away they go, in Chaise and one
Or to undo, or be undone
56. p. 167. Your crabbed Dad is just gone Home
And now we look for Joys to come
57. p. 173. It is in vain that you decide
Death claims you as his destin'd Bride
58. p. 199. "The End of Life" the Chairman cries
'Tis drank—and many a Toper dies
59. p. 204. The carefull, and the careless led
To join the living and the Dead
60. p. 210. The Serjeant's Tongue will cease to brawl
In ev'ry Court of yonder Hall
61. p. 222. All Fates he vow'd to him were known,
And yet he could not tell his own
62. p. 230. To trust to Fortune's Smiles alone
Is the High Road to be undone
63. p. 236. Death, without either Bribe or Fee
Can set the Hopeless Pris'ner free
64. p. 241. Th' Assailant does not feel a Wound
But yet he died—for he is drown'd
65. p. 250. 'Tis strange, but true, in this World's Strife
That Death affords the Means of Life
66. p. 256. What heart-felt Tears bedew the Dust
Of Him whose ev'ry Thought was just
67. p. 259. 'Tis not the Time to meet one's Fate
Just ent'ring on a large Estate
68. p. 266. When Doctors three, the Labour share
No wonder Death attends them there
69. p. 271. Death, jealous of his Right, stands Sentry
Over the strange burglarious Entry
70. p. 275. This fine, hot Feast's a Preparation
To some, for Death's last cold Collation
71. p. 283. From Hour to Hour, from Youth to Age
Life's Traveller takes th' uncertain Stage
72. p. 290. The song now busts beyond the Bounds of Time
And Immortality concludes the Rhyme.

RÉSUMÉ.—Frontispiece, engraved title and 72 plates.

Published originally in 24 monthly numbers (3 plates to each part) and on completion issued in two volumes, royal octavo, boards, for 3 guineas.   The text is by William Combe.

Indispensable to any Rowlandson collection, one of the essential pivots of any colour plate Library, being one of the main works of Rowlandson.

412 Rowlandson (T.)

To Grand Master or Adventures of Qui Hi in Hindostan a Hudibrastic Poem in Eight Cantos by Quiz. Illustrated with Engravings by Rowlandson London Printed by Thomas Tegg, No 111, Cheapside.

Royal Octavo. 1816

COLLATION.—Engraved title as above (E. Gullen sc.) within decorated border Quiz fecit Rowlandson sc. (v. blank) + Preface pp. iii–viii + Invocation to Butler ix–x + Errata slip + pp. 1–252 (pp. 73–4 repeated) + 25 coloured and 1 uncoloured plate (Engraved title, front., and 26 plates making 28 in all).

Plates dated October 1 1815.

1. Title.
2. Front. (Folding) A New Map of India from the latest authority   Rowlandson sc.   Quiz fecit.
3. p.   16. A Scene in the Channel   Rowlandson sc   Quiz fecit.
4. p.   46. The Modern Idol Juggernaut   Rowlandson del et sc.
5. p.   52. Miseries of First of the Month   Rowlandson sc   Quiz fecit.
6. p.   54. The Burning System Illustrated   Rowlandson sc   Quiz fecit.
7. p.   68. Missionary Influence or How to make converts   Rowlandson sc.   Quiz fecit.
8. p.   72. An extraordinary Eclipse   Rowlandson sc   Quiz fecit.
9. p.   82. Labour in vain or his reverence confounded   Rowlandson sc   Quiz fecit.
10. p.   92. Hindoo prejudices   Rowlandson sc   Quiz fecit.
11. p.   124. John Bull converting the Indians   Rowlandson sc   Quiz fecit.
12. p.   128. More Incantations or a Journey to the interior   Rowlandson sc   Quiz fecit.
13. p.   140. Miseries in India   Rowlandson sc   Quiz fecit.
14. p.   178. The Bear & Ragged Staff   Rowlandson sc   Quiz fecit.
15. p.   194. Hindoo Incantations a View in Elephanta   Rowlandson sc   Quiz fecit.
16. p.   196. Phantasmagoria a View in Elephanta   Rowlandson sc   Quiz fecit.
17. p.   198. Modern Phaeton or Hugely in Danger   Rowlandson sc   Quiz fecit.
18. p.   206. Qui Hi arrives at the Bunder Head   Rowlandson sc   Quiz fecit.
19. p.   208. Qui Hi in the Bombay tavern   Rowlandson sc   Quiz fecit.
20. p.   214. Pays a nocturnal visit to Dungaree   Rowlandson sc   Quiz fecit.
21. p.   220. Attends Gen. Koir Wigs Levee   Rowlandson sc   Quiz fecit.
22. p.   225. Qui Hi's Introduction & cool reception Rowlandson sc   Quiz fecit.
23. p.   228. Qui Hi shows off at Bobbery Hunt   Rowlandson del et sc.
24. p.   230. Qui Hi at Bobbery Hall   Rowlandson sc   Quiz fecit.
25. p.   236. All Alive in the Chokee   Rowlandson sc   Quiz fecit.
26. p.   242. Last Visit from Doctors Assistant   Rowlandson sc   Quiz fecit.
27. p.   250. Qui Hi's last march to Padree Burrows Go Down   Rowlandson sc   Quiz fecit.
28. p.   252. Strange figures near the cave of Elephanta   Rowlandson sc   Quiz fecit.

A satire against the Marquis of Hastings the Governor General.   There is a cancel leaf c 8. This is frequently missing, likewise the errata slip.   The text is by W. Combe.

413 ROWLANDSON (T.)

The History of Johnny Quae Genus, the Little Foundling of the late Doctor Syntax: A Poem, By the Authors of the Three Tours. (thick and thin rule)

**What various views of our uncertain State
These playful, unassuming Rhymes relate! Anon.**

(thin and thick rule) London: Published by R. Ackermann, At the Repository of Arts, 101, Strand, London; and to be had of all the Booksellers in the United Kingdom. (short thick and thin rule).

Royal 8vo. 1822

Rowlandson's Quae Genus (*contd.*)

COLLATION.—Title as above (v. Diggins, Printer, St. Ann's Lane, London) + Introduction 2 pp. + pp. 1–267 (p. 268 Directions to Binder) + Narrow warning slip to Reader + 24 coloured plates, each marked, Drawn by Rowlandson. Pubd. [date] by R. Ackermann, 101 Strand.

1. Front. Quae Genus on his Journey to London (March 1 1821).
2. p. 14. Quae Genus in search of Service (Augt. 1 1821).
3. p. 18. Quae Genus reading to Sir Jeffrey Gourmond (March 1 1822).
4. p. 45. Quae Genus at Oxford (Novr 1 1821).
5. p. 47. Conflict between Quae Genus & Lawyer Gripe-All (Octr. 1 1821).
6. p. 63. Quae Genus at a Sheep Shearing.
7. p. 66. Quae Genus assisting a Traveller (March 1 1821).
8. p. 80. Quae Genus in the Sports of the Kitchen (Augt. 1 1821).
9. p. 86. Quae Genus in the service of Sir Jeffery Gourmond (Augt. 1 1821).
10. p. 147. Quae Genus with a Quack Doctor (Octr 1 1821).
11. p. 159. Quae Genus with a Spendthrift (Septr 1 1821).
12. p. 171. Quae Genus attending on a Sporting Finale (Decr 1 1821).
13. p. 185. Quae Genus in the Service of a Miser (Octr 1 1821).
14. p. 190. Quae Genus and the Money Lenders (1st Septr 1821).
15. p. 192. Quae Genus officiating at a Gaming Table (Novr 1 1821).
16. p. 200. Quae Genus with a Portrait Painter.
17. p. 213. Quae Genus gives a grand Party (Feb 1 1822).
18. p. 216. Quae Genus interrupts a Tete a Tete (Jany 1 1822).
19. p. 225. Quae Genus committed with a riotous Dancing Party to the Watch House (Novr 1 1821).
20. p. 227. Quae Genus engaged with Jovial Friends or who sings best (Jany 1 1822).
21. p. 234. The Party breaking up and Quae Genus breaking down (Decr 1 1821).
22. p. 236. Quae Genus turned out of a House which he mistakes for his own (Feb. 1 1822).
23. p. 243. Quae Genus and Creditors (Dec 1 1821).
24. p. 255. Quae Genus discovers his Father (Jany 1 1822).

Issued in eight monthly parts at 2s. 6d. per part (each part with 3 coloured plates and 32 pp. of text) or as above in boards at £1 1s. The text is by W. Combe.

414 ROWLANDSON (T.)

Hungarian & Highland Broad Sword Twenty Four Plates, designed and etched by T. Rowlandson, under the direction of Messrs. H. Angelo and Son, Fencing Masters to the Light Horse Volunteers of London and Westminster dedicated to Colonel Herries (the above lettering on a slab with an arch on either side containing a mounted and foot volunteer respectively, military frieze trophies &c. below) Aquatinta by I. Hill. Published as the Act directs Feb. 12th 1799 by H. Angelo, Curzon Strt. May Fair.

Oblong Folio. 1799

COLLATION.—Title as above (v. blank) + Printed Dedication to Col. Herries 3 pp. (i–iii) (p. iv blank) + Subscribers 3 pp. + 23 plates (24 including title).

Each plate bears Angelo's imprint with the date Sept. 1 1798 (with the exception of plates 8 and 9 which bear no imprint).

1. Prepare to Guard.
2. Guard.
3. Horses Head, near Side, Protect.
4. Off Side Protect New Guard.
5. Left Protect.
6. Right Protect.
7. Bridle Arm Protect.
8. Sword Arm Protect.
9. St Georges Guard.
10. Thigh Protect, New Guard.
11. Give Point, and Left Parry.
12. Cut One, and Bridle-Arm Protect.

Rowlandson's Hungarian and Highland Broad Sword (*contd.*)

13. Cut Two & Right Protect.
14. Cut one and Horses Head near Side Protect.
15. Cut Six, and Sword Arm Protect.
16. Cut Two and Horse's Off Side Protect, New Guard.
17. Cut One, and Thigh Protect, New Guard.
18. On the Right to the Front, Parry against Infantry.
19. Outside Guard, St. Georges Guard, Inside Guard.
20. Outside Half Hanger, Hanging Guard Inside Half Hanger.
21. Half Circle Guard Medium Guard.
22. The Consequence of not shifting the Leg.
23. The Advantage of Shifting the Leg.
24. Title.

415 ROWLANDSON (T.)

Journal of Sentimental Travels in the Southern Provinces of France, shortly before the Revolution; embellished with Seventeen coloured engravings, from designs by T. Rowlandson, Esq. (swelled rule) 2½ line quotation from Lady Montagu's Letters (swelled rule) London: Published by R. Ackermann, 101, Strand; and may be had of all the Booksellers in the United Kingdom. (small swelled rule).

Octavo. 1821

COLLATION.—Title as above (v. blank) + Address 2 pp. (i–ii) + pp. 1–291 (p. 292 Directions to Binder) + 18 plates + 2 ll. of Advertisement at end.

Each plate bears imprint, Pubd. at R. Ackermann's Repository of Arts No 101 Strand date 1820 or 1821.

1. Front. Before the Tribunal at Avignon.
2. p. 5. Table D'hote.
3. p. 12. Searched by the Douaniers on the French Frontiers.
4. p. 22. Consulting the Prophet.
5. p. 37. The Prophet discovering himself and exposing the deception.
6. p. 51. The Arrival in Paris.
7. p. 58. Liberality to infirm beggars on leaving Yvri.
8. p. 73. Rural Happiness at Caverac.
9. p. 74. Pleasures of a Poste aux Anes.
10. p. 87. The Embrace.
11. p. 127. At Avignon First Sight of Clare.
12. p. 137. At the Tomb of Laura.
13. p. 155. Auction of Relics at Avignon.
14. p. 175. A Prisoner at Avignon.
15. p. 186. Mistakes at Cavaillon.
16. p. 189. A Tragic Story at Avignon.
17. p. 223. The Sacred Page Displayed.
18. p. 226. The Inn at Marseilles.

The title only calls for 17 plates but there should be 18, including front. The advertisements at end are usually missing. The work first appeared in the Repository during the years 1817–20.

416 ROWLANDSON (T.)

Loyal Volunteers of London & Environs, Infantry & Cavalry, in their respective Uniforms. Representing the whole of the Manual, Platoon, & Funeral Exercise in 87 plates. Designed & Etch'd by T. Rowlandson and Dedicated by Permission to His Royal Highness the Duke of Glocester (Lettering as above on oval shield surrounded by engraved design of military trophies, cupids &c.).

Quarto. [1798–9]

COLLATION.—Title as above (v. blank) + Printed Dedication 1 p. (v. blank) + Preface 6 pp. (iii–viii) + List of Subscribers 3 pp. + Contents 1 p. + Index 1 p. + 86 plates [87 including title] with descriptive text to each plate.

Each plate marked, "Rowlandson delin" and bearing Ackermann's imprint with date.

Rowlandson's Loyal Volunteers (*contd.*)

1. St. James's Volunteer   Stand at Ease   June 1 1798.
2. Westminster Volunteer Attention   June 1 1798.
3. Broad St. Ward Volunteer   Fix Bayonets 1st motion   June 1 1798.
4. St. Mary Islington Volunteer   Fix Bayonets 2nd motion   June 1 1798.
5. St. Mary-le-Strand and Somerset House Volunteer   Fix Bayonets 3rd motion   June 1 1798.
6. London & Westminster Dismounted Light Horse Volunteer   Shoulder Arms 1st motion   June 1 1798.
7. St. Clement Danes Volunteer   Shoulder Arms 2nd motion   June 1 1798.
8. Bloomsbury & Inn's of Court Volunteer   Recover Arms   June 1 1798.
9. St. George's Hanover Sqr. Light Infantry   Shoulder Arms (from recover) 1st motion   June 1 1798
10. St. George's Hanover Square Volunteer   Charge Bayonet 2nd Motion   June 1 1798.
11. St. Martin's in the Fields Volunteer   Charge Bayonet 1st motion   June.1 1798.
12. Temple Bar and St. Paul's Volunteer   Present Arms 1st motion   June 1 1798.
13. Cornhill Volunteer   Present Arms 2nd motion   June 16 1798.
14. Temple Association   Present Arms 3rd motion   June 16 1798.
15. Bethnal Green Volunteer Light Infantry   Support arms 1st motion   June 16 1798.
16. Bethnal Green Battalion Volunteer   Support arms 2nd motion   June 16 1798.
17. Hans Town Association   Stand at ease supporting arms   July 1 1798.
18. Deptford Volunteer   Slope arms   July 1 1798.
19. Westminster Lt. Infantry   Order arms 1st motion   June 16 1798.
20. Artillery Company   Order arms 2nd motion   July 1 1798.
21. Pimlico Volunteer   Unfix Bayonets 1st motion   July 10 1798.
22. Richmond Volunteer   Unfixed bayonets 2nd motion   July 1 1798.
23. Covent Garden Volunteer   Unfix bayonets 3rd motion   July 10 1798.
24. East India Compy Volunteer   An officer saluting   July 10 1798.
25. Bishopsgate Volunteer   Handle arms   July 16 1798.
26. Brentford Association   Ground Arms 1st Motion   July 18 1798.
27. Fulham Volunteer   Ground arms 2nd motion   July 18 1798.
28. St. Andrew Holborn, and St. George the Martyr Association   Ground arms 3rd motion   July 18 1798.
29. Castle Baynard Volunteer   Secure arms 1st motion   August 1 1798.
30. Finsbury Volunteer   Secure arms 2nd motion   August. 1 1798.
31. Newington Surry Volunteer   Secure arms 3rd motion   Augt. 1 1798.
32. Knight Marshall Volunteer   Prime and load 1st priming motion front rank   Augst. 1 1798.
33. Guildhall Lt. Infantry Volunteer   Prime and load 2nd priming motion   Augt 7 1798.
34. Cheap Ward Volunteer   Prime and load 3rd priming motion   Aug 1 1798.
35. Chelsea Volunteer   Prime and load 4th priming motion   Aug 7 1798.
36. Marylebone Volunteer   Prime and load 5th priming motion   Aug 1 1798.
37. Coleman Street Ward   Prime and load 6th priming motion   Aug 14 1798.
38. St. Pancras Volunteer   Prime and load 7th priming motion   Aug 20 1798.
39. Cordwainers Ward Volunteer   Prime and load 1st loading motion   Aug 20 1798.
40. St. Margaret & St. John, Westr Volunteer   Prime and load 2nd loading motion   Aug. 20 1798.
41. Lambeth Volunteer   Prime and load 3rd loading motion.   Sepr 7 1798.
42. St. Georges Southwark Volunteer   Prime and load 4th loading motion   Sepr 7 1798.
43. St. Saviour Southwark Volunteer   Prime and load 5th loading motion   Sepr 7 1798.
44. St. Olave Southwark Volunteer   Prime and load 6th loading motion   Sepr 7 1798.
45. Poplar and Blackwall Volunteer   Prime and load last motion   Sepr 21 1798.
46. Sadlers Sharp Shooters   A Light Infantry Man defending himself with Sadlers patent gun and long cutting bayonet   Sept. 14 1798.
47. Radcliff Volunteer   Make ready front rank   Sept. 21 1798.
48. Union Wapping Volunteer   Present front rank   Sept 21 1798.
49. Hackney Volunteer   Fire front rank   Oct 5 1798.
50. Bermondsey Volunteer   Front rank kneeling make ready   Oct 5 1798.
51. St. John Southwark Volunteer   Present (as front rank kneeling)   Oct 5 1798.
52. Langbourn Ward Volunteer   Prime and load (as centre rank)   Oct 5 1798.
53. St. Georges Hanover Square Association   Make ready (as centre rank)   Oct 5 1798.
54. St. Sepulchre Middx Volunteer   Present as centre rank   Oct 25 1798.
55. Farrington Ward Within Volunteer   Prime and load as a rear rank   Oct 25 1798.

Rowlandson's Loyal Volunteers (*contd.*)

56. Aldgate Ward Association   Make Ready as a rear rank   Nov 1 1798.
57. Walbrook Ward Volunteer   Present as a rear rank   Nov 1 1798.
58. Clerkenwell Association   Advance Arms   Nov 16 1798.
59. Westminster Grenadier   Advance Arms 4th motion   Nov 16 1798.
60. Bread Street Ward Volunteer   Shoulder Arms from advance first motion.   Nov 16 1798.
61. Vintry Ward Volunteer   Club Arms (1st motion)   Dec 20 1798.
62. Portsoken Ward Volunteer   Club Arms 2nd motion   Dec 20 1798.
63. St. Catherine's Association   Club Arms 3rd motion   Dec 20 1798.
64. Farrington Ward without Volunteer   Club Arms 4th motion   Dec 20 1798.
65. Bridge Ward Volunteer   Mourn arms 1st motion   Jan 1 1799.
66. Tower Ward Association   Mourn arms 2nd motion   Dec 18 1798.
67. Christ Church Surry Association   Mourn arms 3rd motion   Jan 1 1799.
68. Loyal Bermondsey Volunteer   Present arms 1st motion from mourn arms   Dec 18 1798.
69. Billingsgate Association   Present arms from mourn arms 2nd motion   Jan 1 1799.
70. An officer of the Highland Association   Jan 1 1799.
71. Whitechapel Association   Present arms 2nd Flagel Motion   Feby 15 1799.
72. Bank of England Light Infantry   Order Arms 2nd Flagel Motion   Feby 15 1799.
73. Candlewick Ward Association   Support arms 1st Flagel Motion   April 20 1799.
74. Queenhythe Ward Volunteer   A Sergeant with Arms Advanced   May 6 1799.
75. Cripplegate Ward without Volunteer   Order arms from advance 1st motion   April 20 1799.
76. Dowgate Ward Volunteer   Order Arms from advance 2nd motion April 20 1799.
77. { Mile End / Shoreditch Volunteer / Trinity Minories Volunteer } together on 1 plate Pile Arms   May 20 1799.

Cavalry.

78. London and Westminster Light Horse Volunteer   June 24 1798.
79. Surry Yeomanry   July 1 1798.
80. Deptford Cavalry   June 24 1798.
81. Westminster Cavalry   July 1 1798.
82. Middlesex Cavalry   Oct 1 1798.
83. Southwark Cavalry   Nov 1 1798.
84. Clerkenwell Cavalry   Nov 1 1798.
85. Lambeth Loyal Cavalry   Nov 1 1798.
86. Loyal Islington Volunteer Cavalry   24 July 1799.

RÉSUMÉ.—*87 plates including the engraved title. In addition there are two additional plates which are rare, but are found bound in a few copies, viz. Expedition or Military Fly and Sadler's Flying Artillery. Sometimes the plates are heightened with silver and gold.*

417 ROWLANDSON (T.)

The Military Adventures of Johnny Newcome, with an account of his Campaigns on the Peninsula and in Pall Mall: with Sketches by Rowlandson; and Notes (swelled rule) "He jests at Scars who never felt a wound." Shakespeare (swelled rule) By an Officer (thick and thin rule) London: Printed for Patrick Martin, 198, Oxford Street, corner of Orchard Street (rule).

Octavo.   1815

COLLATION.—Title as above (v. W. Wilson, Printer, 4 Greville-Street, Hatton Garden London) + Dedication 1 p. (v. blank) + pp. 1–188.

Each plate marked, Drawn & Etch'd by Rowlandson and imprint London Pubd. Feby. 1st 1815 by P. Martin 198 Oxford Street.

1. Frontispiece. (Johnny Newcome starting to join his Regiment).
2. p. 28. Johnny Newcome going to lay in Stock.

Rowlandson's Johnny Newcome (*contd.*)

3. p. 33. Getting into his billet.
4. p. 40. Taking his Breakfast.
5. p. 51. Introduced to his Colonel.
6. p. 60. Smells powder for the first time.
7. p. 62. Half Rations.
8. p. 63. Johnny writes an account of the Action to his Mother, which afterwards appears in the Star.
9. p. 64. Learning to Smoke and drink Grog.
10. p. 66. Poor Johnny on the Sick List.
11. p. 67. Going Sick to the Rear.
12. p. 73. Johnny safe returned to his Mama.
13. p. 116. Dash'd with his Suite for Santarem that Night.
14. p. 121. Johnny on Duty with his Chief.
15. p. 180. Presenting the Trophies.

First Edition Text by Col. David Roberts, Reprinted the following year. Imitated by Heath (W.) "Life of a Soldier London Sams 1823."

418 ROWLANDSON (T.)

Military Adventures of Johnny Newcombe. . . . Second Edition

Octavo.   1816

COLLATION.—As for the first edition, with the exception of the title page that bears the words Second Edition above the imprint and verso of title, W. Smith & Co. Printers, King Street, Seven Dials.

419 ROWLANDSON (T.)

Naples and the Campagna Felice (short thick and thin rule) In a Series of Letters, addressed to a Friend in England in 1802 (short thick and thin rule) London: Published by R. Ackermann, 101 Strand (short thick and thin rule).

Octavo.   1815

COLLATION.—Engraved title + Title as above (v. J. Diggins, Printer, St Ann's Lane, London.) + Preface 2 pp. (3–4) + pp. 1–400 + Index 5 unnumbered leaves + List of Plates 1 p. (v. blank) + 2 Maps + 16 plates.
Each plate bears Ackermann's Imprint.

1. Front. "If while entranced in balmy rest" &c. T. Rowlandson delt. et sculpt. Letter xii p. 196.
2. Engraved Title "Naples and the Campagna Felice in a Series of Letters Published at R. Ackermanns 101 Strand London June 1 1815." the above on an Etruscan frame in black and bistre with small coloured oval vignette view in lower half.
3. p.   1. Map of the Country, Islands, &c in the Vicinity of Naples I. Girtin sc 8 Broad Str Golden Sqr.
4. p.   3. Don Luigi's Baggage seized by Four Lazzaroni.
5. p. 103. Plan of the Barracks, Theatres &c of Pompeii.
6. p. 107. View of the Temple of Isis in Pompeii (v. Pl iv No 5).
7. p. 124. View of the Gate & High Street of Pompeii.
8. p. 166. Ancient Greek Paintings from Herculaneum.
9. p. 176. Don Luigi meets Donna Anna in the Museum.
10. p. 178. Ancient Greek Paintings from Herculaneum.
11. p. 195. Sleeping Tete a Tete at a first visit of Don Luigi's.

Rowlandson's Naples (*contd.*)

12. p. 215. Map of the Island of Capri E. Gullan sculp.
13. p. 323. Don Michele getting up the ship's side.
14. p. 343. Don Luigi's Ball.
15. p. 343. A Bacchanalian Scene at Don Luigi's Ball.
16. p. 350. A View near Naples.
17. p. 366. Don Michele preparing for his triumphal expedition.
18. p. 375. The Letter Writer.

This work first appeared in Ackermann's Repository during years 1809–13 as " Letters from Italy." The text is by Lewis Engelbach.

420 ROWLANDSON

[Naval Costumes]

Set of 10 plates, all marked, Rowlandson delin., Merks sculp., London, Pub. Feb. 15 1799, by R. Ackermann, 101 Strand.

1. Cabin Boy.
2. Sailor.
3. Carpenter.
4. Cook.
5. Midshipman.

6. Purser.
7. Lieutenant.
8. Captain.
9. Admiral.
10. Captain of Marines.

421 ROWLANDSON (T.)

Poetical Magazine: Dedicated to the Lovers of the Muse, By the Agent of the Goddess, R. Ackermann Vol. I E. Gullan Sculpsit London: Pub. Nov. 1 1809 at R. Ackermann's Repository of Arts, 101, Strand.

4 vols.   Octavo.   1809[–11]

COLLATION VOL. I.—Engraved title lettered as above with vignette of the muses at head (v. blank) + Introductory Address pp. i–iv + pp. 5–404 + Index 4 pp. (unnumbered) Also 1 leaf of rhymed advertisement between pp. 112 and 113 + 14 coloured plates.

Each volume has a Supplement at the end (included in the pagination) and each plate has an imprint No [ ] of the Poetical Magazine Pub. [date] at R. Ackermann's Repository of Arts 101, Strand.

Plate 1. p. 10. Doctor Syntax, setting out on his Tour of the Lakes.   No. 1 . . . 1st May 1809.
„ 2. p. 11. View in Itlay.   No 1 . . . 1st May 1809.
„ 5. p. 57. Mansion House Monitor   No 2 . . . 1st June 1809.
„ 3. p. 64. Doctor Syntax loosing his way   No 2 . . . 1st June 1809.
„ 4. p. 66. Doctor Syntax stopt by Highwaymen   No 2 . . . 1st June 1809.
„ 6. p. 116. Doctor Syntax bound to a tree by a Highwaymen   No 3 . . . July 1st 1809.
„ 7. p. 120. View near Seville in Spain By Moonlight   No 3 . . . July 1st 1809.
„ 8. p. 173. Doctor Syntax disputing his bill with the Landlady   No 4 . . . Augt 1st 1809.
„ 9. p. 174. A View near Naples.   Freebairn delt.   No 4 . . . Augt. 1st 1809.
„ p. 182. Woodcut vignette "The Last Drop."
„ 10. p. 222. Doctor Syntax copying the Wit of the Window   No 5 . . . Septr 1st 1809.
„ 11. p. 223. A View on the Lake of Como   No 5 . . . Septr 1st 1809.
„ 12. p. 278. Doctor Syntax entertained at College   No 6 . . . Octr 1st 1809.
„ 13. p. 280. Doctor Syntax pursued by a bull   No 6 . . . Oct 1st 1809.
„ 14. p. 315. Conway Castle Carnarvonshire   No 5 [misprint for 6] Octr 1st 1809.

Rowlandson's Poetical Magazine (*contd.*)

VOL. II.—Engraved title as before but without imprint at foot and with a new vignette at head (v. blank) + pp. 1–372 + Index 2 ll. (unnumbered).

Plate	2.	Vol. II.	p.	9.	Doctor Syntax mistakes a Gentlemans House for an Inn No 7 . . . Novr 1st 1809.
,,	3.	,,	p.	34.	The Castle of Baron Hulembert No 7 . . . Novr 1st 1809.
,,	4.	,,	p.	52.	Doctor Syntax, meditating on the Tomb Stones No 8 . . . Decr 1st 1809.
,,	5.	,,	p.	68.	Edwin & Matilda No 8 . . . Decr. 1st 1809.
,,	6.	,,	p.	103.	Doctor Syntax tumbling into the Water No 9 . . . Jan 1 1810.
,,	7.	,,	p.	112.	The Beach King discovering himself to Matilda No 9 . . . Jan 1 1810.
,,	8.	,,	p.	150.	Doctor Syntax loses his money on the Race Ground at York No 10 . . . Feb 1 1810.
,,	9.	,,	p.	164.	Tintern Abbey No 10 . . . Feb 1 1810.
,,	10.	,,	p.	198.	Doctor Syntax at a Review No 11 . . . March 1 1810.
,,	11.	,,	p.	203.	View of a Cottage in Wales. Sutherland fec. No 11 . . . March 1 1810.
,,	12.	,,	p.	247.	Doctor Syntax with my Lord No 12 . . . April 1 1810.
,,	13.	,,	p.	248.	Doctor Syntax made free of the cellar No 12 . . . April 1 1810.
,,	14.	,,	p.	249.	A View near Berwick upon Tweed No 12 . . . April 1 1810.

VOL. III.—Engraved title as before but without imprint and Gullan's name omitted after vol. iii, and a new vignette at head J. Thurston delt.   Thos Williamson sculpt. (v. blank) + pp. 1–364 + Index 2 ll. unnumbered.

Plate	1.	Vol. III.	p.	8.	Doctor Syntax Sketching the Lake No 13 . . . May 1 1810.
,,	2.	,,	p.	9.	Castle of Caldwal Scotland No 13 . . . May 1 1810.
,,	3.	,,	p.	56.	Doctor Syntax drawing after nature No 14 . . . June 1 1810.
,,	4.	,,	p.	57.	Dover Castle No 14 . . . June 1 1810.
,,	5.	,,	p.	102.	Dr. Syntax Robb'd of his Property No 15 . . . July 1 1810.
,,	1 [mispt]	Vol. III.	p.	124.	Abbey Ruin No 15 . . . July 1 1810.
,,	7.	Vol. III.	p.	152.	Doctor Syntax sells Grizzle No 16 . . . Augt. 1 1810.
,,	8.	,,	p.	154.	Harleigh Castle, Merionethshire No 16 . . . Augt. 1 1810.
,,	9.	,,	p.	200.	Doctor Syntax, Rural Sport No 17 . . . Septr 1st 1810.
,,	10.	,,	p.	201.	A Cornish Cottage. Sutherland f. No 17 . . . Septr 1st 1810.
,,	11.	,,	p.	246.	Doctor Syntax & Dairy Maid No 18 . . . Oct 1 1810.
,,	12.	,,	p.	248.	Denbigh Castle. Sutherland f. No 18 . . . Oct 1 1810.

VOL. IV.—Engraved title, vignette figure of Apollo in a frame lettered Poetical Magazine G. B. Cipriani Inv.   F. Bartolozzi sculp.   Dedicated to the Lovers of the Muse By their Humble Servant, R. Ackermann Vol. IV London: Pub. May 1 1811 at R. Ackermann's Repository of Arts 101 Strand (v. blank) + pp. 1–342 + Index 2 ll. (unnumbered).

Plate	1.	Vol. IV.	p.	8.	Doctor Syntax at Liverpool No 19 . . . Novr 1 1810.
,,	2.	,,	p.	12.	A View on the Thames near Vauxhall No 19 . . . Novr 1 1810.
,,	3.	,,	p.	48.	Doctor Syntax reading his Tour No 20 . . . Decr 1 1810.
,,	4.	,,	p.	49.	Abbey Church Bath No 20 . . . Decr 1 1810.
,,	5.	,,	p.	94.	Syntax preaching No 21 . . . Jany 1 1811.
,,	6.	,,	p.	102.	College Green Bristol No 21 . . . Jany 1 1811.
,,	7.	,,	p.	150.	Doctor Syntax & Bookseller No 22 . . . Feby 1 1811.
,,	8.	,,	p.	152.	Equality (uncoloured) No 22 . . . Feby 1 1811.
,,	9.	,,	p.	194.	Doctor Syntax at Covent Garden Theatre No 23 March 1 1811.
,,	10.	,,	p.	196.	Affection (uncoloured) No 23 March 1 1811.
,,	11.	,,	p.	242.	Doctor Syntax return'd from his Tour No 24 April 1 1811.
,,	12.	,,	p.	244.	Netley Abbey Engraved by J. Hassell No 24 April 1 1811.
,,	28. [mispt]	Vol. IV.	p.	292.	Doctor Syntax taking possession of his Living No 25 . . . May 1 1811.

Contains the original issue of Combe's Tours of Dr. Syntax under the Title of "The Schoolmaster's Tour."

422 ROWLANDSON (T.)

Poetical Sketches of Scarborough: illustrated by Twenty-one Engravings of Humourous Subjects, coloured from original designs, made upon the spot by J. Green, and etched by T. Rowlandson (small line ornament) London: Printed for R. Ackermann, 101, Strand, by J. Diggins, Saint Ann's Lane (small line ornament).

Octavo.   1813

COLLATION.—Title as above (v. blank) + Advertisement 1 p. (v. blank) + Some Account of Scarborough pp. i–xv (xvi blank) + Text pp. 1–215 + 21 coloured plates, each plate bearing imprint, Pub. 1813, by R. Ackermann, 101, Strand.

    1. Front.   Widow Ducker & her nymphs J. Green delt.
    2. p.   6. A trip to Scarbro' J. Green delt. J. Bluck sculpt. [J. Papworth].
    3. p.   15. The Breakfast J. Green delt. J. Bluck sculpt. [J. Papworth].
    4. p.   25. The Spa Js. Green delt J. C. Stadler sculpt. [J. Papworth].
    5. p.   36. Spa Terrace J Green delt J. C. Stadler sculpt. [J. Papworth].
    6. p.   49. Boot & Shoe Shop J. Green delt J. C. Stadler sculpt [J. Papworth].
    7. p.   53. The Castle J Green delt [Wrangham].
    8. p.   81. The Warm Bath J Green delt. J. Bluck sculpt. [Wrangham].
    9. p.   97. Cornelian Bay Js. Green delt J. C. Stadler sculpt. [Wrangham].
   10. p. 106. Sea Bathing. J Green delt. J. C. Stadler sculpt. [Coombe].
   11. p. 116. The Sands. J Green delt [J. Papworth].
   12. p. 124. The Church. J Green delt Stadler sculpt. [J. Papworth].
   13. p. 138. Shower Bath. J Green delt Stadler sculpt. [Coombe].
   14. p. 144. The Library J Green delt [J. Papworth].
   15. p. 157. The Terrace J. Green delt J Stadler aquat [Coombe].
   16. p. 161. The Theatre J Green delt. [J. Papworth].
   17. p. 176. The Ball Room J. Green delt [Wrangham].
   18. p. 183. Terrace Steps. J. Green delt. J. C. Stadler sculpt. [J. Papworth].
   19. p. 194. Wet Quakers Js. Green delt. J. C. Stadler sculpt. [J. Papworth].
   20. p. 201. The Post Office J. Green delt. J. C. Stadler sculpt. [J. Papworth].
   21. p. 214. The Departure J. Green delt. Stadler sculpt. [J. Papworth].

"*The originals of the plates introduced in this volume were sketches made as souvenirs of the place during a visit to Scarborough. 1812. They were not intended for publication, but being found to interest many persons of taste, several of whom expressed a desire to possess engravings of them, and some gentlemen having offered to add metrical illustrations to each the present form of publication has been adopted*" Advertisement. The gentlemen supplying the Text to the various episodes evolved from each plate are given in the square brackets.

Issued in octavo in boards for 1 guinea, and in green cloth with paper label at a later date.

It is claimed that plate 13 "Shower Bath" is rare but in none of the numerous copies I have examined has it been missing. Plate 8 The Warm Bath is said to contain the portrait of Mrs. Robinson, George IV's mistress.

423 Poetical Sketches of Scarborough Second Edition.   1813

COLLATION.—Title exactly as in First Edition with the exception of the addition of the words Second Edition printed between 2 short double ruled lines immediately over the imprint + Dedication signed James Green 1 p. (v. blank) + Advertisement 1 p. (v. blank) + Contents 1 p. (v. blank) + pp. i–xv + pp. 1–215 + 21 coloured plates as in the First Edition.

POINTS.—*The Dedication and Contents appear for the first time in this Second Edition.*

Rowlandson's Scarborough (*contd.*)

The Dedication is addressed to Rev. Francis Wrangham (one of the contributors). This edition is "corrected of errors." The type is differently set up and the initials of the various authors (with the exception of Coombe's contribution) are added at end of each episode and there are changes in the footnotes.

Published in octavo in "boards" for 1 guinea.

424 ROWLANDSON (T.)

Rowlandson's Characteristic Sketches of the Lower Orders, intended as a companion to the New Picture of London: consisting of Fifty-four plates, neatly coloured (rule) London: Printed for Samuel Leigh, 18, Strand. (rule) 1820 Price 7s. half bound.

Duodecimo. 1820

COLLATION.—Title as above (v. London W. Clowes, Northumberland Court) + Advertisement 2 pp. (iii–iv) + 54 plates.

1. Menagerie. A Beef-eater exhibiting the Royal Wild Beast Show at the Tower.	18. Oysters.	37. Flounders.
2. Drayman.	19. Cooper.	38. Baskets.
3. Chairs to mend.	20. Sweet Lavender.	39. Milk.
4. Cherries.	21. Last Dying Speech.	40. Hot Cross Buns.
5. Wine Coopers.	22. Old Clothes.	41. Walnuts to Pickle.
6. Cucumbers.	23. Curds and Whey.	42. Hackney Coachmen.
7. Singing Birds.	24. "Pray remember the poor Sweeper."	43. Buy my sweet Roses.
8. A Peep at the Comet.	25. Butcher.	44. Poodles.
9. Grinder.	26. Itinerant Musicians.	45. Firemen.
10. Bagpipes.	27. Door Mats.	46. Ballad Singer.
11. Roasted Apples.	28. Earthenware.	47. Shoeblack.
12. Distressed Sailors.	29. Raree Show.	48. Placard (Lottery Prizes).
13. Roasting Jacks &c.	30. Images.	49. "Past One o'clock" (watchman).
14. Gardener.	31. All Hot.	50. Postman.
15. Sweeps.	32. Strawberries.	51. Billet doux.
16. Matches.	33. Dog's Meat.	52. Band boxes.
17. Coal Heavers.	34. Rhubarb.	53. Great News.
	35. Baker.	54. Saloop (Stall of Saloop tea seller).
	36. Tinker.	

Published at 7s. as a Supplement to S. Leigh's New Picture of London.

425 ROWLANDSON (T.)

[A Series of Views at Oxford and Cambridge.] 1809–11

COLLATION.—12 coloured aquatint plates without title or text.

1. Magdalen College, Oxford London Pub Novr 1st 1809 at R. Ackermann's Repository of Arts 101 Strand.
2. The Entrance to the Cloister at Magdalen College—Oxford Published Octr 31, 1811 at R. Ackermann's Repository of Arts 101 Strand London.
3. View of Merton College Oxford.
4. St. Mary's Church & Radclivian Library Published Octr. 31 1811 at R. Ackermann's Repository of Arts 101 Strand London.
5. Front View of Christ Church Oxford London Published May 1 1810 at R. Ackermanns Repositary of Arts 101 Strand.

Rowlandson's Oxford and Cambridge (*contd.*)

6. View of the Theatre, Printing House &c Oxford Published at R. Ackermann's Repository of Arts 101 Strand.
7. View of the Observatory, Oxford London Published May 1 1810 at R. Ackermann's Repository of Arts 101 Strand.
8. View of Oxford Castle London Publish'd Novr 1st 1809 R. Ackermann's Repository of Arts, 101 Strand.
9. Emanuel College, Cambridge Published Octr 31, 1811 at R. Ackermann's Repository of Arts 101 Strand London.
10. Emanuel College Garden Cambridge Published at R. Ackermann's Repository of Arts 101 Strand.
11. Quadrangle of King's College, Cambridge Published Octr 31 at R. Ackermann's Repository of Arts, 101 Strand London.
12. Inside View of the Public Library Cambridge London Pub Nov 1st 1809 at R. Ackermanns Repository of Arts 101 Strand.

Rare.

426 ROWLANDSON (T.)

Rowlandson's Sketches from Nature [no Printer given]

Quarto. [1822]

COLLATION.—Title as above + 18 plates each marked, Drawn and Etched by Rowlandson and each (with the exception of Nos. 7, 10, 13 and 16) Stadler Aquatinta.

1. White Lion Inn, Ponder's End, Middlesex (Dated 1822).
2. A View near Richmond.
3. View near Newport Isle of Wight.
4. Temple at Strawberry Hill (Dated 1822).
5. Stamford Lincolnshire.
6. Taunton Vale Somersetshire.
7. View near Bridport Dorsetshire.
8. A View in Devonshire.
9. Village of St Udy Cornwall.
10. West Loo Cornwall.
11. The Seat of Mr Mitchell Esq Hengar Cornwall.
12. Fowey Cornwall.
13. View on River Camel Cornwall.
14. A View in Camelford, Cornwall.
15. A Cottage in the Dutchy of Cornwall.
16. View at Blisland, near Bodmin Cornwall.
17. Clearing a Wreck on N. Coast of Cornwall.
18. Rouler Moor.

Grego cites only 17 plates omitting the first and slightly varying the sequence of the others.

427 ROWLANDSON (T.)

The Tour of Doctor Syntax, In Search of the (coloured vignette containing the word Picturesque) A Poem. (thick and thin rule) Ut Pictura, Poesis erit, quae, si propius stes, te capiat magis: et quaedam, si longius abstes.   Haec amat obscurum; volet haec sub luce videri judicis argutum quae non formidat acumen: Haec placuit semel, haec decies repetita placebit.   Harat., Ars Poet.

Octavo. 1812

COLLATION.—Title as above + Advertisement 2 leaves (i–iii, p. iv Diggins, Printer, St. Ann's Lane, London) + pp. 1–275 + Directions to Binder 1 leaf + 30 coloured plates designed and etched by Rowlandson.

1. Front.   Rev Doctor Syntax.   May 1st 1812.
2. p.   6.   Dr Syntax setting out on his Tour of the Lakes.
3. p.   10.   Dr Syntax losing his way.
4. p.   12.   Dr Syntax stopt by highwaymen.
5. p.   14.   Dr Syntax bound to a tree by highwaymen.
6. p.   22.   Dr Syntax disputing his bill with landlady.

Rowlandson's Syntax, First Tour (*contd.*)

7. p. 32. Dr Syntax copying the wit of the window.
8. p. 38. Dr Syntax entertained at college.
9. p. 40. Dr Syntax pursued by a bull.
10. p. 50. Dr Syntax mistakes a gentlemans house for an inn.
11. p. 56. Dr Syntax meditating on the Tombstones.
12. p. 70. Dr Syntax tumbling into the water.
13. p. 80. Dr Syntax loses his money on race ground at York.
14. p. 88. Dr Syntax at a Review.
15. p. 100. Dr Syntax with My Lord.
16. p. 102. Dr Syntax made free of the cellar.
17. p. 110. Dr Syntax sketching the Lake.
18. p. 120. Dr Syntax drawing after nature.
19. p. 130. Dr Syntax Robbd of his Property.
20. p. 140. Dr Syntax sells Grizzle.
21. p. 150. Dr. Syntax rural Sport.
22. p. 156. Dr Syntax & Dairy Maid.
23. p. 166. Dr Syntax at Liverpool.
24. p. 180. Dr Syntax, reading his tour.
25. p. 184. Dr Syntax preaching.
26. p. 205. Dr Syntax and Bookseller.
27. p. 222. Dr Syntax at Covent Garden Theatre.
28. p. 238. The Doctors Dream.
29. p. 256. Dr Syntax returned from his Tour.
30. p. 274. Dr Syntax taking possession of his living.

Size of uncut copy in boards 10 by 6¼ inches. The text is by Wm Combe. First Edition (in book form) Published in boards with paper label at one guinea. This celebrated work first appeared in the Poetical Magazine under the title "The Schoolmasters Tour," and the illustrations are the same but retouched and re-engraved by Rowlandson, with 3 additional illustrations, viz. Frontispiece, vignette title, and plate 28 The Doctors Dream or the Battle of the Books. Enormously popular from the outset Dr. Syntax went into many editions, no less than 2 in 1812, 3 in 1813, others in 1815, 1817 and 2 in 1819.

A German Edition was published in Berlin, "Die Reise des Doktor Syntax" with lithograph reproductions of the plates by F. E Rademaker 1822, and a French Edition, "Le Don Quichotte Romantique ou Voyage du Docteur Syntaxe," Paris 1821, with coloured lithographs by Malapeau.

Numerous imitations and Parodies appeared, including Tour of Doctor Syntax through London, 1820; Doctor Syntax in Paris in search of the Grotesque, 1820; Tour of Doctor Prosody, 1821; Sentimental Tour through Margate and Hastings by Doctor Comparative Junior; Doctor Syntax's Life of Napoleon, 1815; The Adventures of Doctor Comicus, by a modern Syntax; The History of Johnny Quae Genus the Little Foundling of the late Dr. Syntax, 1822; The Political Doctor Syntax designs by I. R. Cruikshank, 1820; Wars of Wellington or Narrative Poem in 15 Cantos by Doctor Syntax, 1819, &c.

ISSUES.—There are two issues of text. First issue is headed Chapter I and the Second issue is headed Canto I, Plate 5, p. 14, Doctor Syntax bound to a tree by highwaymen also exists in two states. In the first state the girl riding the donkey has her right arm straight, in the second state she has it raised and bent. The first edition of First Tour is the rarest of the 3 volumes.

428 ROWLANDSON (T.)

The Second Tour of Doctor Syntax, in Search of Consolation; A Poem (rule) volume second (rule) (5 line quotation from Horace as before) (small decorated rule) Published

Rowlandson's Syntax, Second Tour *(contd.)*

by R. Ackermann, At the Repository of Arts, 101, Strand, London: and to be had of all booksellers in the United Kingdom (thick and thin rule).

Octavo.   1820

COLLATION.—Title as above (v. Printed by J. Diggins, St. Ann's Lane, London) + Introduction 1 leaf + pp. 1–277 + Directions to Binder 1 leaf + 24 coloured plates drawn by Rowlandson.

1. Front.   Dr Syntax & his Counterpart.
2. p.   10. Dr Syntax lamenting loss of his wife.
3. p.   24. Dr Syntax at the Funeral of his wife.
4. p.   51. Dr Syntax setting out on his second tour.
5. p.   80. Dr Syntax and the Gypsies.
6. p. 101. Dr Syntax loses his wig.
7. p. 131. Dr Syntax Visit to Widow Hopefull at York.
8. p. 153. Dr Syntax amused with Pat in the Pond.
9. p. 158. Dr Syntax in the Glass House.
10. p. 161. Dr Syntax visits Eaton Hall Cheshire.
11. p. 171. Dr Syntax making his Will.
12. p. 177. Dr Syntax in a Court of Justice.
13. p. 180. Dr Syntax present at Coffee House quarrel at Bath.
14. p. 185. Dr Syntax & superannuated Foxhunter.
15. p. 198. Dr Syntax with the Skimmington Riders.
16. p. 220. Dr Syntax and the Bees.
17. p. 225. Dr Syntax visits a boarding school for young ladies.
18. p. 239. Dr Syntax making a discovery.
19. p. 242. Dr Syntax painting a portrait.
20. p. 250. Marriage of Dr Dicky Bend.
21. p. 256. Dr Syntax at an Auction.
22. p. 266. Dr Syntax & Bookseller.
23. p. 270. Dr Syntax at Freemason Hall.
24. p. 276. Miss Worthys Marriage Dr Syntax in chair.

Appeared originally in eight monthly parts at 2s. 6d. a part, and on completion at 21s. in boards. The text is by W. Combe.

There are two states of plate 15, in the first state the plate being marked Skimerton Riders.

429 ROWLANDSON (T.)

The Third Tour of Doctor Syntax, In Search of a Wife. A Poem (coloured vignette) (5 line verse from Horace as before) (line) London. Published at R. Ackermann's Repository of Arts 101 Strand, and to be had of all Booksellers.   (1821)

COLLATION.—Title as above + Preface 1 leaf (dated 1821) (v. Printed by J. Diggins, St. Ann's Lane, London) + Directions to Binder 1 leaf + pp. 1–279 + 24 plates drawn by Rowlandson.

1. Front.   Dr Syntax setting out in search of a wife.
2. p.   10. Dr Syntax soliloquising.
3. p.   32. Dr Syntax turned nurse.
4. p.   84. The Banns Forbidden.
5. p.   95. Dr Syntax with Blue Stocking Beauty.
6. p. 126. The Cellar Quartetto.
7. p. 136. Dr Syntax presenting a floral offering.
8. p. 139. The Billiard Table.
9. p. 140. Misfortunes at Tulip Hall.
10. p. 145. The Harvest Home.
11. p. 158. The Garden Trio.
12. p. 163. Dr Syntax at Card Party.
13. p. 164. Dr Syntax star gazing.
14. p. 191. Dr Syntax in the wrong Lodging House.

Rowlandson's Syntax, Third Tour (*contd.*)

15. p. 204. Dr Syntax recd. by maid instead of mistress.
16. p. 208. The Artists room.
17. p. 213. Death of Punch.
18. p. 220. The Advt. for a Wife.
19. p. 224. Dr Syntax & the Foundling.
20. p. 233. Result of purchasing a blind horse.
21. p. 255. Noble Hunting Party.
22. p. 263. Introduction to Courtship.
23. p. 276. Dr Syntax in Danger.
24. p. 277. Funeral of Syntax.

Issued in eight monthly parts in printed wrappers, and on completion in boards at 21s. The text is by W. Combe.

430 ROWLANDSON (T.)

Syntax's Tours Miniature Edition 3 vols. 16mo.
The Tour of Doctor Syntax in Search of the (vignette containing the word Picturesque) A Poem (rule) 5 line quote from Horace Pubd. by R. A. Ackermann, London.

Duodecimo. 1823

COLLATION.—Engraved title as above (v. blank) + Preface 2 pp. + Directions to Binder 1 p. (v. blank) + pp. 1–276 + 30 coloured plates (including front.) as in the first edition, each plate bearing imprint, Pubd. by R. Ackermann, London 1823.

30. Front. The Revd Doctor Syntax.
1. p. 6. Doctor Syntax setting out on his Tour of the Lakes.
2. p. 10. Doctor Syntax losing his way.
3. p. 12. Doctor Syntax stopt by Highwaymen.
4. p. 15. Dr Syntax bound to a tree by Highwaymen.
5. p. 23. Dr. Syntax disputing his bill with his landlady.
6. p. 32. Dr. Syntax copying the Wit of the Window.
7. p. 38. Dr. Syntax entertained at College.
8. p. 40. Dr Syntax pursued by a Bull.
9. p. 50. Dr Syntax mistakes a Gentlemans House for an Inn.
10. p. 56. Dr Syntax meditating on the Tombs.
11. p. 71. Dr Syntax Tumbling into the Water.
12. p. 80. Dr Syntax loses his Money on the Race Ground.
13. p. 89. Dr Syntax at a Review.
14. p. 101. Dr Syntax with my Lord.
15. p. 102. Dr Syntax made free of the cellar.
16. p. 111. Dr Syntax sketching the Lake.
17. p. 121. Dr Syntax drawing after Nature.
18. p. 130. Dr Syntax robbed of his Property.
19. p. 140. Dr Syntax sells Grizzle.
20. p. 150. Dr Syntax & Rural Sports.
21. p. 157. Dr Syntax & Dairy Maid.
22. p. 166. Dr Syntax at Liverpool.
23. p. 181. Dr Syntax reading his Tour.
24. p. 184. Dr Syntax Preaching.
25. p. 205. Dr Syntax and Bookseller.
26. p. 223. Dr Syntax at Covent Garden Theatre.
27. p. 238. The Doctors Dream.
28. p. 286. Dr. Syntax returned from the Tour.
29. p. 275. Dr Syntax taking possession of his Living.

The Second Tour of Doctor Syntax In Search of Consolation; A Poem (rule) Volume Second (rule) 5 line quote Horace (ornament rule) London: Published by R. Ackermann, At the Repository of Arts, 101, Strand; and to be had of all the booksellers in the United Kingdom (thick and thin rule).

Duodecimo. 1823

Rowlandson's Miniature Syntax (*contd.*)

COLLATION.—Title as above (v. Diggins, Printer, St. Ann's Lane, London) + Introduction 2 pp. + Directions for placing Plates 1 p. (v. Diggins, Printer, St. Ann's Lane, London) + pp. 1–277 + 24 coloured plates (including front.) each bearing imprint, Pub. by R. Ackermann, London 1823.

1. Front. Dr Syntax and his Counterpart.
2. p. 10. Dr Syntax lamenting the loss of his wife.
3. p. 24. Dr Syntax at the Funeral of his Wife.
4. p. 51. Dr. Syntax setting out on his Second Tour.
5. p. 80. Dr Syntax and the Gypsies.
6. p. 101. Dr Syntax loses his Wig.
7. p. 131. The visit of Dr Syntax to the Widow Hopefull at York.
8. p. 153. Dr Syntax amused with Pat in the Pond.
9. p. 158. Dr Syntax in the Glass House.
10. p. 161. Dr Syntax visits Eaton Hall Cheshire.
11. p. 171. Dr Syntax making his Will.
12. p. 177. Dr Syntax in a Court of Justice.
13. p. 180. Dr Syntax present at a Coffee House Quarrell at Bath.
14. p. 185. Dr Syntax and the Superannuated Fox Hunter.
15. p. 198. Dr Syntax with the Skimerton Riders.
16. p. 220. Dr Syntax and the Bees.
17. p. 225. Dr Syntax visits a Boarding School for Young Ladies.
18. p. 239. Dr Syntax making a Discovery.
19. p. 242. Dr Syntax painting a portrait.
20. p. 250. Marriage of Dr Dicky Bend.
21. p. 257. Dr Syntax at an Auction.
22. p. 266. Dr Syntax and Bookseller.
23. p. 270. Dr Syntax at Free Masons Hall.
24. p. 276. Miss Worthy's Marriage—Dr Syntax in the Chair.

The Third Tour of Doctor Syntax In Search of a Wife. A Poem. (vignette followed by 5 line quote Horace) (rule) London Pubd. 1823 by R. Ackermann 101 Strand.

Duodecimo.

COLLATION.—Engraved title as above (v. blank) + Preface 1 p. (v. Printed by J. Diggins, St. Ann's Lane, London) + Directions for placing Plates 1 p. (v. blank) + pp. 1–279 + 24 coloured plates each bearing imprint, Pub. by R. Ackermann, London 1823.

1. Front. Dr Syntax setting out in search of a wife.
2. p. 10. Dr Syntax Soliloquising.
3. p. 32. Dr Syntax turn'd Nurse.
4. p. 84. The Banns Forbidden.
5. p. 95. Dr Syntax with a Blue Stocking Beauty.
6. p. 126. The Cellar Quartetto.
7. p. 136. Dr Syntax Presenting a Floral Offering.
8. p. 139. The Billiard Table.
9. p. 140. Misfortune at Tulip Hall.
10. p. 145. The Harvest Home.
11. p. 158. The Garden Trio.
12. p. 163. Dr Syntax at a Card Party.
13. p. 168. Dr Syntax Star Gazing.
14. p. 191. Dr Syntax in the wrong Lodging House.
15. p. 204. Dr Syntax received by the Maid instead of the Mistress.
16. p. 208. The Artists Room.
17. p. 218. Death of Punch.
18. p. 220. The Advertisement for a Wife.
19. p. 224. Dr Syntax & the Foundling.

Rowlandson's Miniature Syntax (*contd.*)

20. p. 233. The Result of Purchasing a Blind Horse.
21. p. 255. A Noble Hunting Party.
22. p. 263. Introduction to Courtship.
23. p. 276. Dr Syntax in Danger.
24. p. 277. Funeral of Dr. Syntax.
    p. 279. Coloured vignette as tailpiece.

Issued in boards with printed labels at 7s. a volume.   Fresh plates were re-engraved for this edition, one-third the size of the originals.   I have examined a copy in boards with 18 pages of advertisement at end of Vol. I, and 4 pages at end of Vol. III.

431 ROWLANDSON (T.)

Syntax Imitation

The Adventures of Doctor Comicus or the Frolicks of Fortune A Comic Satirical Poem for the Squeamish & the Queer (rule) In Twelve Cantos, by a Modern Syntax (rule) (4 line verse and 1 line verse) (the whole of the above within rococo woodcut border) London: Printed for B. Blake No 13, Bell Yard, Temple Bar.

Octavo. [1815]

COLLATION.—Frontispiece (Illman sculpt.) + Engraved title "Dr. Comicus or the Frolics of Fortune" (coloured vignette of Doctor riding up to a public house) Published by B. Blake, Bell Yard Temple Bar (v. blank) + Title as above (v. Printed by J. M'Gowan and Son Great Windmill Street) + pp. 1–269 + 13 plates.   The plates bear the imprint of Jacques & Wright Pater Noster Row.

1. Front. Dr Comicus resolves to travel   Illman sculpt.
2. Engraved Title with large vignette.
3. p. 29. Dr Comicus selling his Pills.
4. p. 42. The Doctor and his Wig
5. p. 56. Dr. C. The Parson Clerk & Sexton   Illman sculpt.
6. p. 73. Attacked by Robbers   Illman sculpt.
7. p. 78. The Ghost Scene.
8. p. 88. Drowning of Tip.
9. p. 100. Interview with the Cobbler   Illman sculp.
10. p. 104. Shaving the Doctor.
11. p. 132. Upset of the Night Coach.
12. p. 154. The Doctor and Attorney.
13. p. 166. Presenting a Rose.
14. p. 247. The Doctors Second Marriage.
15. p. 219. Dr C buying a Horse.

Issued in boards with printed label at £1 1s.   Size of uncut copies 8¾ × 5½ inches.
This is the first of many imitations of Dr. Syntax.   Another Edition was published in 1820 with only 12 coloured plates.

432 ROWLANDSON (T.)

Syntax Imitation.

Doctor Syntax in Paris or a Tour in search of the (Grotesque) (coloured vignette depicting a crowd before a stage, a flag with the letters Gro, and 6 players forming the letters tesque) A Humorous and Satirical Poem (2 line quotation from Ovid and 4 line quotation from Horace) London: Printed for W. Wright, 46, Fleet Street.

Octavo. 1820

Rowlandson's Syntax Imitation [1820] (*contd.*)

COLLATION.—Engraved title as above (v. blank) + Advertisement, Episode and Finale pp. iii–viii + pp. 1–318 + 18 coloured plates (including the title).

1. Front. Doctor Syntax reading his Tour.
2. Title as above.
3. p. 1. Doctor Syntax embarking at Dover.
4. p. 1. Doctor Syntax landing at Calais.
5. p. 45. Doctor Syntax on the Road to Paris.
6. p. 56. Doctor Syntax arrives at Paris.
7. p. 61. Doctor Syntax at the Decroteurs or Shoe-Blacks'.
8. p. 84. Doctor Syntax and the Female Tonsor.
9. p. 112. Doctor Syntax at the Opera.
10. p. 127. Doctor Syntax looking at lodgings.
11. p. 137. Doctor Syntax chatting with the Bar Maid—Cafe des Mille Colonnes.
12. p. 184. Doctor Syntax conducted to the Prefecture on a charge of Liberalism.
13. p. 198. Doctor Syntax discovered by his wife.
14. p. 206. Doctor Syntax producing his certificate of marriage to his hostess.
15. p. 210. Doctor Syntax and his wife, descending the Russian Mountains.
16. p. 259. Doctor Syntax alarmed at a domiciliary visit.
17. p. 309. Doctor Syntax and his Wife inspecting the Catacombs.
18. p. 315. Doctor Syntax and his wife making an Experiment in Pneumatics.

Issued in parts and on completion in boards, size 10 × 16¼ *inches. Imprint on last page of text reads, Printed by S. & R. Bentley Dorset Street, Fleet Street, London.*

433 ROWLANDSON (T.)

Syntax Imitation

The Tour of Doctor Prosody, in search of the Antique and Picturesque, through Scotland, the Hebrides, the Orkney and Shetland Isles; illustrated by Twenty Humourous Plates.

> **"Hear, Land o' Cakes, and brither Scots,**
> **Frae Maidenkirk to Johnny Groats,**
> **If there's a hole in a' your coats**
> **I rede you tent it.**
> **A chiel's amang you taking notes,**
> **And, faith, he'll prent it."—Burns.**

London: Mathew Iley, Somerset Street. Edinburgh: Bell and Bradfute, and W. Blackwood. Glasgow: W. Turnbull.

Octavo. 1821

COLLATION.—Title as above (v. London Shackell and Arrowsmith, Johnson's Court, Fleet Street). Advertisement to Reader 1 leaf + pp. 1–251 + 20 coloured plates.

1. Dr. Prosody arrives in the vicinity of Edinburgh.
2. Doctor Prosody discovers a curious relic of antiquity. Drawn & engraved by C. Williams.
3. Doctor Prosody entertained after manner ancients. Drawn & engraved by C. Williams.
4. Doctor Prosody tries his friends at Falls of Clyde. Drawn & engraved by C. Williams.
5. Doctor Prosody visits the Scotch Regalia. Drawn & engraved by C. Williams.
6. Doctor Prosody doing penance on drunken Island Loch Lomond. Drawn & engraved by C. Williams.
7. Doctor Prosody parading on Lochleven is challenged to name his chief. Drawn & engraved by C. Williams.
8. Doctor Prosody taken for a poacher in neighbourhood of Stirling. Drawn & engraved by C. Williams.
9. Doctor Prosody's disaster in Ossian's Hall, Dunkeld. Drawn & engraved by C. Williams.

Rowlandson's Doctor Prosody (*contd.*)

10. Doctor Prosody reproves the audacity of a Highland host.   Drawn & engraved by C. Williams.
11. Doctor Prosody in peril at Corryvreckan.   Drawn & engraved by W. Read.
12. Doctor Prosody visits a chieftain of Isle of Mull.   Drawn & engraved by C. Williams
13. Doctor Prosody proves the inconvenience of a timid companion at Staffa.   Drawn & engraved by W. Read.
14. Doctor Prosody fishing for pearls in the Isle of Sky.   Drawn & engraved by W. Read.
15. Doctor Prosody clears up the antiquities of Iona.   Drawn & engraved by C. Williams.
16. Doctor Prosody correcting his proof in printing office.   Drawn & engraved by W. Read.
17. Doctor Prosody meets a Highland Wedding on the Calidonian Canal.   Drawn & engraved by W. Read.
18. Doctor Prosody and the Smugglers in the Shetlands.   Drawn & engraved by W. Read.
19. Doctor Factobend's recantation in the Bird Basket, St. Kilda.   Drawn & engraved by W. Read.
20. Doctor Prosody attacked by Soland Fowl in the Orkneys.   Drawn and engraved by W. Read.

434 ROWLANDSON (T.)

Syntax Imitation

The Tour of Doctor Syntax through London, or the Pleasures and Miseries of the Metropolis.   A Poem (coloured vignette) London Published by J. Johnston, Cheapside

Octavo.   1820

COLLATION.—Engraved title as above (v. blank) + Preface 2 pp. (iii–iv) + List of Plates
1 p. (v. blank) + pp. 1–319 + 19 coloured plates (20 including Frontispiece and Engraved title).

1. Frontispiece.   The Revd. Doctor Syntax and his Spouse   London Published by J. Johnson, Cheapside   1820.
2.   Engraved Title as above with coloured vignette.
3. p.   9. Doctor Syntax setting out for London   Williams Det F.
4. p.   39. Doctor Syntax arriving in London.
5. p.   59. Doctor Syntax robbed in St. Giles's.
6. p.   62. Doctor Syntax behind the Scenes at the Opera.
7. p.   90. Doctor Syntax at a Masquerade.
8. p.   120. Doctor Syntax reading his play in the green room.
9. p.   127. Doctor Syntax in Hyde Park.
10. p.   148. Doctor Syntax at the Exhibition.
11. p.   165. Doctor Syntax going to Richmond in the Steam Boat.
12. p.   186. Doctor Syntax at Vauxhall Gardens.
13. p.   193. Doctor Syntax shoots London Bridge and pops overboard.
14. p.   207. Doctor Syntax at the London Institution.
15. p.   232. Doctor Syntax at the House of Commons.
16. p.   238. Doctor Syntax at a Gaming House.
17. p.   250. Doctor Syntax in St. Paul's Church Yard—Wet & Windy Day.
18. p.   253. Doctor Syntax inspecting the Bank.
19. p.   295. Doctor Syntax presented at Court.
20. p.   318. Doctor Syntax witnessing the fate of his play.

*Issued in eight parts in printed paper wrappers at 2s. 6d. per part, with 2 coloured plates per
part.   Part II bears an advertisement promising to give 3 plates in Part III, and advertises the
New Bon Ton Magazine.   Part III bears a slip note postponing the promised extra plate to
Part IV and promising an extra plate for Part VI, and mentions the indisposition of one of the
artists engaged on the plates, dated May 1819.   The two extra plates to make up the correct number
are found in Parts V and VI.   Size of Parts 10 × 6⅜ inches.*

*On the completion of the parts the book was issued in boards.   Both Rowlandson and I. R.
Cruikshank are credited with the designs for the plates, the balance of opinion favouring Cruikshank*

Rowlandson's Syntax Imitation [1820] (*contd.*)

but according to the advertisement above more than one artist was employed, or at least a different engraver to the artist.

A Third Edition was issued in 1820, identical with the above with the exception that the words Third Edition were printed immediately above the imprint.

435 Tour of Dr Syntax through London, 1820

COLLATION OF PARTS.—Issued in 8 parts, paper wrappers at 2*s.* 6*d.* per part. Printed title on p. 1 of each wrapper, within an Etruscan border, a note, To The Public, taking the place of the vignette. London: Published by J. Johnston, Cheapside; Sherwood, Neely and Jones, Paternoster Row; Simpkin and Marshall, Stationer's Court; and William Clarke, Royal Exchange; R. Millikin, Dublin; and sold by all booksellers. W. Shackett, Printer, Johnson's-court, Fleet Street, London.

Part   I. pp. 1–40, plates 3 & 4. Three-page insert of advts., Pilgrimage to the Holy Land &c., Wrappers, p. 2 advt. Johnny Newcombe in the Navy &c., p. 3 Adventures of a Post Captain &c., p. 4 New Bon Ton Magazine.

,,   II. pp. 41–80, plates 4 & 6, Wrappers, p. 2 Advts. New Bon Ton Magazine, p. 3 Adventures of a Post Captain &c., p. 4 Johnny Newcome in Navy &c.

,,   III. pp. 81–120, plates 7 & 8, Wrappers, p. 2 advt. Johnny Newcome in Navy, p. 3 Adventures of a Post Captain, p. 4 Bon Ton Magazine.

,,   IV. pp. 121–160, plates 9 & 10, & 12, Wrappers, p. 2 advt. Johnny Newcome, p. 3 Adventures of Post Captain &c., p. 4 New Bon Ton Magazine.

,,   V. pp. 161–200, plates 11 & 14, Wrappers, p. 2 blank, p. 3 blank, p. 4 Bon Ton Magazine.

,,   VI. pp. 201–240, plates 13, 17, & 18, Wrappers, p. 2 advt. New Bon Ton Magazine, p. 3 Adventures of a Post Captain, p. 4 Johnny Newcome.

,,   VII. pp. 241–280, plates 15 & 16, Wrappers, p. 2 New Bon Ton Magazine, p. 3 Adventures of a Post Captain, p. 4 Johnny Newcome.

,,   VIII. pp. 281–319, +Preface pp. iii–iv + List of Plates 1 p. + Frontispiece + Engraved Title + Plates 19 & 20, Wrappers, p. 2 New Bon Ton Magazine, p. 3 Adventures of a Post Captain, p. 4 Johnny Newcome.

In above copy, formerly in my possession, Parts I and II, over-printed Third Edition above Etruscan border, Parts 3, 4, 5, 6 and 7. Second Edition, Part 8, unmarked.

436 ROWLANDSON (T.)

The Vicar of Wakefield; a Tale by Doctor Goldsmith. (swelled rule) Illustrated with Twenty-four Designs, by Thomas Rowlandson. (two line rule) Sperate, miseri, cavete, felices. (two line rule) London: Published by R. Ackermann, at the Repository of Arts, 101 Strand. Printed by W. Clowes, Northumberland Court (rule).

Octavo.   1817

COLLATION.—Title as above (v. blank) + Advertisement 1 p. (v. blank) + Memoirs of Goldsmith, pp. 5–8 + Text pp. 1–254 + 24 coloured aquatint plates.

Plates bear imprint, London Published May 1st 1817, at R. Ackermanns, Repository of Arts, 101 Strand.

1. Front. The Vicar of Wakefield. A character eminently calculated to inculcate benevolence, humanity, patience in sufferings, and reliance on Providence.	2. p. 9.	The Social Evening.
	3. p. 15.	The Departure from Wakefield.
	4. p. 21.	Sophia rescued from the water.
	5. *ibd.*	The Welcome.
	6. p. 27.	The Esquire's Intrusion.

Rowlandson's Vicar of Wakefield (*contd.*)

7. p. 33. Mr. Burchells first visit.
8. p. 51. The Dance.
9. p. 57. Fortune Telling.
10. p. 61. The Vicar's Family on their Road to Church.
11. p. 63. Hunting the Slipper.
12. p. 73. The Gross of Green Spectacles.
13. p. 81. The Vicar selling his horse.
14. p. 97. The Family Picture.
15. p. 117. The Vicar in Company with Strolling Players.

16. p. 127. The Surprise.
17. p. 129. The Stage.
18. p. 141. Attendance on a Nobleman.
19. p. 147. A Connoisseur.
20. p. 155. The Scold with News of Oliver.
21. p. 173. The Fair Penitent.
22. p. 187. Domestic Arrangement in Prison.
23. p. 189. The Vicar Preaching to the Prisoners.
24. p. 251. The Weddings.

Issued in boards. Re-issued 1823 with the same plates.

437 ROWLANDSON (T.)

The World in Miniature, consisting of a Group of Figures for the Illustration of Landscape, Scenery (rule) Drawn and Etched by T. Rowlandson (rule) London Published by R. Ackermann, 101 Strand: Sold by all Respectable Book and Printsellers in the United Kingdom (rule) 1817. L. Harrison, Printer, 733 Strand.

Quarto. 1817

COLLATION.—Title as above (v. blank) + 40 coloured plates, numbered 1–40 without titles, each bearing Ackermann's imprint.

438 RUTLAND

Journal of a Trip to Paris by the Duke and Duchess of Rutland. July MDCCCXIV

Quarto. 1825

COLLATION.—Half-title "Journal of a Trip to Paris" (v. printed by T. Bensley, Bolt Court, Fleet Street, London.) + Title as above (v. Printed by T. Bensley, Bolt Court, Fleet Street, London.) + pp. 1–30 + 3 coloured plates + Title "Journal of a short trip to Paris during the Summer of MDCCCXV" + pp. 1–59.

1. p. 6. On the Lower Road from Rouen to Paris.
2. p. 7. On the Upper Road from Rouen to Paris.
3. p. 29. Between Borduin and Ecousi.

439 ST. CLAIR (Major T.)

"A Series of views of the Principal Occurrences of the Campaigns in Spain and Portugal."

Published in London 1812–1815 by C. Turner, Colnaghi etc.

1. "View of the Fording of the River Mondego by the Allied Army on the 21st Sept. 1810."
2. "View of the Pass of the Tagus at Villa Velha into the Alemtejo, by the Allied Army, on the 20th May 1811."
3. "Battle of Fuentes D'Onor, taken from the right of the position occupied by the 1st, 3rd and 7th Divisions on the 5th May, 1811."

St. Clair's Campaigns in Spain and Portugal (*contd.*)

4. "Badajos During the Siege of June 1811. Shewing the working parties of the 3rd Division British and General Hamilton's Portuguese Division opening the first parallel on the left bank of the Guadiana and the Batteries erected by the 7th Division on the right of the River against Fort St. Christopher."
5. "Troops Bevouack'd near the Village of Villa Velha, on the Evening of the 19th of May, 1811. Shewing the various Occupations of an Encampment."
6. "A View of the Sierra de Busaco at St. Antonio de Cantaro, shewing the attack by Marshal Reigniers upon that part of the Position occupied by the 3rd Division British and Portuguese under Lt. Genl. Sir Thomas Picton, 27th Sept. 1810. The 88th British and 8th Portuguese Regts in the act of engaging with the enemy."
7. "The Village of Pombal in flames, as evacuated by the French Army under Marshal Massena, and the advance of the Allied Army on the morning of the 11th of March, 1811; Lord Wellington in person directing the movement."
8. "City of Coimbra."
9. "Subugal on the River Coa."
10. "A distant view of Ciudad Rodrigo, taken from the Oak-Wood, near the Village of Espelja, with a Troop of Spanish Guerillas."
11. "Serra de Estrella or de Neve. The March of Baggage following the Army—May 16th 1811."
12. "Pena Macor, an ancient Fortress on the Frontier of Portugal. Portuguese Troops on the march to Castello Branco, 18th March, 1811."

A rare work, not personally examined by me, the above being a list of the plates.

440 SALT (Henry)

To Richard Marquis Wellesley K. St. P. & K.C. late Governor General of the British Possessions and Captain General of the British Forces serving in the East Indies These Twenty Four Views taken in St. Helena, the Cape, India, Ceylon, Abyssinia & Egypt, are by Permission most humbly dedicated by his Grateful & most devoted humble servant Henry Salt (the above on architectural slab with ruins and Landscape background printed in sepia, or coloured) Engraved from the Drawings of Henry Salt by & under the inspection of Robt. Havell Published May 1 1809 by William Miller Albemarle Street London.

Oblong Folio. 1809

COLLATION.—Title Dedication as above (v. blank) + 24 coloured aquatint plates.

Each plate is numbered and marked, "Drawn by Henry Salt" Published as the Act Directs, by William Miller, Albemarle Street May 1st 1809 (with the exception of plate xx which is dated Jany. 1 1809 and plate xii dated May 1st 1808 this last a misprint?)

1. Sandy Bay Valley in the Island of St. Helena Engraved by D. Havell.
2. (misnumbered iii) A View near the Roode Sand Pass at the Cape of Good Hope Engraved by I. Bluck.
3. Calcutta Engraved by D. Havell.
4. A View within the Fort at Monghyr Engraved by D. Havell.
5. (misnumbered vi) Mosque at Lucknow Engraved by I. Hill.
6. A View at Lucknow Engraved by D. Havell.
7. Ruins of the Fort at Juanpore on the River Goomtee Engraved by I. Havell.
8. View near Point de Galle, Ceylon Engraved by D. Havell.
9. Pagoda at Ramisseram Engraved by I. Bluck.
10. Pagoda at Tanjore Engraved by I. Bluck.
11. (misprinted xii) Pagodas at Trinchicunum Engraved by D. Havell.
12. Riacotta in the Baramahal Engraved by D. Havell.
13. Poonah Engraved by D. Havell.
14. Ancient Excavations at Carli Engraved by D. Havell.

Salt's St. Helena, Cape, etc. (*contd.*)

15. (misprinted xvii) The Town of Dixan in Abyssinia Engraved by D. Havell.
16. (misprinted xviii) The Town of Abha in Abyssinia Engraved by I. Bluck.
17. View near the Village of Asceriah, in Abyssinia Engraved by D. Havell.
18. Muculla in Abyssinia Engraved by D. Havell.
19. The Pass of Atbara in Abyssinia Engraved by D. Havell.
20. The Obelisk at Axum Engraved by D. Havell.
21. The Mountains of Samayut Engraved by D. Havell.
22. The Vale of Calaat Engraved by D. Havell.
23. View of Grand Cairo Engraved by D. Havell.
24. The Pyramids at Cairo Engraved by D. Havell.

A text exists as follows: "Twenty-Four Views, in St. Helena, the Cape, India, Ceylon, the Red Sea, Abyssinia, and Egypt. From Drawings, by Henry Salt, Esq. London: (thin and thick rule) Published by Thomas M'Lean, 26, Haymarket. (rule) 1822". Collation Title as above + List of Plates 1 leaf + 24 leaves of Text, i.e. 1 leaf printed on 1 side only of description to each plate. This text is not important and the work is usually to be found without it.

441 SAMS (W.)

Fashion and Folly or the Buck's Pilgrimage. London: Published 1822 by William Sams, Royal Library, 1 St James's Street.

Oblong Octavo.   1822

COLLATION.—Engraved pictured title with a clown holding a sheet bearing the title, a Buck either side, with various objects in foreground, depicting the amusements of The Capitol, and 24 plates.

Each plate with two 4 line verses underneath.

1. Fired with the Folly of his London Friend.
2. High raised in telegraphic tandem state.
3. Lo! Dashalls uncouth importation sits.
4. This recommendatory work at end.
5. Next Tattersalls the Tutor's care invites.
   (Another issue same plate with 3, 8 line verses beneath commencing, He here finds out what 'tis to have a friend. watermark 1828.)
6. Blessed with progressive love, and bosom sear.
   (Another issue of this plate with 7 line verse and 2, 14 line verses commencing, Now to the Park the Nimrod hies.)
7. Next to the Drama; where its patron draws.
8. Developed True to Lubin's wondering mind.
9. Won by the thirst of Knowledge, not of gin.
10. Protected by the name of Porson still.
11. Scot free they do the Jarvis for a spree.
12. Mid this assertion of the Fancy's laws.
13. The Messieurs Dogberry & Verges tribe.
14. Now the par nobile are placed before.
15. The exhibition next to Lubins eyes.
16. Here revel They who come the knowing rig.
17. Oh sweet variety of Life! how tame.
18. Dashall and Lubin, at a masquerade.
19. It seems as if some Argosy had thrown.
20. Oh pleasure thou'rt indeed a pleasant thing.
21. Here are they come at last; let laughter here.
22. Sic transit gloria mundi, some one saith.
23. Lubin and Dashall and their light career.
24. How far more free is individual man.

442 SAMS (W.)

Studies from the Stage, or the Vicissitudes of Life London Pubd. by W. Sams, 1 St. James Street.

Oblong Quarto.   [1823]

COLLATION.—Pictured title with lettering on a draped cloth (v. blank) + 20 coloured plates, each plate consisting of several groups of figures and each bearing Sams' imprint.

443 SAMS (W.)

A Tour through Paris, illustrated with Twenty-one coloured plates, accompanied with descriptive letter-press. (thin and thick rule) London: Published by William Sams, St. James's Street.

Folio.   [1822]

COLLATION.—Title as above (v. blank) + 21 coloured plates each with 1 leaf of Text (including front.) + 1 blank leaf [to complete sign. L].

Each plate marked London, Published by W. Sams, 1 St. James's Street 1822 [for the 1st 16 plates, 1824 for last 5 plates].

1. Distribution of Wine on the Morning of St. Louis.
2. The Voitures of Versailles.
3. The Blind Man of the Bridge of Arts.
4. Dancers on Stilts, in the Champs-Elysèes.
5. Office of Nurses.
6. Porters and Fishwomen, revelling round the Statue of Henry IV.
7. Interior of a Swimming School.
8. Parisians reading the Public Prints in the Garden of the Tuilleries.
9. The Catacombs.
10. The Chamber of Deputies.
11. Parisian Street Characters.
12. Itinerants on the Boulevards.
13. Military Degradation in the Place Vendome.
14. The Juggler of the Chateau d'Eau.
15. La Morgue.
16. The Flower Market.
17. The Meridien of the Palais Royal.
18. The Charcoal Porters.
19. Procession of the Fete-Dieu Parish Saint Germain L'Auxenois.
20. A Corps de Garde of the Garde Nationale.
21. Promenade of Her Serene Highness the Duchess of Berri, and the Younger Branches of the Royal Family of France, on the Terrace of the Tuileries.

444   Another Edition, Title as before (with the exception of word Seventeen instead of Twenty-one plates) v. blank + Contents 1 p. (v. blank) + pp. 5–55 + 17 plates only, plates 9, 11, 12 & 15 being omitted.   Otherwise the plates are as in preceding edition.

445 SAUVAN (M.)

Picturesque Tour of the Seine, from Paris to the Sea: with Particulars Historical and Descriptive (rule) By M. Sauvan. (coloured vignette Chateau de Rosny—Residence of the Dutchess de Berry) illustrated with Twenty-Four Highly Finished and coloured Engravings, from Drawings by A. Pugin and J. Gendall; And accompanied by a Map. (rule) London: Published by R. Ackermann, 101, Strand, Printed by L. Harrison, 373, Strand (rule).

Quarto.   1821

COLLATION.—Title as above (v. blank) + Dedication to Louis XVIII 1 p. (v. blank) + Contents 1 p. (v. List of Plates) + Preface 2 pp. (v–vi) + List of Subscribers 2 pp. (vii–viii) + pp. 1–177 + map + 24 coloured aquatint plates.

All plates bear "London Pubd. [date] at 101 Strand for R. Ackermann Views on the Seine."

Sauvan's Seine (*contd.*)

1. Frontispiece. Le Louvre   A. Pugin delt.   T. Sutherland sculpt.   March 1 1821.
2. p.   9. Pont Notre Dame   Drawn by J. Gendall from a Sketch by A. Pugin   T. Sutherland sculpt. Jany. 1 1821.
3. p. 10. Notre Dame   J. Gendall delt. from a sketch by A. Pugin   D. Havell sculpt.   Feby. 1 1821.
4. p. 63. St Cloud   J. Gendall delt.   Dl. Havell sculpt.   July 1 1821.
5. p. 73. St Denis   J. Gendall delt.   T. Sutherland sculpt.   Feby 1 1821.
6. p. 89. St Germain   J. Gendall delt.   D Havell sculpt.   July 1 1821.
7. p. 94. Poissy   J. Gendall delt.   T. Sutherland sculpt.   Jany. 1 1821.
8. p. 97. Triel   J. Gendall delt.   T. Sutherland sculpt.   May 1 1821.
9. p. 98. Meulan   J. Gendall delt.   T. Sutherland sculpt.   July 1 1821.
10. p. 100. Mantes   J. Gendall delt.   T. Sutherland sculpt.   March 1821.
11. p. 105. Roboise   J. Gendall delt.   D. Havell sculpt.   April 1 1821.
12. p. 106. La Roche [Guyon]   J. Gendall delt.   T. Sutherland sculpt.   May 1 1821.
13. p. 108. Vernon   J. Gendall delt.   T. Sutherland sculpt.   March 1 1821.
14. p. 118. Andely [Chateau Gaillard]   J. Gendall delt.   T. Sutherland sculpt.   May 1 1821.
15. p. 120. Pont de l'Arche   J. Gendall delt.   T. Sutherland sculpt.   April 1 1821.
16. p. 122. Elbeuf   J. Gendall delt.   D. Havell sculpt.   April 1 1821.
17. p. 126. Rouen   J. Gendall delt.   T. Sutherland sculpt.   Jany. 1 1821.
18. p. 151. La Bouille   J. Gendall delt.   D. Havell sculpt.   July 1 1821.
19. p. 154. Jumiège   J. Gendall delt.   T. Sutherland sculpt.   Feby. 1 1821.
20. p. 160. Caudebec   J. Gendall delt.   T. Sutherland sculpt.   March 1 1821.
21. p. 165. Quillebeuf   J. Gendall delt.   T. Sutherland sculpt.   May 1 1821.
22. p. 169. Mouth of the Seine as seen from the Heights of Honfleur   J. Gendall delt.   T. Sutherland sculpt.   Jan. 1 1821.
23. p. 170. Honfleur [from Mont Joli]   J. Gendall delt.   T. Sutherland sculpt.   April 1821.
24. p. 172. Havre   J. Gendall delt.   T. Sutherland sculpt.   Feby. 1 1821.
    p. 174. Map of the course of the Seine from Paris to the Sea.
    p. 177. Coloured vignette at foot of page.

Issued in 6 monthly parts in paper wrappers and on completion in elephant quarto in boards at 4 guineas, 50 copies were printed on large paper (17 × 13 inches). Large-paper copies have remarkably brilliant impressions of the plates and are greatly superior to small-paper copies. The watermark being generally J. Whatman 1820. Later issues of the small paper were issued in red cloth gilt.

446 SCHOBERL (F.)

Picturesque Tour from Geneva to Milan, by Way of the Simplon: illustrated with Thirty Six Coloured Views of the most striking scenes and of the principal works belonging to the new road constructed over that mountain, engraved from designs by J. and J. Lory, of Neufchatel; and accompanied with particulars Historical and Descriptive by Frederic Schoberl (thin and thick rule) London: Published by R. A. Ackermann, at his Repository of Arts, and sold by all the Booksellers in the United Kingdom (ornamental rule).

Imperial Octavo.   1820

COLLATION.—Plan of the Road over the Simplon to face title + Title as above (v. Printed by J. Diggins, St. Ann's Lane, London) + Preface 3 ll. + pp. 1–136 + List of Plates 1 leaf + Prospectus of Johnny Quae Genus + Advertisements of Books by Ackermann 2 ll. + 36 coloured aquatints all bearing Ackermann's imprint dated 1820.

1. p.   1. Lake of Geneva.
2. p. 18. Banks of the Lake of Geneva near St Gingouph.
3. p. 20. Extremity of the Lake of Geneva and the Entrance of the Rhone near Boveret.

Schoberl's Tour (*contd.*)

4. p. 26. The Bridge of St Maurice.
5. p. 40. Waterfall of Pissevache.
6. p. 42. West View of Sion.
7. p. 50. East View of Sion.
8. p. 51. Brieg.
9. p. 61. Gallery and Bridge of the Ganther.
10. p. 67. View on Quitting the Gallery of Schalbet (not from the entrance as inscibed on the plate).
11. p. 68. Gallery of Schalbet from Italian side.
12. p. 70. Gallery of Glaciers.
13. p. 72. Monastery of the Simplon & the Rosboden (not Mount Rosa as on plate).
14. p. 74. Village of Simplon.
15. p. 76. View of the exterior Gallery of Algaby.
16. p. 78. View of Interior of Gallery of Algaby.
17. p. 80. Ponte Alto, or Alto Bridge.
18. p. 82. New Road near the Grand Gallery.
19. p. 84. Interior of the Grand Gallery.
20. p. 86. Entrance of the Grand Gallery towards Italy.
21. p. 88. View near Gondo.
22. p. 91. Gallery of Isella or Issel.
23. p. 93. Entrance to the Valley of Dovedro.
24. p. 95. Bridge of Cherasca.
25. p. 97. Entrance to Gallery of Crevola, or Last Gallery.
26. p. 99. Bridge of Crevola & Valley of Domo D'ossola.
27. p. 105. Bridge of Crevola.
28. p. 107. Villa.
29. p. 109. Bridge of Baveno & Isola Madre.
30. p. 112. Lago Maggiore and Borromean Islands.
31. p. 116. Isola Bella or the Beautiful Island.
32. p. 118. Isola Bella taken from Stressa.
33. p. 121. Arona.
34. p. 125. Sesto.
35. p. 127. Pliniana and Lake of Como.
36. p. 131. Milan.

Issued in ¼ leather with board sides at £2 12s. 6d. Care should be taken to see that all the plates are dated 1820 as the book was issued later in red brown cloth with the title still dated 1820 but the plates of later dates, and the impressions of these later issues are considerably inferior to the originals. This work first appeared in Ackermann's Repository of 1818–20.

447 SCHOMBURGK (Robert H.)

Twelve Views in the Interior of Guiana: from drawings executed by Mr. Charles Bentley, after Sketches taken during the Expedition carried on in the years 1835 to 1839, under the direction of the Royal Geographical Society of London, and aided by Her Majesty's Government. With Descriptive Letter-press, by Robert H. Schomburgk, Esq. Accompanied by Illustrations on Wood. London: Ackermann and Co. 96, Strand

Folio.   1841

COLLATION.—Title as above (v. Whitehead and Co. Printers, 76 Fleet Street, London.) + Dedication to Duke of Devonshire 1 leaf (v. blank) + List of Subscribers 1 leaf + Map 1 leaf + Preface 1 leaf + pp. 1–38 + 13 coloured plates including frontispiece. Each plate bears imprint "London Published by Ackermann & Co. 96 Strand 3rd Augt. 1840" and "Drawn from the Original Sketch by Charles Bentley."

Schomburgk's Guiana (*contd.*)

1. Frontispiece "Views in the Interior of Guiana" (within composite picture) On stone by M. Gauci Printed by P. Gauci 9, North Crest, Bedfd. Sqr.
2. p. 3. The Comuti or Taquiare Rock, on the River Essequibo On stone by George Barnard Printed by C. Hullmandel.
3. p. 5. Ataraipu or the Devil's Rock On Stone by Coke Smith Printed by C. Hullmandel.
4. p. 7. Pirara and Lake Amucu The Site of El Dorado On stone by George Barnard Printed by C. Hullmandel.
5. p. 11. Pure-Piapa On Stone by P. Gauci Printed by P. Gauci.
6. p. 13. Roraima A Remarkable Range of Sandstone Mountains in Guiana On stone by George Barnard Printed by C. Hullmandel.
7. p. 17. Purumama The Great Cataract of the River Parima On stone by George Barnard.
8. p. 19. Junction of the Kundanama with the Paramu On stone by George Barnard Printed by C. Hullmandel.
9. p. 21. Esmeralda, on the Orinoco Site of a Spanish Mission On stone by P. Gauci Printed by P. Gauci.
10. p. 23. Brazilian Fort St. Gabriel on the Rio Negro On Stone by George Barnard Printed by C. Hullmandel.
11. p. 27. Christmas Cataract On the River Berbice On stone by P. Gauci Printed by P. Gauci.
12. p. 33. Watu Ticaba a Wapisiana Village On stone by George Barnard Printed by C. Hullmandel.
13. p. 34. Caribi Village Anai Near the River Rupununi On stone by Coke Smith Printed by C. Hullmandel.

448 SEGARD & TESTARD

Picturesque Views of Public Edifices in Paris (rule) By Messrs. Segard and Testard. Aquatinted in Imitation of the Drawings, by Mr. Rosenberg (rule) London: (thin and thick rule) Printed by J. Moyes, Greville Street; for Gale, Curtis, and Fenner, Paternoster-Row; and Samuel Leigh, in the Strand, (small swelled rule).

Quarto.   1814

COLLATION.—Half-title "Picturesque Views of Public Edifices in Paris" (v. blank) + Title as above (v. blank) + Advertisement 2 pp. (5–6) + Contents (i.e. List of Plates) 1 p. (v. blank) + pp. 1–40 + 20 coloured plates [small circular views].

1. Front. L'Interieur de Notre Dame [not called for in List of Contents].
2. p. 1. Les Tuileries.
3. p. 5. Palais de Bourbon.
4. p. 7. Le Louvre.
5. p. 9. Palais Royal.
6. p. 11. Palais du Luxembourg.
7. p. 13. Pantheon.
8. p. 15. Hotel des Monnoies.
9. p. 17. L'Hotel des Invalides.
10. p. 19. L'Ecole de Chirurgie.
11. p. 21. Halle au Bleds.
12. p. 23. Theatre de l'Ambigu-Comique.
13. p. 24. The Opera.
14. p. 26. Notre Dame.
15. p. 31. L'Eglise de St Jacques, at de St Philippe de Roule.
16. p. 33. St Sulpice.
17. p. 35. L'Eglise de St. Chaumont.
18. p. 36. La Porte St. Martin.
19. p. 38. La Porte St Bernard.
20. p. 39. La Porte St Antoine.

Issued in boards with paper label at 2 guineas.

Selection of Facsimiles of Water Colour Drawings. See under Bowyer (R.).

449 SEMPLE (Miss)

The Costume of the Netherlands, Displayed in Thirty Coloured Engravings after Drawings from Nature by Miss Semple with Descriptions in English and French (coloured

Semple's Costume of the Netherlands (*contd.*)

vignette) London: Published March 1st 1817 at Ackermann's Repository of Arts, 101 Strand   W. Bartlett sculpt.

Small Folio.   1817

COLLATION.—Half-title " Costume of the Netherlands after drawings made from nature, by Miss Semple" (v. London Printed by Schulze and Dean, 13 Poland Street) + Title as above (v. blank) + Note 1 p. (v. blank) + Text pp. 1–30 (in English & French) + 30 coloured aquatint plates each plate with imprint, Published Jany. 1 1817, at R. Ackermann's 101 Strand (except plates 4 and 7 dated March 1).

    1. p.   1. Woman & Boy of the neighbourhood of Amsterdam.
    2. p.   2. Woman & Children of Amsterdam.
    3. p.   3. Lady of Rotterdam.
    4. p.   4. Woman and little Girl.
    5. p.   5. Children going to School.
    6. p.   6. Maidservant of Rotterdam.
    7. p.   7. Boy selling Flowers in the Streets of Rotterdam.
    8. p.   8. Gardiners' Wife of Rotterdam.
    9. p.   9. Milkman of Rotterdam.
   10. p. 10. Woman of the neighbourhood of Rotterdam.
   11. p. 11. Girl selling matches in the Streets of Rotterdam.
   12. p. 12. Group at the Fair at Rotterdam.
   13. p. 13. Maid servant washing the pavement.
   14. p. 14. Woman of Broeck.
   15. p. 15. Women of Williamstadt.
   16. p. 16. Man & Woman of North Holland.
   17. p. 17. Woman of North Holland.
   18. p. 18. Woman & Child of Friesland.
   19. p. 19. Woman of Hinlopen.
   20. p. 20. A Zealander.
   21. p. 21. Woman of the neighbourhood of Antwerp.
   22. p. 22. Woman of Brabant.
   23. p. 23. Girl from the neighbourhood of Mons.
   24. p. 24. Labourer near Valenciennes.
   25. p. 25. Girl of the neighbourhood of Valenciennes.
   26. p. 26. Shepherd near Valenciennes.
   27. p. 27. Milk Woman of Valenciennes.
   28. p. 28. Woman of Valenciennes.
   29. p. 29. Country woman going to Valenciennes.
   30. p. 30. Wife of the Keeper of the Burying Ground near Valenciennes.

450 SERRES (Dominic)

Set of 6 plates of Naval Costume.   Nov. 1777.

   1. An Admiral with a first rate Man of War.
   2. A Post Captain with a Frigate and Ships of the Line.
   3. A Lieutenant with a Cutter.
   4. A Master and Commander with a Sloop of War.
   5. A Midshipman with a Long Boat.
   6. A Seaman with a Man of War's Barge.

Each plate has imprint, Published Nov. 1777.   According to Act of Parliament by D. Serres in Warwick Street, Golden Square.

451 SEYMOUR (R.)

A Search after the "Comfortable" being the adventures of a little Gentleman of small fortune (thick and thin rule) quotation 1 line (thin and thick rule) London: Published by Thomas M'Lean, 26 Haymarket.

Oblong Folio. 1829

COLLATION.—Title as above on wrapper. A series of 6 plates.

1. Search after the "Comfortable."
2. Rural Retirement.
3. Arts & Sciences.
4. Travelling. Pl. 1.
5. Travelling.
6. Courtship.

Each plate includes several small designs. Plate 3 includes an illustration of Ballooning.

452 SHEPHEARD (G.) and BRIGHTY (G. M.)

Vignette Illustrations of Rural and Domestic Scenery (thick and thin rule) By G. Shepheard and G. M. Brighty. (swelled rule) Dedicated, with permission, to the Marchioness of Abercorn. (thick and thin rule) London: Published by G. Shepheard, 17 Great Ormond Street, Queens Square; and G. M. Brighty, 46 Red Lion Street, Red Lion Square. (rule) 1814. (the above within Etruscan border, below) Printed by J. Moyes, Greville Street, Hatton Garden, London.

Oblong Folio. 1814–16

COLLATION.—Engraved Dedication dated Jan. 1st 1814 with coloured vignette, and 16 coloured plates, each plate with 1 leaf of Text. Each plate marked, G. Shepheard, delt. G. M. Brighty, sculpt.

Part I.	I. The Shepherd.	Jan. 1st 1814.
,,	II. The Gleaner.	,, ,,
,,	III. The Fisherman	,, ,,
,,	IV. The Cottage Door	,, ,,
Part II.	V. The Tired Soldier	July 1st 1814
,,	VI. The Village Maid	,, ,,
,,	VII. The Cabin Boy	,, ,,
,,	VIII. The Village Matron	,, ,,
Part III.	IX. The Reapers	Jan. 1st 1815.
,,	X. Patty	,, ,,
,,	XI. The Woodman	,, ,,
,,	XII. Crazy Kate	,, ,,
Part IV.	XIII. The Caledonian Shepherd	Jan. 1st 1816.
,,	XIV. Lavinia	,, ,,
,,	XV. Marian	,, ,,
,,	XVI. Crossing the Brook.	,, ,,

The work was originally advertised in 6 parts, at 1½ guineas, with 50 copies proof impressions, at 2 guineas. Only 4 parts were however issued. Dr Jeffery has a copy in Proof State, signed by Shepheard, with part IV corrected in penhand to be completed in IV parts.

453 Sketches of Portuguese Life, Manners Costume, and Character. Illustrated by Twenty Coloured Plates. (rule) By A.P.D.G. (rule) London: Printed for Geo. B. Whittaker, Ave Maria Lane. (rule).

Octavo. 1826

Sketches of Portuguese Life, etc. (*contd.*)

COLLATION.—Half-title "Sketches of Portuguese Life" (v. blank) + Title as overleaf (v. London Printed by R. Gilbert, St. John's Square) + Introduction pp. v–xi (p. xii blank) + Contents xiii–xxv (xxvi blank) + Directions to Binder 1 p. (v. blank) + Sub-title Chapter I etc. + pp. 3–364 + 1 sheet of music + 20 coloured plates.

I.	Front or p. 3.	Street scene in Lisbon.
II.	p. 31.	Landing place at Belem.
III.	p. 36.	Straw Boat unloading, Black women emptying their pots.
IV.	p. 64.	Bathing in the Tagus.
V.	p. 108.	Day of All Souls, in the Convent of St Joao de Deos.
VI.	p. 138.	Procession of the Senor dos Passos da Graca.
VII.	p. 144.	St Francisco, in the Procession of St Antonio.
VIII.	p. 155.	A Lisbon Chaise (sege).
IX.	p. 175.	Court Day at Rio.
X.	p. 180.	Party at Rio de Janeiro. A Castrate singing.
	p. 220.	Vedegals Modhina (music sheet).
XI.	p. 242.	An Interment.
XII.	p. 254.	Military Execution.
XIII.	p. 264.	Portuguese Dragoons.
XIV.	p. 285.	Begging for the Festival of N.S. Atalata.
XV.	p. 247.	Slave Shop at Rio, a Minas Merchant bargaining.
XVI.	p. 317.	A Saloia retailing fruit.
XVII.	p. 320.	Going Home from the Lisbon Market.
XVIII.	p. 340.	Province of Beija. Inhabitants of Foz de Aronce.
XIX.	p. 349.	Execution of the Conspirators. Plate I.
XX.	p. 358.	Execution of the Conspirators. Plate II.

454 SMIRKE (Miss)

[A Series of Six coloured aquatints of Views in Wales.]

Oblong Folio.

No title.   Issued in wrappers.   6 plates all marked, Drawn by Miss Smirke.   Pub by R. Bowyer   87 Pall Mall, as under

Valle Crucis Abbey Denbighshire.   Engraved J. Harraden.
View near Caernarvon.   Engraved by J. Harraden.
Pont Aberglasslyn.   Engraved by W. Pickett.
Carnarvon Castle.   Engraved by W. Pickett.
Bethgellert Bridge, Carnarvonshire.   Engraved by W. Pickett.
Conway Castle.   Engraved W. Pickett.

455 SMITH (C. H.)

Ancient Costume of England, from the eighth to the sixteenth century; after the designs of Charles Hamilton Smith, Esq. to be executed in aquatinta by Mr. J. A. Atkinson and Mr. J. Hill.   Dedicated, by permission, to His Royal Highness the Prince Regent (swelled rule) London: Printed by W. Bulmer and Co.   Cleveland-Row, for Messrs Colnaghi and Co.   Cockspur-Street

Folio.   1812

COLLATION.—Title as above within patterned border (v. blank) + Dedication 1 p. (v.

Smith's Costume of England (*contd.*)

blank) + coloured plates each with 1 leaf of Text.   Most plates marked, C. H. S. delt.   Etched by J. A. Atkinson and bearing Colnaghi's imprint.

Anglo Saxon King of the Eighth Century   Aquatinted by Hill   July 1 1813.
Anglo Saxon Woman of VIII Century   Aquatinted by Hill   Sept. 1 1812.
Anglo Saxon Lady of the IX Century   Aquatinted by Hill   Oct. 1 1812.
Costume of a Cambrian Prince   Aquatinted by Hill   Mar. 1 1813.
Habit of a Bishop of the 10th Century   Aquatinted by J. Hill   May 10 1812.
King Edgar with an Anglo Saxon Youth of Distinction   J. Merigot sculp.   June 4 1811.
Anglo Saxon Military Chief Trumpeter and Warriors.   Aquatinted by J. Havell   April 1 1812.
Anglo Danish Warriors.   Aquatinted by Hill   Oct. 1 1812.
Ships of William the Conqueror   Aquatinted by Merigot   Augt. 1811.
Richard 1st King of England   Aquatinted by J. Merigot   August 1811.
Sir Hugh Bardolf   J. Merigot sculpt.   June 4 1811.
Alberic de Vere 2nd Earl of Oxford   Aquatinted by J. Hill   April 1 1812.
Costume of a Young Nobleman of the reign of King Henry III   Aquatinted by Havel   Feb. 1 1813.
Habits of Ladies in the reign of Henry III   Aquatinted by Hill   March 1 1813.
Avelina daughter & heir of William de Fortibus   Aquatinted by J. Hill   Dec. 1 1811.
Shipping &c. of the Reign of King Henry III   Aquatinted by Havell   June 1 1812.
Fools or Jesters   Aquatinted by Hill   Oct. 1 1813.
A Scots Knight   Aquatinted by Havell   Sept. 1 1812.
A Knight Templar of the XIV Century   Aquatinted by Havell   Sept. 1 1812.
Thomas Earl of Lancaster   Hill sculpt.   June 1 1812.
A Horse Litter   Anno 1325   Aquatinted by Hill   Oct. 1 1813.
Sir John Sitsylt Knight   Aquatinted by Hill   June 1 1812.
Ships of the 14th & 15th Centuries   Aquatinted by Havell   Novr. 1 1812.
Soldiers & Cannon of the latter end of 14th & beginning of the 15th Centuries   Aquatinted by J. Hill   Dec. 1 1811.
Edward Prince of Aquitaine & Wales   Aquatinted by J. Hill   Dec. 1 1811.
Edward III King of England and France   Aquatinted by R. & D. Havell   May 10 1812.
Joane Plantaganet Princess of Wales   Hill aquatinta   Feb. 1 1813.
Officers of the Court King Richard the Second.   Aquatinted by J. Merigot   August 1811.
Arthur McMurroch King of Leinster   Aquatinted by J. Hill   Dec. 4 1811.
King Richard the Second   Aquatinted by R. & D. Havell   May 10 1812.
Roger Walden Bishop of London   Aquatinted by Hill   July 1813.
Sir William Gascoigne   Aquatinted by Havel   Feb. 1 1813.
Robert Chaumberleyn Esquire to the King   Aquatinted by J. Hill   Feby. 1 1812.
Sir William Beauchamp Lord Bergavenny   I. Merigot sculpt.   June 1811.
A Lady of the Reign of King Henry V   Aquatinted by Hill   Oct. 1 1813.
Ralph Nevill 1st Earl of Westmoreland   Aquatinted by Hill   March 1 1813.
Joan Pickering Lady Gascoyne   Aquatinted by Hill   July 1 1813.
Cecilia Lady of Sir Brian Stapleton   Aquatinted by J. Hill   May 10 1812.
A Sportsman of Quality & Gamekeeper   Aquatinted by Havell   April 1 1812.
Richard Beauchamp Earl of Warwick.   Aquatinted by Hill   Sept. 1 1812.
Jocosa or Joice Lady Tiptoft and Powys [no engraver given]   Feb. 1 1812.
Military Costumes of the Reign of King Henry VI   Aquatinted by Hill   March 1 1812.
Henry VI King of England & France   J. Merigot sculpt.   June 4 1811.
Margaret of Anjou Queen to Henry VI   Aquatinted by J. Merigot   Augt. 1811.
Courtier of the reign of King Henry VI   Aquatinted by Havell   April 1 1812.
A Tournament as practised in the XV Century   Aquatinted by Hill   July 1 1813.
Artillery, Warlike Machines & Soldiers of the XV Century   Aquatinted by Hill   Feb. 1 1813.
A Warder or Porter.   Aquatinted by J. Hill   Oct. 1 1813.
Ship of the Reign of King Edward the 4th [no engraver given]   Feb. 1 1812.
English Archers [no engraver given]   Feby. 1 1812.
A Lady & Gentleman in Summer Dress   Havell sculpt.   June 1 1812.
Sir Rhys ab Thomas   Aquatinted by Havel   Novr 2 1812.

456 SMITH (C. H.)

Costume of the Army of the British Empire, according to the last Regulations, 1814. Designed by an Officer of the Staff (thin and thick rule) London (thin and thick rule) Printed by W. Bulmer and Co. Cleveland Row, for Messrs. Colnaghi and Co. Cockspur Street.

Folio.   1815

COLLATION.—Title as above (v. blank) + Dedication to Duke of York 1 p. (engraved, v. blank) + 61 plates.

All plates marked, Drawn by C.H.S.   Aquatinted by I. C. Stadler and with Colnaghi's imprint.

Front. Costume of the British Army &c. &c. &c. [emblematic].
Full Dress Uniform of a Field Marshall.   1st Apl 1812.
Uniform of a Lieutenant General of Cavalry.   May 1 1813.
First Regiment of Life Guards.   New Uniform.   1st May 1815.
Royal Horse Guards Blues.   23rd Nov. 1814.
A Private of the 1st or Kings Dragoon Guards.   March 1 1812.
A Private of the 2nd or Royal North British Dragoons (Greys)   1st Dec. 1813.
A Private of the 3rd or Kings Own Dragoons.   April 1st, 1812.
Uniform of a Major General of Light Dragoons.   Aug 1st, 1813.
An Aid de Camp, and Brigade Major of Cavalry.   Sept 1 1812.
An Officer of the IX Light Dragoons in Review Order.   March 1 1812.
A Corporal of the 10th or Prince of Wales's own Royal Hussars In Review Order.   Jany 1813.
A Private of the 13th Light Dragoons.   April 1st 1812.
An Officer of the 2nd Regiment of Life Guards in Full Dress   July 1 1812.
An Officer (Lieut. Col) of the 14th Light Dragoons In Parade Dress.   April 1, 1812.
A Private of the XV or Kings Lt. Dns. (Hussars)   Sept. 1, 1812.
A Private of the 18th Light Dragoons (Hussars).   1 May, 1812.
Light Dragoons serving in the East Indies.   2nd July, 1812.
Heavy and Light Cavalry Cloaked.   1st June 1815.
Heavy & Light Cavalry in Watering Order.   1st April 1813.
Grenadiers of the XLIId or Royal and XCIId or Gordon Highlanders   Sept. 1 1812.
Staff of the Army (Q.M.G. &c.)   Jan 1813.
Cavalry Staff Corps 1813   May 1 1817.
Major General of Infantry Knight Commander of the Bath.   April 1815.
An Officer of the Guard in Full Dress.   March 1815.
Grenadier of the Foot Guards in full Dress.   2nd July, 1812.
Privates of the First Regiment of Foot Guards on Service.   March 2nd, 1812.
Soldiers of the 1st Regt. of Foot Guards, in Marching Order.   1st May, 1812.
Infantry Officer in Marching Order.   March 2nd, 1812.
Drum Major of a Regiment of the Line Pioneer of the Grenadier Company of Do.   1st March 1815.
IX or E. Norfolk Regiment of Infantry.   1st Dec. 1813.
A private of the 7th or Queens Own LD (Hussars)   Aug 1 1813.
Battalion Infantry Warwickshire Regt.   Royal Welsh Fusileers.   1st Feb 1815.
Grenadiers & Light Infantry.   Worcestershire Regt.   May 1 1813.
An Officer & Private of the 52nd Regt. of Lt. Infantry.   Nov 1st 1814.
British Rifleman (60th & 95th Regt.)
A Sergeant and Privates of the 87th.   Jany. 1813.
York Light Infantry Volunteers.   1st Dec. 1813.
A Field Officer of Royal Engineers and a Private Sapper.   Jany 2nd. 1815.
Royal Artillery.   Feb 1 1815.
Royal Horse Artillery.   1st Feb. 1815.
Royal Artillery Drivers.   1st June 1815.
An Officer, Private & Driver of the Royal Wagon Train.   Arpil 1 1812.
Royal Artillery Mounted Rocket Corps.   2nd Jan. 1815.
A Private of the Royal Marines.   Jan 2nd 1815.

Smith's Costume of the Army (*contd.*)

3rd Hussars, Infantry & L. Infantry Kings German Legion.   2nd April 1815.
Hussars and Infantry of the Duke of Brunswick Oels Corps.   1st July 1812.
A Private of the 5th West India Regiment.   Jan 2nd 1815.
Native Troops E. India Company's Service.   March 1st 1815.
Native Troops E. India Company's Service.   2nd March 1815.
Native Troops E. India Company's Service.   1st March 1815.
Foreign Corps in the British Service (Greek)   1st Dec. 1813.
Cadets of the Royal Military College at Sandhurst.   Jan 1813.
Children of the Royal Military Asylum Chelsea.   Aug 1st 1813.
Chelsea Pensioners Cavalry & Infantry.   Nov 1st 1814.
British Cavalry.   1812.
British Infantry of Line.   1812.
Regular Infantry continued.
Facings of the Militia of Great Britain & Ireland.   1814.
Foreign Corps.   1813 & 1814.
Facings of the Honourable United East India Company's Regular Army   Jany 1814.

457 SMITH (Charles Hamilton)

Selections of the Ancient Costume of Great Britain and Ireland, from the Seventh to the Sixteenth Century, out of the Collection in the possession of the author (thick and thin rule) By Charles Hamilton Smith, Esq. (thin and thick rule) "Omnes artes quae ad humanitatem pertinent habent quoddam commune vinculum et quasi cognatione quadam inter se continentur" Cicero (thin and thick rule) + London: (thin and thick rule) Printed by William Bullmer & Co. Shakspeare-Press, for Messrs. Colnaghi and Co. Cockspur-Street

Folio.   1814

COLLATION.—Half-title + Title as above (v. blank) + Engraved Dedication to Prince Regent (v. blank) + Preface 4 pp. (v–viii) + Frontispiece and 60 coloured plates each with leaf of Text + Directions to Binder 1 p. (v. Errata) + List of Subscribers 2 pp.

All the plates bear "C. H. S. delt." and imprint, "Pub [date] by Colnaghi & Co. 23 Cockspur Street London," and all with the exception of Nos. 6, 11, 17, 29, 30, 35, 45, 49 and 58, "Etched by I. A. Atkinson."

Frontispiece.   Composite, William Bruges Garter King of Arms in 1420 pointing to materials used in compilation of this work   Aquatinted by R. Havell   Feby. 1, 1815.
  1. Anglo Saxon King of the Eighth Century & his armour bearer Equipped for Battle   Aquatinted by Hill   July 1 1813.
  2. Anglo Saxon Woman of the VIII Century   Aquatinted by Hill   Septr. 1 1812.
  3. Anglo Saxon Lady of the IX Century   Aquatinted by Hill   Oct. 1 1812.
  4. Costume of a Cambrian Prince presumed to represent Hywel dda or Hywel the good King of Wales   Aquatinted by Hill   March 1 1813.
  5. Habit of a Bishop of the 10th Century   Aquatinted by J. Hill   May 10 1812.
  6. King Edgar with an Anglo Saxon youth of distinction   J. Merigot sculpt.   June 4 1811.
  7. Anglo Saxon Military Chief Trumpeter and Warriors   Aquatinted by J. Havell   April 1 1812.
  8. Anglo Danish Warriors of the reign of King Cnute   Aquatinted by Hill   Octr. 1 1812.
  9. Ships of William the Conqueror   Aquatinted by Merigot   Augt. 1811.
 10. Richard 1st King of England, Duke of Normandy & Aquitaine and Earl of Anjou surnamed Coeur de Lion   Aquatinted by J. Merigot.
 11. Sir Hugh Bardolf   J. Merigot sculpt.   June 4 1811.
 12. Alberic de Vere 2nd Earl of Oxford Lord High Chamberlain of England and Adelisia his Countess   Aquatinted by J. Hill   April 1 1812.
 13. Costume of a Young Nobleman of the reign of King Henry III in a Summer dress   Aquatinted by Havel   Feby. 1 1813.

Smith's Costume (*contd.*)

14. Habits of Ladies in the reign of Henry III   Aquatinted by Hill   March 1 1813.
15. Costume of the Reign of King Henry 3rd Anno 1250   Aquatinted by Hill   March 1 1814.
16. Soldiers of the Reign of King Henry 3rd   Aquatinted by Havell   Feby. 1 1814.
17. Avelina, Daughter & heir of William de Fortibus Earl of Albemarle, First Wife of Edmund Crouch-back Earl of Lancaster   Aquatinted by J. Hill   Decr. 1 1812.
18. Shipping &c. of the reign of King Henry 3rd   Aquatinted by Havell   June 1 1812.
19. Fools, or Jesters   Aquatinted by Hill   Octr. 1 1813.
20. Sir Roger de Trumpington   Aquatinted by Havell   May 21 1814.
21. A Scots Knight supposed to represent the person of a chief of the Isles   Aquatinted by Havell   Septr. 1 1812.
22. A Knight Templar of the XIV Century in his military habit   Aquatinted by Havell   Sept. 1 1812.
23. Thomas, Earl of Lancaster, Leicester, Derby & Lincoln & Steward of England   Hill sculpt.   June 1 1812.
24. A Horse Litter Anno 1325.   Aquatinted by Hill   Octr. 1 1813.
25. Sir John Sitsylt Knight   Aquatinted by Hill   June 1 1812.
26. Philippa of Hainault Queen of England   Aquatinted by Havell   Feb. 1 1814.
27. Trumpeters performing in Concert   Aquatinted by Havell   May 12 1814.
28. Ships of the 14th & 15th Centuries   Aquatinted by Havell   Novr. 1 1812.
29. Soldiers & Cannon of the latter end of the 14th & beginning of the 15th Centuries   Aquatinted by J. Hill   Decr. 1 1811.
30. Edward Prince of Aquatain & Wales Duke of Cornwall & Earl of Chester surnamed Woodstock.   Aquatinted by J. Hill   Decr. 1 1811.
31. Edward III King of England and France & Lord of Ireland surnamed of Windsor   Aquatinted by R. & D. Havell   May 10 1812.
32. Joane Plantagenet Princess of Wales and Countess of Kent surnamed the Fair Maid of Kent   Hill aquatinta   Feby. 1 1813.
33. Officers of the Court of King Richard the Second   Aquatinted by J. Merigot   August 1811.
34. Sir William Beauchamp Kt. Gr. Lord Bergavenny Captain of Calais Custos of the County of Pembroke   1811.
35. Arthur McMurroch King of Leinster   Aquatinted by J. Hill   Dec. 4 1811.
36. King Richard the Second betrayed by the Earl of Northumberland   Aquatinted by R. & D. Havell   May 10 1812.
37. Roger Walden Bishop of London   Aquatinted by Hill   July 1 1813.
38. John Crosbie Prior of Coventry   Aquatinted by Havell   Feb. 1 1814.
39. Sir William Gascoigne Kt. Chief Justice of the Kings Bench   Aquatinted by Havell   Feby. 1 1813
40. Robert Chamberleyn Esquire to the King   Aquatinted by J. Hill   Feby. 1 1812.
41. A Lady of the reign of King Henry V   Aquatinted by Hill   Oct. 1 1813.
42. Ralph Nevil 1st Earl of Westmoreland, Lord of Raby Castle Earl Marshall Kt. of the Garter &c. &c. and his second wife Joan Beaufort   Aquatinted by Hill   March 1 1813.
43. Joan Pickering Lady Gascoyne   Aquatinted by Hill   July 1 1813.
44. Cecilia Lady of Sir Bryan Stapleton K.G.   Aquatinted by J. Hill   May 10 1812.
45. A Sportsman of Quality and Gamekeeper of the reign of King Henry V   Aquatinted by Havell.   April 1 1812.
46. Richard Beauchamp K.G. Earl of Warwick Regent of France, Governor of Normandy and Captain of Calais   Aquatinted by Hill   Septr. 1 1812.
47. Jocosa or Joice Lady Tiptoft and Powys   Feb. 1 1812.
48. Military Costumes of the reign of King Henry VI   Aquatinted by Hill   March 1 1812.
49. Henry VI King of England & France and Lord of Ireland, surnamed of Windsor   J. Merigot sculpt.   June 1 1811.
50. Margaret of Anjou, Queen to King Henry the 6th   Aquatinted by J. Merigot   Augt. 1811.
51. Courtier of the reign of King Henry VI supposed to represent John Viscount Beaumont K.G. Earl of Boulogne Constable and Lord High Chamberlain of England   Aquatinted by Havell   April 1 1812.
52. A Tournament as practised in the XV Century   Aquatinted by Hill   July 1 1813.
53. A Fisherman of XIV Century   Aquatinted by Havell   Feby. 1 1814.
54. Artillery, Warlike Machines and Soldiers of 15th Century   Aquatinted by Hill   Feb. 1 1813.
55. Costumes of Pages & Valets in the reign of King Edward the 4th   Aquatinted by J. Hill   March 1 1814.

Smith's Costume (*contd.*)

56. A Warder or Porter Aquatinted by J. Hill.
57. Ships of the Reign of King Edward the 4th Feb. 1812.
58. English Archers of the reign of King Edward IV Feb. 1 1812.
59. A Lady & Gentleman in Summer Dresses [Anno 1500] Havell sculpt. June 1 1812.
60. Sir Rhys ab Thomas Knight Banneret & K.G. Governor of all Wales. Aquatinted by Havell Novr. 2 1812.

Plates 6, 30, 34 and 49 were redrawn and these though 2nd are the best issue, being superior both in drawing and engraving. They are as follows:

6. King Edgar with an Anglo Saxon Youth of distinction Aquatinted by R. Havell Feb. 1 1815
   [in this plate the King's left-hand is on the youth's shoulder in the first issue it is on his own hip].
30. Edward Prince of Aquitain &c.
   [this 2nd issue differs only from the first in the prince being without a gold chain round his neck, and his helmet is pointed].
34. Sir William Beauchamp Kt. &c. Aquatinted by R. Havell Feb. 1 1815
   [there are 6 clasps to the chain in this plate in first issue there are 8 clasps].
49. Henry VI Aquatinted by R. Havell Feby. 1 1815
   [in 2nd issue the 2nd figure holds his book open, in first issue he holds it closed].

Another edition was published in 1815 and further edition undated.

Smith (Charles Hamilton.) See also under Meyrick.

458 SMITH (Capt. Robert)

[A Series of 11 Views of Prince of Wales Island.]

Large Folio.

COLLATION.—Each plate marked, Painted by Capt. Robert Smith of Engineers. Wm. Daniell sculpt (except for the eighth plate changed to Engraved Wm. Daniell). Published by Wm. Daniell 9 Cleveland Street, Fitzroy Square, London, Jany 1 1821.

Panoramic View of Prince of Wales Island and opposite Malayan Shore.
View of Mount Erskine and Pulo Ticoose Bay, Prince of Wale's (sic) Island Inscribed to the Proprietor, John Jas. Erskine Esq. &c. &c. R.S.
View from Halliburton's Hill, Prince of Wale's (sic) Island inscribed to Sir Ralph Rice Kt. &c. &c. R.S.
View from the Convalesent Bungalow Prince of Wale's Island Inscribed to Major J. MacInnes B.A. &c. &c. R.S.
View from Strawberry Hill, Prince of Wale's Island Inscribed to Sir Charles D'Oyly Bart. &c. &c. R.S.
View of Glugor House and Spice Plantations, Prince of Wale's Island Inscribed to the Proprietor David Brown Esqr. R.S.
View of the North Beach from the Council House, Prince of Wale's Island. Inscribed to Lieut General Alexr. Kyd &c. &c. R.S.
View of the Chinese Mills Penang.
View of Suffolk House, Prince of Wale's Island. Inscribed to the Honble the Governor W. E. Phillips Esqr. R.S.
(½ size) View of the Great Tree, Prince of Wale's Island Inscribed to Capt. Thos. Maddock B.A. &c. &c. R.S.
(½ size) View of the Cascade Prince of Wale's Island Inscribed to George Chinnery Esqr. R.S.

A Rare Series complete.

459 SMITH (T.)

The Art of Drawing in its various branches, exemplified in a course of Twenty-eight progressive lessons, calculated to afford those who are unacquainted with the art, the

Smith's Art of Drawing (*contd.*)

means of acquiring a competent knowledge, without the aid of a master; being the only work of the kind, in which the principles of Effect are explained in a clear, methodical, and at the same time, familiar style. (rule) By Thomas Smith. (rule) Illustrated with coloured designs and numerous wood engravings (rule) London: Printed for Sherwood Jones and Co., Paternoster Row (rule).

Octavo. 1825

COLLATION.—Title as above (v. London Printed By William Clowes, Northumberland Court) + Index to Illustrations 1 p. (v. blank) + Introduction pp. v–xiii + Contents 1 p. (v. Advertisement) + pp. 1–121 + 17 plates.

1. p. 35. Indian Ink (uncoloured).
2. p. 40. Sketch on colored (sic.) Paper (uncoloured).
3. p. 58. Cottage Plate 1st (coloured), unfinished.
4. p. 63. Cottage Plate 2nd (coloured), finished.
5. p. 64. Siene Boat Plate 1st (coloured), unfinished.
6. p. 65. Siene Boat Plate 2nd (coloured), finished.
7. p. 68. Marine (coloured) (Castle).
8. p. 71. Marine (coloured) (Cock).
9. and 10. p. 72. Flowers (1 coloured, 1 partly).
11. p. 75. Fruit (coloured).
12. p. 78. Still Life (coloured).
13. p. 83. Figure Drawing (uncoloured).
14. p. 89. Figure Drawing (coloured).
15. p. 94. Stag (uncoloured).
16. p. 95. Animal Painting (coloured).
17. p. 97. Animal Painting (coloured).

460 SMYTH (Coke)

Sketches in the Canadas. (vignette) By Coke Smyth London: Published by Thos. McLean, 26 Haymarket. Printed at A. Ducotes Lithographic Establishment, 70 St Martins Lane.

COLLATION.—Title as above + Dedication to Earl of Durham 1 p. (v. List of Plates) + 22 lithographs (23 including title).

1. Vignette on title.
2. Falls of Niagara.
3. Indians of Lorethe.
4. Cape Tourment from Chateau Richet.
5. Quebec.
6. Quebec from the Chateau.
7. Falls of Montmorency from St Joseph's.
8. Citadel Quebec.
9. Zitya Huron Indian.
10. Huron Indian.
11. Church at Beauharnois.
12. Falls of Montmorency.
13. Attack and Defeat of Rebels. Dickinson landing at Upper Canada.
14. Buffalo Hunting.
15. Engagement in the Thousand Islands.
16. Rapids of St. Lawrence.
17. Posting on the St during Winter.
18. Indians bartering.
19. Montreal.
20. America Fort Niagara River.
21. Entrance to Toronto.
22. Moos Hunter.
23. The Private Chapel of the Ursuline Convent, Quebec.

Most copies are to be found plain, but some were issued in colour.

461 SOLVYNS (B.)

The Costume of Indostan, elucidated by Sixty coloured Engravings; with Descriptions in English and French, taken in the years 1798 and 1799. (rule). By Bart. Solvyns, of Calcutta. (rule) London: (thin and thick rule). Published by Edward Orme, Printseller to His Majesty and the Royal Family, 59 New Bond Street.

Folio. [1804–5]

Solvyns's Costume of Indostan (*contd.*)

COLLATION.—Title as above (v. blank) + Title in French 1 p. (v. blank) + Dedication 1 p. (v. blank) + Dedication in French 1 p. (v. blank) + Preface in English 2 pp. + Preface in French 2 pp. + 60 coloured plates, each with 1 leaf of Text.

Each plate is marked, Bart. Solvyns pinx., Calcutta. Sold and Published [date] by Edwd. Orme, His Majesty's Printseller, 59 New Bond Street, London. The Plates do not actually bear titles, but are numbered throughout, 1–60.

1. (An Ooria or Orissa Brahman)	Scott sculp., Jany, 1804.
2. (A Chittery)	Scott sculp. Jany. 1st 1804.
3. (A Dybuck)	Scott sculpt. Jany. 1st 1804.
4. (An Auhheer)	Scott sculpt., Jany. 1st 1804.
5. (Rowanny Bearers, or Chairman)	Scott sculp., Jany 1st 1804.
6. (Tauntees, or Weavers)	Scott sculp. Jany 1st 1804.
7. (B'Haut)	Scott sculp., Jany 1st 1804.
8. (A Dandy or Boatman)	Scott sculp., Jany 1st 1804.
9. (A Jellee-a, or Fisherman)	T. Vivares sculp., Jany. 1st 1804.
10. (Brijbasi)	Scott sculp. Jany 1st 1804.
11. (Kawra, or Hog-Keepers)	Jan 1st 1804.
12. (Puckimar, or Bird-Catcher)	Scott sculp Jany. 1st 1804.
13. (Sircar)	Jany 1st 1804.
14. (A Jummadar)	Jany 1st 1804.
15. (A Choobdar, or Assahburdar)	Jany 1st 1804.
16. (Kherch-Burdar or House Purveyor)	Scott sculp., Jany. 1st 1804.
17. (A B'Heeshty or Waterman)	Scott sculp., Jany 1st 1804.
18. (Hooka-Burdar, or Hooka Purveyor)	Jany 1st 1804.
19. (A Durzee, or Taylor)	Jany 1st 1804.
20. (A Baulber)	Jany 1st 1804.
21. (A Hircarrah)	Jany 1st 1804.
22. (A Peada, or Footman)	Jany 1st 1804.
23. (Native Coachman to a European)	Jany 1st 1804.
24. (A Syce, or Groom)	Jany 1st 1804.
25. (An Aubdar)	Jany 1st 1804.
26. (Corah—Burdar)	Jany 1st 1804.
27. (A Doorea -a, or Dog Keeper)	Jany 1st 1804.
28. (A Bansee)	Jany 1st 1804.
29. (A Man of Distinction)	March. 1804.
30. (A Sircar) (different from plate 13)	Jany 1st 1804.
31. (Bauluck)	June 4th 1804.
32. (A Behaleea)	Scott sculp., Jany 1st 1804.
33. (A Seapoy)	March 1804.
34. (A Seapoy)	March 1804.
35. (A Brigbasi)	Vivares sct., Jany 1st 1804.
36. (A Woman of Distinction)	June 4th 1804.
37. (A Gwallin, or Milk Woman)	June 4th 1804.
38. (A Woman of Inferior Rank)	June 4th 1804.
39. (A Hidgra or Hermaphrodite)	Vivares sct., Jany 1st 1804.
40. (A Ramganny, or Dancing Girl)	June 4th 1804.
41. (A Polye, or Fishwoman)	June 4th 1804.
42. (Beeshnub)	June 4th 1804.
43. (An Oordabahoo)	June 4th 1804.
44. (Nariel, or Cocoa-nut Hooka)	June 4th 1804.
45. (The Hindoo Method of Eating the Paun)	June 4th 1804.
46. (A Sunk or Chank)	Augt 1st 1804.
47. (A Tumboora)	Augt 1st 1804.
48. (A Sittara, or Guitar)	Augt 1st 1804.
49. (A Sarinda or Violin)	Augt 1st 1804.
50. (Pennauck or Been)	Vivares sct. Jany 1st 1804.

Solvyns's Costume of Indostan (*contd.*)

51. (Saringee)		Augt 1st 1804.
52. (A Tubla)		Augt 1st 1804.
53. (A D'Holuc)		Augt 1st 1804.
54. (Jultrung)		Sept 29th 1804.
55. (D'Hauk)		Jany 1st 1805.
56. (Nagra)		Jany 1st 1805.
57. (Kaura)		Sept. 29th 1804
58. (Pukwauz)	Scott sculp.	Jany 1st 1804.
59. (Jugo Jhumpo)		Jany 1st 1805.
60. (Surmungla)		Jany 1st 1805.

462 SOTHEBY (W.)

A Tour through Parts of Wales. Sonnets, Odes, and other Poems. With Engravings from Drawings taken on the Spot, By J. Smith. (thick and thin rule) By W. Sotheby, Esq. (thin and thick rule) London: Printed by J. Smeeton, in St Martin's Lane, for R. Blamire, Strand, near Charing Cross.

Quarto.   1794

COLLATION.—Half-title "Poems" (v. blank) + Title as above (v. blank) + Preface 1 p. (v. blank) + Contents 1 p. (v. blank) + sub-title, "Tour through Parts of South and North Wales," 1 p. (v. blank) + Book the First Contents 1 p. (v. blank) + pp. 5–120 + 13 coloured plates. Each plate marked, J. Smith, delt. S. Alken, fecit.

I. p. 7.	Remains of the Castle at Abergavenny.	VIII. p. 29. Neivegal Sands, St Brides Bay.
II. p. 11.	Caerfily Castle.	IX. p. 33. Pont-aberglaslyn.
III. p. 13.	Pont-y-prid.	X. p. 35. Snowdon from Capel Careig.
IV. p. 17.	Melincourt Cascade.	XI. p. 37. The Eagle Tower, Caernarvon Castle.
V. p. 19.	Caraig—connin Castle.	
VI. p. 20.	Dinevawr Castle.	XII. p. 39. Druidical Remains in Anglesey.
VII. p. 27.	Haverford West Castle.	XIII. p. 105. Llangollen.

463 SOUTHEY (R.)

Views of the Lake and of the Vale of Keswick. Drawn and Engraved by William Westall, A.R.A. (thick and thin rule) London: Published by Rodwell and Martin, New Bond Street (short rule).

Quarto.   1820

COLLATION.—Title as above (v. W. Wilson Printer, 4 Greville Street, Hatton Garden, London) + Text pp. 3–8 + 6 coloured plates, each plate marked, Drawn and Engraved by W. Westall A.R.A.

1. Keswick Lake from Applethwaite.	4. Keswick Lake from Barrow Common.
2. Keswick and Grisedale Pike.	5. Keswick Lake seen from above Lowdore.
3. Lowdore Waterfall.	6. Skiddaw.

Plates 1 and 6 bear Rodwell and Martin's imprint, the others Hurst Robinson & Co. Cheapside.

464 SPILSBURY (F. B.)

Picturesque Scenery in the Holy Land and Syria, delineated during the campaigns of 1799 and 1800. (thick and thin rule). By F. B. Spilsbury, of His Majesty's Ship, Le Tigre: Surgeon in that Expedition during both campaigns. (thick and thin rule) Second Edition (thin and thick rule) London: (thick and thin rule) Printed for Thomas M'Lean, Bookseller and Publisher, by B. R. Howlett, 101 Frith Street, Soho.

Folio.   1819

> *COLLATION.*—Title as above (v. blank) + Dedication 1 p. (v. blank) + Preface pp. i–iv + Text pp. 1–42 + 19 coloured aquatint plates.   Each plate marked, Sketched on the Spot, by F. B. Spilsbury, and Drawn by Danl Orme.

I.	p. 1. View of Acre and H M. S. Le Tigre. Edwd Orme Excudit. Jukes aquatinta.
II.	p. 5. Jezzar Pacha Condemning a Criminal Edward Orme Excudit.
III.	p. 9. Sidon.
IV.	p. 10. Tyre H Merke aquatinta.
V.	p. 11. Daniel Bryan, The Sailor who nobly Volunteered, at the risk of his life to bury the French General, during the Siege of Acre. Edwd Orme Excut J. Vivares scuplt.
VI.	p. 14. A Market in Acre. Edwd Orme Excut. I. C. Stadler aquatinta.
VII.	p. 15. A Burial Place at Beirout. Edwd Orme Excudt Jukes aquantinta.
VIII.	p. 20. Zeta near Jaffa in Syria Edwd Orme Excut. I. C. Stadler aquatinta.
IX.	p. 20. Arab Huts at Zeta Edwd Orme Excut.
X.	p. 22. A Dance at Genin Etched by Vivares.
XI. (misptd. XII).	p. 23. Mount Tabor Edwd Orme Excut I. C. Stadler aquatina.
XII.	p. 25. Joseph's Pit and Well. Edwd Orme Excut. I. C. Stadler aquatinta.
XIII. (XIV)	p. 27. The Lake of Tiberia Edwd Orme Excudit I. C. Stadler aquatinta.
XIV.	p. 28. Jacob's Bridge Edwd Orme Excut I. C. Stadler aquatinta.
XV. (XVIII)	p. 30. Tripoli I. C. Stadler aquatinta.
XVI. (XIX)	p. 32. Caesaria I. C. Stadler Aquatinta.
XVII.	p. 32. The Pilgrims Castle Edwd Orme Excut. Merke aquatinta.
XVIII. (XX) *ibd.*	Dede, near Tripoli I. C. Stadler aquatinta.
XIX. (XVI)	p. 33. The Grand Vizier's Tent Edwd Orme Excudit Merke aquatinta.

> *Issued in boards, with printed label, "Spilsbury's Holy Land: Illustrated with* 19 *plates, coloured. (rule) Five Guineas."*

465 SPOONER & CO.

Costume of the Royal Navy & Marines.

Series of 16 plates by L. Mansion and St. Eschauzier, coloured by C. H. Martin.   Printed by Lefevre & Co., London, Published by Andrews & Co., Ornamental & General Stationers to their Majesties and the Royal Family, 88 Piccadilly facing the Green Park.

Portrait of His Most Excellent Majesty King William the Fourth.	Captain, Flag Officer and Commander (Undress).
Lieutenants.	Masters.
Royal Marines Field Officers.	Gunners, Boatswains and Carpenters.
Midshipmen.	Mates.
Flag Officers.	Master of the Fleet and Physicians.
Captains.	Volunteers of the First Class and Volunteer of the Second Class.
Surgeons.	
Pursers and Captain's Clerk.	Royal Marines (Subalterns). Ensign carrying Divisional Colours.
Royal Marine Artillery (Officers).	

Spooner's Costume of the Royal Navy & Marines (*contd.*)

Each plate is marked at head, Dedicated by permission to the King's Most Excellent Majesty, and at foot Costume of the Royal Navy and Marines. Each marked, Coloured by C. H. Martin, Printed by Lefevre, Mansion & Eschauzier inv. et del. and each with Andrews's imprint.

466 SPOONER (W.)

(Fancy Ball Dress)

Folio.   1832

A Series of 30 fine coloured lithographs of National Costume, each plate marked, Fancy Ball Dress. No. 1 [to 30]. Published by W. Spooner with the Imprints of Engelmann and Co., C. Hullmandel, Mefred Lemercier & Co., or Lefevre. The 30 plates are all by L. Mansion, except plate 16, which is marked, R. Buss pinxt., T. Fairland delt.

1. Ragusa. Engelmann.
2. France (Loire Inferieure). Engelmann.
3. North Holland.
4. Illyrian. Hullmandel.
5. Poland. Hullmandel.
6. Alps. Hullmandel.
7. Spain Catalonia. Hullmandel.
8. Neapolitan. Hullmandel
9. Saxony. Hullmandel.
10. Tyrolean. Hullmandel.
11. Upper Carniola. Hullmandel.
12. France (Provence). Hullmandel.
13. Caucasus. Hullmandel.
14. Greece. Hullmandel.
15. Archangel (Russia). Hullmandell.
16. Hungary (Nograd). Engelmann.
17. Switzerland—Canton of Lucerne. Engelmann.
18. Grecian Archipelago—Milo. Lermecier.
19. Hungarian. Lefevre.
20. Wallachia. Lefevre.
21. Italy—Villa Badissa Matera, Royaume de Naples. Lefevre.
22. Spain—Murcia. Lefevre.
23. Finland. Lefevre.
24. Asiatic Turkey—Diarbekir. Lefevre.
25. Russia Novogorod. Lefevre.
26. Corfu. Lefevre.
27. Tartary—Tchouvache. Lefevre.
28. Spain Madrid. Lefevre.
29. Tyrol—Zillerthal. Lefevre.
30. Persia. Lefevre.

467 SPORTING REPOSITORY

The Sporting Repository, containing Horse Racing, Hunting, Coursing, Shooting, Archery, Trotting and Tandem Matches, Cocking, Pedestrianism, Pugilism. Anecdotes on Sporting Subjects interspersed with Essays, Tales and a Great Variety of Miscellaneous Articles London: Printed by W. Lewis, 21 Finch Lane: for Thomas M'Lean 26 Haymarket

Octavo.   1822

COLLATION.—Title (v. blank) + Contents and Direction to Binder 4 leaves + 540 pp + 19 coloured plates by H. Alken & I. Barenger engraved by G. Hunt lithographed H. la Ree.

1. Front. Meeting at Cover, Holywell Park Wood.
2. p. 29. Claret.
3. p. 38. A Hawk.
4. p. 78. Herefordshire Ox.
5. p. 81. The Coachman.
6. p. 93. Rubens.
7. p. 126. Jacko Macacco or the Game Monkey.
8. p. 160. Merino Sheep.
9. p. 177. Tandem Driving.
10. p. 218. Running.
11. p. 231. Greyhounds.
12. p. 320. The Favourite between the Heats.
13. p. 343. Grouse Shooting.
14. p. 357. Gone Away.
15. p. 380. Gamekeepers & Poachers
16. p. 429. Wild Fowl Shooting.
17. p. 449. The Whipper In.
18. p. 513. The Death.
19. p. 515. Pointers.

468 STRUTT (J. Junior)

Twelve Views on the River Teign Drawn from Nature by J. Strutt Jun. (rule).

1. Teignmouth.
2. The Ness.
3. Smugglers Lane.
4. The Bridge.
5. Entrance to the Harbour.
6. Ringmore.
7. Coombe Cellars.
8. Kingsteignton.
9. Newton.
10. Fingle Bridge.
11. The Logan Stone.
12. The Source of the River.

(two line rule) Published by W. T. Strutt and Son of Exeter and Teignmouth.

Oblong Folio.   [1828]

A series of 12 coloured aquatint plates as above, with descriptions beneath, no date given in imprints, watermark J. Whatman 1828.

469 SULLIVAN (Dennis)

A Picturesque Tour through Ireland (rule) By Dennis Sullivan Esq. (rule) illustrated with numerous coloured views of the most interesting scenery (2 rules) London: Published by Thomas M'Lean, 26, Haymarket

Quarto.   1824

COLLATION.—Title as above (v. London: Printed by W. Lewis 21 Finch-Lane Cornhill) + List of Plates 1 leaf + Introduction 1 leaf + 25 coloured plates, each with 1 leaf of Text.

1. Irish Cottages Wicklow.
2. Stone Cross Uilcullen.
3. Wicklow Gold Mines.
4. Mountains of Lugnaquilla.
5. Lough Erne & Isle of Devenish.
6. Part of the Abbey of Monaincha.
7. Principal Lake at Killarney.
8. Abbey of Aghaboe.
9. Trim Castle East Meath.
10. Giant's Causeway.
11. Ballrichan Castle.
12. Roche Castle.
13. Belfast.
14. Lough of Belfast.
15. View on River Shannon.
16. Downpatrick.
17. Part of Loch Neagh.
18. Carlingford Castle.
19. Waterfall near Bantry.
20. Salmon Leap at Leixlip.
21. Dunamase Castle.
22. Bray Head.
23. View on the River Blackwater.
24. Limerick.
25. Mountains of Morne.

470 [SURTEES R. S.)]

The Analysis of the Hunting Field; being a Series of Sketches of the Principal Characters that Compose One.   The whole forming a slight Souvenir of the Season 1845-6 (rule) With numerous illustrations by H. Alken (rule) London: Published by Rudolph Ackermann, 191 Regent Street (short rule).

Octavo.   1846

COLLATION.—Half-title "The Analysis of the Hunting Field" (v. blank) + Engraved coloured title + Printed title as above (v. London: Cook and Co. Printers and Engravers, 76

Surtees's Analysis of the Hunting Field (*contd.*)

Fleet Street) + Contents 1 p. (v. List of Plates) + Preface 1 p. dated 1846 (v. blank) + pp. 1–326 + Advertisements of R. Ackermann 2 leaves + 6 coloured plates [7 including engraved title] + 43 woodcuts in Text.

Each plate bears imprint, London Published Novr. 19th 1846 by Rudolph Ackermann at his Eclipse Sporting Gallery 191 Regent Street, and each is engraved by J. Harris after H. Alken.

1. Front. The Meet "With Bright faces and merry hearts."
2. Engraved Title. Analysis of the Hunting Field [consisting of 8 small vignette views of various scenes in Hunting].
3. p. 80. Getting Away "Let's take the lead."
4. p. 156. Full Cry "Let's keep the lead."
5. p. 205. The Check "What the devil do you do here."
6. p. 241. The Leap "That will shut out many and make the thing select."
7. p. 290. Whoo-hoo-o-o-p "A chosen few alone the Death survey."

This work first appeared in Bell's Life, and the first edition in book form as above at 31s. 6d. in green cloth with a blind key pattern side borders and gilt design on upper cover of hunting paraphernalia with a fox in centre and same design in blind on back cover. Lettered in gilt on spine Analysis of Hunting Field with fox's paws and crossed tails, yellow ends with binder's ticket of Westley and Clark, gilt edges.

There are two issues. First issue in green cloth with both titles and the preface dated 1846. Second issue in red cloth, with the preface dated occasionally 1846 but usually 1847. Some copies have both the prefaces, the cancel 1846 and the 1847. Issued with gilt edges and ungilded edges, the former being superior.

There are early states of some of the plates with imprint dated Nov. 9th not Nov. 19th.

The following work is placed out of its strict alphabetical order so as not to divide the uniform series of Surtees Sporting Novels.

471 [SURTEES (R. S.)]

Jorrock's Jaunts and Jollities; being the Hunting, Shooting, Racing, Driving, Sailing, Eating, Eccentric and Extravagant Exploits of that renowned Sporting Citizen, Mr. John Jorrocks, of St. Botolph Lane, and Great Coram Street. With Fifteen coloured illustrations by Henry Alken. Second Edition. London: Rudolph Ackermann, Eclipse Sporting Gallery, 191, Regent Street. (rule).

Octavo.   1843

COLLATION.—Engraved title "The Jaunts and Jollities of that Renowned Sporting Citizen Mr. John Jorrocks of St. Botolph Lane & Great Coram St." (the above lettering split up and surrounded by 11 miniature vignettes, with large vignette at foot of a convivial gathering round a punch bowl) Second Edition London: R. Ackermann, Eclipse Sporting Gallery, 191, Regent Street (v. blank) + Printed title as above (v. blank) + Preface to the First Edition 1 p. + Preface to Second Edition 3 pp. (iv–vi) + Contents 1 p. (v. illustration) + Sub-title "No. I. Swell and the Surrey" (pp. 1–2) + pp. 3–358 + Imprint 1 p. "Printed by Walter Spiers, 399, Oxford Street" (v. blank) + 8 pp. of Advertisement by Ackermann + 15 coloured plates.

Each plate marked, Drawn & Etched by H. Alken (except the title which does not bear the artist's name) London Published by R. Ackermann, at his Eclipse Sporting Gallery, 191, Regent St. 1843.

Surtees's Jorrock's Jaunts (*contd.*)

1. Front.   Mr Jorrocks Telegraphs the Fox.
2. Engraved Title.
3. p.   14. The appearance of Swell astonishes the Surrey Hunt.
4. p.   45. Mr Jorrocks introduces the Yorkshireman to the Surrey.
5. p.   79. Squire Cheatum's Keeper attacks the Murderer of Old Tom.
6. p. 108. Mr Jorrocks declares his inability to Subscribe to the Surrey Staghounds.
7. p. 142. The Baron "Vills his wet."
8. p. 147. Mr Jorrocks makes his entree into the Newmarket Betting Ring.
9. p. 195. "Oh Gentlemen!   Gentlemen! here's a lamentable occurrence."
10. p. 249. "Water I do declare—with worms in it."
11. p. 263. Mr Jorrocks renounces the acquaintance of the Yorkshireman.
12. p. 279. Mr Jorrocks makes a Faux Pas.
13. p. 308. Mr Jorrocks beats the Baron for Speed.
14. p. 313. Mr Jorrocks takes a ride at St. Cloud.
15. p. 358. "Lift me up!   Tie me in my chair!   Fill my glass."

First appeared in Vols. I–VII of New Sporting Magazine and then in book form in 1838 with 12 plates by Phiz. and again in 1839.   First edition with coloured plates by Alken as above, issued in green cloth with gilt design at 15s.   The Suzannet copy had an additional plate bound in as frontispiece viz. John Jorrocks Esqre. M.S.H. &c. &c. &c.   A Citizen of Credit and Renown, Drawn and Etched by H. Alken, London Published by R. Ackermann at his Eclipse Sporting Gallery 191 Regent Street 1843.   This plate was for some reason withdrawn and does not form part of the work.

A reissue by Routledge appeared in 1869 with an additional plate Jorrock's Hunt Breakfast. A Terrible Surprise.   Its value is small.   A fourth edition was published in 1874.

The first issue should have advertisements showing Second Edition of Mytton and forthcoming new issue of Jorrocks Jaunts.   The second state advertises the Third Edition of Mytton.   Jorrocks was reissued at later dates, and the watermarks should be examined to see that they are pre-publication.

The following six works [or five, Hillingdon Hall being sometimes omitted] are frequently sold together, and no finer series of Sporting Novels exists in the English language.   As is so rarely the case in colour plate books, the text is as important as the illustrations.   They were reprinted in an undated issue by Bradbury Agnew & Co. in 1888 and subsequently at various times, an edition being still in print.

472 [SURTEES (R. S.)]

"Ask Mamma"; or, the Richest Commoner in England.   By the Author of "Handley Cross," "Sponge's Sporting Tour," etc. etc. (vignette of dog as huntsman) With illustrations by John Leech.   London: Bradbury and Evans, 11, Bouverie Street

Octavo.   1858

COLLATION.—Title as above (v. London: Bradbury and Evans, Printers, Whitefriars) Dedication to Hon. Mrs. Coventry 1 p. (v. blank)+Preface 1 p. (v. blank)+Contents 4 pp. (vii–x)+Engravings on Steel 1 p. (v. Engravings on wood)+pp. 1–412+coloured frontispiece and 12 coloured plates.

13 coloured plates and 69 wood engravings by Leech.

Front.   The Ancesters of our Hero.
1. p.   52. Miss De Glancey captivates the Earl.
2. p.   81. The Richest Commoner's first Jump.
3. p. 119. A Lee-tle Contre-temps—Jack Rogers and the Glove.

Surtees's Ask Mamma (*contd.*)

4. p. 148. Billy is introduced to the Major's Harriers.
5. p. 192. Sir Moses and Mrs Turnbull.
6. p. 230. Jack Rogers putting his nerves to rights.
7. p. 240. Imperial John's attempt to show the Way.
8. p. 289. The great Match between Mr Flintoff & Jack Rogers.
9. p. 315. The Gift Horse.
10. p. 351. Fine Billy quite at home.
11. p. 366. Old Wotherspoon's Hare!
12. p. 398. The Hunt Ball——"Ask Mamma" Polka.

First Edition Published originally in 13 monthly parts in red pictorial wrappers by Leech and on completion issued in red cloth with a gilt design on upper cover of cupid dressed as huntsman and mounted on horseback, lower cover undecorated save for blind side border design, the back strip bears lettering Ask Mamma or the Richest Commoner in England, Illustrated by John Leech, with 3 gilt designs at top, Cupid as hunstman in centre, huntsman on foot at base, huntsman mounted. All edges uncut pale yellow ends.

In the paper wrappers, each of the 13 parts has a vignette of a lady and gentleman dressing and advertisements of Revalenta Arabica Food, Mappins Razor & Edmiston's Waterproof.

Part I in 1st issue has the words Ask Mamma in outline letters, in 2nd issue has the words Ask Mamma in solid letters.

Parts I–X and part XIII, each contain Ask Mamma Advertiser 4 pp.

Part III contains 2 pp. advertisement of English Encyclopedia.

Part VII contains a white slip, The Lazy Tour, and a yellow slip the Virginians.

Part VIII contains advertisement of works of Dickens 2 pp., and a yellow slip of Virginians.

Part IX contains a white slip, Perils of Certain English Prisoners, and a yellow slip, Virginians.

Parts XI and XII contain no advertisement.

473 [SURTEES (R. S.)]

Handley Cross; or, Mr. Jorrocks's Hunt. By the Author of "Mr. Sponge's Sporting Tour," "Jorrocks's Jaunts," etc. etc. (vignette of huntsman holding fox) (thin rule) With Illustrations by John Leech (thin rule) London: Bradbury and Evans, 11, Bouverie Street

Octavo. 1854

COLLATION.—Title as above (v. London: Bradbury and Evans, Printers, Whitefriars) + Dedication to Rt. Hon. Lord John Scott 1 p. (v. blank) + Preface 1 p. (v. blank) + Contents 2 pp. (vii–viii) + Engravings on steel 1 p. (v. engravings on wood) + pp. 1–550 + 17 coloured plates and 84 wood engravings by J. Leech.

1. front. Michael Hardey.
2. p. 57. Mr. Jorrocks starting for "The cut me down Countries."
3. p. 81. Mr. Jorrocks enters into Handley Cross.
4. p. 106. Mr. Jorrocks (loq.)—"Come hup! I say. You ugly Beast!"
5. p. 129. Mr Jorrocks's Lecture on "Unting."
6. p. 187. Mr Jorrocks has a Bye Day.
7. p. 197. Mr. Jorrocks's Bath.
8. p. 243. The Handley Cross Fancy Ball.
9. p. 279. The Kill, on the Cat & Custard Pot Day.
10. p. 325. The Meet at Mr. Muleygrubs.
11. p. 343. "Mind the Bull."
12. p. 362. The Pomponius Ego Day.

Surtees's Handley Cross (*contd.*)

13. p. 407. Mr Jorrocks wants twenty.
14. p. 439. Sir Thomas Trout & The Bloomer.
15. p. 451. Mr Barege and The Draft.
16. p. 485. Pigg in the Melon Frame.
17. p. 532. Mr Jorrock's Return to his Family.

Originally published in 3 vols., octavo, in 1843, unillustrated, then in 17 monthly parts from March 1853 to October 1854, and on completion in volume form as above in red cloth "in one large Volume, 8vo., price 18s."

The upper cover bears a design in gilt repeating the vignette of the title page within a huntsman's crop, the lower cover undecorated save for blind border design, the back strip bears lettering, Handley Cross or Mr. Jorrocks's Hunt Illustrated by John Leech with 3 gilt figures, at top Jorrocks mounted, in centre Huntsman holding up a fox to hounds, at foot Hounds and Huntsman. Edges uncut, yellow ends with advertisement printed in black upon them.

There are 3 issues of this first edition. The first issue bears the words "Illustrious Leech" in preface, the second issue does not bear these words and the third issue does not mention Jorrocks Jaunts on the title.

The parts were issued in red paper wrappers, each wrapper containing a portrait of Jorrocks with a waitress, besides the title, and advertisements as follows.

Part   I. Knights Georgr. of Brit. Empire, Watherston's & Brogden's Gold Chains and Edmiston's Pocket Siphonia & 4 pp. Handley Cross Advertiser   Mar. 1853.

,,   II. The Field, The Angler's Guide, & Edmiston + 2 pp. English Encyclopedia insert.

,,   III. English Cyclopaedia, Breidenbach's Perfumery and Edmiston.

,,   IV. Ditto.

,,   V. New Serial by W. M. Thackeray, Breidenbach & Edmiston + insert on green paper The Field 1 lf.

,,   VI. Piesse's Complexion Powder English Cyclopaedia & Edmiston.

,,   VII. New Elegant Ballads Bank of Deposit & Edmiston + insert yellow slip advt. No. 1 of Newcomes.

,,   VIII. The Respirator Soyer's Pantropheon & Edmiston.

,,   IX. The Respirator Breidenbach & Edmiston.

,,   X. Civil Service Gazette The Respirator.

,,   XI. Bank of Deposit, Respirator, Edmiston + insert 4 pp. Foreign Tour.

,,   XII. Bank of Deposit, British Game Birds, Edmiston.

    XIII. Forster's Life of Goldsmith, Dickens Hard Times, Edmiston.

,,   XIV. Guides & Handbooks, Dickens Hard Times.

,,   XV. Passam Smith & Co's Teas, Dejongh's Cod Liver Oil, Edmiston + insert 2 or 4 pp. English Cyclopaedia.

,,   XVI. Reduction of Tea Duty &c.

,,   XVII. Handley Cross Dejongh and Edmiston

474 [SURTEES (R. S.)]

Hillingdon Hall; or, the Cockney Squire: A Tale of Country Life by Author of "Handley Cross" "Jorrocks's Jaunts and Jollities," &c. (vignette) With Twelve Illustrations By Wildrake—Heath—Jellicoe coloured by hand London John C. Nimmo 14 King William Street, Strand

Octavo.   1888

COLLATION.—Half-title "Hillingdon Hall or The Cockney Squire" (v. Publishers Note) + Title as above (v. Ballantyne Press Ballantyne; Hanson and Co. Edinburgh and London) + Dedication to Royal Agricultural Society (v. Preface) + List of Illustrations 1 p. (v. blank) + pp. 1–519 + 24 numbered pp. of Nimmo advertisements + 12 coloured plates.

Surtees's Hillingdon Hall (*contd.*)

1. Mr Jorrocks's Arrival astonishes the village of Hillingdon front.
2. Mr Jorrocks accosts Hercules Strong p. 34. Wildrake.
3. The Duke of Donkeyton calls on Mr Jorrocks p. 56.
4. The Guests depart from Donkeyton Castle p. 112.
5. The Surprise p. 246.
6. The Harvest Home Ball p. 270.
7. It's Sir Robert Peel's Grand Bull p. 284.
8. The Marquis of Bray Kisses Emma p. 330.
9. Mr Jorrocks starts the hare p. 342 J. Jellicoe.
10. The Duke's horror at the Marquis marrying a commoner p. 292 J. Jellicoe.
11. Mr Bowker's Personal Canvas p. 458. J. Jellicoe.
12. Mr Jorrocks addressing the crowd p. 502 J. Jellicoe.

Originally appeared in New Sporting Magazine, Vol. V–VII, and was first issued in book form in 3 vols., octavo, in 1844, by Henry Colburn, unillustrated. The least popular and valuable of Surtees novels.

475 [SURTEES (R. S.)]

Mr. Facey Romford's Hounds. By the Author of "Handley Cross," "Mr. Sponge's Sporting Tour," "Ask Mamma," etc. etc. (vignette) (rule) With illustrations by John Leech and Hablot K. Browne (rule) London: Bradbury and Evans, 11 Bouverie Street.

Octavo.   1865

COLLATION.—Half-title "Mr. Facey Romford's Hounds" (v. blank) + Title as above (v. London: Bradbury and Evans, Printers, Whitefriars) + Contents 2 pp. (v–vi) + Engravings on Steel 1 p. (v. blank) + pp. 1–391 (p. 392 blank) + Frontispiece and 23 coloured plates.

24 coloured plates by Leech and H. K. Browne.

1. Front. Simon Heavy-side and his Hounds.
2. p.   6. "Who am I! I'm the Mistress of this ere ouse—and this is the young Squire!"
3. p. 43. Romford disturbs the dignity of his Huntsman.
4. p. 60. Madame de Normanville and the Squire.
5. p. 71. "Let me try then" said Lucy.
6. p. 73. The View.
7. p. 103. Mrs. Somerville (!) thinks Beldon Hall will do.
8. p. 121. Mr Muffington on "Placid Joe" (late Pull Devil).
9. p. 132. "The Ladies."
10. p. 156. Captain Spurrier "cut down" by Romford.
11. p. 165. Billy Balsam in his new Livery.
12. p. 185. Mr Romford at Dalberry Lees.
13. p. 202. This is a pretty present for a Master of Hounds to receive.
14. p. 209. "Fresh as a Four year old—Went off like a shot!"
15. p. 226. The Loose-Box door was opened, out came the hounds with a cry.
16. p. 255. What matter did it make to him how she rode confound this ugly place!
17. p. 272. Mr. Stotfold—Master of Staghounds.
18. p. 284. The "Benicia Boy" astonishes Miss Birches Establishment.
19. p. 298. "Rot the beggar!" exclaims Romford.
20. p. 306. Miss Shannon's arrival at Baldon Hall.
21. p. 330. The Invasion.
22. p. 338. Sink! ar always said ar could polish him off.
23. p. 352. The Baronet.
24. p. 377. "Most pernicious woman!"

FIRST EDITION.—*Published in 12 parts in red pictorial wrappers by Leech, and on completion issued in red cloth as above with gilt design on upper cover of Huntsman and Hound, lower*

Surtees's Romford's Hounds (*contd.*)

cover undecorated except for blind side border design. Spine lettered Mr Romford's Hounds Illustrated by John Leech and H. K. Browne, with 3 designs in gilt, at top mounted huntsman, in centre lady and gentleman, at foot hounds and keepers. All edges uncut, plain yellow ends.

The first 14 plates and the cover illustration are by Leech, and the other coloured plates and the title vignette by Phiz. Plate 10 in proof state is lettered " Capt. Spurrier " only.

ISSUE OF PARTS.—There are 3 issues of Part I. One is simply lettered " Mr. Romford's Hounds," a second lettered Mr. Facey Romford's Hounds in outline lettering, and a third Mr Facey Romford's Hounds in solid lettering. All the remaining parts are as the last.

The advertisements of the parts are as follows:

Part | I. Callaghans Opera Glasses, Burrows Binoculars, and H. J. & D. Nicoll Court Taylors + insert Facey Romford Advertiser 8 pp. May 1864 + Important Family Medicine 4 pp.

„ | II. ditto, but Facey Romford Advertiser 8 pp. dated June 1864 and in addition The Temple Anecdotes 4 pp. 12mo.

„ | III. Callaghans Opera Glasses, Burrows Binoculars, H. J. & D. Nicoll Court Taylors + insert Facey Romford Advertiser 8 pp. July 1864.

„ | IV. Revalenta Arabica Food takes the place of Callaghan's advt. otherwise as in part III, but Facey Romford Advertiser 8 pp. dated Aug. 1864.

„ | V. ditto but Facey Romford Advertiser 4 pp. dated Sept. 1864.

„ | VI. Allnutt's Fruit Lozenges, Brown & Polsons Patent Corn Flour Nicoll + insert Note of Lever's Martin of Cro Martin + Liverpool & London & Globe Insurance Co. 4 pp.

„ | VII. Silver & Co., Allnutt, Nicoll + insert slip " Just Published . . . The Belle of the Village."

„ | VIII. Edmiston, Allnutt, Nicoll.

„ | IX. ditto.

„ | X. ditto + insert Liverpool London & Globe Insurance Co. 4 pp. (blue).

„ | XI. ditto.

„ | XII. ditto + insert Liverpool London & Globe Insurance Co. 4 pp. (pink) + slip " Sporting Works by the same author."

476 [SURTEES (R.)]

Mr. Sponge's Sporting Tour. By the Author of "Handley Cross," "Jorrocks's Jaunts," etc., etc. (vignette) (rule) With Illustrations by John Leech (rule) London: Bradbury and Evans, 11, Bouverie Street

Octavo. 1853

COLLATION.—Half-title " Mr. Sponge's Sporting Tour " (v. blank) + Title as above (v. London: Bradbury and Evans, Printers, Whitefriars) + Dedication to Rt. Hon. Lord Elcho 1 p. (v. blank) + Preface 1 p. (v. blank) + Contents 2 pp. (ix–x) + Engravings on Steel 1 p. (v. Engravings on wood) + pp. 1–408 + 18 coloured plates + 8 pp. of advertisement by Bradbury & Evans at end.

13 coloured plates and 84 wood engravings by J. Leech.

1. p. 12. Mr. Sponge is introduced to "'Ercles."
2. p. 56. Hercules "takes" a Draper's Shop.
3. p. 80. Mr. Sponge at Jawleyford Court.
4. p. 102. One of Multum in Parvo's "going" days.
5. p. 160. Sudden appearance of Mr. Sponge at Farmer Springwheat's—Horror of Lord Scamperdale.
6. p. 181. Mr. Sponge completely scatters his Lordship.
7. p. 213. Mr. Bragg's Equestrian Portrait.
8. p. 227. A Day with Puffington's Hounds.
9. p. 288. Hunting the Hounds.
10. p. 299. Mr. Sponge arrives at Sir 'Arry's.
11. p. 330. Mr Jogglebury Crowdey with his dog and his gun.
12. p. 379. Lucy Glitters showing the way.
13. p. 385. Mr Sponge declares himself [often used as a frontispiece].

Surtees's Sponge's Sporting Tour (*contd.*)

FIRST EDITION.—Published originally in 13 monthly parts in red paper wrappers designed by Leech, and on completion issued in book form as above " handsomely bound in [red] cloth price 14s. or with gilt edges price 15s."   The upper cover bears a design of gentleman kneeling and offering fox's brush to lady the whole within a harness frame with fox head at foot, the lower cover is un-decorated save for blind border design, the spine strip bears lettering " Mr. Sponge's Sporting Tour illustrated by John Leech" with 3 gilt designs, at top huntsman's cap, crop, spurs and fox's brush, in centre fox's head and girth, at foot horse on pedestal with hounds at base.   Edges uncut, yellow end papers the first bearing advertisement of Handley Cross, second Child's History of England &c., third Vanity Fair &c., the fourth Illustrated Works suitable presents.   +

There are two issues of this First Edition.   The first issue is dedicated to Lord Elcho [Later issues to Earl Elcho] p. 95 is headed Mr Sponge's sorting Tour, p. 229 has a woodcut and the advertisements on the end papers are printed in red.   In the second issue of first edition, the spelling on p. 95 is corrected, the woodcut is on p. 230 instead of p. 229 and the advertisements on the end papers are printed in black.

The wrappers bear title and vignette of huntsman offering fox's brush to Lady with following advertisements.

Part   I. Locock's Pulmonic Wafers, Poulsons Patent Self Colour Cloth, and Edmistons Pocket Siphonia.
„   II. Pulvermacher's Hydro Electric Chain, Poulson & Edmiston.
„   III. Bleak House, Pulvermacher & Edmiston.
„   IV. Bleak House, Childs History of England & Edmiston + Insert Peoples Illus. Journal 2 pp.
„   V. Registered Aerial Pardessus, Harris & Son's Opera Glasses, Edmiston.
„   VI. Registered Aerial Pardessus, Peoples Illust Journal, Edmiston + insert.   Chapman & Halls notice of Dickens works.
„   VII. Aerial Pardessus, Allsopps Pale Ale, Edmiston + insert 4 pp. slip Allsopp's Ale.
„   VIII. Poulson Aerial Pardessus, Harris & Son, Edmiston.
„   IX. Poulson, Self Colour Cloth, Vegetable Kingdom, Edmiston.
„   X. ditto.
„   XI. Poulsons, Cloth, Rowlands Macassar Oil & Edmiston + insert 8 pp. Allsopp's Pale Ale.
„   XII. and XII ditto + 4 pp. insert Handley Cross, Childs History, Punch Pocket Book, Brit Winter Garden, Sponge Sporting Tour.

Reprinted by Bradbury Agnew & Co. (1888) with coloured plates by Wildrake, Heath & Jellicoe.

477 [SURTEES (R. S.)]

"Plain or Ringlets?"   By the Author of "Handley Cross," "Sponge's Sporting Tour," "Ask Mamma" etc. etc. (vignette of hound jumping fork of tree) With Illustrations by John Leech.   London: Bradbury and Evans, 11, Bouverie Street

Octavo.   1860

COLLATION.—Engraved title "Plain or Ringlets" (coloured vignette of Cupid dressing young lady's hair) London: Bradbury & Evans, 11, Bouverie Street 1860 + Printed title as above (v. London: Bradbury and Evans, Printers Whitefriars) + Dedication to his son 1 p. (v. blank) + Contents 4 pp. (v–viii) + Steel Engravings 1 p. (v. Wood Engravings) + pp. 1–406 + 12 numbered pp. of Advertisements of Bradbury and Evans + Frontispiece and 12 coloured plates.

13 coloured plates and 44 wood engravings by J. Leech.

Front.   Plain or Ringlets [the engraved title].
1. p.   15. The Gypsey's Prophecy.
2. p.   48. Mr. Bunting on his way to the Picnic.
3. p.   77. The Two Strings.

Surtees's Plain or Ringlets (*contd.*)

4. p. 127. Rosa at Mayfield.
5. p. 157. Rosa & the Earl.
6. p. 174. The Mere Matter of Form.
7. p. 205. The Foreign Prince distinguishes himself.
8. p. 260. Mr. Bunting's Shocking Bad Horse!
9. p. 262. Who would have thought of seeing you.
10. p. 306. Appleton Hall.
11. p. 339. The Jug and his Juvenile Field.
12. p. 385. Mr Bunting rejected [frequently used as additional frontispiece].

FIRST EDITION.—Published originally in 13 monthly parts in red pictorial wrappers by Leech, and on completion issued in red cloth as above with gilt design on upper cover repeating the vignette of the engraved title, lower cover undecorated save for blind side border design, the back strip bearing lettering, Plain or Ringlets Illustrated by John Leech, with 3 gilt designs, at top, Lady on Horse, in centre 2 cupids at foot, huntsman mounted on steam engine.

The 13 parts in red paper wrappers each bear the title and advertisements of Rowlands, Kalydor, Samuel Bros. and Mappins Cutlery. Part XII contains a 12-pp. List of Works published by Bradbury and Evans.

478 [SVININE (Paul)]

Sketches of Russia; illustrated with Fifteen Engravings (small swelled rule) London: Printed for R. Ackermann, 101 Strand by J. Diggens, St Ann's Lane (small rule).

Octavo.   1814

COLLATION.—Title as above (v. blank) + Dedication 1 p. (v. blank) + List of Plates and Contents 2 pp. + To the Editor pp. i–x + Text pp. 1–112 + 15 coloured aquatint plates, each plate (except the two portraits) marked, P. Svinine [or Swinie] delt.   J. Bluck sct.   Published at R. Ackermann's 101 Strand.

1. Front. Empress of Russia.
2. p.   1. Emperor Alexander.
3. p. 12. The Monument of Peter the Great in St Petersburgh.
4. p. 30. The Mansion of Mr Paschcott at Moscow.
5. p. 47. A Cozak Killing a Tiger in Siberia in 1810.
6. p. 59. New Cazan church in St Petersbourg.
7. p. 67. The Field of Mars in St Petersburg.
8. p. 72. Circassian.
9. p. 81. A general view of the Kremlin.
10. p. 83. View of the Ancient Palace of the Kremlin.
11. p. 93. The New Exchange in St Petersburg.
12. p. 97. The amusement on the ice.
13. p. 102. Summer Travelling in Russia.
14. p. 104. Winter Travelling in Russia.
15. p. 106. The Public Garden in St Petersburgh.
    p. 106. Two pages of Music.

A scarce book with very charming plates.

479 Swiss Costume.   London   Published by Rodwell & Martin   New Bond Street

Duodecimo.   1824

A series of 24 plates without title or text, except for buff wrapper which bears title and imprint as above upon a scenic design.

Swiss Costume (*contd.*)

The 24 plates are each marked, G. Scharf Delt and are as follows:

Berne.
Soleure.
Zurich (Wenthal).
Berne.
Haut Valais.
Zurich.
Appenzel (Rhode exterieur).
Neufchatel.

Geneva.
Berne.
Berne (Gougisberg).
Unterwalden (Engelberg).
Unterwalden.
Soleure.
Appenzel.
Argovie.

Berne.
Uri.
Vaud.
Turgovie.
Schaffouse.
Fribourg.
Basle.
Argovie.

480 TAYLOR (W. B.)

History of the University of Dublin   By W. B. Taylor   Augt. 5 1819.

Quarto.

COLLATION.—No printed title, but buff wrapper with engraved lettering as above upon a large arch, with Minerva above, and three students below, with a view of rocky shore and temple, through the archway, and tesselated foreground initialed W.B.T. (v. blank) + List of Subscribers' Names 1 p. (v. blank) + Preface 1 leaf (p. i–ii) + Introduction pp. iii–xi (p. xii blank) + Text pp. 13–72 + 7 coloured aquatint plates + 2 coloured etchings.

1. The College Park, Trin. Coll. Dublin   Drawn and Etched by W. B. Taylor   Engraved by R. Havell & Son.
2. N.E. View of the College Observatory, at Dunsinok Co. Dublin.   Drawn & Etched by W. B. Taylor. Aquatinted by R. Havell & Son.   Published 1st Jany. 1820, for Taylor's History of the University of Dublin.
3. S.W. View of the Library, Trin. Coll. Dublin.   Drawn & Etched by W. B. Taylor.   Aquatinted by R. Havell & Son.   Published 1st Jany. 1820, for Taylor's History of the University of Dublin.
4. A Fellow of T.C.D.   Drawn by W. B. Taylor.   Engraved by B. Del Sarto.
5. The Grand Square. T.C.D. at the quarterly examination.   Drawn & Etched by W. B. Taylor. Aquitented (*sic*) by Bluck.
6. Museum of T.C.D.   Drawn & Etched by W. B. Taylor.   Engraved by R. Havell & Son.
7. A Fellow Commoner of T.C.D.   Drawn by W. B. Taylor (*sic*)   Etched by B. Del Sarto.   London, Published Augt. 10th by W. B. Tayler (*sic*).
8. View of the Dining Hall, &c.   From the Provost Garden.   Drawn & Etched by W. B. Taylor.   Engraved by R. Havell.   London Published Augt. 6th 1819, by W. B. Taylor.
9. Front of Trinity College, Dublin.   Drawn & Etch'd by W. B. Taylor.   Engraved by Bluck.   London, Published Augt. 6th 1819, by W. B. Taylor.

REMARKS.—"*the whole plan arranged as nearly as possible to correspond with that adopted by Mr Ackermann, in his Description of the English Universities.*"   *There were 122 subscribers, 24 for large-paper copies, twelve copies each being taken by Ackermann, Allen & Sons, Longman & Co., and Mr Milliken, and 6 by Mr Keene. That is 160 were subscribed. The work however was not a success, as it was never completed, the text stopping at p. 72 in the middle of a word.   Issued at 12s. per part.*

Extremely rare.   I only know of three copies, one in Trinity College Dublin, one in the possession of D. M. Colman Esq., one in the Athenaeum, the above collation being taken from Mr. Colman's copy by the kind permission of the owner.

481 TEMPLE (R.)

Eight Views of the Mauritius comprising the Positions of the British Army, Commanded by the Honble. Majr. Genl. J. Abercrombie, on the 29th & 30th of Novr. & 1st of

Temple's Mauritius (*contd.*)

Decr 1810, also of the Town and Harbour of Port Louis. Most Respectfully dedicated to Lieut. Col. L. Smith & the Officers of H.M. 65th Regt. by their most Obedient Humble Servant, R. Temple. Bombay 1811 H.M. 65th Regt.

Oblong Folio 1811

COLLATION.—Title as above (v. blank) + 8 coloured aquatint plates. Each plate marked at head, Isle of France No. 1 (–8) and below, R. Temple, H.M. 65th Regt. delt. J. Clark sculp. Published April 1813 by W. Haines, 10 South Molton St, London.

1. View from the Deck of the Upton Castle Transport, of the British Army Landing. 29th Nov 1810.
2. A West View of the Moulin à Poudre, where the British Army halted 30th Novr 1810.
3. Part of the British Army, forming before Port Louis 1st Decr 1810.
4. Port Louis from the Champs de Mars.
5. The Town, Harbour and Country, Eastward of Port Louis.
6. The Town of Port Louis, from the West of the Harbour.
7. The West of Port Louis, from the Harbour.
8. Port Louis, about one Mile distant from the Shore.

Beside the published date at foot, plates 4 to 8 have the date of drawing after the artist's name, as follows: (4) *Dec 10th* 1810, (5) *Dec 10, 1810,* (6) *Dec 23, 1810,* (7) *Jan 2, 1811,* (8) *Dec 1, 1810.*

482 TEMPLE (R.)

Sixteen Views of Places in the Persian Gulph, taken in the years 1809–10. Illustrative of the Proceedings of the Forces employd in the Expedition sent from Bombay, under the Command of Captn. Wainwright of H.M. Ship Chiffone, and Lieut. Coll. Smith of H.M. 65th Regiment, against the Arabian Pirates, most Respectfully Dedicated to Lieut. Coll. L. Smith & the Officers of H.M. 65th Regt., by their most obedt. humble servt., R. Temple, H.M. 65th Regt. Bombay.

Oblong Folio. 1811

COLLATION.—Title as above (v. blank) + 16 coloured plates marked at head, No. 1[–16] and below R. Temple, H.M. 65th Regt. delt. J. Clark sculp., Published April 1813 by W Haines 10 South Molton St, London.

1. The Fleet under Convoy of H. Mys. Ship Chiffone, Captn. Wainwright, leaving Bombay Sept 14th 1809, from the Apollo Gate.
2. Muskat Harbour from the Fishermens' Rock.
3. Muskat, from the Harbour.
4. A View of Mutra from the East.
5. Rus al Khyma with the attack of H C's Cruisers on the Eveng. of 11th Nov, 1809.
6. The Wall & Beach near Rus al Khyma, with the Troops preparing to land on the morning of the 13th Nov, 1809.
7. The Troops landing at Rus al Khyma at Sunrise. 13th Novr 1809.
8. The Storming of a large Storehouse near Rus al Khyma where Capt. Dancey of H.M. 65th Regt. was killed Novr 18th 1809.
9. Rus al Khyma from the S.W. and the situation of the Troops at ½ past 2 p.m. Novr 13th 1809.
10. A View of Linga or Lung from the Sea during the destruction of the Dow's &c., Nov. 16th 1809.
11. A View of Luft 20th Nov 1809.
12. The Attack on the Fort of Luft Novr 17th 1809.
13. Schinaass from the Sea.
14. The Attack of the Enemy's Cavalry at Schinaass Jan 2nd 1810.
15. Schinaass from the right of the Encampment on the morning of the 3rd Jany 1810.
16. The Storming of Schinaass Jan 5th 1810.

483 TERRY (D.)

British Theatrical Gallery, A Collection of Whole Length Portraits, with Biographical notices, by D. Terry, Esq., (rule) Published by H. Berthoud, 65 Regents Quadrant, Piccadilly. (rule).

Folio.   1825

COLLATION.—Title as above (v. blank) + Table of Contents 1 p. (v. blank) + 34 unnumbered leaves of Text + 20 portraits.   Each plate bears Berthoud's imprint and is marked, Engraved by R. Cooper.

1. Mr Kean (in Richard III).   Painted by G. Clint A.R.A.
2. Mrs Siddons (as Lady Macbeth).   Painted by Harlowe.
3. Mr C. Young (as the Stranger).   Painted by M. W. Sharp.
4. Mr Harley (as Caleb Quotem).   Painted by M. W. Sharp.
5. Mr Knight (as Hodge).   Painted by G. Clint, A.R.A.
6. Mr Gattie (as Mons. Morbleu).   Painted by M. W. Sharpe.
7. Mr Dowton (as Doctor Cantwell).   Drawn by De Wilde.
8. Mr Willkinson (as Michael)   Painted by G. Clint. A.R.A.
9. Mr Fitzwilliam (as Looney Mactwolter)   Drawn by F. Waldeck.
10. Mr Cooper (as Clement Cleveland)   Painted by M. W. Sharpe.
11. Mr G. Smith (as Robin)   Drawn by De Wilde.
12. Mr Simmons (as Baron Munchausen).   Drawn by De Wilde.
13. Signor de Begnis (as Don Geronio).   Drawn by F. Waldeck.
14. Monsr. Le Blond (Kings Theatre).   Drawn by F. Waldeck.
15. Mrs Bland (as Mme Morbleu).   Drawn by De Wilde.
16. Miss S. Booth (as Christine).   Painted by M. W. Sharp.
17. Miss Smithson (as Miss Dorillon).   Painted by G. Clint, A.R.A.
18. Miss Copeland (as Fanny).   Drawn by F. Waldeck.
19. Mile Noblet (In the Ballet of La Paysanne Supposée).   Painted by F. Waldeck.
20. Mlle Hullin (Kings Theatre).   Drawn by F. Waldeck.

Issued in boards with printed paper label at 4/14/6.
There are plain and coloured copies.

484 [THORNTON (A.)]

The Adventures of a Post Captain: by a Naval Officer.   With characteristic engravings. by Mr. Williams (thick and thin rule) London: Published by J. Johnston, Cheapside: Simpkin and Marshall, Stationers' Court; Sherwood, Neely, and Jones, Paternoster-Row; S. W. Forces, 50, Piccadilly, and 312, Oxford Street; Macredie and Co. Edinburgh; Milliken, Dublin; and sold by all booksellers

Octavo.   [1817]

COLLATION.—Engraved title + Printed title as above (v. J. & T. Agg 21 Water Lane, Fleet Street, London) + Dedication to the British Navy 1 p. (v. blank) + pp. 1–282 + Guide to the Binder 1 leaf + 25 coloured plates, including the engraved title.

Plates 1 to 7 marked, Williams fecit, the remainder without artist's name.

1. Front.   But when he heard the magic word,
      The loyal tar let fall his sword:
2. Engraved Title—"The Post Captain or Adventures of a True British Tar by a Naval Officer."   The preceding lettering on a sail with figure of Britannia Jack Tars and British lion, with 4 line verse beneath, and imprint, London Published by J. Johnston Cheapside.
3. p.   4. Kept the gay captain right ahead
      and steer'd him safely into bed

Thornton's Post Captain (*contd.*)

4. p. 34. In sulky dudgeon the two tars,
Cover'd with shame much more than scars
Walked side by side.

5. p. 37. "Lock'd in a room, securely barr'd
To taste their valours sad reward
Sat the two heroes mute and Pale

6. p. 55. "The haughty commandant now came,
His visage ruddied o'er with shame,
With whisker'd cheeks, and lengthen'd chin,
And rage and hatred in his grin.

7. p. 69. Poor Mizzen tho no melting lubber
Spite of himself, began to blubber
And whimper'd out his honest wishes
That Bowsprit yet might cheat the fishes.

8. p. 80. "Now sweeter tasks await each tar,
Mercy usurps the seat of war:
And many a struggling boat now braves
The tempered fury of the waves

9. p. 85. In chaise and four now gaily seated,
By giddy crowds most loudly greeted,
Bowsprit his rapid course pursu'd
And soon outstripp'd the multitude.

10. p. 103. But callous to the sordid crew,
Reckless of prayer and menace too,
The gallant sailor made retreat,
Safe to the shelter of his fleet

11. p. 114. The maiden listend, blush'd and look'd
As she would have the Words rebuk'd
But there was something in her eye,
Which seem'd to give the words the lie.

12. p. 131. "At length they reached the palace where,
Enthron'd and guarded with much care,
The chieftain sat a turban'd sage,
Rever'd for length of beard and age.

13. p. 140. The frighted slaves, the harem dames,
Scar'd by the progress of the flames,
Ran to and fro and all deplor'd,
The sudden ruin of their lord.

14. p. 152. The chief had perish'd but a tar,
Pushing the gaping moors afar,
Leap'd boldly in the ranging wave,
And snatched the chieftain from the grave.

15. p. 161.   . . . She was alone,
and seated on a rugged stone,
Her head upon her hand reclin'd,
As tho to wretchedness resign'd.

16. p. 170. And vainly now the Arabs pour'd,
Along the beach and promptly scour'd,
With flaming torch each rocky cave,
That grac'd the margin of the wave.

17. p. 177. Two of the dark assassins fell,
And died with horrifying yell,
The third was seiz'd and led away,
T' explain the causes of the fray.

18. p. 194. There sat and more terrific sprite
Ne'er rode upon the wing of Night
His foul desertion to upbraid
The lorn and lost Castilian maid

Thornton's Post Captain (*contd.*)

19. p. 214. And now his confidence all flew,
To hope he bade a last adieu,
The trigger pulled and at the sound,
Fell prone and senseless on the ground

20. p. 232. His eye shot forth a withering look
Which e'en the harpy scarce could brook
Then from the scabbard with firm hand
He swiftly drew his glittering brand.

21. p. 240. His brow relax'd its gloomy frown
As, without pause, the kind unknown
To the bail bond affix'd a name
which oft had been proclaim'd by fame.

22. p. 256. Then sudden starting from his stare
He cry'd 'where is my daughter where?
Here Ellen cry'd banish all fear!
Your happy, long lost girl is here!

23. p. 259. The tar just paus'd as if to trace
The features of his time worn face,
And rushing tow'rds him loudly roar'd—
It is my father by the Lord!

24. p. 272. He seem'd as one by fortune crost,
In battle half his limbs were lost,
A leg and arm were all remained,
Of those which he from nature gain'd.

25. p. 279. The two old men their bumpers quaff'd
And over ancient stories laugh'd,
Till fumes o'erpower'd each aged head,
And both were carried off to bed.

Published in 1 Elegant Volume, royal octavo, 12 monthly or weekly numbers, price 2s.
Issues.—There are two issues of this book.
First issue as above, Printed by J. and T. Agg.
Second issue printed by W. Lewis.

485 *Collation of 2nd issue.—Printed title as in 1st issue but with a rule each side of " by a Naval Officer," and the imprint on the reverse is changed to London: Printed by W. Lewis, 21 Finch-Lane Cornhill + Dedication (v. List of Plates) + pp. 1 –280 + 25 plates as in first issue.   Issued in 12 parts at 2s. per part.*

486 THORNTON (Alfred)

Don Juan. Volume the First. By Alfred Thornton, Esq. (thick and thin rule) With fifteen coloured engravings (rule) London: Printed for Thomas Kelly, 17, Paternoster Row (rule)

2 vols. Octavo.   1821

COLLATION VOL. I.—Title as above (v. (rule) Entered at Stationers Hall (rule) London: Printed by W. Clowes Northumberland Court) + Advertisement 2 pp. (iii–iv) + Contents 8 pp. (v–xii List of Plates also on p. xii) + pp. 1–619 + 15 coloured plates each marked London Published [date] by Thos. Kelly 17 Paternoster Row.

1. Front. Don Juan and his Man Leporello   May 5 1821.
2. p. 15. The Alguazils seeking Juan in the Cottage of Dame Ursula   May 5 1821.
3. p. 33. Don Juan's Extraordinary Dream   May 5 1821.
4. p. 118. Don Juan's insolent intrusion into the Bed Chamber of Donna Aurelia   Aug. 1821.
5. p. 156. Fatima seeking the protection of Juan, after the Murder of her Father   May 5 1821.

Thornton's Don Juan (*contd.*)

6. p. 169. Don Juan's First Introduction to the King of Faisan   May 5 1821.
7. p. 195. Don Juan receiving the Dying Commands of Queen Naama   May 5 1821.
8. p. 222. Horrible Exhibition of the Egyptian Serpent Charmer.   May 5 1821.
9. p. 251. The Dancing Girls exhibiting before Don Juan and Zaide in the Harem of Sidi Bey   May 5 1821.
10. p. 273. Don Jaun escaping from the Shipwreck   Aug. 18 1821.
11. p. 317. Odyssas presenting the dead body of his Sister to Ali Pacha   May 5 1821.
12. p. 351. Duel between the Woman Hater and the Marquis Filipopoli   May 5 1821.
13. p. 433. A Sledge Party on the Danube by Torchlight   May 5 1821.
14. p. 561. Leperello receiving the Village Deputation at Juan's Castle   Aug. 18 1821.
15. p. 614. Don Juan threatened with Torture in the Cells of the Inquisition   May 5 1821.

VOL. II.—Title "Don Juan; Volume the Second: containing his Life in London, or, a True Picture of the British Metropolis.   By Alfred Thornton, Esq." (rule) 8 line quotation from Boswell's Life of Johnson commencing How different a place is London (rule) With Coloured Engravings.   "London Printed for Thomas Kelly, 17, Paternoster-Row (rule) 1832" (v. as in Vol. I) + Reader 2 pp. + Contents pp. v–xi (p. xii Arrangement of Plates) + pp. 1–660 + 16 coloured plates.

1. Front.   The Wellington Statue and relief of the Guard.   Sept. 21, 1822.
2. p.   1. Procession of the Lord Mayor of London on the 9th of November   Feb. 1822.
3. p. 116. Mr Belzoni's Exhibition of an ancient Egyptian Tomb   Decr. 1 1821.
4. p. 156. Untimely irruption of the Police into a Fashionable Gaming House   Jan. 12 1822.
5. p. 193. Scene at the Breaking-up of a Fashionable Rout   July 6th 1822.
6. p. 220. A "Set-to" at the Fives Court for the benefit of "One of the Fancy"   Octo. 23 1821.
7. p. 268. A Masquerade at the King's Theatre, Opera House   Nov. 17 1821.
8. p. 286. A Notorious Hotel on Fire at Midnight   April 18 1822.
9. p. 315. Coronation of George the Fourth in Westminster Abbey   Nov. 1821.
10. p. 366. The King conferring the Honour of Knighthood   Sept. 7 1822.
11. p. 448. A noted Oyster Room near the Theatres—Time 3 o'Clock in the Morning   Feb. 23 1822.
12. p. 492. Descent of Madame Saqui surrounded by Fireworks   May 18 1822.
13. p. 578. The notorious Black Billy "At Home" to a London Street Party   March 1822.
14. p. 593. Royal Armoury in the Tower of London   April 2 1822.
15. p. 601. The Westminster Pit A "Turn up" between a Dog & Jacco Macacco the Fighting Monkey   January 1 1822.
16. p. 658. A few knowing Fanciers at an Evening Pigeon-show   Jan. 26 1822.

Issued in parts, numbers or in boards.   The 31 plates are by Atkinson.   The first volume consists of a mixture of Byron's Don Juan and the opera Don Giovanni.   The second volume was inspired from Egan's Life in London, some of the same incidents being depicted in the plates, for example plate 15, Vol. 2.

487 Don Juan.

Another Edition was published in 1825–36.   The collation is the same as in the first edition above.   The imprint on verso of title of Vol. I is changed to London: Printed by W. Clowes and Sons, Stamford Street.   The verso of title of Vol. II is blank.

488 THORNTON (Colonel)

A Sporting Tour through Various Parts of France, in the year 1802: including a concise description of the Sporting Establishments, mode of Hunting, and other field amusements, as practised in that country, with general observations on the Arts, Sciences,

Thornton's Sporting Tour in France (*contd.*)

Agriculture, Husbandry, and Commerce: strictures on the customs and manners of the French People: with a view of the comparative advantages of Sporting in France and England. In a series of letters to the Right Hon., the Earl of Darlington. To which is prefixed, an account of French Wolf Hunting. (rule) By Colonel Thornton, of Thornville-Royal, Yorkshire. (double rule). Illustrated with upwards of eighty correct and picturesque delineations from original drawings from nature, by Mr Bryant, and other eminent artists. (rule). In Two Volumes, Vol. I [II]. (thin and thick rule). Albion Press Printed: By James Cundee, Ivy Lane: for Longman, Hurst, Rees and Orme, Paternoster-Row, and C. Chapple, Pall Mall. (2 line rule).

Quarto.   1806

COLLATION VOL. I.—Engraved title with vignette of Wolf + Printed title as above (v. blank) + Dedication 1 p. (v. blank) + Preface vii–x + Contents xi–xvii (xviii blank) + sub title "Wolf Hunting" 1 p. (v. blank) + Wolf Hunting pp. xxi–xxxix + List of Illustrations pp. xli–lv + List Illustrations to Vol. II pp. lvii–lxvi + Text pp. 1–168 + Index to Vol. I 3 pp. + 24 plates by Bryant, engraved by Merigot.

 1. Front.   Portrait of Author.
             Engraved Title.
 2. p.   8. A little cabin with 2 Hammocks.   The Ship's Steward.   (Together on one plate.)
 3. p. 11. View from the Hotel du Pacquet Boat at Dieppe, looking towards the Harbour.   Bryant delt. Merigot sc.
 4. p. 14. Opposite the Inn at Dieppe, High Water.   Bryant delt.   Merigot sc.
 5. p. 15. Portrait of a Farmers Daughter near Dieppe.   Character taken at Dieppe.   Bryant del.
 6. p. 16. The Powder Magazine at Dieppe.   Bryant delt., Merigot sc.
 7. p. 17. French Diligence.   Horse rode by Col. Thornton when on a Hunting Party.   Bryant delt.
 8. p. 21. Rouen from the Chartreuse.   Bryant del., Merigot sc.
 9. p. 23. View from the middle of the Bridge of Boats at Rouen.   Bryant del., Merigot sc.
10. p. 25. View of Rouen, from Mount au Malade.   Bryant del., Merigot sc.
11. p. 44. View on the Loire, near Rouen.   Bryant del., Merigot sc.
12. p. 48. Chateau of the Marquis de Conflans.   Bryant del., Merigot sc.
13. p. 50. Le Chateau de Navarre.   Bryant del., Merigot sc.
14. p. 54. View at Vernon.   Bryant del., Merigot sc.
15. p. 56. French Dragoon.   Market Woman at Vernon.   Bryant del., Merigot sc.
16. p. 58. From the Terrace of the Palace at St Germains.   Bryant del., Merigot sc.
17. p. 62. View of Versailles, coming from St Germains.   Bryant del., Merigot sc.
18. p. 66. Chateau at Versailles, from the Terrace.   Bryant del., Merigot sc.
19. p. 70. Sporting Apparatus.   Bryant del., Merigot sc.
20. p. 87. Tomb of Rousseau on the Island of Poplars.   Bryant del., Merigot sc.
21. p. 130. The Great Lake at Eremonvilliers.   Bryant del., Merigot sc.
22. p. 145. Le Chateau de Mereville.   Bryant del., Merigot sc.
23. p. 146. Chateau de Mereville from the Top of the Pillar.   Bryant del., Merigot sc.
24. p. 165. The Bridge at Blois.   Bryant del., Merigot sc.

VOLL. II.—Engraved title with Vignette of Pointers &c. + Printed title + Contents of Vol. II pp. v–xii + pp. 1–260 + Index 3 leaves + Directions to Binder 1 leaf + 28 plates.

25. Front.   Chanteloup, the Seat of the Duke of Choiseul.   Bryant de., Merigot sc.
             Engraved Title with vignette of Partridge Shooting.
26. p.   8. Part of Tours on coming in from Vendome.   Bryant del., Merigot sc.
27. p. 12. View and Castle of Mont-bazon.   Bryant del., Merigot sc.
28. p. 22. Horses drinking from a picture of Paul Potter's, in the Louvre, with a distant view of Tours.
29. p. 24. View on the side of the Loire.   Bryant del., Merigot sc.
30. p. 34. Chateau of M. Le Mercier near Blois.   Bryant del., Merigot sc.
31. p. 38. Lake near Cheverney.   Bryant del., Merigot sc.

Thornton's Sporting Tour in France (*contd.*)

32. p. 43. In the Forest of Fontainbleau. Bryant del., Merigot sc.
33. p. 44. Coming out of Fontainbleau. Bryant del., Merigot sc.
34. p. 60. Specimen of Cattle taken near Fontainbleau. Bryant del., Merigot sc.
35. p. 61. View from the Bois de Boulogne. Bryant del., Merigot sc.
36. p. 86. Chateau Thierry on the Road to Trois Fontaine. Bryant del., Merigot sc.
37. p. 102. Convent des Trois Fontaine, and Chateau de Jaegersbourg. Bryant del., Merigot sc.
38. p. 152. Sporting Scene in the Forest of Trois Fontaine. Bryant del., Merigot sc.
39. p. 126. On the Road to Trois Fontaine. Bryant del., Merigot sc.
40. p. 128. Environs of Beaulieu, and Entrance of the Convent of Trois Fontaine. Bryant del., Merigot sc.
    p. 130. Two sheets of music. "The Horns."
41. p. 140. Jack Boots. Bryant del., Merigot sc.
42. p. 157. View of the Chateau at Chantilly. Bryant del., Merigot sc.
43. p. 165. Entrance of the Chateau at Chantilly. Bryant del., Merigot sc.
44. p. 179. Woodcutter, Watercarrier, Fishwoman, Flour Porter.
45. p. 181. The Market of La Halle in Paris. Bryant del., Merigot sc.
46. p. 183. Itinerant Musicians. Shoe Black. Chestnuts, Washerwomen (on 1 sheet). Bryant del., Merigot sc.
47. p. 184. Stocking Mender. Ptisan Grapes, Porter.
48. p. 191. Parisian Costume. (Headdresses.)
49. p. 192. French costume taken from Life.
50. p. 228. Front view of Thornville Royal.
51. p. 229. Library at Thornville Royal.
52. p. 230. Hawk Houses at Thornville Royal. Temple of Victory in Thornville Park.
53. p. 237. Pheasant Shooting.

489 TITSINGH (M.)

Illustrations of Japan; consisting of Private Memoirs and Anecdotes of the Reigning Dynasty of the Djogouns, or Sovereigns of Japan a description of the Feasts and Ceremonies observed throughout the year at their court; and of the ceremonies customary at Marriages and Funerals: to which are subjoined, observations on the legal suicide of the Japanese, Remarks on their Poetry, an Explanation of their mode of reckoning time, particulars respecting the Dosia Powder, the Preface of a work by Confoutzee on Filial Piety &c. &c. By M. Titsingh formerly chief agent to the Dutch East India Company at Nangasaki (rule) Translated from the French, by Frederic Shoberl (rule) with Coloured Plates, faithfully copied from Japanese original designs (rule) London Printed for R. Ackermann, 101, Strand (rule).

Quarto.   1822

COLLATION.—Title as above (v. London: Printed by William Clowes, Northumberland-court) + Address 2 pp. (iii–iv) + Contents 2 pp. (v–vi) + Advertisement respecting MSS. of M. Titsingh pp. (vii–x) + Preliminary Remarks by M. Abel Remusat pp. (xi–xvi) + sub-title "Japan," Part I, &c. (v. blank) + pp. 3–325 + 13 coloured aquatint plates.

Each plate bears Ackermann's imprint with date.

1. Front. Residence of the Djogoun at Yedo.
2. p. 100. Earthquake & Eruption of the Mountain of Asama-yama, in the Province of Sinano   J. C. Stadler sculpt.
3. p. 112. Earthquake, Volcanic Eruption & Inundation in the Province of Simahara.
4. p. 166. Plan of the Dutch Factory in the Island of Desima at Nangasaki.
5. p. 169. House of the Chief of the Dutch Company.
6. p. 170. The Chinese Factory in the Street of Teng-chan at Nangasaki founded in 1688.
7. p. 224. [Marriage Ceremony].

Titsingh's Japan (*contd.*)

8. p. 244. [Domestic Furniture &c.].
9. *ibd.* [Bride visiting &c.].
10. *ibd.* [Appartment prepared for wedding &c.]
11. *ibd.* Different Ways of folding paper &c.
12. p. 243. Tomb of the Governor of Nangasaki &c.
13. p. 250. Funeral Procession of the Governor of Nangasaki (long folding view, or 3 plates 13–18).

490 TOD (G.)

Plans, Elevations and Sections, of Hot Houses, Green-Houses, an Aquarium, Conservatories, &c., recently built in different parts of England, for various Noblemen and Gentlemen. (2 line rule) By George Tod Surveyor and Hot House Builder (2 line rule) Including a Hot House and Green House in Her Majesty's gardens at Frogmore. (2 line rule) Engraved on 27 plates, with descriptions to each. (2 line rule) London: Published by J. Taylor, at the Architectural Library, 59, High Holborn. (rule)

Folio. 1807

COLLATION.—Half-title (v. blank) + Title as above (v. T. Bensley Printer, Bolt Court, Fleet Street) + Preface pp. 4–8 + pp. 9–23 + 27 coloured aquatint plates. There is 1 plate in Introduction (starred), the remainder of the plates are marked, Plate 1 (to 26) each has imprint, London Published, Septr. 1st. 1806, by J. Taylor, 59 High Holborn.

1. p. 8. Intro. Various Flues to a large scale.
1. A Green House and Exotic House executed for Willm. Linwood, Esq. at Hackney, Middx.
2. A Green House executed for John Elliot esq. at Pimlico.
3. A Green House executed for J. E. Liebenrood Esq. at Prospect Hill, Berks.
4. A Green House executed for Geo. Farrant at Upper Brook St.
5. A Green House executed for Thos. Caldecott Esq. at Dartford, Kent.
6. A Green House executed for Richd. Dickinson Esq., at Hendon Middx.
7. A Green House executed for Marquis of Blandford at White Knights Berks.
8. Two Conservatories executed for John Jackson Esq. North End Hammersmith.
9. A Conservatory executed for William Gosling Esq. Roehampton Surrey.
10. A Conservatory executed for Lord Viscount Courtenay, Powderham Castle, Devon.
11. A Pinery executed for Sir Joseph Banks Bart. Smallbury Green, Middx.
12. A Pinery executed for Sir Lionel Darell Bart. Richmond Hill, Surrey.
13. A Vinery executed for Earl of Coventry at Croome, Worcestershire.
14. A Pine House executed for Lord Heathfield at Nutwell Court Devon.
15. A Hot House executed for Duke of Bedford at Woburn Abbey.
16. An Aquarium executed for Marquis of Blandford at Whiteknights Berks.
17. A Green House & Hot House executed for Earl Chesterfield at Baylis Bucks.
18. A Range of Hot House executed for John Anthony Rucker Esq. Wandsworth Hill (folding).
19. A Green House and Hot House executed for Her Majesty at Frogmore.
20. Two Peacheries and a Green House. Lord Heathfield at Nutwell Court Devon.
21. A Green House, & Two Peach Houses. Lady Jennings Clarke at Holy Grove, Windsor Forest.
22. Peach House, Green House & Pinery executed for Hon. Champion Dymoke at Scrivelsby Lincs.
23. A Green House & Rosery executed for Earl of Upper Ossory at Ampthill Park Beds.
24. Two Pineries & a Peachery executed for Thomas Porter Esq. at Rockbear House Devon.
25. A Pinery & Orangery executed for John Walter Esq. at Teddington Middx.
26. A Peachery & Green House executed for Rev. Primatt Knapp at Shenley End Bucks.

491 *Reissued in 1823, the printer being J. Moyles, Greville Street, the title altered to read, Her late Majesty. The plates are the same.*

Tom Raw the Griffin, 1828. See under [Doyley (Sir Charles)].

Tour of Doctor Prosody.   See under Rowlandson Syntax Imitation.

Tour of Dr. Syntax through London.   See under Rowlandson Syntax Imitation.

Tour through Paris.   See under Sams (W.).

492 TRESHAM & OTTLEY

The British Gallery of Pictures, selected from the most admired productions of the Old Masters, in Great Britain; accompanied with descriptions, historical and critical. (swelled rule).   By the late Henry Tresham, R.A. professor of painting in The Royal Academy, and William Young Ottley, Esq. F.S.A. the Executive part under the management of Peltro William Tomkins, Esq. Historical Engraver to Her Majesty. (swelled rule) London: Printed by Bensley and Son, Bolt Court, Fleet Street; for Longman, Hurst, Rees, Orme, and Brown, Paternoster Row; Cadell and Davies, Strand; and P. W. Tomkins, New Bond Street. (rule).

Folio.   1818 (1808–1820)

> *COLLATION.*—Half-title "The British Gallery of Pictures" (swelled rule) (v. blank) + Title as above (v. blank) + "To the King" 1 p. (v. blank) + Dedication to King, Prince of Wales, Earl of Dartmouth &c., 1 p. (v. blank) + 25 coloured plates, each plate with 2 pp. of Text (with exception of plate 9, which has 3 pp.) + List of Engravers 1 p. (v. blank).   (Some copies have leaf to Subscribers and Prospectus pp. iii–viii.)

1. Heads of Apostles by Giotto di Bondone.   Drawn by Satchwell, engraved by T. Cheeseman March 1, 1819.
2. The Nativity by Ghirlandajo.   Drawn by W. W. Hodgson, engraved by Mary Ann Bourlier   July 1st 1815.
3. Madonna and Child by Raphael.   Engraved by P. W. Tomkins Nov 9th 1808.
4. La Belle Vierge by Raffaello.   Drawn and Engraved by P. W. Tomkins.   Jany. 31st 1820.
5. The Madonna, Infant Christ and St John by Raffaello.   Drawn by P. W. Tomkins   Engraved by Freeman.   March 1st 1815.
6. The Holy Family with the Infant St John by Giulio Romano.   Engraved by P. W. Tomkins   Octr 10th 1820.
7. The Virgin and Child, Elizabeth and St John by Andrea del Sarto.   Drawn and Engraved by P. W. Tomkins   Sepr 22nd 1808.
8. Gaston de Foix by Giorgione.   Drawn by W. W. Hodgson   Engraved by A. Cardon   Feb. 28th 1811.
9. The Vision of St Augustine by Benvenuto da Garafolo.   Drawn by W. W. Hodgson   Engraved by P. W. Tomkins   Novr 1st 1816   (3 pp. text, p. 4 blank).
10. La Madonna dell Gatto by Baroccio.   Drawn by P. W. Tomkins   Engraved by A. Cardon.   Jany. 5th 1810.
11. Children at Play by Nicolo Poussin.   Drawn by P. Violet,   Engraved by R. Woodman.   March 1st 1816.
12. Mid-Day . . . by Claude Lorraine.   Drawn by W. M. Craig, engraved by J. H. Wright.   August 15th 1809.
13. The Marriage of St Catharine . . . by Parmigiano.   Drawn by W. W. Hodgson, engraved by J. S. Agar.   April 1st 1814.
14. The Horn Book . . . by Schidone.   Drawn by P. W. Tomkins, engraved by Robert Cooper.   Jany 1st 1816.
15. Lot and his Daughters . . . by Guido Reni.   Drawn by Hodgson and P. W. Tomkins and engraved by Schiavonetti & Tomkins   Novr. 1st 1813.
16. Christ in the Sepulchre . . . by Guercino.   Drawn by P. Violet, engraved T. Cheeseman.   Feby. 1st 1813.
17. The Woman taken in Adultery . . . by Rubens.   Drawn by T. Uwins, engraved A. Cardon.   April 6th 1807.

Tresham & Ottley's Gallery of Pictures (*contd.*)

18. The Incredulity of St Thomas . . . by Chevalier Adrian Vander Werff. Drawn by L. Eusebi, engraved E. Scriven. Octr. 27th 1817.
19. An Aquatic Fete at Dort by Cuyp. Drawn by Wm. Westall, engraved T. Medland. March 31st 1813.
20. The Interior of a Cottage . . . by Ad Ostade. Drawn by T. W. Strutt, engraved by A. Cardon and Wm. Bland. Septr 1st 1814.
21. Le Bonnet Vert . . . by D. Teniers. Drawn by T. W. Strutt, engraved by R. Cooper. Novr. 1st 1813.
22. Gerhard Dow (self portrait). Drawn by W. M. Craig, engraved E. Scriven. Augt. 17th 1810.
23. The Village Festival . . . by P. Wouwerman. Drawn by W. M. Craig, engraved J. Scott. November 1st 1816.
24. The Happy Shepherds . . . by N. Berghem. Drawn by W. M. Craig, engraved J. Scott. July 1st 1815.
25. Evening . . . by Paul Potter. Drawn by W. M. Craig, engraved J. Scott June 1st 1814.

An exceedingly fine example of coloured stipple engravings, partly printed in colour, partly finished by hand. Landseer thought so highly of this work, that he paid £50 for a copy in 1847, and thought it cheap.

493 TULLY (Richard)

Narrative of a Ten Years' Residence at Tripoli in Africa: from the original correspondence in the possession of the family of the late Richard Tully, Esq., the British Consul. Comprising Authentic Memoirs and Anecdotes of the Reigning Bashaw, his Family, and other persons of distinction; also, an account of the domestic manners of the Moors, Arabs, and Turks. (rule). Illustrated with a Map, and several coloured Plates. (rule) 2 line quotation Gier Liber XV. 38. (thick and thin rule) London: Printed for Henry Colburn, British and Foreign Public Library, Conduit Street, Hanover Square.

Quarto. 1816

COLLATION.—Title as above (v. Printed by Cox and Bayliss, Great Queen Street, Lincoln's Inn—Fields.) + Preface 2 leaves (pp. iii–vi) + Contents 4 leaves pp. (vii–xiii) (p. xiv blank) + Royal Family of Tripoli 1 p. (v. List of Plates) + pp. 1–370 (including index) + List of Advertisements by Colburn 1 leaf (this is necessary to complete signature) + Map + 5 coloured aquatint plates.

Each plate with imprint, Publish'd May 1, 1816 by Henry Colburn. Conduit Street, London.

1. Front. Sidy Hassan, late Bey of Tripoly.
   p. 1. Map of the Regencies of Tripoly & Tunis.
2. p. 2. Aqueduct near the City of Tripoly.
3. p. 21. Arabs recreating in the Desert. Engraved by R. Havell & Son.
4. p. 35. Officers of the Grand Seraglio regaling. Engraved by R. Havell & Son.
5. p. 35. An Egyptian Puppet Shew. Engraved by Havell & Son.

494 *SECOND EDITION.*—Imprint changed to London: Printed for Henry Colburn, Conduit Street, Hanover Square. Sold also by J. Cumming, Dublin, and Bell and Bradfute, Edinburgh. 1817.

COLLATION.—XVI pp. (including List of Plates) + pp. 1–376 including Index + Maps + 7 coloured plates (4 as in 1st Edition and 3 additional as follows).

p. 8. Triumphal Arch at Tripoly.
p. 22. A Bedouin Peasant Woman.
p. 95. A Cologee or Guard of Tripoli.

(Plate 2 in the 1st Edition, not included.)

495 VIDAL (E. E.)

Picturesque Illustrations of Buenos Ayres and Monte Video, consisting of Twenty-four Views: accompanied with Descriptions of the Scenery, and of the Costumes, Manners, &c. of the inhabitants of those cities and their environs. By E. E. Vidal, Esq. (rule) London: Published by R. Ackermann, 101 Strand. Printed by L. Harrison, 373, Strand (rule).

Folio.   1820

COLLATION.—Title as above (v. blank) + Preface 1 leaf + Introduction pp. v–xxviii + pp. 1–115 (p. 116 blank) + 24 coloured plates.

Each plate bears E. E. Vidal Esq. delt. and the imprint, London Published (date) at R. Ackermann's 101 Strand.

1. Frontispiece General View of Buenos Ayres, from the Plaza de Toros   G. Maile & T. Sutherland sculpt.   Octr. 1 1820.
2. p.   1. Two Views on 1 long folding sheet "Monte Video from the Anchorage outside the Harbour and Buenos Ayres, from the Bank between the Outer and Inner Roads   T. Sutherland sculpt.   May 1820."
3. p.   15. Landing Place   G. Maile & J. Bluck sculpt.   Septr. 1 1820.
4. p.   17. Fort T.   Sutherland sculpt.   July 1 1820.
5. p.   19. Water Cart   G. Maile & J. Bluck sculpt.   Augt. 1 1820.
6. p.   23. Market Place   D. Havell sculpt.   May 1 1820.
7. p.   27. Plaza   G. Maile & J. Bluck sculpt.   Septr. 1 1820.
8. p.   33. Milk Boys   T. Sutherland sculpt.   May 1 1820.
9. p.   35. South Matadero (Public Butchery)   Maile & Sutherland sculpt.   July 1 1820.
10. p.   41. Fishing   G. Maile and J. Bluck sculpt.   Augt. 1 1820.
11. p.   45. Church of San Domingo   J. Bluck & G. Maile sculpt.   July 1 1820.
12. p.   51. Beggar on Horseback   J. Bluck sculpt.   June 1 1820.
13. p.   53. Pampa Indians   J. Bluck sculpt.   June 1 1820.
14. p.   61. Shipping Hides at the Custom House   G. Maile & J. Bluck sculpt.   Octr. 1 1820.
15. p.   67. A Country Public House & Travellers   G. Maile & J. Bluck sculpt.   Octr. 1 1820.
16. p.   71. Estantia (Farm) on the River San Pedro   Maile & Sutherland sculpt.   Septr. 1 1820.
17. p.   85. Balling Ostriches   T. Sutherland sculpt.   May 1 1820.
18. p.   89. Guachos (Rustics) of Tucuman   G. Maile & J. Bluck sculpt.   Septr. 1 1820.
19. p.   91. Convoy of Wine Mules   G. Maile & T. Sutherland sculpt.   Augt. 1 1820.
20. p. 101. Travelling Wagon in a Pontano (Morass)   J. Bluck sculpt.   June 1 1820.
21. p. 105. Travelling Post (folding plate)   T. Sutherland sculpt.   June 1 1820.
22. p. 107. Paolistas, Soldiers of the East Bank of the Plata   G. Maile & J. Bluck sculpt.   Octr. 1 1820.
23. p. 111. A Quinta (Farm)   Sutherland & Maile sculpt.   Augt. 1 1820.
24. p. 113. A Horse Race   G. Maile & T. Sutherland sculpt.   July 1 1820.

750 copies were published in elephant 4to. for £3 13s. 6d. and 50 large-paper copies on Atlas Folio for £6 6s.   Issued in 4 ways, first in 6 monthly parts in brown paper wrappers with a specially drawn design by Vidal repeated on each cover.   On completion issued in plain boards, also in a publishers binding of half leather with board sides bearing a pictured label of Vidal, entirely different in design to the wrapper bindings.   And later it was issued in red cloth.

Not an uncommon book, but owing to the importance of its subject and the fact of its being the only notable colour plate book in English dealing with the Argentine, it always commands a high price.

A reprint was issued in 1929.

Views in West Indies 1827.   See under Johnson (J.).

496 WALES (J.)

Views of Bombay.

12 coloured aquatints ($25\frac{1}{2} \times 15$ inches) drawn and engraved by James Wales. London R. Cribb, 1820.

1. View of Bombay Harbour.
2. View of Bombay Harbour.
3. View from Malabar Hill.
4. View from Malabar Hill.
5. View of the Breach Causeway.
6. View of the Breach from Love Grove.
7. View of Belmont.
8. View of Belmont.
9. View of Belmont.
10. View from Sion Fort.
11. [View from Sion Fort.]
12. View from the Island of Elephanta.

497 WALKER (Mrs. A.)

Female Beauty, as preserved and improved by Regimen, Cleanliness, and Dress; and especially by the adaptation, colour and arrangement of dress, as variously influencing the Forms, Complexion, & Expression of each individual, and rendering cosmetic impositions unnecessary. (waved rule) By Mrs. A. Walker (waved rule) and that regards Regimen and Health being furnished by medical friends, and revised by Sir Anthony Carlisle, F.R.S. vice president of the college of Surgeons &c, &c., &c., Illustrated by coloured drawings of Heads by J. W. Wright, and of figures by E. T. Parris. London: Thomas Hurst, 65, St Paul's Churchyard.

Octavo.   1837

COLLATION.—Half-title "Female Beauty as preserved and improved by Regimen, Cleanliness and Dress" (v. blank) + Title as above (v. Printed by J. & C. Adlard, Bartholomew Close) + Dedication 1 p. (v. blank) + Advertisement pp. vii–x + Contents pp. xi–xxi (p. xxii blank) + List of Plates 1 p. (v. blank) + Advertisements of works published by Hurst pp. xxv–xxxvi + Preface pp. 1–46 + Text pp. 47–432 + coloured front. + uncoloured diagram + 10 coloured plates, each with cut out overlay, each plate marked, On Stone by M. Gauci, from a drawing by F. T. Paris (or Wright) and bearing Hurst's imprint.

Front. Mrs Nicholas Geary's Corsets.
p. 239. Diagram of Colours, comb &c., uncoloured.
p. 291. Management of Yellow Complexion.   J. W. Wright.
p. 292. Management of Red Complexion.   J. W. Wright.
p. 298. Management of Pale Dark Complexion.   J. W. Wright.
p. 354. Management of Thick Waist.   F. T. Parris.
p. 355. Management of Short Limbs.   F. T. Paris.
p. 361. Management of Broad Jaws.   W. Wright.
p. 363. Management of Short Neck.   W. Wright.
p. 387. Production of character in Dress.   W. Wright.
p. 392. Simplicity & Ornament Compared.   F. T. Parris.
p. 393. Different Character in Ornament.   F. T. Paris.

498 WALKER (G.)

The Costume of Yorkshire, illustrated by a Series of Forty Engravings, being Facsimiles of Original Drawings.   With Descriptions in English and French (swelled rule) London: Printed by T. Bensley, Bolt Court, Fleet Street, for Longman, Hurst, Rees, Orme, and Brown, Paternoster Row; Ackermann, Strand; and Robinson, Son, and Holdworth, Leeds

Quarto.   1814

Walker's Costume of Yorkshire (*contd.*)

COLLATION.—Title as above (v. blank) + Title in French (v. blank) + Table of Contents 1 p. (v. blank) + ditto in French (v. blank) + Introduction 1 p. (v. ditto in French) + pp. 3–96 + frontispiece and 40 coloured plates.

Each plate is marked, G (or Geo) Walker del Engraved by R (or R & D) Havell Published by Robinson & Son, Leeds (and date).

Frontispiece (Horse dealer mounted with 2 led horses, York in background) Oct. 1 1814.

1. The Horse Dealer Aug. 1 1813.	21. The Preemer Boy Jany. 1 1814.
2. Cloth Makers Augt. 1 1813.	22. Thirty third Regiment Jany. 1 1814.
3. The Collier Augt. 1 1813.	23. Teasel Field Jany. 1 1814.
4. The Dog Breaker Aug. 1 1813.	24. Line Swinglers Jany. 1 1814.
5. Fisherman Sept. 1 1813.	25. Grenadier of the First West York Militia Feby. 1 1814.
6. The Cloth Dresser Sept. 1 1813.	
7. Lowkers Sept. 1 1813.	26. Riding the Stang Feby. 1 1814.
8. Stonebreakers on the Road. Sept. 1 1813.	27. Peat Cart Feby. 1 1814.
9. Woman making Oatcakes Octr. 1 1813.	28. The Cloth Hall Feby. 1 1814.
10. The Ruddle Pit Oct. 1 1813.	29. Woman Spinning March 1 1814.
11. The Fool Plough Oct. 1 1813.	30. Hawking March 1 1814.
12. Nor and Spell Octr. 1 1813.	31. North York Militia March 1 1814.
13. The Cranberry Girl Novr. 1 1813.	32. Alum Works March 1 1814.
14. The Milk Boy Novr. 1 1813.	33. East York Militia April 1 1814.
15. Rape Threshing Novr. 1 1813.	34. Midsummer Eve April 1 1814.
16. The East Riding or Wolds Waggon Nov. 1 1813.	35. Leech Finders April 1 1814.
	36. Factory Children April 1 1814.
17. Sea Bathing Decr. 1 1813.	37. Bishop Blaize June 1 1814.
18. Whalebone Scrapers Decr. 1 1813.	38. Wensley Dale Knitters June 1 1814.
19. Farmers Decr. 1 1813.	39. Sheffield Cutler June 1 1814.
20. Moor Guide Decr. 1 1813.	40. Jockies June 1 1814.

Issued in boards at £6. A few copies were issued on large paper (folio) with the plate proofs before titles and a duplicate set of the plates in etched outline.

Plate 3, the Collier, Aug. 1st 1813, is the first English plate to show a steam engine.

Another Edition was published in 1885.

499 WALPOLE (Horace)

Observations on Modern Gardening, and laying out Pleasure Grounds, Parks, Farms, Ridings, &c, illustrated by descriptions. To which is added an Essay on the different natural situations of gardens. (thick and thin rule) A New Edition: with notes by Horace (late) Earl of Orford; and ornamented with plates, chiefly designed by Mr Woollet (thin and thick rule) 6 line verse (2 line rule) London, Printed for West and Hughes, Pater-Noster Row. (small swelled rule)

Quarto.   1801

COLLATION.—Half-title "Observations on Modern Gardening &c, &c, &c," (between rules). Price One Pound Seven Shillings Boards (rule). Printed by W. Blackader, Tooks Court, Chancery Lane (v. blank) + Title as above (v. blank) + Contents 2 ll. (pp. v–viii) + pp. 1–155 + 6 coloured plates.

1. front.   A View of part of the Garden, at Hall Barn, near Beaconsfield, Bucks, as laid out by Edmond Waller Esqr. Woollet Delint.   Willm. Wise sculpt.   Jany 1 1798.
2. p.   30.   Esher in Surry, the Seat of the Rt. Hon. Henry Pelham: as laid out by Mr Kent.   W. Woollet delt.   J. Walker sculpt.   March 1798.

Walpole's Modern Gardening (*contd.*)

3. p. 34. View of the Garden &c at Carlton House, the Residence of H.R.H. the Prince of Wales. May 1799.

4. p. 98. The House and Gardens at Woobourn in Surry, as laid out by Philip Southcote Esqr. Woollet Delint. J. Walker sculpt. Jany. 1st 1798.

5. p. 104. View of the West side of the Island in the Gardens at Pains Hill Surrey, as laid out by the Honble. Charles Hamilton. Wm. Wise sculpt. Jany 1st 1798.

6. p. 108. A View of Hagley Gardens &c. from Thomson's Seat. Woollet delt. Le Couer sculpt. May 1st 1800.

Size 11¾ × 8⅞ *inches for uncut copies.*

500 WARRE (Capt. H.)

Sketches in North America and the Oregon Territory. By Captain H. Warre, (A.D.C. to the late Commander of the Forces) Lithographed, Printed and Published by Dickinson & Co., 114, New Bond Street.

Folio. [1848]

COLLATION.—Title as above (v. blank) + Sketch of the Journey across the Continent of America pp. 1–5 (p. 6 blank) + 16 lithograph plates, each plate marked, H. J. Warre del. Dickinson & Co. Lith.

1. Fort Garry.
2. {Buffalo Hunting on the W. Prairies. / Forcing a passage through the burning Prairie.
3. Falls of the Kamanis Taquoin River.
4. Distant View of the Rocky Mountains.
5. The Rocky Mountains.
6. Source of the Columbia River.
7. {Fort Vancouver. / Indian Tomb.
8. {Mount Baker. / Cape Disappointment.
9. Valley of the Williamette River.
10. The American Village.
11. {Fort George formerly Astoria. / McGillivray or Kootoonai River.
12. Mount Hood from Les Dalles.
13. Les Dalles Columbia River.
14. Mount Hood.
15. Fall of the Peloos River.
16. The Rocky Mountains from the Columbia River looking N.W.

Map in outline.

501 WEBBER (J.)

Views in the South Seas, from Drawings by the late James Webber, draftsman on board the Resolution, Captain James Cooke, from the year, 1776 to 1780 with Letterpress Descriptive of the various Scenery, &c. These Plates form a New Series, and are of the same size as those engraved for Captain Cooke's last Voyage (thin and thick rule) The Drawings are in the possession of the Board of Admiralty. London: (thin and thick rule) Published by Boydell and Co. No. 90 Cheapside. Printed by W. Bulmer and Co. Cleveland Row

Folio. 1808

Webber's Views in the South Seas (*contd.*)

COLLATION.—Title as above (v. blank) + 16 coloured plates, each with 1 leaf of Text. Each plate marked, "J. Webber fecit" London Pubd. April 1 1809 by Boydell & Compy. No. 90 Cheapside.

1. View in Queen Charlottes Sound, New Zealand.
2. Boats of the Friendly Islands (the text to this plate is included with text to plate 3).
3. A Sailing Canoe of Otahaite.
4. The Plantain Tree in the Island of Cracatoa.
5. A View in Oheitepeha Bay in the Island of Otaheite.
6. Waheiadora Chief of Oheitepeha lying in state.
7. View of the Harbour of Taloo, in the Island of Eimeo.
8. A Toopapaoo of a Chief with a Priest making his offering to the Morai in Huoheine.
9. The Resolution beating through the Ice with the Discovery in the most eminent danger in the Distance.
10. The Narta of Sledge for Burdens in Kamtchatka.
11. Balagans or Summer Habitations, with the method of Drying Fish at St Peter & Paul Kamtschatka.
12. View in Macao Including the Residence of Camoens, when he wrote his Lusiad.
13. View in Macao.
14. A View in the Island of Pulo Condore.
15. View in the Island of Cracatoa.
16. The Fan Palm in the Island of Cracatoa.

502 WESTALL (R.)

Victories of the Duke of Wellington, from Drawings by R. Westall, R.A. (large woodcut vignette of military trophies) London: Printed for Rodwell and Martin, New Bond-Street (short rule).

Quarto.   1819

COLLATION.—Title as above (v. London: Printed by Thomas Davison, Whitefriars) + Preface 1 leaf (pp. iii–iv) + pp. 1–47 + 12 coloured plates.

Each plate marked, Drawn by R. Westall R.A.   Engraved by T. Fielding [except plate 6 which is engraved by Heath] and imprint of Rodwell & Martin 1819.

1. p. 1. Vimiera.	5. p. 18. Badajoz.	9. p. 33. Pyrenees.
2. p. 5. Oporto.	6. p. 23. Salamanca.	10. p. 37. St. Sebastians.
3. p. 10. Talavera.	7. p. 27. Madrid.	11. p. 40. Toulouse.
4. p. 14. Busaco.	8. p. 29. Vittoria.	12. p. 43. Waterloo.

503 WESTALL (W.) & SAMUEL OWEN

Picturesque Tour of River Thames; illustrated by Twenty-Four coloured Views, a Map, and Vignettes, from original drawings taken on the spot by William Westall and Samuel Owen (coloured vignette "Source of the Thames" S. Owen del) Published 1828 by R. Ackermann 96 Strand London.

Folio.

COLLATION.—Title as above (v. blank) + Preface 1 leaf (iii–iv) + Contents 1 p. (v. List of Plates) + pp. 1–169 + Index 1 leaf + Map and 24 coloured aquatint plates.

Each plate bears imprint, Published 1828 by R. Ackermann 96 Strand London.   Plates 1–19 are marked, W. Westall A.R.A. delt. plates 20–24 S. Owen delt.

   p. 1. Folding Map "River Thames from Oxford to its mouth"   J. & J. Neale sc.
1. p. 35. Oxford   R. G. Reeve sculpt.

Westall & Owen's Tour of River Thames (*contd.*)

2. p. 76. Park Place Henley-on-Thames Seat of Fuller Maitland Esqr. M.P. R. G. Reeve sculpt.
3. p. 83. Callum Court Henley-on-Thames Seat of Honble Fredk West R. G. Reeve sculpt.
4. p. 90. Maidenhead Bridge J. Bailey sculpt.
5. p. 93. Windsor Castle from Eton R. G. Reeve sculpt.
6. p. 106. Eton College from the River J. Fielding sculpt.
7. p. 110. Beaumont Lodge—Old Windsor, The Seat of Viscount Ashbrooke C. Bentley sculpt.
8. p. 112. Staines Bridge C. Bentley sculpt.
9. p. 117. Hampton House, the Seat of Thomas Carr Esqre. R. G. Reeve sculpt.
10. p. 128. Pope's Villa Twickenham C. Bentley sculp.
11. p. 130. Twickenham R. G. Reeve sculpt.
12. p. 131. View from Richmond Hill R. G. Reeve sculpt.
13. p. 133. Richmond R. G. Reeve sculpt.
14. p. 134. St Margarets, Twickenham Seat of the Earl of Cassillis C. Bentley sculpt.
15. p. 136. Sion House Seat of His Grace the Duke of Northumberland J. Bailey sculpt.
16. p. 139. Suspension Bridge Hammersmith J. Baily sculpt.
17. p. 148. Westminster Bridge R. G. Reeve sculpt.
18. p. 150. Waterloo Bridge R. G. Reeve sculpt.
19. p. 152. Southwark Bridge C. Bentley sculpt.
20. p. 154. The Custom House R. G. Reeve sculpt.
21. p. 156. Greenwich Hospital R. G. Reeve sculpt.
22. p. 161. Gravesend S. Owen delt. R. G. Reeve sculpt.
23. p. 164. Tilbury Fort. S. Owen delt. R. G. Reeve sculpt.
24. p. 166. Sheerness. S. Owen del. R. G. Reeve sculpt.
    p. 169. Coloured Vignette "The Crow Stone" S. Owen delint.

Issued in 6 monthly parts in paper wrappers, and on completion in volume form as above in boards. A few copies were done on large paper, and the plates were also issued on India paper proofs uncoloured. Messrs. Batsford had a fine large-paper copy with the plates in two states.

Westall (W.). See also under Southey (R.).

504 [WESTMACOTT (Charles Molloy)]

The English Spy: An Original Work, Characteristic, Satirical, and Humourous. Comprising Scenes and Sketches in Every Rank of Society, being Portraits of the Illustrious, Eminent, Eccentric, and Notorious. Drawn from the Life By Bernard Blackmantle. The illustrations designed by Robert Cruikshank. (woodcut vignette)

> **By Frolic, Mirth, and Fancy gay,**
> **Old Father Time is borne away.**

(rule) London: Published by Sherwood, Jones, and Co. Paternoster-Row (short rule)

2 Vols. Octavo.   1825(6)

COLLATION.—Title as above (v. London Printed by Thomas Davison, Whitefriars) + Bernard Blackmantle to the Reviewers 3 pp. (iii–v) (p. vi blank) + Contents 6 pp. (vii–xii) + Illustrations in the English Spy 11 pp. (xiii–xxiii) (p. xxiv blank) + sub-title "The English Spy" &c. 1 p. (v. blank) + Introduction 2 pp. (3–4) + Preface 2 pp. (5–6) + pp. 7–417 + 35 coloured plates + 49 woodcuts in Text (including vignette on title).

Each plate bears imprint, Published [date] by Sherwood Jones & Co.

1. Front. (Gothic Temple supporting small vignettes of King, Lords, Commons, Oxford, Cambridge, Terrestrial Heaven, Hell, Misery, Death, Poetry, Painting Greenwich, Chelsea &c.) Designed by Robt. Cruikshank Jan. 1 1825.
2. p. 3. The Five Principal Orders of Society (uncoloured woodcut).

Westmacott's English Spy (*contd.*)

3. p. 29. First Absence, or Etonians answering Morning Muster Roll Drawn & Engraved by R. Cruikshank March 1 1824.

4. p. 57. The Oppidan's Museum or Eton Court of Claims at the Christopher Drawn & Engraved by R. Cruikshank March 1 1824.

5. p. 109. Eton Montem, and the Mount—Salt Hill. Drawn & Engraved by R. Cruikshank June 10 1824.

6. p. 127. First Bow to Alma Mater or Bernard Blackmantle's introduction to the Big Wig, Drawn & Engraved by R. Cruikshank June 10 1824.

7. p. 147. Flooring of Mercury, or Burning the Oaks, a Scene in Tom Quadrangle Drawn & Engraved by R. Cruikshank May 1 1824.

8. p. 169. College Comforts, A Freshman taking possession of his Rooms Drawn & Engraved by Cruikshank June 1 1824.

9. p. 170. Capping a Proctor, or Oxford Bull-dogs detecting Brazen Smugglers Drawn & Engraved by R. Cruikshank March 1 1824.

10. p. 185. The Arrival, or Western Entrance to Cockney Land Drawn & Engraved by R. Cruikshank March 1 1824.

11. p. 225. The Opera Green Room, or Noble Amateurs viewing Foreign Curiosities Drawn & Engraved by R. Cruikshank March 1 1824.

12. p. 233. The Royal Saloon Piccadilly Engraved by R. Cruikshank Sep. 1 1824.

13. p. 267. Oxford Transports, or Albanians doing Penance for Past offences Drawn & Engraved by R. Cruikshank March 1 1824.

14. p. 278. Shew Sunday, Sketches of Character, in the Broad Walk, Christ Church Meadows, Oxford Engraved by R. Cruikshank Sep. 1 1824.

15. p. 280. Town and Gown or the Battle of the Togati and the Town Raff in the High Street Oxford Drawn & Engraved by R. Cruikshank Augt. 2 1824.

16. p. 305. Black Matins, or the Effect of Late drinking upon Early Risers Drawn & Engraved by R. Cruikshank March 1 1824.

17. p. 309. Golgotha or the Place of Sculls—Tom Echo receiving sentence of Rustication Drawn & Engraved by Cruikshank June 1 1824.

18. p. 335. The Evening Party in the Yellow Room, at the Pavilion, Brighton. Designed by G. M. Brighty Octr. 1 1824.

19. p. 337. The King at Home, or Mathews at Carlton House. Engraved by R. Cruikshank Sep. 1 1824.

20. p. 342. A Frolic in High Life, or a Visit to Billingsgate Drawn & Engraved by Robt. Cruikshank Dec. 1 1824.

21. p. 348. Characters on the Steyne Brighton Drawn & Engraved by Robt. Cruikshank Nov. 1 1824.

22. p. 365. Tom Echo laid up with the Headinton Fever or an Oxonian very near the Wall Drawn & Engraved by R. Cruikshank June 10 1824.

23. p. 370. Monday after the "Great St Leger" or Heroes of the Turf paying & receiving at Tattersalls Drawn & Engraved by R. Cruikshank March 1 1824.

24. p. 373. Exterior of Fishmongers Hall, a Regular break down Drawn & Engraved by Robt. Cruikshank Dec. 1 1824.

25. p. 376. The Interior of Modern Hell. Vide—the Cogged Dice Drawn & Engraved by Robt. Cruikshank Nov. 1 1824.

26. p. 381. The Daffy Club, or a Musical Muster of the Fancy Drawn & Engraved by R. Cruikshank March 1 1824.

27. p. 385. Peep o'day Boys & Family Men at the Finish a Scene near Covent Garden Drawn & Engraved by Cruikshank June 1 1824.

28. p. 389. Family Men at Fault or an unexpected Visit from the Bishop and his Chaplains Drawn & Engraved by R. Cruikshank Augt. 2 1284 (*sic*).

29. p. 399. The Hall of Infamy, Alias the Oyster Saloon in Bridges St. or New Covent Garden Hell Drawn by Rt. Cruikshank Jan. 1 1825.

30. p. 407. The Maiden Brief, Dick Gradus's first appearance among the worthies of Westminster Hall Drawn & Engraved by R. Cruikshank Augt. 2 1824.

31. p. 410. Surry Collegians giving a lift to a limb of the Law Drawn & Engraved by Robt. Cruikshank Jany. 1 1825.

32. p. 411. RA's of Genius reflecting on the true line of Beauty, at the Life Academy Somerset House J. Rowlandson June 1 1824.

Westmacott's English Spy (*contd.*)

33. p. 412. Bernard Blackmantle reading his Play, in the Green Room of Covent Garden Theatre. Drawn & Engraved by R. Cruikshank   June 10 1824.

34. p. 413. Bernard Blackmantle reading his Farce in the Green Room of the Theatre Royal Drury Lane. Drawn by T. Wageman   Sep. 1 1824.

35. p. 415. City Ball at the Mansion House   Drawn & Engraved by Robt. Cruikshank   Nov. 1 1824.

36. p. 416. Jemmy Gordon's Frolic, or Cambridge Gambols at Peter House   Drawn by T. Rowlandson   Dec. 1 1824.

The 49 woodcuts are on pp. 4, 7, 14, 17, 19, 24, 28, 36, 37, 48, 49, 56, 68, 69, 77, 100, 108, 109, 119, 121, 124, 125, 127, 144, 145, 147, 153, 175, 177, 183, 185, 224, 250, 265, 273, 277, 279, 297, 310, 311, 324, 329, 343, 353, 366, 367, 409, 417, *and on title page.*

VOL. II.—Title as in Vol. I (with the addition of the words vol. II between single rules after the word Cruikshank) The Imprint being altered to "London: Published by Sherwood, Gilbert, and Piper, Paternoster-Row (short rule) 1826" (v. London: Printed by Thomas Davison, Whitefriars) + Contents 6 pp. (iii–viii) + Illustrations in the English Spy 6 pp. (ix–xiv) + Engravings on wood 1 p. (xv, verso blank) + sub-title "The English Spy &c." Vol. II 1 p. (v. blank) + Introduction to the Second Volume 2 pp. (3–4) + Ode to Blackmantle pp. 5–10 + pp. 11–399 (p. 400 London: Printed by Thomas Davison, Whitefriars) + 36 coloured plates. Each plate bears imprint, Pubd. by Sherwood Jones & Co. (and date).

1. p. 16. A Short Set to at Long's Hotel, or Stop-Ford, not getting the Best of it   Drawn & Engraved by Robt. Cruikshank   March 1 1825.

2. p. 32. Courtiers Carousing in a Cadgers Ken   Drawn & Engd. by R. Cruikshank   Feby. 1 1826.

3. p. 34. The Wake,—or last appearance of Teddy O'Rafferty, a scene in Holy Land   Drawn & Engraved by Robt. Cruikshank   March 1 1825.

4. p. 48. The Cyprians Ball, at the Argyle Rooms   Drawn & Engraved by Robt. Cruikshank   March 1 1825.

5. p. 66. Liston and the Lambkins or the Citizens Dinner Party   Drawn & Engraved by R. Cruikshank   Feby. 1 1826.

6. p. 72. The Great Actor, or Mr Punch in all his Glory   Drawn & Engd. by R. Cruikshank   May 2 1825.

7. p. 76. Westminster Frolics   Drawn & Engraved by Robt. Cruikshank   Nov. 1 1825.

8. p. 78. The Marigold Family on a Party of Pleasure, or effect of a Storm in the little Bay of Biscay vide Chelsea Reach   Drawn & Engd. by Robt. Cruikshank   April 2 1825.

9. p. 84. The Epping Hunt or Cockney Comicalities in full Chace   Drawn & Engd. by R. Cruikshank   June 1 1825.

10. p. 94. The Tea Pot Row at Harrow, or the Battle of Hog Lane   Drawn & Engd. by R. Cruikshank   May 2 1825.

11. p. 104. The Cits Ordinary at the Gate House Highgate, or every Hog to his own Apple   Drawn & Engraved by Robt. Cruikshank   April 2 1825.

12. p. 144. Bulls and Bears in High Bustle, or Billy Wright's Poney, made a Member of the Stock Exchange   Drawn & Engd. by R. Cruikshank   May 2 1825.

13. p. 188. The Promenade at Cowes, with Portraits of Noble Commanders & members of the Royal Yacht Club   Drawn & Engraved by Robt. Cruikshank   Oct. 1 1825.

14. p. 214. A Jollification on board the Peranga   Drawn & Engraved by Robt. Cruikshank   Novr. 1 1825.

15. p. 218. Point Street, Portsmouth, or the Coxswain's Carousal   Drawn & Engraved by Robt. Cruikshank   Nov. 1 1825.

16. p. 222. Evening and in High Spirits—a Scene at Long's Hotel   Drawn and Engraved by Robt. Cruikshank   July 1 1825.

17. p. 240. Morning and in Low Spirits—a Scene in the Lock up House   Drawn & Engraved by Robt. Cruikshank   July 1 1825.

18. p. 244. The House of Lords   Drawn & Engd. by Robt. Cruikshank   June 1 1825.

19. p. 248. The Point of Honor decided, or the Leaden argument of a Love affair   Drawn & Engraved by Robt. Cruikshank   April 2 1825.

20. p. 252. The Great Subscription Room at Brooks's or Opposition Members engaged upon Hazardous Points   Drawn & Engraved by Robt. Cruikshank   July 1st 1825.

Westmacott's English Spy (*contd.*)

21. p. 254. The Circular Room, or a Squeeze at Carlton Palace   Drawn & Engrad. by Robt. Cruikshank
June 1 1825.

22. p. 258. Eccentrics in the High Street, Cheltenham   Drawn & Engraved by Robt. Cruikshank
Dec. 1 1824.

23. p. 262. Going out, View of the Berkeley Hunt Kennel, Cheltenham   Drawn & Engraved by Robt.
Cruikshank Octr. 1 1825.

24. p. 284. The Royal Wells, Cheltenham or Spasmodic affections from Spa Waters   Drawn & Engraved
by Robt. Cruikshank   August 1 1825.

25. p. 288. The Bags Mens Banquet, at the Bell Inn Cheltenham   Drawn & Engraved by Robt. Cruikshank   Novr. 1st 1825.

26. p. 310. The Oakland Cottages, Cheltenham, or Fox Hunters & their Favourites   Drawn & Engraved by Robt. Cruikshank   August 1 1825.

27. p. 312. Doncaster, Great St. Leger Race, & Characters on the Turf   Drawn & Engd. by R. Cruikshank   Jany. 2 1826.

28. p. 334. The Comical Procession from Gloucester to Berkeley   Drawn & Engraved by Robt. Cruikshank   Feby. 1826.

29. p. 340. The Post Office Bristol, Arrival of the London Mail   Drawn & Engraved by Robt. Cruikshank   Septr. 1 1825.

30. p. 352. The Fancy Ball at the Upper Rooms Bath   Drawn & Engraved by Robt. Cruikshank   Octr. 1
1825.

31. p. 362. Well known characters in the Pump Room, Bath taking a sip with King Bladud   Drawn &
Engraved by Robt. Cruikshank   Octr. 1 1825.

32. p. 368. A Bath Beau, and Frail Belle or Mr. B and Miss L.   Drawn & Engraved by R. Cruikshank
Jany. 2 1826.

33. p. 372. Public Bathing at Bath, or Stewing Alive   Drawn & Engraved by Robt. Cruikshank
August 1 1825.

34. p. 380. Milsom Street & Bond Street with Portraits of Bath Swells   Drawn & Engraved by Robt.
Cruikshank   Novr. 1 1825.

35. p. 386. The Buff Club, or the Pig & Whistle Avon Street Bath   Drawn & Engraved by Robt. Cruikshank   Septr. 1 1825.

36. p. 390. The Bowling Alley Worcester, or characters of the Hand and Glove Club   Drawn & Engraved
by Robt. Cruikshank   August 1 1825.

With Twenty-five woodcuts on pp. Title, 4, 10, 24, 38, 63, 76, 104, 127, 162, 208, 221, 258,
288, 312, 327, 337, 339, 342, 343, 349, 356, 362, 393, 399.

RÉSUMÉ.—71 coloured aquatints by, Robert Cruikshank (68), T. Rowlandson (2), T. Wage-
man (1), and G. M. Brightly (1), and 74 woodcuts in Text and 1 full page.

Issued in 24 monthly parts in paper wrappers.   In the first issue plate 28, p. 389, Vol. I, is
misdated 1284, and p. 222, Vol. II, is blank.   The leaves of advertisement at end of each volume
are almost invariably missing.   The woodcut, Vol. I, p. 3, "The five Pillars of Society," is also
rare, and care should be exercised to see that it has not been supplied in facsimile.

505 WHITTOCK (N.)

**The Art of Drawing and Colouring from nature, Flowers, Fruit, and Shells; to which
is added, correct directions for preparing the most brilliant colours for Painting on
Velvet, with the mode of using them; also the New Method of Oriental Tinting.   By
Nathaniel Whittock. Esq. author of the Oxford Drawing Book &c. with Plain & Coloured
Drawings.   London: Isaac Taylor Hinton, 4, Warwick Square.**

Quarto.   1829

COLLATION.—Title as above (v. blank) + List of plates 1 p. (v. blank) + text pp. 1–96
+ 24 plain and 24 coloured plates.

Whittock's Art of Drawing (*contd.*)

1. p. 1. (Fuschia & Jasmine) (numbered Lesson 1 & 2) on 1 plate.	14. p. 57. (Grapes).
	15. p. 58. (Hyancith).
3. p. 12. (Fuschia).	16. p. 59. (Auricula).
4. p. 16. (Leaves).	17. p. 60. (Single Anemones).
5. p. 21. (China Asters).	18. p. 63. (Full Blown Moss Rose).
6. p. 27. (Honeysuckle).	19. p. 65. (Two Shells).
7. p. 30. (Moss Rose Buds).	20. p. 68. (Three Shells).
8. p. 36. (Major Convolvulus).	21. p. 80. (Oriental Tinting).
9. p. 39. (Apple Blossom).	22. p. 70. (Velvet Painting).
10. p. 44. (South American Passion Flower).	23. p. 73. (Dahlias) (not included in List of Plates, but making 24th).
11. p. 49. (Plums).	
12. p. 53. (Peaches).	24. p. 90. (Group of Fruit).
13. p. 55. (Currants).	25. p. 93. (Group of Flowers).

506 WHITTOCK (N.)

The Art of Drawing and Colouring, from Nature, Birds, Beasts, Fishes, and Insects. By Nathaniel Whittock, Esq. Author of the Oxford Drawing Book, Painters and Glaziers' Guide etc. with Plain and Coloured Drawings, from Original Paintings by Morland, Vernet, Howet (sic) Le Cave, &c. (rule) London Isaac Taylor Hinton 4 Warwick Square.

Quarto. 1830

COLLATION.—Title as above (v. London: R. Clay Printer, Bread Street Hill, Cheapside) + List of Plates (v. blank) + pp. 1–100 + 24 plain + 24 coloured plates.

1. p. 3. Cat and Kittens.
2. p. 6. Group of Sheep, from Barrett.
3. p. 11. Tom Tit and Robin Redbreast.   (Lettered on plate 1 Red Pole (not Robin), 2 Tom Tit.)
4. p. 17. Goats Male & Female.
5. p. 23. Rabbit and Squirrel.
6. p. 28. (Deer).
7. p. 32. 1. The Gold Pheasant.   2. The Silver Pheasant.
8. p. 36. Wild Boar and Lion from Howitt.
9. p. 40. Puppies Playing.   Painted by S. Taylor.   N. Whittock Lithog.   44 Paternoster Row.
10. p. 43. (Setters, from Morland).
11. p. 46. The Stag Entangled by his horns (from Howit).
12. p. 48. Dog of the Convent of St Bernhard.
13. p. 62. Green Fly Catchers Male & Female.
14. p. 68. 1. Male & Female humming Birds.   2. Butterflies.
15. p. 70. Groupes of Horses.   N. Whittock delt.
16. p. 71. 1. Magnificent Bird of Paradise.   2. King Bird of Paradise.
17. p. 73. Wounded Tiger and Fox   Painted by Howitt.   N. Whittock Lith.   44 Paternoster Row.
18. p. 74. 1. Paradise Bunting.   2. Rice Bird.
19. p. 77. The Camelopard.
20. p. 78. Eagle Hare Hawk & Sparrow from Howitt.
21. p. 89. Dragon Flies.
22. p. 93. Gold & Silver Fish.
23. p. 97. Girl & Poultry.
24. p. 99. Ass and Foal.

507 WHITTOCK (N.)

A Topographical and Historical Description of the University and City of Oxford, with Views of the Churches, Colleges, Halls, and other Public Buildings in the Vicinity

Whittock's Oxford (*contd.*)

of Oxford; to which is added correct delineations of the Costume of the Members of the University, By Nathaniel Whittock, lithographer to the University of Oxford. London. Published by Isaac Taylor Hinton, 4 Warwick Square.

Quarto.   1828

COLLATION.—Lithograph title with vignette + Printed title as above (v. I. T. Hinton Printer, 4 Warwick Square) + Preface 1 leaf + Contents 1 leaf + pp. 1–102 + List of Plates + 43 litho. plates (p. 87 St Bartholomew's Chapel not in list) 5 of the plates are coloured and marked, J. Whittock delt. 14 Patenoster Row.

p. 41. Proctor Doctor of Divinity full Dress. Doctors of Civil Law in Dress (*sic*) Gown, this is also the dress of an M.D.

p. 41. Doctor of Music Undress Gown, Doctor of Divinity undress Gown, Master of Arts and Pro Proctor.

p. 42. Master of Arts, Bachelor of Arts, Bachelor Civil Law.

p. 43. Nobleman in Dress and Undress Gowns, Gentleman Commoner Dress Gown.

p. 43. Commoner, Gentleman Commr. Undress Gown, Scholar.

508 WILLIAMSON (Capt. Thomas)

Oriental Field Sports; being a complete, detailed, and accurate description of the Wild Sports of the East; and exhibiting, in a novel and interesting manner, the Natural History of the Elephant, the Rhinoceros, the Tiger, the Leopard, the Bear, the Deer, the Buffalo, the Wolf, the Wild Hog, the Jackall, the Wild Dog, the Civet and other undomesticated animals; as likewise the different species of feathered game, fishes, and serpents. The whole interspersed with a variety of Original, Authentic, and curious Anecdotes, which render the work replete with information and amusement. The scenery gives a faith-full representation of that picturesque country, together with the Manners and Customs of both the native and European Inhabitants. The narrative is divided into forty heads, forming collectively a complete work, but so arranged that each part is a detail of one of the Forty Coloured Engravings with which the publication is embellished. The whole taken from the manuscript and designs of Captain Thomas Williamson, who served upwards of Twenty years in Bengal; the Drawings by Samuel Howett made uniform in size, and engraved by the first artists, under the direction of Edward Orme. London: (thin and thick rule) Printed by William Bulmer and Co. Shakespeare Printing-Office, for Edward Orme, Printseller to His Majesty, Engraver and Publisher, Bond Street, the Corner of Brook Street

Oblong Folio.   1807

COLLATION.—Pictured title [Tiger on Rock bearing words "Wild Sports of the East" Pub by Edwd Orme 59 Bond Street] + Printed Title as above (v. blank) + Dedication to George III 1 leaf (v. blank) + Preface 1 leaf + Text pp. 1–146 + Index pp. 147–150 + List of Plates 1 leaf + 40 coloured plates.

Each plate bears words Saml Howett del from the original design of Capt Thos Williamson H. Merke sculp (with the exception of plates 27, 31 and 34 which are engraved by J. Hamble, Vivares & J. Hamble respectively) Edwd Orme Excudit and Imprint Published & Sold [date] by Edwd Orme Printseller to His Majesty 59 Bond Street London.

1. Hunters going out in the morning June 4th 1805.

2. Beating Sugar Canes for a Hog June 4 1805.

Williamson's Oriental Field Sports, 1807 *(contd.)*

3. The Chase after a Hog   Septr. 1 1805.
4. Hog Hunters meeting by Surprise a Tigress and her cubs   June 4 1805.
5. The Hog at Bay   April 1 1806.
6. The Dead Hog   Novr. 1 1805.
7. The Return from Hog Hunting   Novr. 1 1805.
8. Driving Elephants into a Keddah   June 4 1805.
9. Decoy Elephants catching a Male   Novr. 1 1805.
10. Decoy Elephants leaving Male fastened to tree   Septr. 1 1805.
11. A Rhinoceros hunted by Elephants   Jany. 1 1806.
12. A Tiger Prowling through a Village   April 1 1806.
13. Shooting a Tiger from a Platform   Sept 1st 1805.
14. A Tiger seizing a Bullock in a Pass   Jan. 1st 1806.
15. Driving a Tiger out of a Jungle   Jany. 1 1806.
16. Chasing a Tiger across a River   June 4th 1805.
17. The Tiger at Bay   Septr. 1 1805.
18. A Tiger springing upon an Elephant   June 4th 1806.
19. The Dead Tiger   June 4th 1806.
20. Shooters coming by Surprise upon a Tiger   Jany. 1 1807.
21. A Tiger hunted by wild dogs   June 4th 1805.
22. A Tiger killed by a poisoned arrow   Jany. 1 1807.
23. Shooting a Leopard   June 4th 1806.
24. Exhibition of a Battle between a Buffalo & a Tiger   Jany. 1 1807.
25. Hunting an old Buffalo   Jany. 1 1807.
26. Peacock shooting   June 4th 1805.
27. Shooting at the edge of a Jungle   J. Hamble sculpt.   September 1st 1806.
28. Driving Bear out of Sugar Canes   April 1 1806.
29. Death of the Bear   June 4th 1806.
30. Hunting a Kuttauss, or Civet Cat   April 1 1806.
31. Jackals rescueing a hunted brother   Vivares sculpt.   Jany. 1st 1st 1806.
32. Chase after a wolf   Jany. 1st 1807.
33. The common wolf trap   Jany. 1st 1806.
34. Smoking Wolves from their Earths   J. Hamble sculpt.   September 1st 1806.
35. The Ganges breaking its Banks, with Fishing &c.   Sept. 1 1805.
36. Killing Game in Boats   Sept. 1 1806.
37. Dooreah or Dog Keepers leading out dogs   June 4 1805.
38. Syces, or Grooms leading out horses   Novr. 1 1805.
39. Hunting a Hog Deer   April 1 1806.
40. The Hog Deer at Bay   Jany. 1 1807.

Issued in 20 monthly parts in blue paper wrappers with design of tiger on a rock on front cover, the last part containing a slip note advertising Howitts British Field Sports. In parts it is extremely rare, no copy has appeared in auction, and I have only seen one copy in this state, in the possession of Messrs. Robinson. It is a subscribers copy, and contains the finest impressions of the plates. Plate 31 is lettered Hunting Jackalls and this must be the first issue of the plate. It is rare. The second and usual issue is lettered Jackals rescueing a hunted brother.

509   *Another edition was published in 1808. It is greatly inferior to the first edition.*

510 WILLIAMSON (Capt. T.)

Oriental Field Sports; being a complete, detailed, and accurate description of the Wild Sports of the East; and exhibiting, in a Novel and interesting manner, the Natural History of the Elephant, the Rhinoceros, the Tiger, the Leopard, the Bear, the Deer, the Buffalo, the Wolf, the Wild Hog, the Jackall, the Wild Dog, the Civet, and other un-domesticated Animals: as likewise the Different Species of Feathered Game, Fishes,

Williamson's Oriental Field Sports, 1819 (*contd.*)

and Serpents.   The whole interspersed with a variety of Original, Authentic, and Curious Anecdotes, taken from the Manuscript and Designs of Captain Thomas Williamson, who served upwards of Twenty Years in Bengal; The Drawings by Samuel Howitt, made Uniform in Size, and Engraved by the First Artists (rule) In Two Volumes—Vol. I [II] (rule) Second Edition (thick and thin rule) London: Printed for H. R. Young, 56 Paternoster-Row; By J. M'Creery, Black-Horse-Court.

2 vols.   Quarto.   1819

COLLATION VOL. I.—Frontispiece in sepia of tiger + Title as above (v. blank) + Dedication to George III 1 p. (v. blank) + Preface pp. v–xiv + List of Plates 1 p. (v. blank) + pp. 1–306 + 20 coloured plates.

Each plate bears imprint, "Published by Edwd. Orme Bond Street [date] & by B. Crosby & Co. Stationers Court" and Williamson & Howitt in left-hand corner, J. Clark Etched in right-hand corner.   The plates which are not titled, are as follows:

1. p.   1. Hunters going out in the Morning   Septr. 1st 1807.
2. p.   15. Beating Sugar Canes for a Hog   Septr. 1st 1807.
3. p.   30. The Chase after a Hog   June 4th 1807.
4. p.   45. Hog-Hunters meeting by surprise a Tigress and her Cubs   June 4th 1807.
5. p.   61. The Hog at Bay   Septr. 1st 1807.
6. p.   76. The Dead Hog   June 4th 1807.
7. p.   92. The Return from Hog Hunting   Septr. 1st 1807.
8. p. 108. Driving Elephants into a Keddah   Augst. 1st 1807.
9. p. 126. Decoy Elephants catching a Male   Septr. 1st 1807.
10. p. 144. Decoy Elephants leaving the Male fastened to a Tree   Septr. 1st 1807.
11. p. 163. A Rhinoceros hunted by Elephants   Augst 1st 1807.
12. p. 178. A Tiger prowling through a Village   June 4th 1807.
13. p. 209. A Tiger seizing a Bullock in a Pass   June 4th 1807.
14. p. 194. Shooting a Tiger from a Platform   Septr. 1st 1807.
15. p. 223. Driving a Tiger out of a Jungle   Septr. 1st 1807.
16. p. 238. Chasing a Tiger across a River   June 4th 1807.
17. p. 252. The Tiger at Bay   Septr. 1st 1807.
18. p. 266. A Tiger springing upon an Elephant   June 4th 1807.
19. p. 281. The dead Tiger   June 4th 1807.
20. p. 295. Shooters coming by Surprise upon a Tiger   Augst. 1st 1807.

VOL. II.—Frontispiece Two Leopards + Title as before + List of Plates 1 p. (v. blank) + pp. 1–239 + Index 6 leaves unnumbered + 20 coloured plates.

Plates bear same imprint and artists' names as before.

21. p.   1. A Tiger hunted by Wild Dogs.   Septr. 1st 1807.
22. p.   13. A Tiger killed by a poisoned Arrow   Augst. 1st 1807.
23. p.   25. Shooting a Leopard in a Tree   Augst. 1st 1807.
24. p.   37. Exhibition of a Battle between a Buffalo and a Tiger   Augst. 1st 1807.
25. p.   49. The Buffalo at Bay   Augst. 1st 1807.
26. p.   61. Peacock Shooting   Augst. 1st 1807.
27. p.   74. Shooting at the Edge of a Jungle   June 4th 1807.
28. p.   86. Driving a Bear out of Sugar Canes   Augst. 1st 1807.
29. p.   98. Death of the Bear   Augst. 1st 1807.
30. p. 109. Hunting a Kuttauss, or Civet Cat   July 1st 1807.
31. p. 121. Hunting Jackalls   Septr. 1st 1807.
32. p. 133. Chasing a Wolf   Augst. 1st 1807.
33. p. 145. The Common Wolf Trap   Septr. 1st 1807.
34. p. 156. Smoking Wolves from their Earths   Augst. 1st 1807.
35. p. 168. The Ganges breaking its Banks; with Fishing, &c.   Septr. 1st 1807.
36. p. 181. Killing Game in Boats   June 4th 1807.

Williamson's Oriental Field Sports, 1819 (*contd.*)

37. p. 194. Dooreahs, or Dog keepers, leading out Dogs   Augst. 1st 1807.
38. p. 206. Syces, or Grooms, leading out Horses   Sept. 1st 1807.
39. p. 218. Hunting a Hog Deer   Augst. 1st 1807.
40. p. 230. The Hog Deer at Bay   July 1st 1807.

Costume & Custom of Modern India.   See under Doyley (Charles).

Costume & Custom of European in India.   See under Doyley (Charles).

511 WILLYAMS (Rev. C.)

A Selection of Views in Egypt, Palestine, Rhodes, Italy, Minorca, and Gibraltar, from the original drawings, executed during a visit to those places: by the Rev. C. Willyams A.M. with a Geographical and Historical Description to each view, in English and French (thin and thick rule) London: Printed for John Hearne, 218 Tottenham Court Road; by J. F. Dove, St. John's Square, Clerkenwell.

Folio.   1822

COLLATION.—Title as above (v. blank) + List of Plates in English and French 1 p. (v. blank) + pp. 1–36 + 36 Coloured plates.

1. View of the Procession of the Sacred Camel preparatory to the Annual Pilgrimage to Mecca & Medina.
2. View of the Grand Procession of the Sacred Camel through the Streets of Cairo on their Pilgrimage to Mecca & Medina.
3. Perspective View of Cairo.
4. View of Old Cairo opposite Mokkias towards Boulac.
5. The Pharos at Alexandria.
6. A Street in Caiffe.
7. The Bay of Acre, from the top of Carmel.
8. Caiffe and Mount Carmel.
9. Agriculture in Syria.
10. The Arsenal at Rhodes.
11. Hassan Bey's Palace at Rhodes.
12. Mount Pelegrino near Palermo.
13. Scylla, on the Coast of Calabria.
14. Landing place at Syracuse.
15. Temple of Minerva Syracuse.
16. Entrance into Dionysius' Ear.
17. Caverns near Syracuse.
18. Inside of a Cavern near Syracuse.
19. Grand place at Syracuse.
20. Garden and Monastery of the Capuchins near Syracuse.
21. Curious Cemetry under the Capuchin Monastery near Syracuse.
22. The Castle and Town of Ischia.
23. View at Lago, in the Island of Ischia.
24. Palazzo di Aqua viva, near Lago.
25. Val Ombrosa, on the Appenines.
26. Cubillario on the Appenines.
27. Grand Canal and the Rialto, Venice.
28. View on Lago di Guarda.
29. Flying Bridge on the Po.
30. Grand Parade Mahon.
31. Inhabitants of Minorca.
32. The Bay of Fournelles.
33. Entrance to the Spanish Church Gibraltar.
34. Inside of a Gallery Gibraltar.
35. Interior of Poco Roca Cave.
36. St Michael's Cave Gibraltar.

Plates 1–4 are marked, Pub. by Hearne but without artist's or engraver's name.   Plates 5–36 are marked, Revd. C. Willyams delt.   J. C. Stadler sculpt. but without publisher's imprint.
Only 32 plates are given in the List but the correct number is 36 as above.

512 [WINSTON (J.)]

The Theatric Tourist; being a genuine collection of correct views, with brief and authentic historical accounts of all the Principal Provincial Theatres in the United Kingdom.   Replete with useful and necessary information to theatrical professors,

Winston's Theatric Tourist (*contd.*)

whereby they may learn how to chuse and regulate their country engagements; and with numerous anecdotes to amuse the reader (2 line rule) By a Theatric Amateur. (2 line rule) London: Printed by T. Woodfall, No 21 Villiers-Street, Strand and sold by H. D. Symonds, Paternoster-Row; Vernor and Hood, Poultry; Lindsell, Wigmore-Street, Oxford-Road, E. Kerby, Stafford-Street, Bond Street; Sylvester, Strand; C. Chapple, No. 66 Pall Mall, and No. 30, Southampton-Row, Russell-Square; and by all the principal booksellers in town and country (short rule).

Quarto.   1805

COLLATION.—Title as above (v. blank) + pp. 1–72 + 24 coloured aquatint plates.
Each plate bears imprint, London Published [date] by T. Woodfall Villiers St Strand.

1. p. 7. Bath 1 March 1804.	13. p. 44. Newcastle Oct. 1 1804.
2. p. 10. Andover 1 March 1804.	14. p. 46. Edmonton 1 Jan. 1805.
3. p. 14. Margate 1 March 1804.	15. p. 48. Maidstone Dec. 1 1804.
4. p. 16. Tunbridge Wells 1st April 1804.	16. p. 52. Liverpool Dec. 1 1804.
5. p. 18. Reading 1st April 1804.	17. p. 54. Windsor 1 Feb. 1805.
6. p. 22. Brighton 1st April 1804.	18. p. 56. Chichester 1 Jan. 1805.
7. p. 28. Richmond Feby. 1 1804.	19. p. 60. Birmingham 1 Feb. 1805.
8. p. 30. Newbury Nov. 17 1803.	20. p. 62. Manchester 1 Feb. 1805.
9. p. 34. Portsmouth Nov. 17 1803.	21. p. 64. Southampton 1 Feb. 1805.
10. p. 38. Grantham 1 Dec. 1804.	22. p. 70. Plymouth 1 Feb. 1805.
11. p. 40. Lewes 1 June 1804.	23. p. 71. Winchester 1 Feb. 1805.
12. p. 42. Exeter 1 May 1804.	24. p. 72. Norwich 1 April 1805.

513 WOOD (I. G.)

Views of the Noblemen's and Gentlemen's Seats of Kent
Oblong Folio.   1800

COLLATION.—37 coloured aquatints measuring 16 × 14 inches (engrd. surface) Drawn by J. G. Wood   Engraved by Wm. Green.

1. Hall Place in Kent The Residence of Geo. Gipp Esqr.
2. Lees Court in Kent The Seat of the Right Honble. Lord Sondes.
3. Surrenden-Dering in Kent The Seat of Sir Edward Dering Bart.
4. The Mote in Kent The Seat of the Right Honble. Lord Romney.
5. Hempstead Place in Kent The Seat of Thomas Hallett Hodges Esqr.
6. Lullingstone Castle in Kent The Seat of Sir John Dixon Dyke Bart.
7. Preston Hall in Kent The Seat of Charles Milner Esqr.
8. Oxenhoath in Kent The Seat of Sir William Geary Bart.
9. Kenward in Kent The Seat of Sir John Gregory Shaw Bart.
10. Belvidere in Kent The Seat of the Right Honble. Lord Eardley.
11. Godmersham Park in Kent The Seat of Mrs Knight.
12. Updown in Kent The Seat of John Fector Esqr.
13. Nackington House in Kent The Seat of Richard Milles Esqr.
14. South Park in Kent The Seat of Richard Allnutt Esqr.
15. Fredville in Kent The Seat of John Plumtre Esqr.
16. Clare House in Kent The Seat of John Larking Esqr.
17. Penshurst Castle in Kent The Seat of John Shelley Sidney Esqr.
18. St. Albans Court in Kent The Seat of William Hammond Esqr.
19. Cobham Hall in Kent The Seat of the Earl of Darnley.
20. Mereworth Castle in Kent The Seat of the Rt. Honble. Lord le Despencer.
21. Vinters in Kent The Seat of James Whatman Esqr.
22. Court Lodge in Kent The Seat of William Alexander Morland Esqr.

Wood's Seats in Kent (*contd.*)

23. Egerton Farm in Kent The Seat of Sir Horace Mann Bart.
24. Lee in Kent The Seat of Thos. Barrett Esqr.
25. Kippington in Kent The Seat of Francis Motley Austen Esqr.
26. Broome in Kent The Seat of Sir Henry Oxenden Bart.
27. Leybourne Grange in Kent The Seat of Sir Henry Hawley Bart.
28. Woodstock House in Kent The Seat of Samuel Chambers Esqr.
29. Ash Grove in Kent The Seat of Miss Otways.
30. Sandling in Kent The Seat of William Deedes Esqr.
31. Chilham Castle in Kent The Seat of James Wildman Esqr.
32. Horsmonden Rectory Belonging to the Revd. Dr Marriott.
33. Eastwell Park in Kent The Seat of George Finch Hutton Esqr.
34. Canterbury Cathedral Jno. Geo Wood delt. W. Green sculpt. Feby. 1 1800.
35. Mystole in Kent the Seat of Sir John Fagg Bart.
36. Godinton in Kent, The Seat of Jno. Toke Esq.
37. Bradbourn in Kent the Seat of Sir John Papillon Twisden Bart.

Prideaux gives the number of plates as 24. I have examined 2 copies, one with 33 plates, and one, the most extensive, in the possession of Messrs. Joseph with 37 plates as above. The plates are not necessarily in the above order. The work is rare.

514 WOODHOUSE (F. W.)

Representation of the Brigade Field Day in Ware Park, on the 11th of June, 1853 Consisting of the Hertfordshire Militia, under the command of Colonel Most Noble the Marquis of Salisbury & the Essex Yeomanry Cavalry and Artillery, commanded by Major Palmer, upon which occasion the Hertfordshire Regiment of Militia was officially inspected by Colonel Thornton of the Grenadier Guards. These plates are most respectfully dedicated to the Right Honble The Viscount Palmerston, Her Majesty's Secretary of State for the Home Department The Right Honble the Earl of Verulam, Lord Lieutenant of the County of Herts and the Right Honble the Viscount Maynard, Lord Lieutenant of the County of Essex. By their obedient servant F. W. Woodhouse.

Folio.

COLLATION.—Title Dedication as above with coloured vignette at foot and imprint Stannard & Dixon, 7 Poland St. (v. blank) + 8 coloured lithographs.

Each plate marked, F. W. Woodhouse pinxt. Ploszczynski lith. (except 6 which bears no lithographer's name). Stannard & Dixon, 7 Poland St.

1. Essex Artillery supported by Cavalry & the Herts Militia in action towards the Town of Ware.
2. Herts Militia firing by Companies. Preparing to charge with fixed bayonets.
3. Herts Militia forming Square. After charging.
4. Herts Militia Retiring. Covered by the Essex Artillery & Cavalry.
5. The Essex Cavalry & Artillery advancing in Line—and Herts militia formed upon the original ground in close column of companies.
6. Essex Cavalry retiring by alternate Troops—supported by their artillery & Herts Militia forming line to the rear of their original position.
7. Herts Militia Firing on the Enemy, to the rear of the original position supported on the right & left by the Essex Artillery & Cavalry.
8. The United Brigade advancing in Parade Order.

515 World in Miniature, 43 Vols, Duodecimo, as under

The World in Miniature; edited by Frederic Shoberl (thick and thin rule) Africa, containing a description of the Manners and Customs with some historical particulars of

World in Miniature—Africa (*contd.*)

the Moors of the Zahara, and of the Negro Nations between the Rivers Senegal and Gambia: Illustrated with Two Maps, and Forty-Five Coloured Engravings (rule) Vol. I [II, III, IV] (rule) London: Printed for R. Ackermann, 101 Strand, And to be had of all Booksellers

4 vols.   Duodecimo.   (1821)

> COLLATION VOL. I.—Title as above (v. London C. Green, Leicester Street, Leicester Square) + Advertisement 2 pp. (iii–iv) + Preface 8 pp. (v–xii) + Contents 3 pp. (unnumbered) + List of Plates 3 pp. (unnumbered) + pp. 1–180 + Map + 10 coloured plates.

1.	Front.	Moor & Moorish Woman.
2.		Engraved Title.
	p. 1.	Map of the Country of the Moors.
3.	p. 22.	Chief of the Assounas.
4.	p. 44.	Moorish Chief & Wife.
5.	p. 48.	Moorish Adouar or Camp, with tent of a chief.
6.	p. 54.	Moorish Princess going abroad on a Dromedary.
7.	p. 62.	Talbe or Moorish Priest in his ordinary dress.
8.	p. 140.	Moors surprising a Negro Village.
9.	p. 146.	Negro & Moor of Gum Caravan.
10.	p. 155.	Grisgris, Waterbottle & Pouch.

> VOL. II.—Title as before + pp. 1–170 + Map + 12 coloured plates.

11.	Front.	A Felup.
	p. 1.	Map of the Countries inhibited by the Woloes.
12.	p. 28.	View of St. Louis.
13.	p. 31.	A Signara or Woman of colour of St. Louis.
14.	p. 41.	A Negro Foot Soldier.
15.	p. 56.	A Negro Horse Soldier.
16.	p. 66.	View of Goree (folding).
17.	p. 64.	View of the Village of Ben in Cayor.
18.	p. 70.	Canoes of the Negroes.
19.	p. 89.	View of Guisala or Joal.
20.	p. 100.	Apartment of the King of Salurn.
21.	p. 114.	A Mandingo.
22.	p. 165.	Negro method of attacking the Crocodile.

> VOL. III.—Title as before + pp. 1–168 + 15 coloured plates.

23.	Front.	Head Dress & Ornaments of the Negro Women.
24.	p. 63.	Temple of the Talbes or Marabouts.
25.	p. 81.	Negro Women washing themselves.
26.	p. 88.	Graves of the Severes.
27.	p. 101.	Plan of the Residence of the Bour Sine at Joal.
28.	p. 105.	Town & Plantation of the Fulahs (folding).
29.	p. 107.	[Domestic Implements].
30.	p. 134.	A Negro ascending a Palm for its Wine.
31.	p. 153.	[Implements].
32.	p. 155.	A Goldsmith.
33.	p. 157.	Beating Cotton.
34.	p. 158.	Negress spinning cotton.
35.	p. 161.	A Weaver.
36.	p. 165.	[Weapons &c.]
37.	p. 167.	A floating bridge.

> VOL. IV.—Title as before + pp. 1–184 + 8 coloured plates.

38.	Front.	Negro girl studying the Game of Ourri.
39.	p. 47.	A Chain of Slaves Travelling from the interior.

World in Miniature—Africa (*contd.*)

40. p. 72. The Slave Ship.
41. p. 119. A Negro playing on the Balafo.
42. p. 120. African Airs.
43. p. 154. The Galago of the Senegal.
44. p. 159. The Termite.
45. p. 165. Nest of the Termites (folding).

Issued in pink boards with yellow printed labels at £1 1s.

The World in Miniature: edited by Frederic Shoberl. (thick and thin rule) The Asiatic Islands and New Holland: being a description of the Manners, Customs, Character, and State of Society of the various tribes by which they are inhabited: illustrated by Twenty-Six Coloured Engravings (rule) In Two Volumes (rule) Vol. I [II] (rule) "The proper study of mankind is man . . . Pope" (rule) London: Printed by R. Ackermann Repository of Arts, Strand: and to be had of all Booksellers

2 vols. Duodecimo.   (1824)

COLLATION VOL. I.—Title as above (v. London: Green, Leicester Street, Leicester Square) + Advertisement 1 p. (v. blank) + Preface 5 pp. (iii–vii) (p. viii blank) + Contents 1 p. + Directions for placing plates 1 p. + pp. 1–291 + 14 coloured plates, each plate bearing imprint, "Pub by R. Ackermann 1824."

 1. Front. Man of the Island of Luzon.
 2. p. 34. Girl of the Mountains of Luzon.
 3. p. 41. Woman of the Island of Luzon.
 4. p. 51. Woman of the Marian Islands.
 5. p. 52. Man of the Marian Islands.
 6. p. 76. View of the Padang Sumatra.
 7. p. 88. A House in Sumatra.
 8. p. 186. Natives of Java.
 9. p. 193. A Javanese Chief in his ordinary dress.
10. p. 195. Javanese Mantri.
11. p. 198. Javanese in War Dress.
12. p. 200. Court Dress of Java.
13. p. 255. Rongging, or Dancing Girl of Java.
14. p. 258. Musical Instruments of the Javanese.

VOL. II.—Title as before + pp. 1–289 + 12 coloured plates, each bearing imprint, "Pub by R. Ackermann 1824."

15. Front. Girl of Timor.
16. p. 66. Man of Timor.
17. p. 109. Man of Ombay (No 1).
18. p. 111. Man of Ombay (No 2).
19. p. 186. Woman of Amboyna.
20. p. 196. A Man of Rawak.
21. p. 215. Man of New Holland.
22. p. 226. Native of the East Coast of New Holland.
23. p. 235. Native of New South Wales dancing.
24. p. 237. Musician of New Holland.
25. p. 264. Man of Van Diemans Land.
26. p. 270. Woman of Van Diemans Land.

Issued in mauve boards at 12s.

The World in Miniature; edited by Frederick Shoberl (thick and thin rule) Austria, containing a description of the Manners, Customs, Character, and Costumes of the People of that Empire, Illustrated by Thirty-Two Coloured Engravings (rule) In Two Volumes (rule) Vol. I [II] (rule) The proper study of mankind is man—Pope (rule) London: Printed for R. Ackermann, Repository of Arts, Strand; And to be had of all Booksellers N.D.

2 vols. Duodecimo.   [1823]

COLLATION VOL. I.—Title as above (v. London: Green, Leicester Street, Leicester Square) + Preface pp. iii–vi + Contents pp. vii–ix (p. x blank) + List of Plates 2 pp. (xi–xii) + Text pp. 1–161 [p. 162 blank] + 10 leaves of Ackermann Advertisements.

World in Miniature—Austria (*contd.*)

1. Frontispiece. Anachian Woman of Moravia.
2. p. 81. Fireman of Vienna.
3. p. 83. Country-woman of Upper Austria.
4. p. 93. Peasant of Egra in Winter Dress.
5. p. 95. Female Peasant of Egra in Winter Dress.
6. p. 103. Peasant of the Mountains of Moravia.
7. p. 119. Tyrolese Wrestler.
8. p. 122. Tyrolese Hunter.
9. p. 136. Tyrolese Woman.

VOL. II.—Title as before + Text pp. 1–200 + 22 coloured plates.

10. Frontispiece. Women of Slavonia.
11. p. 52. Hungarian Peasant of the County of Szolnok-Weszprim.
12. p. 54. Unmarried Female of the County of Weszprim.
13. p. 56. Tsikoshes of Mezohegyes.
14. p. 66. Peasant of Bocsko.
15. p. 68. Unmarried Female of Bocsko.
16. p. 70. Married Female of Bocsko.
17. p. 100. Unmarried Female of Torotzko.
18. p. 102. Unmarried Female of Oberascha.
19. p. 104. Young Man of Oberascha.
20. p. 106. Armed Plajash.
21. p. 111. Boyar of Seret.
22. p. 113. Peasant of Bukowina.
23. p. 117. Woman of Szutzawitza.
24. p. 118. Unmarried Female of Jackoberg.
25. p. 122. Female Peasants of Phillippowan.
26. p. 133. Tanaszia Dorojevich vice Harom Bassa of the Serischans.
27. p. 139. Unmarried Female of Dragathal.
28. p. 146. Unmarried Female of Ottochace.
29. p. 152. Unmarried Female of Glina.
30. p. 154. Woman of Dubitza.
31. p. 165. Man of the Frontiers of Bannat.
32. p. 168. Woman of Almasch in the Bannat.

Issued in blue boards with brown label at 12s.

The World in Miniature; edited by Frederic Shoberl. (thick and thin rule) China, containing illustrations of the Manners, Customs, Character and Costumes of the People of that Empire. Accompanied by Thirty Coloured Engravings (rule) In Two Volumes (rule) Vol. I [II] (rule) The proper study of mankind is man—Pope (rule) London: Printed for R. Ackermann, Repository of Arts, Strand; And to be had of all Booksellers

2 vols. Duodecimo. [1823]

COLLATION VOL. I.—Title as above (v. London: Green, Leicester Street, Leicester Square) + Preface pp. iii–x + Contents pp. xi–xii + Directions for placing plates pp. xiii–xiv + p. 1–208 + 15 coloured plates, each bearing imprint, Pub by R. Ackermann London 1823.

1. Front. Confectioner.
2. p. 63. Mandarin.
3. p. 91. Mandarin's Officer.
4. p. 94. Lady of Rank.
5. p. 128. Sedan Bearer.
6. p. 130. Female Bonze.
7. p. 149. Watchman.
8. p. 157. Soldier with Matchlock.
9. p. 166. Tiger of War.
10. p. 170. Juggler.
11. p. 178. Tradesman with an Umbrella.
12. p. 186. Seamstress.
13. p. 188. Waterman.
14. p. 195. Itinerant Fruit Seller.
15. p. 203. Fruit Stall.

VOL. II.—Title as before + pp. 1–257 + 15 coloured plates imprint as before.

16. Front. Bookseller.
17. p. 44. Flower Seller.
18. p. 54. Pedlar.
19. p. 60. Dog Seller.
20. p. 76. Fishing Cormorant.
21. p. 86. Countryman with Cloak made of Rice Straw.
22. p. 88. Barber.
23. p. 96. Viper Seller.
24. p. 100. Pigeon Merchant.
25. p. 108. Puppet Show.
26. p. 121. A Miao Tse.
27. p. 126. A Miao Tse Woman.
28. p. 142. Chinese Mahometan.
29. p. 175. Eleuth Tartar.
30. p. 184. Corean Mandarin.

Issued in buff boards with pink printed labels at 12s.

World in Miniature—England

The World in Miniature; (thin and thick rule) England, Scotland, and Ireland, edited by W. H. Pyne. Containing a description of the character, manners, customs, dress, diversions, and other peculiarities of the inhabitants of Great Britain (rule) In Four Volumes; illustrated with Eighty-Four Coloured Engravings. (rule) Vol. I [II, III, IV] (rule) "The proper study of mankind is man"—Pope (rule) London 1827: Printed for R. Ackermann, Repository of Arts, Strand; And to be had of all Booksellers.

4 vols. Duodecimo. 1827

COLLATION VOL. I.—Title as above (v. Shackell and Co., Johnson's Court, Fleet-street) + Preface 6 pp. (iii–viii) + Index (being List of Plates) 4 pp. + pp. 1–288 + 21 coloured plates.

Each plate bears imprint, "Pub by R. Ackermann London."

1. Frontispiece Watchman.	12. p. 172. Yeoman Guard.
2. p. 22. Lord Mayor.	13. p. 184. Fireman.
3. p. 42. Alderman.	14. p. 196. Life Boat.
4. p. 52. City Marshal.	15. p. 210. Shrimper.
5. p. 58. Blue Coat Boy.	16. p. 216. Milk Girl.
6. p. 76. Knight of the Garter.	17. p. 226. Bill Sticker.
7. p. 91. Mail Coach.	18. p. 242. Chimney Sweep.
8. p. 101. General Postman.	19. p. 251. Charity Children.
9. p. 113. British Peer.	20. p. 266. Knife Grinder.
10. p. 127. Bishop.	21. p. 273. Newsman.
11. p. 156. Herald.	

VOL. II.—Title as before + pp. 1–288 + 20 coloured plates.

22. Frontispiece Councellor.	32. p. 173. Coal Porters.
23. p. 1. Common Council-man.	33. { p. 185. Fisherwoman. } { p. 196. Dustman. }
24. p. 41. Gentleman Pensioner.	
25. p. 66. Doctor in Music, Oxford.	34. p. 203. Brickmakers.
26. p. 75. Huntsman.	35. p. 214. Stage Coach.
27. p. 97. Race Course.	36. p. 224. Pedlar.
28. { p. 120. Chelsea Pensioner. } { p. 129. Greenwich Pensioner. }	37. p. 253. Cat's-meat Woman.
	38. p. 242. Jew Old Clothes' man.
29. p. 137. Parish Beadle.	39. p. 257. Link man.
30. p. 153. Coachman.	40. p. 269. Match Girl.
31. p. 161. Baker.	41. p. 279. Tread Mill.

VOL. III.—Title as before + pp. 1–288 + 24 coloured plates.

42. Frontispiece Lamp Lighter.	54. p. 115. Steam Boat.
43. p. 14. Barrow Woman.	55. p. 131. Inland Navigation.
44. p. 27. Scavengers.	56. p. 149. Ticket Porter.
45. p. 42. Hawkers.	57. p. 154. Porter Brewers Drayman.
46. p. 60. Bachelor of Laws Oxford.	58. p. 160. Ale Brewers Drayman.
47. p. 64. Nobleman Oxford.	59. p. 167. House Maid.
48. p. 81. Scholar Oxford.	60. p. 176. English Peasant.
49. p. 82. Servitor Oxford.	61. p. 197. Butchers Boy.
50. p. 84. Commoner—Oxford.	62. p. 224. Fisherman.
51. p. 89. Collector Oxford.	63. p. 242. Smithfield Drover.
52. p. 92. Westminster Scholar.	64. p. 253. Hackney Coachman and Cad.
53. p. 103. Quakers.	65. p. 261. Boxers.

VOL. IV.—Title as before + pp. 1–252 + Errata 1 p. (v. blank) + 16 coloured plates.

66. Frontispiece Knight of St Patrick.	69. p. 50. Pensioner Trin. College, Master of Arts, Sizar Cambridge.
67. p. 1. Knight of the Bath.	
68. p. 49. Fellow Commoner Cambridge.	70. p. 59. Proctor Cambridge.

World in Miniature—England (*contd.*)

71. p. 61. Esquire Beadle Yeoman Beadle Cambridge.
72. p. 68. Doctor of Divinity Cambridge.
73. p. 74. Doctor in Law or Physic Cambridge.
74. p. 80. Wine Coopers.
75. p. 89. Irish Pavior.

76. p. 119. Bricklayers Labourer.
77. p. 126. Scotch Peasant Girl.
78. p. 132. Scotch Piper.
79. p. 138. Scotch Shepherd.
80. p. 153. Campbell of Breadalbane.
81. p. 167. Frazer of Lovat.

Issued in white boards with yellow labels at £1 12s.

The World in Miniature; edited by Frederic Shoberl; (thick and thin rule) Hindoostan, containing a description of the religion, manners, customs, trades, arts, sciences, literature, diversions, &c. of the Hindoos. Illustrated with Upwards of One Hundred Coloured Engravings (rule) in Six Volumes (rule) Vol. I [II, III, IV, V, VI] (rule) The proper study of mankind is man—Pope (rule) London: Printed for R. Ackermann, Repository of Arts, Strand; And to be had of all Booksellers.

6 vols. Duodecimo.   [1822]

COLLATION VOL. I.—Title as above (v. Green, Leicester Street, Leicester Square) + Advertisement 2 pp. (numbered) + Preface pp. v–xxviii + Contents pp. xxix–xxxiii + List of Plates pp. xxxv–xxxix + pp. 1–187 + 8 coloured plates.

All plates bear imprint, "Pubd. by R. Ackermann London 1822."

1. Frontispiece Trimurti the Indian Trinity.
2. p. 28. Brama.
3. p. 38. Dourga killing Maissassour.
4. p. 45. Ganesa God of Wisdom.
5. p. 49. Supramania Second son of Sheeva.
6. p. 67. Manmadin the Indian Cupid.
7. p. 83. Vishnu reclined on the Serpent Adissechan.
8. p. 84. Vishnu in his third Incarnation as a Wild Boar.

VOL. II.—Title as before + pp. 1–273 + 19 coloured plates.

 9. p. 61. Malabar Writer.
10. p. 65. Wives of Bramins.
11. p. 76. A Mahometan Officer.
12. p. 80. Sujah Dowlah, Vizir of the Mogul Empire, Nabob of Oude, & his ten Sons (folded).
13. p. 105. Hindoo Ladies paying a visit to a Persee Lady.
14. p. 181. A Brahmin who teaches the days & His Wife.
15. p. 186. A Pandidapan Bramin & his Wife.
16. p. 188. A Papan Vaichenaven Bramin A Tatoidipapan Bramin.
17. p. 210. The Fakir Praoun Poury.
18. p. 212. The Fakir Perkasamund.
19. p. 216. Ter, or Sacred Chariot.
20. p. 219. Tadin playing with fire Ariganda Pandaron Tadin with a padlock to his mouth.
21. p. 223. Pandarous Penitents of the Sect of Sheeva.
22. p. 229. A Poojaree singing the history of Mariatta.
23. p. 231. Mariatta Codam or manner of dancing in honour of the Goddess Mariatta.
24. p. 233. Nemessura Cavadi or Woman carrying the Water of the Ganges.
25. p. 243. A Rajah & his wives celebrating the Festival of Kishna (folded).
26. p. 250. A Religious Procession.
27. p. 252. Ceremony of throwing the colossal statue of the Goddess Cali into the water.

VOL. III.—Title as before + pp. 1–324 + 22 coloured plates.

28. Frontispiece A Hindoo Cradle.
29. p.   1. Hindoos throwing themselves on Mattresses covered with sharp Instruments.
30. p.   8. A species of Penance practised at the Festival of the Goddess Bhavani (folded).

World in Miniature—Hindustan (*contd.*)

31. p. 18. Musical Instruments Plate I.
32. p. 22. Musical Instruments Plate II.
33. p. 27. Musical Instruments Plate III.
34. p. 32. A Mahometan beating the Nagabotte.
35. p. 44. A Hindoo Dancer called Baloks.
36. p. 50. Devedassis or Bayaderes.
37. p. 67. The Father of the Bride going with the Nuptial Presents to the Bridegroom (folded).
38. p. 72. The Bridegroom conducted in state to the house of the Bride (folded).
39. p. 77. The husband swearing in the presence of a Bramin to take care of his wife (folded).
40. p. 90. Funeral of a Hindoo.
41. p. 99. A Hindoo Widow burning herself with the Corpse of her Husband.
42. p. 242. A Rajah giving audience.
43. p. 248. Dress & Ornaments of Hindoo Ladies.
44. p. 262. A Rajpoot.
45. p. 264. A Mahratta.
46. p. 303. Pecali or Water carrier attending the Army.
47. p. 306. 1, 2 Seapoy Officers   3 A private Seapoy.
48. p. 308. A Seik   A Seapoy in the French service.
49. p. 313. A Seapoy in the native dress   A Hindoo soldier   A Brigbasi.

VOL. IV.—Title as before + pp. 1–216 + 23 coloured plates.

50. Frontispiece Basket Maker & his Wife.
51. p. 31. Sugar Mill.
52. p. 63. Hindoo Ploughman & Herdsman.
53. p. 86. A Sourer & his Wife.
54. p. 90. Apparatus for Distillation.
55. p. 102. Carpenter Mason.
56. p. 125. A Column from a Temple at Benares.
57. p. 146. A Choultry (folding).
58. p. 151. Taje Mahl (folding).
59. p. 164. Beater of Cotton & his Wife.
60. p. 168. Cotton Spinning.
61. p. 169. Winding Cotton.
62. p. 170. Preparation of the Warp for Weaving.
63. p. 172. Weaver joining the broken Threads.
64. p. 174. Weaving.
65. p. 176. Cloth-Beater.
66. p. 179. Cloth Painter.
67. p. 181. Dyer.
68. p. 192. Silk Dyer.
69. p. 193. Winding Silk.
70. p. 197. Ironer.
71. p. 199. Malabar Tailor.
72. p. 210. School-Master.

VOL. V.—Title as before + pp. 1–234 + 16 coloured plates.

73. Frontispiece Potters Wife.
74. p. 2. Potter.
75. p. 9. Horse Breaker Smith.
76. p. 15. Gold-Beater.
77. p. 17. Goldsmith.
78. p. 22. Gilder.
79. p. 24. Brazier.
80. p. 26. Brazier's Wife.
81. p. 27. Shell-Cutter.
82. p. 30. Water Carriers.
83. p. 32. Telinga Barber Malabar Barber.
84. p. 60. Mahratta Shoe-maker   Shoe maker.
85. p. 70. Catamaran Chelingh.
86. p. 74. Perfumer.
87. p. 85. Dealer in Betel, Areca &c.
88. p. 92. Dealer in Pearls.

VOL. VI.—Title as before + pp. 1–240 + Advertisement "Books &c. Published by R. Ackermann" pp. 1–18 + 15 coloured plates.

89. Frontispiece Mahometan Woman travelling.
90. p. 34. Chess Board & Spring Bow for shooting Tigers.
91. p. 39. Tumblers.
92. p. 42. Interior of Fort St. George with Rope-dancers, Tumblers &c.
93. p. 46. Hindoo Jugglers, swallowing a Sword & balancing a Buffalo.
94. p. 52. Conjurer & Juggler with Cups & Balls.
95. p. 65. Snake Charmer.
96. p. 90. Wrestlers.
97. p. 105. Tiger Hunt (folding).
98. p. 175. Bengal Palanquin.
99. p. 182. Mogul Palanquin.
100. p. 184. Dolee.
101. p. 190. Gadee.
102. p. 197. Peon.
103. p. 199. Head Peon.

Issued in buff coloured boards at £2 8s.

World in Miniature—Illyria and Dalmatia

The World in Miniature (thick and thin rule) Illyria and Dalmatia; containing a description of the Manners, Customs, Habits, Dress, and other peculiarities characteristic of their Inhabitants and those of Adjacent Countries; illustrated with Thirty-Two Coloured Engravings. (rule) Vol. I [II] (rule) "The proper study of mankind is man" Pope. (rule) London: Printed for R. Ackermann, 101 Strand; And to be had of all Booksellers

2 vols.   Duodecimo.   [1821]

COLLATION VOL. I.—Title as above (v. C. B. Green, Leicester Street, Leicester Square) + Contents 2 pp. + Order of the Plates 2 pp. + Advertisement 4 pp. (vii–x) + Introduction 8 pp. (xi–xviii) + pp. 1–146 + 11 coloured plates.

Plates bear imprint, "Pubd. at R. Ackermann's London 1821."

1. Frontispiece Slavonian, Wende, & Illyrian.	7. p. 86. A Wipachian Woman.
2. p. 5. A Man of the Geilthal.	8. p. 95. A Gothscheer Woman.
3. p. 12. A Woman of the Geilthal.	9. p. 105. A Liburnian.
4. p. 41. A Woman of Carniola.	10. p. 109. A Liburnian Woman.
5. p. 51. A Woman of Istria.	11. p. 136. A Morlachian.
6. p. 77. A Japide Woman.	

VOL. II.—Title as before (with addition of words "edited by Frederic Shoberl") + pp. 1–166 + 21 coloured plates.

12. Frontispiece A Morlachian Woman. A Married Morlachian.	22. p. 97. A Dalmatian Woman.
	23. p. 101. An Inhabitant of Bocca di Cattaro.
13. p. 13. A Morlachian Woman.	24. p. 102. A Woman of Sabioncello.
14. p. 33. A Croation Woman.	25. p. 110. A Montenegrin Woman.
15. p. 36. An Uscoke Woman.	26. p. 120. The Rector of Ragusa.
16. p. 45. An Uscoke.	27. p. 121. A Montenegrin.
17. p. 46. An Uscoke Woman.	28. p. 122. A Woman of Canali.
18. p. 67. An Inhabitant of Juppa.	29. p. 137. A Slavonian Woman.
19. p. 69. A Likanian.	30. p. 147. A Clementinian.
20. p. 81. A Likanian Woman.	31. p. 152. A Clementinian Woman.
21. p. 83. A Dalmatian.	32. p. 164. A Rascian Woman.

Issued in light blue boards with yellow labels at 12s.

The World in Miniature; edited by Frederic Shoberl (thick and thin rule) Japan, containing illustrations of the Character, Manners, Customs, Religion, Dress, Amusements, Commerce, Agriculture, &c. of the people of that Empire.   With Twenty Coloured Engravings. (rule) "The proper study of mankind is man" Pope (rule) London: Printed for R. Ackermann, Repository of Arts, Strand; And to be had of all Booksellers.

Duodecimo   [1823]

COLLATION.—Title as above (v. London: Green, Leicester Street, Leicester Square) + Preface 7 pp. (iii–ix) p. x blank + Contents 3 pp. (xi–xiii) + Directions for placing the plates 1 p. + pp. 1–286 + 20 coloured plates.

20 plates bearing imprint, "Pub by R. Ackermann London 1823."

1. Frontispiece Lady in a Car.	7. p. 127. Mechanic in Winter Dress.
2. p. 56. Soldier of Nangasaki.	8. p. 130. Japanese in Dress of Ceremony.
3. p. 59. Japanese Soldier.	9. p. 135. Civil Officer.
4. p. 64. Seaman.	10. p. 138. Lady in a Dress of Ceremony.
5. p. 85. Monk of the Sect of Rokubo.	11. p. 141. Woman & Child.
6. p. 110. (misprinted p. 144) Bonze.	12. p. 190. Implements for Writing.

World in Miniature—Japan (*contd.*)

13. p. 210. Servant, carrying his Masters effects.
14. p. 212. Lady walking abroad.
15. p. 234. Wrestler.
16. p. 244. Peasant pounding rice.
17. p. 250. Fisherman.
18. p. 255. Fisherman's Wife.
19. p. 279. An Inhabitant of Jesso.
20. p. 284. Superior of the Tartar Establishment in the Island of Sakhalin.

Issued in yellow boards with pink label at 8s.

The World in Miniature; edited by Frederick Shoberl (thick and thin rule) The Netherlands; containing a description of the character, manners, habits, and costumes of the inhabitants of the late Seven United Provinces, Flanders and Brabant. Illustrated with Eighteen Coloured Engravings (rule) "The proper Study of mankind is man" . . . Pope **London: Printed for R. Ackermann, Repository of Arts, Strand; And to be had of all Booksellers**

Duodecimo. [1823]

COLLATION.—Title as above (v. London: Green, Leicester Street, Leicester Square) + Preface 3 pp. (iii–v) p. vi blank + Contents 2 pp. (vii–viii) + Directions for placing the Plates 1 p. (v. blank) + pp. 1–241 + 18 coloured plates.

1. Frontispiece Coal Girl of Brabant.
2. p. 133. A Woman and boy of the neighbourhood of Amsterdam.
3. p. 137. Match-girl of Rotterdam.
4. p. 139. Woman of the neighbourhood of Rotterdam.
5. p. 145. Woman of North Holland.
6. p. 147. Fish-Woman of Schevening.
7. p. 153. Man of Zuid Beveland.
8. p. 154. Woman of Zuid Beveland.
9. p. 157. A Woman of Zealand (of Walcheven in list of plates).
10. p. 164. Woman of the Island of Schokland.
11. p. 166. Man of the Island of Schokland.
12. p. 177. Bride of Marken.
13. p. 183. Country woman of Guelders.
14. p. 186. Villager of Guelders.
15. p. 192. Lady of Leeuwarden.
16. p. 195. Skipper of Friesland.
17. p. 197. Skipper's Wife.
18. p. 201. Woman of Hinlopen.

Issued in pink boards with yellow printed label at 8s.

The World in Miniature; edited by Frederic Shoberl (thick and thin rule) Persia, containing a brief description of the country; and an account of its government, laws and religion, and of the character, manners and customs, arts, amusements, &c. of its inhabitants (rule) In three volumes. Illustrated with Thirty Coloured Engravings (rule) Vol. I [II, III] (rule) London: Printed for R. Ackermann, Repository of Arts, Strand; And to be had of all Booksellers

3 vols. Duodecimo. 1822

COLLATION VOL. I.—Advertisement of part of the series 1 p. (v. blank) Title as above (v. London: Green, Leicester Street, Leicester Square) + Preface 6 pp. (v–x) + pp. 1–240 + small slip Directions to Binder.

All plates bear imprint, "Pubd. by R. Ackermann, London 1822."

1. Frontispiece Futteh Ali Shah, King of Persia.
2. p. 94. Master of the Ceremonies.
3. p. 100. Woman of the Harem.
4. p. 103. Female Slave of the Seraglio.
5. p. 109. Eunuch of the Seraglio.
6. p. 111. Queen of Persia travelling in her litter.
7. p. 114. Attendants on the Queen of Persia.
8. p. 127. Officer of the Guards.
9. p. 198. A Foot Soldier.
10. p. 204. A Camel Artilleryman.

VOL. II.—Title as before + pp. 1–236 + Directions to Binder 1 p. (v. blank) + 10 coloured plates.

417

World in Miniature—Persia (*contd.*)

11. Frontispiece Persian Smoking.
12. p. 10. High Priest.
13. p. 12. Doctor in Divinity.
14. p. 72. Persian at Prayers.
15. p. 77. Persian Lady at Prayers.

16. p. 180. Persian of High Rank.
17. p. 186. Ambassador.
18. p. 223. Persian Female (indoor dress).
19. p. 225. Persian Female (outdoor dress).
20. p. 230. Grandee, smoking on Horseback.

VOL. III.—Title as before + pp. 1–233 + Contents pp. xi–xv + List of Plates to all 3 vols. 2 pp. (xvii–xviii) + 10 coloured plates.

21. Frontispiece Geber Female.
22. p. 46. Village Dancing Girl.
23. p. 138. Armenian.
24. p. 142. Armenian Lady.
25. p. 145. Banian.

26. p. 147. Banian Female.
27. p. 159. Well & Agricultural Instruments.
28. p. 190. Musical Instruments Plate A.
29. p. 193. Musical Instruments Plate B.
30. p. 213. Takhti Cadjar.

Issued in yellow boards with white labels at 5s. 6d. a volume.

The World in Miniature; edited by Frederic Shoberl. (thick and thin rule) Russia, being a description of the character, manners, customs, dress, diversions, and other peculiarities of the different nations, inhabiting the Russian Empire (rule) in Four Volumes. Illustrated with Seventy-Two Coloured Engravings (rule) Vol. I [II, III, IV] (rule) London: Printed for R. Ackermann, Repository of Arts, Strand; And to be had of all Booksellers.

4 vols. Duodecimo. (1822–3)

COLLATION VOL. I.—Title as above (v. London, Green, Leicester Street, Leicester Square) + Preface 5 pp. (iii–vii) p. viii blank + pp. 1–181 + Plates in Vol. I 1 p. (v. blank) + Advertisements 2 leaves unnumbered followed by 9 leaves numbered 1–18 + 18 coloured plates.

All plates bear imprint, Pubd. by R. Ackermann, London 1822 [or 1823].

1. Frontispiece Tradesman—Peasant.
2. p. 52. Tradesman's Wife in her Holiday Dress.
3. p. 80. Egg Seller.
4. p. 82. Washerwoman.
5. p. 84. Peasant of Livonia.
6. p. 87. Woman of Valday.
7. p. 88. Female Gardener of Tula.
8. p. 90. Tradesman's Wife of Yaroslaw.
9. p. 115. Finlander going to market.

10. p. 119. Sledge of the Russian Peasants.
11. p. 127. Vender of Spirituous Liquors.
12. p. 141. Travelling Sledge.
13. p. 144. Droschki.
14. p. 148. Butcher of Moscow.
15. p. 150. Itinerant Poulterer.
16. p. 167. Old Woman of Little Russia.
17. p. 168. Villager of Little Russia.
18. p. 174. Regular Monk.

VOL. II.—Title as before + pp. 1–294 + 18 coloured plates.

19. Frontispiece Moldavian Prince and Princess.
20. p. 65. Nogay Musician.
21. p. 67. Tartar Musician.
22. p. 127. Cossack.
23. p. 187. Pole in his Dress of Ceremony.
24. p. 190. Pole in his usual Dress.
25. p. 205. Finland Woman.
26. p. 207. Finland Girl.
27. p. 210. Finlander attacking a Bear.
28. p. 219. Female Peasant of Ingria.

29. p. 229. Tshuwash Women.
30. p. 243. Tsheremiss Woman in her summer dress.
31. p. 245. Tscheremiss Woman in her winter dress.
32. p. 251. Morduan Girl.
33. p. 254. Woman of Pensa.
34. p. 257. Wotyak Woman.
35. p. 283. Ostiak.
36. p. 288. Ostiak woman.

VOL. III.—Title as before + pp. 1–204 + Plates to Vol. III (v. blank) + 20 coloured plates.

World in Miniature—Russia (*contd.*)

37. Frontispiece Circassian Prince and Princess.	48. p. 65. Condour Tartar Girl.
38. p. 12. Tartar of Cazan.	49. p. 82. Bashkir Man.
39. p. 14. Tartar Female of Cazan.	50. p. 84. Bashkir Woman.
40. p. 15. Woman of Azamar.	51. p. 86. Bashkir Chief.
41. p. 27. Tartar Girl of Katchin.	52. p. 98. Kirghises.
42. p. 33. Mursa or Gentleman.	53. p. 143. Yakout Priest.
43. p. 34. Judge of the Crimea.	54. p. 160. Circassian Warrior.
44. p. 36. Tartar Woman.	55. p. 196. Tartar of the Cuban (misprint for
45. p. 47. Tartar of the Mountains.	Tcherkassian Prince).
46. p. 48. Tartar of the Mountains.	56. p. 201. Woman of Georgia.
47. p. 61. Condour Tartar Woman.	

VOL. IV.—Slip advertisement for "Austria" of same series + Title as before + pp. 1–267 + Contents pp. ix–xiii + List of Plates to the 4 vols. 4 pp. (xv–xvii) + 16 coloured plates.

57. Frontispiece Woman of Archangel.	65. p. 191. Women of Archangel.
58. p. 70. Calmuck.	66. p. 197. Tshuktshi Hunter.
59. p. 111. Bratskian Woman.	67. p. 200. Tshuktshi Man.
60. p. 117. Husbandman of the Frontiers of China, Mongol Tartar.	68. p. 201. Tshuktshi Woman.
	69. p. 202. Kamtschadale in Snow Shoes— Sledge of Kamtschatka.
61. p. 154. Tungusian Shaman.	70. p. 257. Native of the Fox Island.
62. p. 162. Tungusian Sorceress.	71. p. 258. Woman of Oonalashka.
63. p. 168. Samoyede.	72. p. 263. Canoes of Oonalashka.
64. p. 183. Samoyede Woman.	

The 4 vols. issued in green boards with orange labels at 8s. per vol.

The World in Miniature; edited by Frederic Shoberl. (thick and thin rule) Spain and Portugal, containing a description of the Character, Manners, Customs, Dress, Diversions, and other peculiarities of the inhabitants of those countries (rule) In Two Volumes; illustrated with Twenty-Seven Coloured Engravings (rule) Vol. I [II] (rule) "The proper study of mankind is man" . . . Pope (rule) London: Printed for R. Ackermann, Repository of Arts, Strand; And to be had of all Booksellers

2 vols.   Duodecimo.   [1825]

COLLATION VOL. I.—Title as above (v. London: Green, Leicester Street, Leicester Square) + Preface 2 pp. (iii–iv) + Contents 4 pp. (v–viii) + List of Plates 2 pp. + pp. 1–303 + 11 coloured plates, each plate bearing imprint, "Pub By R. Ackermann London 1825."

1. Front. Bull Fighter of Seville.	8. p. 285. Peasants of the Environs of Toro, Leon.
2. p. 16. Lady of Madrid.	
3. p. 123. Gipsy Dance.	9. p. 287. Villages of the Environs of Astorga.
4. p. 185. Infant Capuchin.	10. p. 289. Villager of the Environs of Salamanca.
5. p. 231. Courier.	
6. p. 265. Watchman of Madrid.	11. p. 291. Villager of the Environs of Salamanca (female.)
7. p. 275. Goat herd of the Environs of Valladolid.	

VOL. II.—Title as before + pp. 1–281 + 16 coloured plates with imprint as before.

12. Front. Villager of the District of Mequinenza.	20. p. 56. Gardener of Valencia.
13. p. 22. Villagers of Navarre.	21. p. 97. Peasant of the Mountains of Sagra
14. p. 28. Peasant of the Environs of Saragossa.	22. p. 100. Carter of Lorea.
15. p. 42. Peasant of Majorca.	23. p. 122. Lady of Cadiz.
16. p. 44. Lady of Majorca.	24. p. 129. Majo of Coldova.
17. p. 46. Villager of the Island of Iviza.	25. p. 152. Woman of Lisbon.
18. p. 48. Female Peasant of the Island of Iviza.	26. p. 159. Peasant in a Straw Cloak.
19. p. 52. Fisherman of Iviza.	27. p. 160. Girl of Guarda.

Issued in pink boards with green printed labels at 12s.

World in Miniature—South Seas

The World in Miniature; edited by Frederic Shoberl. (thick and thin rule) South Sea Islands: being a description of the Manners, Customs, Character, Religion and State of Society among the various tribes scattered over the Great Ocean, called the Pacific, or the South Sea: illustrated with Twenty Six Coloured Engravings (rule) In Two Volumes (rule). Vol. I [II] (rule) "The proper study of mankind is man" . . . Pope (rule) London: Printed for R. Ackermann, Repository of Arts, Strand; And to be had of all Booksellers

2 vols.   Duodecimo.   [1824]

COLLATION VOL. I.—Title as above (v. London: Green, Leicester Street, Leicester Square) + Advertisement 1 p. (v. blank) + Preface 10 pp. (iii–xii) + Contents 1 p. (v. blank) + Directions for placing plates 2 pp. (xv–xvi) + pp. 1–320 + 11 coloured plates.

1. Frontispiece Dance of the Friendly Islands.
2. p. 185. Sandwich Islander.
3. p. 190. Woman of the Sandwich Islands.
4. p. 211. Morai of the King of the Sandwich Islands.
5. p. 228. Dancer of the Sandwich Islands.
6. p. 274. Native of La Magdalena (Marquesas Islands) with a Club.
7. p. 280. Young man of the Marquesas not completely tatowed.
8. p. 283. Jean Baptiste Cabri.
9. p. 286. Man of Distinction of the Marquesas.
10. p. 288. Native of La Magdalena (Marquesas Islands) with a Sling.
11. p. 297. Native of La Magdalena (Marquesas Islands) with a Fan.

VOL. II.—Title as before + pp. 1–325 + 15 coloured plates.

12. Frontispiece Cheif (*sic*) of the Romanzoff Islands.
13. p.   11. Man of Easter Island.
14. p.   12. Woman of Easter Island.
15. p. 103. Man of the Feejee Islands.
16. p. 130. Man of New Zealand.
17. p. 136. Girl of New Zealand.
18. p. 205. Woman of the Saltikoff Islands.
19. p. 207. Man of Radack Islands.
20. p. 209. Woman of the Tchichagoff Islands.
21. p. 221. Labeleoa Chief of the Kotousoff Islands.
22. p. 234. King of the Caroline Islands.
23. p. 237. Woman of the Caroline Islands.
24. p. 254. Letter from a native of the Caroline Islands.
25. p. 256. Kadoo, a native of the Caroline Islands.
26. p. 282. Double Canoe of New Caledonia.

Issued in green boards with brown paper labels at 12s.

The World in Miniature; edited by Frederic Shoberl (rule) Switzerland; containing a description of the character, manners, customs, diversions, dress &c. of the people of that country in general and of the inhabitants of Twenty-two Cantons in Particular (rule) Illustrated by Eighteen Coloured Engravings (rule) "The proper study of mankind is man"—Pope (rule) London: Printed for R. Ackermann, Repository of Arts, Strand; And to be had of all Booksellers

Duodecimo.   [1823]

COLLATION.—Title as above (v. blank) + Preface pp. iii–vi + Contents 1 p. + List of Plates 1 p. + Text pp. 1–287 (p. 288 London: Printed by William Clowes, Stamford-street) + Advertisements of Ackermann 4 pp. + 18 coloured plates.

World in Miniature—Switzerland (*contd.*)

1. Frontispiece Women of Berne-Guggisberg-OberHasli.
2. p. 114. Man and Woman of Aargau.
3. p. 116. Women of the Canton of Zurich.
4. p. 119. Girl of Zurich.
5. p. 123. Man & Boy of the Canton of Zurich.
6. p. 137. Woman of St. Gall.
7. p. 151. Woman of Appenzell.
8. p. 154. Man & Woman of Schwytz.
9. p. 167. Women of Lucerne.
10. p. 180. Woman of Soleure.
11. p. 198. Woman of the Pays de Vaud.
12. p. 207. Man of Unterwalden.
13. p. 213. Woman of Unterwalden.
14. p. 218. Man of Uri.
15. p. 245. Woman of German Friburg in Bridal Costume.
16. p. 249. Lady of French Friburg.
17. p. 252. Woman of German Friburg in Funeral Costume.
18. p. 279. Woman of the Tessin.

The rarest volume of the series. Issued in pink boards with yellow labels at 8s.

The World in Miniature; edited by Frederic Shoberl (thick and thin rule) Tibet, and India beyond the Ganges; containing a description of the character, manners, customs, dress, religion, amusements, &c. of the nations inhabiting those countries: illustrated with Twelve Coloured Engravings. (rule) "The proper study of mankind is man"... Pope (rule) London: Printed for R. Ackermann, Repository of Arts, 101 Strand; And to be had of all Booksellers

Duodecimo [1824]

COLLATION.—Title as above (v. London: Green, Leicester Street, Leicester Square) + Preface 6 pp. (iii–viii) + Contents 3 pp. (ix–xi) + p. xii Directions for placing plates + pp. 1–352 + 12 plates.

12 coloured plates, each bearing imprint, "Pub. by R. Ackermann London 1824."

1. Frontispiece Cassay Horseman.
2. p. 117. A Woongee.
3. p. 121. Wife of a Woongee.
4. p. 123. Female Birman Peasant.
5. p. 125. Birman Peasant.
6. p. 149. A Rhahaan or Priest.
7. p. 209. Man of the Mountains of Arracan.
8. p. 211. Woman of the Mountains of Arracan.
9. p. 225. Mandarins of Tonquin.
10. p. 246. Soldier of Cochin China.
11. p. 281. Woman of Siam.
12. p. 283. Mandarin of Siam.

Issued in pink boards with yellow title label at 6s. 6d.

The World in Miniature; edited by Frederic Shoberl (thick and thin rule) Turkey, being a description of the Manners, Customs, Dresses, and other Pecularities characteristic of the inhabitants of the Turkish Empire; to which is prefixed a sketch of the History of the Turks: translated from the French of A. L. Castellan, Author of Letters on the Morea and Constantinople, and illustrated with Seventy-Three Coloured Engravings, containing Upwards of One Hundred and Fifty Costumes (rule) In Six Volumes (rule) (Vol. I [II, III, IV, V, VI]) (rule) London: Printed for R. Ackermann, 101 Strand, And to be had of all Booksellers.

6 vols. Duodecimo. (1821)

COLLATION VOL. I.—Title as above (v. Green, Leicester Street, Leicester Square) + Advertisement 4 pp. (i–iv) + Contents 6 pp. (v–x) + List of Plates 5 pp. (xi–xv) p. xvi blank + Preface pp. 1–14 + pp. 15–211 + 2 coloured plates.

All plates bearing imprint, "Pubd. by R. Ackermann London 1821."

1. Frontispiece Death of Sultan Amurat I.
2. p. 57. Othman I First Emperor of the Turks.

VOL. II.—Title as before + pp. 1–237 + 2 coloured plates.

World in Miniature—Turkey (*contd.*)

3. Frontispiece Discovery of the Sultana Kieuzel.
4. p. 227. Portrait of Mahmud II the reigning Emperor.

VOL. III.—Title as before + pp. 1–264 + 16 coloured plates.

5. Frontispiece The chief Khatoun or Favourite Sultana and the Heir-apparent to the Throne.
6. p. 7. The Sultan or Grand-Signor and Vizir.
7. p. 67. Musician-Dancer Khouzmat-Kar-Seray Governess of the Harem.
8. p. 114. Qyzlar-Agha, Chief of the Black Eunuchs,—Odahlye, or Woman of the Harem.
9. p. 124. Capou-Aghacy, Chief of the White Eunuchs.
10. p. 147. Itch-oghlan, Page of the Chamber—Rekabdar-agha, Stool Bearer.
11. p. 150. Itch-oghlan writing with the Calam—Writing Master.
12. p. 152. Instruments for Writing Plate A.
13. p. 154. Instruments for Writing Plate B.
14. p. 177. Dulbenddar-Agha, Turban Bearer-Silehh-dar-Agha, Sword Bearer to the Sultan.
15. p. 183. Itch-oghlan-aghacy, Page to the Sultan—Tezkierchdjy-bachy, Secretary to the Grand Signor.
16. p. 198. Sazend-bachy, Music Master to the Seraglio—Hhlavahdjy, Confectioner to the Seraglio.
17. p. 201. Musical Instruments Plate C.
18. p. 203. Musical Instruments Plate D.
19. p. 207. Tchenguy, Avrety A Female Dancer Tchenguy A Dancer.
20. p. 226. Copydjy-bachy Chief of the Porters.

VOL. IV.—Title as before + pp. 1–300 + 17 coloured plates.

21. Frontispiece Mamelukes.
22. p. 2. The Grand Vizir with the Army.
23. p. 6. Vezyri-Khousmet-Kiarycy, and Tchocah-dar, Attendants of the Vizir.
24. p. 20. A Spahy-A Dely.
25. p. 115. Reis Effendy, Minister for Foreign Affairs—Drogman, Interpreter.
26. p. 129. Tchaouch-bachy, Chief Introducer of Ambassadors—Tchaouch a common Tchaouch.
27. p. 163. Sekban-bachy, Third Officer of the Janissarie—Tegnytschery a Janissary in his State Dress.
28. p. 174. Achdjy, Cook—Achdjy-bachy, Head Cook of the Janissaries.
29. p. 176. Cazan, Kettle of the Janissaries—Tchorbadjy, Ladle-bearer, or Captain of Janissaries.
30. p. 188. Coulloucdjy, Inferior Officer of Janissaries in his ordinary dress—Bach-Tchaouch, Serjeant-Major of Janissaries.
31. p. 193. Thopdjy, gunner of the Nizam Djedyd-Nefer, a soldier of the Nizam-djedyd.
32. p. 202. Hammal a Porter Sacca a Water Carrier.
33. p. 251. Trumpets, Bits, Stirrups &c. Plate H.
34. p. 252. Standards Plate E.
35. p. 259. Arms, Offensive & Defensive.
36. p. 264. Drum, Kettle Drums, Fire Javelins &c. Plate G.
37. p. 274. Levanty-roumy a Greek Sailor—Levanty, a Turkish Marine.

VOL. V.—Title as before + 1–234 + 9 coloured plates.

38. Frontispiece Turbeh, or Tomb of a Sultan-Mufty, Chief Officer of the Law.
39. p. 24. Ulema or Molla—Istam ̣ol-Cadhycy, Judge of Constantinople.
40. p. 72. Turning Dervises.
41. p. 74. Dervise of Constantinople—Dervise of Syria.
42. p. 108. Postures of Prayer.
43. p. 141. A Mosque.
44. p. 154. A Fountain.
45. p. 207. A Carriage called Arabah.
46. p. 280. A Turkish Tomb.

VOL. VI.—Title as before + pp. 1–244 + Advertisements pp. 1–18 + 27 coloured plates.

47. Frontispiece Woman of Aleppo—Woman of Antioch.
48. p. 12. A Turk in a pelisse—a Turk in a Shawl.
49. p. 19. Turbans Plate A.
50. p. 22. Turbans Plate B.

World in Miniature—Turkey (*contd.*)

51. p. 25. Turbans Plate C.
52. p. 27. Turkish Woman of Constantinople—Turkish Woman from the Country.
53. p. 41. Greek Women—Turkish Women in the Town Dress.
54. p. 49. Bedouin Arab and his Wife.
55. p. 52. Bedouin woman making butter.
56. p. 54. Turk of St Jean d'Acre Arab woman of the Desert.
57. p. 63. A Syrian—an Egyptian Woman.
58. p. 72. Kurds.
59. p. 84. Turkish women of Asia making Bread.
60. p. 86. Drusian Women grinding corn.
61. p. 88. Turk of Tunis—Turk of Damascus.
62. p. 92. A Bosniac—a Tartar.
63. p. 102. A Jew—an Armenian.
64. p. 106. Woman of the Island of Simia—Woman of Pera.
65. p. 110. Albanians.
66. p. 114. Women of Scio, Samos and Metelin.
67. p. 117. Women of the Island of Andros.
68. p. 120. Woman of Spra—Woman of Cyprus.
69. p. 122. Woman of Naxos—Woman of Marmora.
70. p. 126. Woman of Argenteria—Woman of Scio.
71. p. 199. A Caimac-seller—Khodjah-baccal, a dealer in Vegetables.
72. p. 207. Turkish Repast.
73. p. 239. Turkish Fishery.

Issued in sap green boards with pink labels at £2 2s.

516 YOUNG (J.)

A Series of Portraits of the Emperors of Turkey, from the foundation of the Monarchy to the year 1815. Engraved from pictures painted at Constantinople. Commenced under the auspices of Sultan Selim the Third, and completed by command of Sultan Mahmoud the Second. With a Biographical account of each of the Emperors (thick and thin rule). By John Young (thin and thick rule).

Folio.   1815

COLLATION.—Title as above (v. blank) + Title in French (v. blank) + Dedication to Prince Regent 1 p. (v. blank) + Preface pp. 1–4 + Origin of Turks pp. 5–7 (p. 8 blank) + Preface in French pp. 9–12 + Origine des Turcs pp. 13–15 (p. 16 blank) + pp. 17–128 (at foot, London Printed by W. Bulmer & Co, Cleveland Row St. James's) + 1 unnumbered leaf of Text + Engraved title and 30 fine coloured mezzotint portraits. The portraits are oval, lettered in French from Ier to Trentieme Empereur Othoman and each has a vignette beneath the portrait.

1. Front. Sultan Mahmoud Khan IInd.	11. p. 53. Sultan Soliman Khan Ier.
2. p. 17. Engraved title within border of trophees.	12. p. 57. Sultan Selim Khan IInd.
	13. p. 61. Sultan Amurat Khan IIIme.
2. p. 17. Sultan Othman Khan Ier.	14. p. 65. Sultan Mahomet Khan IIIme.
3. p. 21. Sultan Orkan Khan.	15. p. 69. Sultan Achmet Khan Ier.
4. p. 25. Sultan Amurat Khan Ier.	16. p. 73. Sultan Mustapha Khan Ier.
5. p. 29. Sultan Bajazet Khan Ier.	17. p. 77. Sultan Othman Khan IInd.
6. p. 33. Sultan Mahomet Khan Ier.	18. p. 81. Sultan Amurat Khan IVme.
7. p. 37. Sultan Amurat Khan IInd.	19. p. 85. Sultan Ibrahim Khan.
8. p. 41. Sultan Mahomet Khan IInd.	20. p. 89. Sultan Mahomet Khan IVme.
9. p. 45. Sultan Bajazet Khan IInd.	21. p. 93. Sultan Soliman Khan IInd.
10. p. 49. Sultan Selim Khan Ier.	22. p. 97. Sultan Achmet Khan IInd.

Young's Turkey (*contd.*)

23. p. 101. Sultan Mustapha Khan IInd.
24. p. 105. Sultan Achmet Khan IIIme.
25. p. 109. Sultan Mahomet Khan Vme.
26. p. 113. Sultan Othman Khan IIIme.

27. p. 117. Sultan Mustapha Khan IIIme.
28. p. 121. Sultan Ab Dal Hamed Khan.
29. p. 125. Sultan Selim Khan IIIme.
30. (no number) Sultan Mustapha Khan IVme.

517 ZIEGLER (H. B.)

The Royal Lodges in Windsor Great Park From Drawings by H. B. Ziegler, executed by L. Haghe in Lithography by express command, for Her Gracious Majesty Queen Victoria. London Ackermann & Coy. Printsellers, Booksellers, Stationers &c. by appointment to Her Majesty and H.R.H. the Duchess of Kent Published November 1st 1839 Day & Haghe Lithrs. to the Queen.

Folio.

1839

COLLATION.—Title as above (v. blank) + Engraved Note 1 p. (v. blank) + 8 coloured plates, each plate with an uncoloured plan facing it.

Each plate bears Day & Haghe Lithr. to the Queen & imprint, R. Ackermann & Co. 96, Strand 1st Oct. 1839.

1. Keeper's Lodge—Bishop's Gate.
2. Keepers Lodge—Forest Gate.
3. Keepers Lodge—Blacknest Gate.
4. Head Keeper's Lodge—On the Road from Windsor.
5. Keepers Lodge—The Double Gates in the Long Walk.
6. Keepers Lodge on the Windsor Road.
7. Keepers Lodge The Sandpit Gate.
8. Royal Lodge Chapel.